D1292715

HAYDN
His Life and Music

HAYDN

His Life and Music

H. C. ROBBINS LANDON

and

DAVID WYN JONES

INDIANA UNIVERSITY PRESS

Bloomington and Indianapolis

Copyright © 1988 by H.C.Robbins Landon and David Wyn Jones

All rights reserved
No part of this book may be reproduced or utilized in any form or by
any means, electronic or mechanical, including photocopying and
recording, or by any information storage and retrieval system, without
permission in writing from the publisher. The Association of American
University Presses' Resolution on Permissions constitutes the only
exception to this prohibition.

Manufactured in the German Democratic Republic

Library of Congress Cataloging-in-Publication Data

Landon, H.C.Robbins (Howard Chandler Robbins), 1926-
   Haydn: His life and music / H.C.Robbins Landon and
  David Wyn Jones
        p.   cm.
   "In this publication the biographical chapters have been abridged and
adapted from those previously published in H.C.Robbins Landon,
Haydn: Chronicle and Works (London and Bloomington, Ind., 1976–80)
and Haydn: a documentary study (London and New York, 1981); the
chapters devoted to Haydn's music have been specially written for this
publication by David Wyn Jones" – T.p. verso.
  Bibliography: p.
  Includes index.
  ISBN 0-253-37265-8
  1.Haydn, Joseph, 1732–1809. 2.Composers—Austria—Biography.
I.Wyn Jones, David. II.Landon, H.C.Robbins (Howard Chandler
Robbins), 1926-   Haydn. III.Landon, H.C.Robbins (Howard
Chandler Robbins), 1926-   Haydn: a documentary study.
IV.Title.
ML410.H4L265 1988
780'.92'4—dc19
[B]   88-2685

1 2 3 4 5 92 91 90 89 88

Contents

Authors' note

Haydn's music

Works referred to in the text are identified in context by their respective numbers in Hoboken's *Haydn Verzeichnis* (see Select bibliography). Vocal music is identified by its customary title. Instrumental works are identified as follows:

Symphonies are referred to by their number in Mandyczewski's list prepared for the publishers Breitkopf & Härtel, which numbering was adopted by Hoboken.
String quartets are identified by their opus number.
Piano sonatas are listed by their chronological numbering in the *Wiener Urtext Ausgabe*, edited by Christa Landon.
Piano trios are identified by the chronological numbering as used in the *Complete Edition of Haydn's Piano Trios*, edited by H. C. Robbins Landon, published by Doblinger.

String trios are identified by the chronological numbering as used in the *Complete Edition of Haydn's String Trios*, edited by H. C. Robbins Landon, published by Doblinger.

Other instrumental works are identified by their customary title. The system of pitch notation used is based on middle C being represented by the symbol *c'*. In the musical examples instruments (in order of their customary appearance in the orchestral score) are abbreviated thus: Fl. - flute; Ob. - oboe; Cor ang. - cor anglais; Clar. - clarinet; Fag. - bassoon; Cor. - horn; Trbe. - trumpet; Trbn. - trombone; Timp. - timpani (kettledrums); V. - violin; Va. - viola; Vc. - violoncello; Cb. (B.) - contrabasso (double bass); Cemb. - cembalo (harpsichord). Other abbreviations used are: Pf. - pianoforte; Bar. - baryton.

Documents

In all documents cited in the text the original orthography - whether in English, German, French or Italian - has been retained. Thus, accents have not been inserted where they were omitted in the original document, notably in passages from the Zinzendorf Diaries. Other contemporary variable usages in German, such as 'Capellmeister' and 'Kapellmeister', have been retained in context. The language of the original document is indicated only in those cases which require clarification. Bibliographical references will be found in an abbreviated form in the text, at the end of quotations and in the footnotes; full titles of works cited are given below.

The abbreviations 'k.k.' and 'I.R.' (meaning *'kaiserlich-königlich'* /'Imperial Royal') are used interchangeably. Austrian money is abbreviated thus: Gulden (gulden; sc. florins) = 'f.' or 'fl.' (or 'F.', 'Fl.'); Kreuzer = 'k.' or 'kr.' or 'xr.' ('K.', 'Kr.', 'Xr.').

The following abbreviations are used for sources referred to frequently in the text and in footnotes:

A.M.   'Acta Musicalia', in the Esterházy Archives housed in the Music Department, National Széchényi Library (Országos Széchényi Könyvtár), Budapest

A.T.   'Acta Theatralia', in the Esterházy Archives (as A.M. above)

C&W I, II, III, IV, V   H. C. Robbins Landon, *Haydn: Chronicle and Works* (5 vols.), London and Bloomington, Ind. 1976-80:
I = *Haydn: the Early Years, 1732-1765*; II = *Haydn at Eszterháza 1766-1790*; III = *Haydn in England 1791-1795*; IV = *Haydn: the Years of 'The Creation' 1796-1800*; V = *Haydn: the Late Years 1801-1809*

Carpani   Giuseppe Carpani, *Le Haydine*, Milan 1812

CCLN   *Collected Correspondence and London Notebooks of Joseph Haydn*, trans. and ed. H. C. Robbins Landon, London 1959

Dies   A. C. Dies, *Biographische Nachrichten von Joseph Haydn*, Vienna 1810; new ed. Horst Seeger, Berlin, n.d. [1959]

EH   Esterházy Archives (now Budapest, Forchtenstein and Eisenstadt); cf. A.M. and A.T. above, and see p. 359 (Chapter I, note 8)

EK   *Entwurf-Katalog*, Haydn's draft catalogue of his own compositions, *c.* 1765 *et seq.*, in the Staatsbibliothek, Berlin

Griesinger   G. A. Griesinger, *Biographische Notizen über Joseph Haydn*, Leipzig 1810; new ed. Franz Grasberger, Vienna 1954

HJB   *Haydn Jahrbuch/Haydn Yearbook*, 1962 *et seq.*

H-S   *Haydn-Studien*, 1965 *et seq.*

HV   *Haydn Verzeichnis* (1805), Haydn's thematic catalogue of works composed between his '18th and 73rd years'

JHW   *Joseph Haydn Werke* (new collected edition of Haydn's works), published by the Joseph Haydn Institut, Cologne

Mozart, *Briefe*   *Mozart Briefe und Aufzeichnungen* (ed. Bauer, Deutsch and Eibl), 6 vols., Kassel 1962 *et seq.*

ÖNB   Österreichische Nationalbibliothek (Austrian National Library), Vienna

Pohl I, II, III   C. F. Pohl, *Joseph Haydn* (3 vols.): I, Berlin 1875; II, Berlin 1882; III (completed by Hugo Botstiber), Leipzig 1927. All three volumes since reprinted

WZ   *Wiener Zeitung*

Zinzendorf   Diaries (ms.) of Count Carl von Zinzendorf, in the Haus-, Hof- und Staatsarchiv, Vienna

Introduction

THE STORY of Joseph Haydn's life is one that he himself thought would be of little interest to anyone; but the history of his single-handed and tremendous conquest of musical Europe during his lifetime, unlike anything that had ever occurred before, the subsequent decline of his reputation almost to oblivion, as well as his rise from the ashes 250 years after his birth – these aspects of Haydn have proved to be unique and curious.

Other composers before Haydn had been popular and venerated during their lifetimes – Palestrina, Monteverdi, Corelli, Handel, Vivaldi; but with the exception of Handel these other composers fell into more or less complete neglect after their respective deaths. Handel (unlike J. S. Bach, who was scarcely known outside German-speaking countries before 1800) had been a spectacular success in Italy when a young man in his early twenties and had gone on to conquer the English, and was to remain a cult-figure in England during the rest of the eighteenth century – he had died in 1759 – and well beyond. But in the year 1750, let us say, Handel's music was practically unknown in many parts of Europe, such as Spain or Hungary or Sweden; in Italy, once the scene of his youthful triumphs, he was already forgotten. Haydn, on the other hand, achieved a total European popularity within his lifetime; by 1790 his music was adored even in the far corners of the Continent such as Seville, St Petersburg, Pest (now Budapest) and Stockholm. Such popularity and, it must be added, profound respect do not happen accidentally, nor was such a position the result of organized propaganda by the composer or his publishers. It was, on the contrary, the result of a deep-seated conviction, of supra-national dimensions, on the part of the public, that Haydn's language was their language; it was a case of total, or near-total, identification of the audience with the composer, on a European scale. Perhaps it has never happened again to that extent *during a composer's lifetime*. The music of Mozart, Beethoven, Schubert, Wagner, Bruckner and Mahler was adored by a segment of their contemporary audiences, but it was not until after the deaths of those six composers that their works achieved the kind of popularity that Haydn had enjoyed during his lifetime. Who, in 1827, knew anything about Beethoven in Palermo, in Toulouse, in Bath, in Madrid?

Any detailed assessment of Haydn and his place in the eighteenth century was hardly possible until very recently. Today, almost the last of Haydn's unpublished œuvre has appeared – the baryton trios, the early operas, much of the early church music and the occasional instrumental work such as the Seitenstetten Minuets (possibly his earliest known orchestral work). Since 1949, then, almost the whole of the 'unknown Haydn' has appeared not only in print but also on gramophone records; for it is now obvious that recordings are of much more importance in the dissemination of the works of a composer like Haydn than the mere printed page can ever be. All the symphonies are available, in two complete recordings, and very shortly to be amplified by a third set played on original instruments by L'Estro Armonico under Derek Solomons; all the piano sonatas in half-a-dozen different versions, all the piano trios in two versions, all the quartets in countless complete sets, all the oratorios and masses in sundry performances, most of the operas in the exemplary Philips sets conducted by Antal Dorati, not to speak of countless single works such as the insertion arias and other numbers in operas by 'foreign' composers which Haydn conducted at Eszterháza. Anyone can now listen to almost the complete major works of Haydn, something that no one except the composer was in any position to do hitherto. And parallel with this explosion of Haydn's music comes what might be called the documentary substructure - all those thousands of contemporary manuscripts from the Esterházy Archives which reveal in a unique way the day-to-day life of the musicians and the *Herrschaft* (gentry), and which are to a large (though not complete) extent now available in publications, foremost in *Haydn-Studien* and the *Haydn Yearbook*. For the first time, in 1959, Haydn's letters were collected and published, and in recent years nearly a dozen previously unknown letters have appeared on the antiquarian market. Some of these letters have not been included in a Haydn biography hitherto, and are printed here for the first time (apart from their appearance in scholarly journals). Even works by Haydn thought to have been lost have suddenly come to the surface: the complete motet 'O coelitum beati' and the *Missa* 'Sunt bona mixta malis' are two examples of works that have never been discussed in any previous biography.

Hence we are for the first time in a position to view that mighty procession of works, the sum total of which is staggering and far beyond that of any other known composer; and this was the collection which, in part and *in toto*, contributed to form the unique position that Haydn enjoyed during his lifetime. Before this mass of supremely professional music was available, how could that position be explained, except by enlightened guesswork? A generation ago, hardly anyone could have imagined the extent to which Haydn's life from 1776 to 1790 was governed by operatic productions at Eszterháza – over a thousand performances of dozens of operas by such composers as Paisiello, Gazzaniga, Dittersdorf, Cimarosa and Anfossi, all of which Haydn not only prepared and conducted, but for which he acted as a rather barbarous musicologist as well - ruthlessly cutting, re-orchestrating, changing tempi, and even adding whole sections of new music, some (such as the terzetto 'Lavatevi presto' of 1789 for *La Circe*) of very substantial dimensions and enchanting musical content.

We are also learning – to remain with the man in his time – of Haydn's fascination with the mechanical aspects and musical possibilities of the instruments with which he worked. This is part and parcel of his supreme professionalism, of course, but was not revealed to us completely until the music became available in scholarly editions: how Haydn's trumpets (before the Concerto for keyed trumpet of 1796) had a mechanical device to enable them to play the written note

by lowering middle *C* (*c'*) in some mysterious fashion - and how this operation took place not only in Eisenstadt in 1798 (*Missa in angustiis*, known as the 'Nelson' Mass) but also in England in 1791 (Symphony no. 95) and in a work destined for a French orchestra whose players were not known personally to Haydn (Symphony no. 86, 1786, for the Loge 'Olympique' in Paris). And we are learning that *c.* 1768 Haydn's oboes and cors anglais were improved technically with an extension that enabled the oboes to play *c sharp'* (by depressing their newly-won B extension and playing on it *d'* which produced the hitherto unplayable *c sharp'*) and the cors anglais to play the sensational low pedal note E flat sounding

at the beginning of the Gloria of the *Missa in honorem B.V.M.* (Great Organ Solo Mass), to the astonishment and delight, no doubt, of the player, the composer and Prince Nicolaus Esterházy (a trained musician who would have heard and understood the innovation at once). And in a recently disovered letter to the Parisian piano-manufacturing firm of Erard, we see that in 1801 Haydn's technical knowledge of the new piano was in fact as profound as the composition of Piano Sonata no. 60 in C (1794?), with its use of the new *sopra una corda* pedal (not known to Viennese pianos of the time), had already suggested.

We are also learning that one of the principal innovations that Haydn carried back to Vienna from England in 1795 was not only the profound effect of great Handelian oratorio as a class of music but its particular and staggering effect when performed with 'monster' forces – a combination that Haydn repeated in both senses with his late oratorios in Vienna. It was for these oratorios that Haydn enlarged the orchestra to the standard proportions of the nineteenth century before Wagner, that is, with three flutes, two oboes, two clarinets, two bassoons, double bassoon (an instrument little used by 1798 except in wind bands), four horns, three trumpets, three trombones (which by 1798 were no longer used in many parts of Europe), timpani, extra percussion, and of course the usual strings. Haydn's forward-looking character – one of the facets by which his extraordinary success was guaranteed – thus created a new and much larger orchestra, but even more the large general effect of massed forces which has ever since remained a source of fascination for the Viennese (for whom the opera, and massive choral/orchestral concerts are the principal bill of fare for the general public).

What were the components that made up Haydn's recipe for success? Put at its most simple, it was the combination of popular language and forms (e.g. the rondo with its catchy, returning tune), together with a highly professional approach and a marked bent for intellectual exploitation of the given material. A particular incentive in the 1770s was the scintillating mixture of Italian *opera buffa* language (a derivative of the old *commedia dell' arte*, and thus stressing the absurd, the exotic, the tender, the quixotic, sometimes the slightly sinister too) with solid Austrian symphonic workmanship. This meant that the tiresomely repetitious language of, let us say, the Overture to Pergolesi's *Il geloso schernito* (Naples 1732) becomes transformed into something as sophisticated as the 'Turkish' overture to *L'incontro improvviso* of 1775 (still with Pergolesi's three-movement form,[1] but with a slow introduction and couched in Viennese symphonic language and orchestration: from Pergolesi's horns and strings with harpsichord continuo to Haydn's oboes, bassoons, horns, trumpets, timpani, extra percussion and strings), and shortly thereafter to the one-movement *sinfonia* to *Orlando Paladino* (1782) and the potpourri overture to *Armida* of 1784. The simplistic language of Pergolesi's overture, authentic or not, cannot have satisfied audiences anywhere in Europe except in the chatter-ridden precincts of the opera house, and in this single example one can see in a dramatic confrontation what it was that raised Haydn above most of his popular Italian precursors and what it was, moreover, that fascinated his contemporaries. It was partly a new way of fusing older styles, partly a heightened sense of intellectual awareness, but it was mainly inspiration combined with an impeccable sense of length. Even short chatter is not interesting, and Haydn's miniatures such as his early *Scherzandi* (*c.* 1760?) already show his highly developed sense of brevity as (one might say) a national virtue. It is characteristic that in 1796, when Haydn was composing his great and humane *Missa Sancti Bernardi de Offida*, the changes that he made in the autograph of the Gloria's opening are all towards *lengthening* the exceedingly pithy musical language.

It is clear, then, that Europe responded with delight to Haydn, to his very personal, positive and indeed sunny message, his nervous masculine style, and his split-level language: in Symphony no. 88 the towering intellectual feat whereby all the first movement's thematic material is able to combine with itself in apparently effortless contrapuntal virtuosity, yet is presented in a seamless and easy style so that a listener less educated than Haydn's ideal was able to appreciate the insouciant progress of the music without understanding its technical complexities. It was the same principle that had guided Mozart when he composed his set of three piano concertos (K.413–5) for Vienna in 1782–3. He wrote to his father on 28 December 1782 about them:[2]

> These concertos are a happy medium between what is too easy and too difficult; they are very brilliant, pleasing to the ear, and natural, without being vapid. There are passages here and there from which connoisseurs alone can derive satisfaction, but these passages are written in such a way that the less learned cannot fail to be pleased though without knowing why.

In considering Haydn's position during his lifetime, scholars and critics have always rightly judged Mozart's arrival on the scene to have been a major influence on the older man's music; but perhaps these same critics have not always placed in perspective: (a) Mozart's effect on music in general during his lifetime and (b) his particular fate in Vienna, where he chose to live during the last decade of his life. As to the first part, it is clear that Mozart's influence was as limited during his own lifetime as it was boundless after his death. This was in the main because most of his music was not published until after his death in 1791. But his peculiar reception by the Viennese has a more direct bearing on Haydn. Everyone knows that, after his initial successes in the Austrian capital (his concerts attended by the cream of society, the Emperor favourably impressed by him), the nobility turned their backs on Mozart and the critics found his music too 'highly spiced'. No one has ever explained satisfactorily why in 1789 Mozart's subscription invitation for concerts in the next season should have come back with one single name (Gottfried van Swieten's) in contrast to the hundreds of a few years earlier. Certainly there is enough contemporary evidence to suggest that the public found the 'dark' side of Mozart's art alarming, to say the least. Possibly the same Viennese (and indeed European) audiences who adored Haydn's message of optimism, faith and cheer were in many cases repelled by the grim power of Mozart's demonic side – the C minor of the Adagio and Fugue (K.546) or of the Piano Concerto (K.491); the G minor of piano quartet, symphony and quintet; the D minor of quartet and concerto. Mozart's depression and anguish, as vividly expressed in this kind of music, patently found little sympathy among the nobility of Austria (most of the bourgeoisie will have known only his operas and some chamber music which they played themselves) or – as far as they knew it – audiences elsewhere, either. In many respects such music was the very opposite of Haydn's art, and whereas the Emperor Joseph II may have derided and disliked Haydn's humour, the Austrian public was clearly of another opinion.

Haydn was, of course, a real connoisseur and his admiration for and love of Mozart's music is well documented. What is amazing is that the two men became great friends (it was amazing to their contemporaries too, as one can sense clearly in Niemetschek's Mozart biography of 1798), although Haydn realized that Mozart was musically his superior and said so on many occasions: in 1791 he told Dr Burney that Mozart 'was truly a great musician. I have often been flattered by my friends as having some genius, but he was much my superior.' It was Mozart's generosity not to brook criticism of Haydn, but Haydn's generosity is even more astonishing. Indeed, he loved the younger man whose music was, sooner or later, destined to diminish his own, a fact which a man of Haydn's knowledge, taste and perception was unlikely to ignore. Then, in 1792, a year after Mozart's death, there arrived on the Viennese scene Haydn's most talented pupil. Haydn's generosity to Beethoven is also well documented: 'Beethoven will in time fill the position of one of Europe's greatest composers, and I shall be proud to be able to speak of myself as his teacher ...' (23 November 1793). But whereas Haydn had managed to survive and even sublimate Mozart – Wagner's perceptive remarks on the subject remain the best summary:

Haydn, inspired after the death of Mozart by the latter's genius, becomes the real predecessor of Beethoven: rich and yet so finely worked orchestration, everything 'speaks', everything is inspiration ...

– Beethoven set about deliberately to topple Haydn's reputation, in which he was eminently successful. In conversation with his pupils and admirers, in the opening years of the new century, Beethoven often discussed the music of his predecessors and 'Haydn seldom escaped without a poke in the ribs' (Ries). Both Mozart and the young Beethoven (post 1792) to a certain extent used Haydn's own language but extended it so that, although similar in many respects in both their hands, the original soon began to seem threadbare. The situation was not helped by the dozens of *seguaci*, those well-meaning but limited followers of Haydn such as Pleyel, Gyrowetz and the Wranitzky brothers, who further debased Haydn's language by constant and partly simplistic over-use. By 1800, according to the *Allgemeine Musikalische Zeitung*, the Berliners, never among Haydn's great admirers, were finding Haydn symphonies 'droll, trifling and irritating', and by 1807 the Viennese 'no longer respected Haydn symphonies according to their value'.

Part of this change vis-à-vis Haydn was simply the reaction against fifty years of popularity, a process accelerated by Haydn's death in 1809, perhaps, but in evidence several years before, when it became clear (after 1804) that he was not going to compose any more music. Yet the decline in Haydn's popularity during the nineteenth century was especially to be noted in his native Austria, and in that case there were possibly other factors involved. Profound changes were taking place in the Austrian character, and indeed even in the Austrian appearance, ever since the Congress of Vienna in 1815. There enters a streak of melancholy in the Austrian character which was hardly to be noticed, if at all, in the eighteenth century before Mozart; for it seems clear that the fatalistic, and indeed sometimes seemingly near-suicidal, tendencies of Mozart's 'black' music were well in advance of their age. To jump to the conclusion of our narrative, what was in 1785 a tendency in one man was to become two hundred years later symptomatic of a nation, reflected in the fact that, after Hungary, Austria now has the highest suicide rate in Europe.

However, this change occurred very slowly, and Schubert's profound pessimism was the exception rather than the rule; indeed, at the time of his death Schubert was hardly known except to connoisseurs, and there is no reason to believe that the post-Congress Viennese were in sympathy with the dark majesty and bleak outlook of his *Winterreise*, nor with the private agonies of the late piano and chamber music. Still, what was a trickle in Mozart and a brook in Schubert soon became a mighty river, nurtured by Brahms, Bruckner and Mahler – all to some extent (Brahms perhaps less so) prophets of doom. As the Industrial Revolution came to Austria, masses of poor Bohemians, Hungarians and Croatians flocked to the capital to become Austria's first industrial proletariat, bringing with them Slav pessimism. Swarms of poor Jews from Galicia also reached Vienna, and their outlook could hardly, given their history and potential future, be called cheerful; the process of their assimilation often caused problems of a special kind, and, being gifted intellectuals, their sarcastic pessimism came to be an important factor in Austrian journalism and art, whether in the *Neue Freie Presse*, or in Hugo Wolf's Lieder and criticisms, the latter violently anti-Haydn, as might be imagined: thus, Haydn symphonies are the typical fare of the Philistine *rentier* 'who likes to talk about the good old wonderful days' and whose 'favourite composer is Haydn' (*C&W*, V, 423). From Wolf to Kafka was not such a big step. Thus, as the century waned, Haydn's smoothly seamed music with its playful intellectualism was as off-putting to the depressive hysterical Viennese as much of Mozart's had been, for other reasons, a hundred years earlier. Even in the greatest of the late Johann Strauss waltzes, such as the Emperor's Waltz, there was a profound streak of melancholy. The Empire was growing old, and it seemed that Haydn had no place in it – or almost none: with a curious tenacity for survival, Haydn's music never quite disappeared from the programmes of the Vienna Philharmonic or the Rosé String Quartet. There were always members of the public who persisted in liking Haydn, and the centenary celebrations of 1909 provided the impetus for starting a *Gesamtausgabe* – very late, after the works of Bach, Handel, Mozart, Mendelssohn and Beethoven were already available in standard critical editions; and very shakily, for by 1933 there had appeared only half-a-dozen further volumes (after the initial three containing the first forty symphonies, which no one played even after their publication). To a certain degree, Haydn's popularity within Austria has never recovered.

Just as this more or less permanent collapse of Haydn's reputation in Austria may be historically explicable, at least up to a point, it is probable that the great renaissance of his music taking place since 1949 (when a new attempt at a *Gesamtausgabe* was begun) was of necessity an Anglo-Saxon operation. Specifically, it has been Britain where the musical renaissance took place and continues to flourish. At the risk of airing an obvious explanation, one might propose that the British character, even during the Industrial Revolution, never showed any marked suicidal tendencies; on the contrary, a certain confidence seemed to go hand in hand with Victorian expansion of territory and business. The confidence of Haydn's music perhaps never quite lost its appeal to the British, though even *The Creation* had its low spot in 1899, when it was judged to be 'a third-rate oratorio, whose interest is largely historic and literary'.[3] Nevertheless, it cannot be an accident that Haydn's appeal today is strongest in Britain and weakest in Austria (obviously we are only counting European countries where Haydn has a potential at all).

As a result of the Haydn renaissance, certain views about the relative importance of his huge output are now gradually making themselves felt. Probably the tried and tested favourites – piano sonatas (on which countless young fingers have found their way to music altogether), symphonies and string quartets – have if anything become even more popular. There are, for example, six complete recordings of the piano sonatas in Christa Landon's edition (Universal Edition) which for some reason has totally dwarfed that of Georg Feder (Henle Verlag). The symphonies and quartets have never left the repertoire, though in the case of the symphonies there were until recently only a handful readily available in print and known to the average concert-goer. The quartets always fared better because they were the only genre of Haydn's music available in their totality since their first complete publication by Haydn's pupil Pleyel at the beginning of the nineteenth century. Although that edition was textually very dubious and included two sextets with horns, a symphony, and six spurious works, it was nonetheless the means of keeping Haydn's quartets alive from then till now: Pleyel's editions were reprinted with slight emendations by Peters and by Breitkopf and – following Pleyel's own initiative – miniature scores were available as soon as that form was re-invented by Payne, and the Eulenburg reprints ensured that the music was always available to students.

The oratorios, especially the late works, also never left the repertoire, but it was not until 1949 that *The Creation* was first recorded (with the Vienna Philharmonic under Clemens Kraus); it had been preceded by a wartime record of a slightly abbreviated *The Seasons* conducted by Vittorio Gui. Meanwhile both these works, as well as *The Seven Words* (for years only performed in the version for string quartet), have gained a new lease of life and are now as popular as the choral music of Bach and Handel. But of all the genres of Haydn's many-sided genius, there is one that has, since 1949, flowered as none other: the mass. Before that date, Haydn's masses were restricted to their liturgical use in south German and Austrian churches, often performed from ancient manuscript material. Such works as the *Missa brevis* in F, the Great Organ Solo Mass (*Missa in honorem B.V.M.*) and the uncut score of the *Missa Cellensis in honorem B.V.M.* begun in 1766 (formerly known as the *Missa Sanctae Caeciliae*) were not available in print until 1950, but it was not until the 1960s that Haydn's masses began to catch the general public's fancy. Since then, their popularity has grown enormously, and such a work as the *Missa in angustiis* ('Nelson' Mass) now rivals in popularity almost any other work by Haydn; not quite any other work – the Trumpet Concerto is now one of the most popular works in the whole repertoire of Classical music, and for a wonder its popularity is justified by its magnificent content.[4] Other Haydn concertos are almost as popular, especially the Piano Concerto in D and the two extant Cello Concertos; and the Violin Concerto in C is fast becoming a regular part of the repertoire, too.

The most interesting experiment of this Haydn renaissance has been the revival of his operas, beginning with *Il mondo della luna*, which Carlo Maria Giulini conducted at the Holland Festival in 1959. Since then most of Haydn's operas have been performed on the stage with varying degrees of success. Haydn as a stage composer is still the subject of passionate controversy, particularly among the Germans (Germany still commands more working opera houses than the rest of Europe combined and, for obvious reasons, most of the performances take place there). The Germans have never really approved of Haydn, even during his lifetime, and it was not surprising that the most widely read magazine dealing with the theatre should recently mount a devastating attack on Haydn's operas.[5] The one Haydn opera that has proved to be a continuing success on the stage (and indeed off it, with three complete recordings) is *L'infedeltà delusa*, another work launched at the Holland Festival, this time in 1963 under Alberto Erede. Haydn's operas are indeed a special problem and hardly anyone expects them – especially after an interval of some 200 years – to rival those of Mozart or even Gluck: of recently relaunched operas, the only ones to have a tentative claim to have become part of the repertoire are those by Monteverdi. Part of the trouble with the survival on the stage of Haydn's operas is that they depend largely upon Germany (and to a lesser extent Austria), where there is little sense of a Haydn style and little sympathy with his music altogether: it is not an accident that the signal success of the Holland Festival performances was because of the fact that the conductors and most of the singers were Italian, in short that the operas were not produced, sung, staged and conducted by Germans or Austrians, which would have ensured their instant failure. For typical productions of Haydn operas sung in German, we may refer our readers to the television programmes of *Lo speziale, Le pescatrici, L'infedeltà delusa, La vera costanza* and *Il mondo della luna*, made at Schloss Hohenems near Bregenz by Austrian Radio and Television (ÖRF) in the 1960s and 1970s. These were enough to put anyone off Haydn operas for life, which in the event they succeeded for many people in doing. A subsidiary benefit of Haydn's interest in the stage is provided by those many insertion arias (and also larger numbers, up to trios) for the operas of other composers performed at Eszterháza. Some have become quite popular, and at least one reveals the experimental and 'quirky' side of the composer's personality *par excellence*: the terzetto 'Pietà di me' for two sopranos, tenor and orchestra with obbligato cor anglais, bassoon and horn (the latter surely the most taxing solo part in the repertoire, rising to an exposed sounding *b flat"*).

What has this enormously increased knowledge of Haydn and his world brought us? It has given us, literally, hundreds of hitherto unpublished or hitherto unavailable works in all kinds of genres. It remains to be seen to what extent these works will become part of the repertoire: their sheer numbers will of necessity prevent that in most cases, as has been proved by the complete publication, since the 1960s, of all the symphonies. It is manifestly impossible for 107 symphonies and the Concertante of 1792 (now one of his most popular pieces, incidentally) to become part of the regular symphonic repertoire. Hence we must return to the vital role which the long-playing record has assumed in the dissemination of Haydn's music. The recording is in some cases – the operas spring to mind immediately – essential if the work in question is to survive at all (where, in America for example, will Haydn's operas ever be staged except in the relative obscurity of colleges or the cellars of Greenwich Village?). A work like the aforementioned 'Pietà di me' not only contains an almost unplayable horn solo but the cor anglais contains those typically Eszterháza low pedal notes (E flat in the middle of the bass clef) which are also unperformable on most present-day instruments, though it is true that the E flat in question is also required by Mahler in his First Symphony; such a work is also a typical candidate for the long-playing record, where it can be studied together with the score which, even in the quite recent past (if it had been printed, which it was not) would never have been performed at all as the composer intended.

Except in England, then, Haydn remains very much a connoisseur's composer. The Haydn renaissance has hardly touched parts of Western Europe and it is unlikely to do so in the foreseeable future. Hence this book, too, addresses itself primarily to English-speaking readers, for whom Haydn is no longer uncharted territory. After the publication of the co-author's *Haydn: Chronicle and Works* in five volumes (1976–80) it was thought that a single-volume work might meet the needs of the student in a more practical way. Rather than attempting to condense some 3,200 pages into manageable length, it was decided to write completely new chapters on the music; this decision was rendered the easier because, in the years since 1980, a quantity of newly discovered music has become available. On the biographical side, apart from newly discovered letters by Haydn, at least two previously unrecorded short 'memoirs', by Haydn's pupils Kalkbrenner and Reicha, here add interesting details to our knowledge of Haydn's life.[6] The present biography may be seen therefore as a kind of 'stocktaking', a summary based on what might be called the collective view of Haydn just over a quarter of a millennium after his birth.

I
The early years,
1732–1765

As THE TURKS were rolled back after their nearly successful siege of Vienna in September 1683, Austria, and very soon large parts of Hungary (sections of which had been under Turkish rule for a century), began a new life. Freed from this foreign oppressor, the Habsburg rulers of Austria could turn their collective attention to another problem which was causing much anguish – the success in Hungary of Lutheran ideas. The Counter-Reformation which took place in the early seventeenth century in Austria and much later in Hungary proved in its way as thorny a problem as the Turkish campaign with which it is chronologically associated in Hungary. As Lutheranism was stamped out in Hungary in the wake of the retreating Turkish armies slowly being forced eastwards, the Counter-Reformation produced a great upsurge of art and architecture (the two in Austria often being very closely allied in propagating 'the cause' and hence each less important intrinsically than, say, in Italy): great pilgrimage churches and monasteries were rebuilt in the Baroque style. Artists like Paul Troger painted stirring frescoes on the ceilings of huge churches, which were in turn part of vast spatial concepts designed by men like Jacob Prandtauer, whose genius and vision have given us Melk Abbey and (at least in large part) St Florian Abbey and the sweeping pilgrimage church of Maria Taferl standing above and overlooking the Danube. It was the symbol of *ecclesia triumphans*, and in this living display of the Counter-Reformation music played almost as decisive a part as art and architecture. Indeed Austria developed a special kind of festive *missa solemnis* language, in C major and with trumpets and timpani, to glorify the church for feasts and solemn occasions. Haydn would write two masses of this kind for the famous pilgrimage church of Mariazell, the large-scale cantata-like *Missa Cellensis in honorem B.V.M.* (begun in 1766) and the other *Missa Cellensis* (of 1782), now known as the 'Mariazellermesse'.

The world into which Franz Joseph Haydn[1] was born in 1732 was, then, an Austria expanding its boundaries and full of religious zeal, under the rule of the talented Habsburgs. The reigning Emperor was Charles VI, who like most of his family was highly musical (as well as being an operatic composer of considerable skill, he was a fine violinist and harpsichordist and also a gifted *Kapellmeister*). The social structure of Haydn's Austria was rigid, and, seemingly, immutable. The gap between the rich, powerful Austrian and Hungarian magnates (Esterházys, Liechtensteins, Schwarzenbergs), with their vast lands, and the minor aristocracy with their small, pretty estates (largely in Bohemia, where they had been wrested from the local Protestant nobility, and in Lower Austria), was as great as that between the small but growing middle class (which flourished largely in the cities and towns) and the mass of peasants whose lot, particularly in Hungary, was hardly better than it had been in the middle ages. The vast riches of Prince Esterházy and the appalling poverty of many of his subjects are graphically illustrated in the richly detailed documents of the Esterházy Archives, now being published (with the accent on the musical aspects, of course) both in the original and in translation in the *Haydn Yearbook*. The peasants could not leave their lands without permission, nor could they marry without their lord's leave; they were obliged to do forced labour (*Robot*) on the lord's estates for a certain period each year, and they paid a fixed tithe to the church as well as another tithe to their lords. Ultimately, their well-being depended entirely on the individual decisions taken by their lords (which decisions were usually suggested by the all-powerful Estates Governor, or *Güter-Regent*). Protestants, Jews and other minorities were second-class citizens, and it was not until the reign of Joseph II (1780–90) that they were granted equal rights under the law.

Yet it was entirely possible for a poor peasant lad to rise to fame and riches – and not only Haydn's but other cases are known to historians, one such being that of Franz Heintl, a child of poor mountain farmers who ended his life as a rich and successful lawyer in Vienna (Diary, discovered by Else Radant; cf. *C&W*, I, 75 f.). Heintl was befriended by Baron Gottfried van Swieten, the patron of Mozart and Beethoven and the author of the librettos for Haydn's oratorios *The Creation* and *The Seasons*. But these were the exceptions, and in general a Hungarian peasant remained a peasant and (obviously) an Esterházy remained, if not a hereditary prince of the Holy Roman Empire of German Nations, then at least a comfortably situated member of the second (cadet) lines with the hereditary title of Count. Intermarriage between these various social classes was almost non-existent. The nobility spoke (and wrote their diaries in) French, while Latin was the *lingua franca* of Hungary for legal documents; it was Joseph II who insisted on German being the official bureaucratic language for the entire monarchy, an edict which met with stiff opposition in Hungary.

Joseph Haydn was born either on 31 March or (in another version; see *C&W*, I, 44) on 1 April 1732, at four o'clock in the afternoon, in the village of Rohrau in Lower Austria, on the domains of the Counts Harrach. Haydn's father was a wheelwright and later became the modern-day equivalent of *Bürgermeister* (the eighteenth-century title Mathias Haydn enjoyed was *Marktrichter*); Joseph's mother, *née* Anna Maria Koller, had been a cook in the Harrach Castle. Joseph was the second of twelve children born to the wheelwright and this, his first wife; most of the other children died in infancy, but two others also became musicians, Johann Michael (born 1737), later a celebrated composer in Salzburg, and Johann Evangelist (born 1743), who later became a tenor in the Esterházy Chapel Choir at Eisenstadt. Joseph was very much attached to his family, kept up with them all his life and left them (or their children, or grandchildren) handsome legacies in his will.

The village of Rohrau has changed somewhat, but not in a very basic sense, from its physical shape of 1732. The church remains; the pious statue that Mathias Haydn erected; the great Castle, now with the magnificent picture gallery from the Harrach Palace in Vienna; and Haydn's house, which has some vague resemblance to the composer's birthplace; it burned down in 1899 and before that had been subjected to floods which twice (1813, 1834) almost totally destroyed everything except the outside walls. Haydn's birthplace is therefore more a 'remembrance' than an actual relic of his youth.

But that which has changed hardly at all is the countryside around Rohrau, with its ancient history of Roman legionaries, migratory peoples from the east, invading Turkish troops and revered Christian traditions, binding people to the Cross and to their country in such ceremonies as Corpus Christi (where Mother Earth was gently combined with Mother Church). And hard by there was the Danube, one of Europe's great rivers, whose swift waters brought ships and men from Germany,

Austria and Hungary to faraway lands at its mouth in the Black Sea. The Danube countryside exerts a peculiar fascination: its surrounding vegetation, the great vineyards which the first Roman settlers had lovingly planted, the texture of the hills and plains through which the river runs, are quite different from those of any other part of Austria. And as the great river debouches on to the great plains, we find ourselves in the former Roman province of Pannonia, on the borders of which Haydn would spend most of his adult life.

He was deeply attached to the region and to its people. He was to be their greatest representative. There is, nowadays, a poster that the Museum of Free-masonry at Schloß Rosenau puts out. It shows the magnificent castle, with its traditional 'Schönbrunn yellow' and white walls, against a deep-blue, almost Mediterranean, sky, and below are the words 'Natur, Kunst, Humanität' ('nature, art, humanity'), the three most important components of Haydn's music, which, we believe, were the great heritage of his country and its peoples.

Our principal knowledge of Haydn's youth comes from four sources: an Autobiographical Sketch that Haydn wrote for an Austrian magazine in 1776;[2] and the three so-called 'authentic' biographies, all based on personal acquaintance and interviews with the aging Haydn – (1) G. A. Griesinger's *Biographische Notizen über Joseph Haydn*, Leipzig 1810 (previously published in part in instalments in the *Allgemeine Musikalische Zeitung* for 1809); (2) A. C. Dies's *Biographische Nachrichten von Joseph Haydn*, Vienna 1810; and (3) Giuseppe Carpani's *Le Haydine*, Milan 1812. Of these Griesinger is by far the most reliable, partly because much of the information in it was gathered when the composer was still in possession of a good memory (i.e. from 1799 onwards); Dies is charming but garrulous and not as reliable as his Saxon contemporary; while Carpani is the least trustworthy of all three, to be used only with extreme caution when his evidence contradicts or supplements that of the others. There are, of course, other sources as well, both contemporary as well as posthumous (among the latter we might single out N. E. Framery's *Notice sur Joseph Haydn*, Paris 1810, based in part on information from Haydn's erstwhile pupil Ignaz Pleyel, who then lived in Paris, and sometimes containing interesting material not found in the other biographies), all of which help us in reconstructing the years of Haydn's youth and early successes.

Here is *Legationsrath* Griesinger's account of Haydn's family background and his early years (pp. 8–11):

… Joseph Haydn was born on 31 March 1732 at Rohrau, a village in Lower Austria, in the district Unter-Wiener-Wald hard by the Hungarian border, not far from the little town of Bruk [*sic*] an der Leitha. Of the twenty [*recte*: seventeen] children from two marriages of his father Mathias, a wheelwright by profession, Joseph was the [second] eldest. As was customary in his trade, the father had seen a little of the world, and during his sojourn in Frankfurt am Mayn he had learned to strum the harp. As a master of his trade at Rohrau, he continued to practise this instrument for pleasure, after work; nature had also endowed him with a good tenor voice, and his wife, Anne Marie,[1] accompanied his playing with her singing. The tunes of these songs were so deeply imprinted in Joseph Haydn's memory that he could recall them even in advanced old age.[2] – One day the school rector from the neighbouring little town of Haimburg [*sic*], a distant relative of the Haydn family, came to Rohrau. Master Mathias and his wife gave their usual little concert, and five-year-old Joseph sat near his parents and sawed at his left arm with a stick, as if he were accompanying on the violin. The schoolteacher noted that the boy marked the time accurately; he inferred from this a natural talent for music, and he advised the parents to send their Sepperl [an Austrian diminutive for Joseph] to Haimburg in order to help acquire an art which in time would without fail open to him the prospect 'of becoming a clergyman'. As ardent admirers of the clergy, the parents jumped at this proposal, and in his sixth year Joseph Haydn went to the school rector at Haimburg. Here he received lessons in reading and writing, in catechism, in singing, and in almost all wind and string instruments, even in playing the timpani. 'I shall owe it to that man even in my grave', Haydn used to say frequently, 'that he taught me so many things, though in the process I received more thrashings than food.'

Haydn, who even then wore a wig for the sake of cleanliness, had been about three years in Haimburg when the Court Chapel Master Reutter from Vienna, who directed the music at St Stephen's Cathedral, came to visit his friend the dean in Haimburg. Reutter told the dean that his older choir-boys, whose voices were beginning to break, were about to become useless, and that he would have to replace them with younger substitutes. The dean proposed the eight-year-old Haydn, and both he and the schoolmaster were at once called for. The badly nourished Sepperl cast hungry glances at the cherries that were sitting on the dean's table; Reutter tossed a few handfuls into his hat, and he seemed quite satisfied with the Latin and Italian strophes that Haydn had to sing. 'Can you also make a trill?' asked Reutter. 'No', said Haydn, 'for even my cousin [*Herr Vetter*] can't do that.' This answer greatly embarrassed the schoolteacher, and Reutter laughed heartily. He showed the mechanical means by which a trill could be produced. Haydn imitated him, and succeeded at the third attempt. 'You shall stay with me', said Reutter. The departure from Haimburg was soon arranged, and Haydn came as a pupil to the Choir School at St Stephen's Cathedral in Vienna, where he remained until he was in his sixteenth year.

Apart from the scanty instruction customary at that time in Latin, religion, arithmetic and writing, Haydn had in the Choir School very capable instructors on several instruments, and particularly in the art of singing. Among the latter were Gegenbauer,[3] a member of the court choir, and an elegant tenor, Finsterbusch.[4] In the Choir School there was no instruction in musical theory, and Haydn recalled having received only two such lessons from the worthy Reutter. But Reutter did encourage him to make whatever variations he liked on the motets and Salves that he had to sing in church, and this discipline soon led him to ideas of his own which Reutter corrected. He also came to know Mattheson's [*Der*] *vollkommene Kapellmeister*,[5] and Fux's *Gradus ad Parnassum*[6] in German and Latin - a book he still in his old age praised as a classic and of which he kept a well-used copy. With tireless exertion Haydn tried to understand Fux's theory; he worked his way right through the whole school, wrote out the exercises, put them by for several weeks and then took them up again, polishing them till he considered them perfect. 'Of course the talent was latent in me: as a result of it, and with great diligence, I made progress.' In his fevered imagination he even ventured into compositions in eight and sixteen parts. 'In those days I used to think everything was fine so long as the paper was well covered. Reutter laughed about my immature products, about movements which no throat and no instrument could have executed, and he scolded me for composing in sixteen parts before I had learned how to write in two.'

At that time many *castrati* were employed at court and in the Viennese churches, and the director of the Choir School no doubt considered that he was about to make the young Haydn's fortune when he brought forth the plan to turn him into a permanent soprano [*ihn sopranisieren zu lassen*], and actually asked the father for his permission. The father, who totally disapproved of this proposal, set forth at once for Vienna and, thinking that the operation might already have been performed, entered the room where his son was and asked, 'Sepperl, does anything hurt you? Can you still walk?' Delighted to find his son unharmed, he protested against any further proposals of this kind, and a *castrato* who happened to be there even strengthened him in his resolve.

The truth of this anecdote was attested by persons to whom Haydn often related it.

Notes:
1 *Recte* Anna Maria.
2 This is confirmed in yet another source, Carl Bertuch's *Bemerkungen auf einer Reise aus Thüringen nach Wien im Winter 1805 bis 1806*, Weimar, im Verlage des Landes-Industrie-Comptoirs 1810, p. 181 (15 April 1805): 'On Sundays he [Mathias Haydn] played his songs, and Haydn's mother sang with him. Even today Haydn knows all those songs by heart. As a lad of five years our Sepperl sat next to his parents, took a piece of wood in his right hand and sawed with it against his left arm, as if he were playing the violin ...'. This raises a rather interesting question: can Griesinger (and Dies?) have garnered this information from Bertuch? It seems possible until we consider that Griesinger was clearly the first to pub-

lish, not as a book, but in the *AMZ*: the passage in question appears in the issue of 12 July 1809. Once again the whole problem of authenticity is raised, and once we know the chronological order, we begin to doubt Bertuch's 'original interview'. Of course, Haydn may well have repeated the story to each of the interviewers.
3 Adam Gegenbauer, died 1753.
4 Ignaz Finsterbusch, also died 1753.
5 It appeared in 1739.
6 It appeared earlier, in 1725. Haydn's copy was seen by C. F. Pohl, who transcribed all the supplementary Latin notes. See A. Mann: 'Haydn as a student and critic of Fux', in *Studies in Eighteenth-Century Music: A Tribute to Karl Geiringer on his Seventieth Birthday* (ed. H. C. R. Landon and R. E. Chapman), London 1970, pp. 323 ff. It was hitherto considered that the many additional notes and commentary in Haydn's copy were made by Haydn himself. But this theory is undermined by the presence of another copy, in the Library of Smith College, which we were shown in 1975, wherein there are almost the identical supplementary ms. comments. Perhaps a revised edition of Fux was in circulation. It is, of course, possible that the Smith copy represents another version of Haydn's own *corrigenda*.

We may flesh out this documentary account by Griesinger with the conclusion of that by Dies: Dies recounts the story of Haydn's composing complicated music, and actually identifies one such work as a *Salve Regina* in twelve parts, and we hear of *Kapellmeister* Reutter saying, 'You silly boy, aren't two parts enough for you?' Dies then continues (pp. 24–32):

Joseph had to content himself, until he was eighteen, with the tossed-off comments, of which the one above serves as an example; his spirit received no nourishment. That which was most embarrassing to him, however, and at his age must have been painful, was the fact that they seemed set on a campaign to starve the body along with the mind. Joseph's stomach had to accustom itself to a perpetual fast, which for a time he attempted to improve by the occasional musical academies [concerts], for which the choir-boys were given refreshments.

As soon as Joseph had made this discovery, so important for his stomach, he developed an insatiable appetite for these musical academies. He concentrated on singing as well as possible so as to become known as a clever singer and – this was his secret motive – would be everywhere in demand, thus finding opportunities to satisfy his nagging hunger. Who would have thought that the old saying, 'Make a virtue of necessity', would have to apply even to a genius? – But what am I saying? Does not everyday experience show that the goddess of hunger seeks out genius everywhere and, unbidden, thrusts herself on him as a companion throughout youth, and often throughout life?

As a choir-boy Haydn had many amusing adventures. Once, when the Court was building the summer castle at Schönbrunn, Haydn had to sing there in the choir during Whitsuntide. Except for the church services, he used to play with the other boys, climbing the scaffolding round the construction and making a terrible racket on the staging. What happened? The boys suddenly beheld a lady. It was the Empress Maria Theresa herself, who ordered someone to get the noisy boys off the scaffolding and to threaten them with a thrashing if they dare to be caught there again. The next day Haydn, driven by curiosity, climbed the scaffolding alone, was caught and collected the promised thrashing [*Schilling*].

Many years later, when Haydn was in the service of Prince Esterházy, the Empress came once to Esterhaz [Eszterháza, 1773]. Haydn presented himself before her and thanked her most humbly for the reward he had received. – He had to tell the whole story, which occasioned much merriment.

In nature there is no standing still. Haydn now had to discover that he was not destined to remain a choir-boy for ever. His beautiful voice, with which he had so often sung for his supper, suddenly betrayed him. It broke, and wavered between two whole notes [*zwischen Doppeltönen*].

The following anecdote Haydn told me at a later time, but it belongs to this period in which his voice broke. At the ceremony performed every year at Klosterneuburg [the celebrated Monastery of the Augustinian Canons on the Danube, upstream from Vienna] in honour of St Leopold, the Empress Maria Theresa usually appeared. The Empress had already let it be said in jest to *Kapellmeister* Reutern, 'Joseph Haydn doesn't sing any more; he crows.' So Reutern had to replace Joseph with another soprano for the ceremony. His choice fell on Joseph's brother, Michael, who sang so beautifully that the Empress had him called before her and presented him with 24 ducats.

'Michael,' Reutern asked him, 'now what will you do with all that money?' Michael thought for a short moment and answered: 'One of our father's animals has just died, so I shall send him 12 ducats; I would ask you to keep the other 12 for me until *my* voice breaks, too.' Reutern took the money but forgot to give it back.

Since Haydn, with his cracked voice, was unfit to be a choir-boy any more and thus had no monetary value for *Kapellmeister* Reutern, the latter found it only quite fair to discharge him.

A piece of mischief on Haydn's part hastened his dismissal. One of the other choir-boys, contrary to the usual custom of a choir-boy at that time, wore his long hair in a pigtail, and Haydn, just for the fun of it, cut it off. Reutern called him to account and sentenced him to a caning on the palm of the hand. The moment of punishment arrived. Haydn tried every way to escape it and finally declared he would rather not be a choir-boy any more and would leave at once rather than be punished. 'That won't help,' answered Reutern, 'first you'll be caned and then march!'*

Reutern kept his word, and so it was that the cashiered choir-boy, helpless, without money, with three mean shirts and a worn coat, stepped into the great world that he knew nothing about. His parents were very upset. Especially the tender motherly heart showed her anxiety with tears in her eyes. She implored her son that 'he might yet accede to the parental desires and prayers and dedicate himself to the priesthood'. This wish had lain slumbering for ten years, and it now awoke, its force undiminished. The parents gave their son no peace; they were sure that they must impose their will on him, but Haydn remained unswerving in his purpose and paid no attention. It is true that he could not provide any reasons for opposing his parents' wishes; he considered that he had explained things clearly enough when he squeezed the force of genius, mysterious even to himself, into the few words, 'I don't want to be a priest'. But how could this answer satisfy his parents? How could they imagine the development of their son's talents, or the future, so fortunate and so full of fame, when Haydn himself entertained no such thoughts, and when he understood just a little as did his parents what genius was, knew nothing of the pride that usually conquers the youthful genius, and was himself blessed with no insight whatever?

* [Original footnote:] Both Joseph and Michael Haydn appear to have vexed *Kapellmeister* Reutern quite often, who punished them frequently. When Michael was in Vienna in 1801, he once passed the Choir School in company with intimate friends. Here he stopped and, with a smile, said: 'In that dear house for many a year I collected a thrashing [*Schilling*] every week.'

Haydn's education was at best patchy: he received a solid grounding in musical performance; at Hainburg he learned to play every instrument, 'even the timpani', and years later in London George Smart, substituting for the absent timpani player in the Haydn–Salomon orchestra of 1794, relates how Haydn afterwards

came to me at the top of the orchestra, praised my beating in time, but observed upon my bringing the drumstick straight down, instead of giving an oblique stroke, and keeping it too long upon the drum, consequently stopping its vibration. 'The drummers in Germany,' he said, 'have a way of using the drumsticks so as not to stop the vibration' – at the same time showing how this was done ...[3]

But if Haydn's practical musical training was in some respects thorough, even that aspect of his education was lacking compositional finesse; although as a young man recently expelled from the Choir School of St Stephen's Cathedral he composed prolifically, as he said himself in his Autobiographical Sketch of 1776, he did so 'not quite correctly, until at last I had the good fortune to learn the true fundamentals of composition from the celebrated Herr Porpora (who was at the time in

Vienna)'. Haydn refers, of course, to Nicola Antonio Porpora (1686–1768), famous for his operas. Georg Reutter, from whom Haydn received some sporadic lessons in composition, was not only Chapel Master at St Stephen's but held several other posts in Vienna as well, as organist and conductor. His church music was very well known, and Haydn undoubtedly profited from it. But altogether, as Haydn himself relates, he had ample opportunity to study a quantity of great music then in vogue, secular and sacred, Italian and local. Italian opera dominated the stage all over Europe and the imperial court in Vienna had always welcomed Italian composers and singers. But there was also a healthy and thoroughly native school which especially produced original instrumental music—touched, no doubt, with the rosy light from south of the Alps, but nevertheless containing markedly Austrian traits – waltz-like minuets and trios, an earthy sense of melody closely allied to the kind of tunes sung in the tavern and in the fields, and a special propensity for exploiting the wind instruments. Horn-playing, a skill imported, like the playing of other wind instruments, from nearby Bohemia, flourished as never in Italy: wind bands were becoming fashionable (again as never in Italy or indeed at that time in other musical centres of Europe such as England). All this Haydn eagerly absorbed; but compared to the Jesuit education which his brother Johann Michael was soon to enjoy in Vienna, Haydn's knowledge of literature (for instance) was limited in the extreme, and this gap in his education was to serve him ill throughout his life. Now let us use the accounts of Griesinger and, after him, Dies once again to flesh out the bare hones of Haydn's existence in the period after he left St Stephen's and his numerous duties there – which seem to have included participating in the funeral services for Antonio Vivaldi, who died in poverty in Vienna in 1741 (*C&W*, I, 58):

... Soon after his departure from the Choir School, Haydn made a pilgrimage to Mariazell.[1] In his pocket he had several motets which he had composed and asked the *Regens chori* there for permission to put out the parts in the church and sing them. This request was refused, and in order to gain a hearing he had recourse to a trick on the following day. He stationed himself behind the boy who was to sing the alto part and offered him a seventeen-kreuzer piece to give up his place to him; but the boy, fearing the director, did not dare make the bargain, whereupon Haydn reached swiftly over the boy's head, seized the music from the stand and sang to general satisfaction. The *Regens chori* made a collection of sixteen gulden and sent the optimistic lad back to Vienna with the sum in his pocket.

Haydn was dismissed from the Choir School in his sixteenth year[2] because his voice had broken; he could not hope for the least support from his poor parents and thus was obliged to make his own way simply by his talents. He took lodgings in a wretched garret (in the house No. 1220 in the Michaelerplatz)[3] in Vienna, without a stove, and where he was barely protected from the rain. Deprived of life's comforts, he divided his whole time among giving lessons, studying his art and performing. He played for money in evening serenades and in the orchestras, and studied composition diligently, for 'when I was sitting at my old, worm-eaten spinet [*Klavier*] I envied no king his lot'. About this time Haydn came upon the first six sonatas of Emanuel Bach;[4] 'I did not leave my clavier until I had played them through, and whoever knows me thoroughly must discover that I owe a great deal to Emanuel Bach, that I understood him and have studied him with diligence. Emanuel Bach once paid me a compliment on that score himself.'

In the same house wherein Joseph Haydn was quartered there also lived the famous poet Metastasio.[5] He was educating a Fräulein Martinez. Haydn had to give her singing and harpsichord lessons, in return for which he received free board for three years. At Metastasio's Haydn was also introduced to the then aged *Kapellmeister* Porpora. Porpora gave voice lessons to the mistress of the Venetian ambassador, Correr, and since Porpora was too grand and too fond of his ease to accompany her on the fortepiano himself, he entrusted this business to our Giuseppe. 'There was no want of *Asino, Coglione, Birbante* and pokes in the ribs; but I put up with all of it because I greatly profited from Porpora in singing, in composition and in the Italian language.' Correr went in the summer with the lady to the then much frequented baths at Mannersdorf,[6] not far from Bruk [*sic*]; Porpora also went there to continue the lessons and took Haydn with him. For three months Haydn acted as Porpora's servant, eating at Correr's officers' table and receiving six ducats a month. Here he sometimes had to accompany on the keyboard [*Klavier*] for Porpora at a Prince von Hildburghausen's,[7] in the presence of Gluck, Wagenseil and other celebrated masters; and the approval of such connoisseurs was a special encouragement to him.

The author was told by a very reliable source that the violinist Misliwezech,[8] a Bohemian by birth, had heard some quartets performed during his stay in Milan; and when they told him that the composer was Johann Baptista Sammartini,[9] then a man of seventy, he had cried out in utter astonishment, 'At last I know Haydn's precursor, and the model on which he patterned himself!' It seemed to me worthwhile to investigate this statement more closely, since I had never heard Haydn's originality doubted, especially in his quartets. So I enquired of Haydn if he had known Sammartini's works in his youth, and what he thought of that *compositeur*. Haydn told me that he had in fact heard Sammartini's music but he had never valued it, 'for Sammartini was a scribbler [*Schmierer*]'. He laughed heartily when I produced Misliwezech's supposed discovery, and said he recognized only Emanuel Bach as his prototype ...   [pp. 11f.]

In the beginning Haydn received only two gulden a month for giving lessons, but gradually the price rose to five gulden, so that he was able to look about for more suitable quarters. When he was living in the Seilerstadt [Seilerstätte], all his few possessions were stolen. Haydn wrote to his parents, asking them to send some linen to make a few shirts; his father came to Vienna, brought his son a seventeen-kreuzer coin and the advice, 'Fear God, and love thy neighbour!' Haydn soon saw his loss restored by the generosity of good friends; one had a dark suit made for him, another gave him shirts [*Wäsche*, also underclothing] etc., and Haydn recovered through a stay of two months with Baron Fürnberg that cost him nothing. In this period Haydn was also leader of the orchestra in the Convent of the Hospitallers [Barmherzige Brüder][10] in the Leopoldstadt, at sixty gulden a year. Here he had to be in the church at eight o'clock in the morning on Sundays and feast days, and at ten o'clock he played the organ in what was then the chapel of Count Haugwitz,[11] and at eleven o'clock he sang at St Stephen's. He was paid seventeen kreuzer for each service. In the evenings, Haydn often went 'gassatim'[12] with his musical comrades, when one of his compositions was usually performed, and he recalled having composed a quintet[13] for that purpose in the year 1753.

Once they went to serenade the wife of Kurz,[14] a comic actor very popular at that time and usually called 'Bernadon'. Kurz came into the street and asked for the *compositeur* of the music just performed. Hardly had Haydn, who was then about nineteen, identified himself when Kurz urged him to write an opera for him. In vain Haydn pleaded his youth; Kurz encouraged him, and Haydn actually composed the opera, *Der krumme Teufel* – a satire on the lame theatre director Affligio,[15] on whose account it was banned after the third performance.

Haydn liked to linger over the history of his first operatic composition, because it reminded him of Bernadon's many comic traits. Harlequin fled from the waves in *Der krumme Teufel*; to illustrate this, Bernadon lay down at full length across several chairs and imitated all the movements of a swimmer. 'See me swimming! See me swimming!', cried Kurz to Haydn, sitting at the keyboard [*Klavier*], who immediately fell into six-eight time, to the poet's great satisfaction. – When Haydn had finished his opera, he brought it to Kurz. The maid wanted to send him away because her master was at his studies. But through a window in the door Haydn, to his astonishment, saw Bernadon standing before a large mirror, grimacing and performing the most ridiculous contortions with his hands and feet. Those were the studies of Herr Bernadon. – Haydn received four and twenty ducats for the opera, a sum which at that time he considered made him a rich man.

Apart from performing and teaching, Haydn was indefatigable in his composing. Many of his easy harpsichord lessons [*Klaviersonaten*], trios, and so on belong to this period, and he generally took into consideration the needs and capacities of his pupils. Only a few of the originals remained in his possession: he gave them away and considered it an honour when they were accepted; he was not aware of the fact that the music dealers were doing a good business with them, and he loitered with pleasure in front of the shops where the one or the other of his works in print were displayed. ...[16]   [pp. 13f.]

Notes:

1 The vast pilgrimage church in Styria, dedicated to Our Lady, is still Austria's most popular. For Haydn's private thank-offerings to the friendly monks at Mariazell, and Our Lady (for Whom the church is named, 'Maria Zell'), see *C&W*, II, 120ff., 467. The *Regens chori* at that time was P. Florian Wrastil (Pohl I, 121).

2 Surely too early (1747/8).

3 The house, next to St Michael's Church, still exists, but has been slightly altered since then.

4 J. F. Rochlitz, in *Für Freunde der Tonkunst*, IV (Leipzig 1832), quotes Haydn as saying, 'I played them over for my own pleasure countless times, especially when I was burdened by cares or discouraged, and they always cheered me up and I left the instrument in a good mood.' In 1742, C. P. E. Bach's so-called 'Prussian' Sonatas, *Sei Sonate per cembalo*, dedicated to Frederick the Great, were published in Nuremberg.

5 Pietro Metastasio (1698–1782), Imperial Court Poet, who lived for fifty-three years in the house and died there. In 1779 Haydn would set to music his text of *L'isola disabitata*. Anna Katharina ('Marianne') von Martinez (Martines) (1744–1812) studied with Haydn and later became a singer, harpsichord player and a successful composer.

6 Bad Mannersdorf is still a modest but successful spa.

7 Joseph Friedrich, Prince von Sachsen-Hildburghausen (1702–87), who befriended the composer Carl Ditters (later von Dittersdorf; 1739–99), and was himself a well-known general and man-of-politics. See Chapter II of Dittersdorf's *Lebensbeschreibung*.

8 Joseph Misliweczek (Mislivecek; 1737–81), whose operas were performed successfully in Italy and who was a friend of the Mozart family.

9 Giovanni Battista Sammartini (1700/01–75), the celebrated Italian composer.

10 The Church and Hospital still flourish.

11 Friedrich Wilhelm, Count Haugwitz, who held a ministerial position at Court.

12 'Gassatim' is believed to have its origin in the word 'Gasse' (little street) and to have been manipulated into the piece of music, 'Gassatio' = 'Cassatio'. The term's origin has been the subject of much speculation, largely idle.

13 Believed to be the Quintet in G (II:2), of which there is a Berlin ms. dated 1754.

14 Johann Joseph Felix Kurz (theatrical name: Bernadon; 1717–84). His first wife was Franziska (died 1755).

15 Giuseppe Afflisio (*recte*; *c.* 1720–1787).

16 Haydn's works were not printed until 1764 – and then, moreover, by publishers in Paris. Perhaps Griesinger means that handwritten copies were placed on display.

Dies provides us with some interesting details not found in the otherwise more reliable account by Griesinger. He recounts, for instance, that such was Haydn's desperate state, and especially his actual hunger, 'that against all inclination he decided to enter the Servite Order simply in order to eat his fill.' Dies (pp. 32–7) also gives us two delightful vignettes of the young composer's rather robust sense of humour (which seems to have prevailed over his momentary ambition to join the Church):

Haydn once took it into his head to invite a number of musicians for an evening serenade [*Nachtmusik*]. The rendezvous was in the Tiefer Graben,[1] where the musicians were to place themselves, some in front of houses and some in corners. There was even a kettledrummer on the high bridge. Most of the players had no idea why they had been summoned, and each had been told to play whatever he wanted. Hardly had this hideous concert begun when the astonished residents of the Tiefer Graben opened their windows and began to scold, to hiss and to whistle at the accursed music from hell. Meanwhile the watchmen, or as they were then called, the *Rumorknechte*,[2] appeared. The players escaped in time, except the kettledrummer and a violinist, both of whom were led away under arrest; however, they were set at liberty after a few days since they could not name the ringleader.

The well-known Ditters[3] and Haydn were youthful friends. Once the two were roaming the streets at night and stopped in front of a common beer hall in which half drunken and sleepy musicians were miserably fiddling away at a Haydn minuet. In those days Haydn composed pieces for the dance halls that, because of their originality, were much in favour.

'Hey, let's go in!', said Haydn.

'In we go!', Ditters agreed.

Into the beer hall they go. Haydn places himself next to the first violinist and asks off-handedly, 'Who wrote that minuet?' The latter answers, still more drily, indeed sharply. 'By Haydn!' Haydn goes and stands in front of him says with feigned wrath, 'That's a pig of a minuet.' – 'What, what, what?' yells the violinist, now in a rage himself, jumping out of his seat, followed by the other players, who are about to break their instruments over Haydn's head; and they would have, too, if Ditters, who was a big man, had not put up his arms to shield Haydn and shoved him out through the door.

Notes:
1 Tiefer Graben is in the old part (inner city) of Vienna and the high bridge still exists.
2 A kind of police force – in modern parlance 'riot squad'.
3 Carl Ditters, later von Dittersdorf.

Another point on which Dies differs from Griesinger is in the section concerning Haydn's study of and admiration for C. P. E. Bach. Griesinger says specifically that Haydn 'came upon the first six sonatas of Emanuel Bach', whereas Dies gives another version, according to which Haydn came upon the theoretical writings of C. P. E. Bach – the famous *Versuch über die wahre Art das Clavier zu spielen* (Berlin 1753) – in a Viennese bookshop. Haydn began to leaf through the book, 'understood that which he had sought, paid for the book, and took it away with great delight'. Haydn also studied the theoretical works of other masters, and Dies cites *inter alia* Haydn's second acquisition as Mattheson's *Der vollkommene Kapellmeister*, which Griesinger also mentions as one of Haydn's theoretical sources. But Dies adds amusingly that although Haydn found the principles good, he considered the written-out examples 'dry and tasteless' and 'set himself the task of rewriting all the examples in this book. He retained the whole framework, even the identical number of notes, and invented new melodies for it.'

Dies then continues with his narration, ending with the story of *Der krumme Teufel*, for which (he relates) 'Haydn received 25 ducats [Griesinger, '24'] and considered himself rich'. From another piece of contemporary evidence, we know that Haydn's *Der krumme Teufel*, of which every scrap of music is lost despite its immediate success and its many repetitions throughout German-speaking Europe until the end of the 1770s, was certainly performed in Vienna at the Kärntnerthortheater on 29 May 1753 and brought in substantial box-office receipts (only four other performances in May earned more). It is, however, likely that Haydn contributed other music to Kurz's operas, of which a substantial amount has survived in one contemporary ms. source (*C&W*, I, 101f.).

On 21 February 1754, Haydn's mother died in Rohrau, aged forty-seven. In 1762 and 1764, Joseph received part of her legacy – it took a long time in those days for such legacies to be put into operation. And in that same year, 1754, we have documentary evidence about Joseph's highly talented brother, Michael (he too hardly used his first given name), who had also been a choir-boy under Reutter and then attended the Jesuit Seminary in Vienna. Michael's first known work, the brilliant *Missa in honorem Sanctissimae Trinitatis* of 1754, with scintillating high trumpets and timpani far outshines the earliest known works of his brother, the *Missae breves* in F and G. From this scarcely documented period we have a charming little note from Father Mathias to 'Hanßmichl' (Johann Michael's nickname), which happily breaks into the poverty-stricken 'years of the galley' (to use the Verdian phrase about *his* similar experience in his youth) of Joseph and, presumably, Michael, and suggests a pleasant weekend party in Rohrau for the two Haydn brothers, their friend 'Ehrrath' and the three young ladies:

Jesus Christ be praised!
My very dearest Hanßmichl, I am herewith sending you a carriage from Rohrau which can bring you and perhaps a good friend back and forth, and the driver will spend the night in the Landstraß at the Falcon or the Angel; you can talk to him and arrange that you and Joseph and perhaps Ehrrath, all three of you, can get on the road early on Saturday. Mistress Nänerl and Mistress Loßl and another young lady will also receive a carriage, but only very early because it's so pitch dark at night, so heartfelt greetings to all of you, and in God's name

Mathias Haydn

Michael Haydn obtained an interesting position with the Bishop of Großwardein (now Oradea Mare in Romania), where in 1760 we find him composing symphonies, concertos and church music – all highly individual works which are in many respects more immediately arresting than those that his brother was composing at the same time. The year before, in 1759, Michael had undertaken the pilgrimage walk to Mariazell and composed an Ave Regina for the Benedictine priory there (*C&W*, I, 80n.).

Gradually, as Joseph Haydn's modest career began to prosper in the capital, we hear, from Griesinger (15), that the young man 'had often received assistance in Vienna (in the Landstraße), at the home of a hairdresser named Keller; he also gave music lessons to their elder daughter, and with closer acquaintance he grew increasingly fond of her. But she entered a nunnery.' In fact, Haydn fell in love with the younger daughter, Therese (born in 1733, she outlived Haydn, reaching the ripe old age of eighty-six). She took her vows on 12 May 1756, and Haydn preserved two of the works he played and conducted for this (for him) sad occasion – the remarkable and poignant Salve Regina in E and the Organ Concerto in C (XVIII:1); possibly he also performed the Double Concerto in F for Organ and Violin (XVIII:6). Four years later, Haydn made the fateful mistake of marrying Therese's sister, who – in Griesinger's phrase – 'kept pressing the matter'. About Haydn's unhappy marriage, we have evidence from Griesinger (who actually met Frau Haydn in 1799). He states (15):

Haydn had no children by this marriage. 'My wife was incapable of having children, and thus I was less indifferent to the charms of other women.' Altogether his choice was not a happy one, for his wife had a domineering, unfriendly character; and he had carefully to hide his income from her since she was a spendthrift. She was also bigoted, and was always inviting clergymen to dinner; she had many masses said and was rather more liberal in her support of charity than her financial situation allowed. Once, when Haydn had done someone a favour for which he would take no recompense, it was suggested that I [Griesinger] offer something to his wife instead; he answered me 'She doesn't deserve anything, for it is a matter of indifference to her whether her husband is a cobbler or an artist.' She died in the summer of 1800 at Baden, near Vienna.

From the marriage documents, dated 17 November 1760 (*C&W*, I, 247f.), we learn that Haydn obligated himself to deposit the huge sum of 1,000 gulden (equivalent to 2¼ years' of his salary at that time) as 'matching sum' (*Wiederlage*) for his wife's dowry. This substantial amount of capital can only represent (unless Haydn borrowed some of the money) a measure of the success with which the composer was now selling manuscript copies of his works; for this was the fashion in which a young Austrian musician made money in those days, not by causing his works to be printed (the trade was in its infancy in Vienna then), but by selling them in manuscript. As for Maria Anna Aloysia Apollonia Haydn, it must be remembered that history has recorded only Joseph's side of the story; certainly Frau Haydn had to put up with many infidelities on her husband's part. But the sources also suggest that Frau Haydn later loved the court painter at Eszterháza, Ludwig Guttenbrunn (whose portrait of Haydn, reproduced in colour in *C&W*, II, is well known). At all events, it was not a good marriage and later reports seem to indicate that Frau Haydn would not have been able to match her husband's meteoric rise in the social scale (she spoke a primitive Viennese dialect and was totally uneducated).

Before Haydn entered into matrimony, however, his life had taken a marked turn for the better. The documents tell us the bare facts of the matter.

(1) Autobiographical Sketch, 1776:
... finally, by the recommendation of the late Herr von Fürnberg[1] (from whom I received many marks of favour), I was engaged as *Directeur* at Herr Count von Morzin's ...

(2) Griesinger (12f.):
... the following purely accidental circumstance had led him to try his hand at the composition of quartets. A Baron Fürnberg had an estate in Weinzierl,[2] several stages from Vienna; and from time to time he invited his parish priest, his estates manager, Haydn and Albrechtsberger (a brother of the well-known contrapuntist,[3] who played the violoncello) in order to have a little music. Fürnberg asked Haydn to write something that could be performed by these four friends of the art. Haydn, who was then eighteen[4] years old, accepted this proposal, and so originated his first quartet[5]

which, immediately it appeared, received such general approval that Haydn took courage to work further in this genre.

Notes:
1 Carl Joseph, *Edler* von Fürnberg, *Regierungsrath* in the Lower Austrian Government and I.R. *Truchseß* (which means, in effect, head of the Imperial Household), who died on 21 March 1767 at the age of forty-seven. His second wife, who was the hostess at Weinzierl in the 1750s, was Marie Antonie, *née* von Germetten; she died on 19 December 1779 at the age of fifty-two. Pohl I, 181.
2 Weinzierl Castle, which still survives more or less intact, is some distance from Melk Abbey and a few miles from the pretty old town of Wieselburg, in Lower Austria. It is now an agricultural school.
3 The contrapuntist and teacher of Beethoven was Johann Georg Albrechtsberger (born at Klosterneuburg 1732, died Vienna 1809); his brother was Antonius Johannes, born at Klosterneuburg on 20 November 1729. Anton Johann was also a composer, like his younger brother, and he became *Kapellmeister* to the Bishop of Wiener Neustadt.
4 It is now generally believed that Haydn was not eighteen but about twenty-five when he wrote these works.
5 Op.1 no.1.

In 1932, a distinguished Austrian art historian, Fritz Dworschak, published a highly important article[5] which did not receive the attention it deserved. In it, Dworschak was able to show that Johann Georg Albrechtsberger was a fellow student of Michael Haydn's in the Jesuit Seminary in Vienna (1753–4). From 1755 to 1756 (or perhaps to 1757) Albrechtsberger was in Raab (Györ, Hungary), but from September 1757 to April 1759 he was organist at Maria Taferl, about a dozen kilometres from Weinzierl Castle, and later he occupied this post at Melk Abbey. Dworschak suggests that the estates' manager was the 'Pfleger' Matthias Leonhard Penzinger and the priest Johann Joseph Fromiller, 'Benefiziat an der Josephskapelle im Schlosse' (St Joseph's Chapel, which still exists). The commemorative tablet that records Haydn's presence in Weinzierl also suggests 1757–9 as the period in question.

Abbé Stadler, Haydn's friend, writes in his ms. memoirs:[6]

> Joseph Haydn, who at this time composed his first divertimenti near Melk at Freyherr v. Firmberg's [*sic*] – at which Albrechtsberger played violoncello – heard him [Albrechtsberger], admired his artistry, and assured him that he had never heard such perfection on an organ.
> [Later, we hear of another group including the composer Florian Leopold] Gaßmann, in whose fugal quartets he [Albrechtsberger] often played the violoncello ...

Obviously with the evidence at our disposal, we cannot solve the problem of the Albrechtsberger brothers, but if we accept Griesinger's statement that the cellist was Anton Johann, then the chronological postulate involving Johann Georg must be dismissed. Nevertheless, we believe that *c.*1757 is the correct date for the first string quartets. First, the Fürnberg/Morzin sources of op. 1 nos. 1, 2, 4 and 6 use the spelling 'Minuet', which Haydn writes only up to (and including) 1760, whereas in the authentic sources of op. 2 nos. 1, 2 and 6, we find 'Menuet', which suggests a slightly later date (1760–2?). Secondly, we have some very early works by Haydn, such as the *Missa brevis* in G, 'Rorate coeli desuper' (see p. 55), or the Cassation in A (II:A1), where there are really serious problems of faulty composition. The quartets, on the other hand, are of flawless construction and cannot be the work of the eighteen-year-old Haydn (1750). Thirdly, there are no dated ms. copies earlier than 1762 and no prints earlier than 1764; it is unlikely that works written in 1750 and achieving instant popularity would have to wait twelve years before circulating to Göttweig and Melk and fourteen years to reach the Paris presses. Finally, we adduce a bit of evidence connected with the Seven Years' War, which was raging in 1757 (Battle of Kolin) and 1758 (Battle of Hochkirch). The Austrians took a number of Prussian prisoners; the officers, considered gentlemen and men of their word, were quartered 'on good behaviour' throughout the estates of the Lower Austrian nobility. One such prisoner was a Prussian major named Weirach. Weirach told the German composer and writer Johann Friedrich Reichardt 'that during the Seven Years' War he was taken prisoner and was quartered with the nobleman on whose estates Haydn was born [i.e. at Rohrau Castle], and he heard that artist, as modest as his genius was great, himself playing his first quartets. Haydn called them Cassatios – a word that means the same as Notturno or Serenada, altogether a "piece of music" that at the same time is suitable for performance outside. The man was modest to the point of timidity, despite the fact that everybody present was enchanted [*entzückt*] by these compositions, and he was not to be persuaded that his works were worthy of being presented to the musical world ...'[7]

Apart from the interesting fact that Haydn was now (1757–8) being invited to musical parties at the castle of his former Lord – which must have been a welcome improvement for his hungry and penniless condition – the story confirms the date of 1757–8 for the performances of Haydn's obviously new quartets, albeit at Rohrau and not at Weinzierl.

About Haydn's second appointment as music director, we hear from Griesinger (14 f.):

> In the year 1759 Haydn was engaged as Music Director to Count Morzin[1] in Vienna at a salary of two hundred gulden, free lodging and board at the officers' table. Here he was finally able to enjoy the happiness of a carefree existence; he was quite contented. He spent the winter in Vienna and the summer in Bohemia near Pilsen.[2] He used to like to relate, in later years, how one day he was sitting at the harpsichord [*Klavier*], and the beautiful Countess

Morzin leaned over him in order to see the notes, when her neckerchief came undone. 'It was the first time I had ever seen such a sight; I became confused, my playing faltered, my fingers became glued to the keys. – What is that, Haydn, what are you doing? cried the Countess; most respectfully I answered: But, Countess, your grace, who would not be undone at such a sight?'

... As Music Director in the service of Count Morzin Haydn composed his First Symphony:[3]

NOTES

1 Ferdinand Maximilan Franz, Count Morzin (1693–1763); for details of the family see *C&W*, I, 235n.
2 In Unter-Lukavec (Dolní-Lukavice), usually referred to simply as Lukavec; the castle, which still stands, is now used as a mental hospital.
3 Griesinger was quite right; Haydn's First Symphony really was the work cited, though it was probably composed earlier than 1759.

Since the discovery of a copy, dated 1758, of Symphony no. 37 in the Schwarzenberg Archives in Český Krumlov, it is thought that Haydn may have erred by a year or two in quoting his engagement with Count Morzin; but the discovery of a whole series of Fürnberg copies of Haydn's early symphonies, numbered by the composer, suggests that no. 1 was indeed the first (*C&W*, I, 240, 250ff., 280ff.). These authentic copies of symphonies suggest in the number of their used duplicate parts (as opposed to what one might call 'archive' duplicate parts) that Fürnberg's band, and possibly therefore Morzin's also, consisted of at least six, possibly eight, violins (two Violin I, two Violin II parts copied), while in the *basso* section (two parts copied) there were at least one cello, one bassoon and one double bass (*violone*). There was also a wind-band sextet (oboes, bassoons, horns). Unfortunately, the Morzin Archives for the relevant period have never been discovered, hence our knowledge of Haydn and his association with the family is based on such evidence as Griesinger's account and on the ms. parts (discovered in a remote Hungarian castle after World War II) containing the only known authentic sources for Haydn's early quartets, string trios and horn sextets.

Dies's description (49) of Haydn's transition from service in the Morzin family to the Esterházys reads as follows:

A year passed without Count Morzin's learning of his *Kapellmeister*'s marriage; but it happened that Haydn's situation took a different turn. The Count found it necessary to reduce his hitherto great expenses. He dismissed his virtuosi and Haydn thus lost his post as *Kapellmeister*.

Meanwhile, public opinion proved to be a great recommendation for Haydn. His attractive character was known. Count Morzin was at pains to be of service. Three circumstances which fortunately occurred simultaneously enabled Haydn, when he ceased being (in the year 1760) *Kapellmeister* to Count Morzin, to become *Vizekapellmeister*, under the direction of *Kapellmeister* Gregorius Werner, in the service of Prince Anton Esterházy de Galantha at Eisenstadt with a salary of 400 fl. [Original footnote: Apart from the salary, persons in princely service enjoy other advantages, such as free lodgings, firewood, etc.] This gentleman gave Haydn the four periods of the day [morning, noon, evening, night] as the theme of a composition; he wrote them in the form of quartets which are very little known. ...

Prince Paul Anton Esterházy, then, was to be Haydn's new patron; he was the head of a family in whose service Haydn would remain until he died (the visits to

England were accomplished 'on leave', as it were, from the family service). Dies finishes the paragraph by suggesting that Paul Anton's first orders to Haydn were for the composition of three (in fact) symphonies. The autograph of one, no.7 in C ('Le midi'), has survived and is dated 1761; the flanking ones, nos. 6 ('Le matin') and 8 ('Le soir'), may be thus assigned to the same year. But before we enter into details, a short survey of the extraordinary family with which Haydn was now associated would be appropriate.

The fortunes of the Esterházys were inexorably intermingled with those of their rulers, the Habsburgs; the Esterházys always proved loyal to the crown, and for that unswerving loyalty they were richly rewarded. Their first rewards came as a result of the crown's war against the Protestants: the Bohemians had been fatally attracted to the new religion and, when the Counter-Reformation had crushed them, Bohemian lands were redistributed to faithful Catholic supporters by the Austrian Emperor, Ferdinand II (reigned 1619–37). The Esterházys were so-called 'new noblemen', having been created barons only in 1613 and counts in 1626. The Esterházy family fortunes were also greatly increased by clever marriages (rather like those famous Habsburg marriages which culminated in the witty saying, 'Tu felix Austria, nube'). That, combined with the expulsion of the Turks, created one of the wealthiest Hungarian noble families almost overnight (the commission entrusted with redistributing former Turkish lands allotted 140,000 acres to the Esterházys). Emperor Leopold I created Count Paul Esterházy (1635–1715) a prince; the next day he (as Palatine of Hungary) and the Archbishop of Gran placed the Hungarian Crown of St Stephen on the Imperial head. Paul had been educated by the Jesuits and led huge processions to the pilgrimage church of Mariazell; he used to call himself 'the lowliest servant of Our Dear Lady'. Paul was also an ardent musician and in 1711 he had printed his famous music collection, entitled 'Harmonia caelestis', which has been revived with great success in our age. It is adroit, civilized music with a genuine melodic flair and sophisticated orchestration.

In 1712, the new Emperor, Charles VI, conferred on the family the hereditary rank of prince, by which the eldest son inherited the title automatically (*primogenitur*). By this time their principal residence was Eisenstadt Castle, which was gradually growing into a provincial music centre. When Prince Michael died on 24 March 1721, there was no direct heir, and the title passed to his half-brother Joseph. Joseph died on 7 June, however, and the title passed to his son, Paul Anton, then only ten years old; hence until he came of age, his mother (Princess Maria Octavia) and his guardian, Count Georg Erdödy, acted as regents. The young prince's guardian was a member of a family with which the Esterházys and also Haydn were to have continuing contact all through the century (culminating in Haydn's dedication of his set of quartets, op.76, published in 1799, to Count Joseph Erdödy). On 10 May 1728, Princess Maria Octavia, probably at her son's instigation, engaged a new *Kapellmeister*, Gregor Joseph Werner, an astute musician who was to head the family's musical activities until his death in 1766. Werner composed enormous numbers of works for the Esterházys, primarily religious music, some of which has been revived with considerable applause in recent years.

Prince Paul Anton and his younger brother, Count Nicolaus (born 18 December 1714), had studied with the Jesuits and both were intensely musical, Nicolaus even more so than his brother. Paul Anton played violin, flute and lute, Nicolaus the viola da gamba and violoncello. Paul Anton studied at the University of Leyden (he was enrolled in the autumn of 1731) and on 26 December 1734 he married a noble Italian lady, Maria Anna, Marchesa di Lunati-Visconti, at Lunéville; the couple had no children. Paul Anton at first pursued a military career and under Empress

Maria Theresa rose to be a Field-Marshal and then (1750–2) became Austrian Minister Extraordinary to the Court of Naples. When he returned, he gave orders for a theatre to be constructed at Eisenstadt Castle, for strolling players to perform comedies and to permit modest operatic performances (often necessitating the importation of part of the ensemble from Vienna) to be staged.

No doubt Haydn's sober conduct and religious fervour were strong factors in his favour with the Esterházy family: the Esterházys were firm patrons of the pilgrimage church of Our Lady at Mariazell, to which Haydn not only made the pilgrimage but also (no doubt with Esterházy support) contributed two masses. Haydn was now to become an Esterházy 'house officer'. He was officially engaged on 1 May 1761, although he already acted for the family in an unofficial capacity before that date. The document has become a classic, and since it has been reproduced countless times, we need only summarize its contents. In the first paragraph it is rather tactfully explained that the old and faithful Gregor Werner will continue to retain his title of Full Chapel Master (*Ober-Capel-Meister*) and will be in charge of the church music, whereas the new Vice Chapel Master (*Vice-Capel-Meister*) will take charge of the orchestra and generally manage the court's musical affairs. Haydn is to be 'considered and treated as a house officer' and is to be temperate and treat the musicians under him 'with mildness and leniency'. Both he and they are to present themselves attired 'neatly in white stockings, white linen, powdered, and with either pigtail or hair-bag, but otherwise of identical appearance'. Haydn is to 'abstain from undue familiarity' with the musicians so as to preserve a distance between them and himself, 'for these subordinates should the more remember their respectful duties if it be considered how unpleasant to the *Herrschaft* must be the consequences of any discord or dispute'. Haydn 'shall be under permanent obligation to compose such pieces of music as his Serene Princely Highness may command,' and these pieces are to be the exclusive property of the court and may not be distributed elsewhere; nor may Haydn compose music for anyone else. 'The said Joseph Heÿden [*sic*] shall appear daily (whether here in Vienna or on the estates) in the *antichambre* before and after midday, and inquire whether a high princely order for a musical performance has been given.' Haydn is not to bother the prince with minor infractions of discipline, etc., but in cases where Haydn is not able to settle a dispute or cannot act as intermediary, 'then his Serene Princely Highness must be respectfully informed'. Haydn is to take charge of 'all the music and musical instruments' and is to 'instruct the female vocalists, in order that they may not again forget (when staying in the country) that which they have been taught with much effort and at great expense in Vienna'. Haydn, who was proficient on various instruments, is enjoined to practise 'on all those with which he is acquainted'. His annual salary was 400 florins, to be paid quarterly, and when 'on the estates' he shall 'board at the officers' table or receive half-a-gulden in lieu therefor'. The contract, drawn up on 1 May 1761, was to hold good for at least three years. If Haydn wished to leave, he should give six months' notice. The final clause of this contract states:

14mo. The *Herrschafft* undertakes not only to retain the said Joseph Heÿden in his service during this period, but should he provide complete satisfaction, he may look forward to the position of *Ober-Capel-Meister*. On the other hand, his Highness is free at all times to dismiss him from his service, also during the period in question. In witness whereof, two identical copies of this document have been prepared and exchanged. Given at Vienna this 1st of Maÿ 1761.

[signed] Joseph Haydn mpria.

This extraordinarily detailed contract has been the subject of widespread comment, but the astonishment expressed concerning its language and supposedly debasing content was perhaps partly because the other contracts with Prince Paul Anton (and later with Prince Nicolaus, where the language was retained) were not available for comparison. Many of the 'debasing' clauses were simply standard procedure for all house officers' contracts with the family. It is certainly not true that Haydn was treated like a servant. On the contrary, there was a vast difference between a real servant (and they, too, were subdivided into classes) and a house officer. The language in which a prince of the Holy Roman Empire expected to be addressed, either *viva voce* or in writing, will be evident from other documents quoted in this biography. The fawning, flattering and demeaning addresses and good wishes for name-days and birthdays strike oddly on the twentieth-century ear, but they were common all over Europe. As a contract, Haydn's was as fair and proper as would have been possible anywhere on the Continent, and there can be no doubt that Haydn signed it with relief, joy and high hopes.

What kind of patrons were Paul Anton and his wife, *née* Marchesa di Lunati-Visconti (who would outlive her husband by two decades, dying on 4 July 1782 at Eisenstadt)? Of the four Esterházy princes under whom Haydn served, Paul Anton and Anton (reigned 1790–4) are the least known, possibly because the former appears in Haydn's life only for some eight-and-a-half months and the latter also rather briefly (and during the time when Haydn was mostly away in England).

The princely couple lived a life of ostentatious magnificence, as might be expected. Their clothes were made in Paris, probably with the aid of dummies (*mannequins*) which the tailors had prepared when the couple visited France, and which could be brought up to date as necessary. The sums for these clothes were astronomical, reaching 11,384 livres – or 4,552 gulden – for the year 1759 alone, which was more than ten times the size of Haydn's salary when he was engaged, and more than one-third of the total budget (12,939 Fl.) for the *Herrschaft* Eisenstadt of the year 1763.

The Prince was a great linguist (German, French, Italian), to which must be added his fluent knowledge of Latin, the language used for much of the official correspondence, particularly with Austrian government officials and even with other Hungarian officials (these outgoing letters have been preserved in enormous bound folio volumes: Esterházy Archives, Budapest, Magyar Országos Levéltár).[8] The Princess also learned good German (not exactly a habit with Italians, even when they lived for years in a German-speaking country, e.g. Pietro Travaglia, the princely stage designer): the *Prothocollum Missilium* of this period (1758–62) contains a series of German letters dictated by Princess Maria Anna, and they reveal a quick and intelligent mind. She retained her good looks until old age.

Prince Paul Anton brought back many books from his travels, the catalogue of which filled a large folio volume as early as 1738. It is interesting to see that he ordered from Holland books by Jean-Jacques Rousseau which the Austrian censor would hardly have allowed to pass into Maria Theresa's dominions, but which the Prince (with his diplomatic connections) managed to have conveyed to Eisenstadt without difficulty (*C&W*, I, 324).

Otherwise, apart from the evidence of their education, breeding, high cultural standards in general and their knowledge and appreciation of music, the princely couple remain a rather shadowy pair in the Haydn literature. But we may assume that it was no accident that Haydn wrote one of his most beautiful and successful operas, *L'infedeltà delusa*, to celebrate the (by then) Dowager Princess's name-day in 1773.

Paul Anton's younger brother, Count Nicolaus, who would be Haydn's princely patron from 1762 to 1790, must now demand our attention. Like Paul Anton, Nicolaus was a good musician and became one of the greatest connoisseurs of *settecento* Central Europe. Like his elder brother, Nicolaus pursued a military career with considerable distinction, particularly as Colonel at the Battle of Kolin (1757) in the Seven Years' War where, with great personal courage, he led the wavering cavalry troops to victory. He was later made a Lieutenant Field-Marshal. On 4 March 1737, he had married *Freiin* Marie Elisabeth, daughter of *Reichsgraf* (Count of the Holy Roman Empire) Ferdinand von Weissenwolf.

Nicolaus returned from the wars to live modestly in a hunting lodge at Süttör on the Neusiedlersee (Lake Neusiedl) in Hungary. The brothers were fond of each other, and Prince Paul Anton took the trouble to write congratulatory letters to his brother (which happen to have survived because, being semi-official, they were entered into the *Prothocollum Missilium*) on the occasion of Nicolaus's birth- or name-day. Here is a specimen from the Esterházy Archives:[9]

To the good Nicolas Esterházy, Brother of the Prince, from Vienna, 5th Xbris [Dec.] 761 autograph letter of congratulation.

Highly respected *H[er]r Bruder*,

Although you are long assured of my unwavering friendship, brotherly love and devotion, it is nevertheless a particular pleasure for me to confirm them to you in writing on the occasion of your name-day, and especially to add the sincere wish, in which my consort, your Princess, joins me, that my highly respected brother [*Herr Bruder*] may enjoy not only the forthcoming name-day, but many more in years to come, in constant good health, and may continue to live in the present prosperity and in the most pleasant satisfaction. With which I remain for my whole life with deepest esteem, my highly respected *H[err] Bruder*'s

most devoted
brother and servant
Anton *Fürst* Esterhazy.

Nicolaus engaged strolling players, marionette troupes and Gypsy dance bands in Süttör. He was always devoted to music, and immediately recognized Haydn's talent. This biography occupies itself in considerable detail with Prince Nicolaus, and we may thus limit ourselves here to pointing out that, with his military education, he sometimes tended to treat his court employees like foot soldiers, and in this army-like discipline he was materially aided by his Estates Manager, Peter Ludwig von Rahier, also a former military man. Nicolaus's love of music amounted almost to an obsession, and there is evidence, especially in the account of him in Framery's *Notice* (1810, based largely on reports from Haydn's former pupil Ignaz Pleyel, who was at Eszterháza, 1772–7), that he had bouts of serious, perhaps even manic, depression. Nicolaus attempted, with all his military severity, to be scrupulously just. Rahier who, judged only from the evidence of his correspondence with and about the musicians, appears to have been a rather cold, despotic official, was in fact an excellent right-hand man for Nicolaus. The hundreds of letters in the Rahier correspondence files of the Esterházy Archives in Budapest show that he made every effort to be impartial, scrupulously correct (though formal and, with his inferiors, *de haut en bas*), often taking immense pains over the fate of his and the Prince's *Unterthanen*. Indeed, this biography will record at least one interesting case of his intervening with Prince Nicolaus on behalf of the musicians (see p. 46). To take a case concerning the Prince's and Rahier's efforts to avoid bribery, corruption and financial inefficency, we may mention a letter in the period under review (30 September 1765) from Nicolaus to Rahier. The first part deals with the bassoon player, Georg Schwenda, who had incurred 'passive debts' with the princely cashier's office ('which was hitherto unknown to me') and had petitioned the Prince to change his mind about fining Schwenda 10 ducats (42 Fl. 20 Kr.), which represented more than two months' salary (20 Fl. per month), no doubt for some misdemeanour. The Prince agreed to this and then went on to the next point: the former Administrator of the Castle and lands at Kreutz (now Deutsch-Kreutz), one Tergovihich (Fergovichi) was caught undertaking dubious financial transactions ('malversationes') by his cashkeeper Zöchmeister who, however, did not report them at once 'but waited until they had multiplied'. The Prince made an example of Zöchmeister, too, dismissing him from service, and, furthermore, Rahier was to dismiss 'not only the Judge at Kreutz but also the other members of the Jury, who certainly knew all about the administrator's *malversationen* and neverthe-less said nothing; and to replace them with others …' (*C&W*, I, 326).

The amount of detailed supervision and decisions required by Rahier and, in turn, the Prince just in the day-to-day management of the huge estates proved to be staggering. We are fortunate in having, in the Esterházy Archives, one of the most complete extant records of a great central European noble house. The *Haydn Yearbook* is currently engaged in publishing the entire 'Acta Musicalia', but among these documents there are also files concerning many non-musical matters – hous-ing problems, agriculture, questions of law and all sorts of disputes. Some of these documents are amusing, some dreadful, some infinitely touching – a large slice of eighteenth-century life in all its manifold aspects.

Haydn, as we know, was in a position of authority with the Esterházy family at least a month before he was contractually engaged on 1 May 1761. In April, he was engaging new musicians and causing others in Eisenstadt to be dismissed (hence he must have gone there to hear them in order to judge their efficiency or lack of the same). The band which was now in Haydn's charge was small but very select; it was not, in fact, an 'orchestra' in the modern sense but rather a chamber group, consisting of one flute, two oboes, two bassoons, two horns, five violinists and viola players (including Haydn himself and the bass singer Melchior Grießler, who is listed as 'Bassist und Violinist'), and one cellist. The second bassoon player, Georg Schwenda, was also a double-bass player, hence there is only one bassoon part in Symphonies nos. 6–8 ('Le matin', 'Le midi', 'Le soir'). In the works of the early 1760s that Haydn composed for the Esterházy family there are never parts for trumpets and timpani in the secular works, though the early Te Deum for Prince Nicolaus (1762 or 1763, perhaps) contains those parts (the players must have been engaged separately, as was frequently the case). There were enough good singers for Haydn to mount a by no means uncomplicated opera, *Acide*, in 1763 using only his own personnel (five soloists). Among the famous virtuosi were Luigi Toma-sini, the leader; Joseph Weigl, cello; and the tenor Carl Friberth, whose Italian was sufficiently good for him later to fashion a libretto for Haydn, *L'incontro improvviso* (1775).

It seems certain that Symphonies nos. 6–8 were first performed in the great hall of the Esterházy palace in the Wallnerstraße, Vienna, in May or June 1761. Prince Paul Anton's health was already undermined by the illness which would prove fatal the following year. A friend of the family, young Carl, Count Zinzendorf (1739–1813), kept a diary from 1761 until his death, and from it we learn a great deal about the Esterházys of this period. On 1 April 1761 he wrote: 'Le Prince Esterhazy étoit encore malade …' (*C&W*, I, 346). Haydn's immediate superior, *Kapellmeister* Gregor Joseph Werner, was at Eisenstadt and directed the church music. Relations between the two men steadily deteriorated, culminating in the bitter letter which marks the end of this period (see p. 47). But at the beginning, all was well, and in a

French report of 1810 (*C&W*, I, 347) we read, 'Werner conceived a liking for Haydn, and gave him lessons and advice ...'; later he would become angry and embittered as a result of his jealousy of Haydn's talents and of his sense of outrage at the younger man's easy-going way with the music library and lack of interest in enforcing strict discipline among the musicians.

In accordance with the terms of his contract, Haydn was expected to present himself daily, in full livery, in the princely antechamber; later he told Griesinger (p. 58) that his habit of being dressed and ready early in the morning dated from the time of his service with the Esterházys, when his Prince often 'called for him unexpectedly'.

Meanwhile, in Eisenstadt, a new theatre was being constructed in the garden behind the Castle, where it was to be placed in a huge glass dome. Count Jacob Durazzo (1717–94) – whose vast music collection later contained all those precious Vivaldiana which form the *corpus* of the composer's works and are now in the Biblioteca Nazionale, Turin – was in charge of the theatrical construction; later he became famous as the protector of Gluck, and still later he went to live in Venice. Haydn later wrote, in a letter dated 20 March 1783, 'I value Count Durazzo's house above all others' (*C&W*, II, 473).

But by the middle of October, Zinzendorf was writing in his diary that Prince Paul Anton 'a l'air d'un mort'. Haydn, meanwhile, was gradually learning to be a courtier, an art in which he soon excelled: for a large part of his activities were those of a skilled diplomat, acting as a buffer between the musicians and the princely administration. This book will show many instances of Haydn rescuing individual musicians from dismissal or punishments. In the process of becoming a courtier, it is always important to know when to remain firm, and Framery (no doubt via Pleyel, Haydn's pupil) tells us of such an instance, where Haydn was 'protected' by the man who drew up his contract, the princely 'secrétaire', Johann Stifftel. The *Haus-Hofmeister* (or major-domo), one J. Neumann, tried to oust Haydn from his newly assigned place at the officers' table. Haydn refused to budge, whereupon Neumann took Haydn's place-setting and moved it down to the end of the table. 'Without saying a word, the Secretary went and took his place next to that now assigned to Haydn; the other officers followed suit' and the furious major-domo was left in solitary splendour at his end of the table. The matter was taken before the Prince, who said to Haydn, 'You have offended an old servant of this House, whom I hold in high regard ...'. Haydn tried to defend his position and ended by saying, 'his pretension and his way of insisting were an insult which your *Capellmeister* found it impossible to tolerate.' The report continues: 'The Prince smiled, and promised to arrange the affair ...; the next day [Neumann] was given another place ...' (*C&W*, I, 365). Thus did Haydn learn the art of diplomacy and courtly intrigue.

One interesting aspect of Haydn's special relationship with his employer was the matter of his salary: officially, this was 400 gulden p. a., but in the Esterházy Archives a document has been discovered, dated 1 November 1761, in which Haydn receives an additional 50 fl. for the quarter 1 August–31 October (facsimile, *CCLN*, facing p. 106) from the privy purse ('Cammer Beutel'). What can this extraordinary state of affairs mean? Apparently, that Haydn was receiving secretly, perhaps so as not to offend Werner (who also received 400 gulden), an additonal 200 gulden p.a. When Prince Nicolaus succeeded to the title, one of his first acts was to make this additional salary official (25 June 1762: *C&W*, I, 372), possibly because he was less inclined to spare Werner's feelings (after all, it was his brother Paul Anton who had engaged Werner).

Count Zinzendorf's diary for March 1762 records the wretched health of Prince Paul Anton, who died at 3 a.m. on 18 March; his widow fled the house and took refuge at her mother-in-law's (Princess Maria Octavia). It must have been during the period of mourning (during which only church music was allowed) that the new Prince, Nicolaus – later known as 'The Magnificent' – reassured his *Kapellmeister* that he and the other musicians would be retained in service.

Prince Nicolaus was to prove an excellent head-of-court. No doubt his military training assisted him in developing the qualities of a leader, but by the time of his death in 1790 he had, by wise financial management, greatly increased the wealth of the family estates. Part of this successful management depended on having scrupulously honest, efficient, humane officials, to which end we find him issuing a detailed printed document to his subordinates (see *C&W*, I, 368f.) which contains all manner of amusing instructions and advice ('locks on the granaries must be subject to checks'; 'officials must be polite'; 'intoxication is the greatest vice'; 'the bee-hives are to be counted'; 'officials must lead God-fearing lives').

On 12 May 1762, an Italian opera company came to visit Eisenstadt. They were under the direction of Girolamo Bon (or Le Bon), whose wife Rosa and daughter Anna also appeared as singers. Carl Friberth had previously been with the company, which obviously had a good reputation, and later it supplied the Esterházys with the tenor Leopold Dichtler (who joined the *Capelle* on 1 March 1763). In 1762 they were put up at the Griffin Inn, remaining to the end of June. It proved to be the end of the little company, however, because Prince Nicolaus liked them so much that he forthwith engaged Bon and his family, as from 1 July. Bon was a man of many talents, an excellent stage-designer and painter, writer of libretti and impresario, also a composer (*Sei facili Sonate*, Nuremberg 1752). He was of great help to the budding Esterházy opera establishment, and it is now thought that he may have fashioned the texts to Haydn's Italian cantatas composed for the Prince in 1763 and 1764.

On 3 July 1762, Haydn's wife Maria Anna became godmother to a daughter of the later famous horn player Joseph (not Ignaz) Leutgeb and his wife in Vienna, at the parish church of St Ulrich. Obviously Haydn could not get away from his duties at Eisenstadt, which were increasingly onerous; but it is thought that for the occasion he wrote the Horn Concerto in D (VIId:3) for his friend Leutgeb to perform; the autograph is dated 1762 and contains, towards the end, the famous mix-up of staves over which Haydn amusingly notes 'In Schlaff geschrieben' ('written while asleep'). It was not the only concerto Haydn was writing in those days: the quickest way to a musician's heart is to write a concerto for him, and Haydn composed in the early 1760s violin concertos for Luigi Tomasini (including the popular C major work), a double-bass concerto for Schwenda in 1763 (alas, lost), as well as concertos for flute (lost) and two for cello (one of these [VIIb:1] now ranks among Haydn's best-loved works; the ms. parts were discovered in Prague in 1961).

It must have been after the accession of Prince Nicolaus that the court painter, Johann Basilius Grundmann, was commissioned to paint Haydn's portrait in his blue livery with silver braid trimmings. It was in this uniform that old Mathias Haydn saw his son when he came to visit him at Eisenstadt; at that time Mathias heard many compliments from Prince Nicolaus about his son's talents (Griesinger, 15f.).

The Esterházy court, in those days, generally spent the summers in Eisenstadt and the winters in Vienna. On 19 February 1763, Zinzendorf reports a large dinner at the palace in the Wallnerstraße; later there was a 'grand Concert' (*C&W*, I, 384).

Two of the symphonies that Haydn wrote in 1763 could have been played at such a concert: no. 12 or no. 40, with its delightful final fugue. In April a brilliant horn player, Carl Franz, was engaged, and – judging from the incredibly difficult music Haydn composed for him – he must have been one of the great horn virtuosi of all time. And on 1 August a new hunting-horn player, Franz Reiner, the fourth of the group, joined the *Capelle*. In a recently discovered document from the Archives, which will be quoted *in extenso* below, the princely copyist lists 'Parts for a new Sinfonia in D with all instruments … 17 [bifolium sheets]', which can only refer to Symphony no. 72, with its improbably difficult four horn parts (rising at once to sounding *f sharp*"), as well as flute, solo violin, solo cello, solo double bass, two oboes, bassoon and strings. Another symphony with four horns was no. 13, using the instruments in a different way, with organ-like sonority in 'holding' notes. Haydn was, like the right by which his Empress ruled, a pragmatist: if four horn players were available, then display their skills to his Prince (and for the players' delight).[10]

Dance music, which of course was a part of all festivities, was always – as far as we can tell from the documents – performed by visiting musicians from the local Eisenstadt *Thurnermeister* (Anton Höld) and his men: they supplied two violins and a double bass for the dance music 'provided at the marriage of His Excellency Anton Esterhazy' (*H-S*, IV, 175f.) and a further two trumpets and timpani used to accompany the fireworks. (Did they perhaps play in the new Haydn setting of the Te Deum?)

Throughout this period, Haydn was sufferng from continual strain: we can see this in the bills in his name at the Hospitallers (Barmherzige Brüder, an Order with which he had been on friendly terms ever since he had been the leader of the orchestra of their Vienna Chapter): in 1763 we find a steady stream of laxatives, purgative medicines, medicines for wind in the stomach, *Electuarium* (a mixture of various medicines with prunes, and sometimes honey, used as a strong laxative), and so on (*H-S*, IV, docs. 85, 89, 102, 113, 175, etc.), so it must have been something of a relief when Prince Nicolaus left for a long journey to Italy (26 April till the end of July). When he returned, he had to deal with one of the grimmer documents now in the Esterházy Archives: it concerns a poor music copyist, who entered the following petition (which was rejected) to the Prince:

Most Serene Highness and Noble Prince of the Holy Roman Empire Gracious and Dread Lord!

It will be known to Your Serene Princely Highness in your infinite grace that I, a poor copyist, Antonj Adolph, have often submissively requested Your Princely Highness in your gracious mercy to improve my yearly salary; for I, a poor man, who is also married, have no more each month than twelve gulden in cash, together with the livery like other servants, and from this my meagre salary I must not only pay for my lodgings but also for wood, candles, and must support myself, miserably, even though I am crushed with work, so that as copyist I work day and night to supply the operas and comedies, as the enclosed list will attest. And not only must I copy all this but even supply my own ink.

Considering that for all this I receive only 12 fl. and the livery (but without coat), it is difficult especially when it rains or snows, which is bad for the paper I take back and forth; that I have to pay for lodgings, wood and especially candles because I have to write so much at night; that my yearly salary, which is anyway not large, is stretched to the utmost; therefore I beg Your Serene Princely Highness on my knees, in humility and submissiveness, that in your graciousness (known to the whole world) you grant me some improvement in my monthly salary, or something towards lodgings, wood or candles; for which act of grace God the Almighty will reward you richly, but I with my poor wife will pray to God every day in our prayers to grant rich blessings to Your Serene Princely Highness. And so I comfort myself that you will heed this request, and remain, Your Serene Princely Highness's

Humble and Submissive Servant,
Antonj Adolph

Specification

What was copied for Your Serene Princely Highness for operas and comedies, paper lined, and copied, from 3 May to the month of August this year 1763, viz.

	Whole Bogen [4 pages]
First. Opera Vocal score, together with the Recitatives for Friedberg [Friberth] of L'Mantile	24.
Sinfonia ex D	14.
paper lined with music staves	96.
Opera vocal score for Bon	40.
lined the paper for composing, 6 books, makes	144.
Music ordered by Your Serene Highness and sent to Italy:	
I^{mo} } written	14.
item }	18.
lined	48.
written	34.
Ditto }	71.
item } written	15.
Ditto }	9.
Opera vocal score L'Mantile for the Italian, written	48.
Ditto, lined, 4 books, makes	100.
written	5.
item for the new Comedy L'Marchese, violin & Bass	18.
Parts for a new Sinfonia ex D with all instruments	17.
Ditto a new Concerto for Schwenda on the double bass	13.
item 6 new Trios, written	18.
Lined	72.
item, ditto, lined	14.

Summa 832.
[*H-S*, IV, 182 f.]

Prince Esterházy (and Rahier) had an open ear for many petitions, but they obviously thought that in this instance Adolph's salary, low though it was, could have been considered what the market would bear. Indeed, after Adolph fled the Prince's service in May 1764, his place was taken by Haydn's principal copyist, Joseph Elssler, who seemed able to manage on the 12 gulden and livery. In the document quoted, the second part provides important evidence for the dating of the works listed: the lost double-bass concerto Haydn composed for Schwenda; the identification of Giuseppe Scarlatti's (or possibly Domenico Fischietti's) *Il mercato di Malmantile* (libretto by Carlo Goldoni), of which Haydn owned a copy of the libretto (with its curious reference to the Baron of Ripafratta of *L'infedeltà delusa* fame: see p. 122); but, most important, a new date for Haydn's delightful *La Marchesa Nespola*. On the autograph of this work (in the Esterházy Archives in Budapest) the date has been heavily altered by Haydn himself (perhaps 1761 at first, then 1762 or even 1763); but surely 'new Comedy' must mean that – although the number of bifolium sheets is only for two of the parts and hence small – the work was 'new' in the late spring and summer of 1763. The first Symphony in D must be no. 13, also with four horn parts; the trios at the end are possibly baryton trios (the baryton being an instrument like the viola da gamba, but with sympathetic vibrating strings; to which Prince Nicolaus was becoming ever more committed).

In the summer Mathias Haydn, now remarried, suffered an accident at Rohrau when a pile of wood collapsed on him; he died on 12 September and it took Joseph until 1787 (!) to receive his share of the inheritance, 67 fl. 21 kr. 3d., which he generously handed over to his brother Johann, the tenor (then in Eisenstadt as a member of the church choir).

Part of Haydn's many duties was the rather boring supervision of all the bills concerning the Esterházys' musical establishment; this supervision also included checking endless bills submitted by instrument makers for repairing harpsichords, supplying strings and horn crooks, etc.; but even these mundane details contribute to our detailed knowledge of life at Eisenstadt and, later, Eszterháza. From bills concerning replacement strings for the double bass (e.g. *C&W*, I, 390 f.) of 1763, we can see that Haydn's double bass was tuned in the fashion of a *Cammer Violon* (small bass)

and indeed this is the tuning that Haydn uses for his double-bass solo in the Trios of Symphonies nos. 6 and 8 (in this group of symphonies, the exception is no. 7, where the low A-string is tuned to the adjacent G, used only once as an open string).

In the spring of 1764, Haydn had another respite from his onerous duties when Prince Nicolaus was sent to the Coronation in Frankfurt of Archduke Joseph as King of the Holy Roman Empire. Nicolaus was the First Ambassador of the Elector of Bohemia, and Goethe, who saw him in Frankfurt, thought Esterházy 'not tall, though well-formed, lively, and at the same time eminently decorous, without pride or coldness' (*C&W*, I, 393). While the Prince was away in March and April, Haydn suddenly renewed his interest in the harpsichord and began to practise, also causing an organ builder from Wiener Neustadt to come in April to tune, string and effect other repairs to the princely harpsichord (the man, Herr Zierengast, was illiterate and Haydn himself wrote out his bill so that it could be paid – a nice touch from the busy *Kapellmeister*). One manifestation of all this sudden preoccupation with the harpsichord is the greatly increased amount of solo keyboard music that Haydn began to write for himself: first the extended solo in the cantata 'Da qual gioja improv(v)iso' (XXIVa:3), which tells us in its libretto (probably fashioned by Le Bon) the occasion for which it was composed and performed: 'Which day is this?'. The answer is our amiable sovereign has returned from that place 'where the [River] Main washes its banks.' Also in 1764, Haydn composed a 'Divertimento per Cembalo' (XIV:4) with accompaniment of strings, another aspect of this renewed interest in harpsichord playing. And for the Prince's nameday on 6 December he wrote another cantata, 'Qual dubbio' (XXIVa:4), with an elaborate harpsichord solo for himself – this perhaps in response to a hint from Esterházy ('Don't you play the harpsichord any more, Haydn?'). In any event, the gain is ours, also in the rich vein of harpsichord sonatas that soon begin to come from Haydn's pen as the 1760s progress.

In the summer of 1764, Haydn and the *Capelle* journeyed to the Esterházy Castle of Kittsee, across the Danube from Pressburg (now Bratislava), where the Hungarian Diet met: hence Emperor Francis Stephen, who had business at Pressburg, came to Kittsee on 1–3 and 26 September. Earlier (beginning at the end of June) there had been opera performances there, and two opera libretti were later printed (order dated 29 December 1764): no copies have survived, but it is thought possible that one opera was a revived version of Haydn's *Acide* which was still in the repertoire in 1773. We have one document about wine consumed at Kittsee and Pressburg on 14 July 1764, and as late as 17 December the musicians were rewarded with six bottles of white wine, one bottle of vermouth, two of champagne, one of Cyprus, half-a-bottle of muscat, three of tokay and twenty-six bottles of officer's wine – not a bad finish to a lively operatic entertainment (*H-S*, IV, 201, 205, 206 f.; *C&W*, I, 399 ff.). But all this frenetic activity took its toll on Haydn's health, and at the end of December he applied to the Prince to receive *gratis* medicine from the Hospitallers, who were financed and supported by the Esterházys. On 27 December Prince Nicolaus allowed Haydn his free medicine, but not the other musicians ('since they are in any case well paid and can secure their own necessary medicines'; *C&W*, I, 401).

From the year 1765 we have the earliest extant letters written by Haydn: the first is dated 23 January, reporting that the horn player Knoblauch had died and suggesting a replacement (interestingly, the player proposed was not accepted: Esterházy had his ideas, too). Haydn, in this same letter, tried once again without success to have free medicine given to his colleagues.

For Carnival, Prince Nicolaus engaged (as was the custom) strolling players from St Pölten; the troupe included the later famous Carl Marinelli, who was to found his own group, and other well-known actors and actresses. It was also the custom for Haydn to supply music (played by the *Capelle*) for the overtures, entr'actes, and so on: probably some of these were turned into symphonies (as was later the case with one known work, no. 60, for a Regnard play, *Le distrait*, 1773). Meanwhile, the four horns were again brought up to full strength (since Franz Reiner had left in December 1763), by engaging Franz Stamitz and Joseph Dietzl, and to celebrate the event Haydn wrote another 'hunting' symphony along the lines of no. 72 (misplaced in the old chronological list): this was no. 31 ('Mit dem Hornsignal') with four glorious horn parts and solo passages as in no. 72 (flute, violin, cello, double bass, but this time no bassoon). The band had grown, too, in other respects since 1761: in the pay-list of 1765 we note, apart from Werner's church music instrumental players, that all the singers (also those in Werner's *Capelle*) are to perform in church and in opera. There were no fewer than eight singers; however, the small group of string players (three violinists and viola players, one cellist, one double-bass player who was also second bassoonist) had not changed, though Haydn often played violin when he was not playing harpsichord (as in the operas and cantatas), and possibly the church musicians (two violinists and a double-bass player) contributed to opera performances when necessary.

On 18 August 1765, Emperor Francis Stephen died suddenly in Innsbruck (where he had gone to attend a family wedding): Prince Nicolaus was also present, faithfully playing the baryton when he had the time (and purchasing a new instrument as well). Joseph II now became co-ruler with his mother as long as she lived, an unhappy alliance (the headstrong Joseph wanting to turn the world upside down with his Enlightenment ideas) which ended only in 1780 with the Empress's death.

The course of Haydn's relations with his Prince had, on the whole, been a smooth one; the composer was certainly overworked, but his music was appreciated and he had a first-rate group of singers and players with whom to experiment and for whom his bold, new ideas must have been most stimulating. But now, in the autumn of 1765, relations between Haydn, Rahier, the Prince and the *Capelle* rapidly degenerated. It all started when the flautist Franz Sigl went out shooting and set the roof of a house on fire. They just managed to put out the fire and avoid an appalling catastrophe: the whole town could have burned down (this did happen three years later, with results that will be recounted below (see p. 105).

Prince Nicolaus at once had Sigl arrested and then dismissed. Haydn considered Sigl's arrest and dismissal wrong and protested to Rahier, who (as will be seen) flew into a rage and apparently put the matter in the darkest terms to the Prince who, in turn, reprimanded Haydn in a (lost) letter of 8 September. But Haydn himself was by now quite shocked by the whole affair, and especially by the conduct of Rahier. In all this Rahier's authority was fully backed by Esterházy, who wrote, 'in case such an occurrence should be repeated in my absence at any time in the future, and the musicians should object to your orders, you yourself, should it become necessary, should also have them arrested by the grenadiers, and I shall support you at all times.' Then came Haydn's amazing letter to the Prince:

SERENE HIGHNESS AND NOBLE PRINCE OF THE HOLY ROMAN EMPIRE, GRACIOUS AND DREAD LORD![1]

I have received with every submissive and dutiful respect YOUR ILLUSTRIOUS AND SERENE HIGHNESS' letter of the 8th inst. addressed to me, and I see from it that your Highness has taken it very amiss that I protested against the detention of the *flauto traverso* player Frantz Sigl to Herr von Rahier, whose commands I am now admonished to follow, in order that I may behave better in the future, on penalty of the dread displeasure of my SERENE HIGHNESS.

MOST SERENE HIGHNESS! GRACIOUS LORD! On behalf of the above-named *flauto traverso* player, because of whom the fire started, I went with the whole band to Herr von Rahier, and it was not on account of the detention, but only on account of the rude detention and the harsh treatment of the subject that I protested, but with all proper respect, to Herr von Rahier. But we could not get anywhere with the administrator, and I even had to put up with his slamming the door in my face, he addressed all the others in the 'Ihr' form[2] and threatened everyone with detention. Similarly, this very day Friberth fled excitedly from the *Regent's* passion (on account of not doffing his hat, which must have been an oversight), and does not dare to come home, because this same *Regent* pretends that the first-mentioned Friberth was rude to him, and that therefore he will mete out his own punishment. But I testify, as do all the other musicians, that Friberth did nothing else except, when the *Regent* threatened all of us with detention – and without any reason – he said he had no other master but HIS SERENE HIGHNESS, PRINCE ESTERHAZY. I myself told the *Regent* to complain to YOUR SERENE AND ILLUSTRIOUS HIGHNESS if he felt his own person to have been insulted, but I was given the answer that the *Regent* is his own judge and will mete out the punishment himself. Everyone is very upset on this account, these honourable men find this treatment very unfair and hope that YOUR SERENE AND GRACIOUS HIGHNESS' intentions certainly do not extend this far, and that for this reason you will graciously put a stop to such exercises of power [*Potere*] whereby anyone can be his own judge without differentiating between guilty and not guilty.

The orders of the oft-mentioned *Regent* (as YOUR SERENE AND GRACIOUS HIGHNESS knows anyway) have been correctly carried out at all times, and as often as I receive through him an order of YOUR SERENE AND GRACIOUS HIGHNESS, I shall always execute it to the best of my ability; if therefore the *Regent* has complained in this regard, it must be the result of his angry pen. But moreover YOUR SERENE AND ILLUSTRIOUS HIGHNESS must yourself remember, in your graciousness, that I cannot serve two masters, and cannot accept the commands of, and subordinate myself to, the administrator, for YOUR SERENE AND ILLUSTRIOUS HIGHNESS once said to me: COME FIRST TO ME, BECAUSE I AM HIS[3] MASTER.

---

1 'Durchleuchtig Hochgebohrner Reichsfürst. / Gnädigst Hochgebiettender Herr Herr!'
2 'die übrige gesamte per Ihr tractiret'. Instead of addressing them as 'Sie' (for the plural of 'Er'), Rahier called them 'Ihr', which is the plural of 'Du', used for menial servants, children, dogs (and, in the concentration camps of our own era, by the S.S. when addressing Jews).
3 'His' = 'your'; again, Haydn tells us that Prince Nicolaus referred to his *Kapellmeister* in the third person singular, 'Er' form (see note 2).

I am therefore confident that YOUR SERENE AND ILLUSTRIOUS HIGHNESS will not receive ungraciously this my most submissive and obedient letter, but will regard me and the whole *Musique* with gracious eyes, and, since everyone is desirous of this grace, that you will watch over us in fatherly protection. I hope for further marks of favour and grace from YOUR HIGHNESS and I remain ever, with every mark of profound respect,

YOUR SERENE AND GRACIOUS HIGHNESS'
most humble and obedient
Josephus Haydn.

Eisenstadt, 9th September 1765

In fact Rahier fully intended to arrest poor Friberth as well, as the following letter shows. But Haydn's intervention on all these levels seems to have had its wished-for effect; perhaps Rahier's anger had died down in the intervening four days, and possibly Prince Nicolaus put in a word to calm the irate spirits, but in any case Rahier's next letter is in a more civilized tone ('as', might have thought Esterházy, 'befits the language of an honourable princely court'). Unfortunately there was no way to save Sigl; but as we shall see, even that part of the story had a happier ending.

Most Serene, Nobly Born Prince of the Holy Roman Empire, Gracious Lord & Sire, etc., etc.

Yesterday *Kapellmeister* Hayden and Friberth were finally here before me; the latter sub-missively apologized for his recent offensive and improper language which was to lead to his arrest, and has asked that he be forgiven. I answered him that I had already informed Your Highness and that any further decision must be awaited from that source, but since he has submissively apologized, I would ask Your Highness with due respect this time graciously to leave it at the submissive apology; and, with respect, I would also ask for a confirmation of this.

This afternoon, in the presence of all the musicians, as was ordered, I had Siegl [*sic*] arrested and dismissed from service, and ordered the *Kapelmeister* [*sic*] to collect everything in the way of clothes, instruments and music which might belong to Your Highness, and finally that Chief Cashier Zoller pay him [Sigl] his final salary up to and including today.

The two hunting-horn players should have left for Süttör today, as Hayden informs me, but because one of them fell ill this morning and had to take some medicine and was therefore unable to travel, they will leave at daybreak tomorrow morning so as to be there at noon; and with this I remain, in profound respect,

Your Highness' etc.
Most obedient servant
P. L. Rahier mpria

Eisenstadt, 13th 7bris 765

On 15 September, Prince Nicolaus, who was staying at Süttör supervising work on the future Eszterháza Castle, replied to Rahier saying that in view of Friberth's apologies he should be retained in princely service,

but he is to be warned not to indulge in any insubordination, bad conduct or to stir up any trouble, as he was hitherto wont to do, otherwise he may be assured that one will not permit his presence in our service for a single moment ...   [*H-S*, IV, 221ff.]

Haydn's troubles were only beginning, however, for towards the end of October Gregor Werner, now old and embittered, wrote to Prince Nicolaus at Süttör:

HIGH BORN PRINCE OF THE HOLY ROMAN EMPIRE, GRACIOUS AND DREAD LORD!

I am forced to draw attention to the gross negligence in the local castle chapel, the un-necessarily large princely expenses, and the lazy idleness of the whole band, the principal responsibility for which must be laid at the door of the present director, who lets them all get away with everything, so as to receive the name of a good Heyden [*sic*]; for as God is my witness, things are much more disorderly than if the 7 children were about; it seems that there are only libertines among the chorus people, who according to their fancy take their recreation for 5 or even 6 weeks at a time: the poor chapel thus has only 5 or six at a pinch, also not one of them pays attention to what his neighbour is playing. Over half the choir's instruments are lost, and they were collected only seven years ago, after many requests, from the late lamented Prince. Apart from all that, now most of the church music itself goes out to all the world; before, the late organist took good care of it, but after his death it had to happen that I gave the key to the present *Capell Meister* to care for; but with the proviso that he should draw up a proper catalogue of the items in the choir-loft, and this should have been copied three times. One for Your Highness; the second for the princely book-keepers; the third deposited in the actual choir-loft. Herr Heyden most willingly agreed, also with the preparation of the catalogues, which he was to bring to my sick bed; but up to now nothing has been done.

The cabinet with the music, however, as true Christian men report to me, has been considerably depleted, which is the more easily credible if one considers that on my sick bed I have already had requests from three parties, asking if I could supply church music for them advantageously, since Vienna at present has a considerable lack of church composers.

I, however, left such letters unanswered. But it is easy to presume that they will have addressed their request to Heyden. Thus the church choir will be meanwhile depleted completely unless Heyden is seriously ordered to prepare a catologue at least of what pieces remain.

Incidentally, it is humbly requested: Your Princely Highness should give him a severe order that he must issue the strictest command to the princely musicians that they appear in the future, all of them without exception, at their duties. And because it is likely that he, Heyden, will try to lie his way out of it, the order must come from on high, that the extant choir instruments be examined, among which there must be 12 old and new violins.

Of the violas, 2 old and 2 new, but 2 Passetel [violoncellos] and 2 good large double basses: all too soon it will be seen where the truth lies.

Under the late lamented Prince, apart from the usual summer *fatigue*, it was ordered that in winter time we were to give two academies [concerts] a week in the princely officers' room, Tuesdays and Thursdays, for which two hours each was required. If this were to be reinstated now, the injurious laziness would be removed, and no longer would such bad practices obtain as, alas, experience has shown to have occurred.

Because today, as a very old man who has borne the title of *Capellmeister* here for 37 years, and because the price of wood has risen considerably, and I as a sick man cannot deal with the heating myself and am forced as a result to get outside people, who do not forget to look after their own interests, to come and do it.

Thus I mòst humbly beg your Princely Highness only out of pity to add two cords of wood to my emoluments [*Deputat*], for my constitution is so weakened by loss-of-weight, that my sick body consists of almost nothing except skin and bones. For such a stroke of generosity I will earnestly pray to God, not only as long as I am alive but also when I am dead, for your long and happy reign and for an increase of your rents and income.

With which I most humbly recommend myself to Your Highness' grace and favour, and remain,

> Your Serene Highness'
> most obedient servant
> Gregorius Werner

1765 in 8ᵇᵉʳ [October]

How much of this diatribe is true? Surely a part of it. Haydn was clearly easy-going, and discipline was probably not rigorous under his sympathetic leadership. Probably, too, the catalogue and condition of the music itself left a good deal to be desired. It is not likely that the masses, etc., were actually taken out and sold, but it is quite possible that some of the manuscripts were lent and never returned. Obviously it was found that no musical instruments were actually missing.

Prince Esterházy, seems to have taken this outburst with a grain of salt, for when he returned it to Rahier, it was accompanied by the following laconic note:

'Moreover, I attach the document of *Kapellmeister* Werner here; as concerns his laments, you will be in the best position to act on them' (Pohl I, 367). Some days went by. Apparently the famous *Regulatio Chori Kissmartoniensis* (cited overleaf) was, in its concept, the work of Rahier, which would explain its peremptory tone. We suspect that clauses 1–6 were *verbatim* the work of Rahier and that the last paragraph (concerning the lack of baryton trios) preceding 'Formulae' was by Prince Nicolaus himself.

It is one of the real tragedies for Haydn scholarship that this thematic catalogue has not survived. However, to redress the balance, it now seems clear that we owe the existence of Haydn's own thematic catalogue known to scholars as *EK* (*Entwurf-Katalog* or Draft Catalogue) to this storm-in-a-teacup. Haydn assembled all the works of which he still owned a copy – perhaps he had made his own lists, too – and had the princely copyist Joseph Elssler draw them up thematically. Haydn himself then added to this *corpus* as time went on, making entries sporadically until after the London journeys. We wonder if in fact *EK* is not Haydn's copy of a similar list presented as part of the (lost) *inventarium* to Prince Nicolaus as a living sign of dutiful and submissive diligence.

It was, of course, a great bore for Haydn to be saddled with all this administrative vituperation. And Rahier was often tediously pedantic: 'As I learn from outside sources, the musicians like to play, sometimes at Countess Lodron's, sometimes at Countess Amour's; if I knew that Your Highness did not approve, I would forbid it ...' (*H-S*, IV, 226). And Prince Nicolaus was not much better: he even occupied himself with the excessive use of wax candles in the Castle Chapel, and suggested that one could have a test case and see how long a wax candle (such as those then in use) actually burned, and expected an answer on the subject from Rahier: all this was hardly a fit subject for one of the great princes of the Holy Roman Empire and his *Regent*.

As far as Haydn's personal life at Eisenstadt is concerned, we know very little. He lived in an apartment in the 'Old Apothecary', and he seems to have employed a boy servant. At least that would appear to be the explanation for an unedifying legal wrangle involving accusations of stolen money recorded in the Town Books, in which Haydn's 'Godless boy', Ludwig Hähnl, is mentioned (*C&W*, I, 424).

Apart from typical manifestations of life in a small town during the period, Haydn had consolidated his position, both financially and in other ways. Despite the *Regulatio*, Haydn enjoyed the greatest confidence of his patron, and, all things considered, the history of Joseph Haydn and Nicolaus Esterházy is one that reflects the greatest credit on both sides. The two (for Esterházy's role cannot be underestimated) made cultural and musical history. Haydn was now sufficiently well situated to ask Prince Nicolaus if his brother Johann might come to Eisenstadt as an unpaid tenor in the *Chor Musique*. The Prince agreed and, in 1765, Johann joined the *Capelle* in an unpaid capacity, being supported by his brother.

About 1765, Haydn began to use the permanent services of Joseph Elssler, the princely copyist. Haydn became a kind of protector to the whole Elssler family, being present at their marriages and christenings, and finally engaging the son Johann as a permanent valet, factotum and copyist (Johann went with Haydn to England in 1794). Joseph Elssler's hand was clear and precise, and Haydn used him for the most important tasks, though of course there had to be many other copyists as well to cope with the enormous amount of scores and parts being produced. Joseph Elssler signed himself on a copy, dated 1771, of Haydn's Salve Regina (XXIIIb:2; the copy owned by the Gesellschaft der Musikfreunde, Vienna), which enables us to identify other examples of his hand.

[To Haydn. Draft of an Order from Prince Nicolaus Esterházy.]

Regulatio Chori Kissmartoniensis

Inasmuch as the musicians of the Eisenstadt Castle Chapel have produced a great disorder in the choir-loft, because of indolence and carelessness, and have neglected the instruments through poor care and storage, *Capellmeister* Hayden [*sic*] is herewith earnestly enjoined,

First, to prepare an inventory, in three identical copies, of all the instruments and music in the choir-loft, according to the enclosed formulae, with indication of the composers, number of parts, etc., to sign it and within eight days from today to deliver one to us, the second to the book-keeper's office, and the third to the choir-loft:

Secondly, the schoolmaster Joseph Diezl is to collect and distribute the necessary music before each choir service, and after the service to collect it and to see that it is properly returned to the cupboards wherein it belongs, locked, so that nothing will be removed or lost:

Thirdly, to see to it that the schoolmaster keeps all the choir instruments constantly in good repair and in proper order, to which end said schoolmaster is ordered to appear in the choir-loft one quarter of an hour before each service:

Fourthly, to take especial pains that all the members of the chapel appear regularly at the church services and fulfil their duty and obligations in a proper and disciplined fashion:

Fifthly, in our absence to hold two musical academies [concerts] each week in the Officers' Room at Eisenstadt, viz., on Tuesdays and Thursdays from two to four o'clock in the afternoon, which is to be given by all the musicians, and in order that

6thly, to assure that in future no one is absent without permission from the church services or the above-mentioned academies (as was the case hitherto), a written report will be delivered to us every fortnight, with the name of, and reason for, anyone presuming to absent themselves from duty.

[Nicolaus, Prince Esterházy]

Süttör, the [blank = 3 November] 1765

Finally, said *Capelmeister* [*sic*] Haydn is urgently enjoined to apply himself to composition more diligently than heretofore, and especially to write such pieces as can be played on the gamba [baryton], of which pieces we have seen very few up to now; and to be able to judge his diligence, he shall at all times send us the first copy, cleanly and carefully written, of each and every composition.

Formulae

Inventarium

Of the music and instruments which are under today's date found in the choir-loft of the Eisenstadt Castle, viz.:

Nro	Musicalien	Stimmen [parts]
I.	Missae Solemniores Missa Primitiva cum Tympanis et Clarinis. Here must follow the *incipit* with 2 or 3 bars of the organ part etc. Auth. Werner. E.g. with . . . . and thus the Masses, Vespers, Litanies, Symphonies, Offertories, etc., whatever is there.	10.

Instrumenten	Number
Violins old	
Violins new	
Violas old	
ditto new	
Bassetlen [violoncellos] old	
ditto new . . . . etc., etc.	

Eisenstadt the [blank] 7̄65̄

In 1765, Haydn is known to have composed at least four symphonies: nos. 28, 29, 30 ('Alleluja') and 31 ('Hornsignal') – not necessarily in that order – and probably many other works as well which cannot be dated precisely. But even these four works reveal a sure hand technically and an inner emotional stability, a maturity, which augured well for the future of the *Capelle*, and the future of music, too, though no one could yet foresee the effect that Haydn would have on that future.

II

Haydn's compositions
up to 1765

THE FIRST EXTANT WORK by Joseph Haydn that can be dated with any measure of certainty is the Mass in F major (XXII:1), composed in 1749. When Haydn rediscovered the mass in 1804–5, he was pleased to note 'a certain youthful fire' and it was probably then that he recalled having composed the work in 1749 (the date, not in Haydn's hand, was added to a manuscript copy of the organ part). Bibliographical information of even such limited certainty is the exception rather than the rule in Haydn's early output. Between 1749 and 1765 Haydn composed, at a conservative estimate, over 170 single works: sacred music, various types of opera, harpsichord sonatas, harpsichord trios, string quartets, miscellaneous divertimentos, dances, concertos and symphonies. Of these no more than approximately three dozen can be ascribed to a particular year. The middle decades of the eighteenth century were still a time when little value was placed on autograph manuscripts and Haydn kept very few from his first decade as a composer. From c. 1760 he seems to have dated his autograph scores as a matter of course and when he came across an early work that did not carry a date he would apply one retrospectively. Very few autographs, however, specify anything but the year.

Until he entered Count Morzin's service in 1759, Haydn had no regular employer, whether aristocratic or ecclesiastical. There was no pattern to Haydn's musical output and no institution to retain his music. Consequently, the vast bulk of his early compositions survive in manuscript copies only, with infrequent indications of date of composition. Unfortunately, as in the case of many other small aristocratic estates of the time, such as Großwardein where Michael Haydn and Dittersdorf each worked for some years, the library of the Morzin family has not survived and very little is known about Haydn's period of employment at Lukavec. From 1761, however, when Haydn was appointed *Vice-Capel-Meister* by Prince Paul Anton Esterházy, an abundance of documentary material is available, thus giving, for the first time in Haydn's career, a vivid picture of his compositional activities. The artistic security which the Esterházy court provided allowed Haydn's creative imagination to flourish, and the disciplined life of a courtier encouraged him to adopt a more orderly attitude to the preservation and dating of his music. No fewer than twenty-two of the twenty-seven surviving autographs up to the year 1765 are of works composed for the Esterházy court. For many early works that survive only in the form of manuscript copies, Haydn's own *Entwurf-Katalog*, begun in 1765, provides the sole proof of authorship, and the year 1765 is therefore a *terminus ante quem* for a large proportion of Haydn's early output; more precise dating within the period c. 1750–1765 is largely a matter of speculation, occasionally supported by snippets of pertinent biographical information.

Sacred vocal music

Given Haydn's constant exposure to church music in his youth, it is not surprising that the Mass in F major is one of his first compositions to have survived. It is a neat, concise work which, one imagines, cost the teenage composer much pains-taking but rewarding labour. A *missa brevis* designed for performance in the normal daily liturgy, its forces are typical of much contemporary Austrian church music: SATB choir with two soprano soloists, and accompaniment of two violins and con-tinuo. With the exception of the Benedictus, all the movements begin without in-strumental introductions and are led by the chorus, the two soloists providing brief melismatic decoration of the predominant homophony. Much of the Credo is polytextual, i.e. several different clauses of the text are sung simultaneously, a time-saving technique frequently encountered in *missa brevis* settings of the time. On reaching the clause 'Et incarnatus est' the declaimed text becomes a single, in-telligible one, the tempo changes from Allegro to Adagio and the harmony dark-ens; Haydn was never to tire of the expressive potential of gently emphasized aug-mented sixth and 4/2 chords in such contexts.

In the mass service the Host was consecrated and exhibited during the Benedic-tus, a spiritual highlight reflected in the musical treatment of the liturgical text by Haydn and his contemporaries. The setting of the single clause 'Benedictus qui venit in nomine Domini' ('Blessed is he that cometh in the name of the Lord') is noticeably expansive in comparison with the restrictive approach of other, sur-rounding movements. The key changes from the F major of the previous four movements to B flat, the tempo is a relaxed Andante, there are lengthy instrumen-tal passages and the word setting is characterized by liberal repetition and decora-tion. The ensuing repetition of the 'Osanna in excelsis' ('Hosanna in the highest') music from the Sanctus provides an uncomfortable jolt which, however, should not be taken as a sign of inexperience; many masses by the mature Haydn, as well as settings by Mozart and others, have this awkward gear-change.

After the customary slow-moving homophonic music in the minor for the Ag-nus Dei, the ensuing 'Dona nobis pacem' is set to the same music as the opening Kyrie (this is possible because the number of syllables and the stress pattern of the two clauses are the same with 'lei' of 'eleison' being treated as one rather than two syllables). Although Haydn employed this convenient framing procedure only once more in his masses, in the *Missa Sancti Nicolai* of 1772, its use was far more commonplace than its occurrence in Haydn's masses suggests.[1] Here, as in the similarly restrained *Missa Sancti Nicolai*, it provides a sense of calm control that would seem unconvincing in his later, emotionally diversified settings of the Ordinary.

Underneath the Mass in F major in the *Entwurf-Katalog*, the composer entered the *incipit* of the Mass in G major (XXII:3) with the title 'Rorate coeli desuper', a quotation from God's command to Cyrus, King of Persia, and the Lord's anointed ('Drop down, ye heavens, from above'; Isaiah xlv, 8); in the *Liber Usualis* this text features in the Introitus for the fourth Sunday in Advent. Whereas the F major Mass circulated quite extensively in the Austro-Hungarian Empire in the second half of the eighteenth century and Haydn himself in 1804-5 added (or supervised the addition of) wind parts, the history of the G major Mass is sketchy in the extreme and fraught with unresolved problems. The only source under Haydn's name is a set of manuscript parts discovered at Göttweig Abbey in 1957, in which the opening music is a little different from the *incipit* given in the *Entwurf-Katalog* and the title does not carry the appellation 'Rorate coeli desuper'. Neither of these discrepancies can be used to disprove Haydn's authorship conclusively. More unsettling is the existence of contemporary manuscript copies of the mass under the names of Georg Reutter and Ferdinand Arbesser (1720/1-95). To the sceptical two related questions pose themselves: can the conflicting attributions be ignored, and is the extant work necessarily the same as the one entered in Haydn's catalogue? Every one of the bibliographical objections can be dismissed reasonably on the grounds of clerical error and inconsistency, yet a glance at the score immediately sets an opposite train of thought in process. One commentator has called the music 'primitive'. Certainly it is *'brevis'* in the extreme; the polytextual Gloria and Credo movements consist of only nine and twenty-four bars respectively, and the normally expansive Benedictus has only eleven bars. There are no soloists and the harmony is marred by some crass errors of part-writing. But it is 'primitive' only in comparison with later and more familiar Haydn and, perhaps, with what we feel ought to be the standard ideally shown in a juvenile work of a great composer. However, similar gaucheries appear in several early compositions by Haydn (e.g. the motet 'Lauda Sion', the 'Seitenstetten' Minuets and the C major Organ Concerto, XVIII:1) and considered in this light the G major Mass appears as an indifferent early attempt at a composition by a student with little formal training. As for the more sure-footed F major Mass, it attains a degree of craftsmanship that was to take the best part of a decade to achieve consistently and with ease.

It is worth recalling that after these 'apprentice' works Haydn did not set the mass text again until seventeen years later, in 1766. Had he been employed in the 1750s at a church or as a *Regens chori* of a monastery (for which no monastic training was necessary), he would have composed several masses and doubtless some examples of the *'solemnis'* or *'longa'* type, but his personal circumstances meant that Haydn's sacred compositions (until he assumed the responsibilities of full *Kapellmeister* at Eszterháza in 1766) were occasional in circumstance and diverse in type. Towards the end of his life, the composition of the six late masses reflects a new energy that was partly the result of coming to the genre afresh after a break of fourteen years; similarly, the freshness and imagination of the masses composed between 1766 and 1775 might well have been less compelling had Haydn been required to contribute regularly to the genre in the 1750s.

Following the two masses, Haydn's next essay in church music was more ambitious, a set of four motets 'de Venerabili Sacramento' designed to be played during the procession of the Host at the Feast of Corpus Christi. In Austria this procession often took place out of doors and Haydn's four motets were probably sung in different locations, each representing one of the four quarters of the globe. Such *al fresco* performance would explain the forthright nature of the music. All the movements are in C major, 3/4 and marked Vivace; the choral writing (with some brief solo writing) is largely syllabic with little decoration; the strings of the orchestra (including a written-out viola part) double the voices, the first violins often heightening the intensity of the singing with measured tremolo; oboes and trumpets provide an additional sonority, the latter cutting through the texture with jubilant fanfares in a manner that can be traced back in Austrian church music to at least the early eighteenth century and one which Haydn was to make distinctly his own. No date of composition is forthcoming, but some awkward part-writing and the occasional unconvincing modulation suggest the early 1750s.

In later life Haydn recognized that some of his early music was technically defective. In the Autobiographical Sketch which he submitted for publication in the *Wiener Diarium* in 1776, he admitted 'I wrote diligently, but not quite correctly, until at last I had the good fortune to learn the true fundamentals of composition from the celebrated Herr Porpora'. The first work of church music that reveals this assurance is a Salve Regina in E major (XXIIIb:1), the first of two appealing settings of the Marian antiphon in Haydn's output. The autograph was retrospectively dated 1756 and the work may have been given its first performance that year at the ceremony in which Haydn's one-time love, Therese Keller, took the veil.

A new refinement and elegance is present throughout the Salve Regina, never more than in the opening orchestral paragraph quoted above. The contrast of register and sonority in the very first bar, the new sense of spaciousness that results from allowing secondary dominants in bars 6 and 8 to make their full impact and the manner in which dynamics help shape the melodic line are all signs of a new sensitivity. The choice of key, too, is notable: E major almost always elicits the best from Haydn at every stage of his career and in all genres. Other memorable E major movements and works include Symphony no. 12, Justice's aria in the 'Applausus' Cantata, Sonata III in the *Seven Words*, the slow movement of the 'Rider' Quartet (op.74 no.3) and the Introduction to Part III of *The Creation*. Haydn's experience with Porpora, the teacher of singing, is reflected in the presence of several vocal tricks of the trade: the long-note, *messa di voce* opening, the gentle florid decoration interposed with affecting rests, the elongated, mainly chromatic descent over an octave in the second movement and the agile *fioriture* of the third movement. The beginnings of the second and fifth movements reveal the broadening horizons of Haydn's musical expression. The initial rising sixth and the pulsating accompaniment in the first of these generate a characteristically hopeful setting of the phrase 'Ad te clamamus' ('To thee we cry'); while in complete contrast the stern dotted rhythms that accompany 'Et Jesum, benedictum fructum ventris tui' ('And Jesus, the blessed fruit of thy womb') are an impressive use of a baroque cliché.[2] Elsewhere, passages of the text are allotted first to the soprano soloist, who sings in an expansive or virtuoso manner, and then to the chorus, who, in contrast, sing in simple and direct homophony. It is the chorus who end the work, with a contemplative plagal cadence on the name 'Maria'. In its emotional control and commitment the Salve Regina represents a major step forward in Haydn's career.

A three-movement Ave Regina in A major (XXIIIb:3) is scored for the same forces as the Salve Regina and reveals also many of the Italianate characteristics and general sophistication, but without the same impressive range of sonority. Though the earliest known reference to the work is from 1763, it probably dates from the same time as Salve Regina, if not before.

Personal circumstances ensured that in the late 1750s and early 1760s Haydn's energies were concentrated on instrumental music. No vocal music seems to have originated during his period of employment at the Morzin court and his duties at Eisenstadt excluded the composition of church music, the sole responsibility of *Kapellmeister* Werner. While he was *Vice-Kapellmeister*, Haydn is known to have composed only one original church work, the Te Deum in C major (XXIIIc:1). Compared with the inventiveness and spontaneity of contemporary instrumental music and, to a certain extent, secular vocal music too, the Te Deum is oddly reserved and conventional and contains nothing that would have shocked Werner. In the customary festive key of C major, it is scored for SATB choir (with some solo sections), violins, continuo, two trumpets and timpani. Like most settings of the text in eighteenth-century Austria – for instance, Michael Haydn's Te Deum dated 1 April 1760 – it is divided into three parts: a vigorous, fully scored Allegro; an Adagio with reduced scoring and softer dynamics for the sentence 'Te ergo quaesumus, tuis famulis subveni, quos pretioso sanguine redemisti' ('Help us, then, we entreat thee: help thy servants whom thou hast ransomed with thy precious blood'); and a brisk Allegro culminating in a resourceful fugue, Haydn's first in a vocal composition, on the words 'In te Domine speravi, non confundar in aeternum' ('In thee, Lord, is my hope. Let me never be put to confusion').

Whether Haydn regretted not having the opportunity to compose original works for the church in the late 1750s and early 1760s is not known. To his contemporaries he had by the mid-1760s established a secure niche as a composer of characterful instrumental music. However, the comparatively small number of original church compositions should not lead to the unqualified assumption that his reputation as a church composer was negligible. Werner's letter of October 1765, in which the *Vice-Kapellmeister* is berated for administrative negligence, accused Haydn specifically of lending church music 'to all the world', suggesting that he kept up his contacts with the churches of Vienna. Moreover, at least seven *contrafacta* pieces of church music date from this time. Substituting alternative texts to existing works to make 'new' church compositions was common practice; Haydn's own Ave Regina circulated also as a Salve Regina. Replacing secular texts normally written in Italian with sacred Latin ones, or, occasionally, German words was also a regular and acceptable manner of supplementing the repertoire of church and monastic choirs. In Haydn's case, the attempt to establish the pedigree of the *contrafacta* is often very difficult. Some seem to have been prepared or sanctioned by Haydn, others not; in many cases the awkwardness of the word setting and the style of the music betray a secular origin, but the sacred version is the only one to have survived; in some works *contrafacta* movements mingle with newly-composed movements. Even if the pedigree of these works is not always impeccable and the music of variable quality judged by the standards set by contemporary works, the existence of these *contrafacta* suggests that Haydn's reputation as church composer in the 1760s was more extensive than might at first seem apparent.

The motet 'O coelitum beati' (XXIIIa:G9) was authenticated only in the spring of 1983; its origins are typical of many Haydn *contrafacta*. It consists of two movements, an Andante aria in G major for soprano and string orchestra, and a chorus (with brief solo passages) in C major accompanied by a string orchestra plus two trumpets; there is a written-out viola part in the aria, none in the chorus. The aria is similar in style to the many virtuoso soprano arias found in the three extant Italian cantatas and the two incomplete operas composed by Haydn in the period 1762–4. Its structure is an amalgam of da capo and ritornello form, such as is found in the concluding chorus of the cantata 'Qual dubbio' (XXIVa:4) and Polyphemus's aria in *Acide*; many features of Haydn's treatment of ritornello form revealed in contemporary concertos are in evidence here too.[3]

RITORNELLO	SOLO I	RITORNELLO II
I	I-V	V
bars 1-22	bars 23-50	bars 51-62
SOLO II	RITORNELLO III	SOLO III
V modulating	I	I
bars 63-91	bars 92-93	bars 94-105
RITORNELLO IV	SOLO ('Middle section')	DA CAPO
I	IV – modulating – vi	concluding with
bars 106-121	bars 122-139	Ritornello IV

As to the origins of the movement, any one of the following lost works from the period *c.*1761-1765 could have been plundered: three (possibly four) comic operas, three secular cantatas and the missing portions of *Acide* and *La Marchesa Nespola*. Of these, the serious-toned *Acide* and cantatas are more likely than the comic works to have contained an aria on such a large scale. Although finely wrought, the soprano writing of the presumed secular original does produce some arbitrary word setting.

The brief chorus, presumably newly composed to make a two-movement work, sets the single word 'Alleluja' in a steady andante tempo. It provides an appropriate contrast to the first movement, with its predominant homophony and diatonic choral writing separated by gently decorative solo sections.

Secular vocal music

One of the most crucial formative influences on the young Haydn was his experience of Viennese *Singspiel* in the 1750s. From 1710 onwards, the Kärntnerthortheater had been the home of this popular type of entertainment, a mixture of spoken dialogue and simple musical numbers. The German comedy was organized and directed from 1744 by Johann Joseph Felix Kurz (usually known as Bernadon), who also appeared regularly as the buffoon character Hanswurst. The plots of the comedies, such as they were, consisted of magic, earthy humour, the antics of stock comic characters (sometimes drawn from the Italian *commedia dell'arte*), crude but never bitter satire of the social conventions of the upper classes and, in the musical numbers, their operatic tastes too. As long as a *Singspiel* was entertaining and provocative, being almost always ridiculous and inconsequential mattered little.

At the age of about nineteen, Haydn is known to have composed the music for one of Kurz's productions, *Der krumme Teufel* ('The crooked devil'). This was revived and probably revised a few years later, appearing under the title *Der neue krumme Teufel*. These two titles provide the only extant evidence of the association between composer and director, but it is likely that Haydn composed, if not complete works, many single arias for other productions by the Kurz company. In the absence of Haydn's music, the nature of his contribution can only be guesswork stimulated by the survival of two printed librettos for *Der neue krumme Teufel*, from 1758 and 1770. The title page of the earlier version reads as follows:

Der neue Krumme Teufel. Eine Opera-Comique von zwey Aufzügen; Nebst einer Kinder-Pantomime, Betitelt: Arlequin der neue Abgott Ram in Amerika. ('The New Crooked Devil. An opera-comique in two acts, including a children's pantomime entitled Arlequin the New Idol Ram in America'.)

Though the work was performed in the German language and is technically a *Singspiel*, Kurz termed it an *'opéra comique'* in deference to the French equivalent of the German *Singspiel*, then very popular in the Viennese theatres. (The term *'Singspiel'* was infrequently used in Vienna, *'komische Oper'* being more common; Haydn himself used the term *'opéra comique'* to describe his later German operas.)

The main characters include Dr Arnoldus who, for all his hard-worn wisdom (expounded in a 'learned' Latin aria), is discontented; Fiametta, a strapping young wench (*Zuchtmädel*) whom the doctor wants to marry; and Asmodeus, the crooked devil, who begins by helping Fiametta but then tranfers his allegiance to the doctor. The action incorporates a pantomime and an Italian intermezzo between the two acts of the *Singspiel*. A note at the end of the 1758 libretto names Haydn as the composer of the music for the Pantomime as well as the 'Opera-Comique', but the composer of the intermezzo *Il vecchio ingannato* ('The old man tricked') is not mentioned; it is possible that Haydn composed the music for this too. The first of these interpolations, the Pantomime, is entitled *Arlequin der neue Abgott Ram in Amerika*. Thus, midway through the evening, the machinations of the deceitful devil and the crafty doctor are suspended and Kurz's audience is treated to the visual spectacle of a shipwreck off the coast of America – the eighteenth-century equivalent in fantasy to the modern preoccupation with crashed space ships on distant inhospitable planets. Harlequin and his master, the ship's captain, Celio, swim for the shore. It is this portion of the action that provides the only hint of Haydn's contribution to the entertainment. Griesinger records Haydn's own recollection of how he provided an appropriate accompaniment, on the harpsichord, to Kurz's swimming movements (see p. 28).

Descriptive writing of this type was commonplace in the genre and *Der neue krumme Teufel* also includes references to fainting, vomiting and boiling, as well as some routine thunder and lightning. Its significance for Haydn's development is that it provides the first instance of the composer's lifelong predilection for simple pictorial writing, a characteristic that appears mainly in opera and oratorio but which is found in his instrumental music too. It is doubly unfortunate that the music of the *Singspiel* is lost, both for its own sake and because its availability might more readily prompt the realization that the characteristics of the genre, in both composition and performance, were important ingredients in Haydn's artistic personality. Many of the 3/8 Allegro themes that rely on spirited rhythms rather than broad cantabile inhabit the comic world of Arnoldus and Fiametta, and the gruff humour of the libretto and (one may assume) the music, together with the general confidence in entertainment that is direct and unsubtle, are characteristics that inform even the most durable of Haydn's mature masterpieces. In the nineteenth and early twentieth centuries, when Haydn's reputation was at its lowest ebb, critics and audiences often adopted a patronizing attitude to this facet of Haydn's art, reducing it to the level of the cute. The willingness to acknowledge the latent power of a direct statement is as essential a prerequisite for the full comprehension of Haydn's personality as are the ability to respond to the sense of joyous Christian faith that informs his church music and the readiness to be fascinated and instructed by the intellectual problems posed and solved in his instrumental music.

Haydn's familiarity with Italian opera at this stage in his career was less extensive than might at first be thought. Though the influence of Porpora is clearly in evidence in the E major Salve Regina, it is doubtful whether Haydn knew much of his operatic music; certainly no operas were composed by Porpora in the 1750s. The theatrical taste of the Viennese aristocracy in that decade followed that of its chancellor, Prince Kaunitz, and was decidedly French. Most evenings at the Burgtheater and the Kärntnerthortheater were taken up by French plays, ballets and *opéra comique*, and Gluck, who was an experienced composer of Italian opera and a prominent figure in the musical life of the court, composed mainly *opéras comiques* in the 1750s. Italian opera began to re-assert itself in Vienna in the early 1760s with works by Tomaso Traetta, Giuseppe Scarlatti and, in 1762, Gluck's *Orfeo ed Euridice*. From a letter written in 1768 it is known that Haydn revered Johann Adam Hasse as a composer and *c.*1759 he recommended that a pupil, Robert Kimmerling, study the score of *Il mondo alla roversa* by Baldassare Galuppi for its 'good cantabile'. But Haydn's familiarity with the music of these two composers was based, in the main, on score-reading, whether silently or at the keyboard; the all important sense of live theatre was absent and would to a large extent remain so until Nicolaus Esterházy's fondness for Italian opera changed the whole direction of Haydn's output in the late 1760s.

In his first five years of service at the Esterházy court Haydn composed four (possibly five) comic operas ('comedia') of which a portion of only one survives, *La Marchesa Nespola*.[4] In addition he wrote an old-fashioned *festa teatrale* on the Acis and Galatea story, *Acide*, which was first performed in 1763 (and revised in 1773); portions of both versions survive. To these may be added three surviving cantatas, written in praise of Nicolaus Esterházy and using the language and structures of Italian opera. The subject matter of these Italian works is extremely diverse, embracing the old-fashioned pastoral idiom of *Acide*, the stultifyingly laudatory texts of the cantatas and the more up-to-date libretto of *La Marchesa Nespola*. For this reason, as well as because of the incomplete state of the operas that survive, it would be unreasonable to draw conclusions about Haydn's handling of operatic language at this stage in his career.

If it were possible to listen to the various Italian works in close succession, the astonishing difficulty of the vocal parts would continually impress; a tribute to Haydn's singers at Eisenstadt, in particular Anna Scheffstoss (soprano), Barbara Fux (alto), Carl Friberth (tenor) and Melchior Griessler (bass). For the soprano and tenor voices, especially, Haydn's demands match anything in contemporary Italian opera and expand on the cliché techniques first used in the E major Salve Regina: long-note, *messa di voce* openings, scales, roulades, trills and climactically placed high notes. Acide in his first aria sings of his love for Galatea, 'the beauty, that fascinates me'; when, in the course of this sturdy C major aria, he mentions his fear that Galatea might leave him, the word fear ('paventar') is singled out for a vigorous display of coloratura.

Displays of vocal prowess form a natural part of the three cantatas: the forces of the Esterházy *Kapelle* assemble to pay homage to their master and flatter his wisdom and munificence through vocal ostentation, the musical equivalent of ceremonial dress. In 'Destatevi, o miei fidi', composed for Nicolaus's name-day in 1763, the second number is a duet for soprano and tenor where the key word 'omaggio' triggers off six-and-a-half bars of coloratura in parallel tenths.

Not all the vocal numbers are of this showy nature. In the only comic work to have survived in part, *La Marchesa Nespola*, several of the arias are sung by the *commedia dell'arte* figures, Colombina, Sganarello and Pantalone, and adopt a predominantly syllabic setting with cheeky folk-like melodies doubled literally by the first violins; the sentiments and style are closer to *Singspiel* than to the respectful Italian cantatas and the result has more personality (see example below).

Many of the arias in these vocal works have lengthy orchestral introductions that show the influence of Haydn's symphonies. Leopoldo's aria 'Trema Tÿrran regnante' ('Tremble, Tyrant') from *La Marchesa Nespola* has an opening orchestral ritornello, twenty-five bars long, with the familiar features of syncopated crotchets

20

cor tut-to è per te, il mio cor, il mio cor tut-to è per te

over Alberti figuration in semiquavers and repeated quavers, unison violin scales and, most tellingly, local excursions to the minor in a reduced orchestral texture at a *piano* dynamic; Symphonies nos. 21, 23, 29 and 31, all dating from within two or three years of the opera, reveal the same features.

If many of the arias reflect Haydn's experience as a composer of orchestral music, one particular aria anticipates a stylistic development that was not to flourish until much later in the decade. In the cantata 'Destatevi, o miei fidi' a soprano propounds the (unlikely) sentiment that, whatever treasures the vast sea may be capable of yielding up, serving Prince Nicolaus Esterházy offers even greater joy. The aria is in D minor and, with its rapidly oscillating busy semiquavers, nervous quavers and wide-leaping melodic line, is a clear precursor of the *Sturm und Drang* orchestral idiom of the late 1760s and the early 1770s that Haydn was to make so much his own. The sinewy and nervous power is an entirely new sonority in Haydn's music and was occasioned, ostensibly, by the reference to the sea. Even allowing for the convention of the simile aria, Haydn's response is oddly one-sided, emphasizing the image of the sea at the expense of the pleasures of duty and service; there is the suspicion that Haydn was more interested in exploring this new sonority than setting the particular text. There is a marked similarity between this music and the D minor finale to Gluck's ballet, *Don Juan* (see overleaf).

Don Juan was first produced in October 1761 at the Burgtheater, Vienna, and Haydn, who was in town, could well have heard a performance. The 'Destatevi' cantata, composed two years later, afforded the first opportunity to compose a movement in a similar style, and only later did Haydn realize that the idiom could be developed independently of a pictorial image. Like Gluck, but using very different means, Haydn sought to create dramatic realism and involvement in his music; it is indicative of their different approaches, as well as ironic, that this direct influence from the older composer should first feature in such a sterile context.

Gluck

Haydn

Haydn was never to be a critical appraiser of dramatic or poetic texts and, at this stage in his career, his subordinate status as well as his lack of direct experience as a dramatic composer discouraged critical evaluation. Throughout these Italian works it is Haydn the resourceful musician who is most apparent. This reveals itself not only in the arias but in accompanied recitatives too.

Most of the recitatives in *Acide* would naturally have been *secco* - none survives - but the extant passages of accompanied recitative show a willingness to comment forcefully on changes of mood. More personal are the accompanied recitatives that open the three cantatas. All three begin with lengthy passages of orchestral writing in a regular allegro tempo; the soloist does not enter until near the end of the movement. The intention in each case is to generate a sense of expectation preceding the formal announcement by the vocal soloist of the purpose of the cantata. In 'Qual dubbio omai' (XXIVa:4) the opening material (see example below) provides the most arresting gesture in all of Haydn's music to date, including his symphonies and quartets.

A two-bar *forte* phrase is followed by a *piano* echo; the whole process is then repeated down a tone beginning on G natural; a third statement begins on D and finishes on the flat submediant, F natural, which leads to a dominant chord and the first perfect cadence in the work; it is only now that the music proceeds fluently. The sudden questioning change of dynamic to *piano*, the presentation of unusual harmonic progressions in bare octave unison rather than with explanatory harmony, and the repeated use of a recurring turn motif, 'a' (also to feature later in the movement), are all staple ingredients of Haydn's mature style. The repetition of the opening three bars down a whole tone is a remarkable anticipation of the beginning of Beethoven's 'Waldstein' sonata, op. 53. But the resemblance is no

66

more than just that, for the Beethoven sonata makes its impact as a parody of a standard opening procedure in the late Classical style, the so-called supertonic gambit (e.g. the first movement of the Notturno in G, II:30; the finale of the last piano sonata; Beethoven's First Symphony, and his aborted Violin Concerto in C), whereas in the 1760s it had not yet been invented.[5] Haydn's opening makes its impact in rhetorical terms only, the listener being disorientated until the arrival in bar II of A major, a full texture and rhythmic continuity. It is empty rhetoric, too, in the sense that it has no consequence in the way that similar harmonic surprises in later Haydn have. In spirit it is close to the strange openings of some of C. P. E. Bach's music, but the whole question of Bach's influence on Haydn is bedevilled by the problem of what music by him was known to Haydn. A more likely source for this strong, inconsequential beginning is the language of accompanied recitative itself, which often relies on the juxtaposition of unrelated material with little or no sense of musical continuity, the text providing the element of control; here it is the steady pulse that provides the necessary control.

'Da qual gioja improviso' (XXIVa:3) and 'Qual dubbio omai' were composed in the same year, 1764, and both feature solo harpsichord writing, in the first cantata as a decorative part of the final chorus and in the second as one of the soloists in what is effectively a double concerto movement for voice, harpsichord and orchestra, a large-scale ritornello with da capo movement. In this way Haydn who, on his own admission, was no wizard on any instrument, impressed his employer both as a performer and a composer.

Harpsichord music (solo and with strings)

Haydn's early instrumental music shows a diversity of genre that is not matched in his output in later life. He composed solo harpsichord sonatas, chamber works for harpsichord and strings, wind-band music, sundry works for mixed string and wind ensembles, string trios, quartets, dances, concertos and symphonies – all, with the celebrated exception of quartets, genres that were well-developed in mid-eighteenth-century Austria. Haydn's unsettled life until the mid–1760s clearly prompted this diversity, in the same way as later in life comparative security enabled him to concentrate on fewer genres. At the same time it is fascinating to note how certain genres seized the creative imagination of the composer, principally the symphony and the quartet and, to a lesser extent, keyboard sonatas and chamber works for keyboard and strings. Other genres, such as the string trio and the concerto, contain some fine individual works, but neither was to exert a continuing hold on Haydn's inspiration. That useful faculty, hindsight, plays only a small part in this assessment, for it is abundantly clear from the evidence of the music itself that symphonies and quartets were destined to play a major part in Haydn's creative life.

Among Haydn's earliest instrumental music were keyboard sonatas. After leaving St Stephen's he earned money by teaching the clavichord and harpsichord and he wrote keyboard music that 'mostly took into account the need and the capacity of his pupils' (Griesinger). Many more works were composed than have survived for, as Griesinger relates, Haydn 'gave them away and felt honoured when they were accepted'. It is probable that keyboard teaching formed part of his duties at the Morzin court; on the other hand it seems that the early years at Eisenstadt did not require the composition of keyboard sonatas. In total, some eighteen sonatas survive from before 1765, but none can be dated more precisely; and even 'before 1765' is in a few cases based on assumption rather than firm evidence.

In 1753 one of the most respected Austrian harpsichord players and composers of the day, Georg Christoph Wagenseil (1715–77), published six divertimentos for harpsichord as his opus 1. They have much in common with Haydn's keyboard sonatas of the 1750s and 1760s. Three movements are the norm for both composers, with a minuet (or a Tempo di minuetto) coming either last or – displacing the slow movement – second in the design. Wagenseil includes only one work in four movements (fast, slow, minuet and fast); similarly there are only two four-movement sonatas by Haydn, nos. 1 and 13. There are many correspondences of style between the two composers, as evidenced by the following pairs of quotations:

Wagenseil, op.1 no.2

The common property of a theme propelled by a turn figure and articulated by a cadential trill is obvious enough; Wagenseil and Haydn also share a fondness for concluding a four-bar phrase with descending melodic motion that comes to a rest on the mediant. In Haydn this feature is almost a mannerism in his early music, more obvious when part of a regular phrase, as here, less so when the phrasing is more irregular, as in Sonata no. 4. Wagenseil's C major opening continues with an echo repetition of the final two bars down an octave, a technique not used in Haydn's C major sonata but which does appear elsewhere (e.g. Sonata no. 11). The openings of the quoted minuets reveal a strong liking for triplet figuration, appoggiatura cadences and bass lines that emphasize the pulse of the dance.

In all movements a two-voice texture is the norm, occasionally expanding to sustained three- or four-part writing; single, full chords are used at the beginnings and ends of major paragraphs as strong punctuation marks. In allegro movements Haydn shares Wagenseil's dislike of persistent automatic accompaniment patterns, such as Alberti or repeated note figuration; these and other cliché patterns do appear, but without the monotonous predictabi'ity that characterizes the sonatas of contemporary Italian composers in particular.

Within a sonata the sound of the minor is most likely to occur in trio sections of minuets, often in the form of some gentle *alla zoppa* (limping) syncopation between the hands producing a dispirited, rather faceless atmosphere. Interestingly enough, the key of G minor elicits a more powerful response from both composers. In Wagenseil's case the slow movement of op. 1 no. 6 uses baroque rhythmic patterns and keyboard figuration to produce a lengthy, dramatic movement. In Haydn's early sonatas two slow movements in G minor are equally forceful, though less dependent on old-fashioned keyboard style than Wagenseil's slow movement. The Largo of no. 11 and the Adagio of no. 13 are effectively slow operatic arias transferred to the medium of the keyboard; over a persistent, comforting accompaniment the right hand spins out a melody using the type of figuration that Haydn had learned from Porpora. It is a concertante approach that occurs with great frequency in slow movements in Haydn's instrumental music.

Wagenseil's six works were published as a set and are roughly of the same size and scope, whereas Haydn's extant sonatas are single works composed over a period of up to fifteen years or more. Consequently, their size and duration vary, though, since didactic utility was their *raison d'être*, it should not be assumed that the smallest and simplest are necessarily the earliest. Those movements that are in sonata form range from a miniature text-book example (but long before any text book defined it) in Sonata no. 7, to the expansive proportions of no. 11 (148 bars).

With the exception of the doubtful no. 7, none of these early sonatas contains a variations movement. Two independent movements exist, however, the Variations in G major (XVII:2) and the Capriccio: 'Acht Sauschneider müßen seyn' (XVII:1). The latter, dating from 1765, is Haydn's most ambitious early work for keyboard. Using a South German folk-song ('Eight castrators must there be'), Haydn constructs a movement of 368 bars elaborating the folk-song. In approach the movement is akin to the free keyboard rondos of C. P. E. Bach and the rhetoric, too, sometimes recalls the North German composer (e.g. bar 165 etc.), but while Bach would have admired these features as well as the extensive modulations of the movement, he would have disdained the frequent passages of routine accompaniment figuration and, perhaps, would have been perplexed by the notion that a serious musical work could be based on such a vulgar source.

In addition to works for harpsichord solo, Haydn composed approximately eighteen trios for harpsichord, violin and cello during the period. Two of these, nos. 3 and 4, exist also as solo harpsichord sonatas; both versions are presumably authentic, and the string parts were probably added to the sonata by Haydn. As trios, the works are typical examples of the accompanied sonata tradition that was so popular with dilettante players and which was voluminously catered for by Parisian publishers. But this approach is not the main one in Haydn's early harpsichord trios. Rather it is the old baroque trio sonata and not the modern keyboard sonata that lies behind the texture of much of the music. The leading lines are shared between the violin and the right hand of the harpsichord, with the cello doubling the left hand as in a basso continuo role; there is not a single, even brief instance of independent writing for the cello. Several allegro movements begin with the common baroque practice of a theme announced in succession by the two melodic lines, and very occasionally the right hand of the keyboard is left unrealized.

As in the keyboard sonatas, Haydn shows a preference for a three-movement design in which a minuet is placed second or third. Though the keyboard writing itself is no more difficult than that encountered in some solo harpsichord works, the trios as compositions are, on the whole, more ambitous and wide-ranging. Trio no. ɪɪ in E major contains much that is representative of Haydn's instrumental style in the late 1750s.

The first movement, an Allegro moderato in 2/4, begins with a double announcement of the main theme and thereafter the melodic material is divided more informally between the right hand of the keyboard and the violin. The moderate tempo and the repeated quavers of the accompaniment keep the music within a narrow emotional range and the full sonata form, though carefully proportioned in terms of thematic outlay and tonality, lacks that intellectual involvement characteristic of later Haydn. The development opens conventionally in the dominant with another double statement of the first subject, after which the music modulates away from B major via a series of Italianate sequences before cadencing in C sharp minor (see example below). The preparation for the return of the tonic makes idiomatic use of the augmented sixth; and the march down the scale from dominant to tonic that leads into the recapitulation is a mannerism in Haydn's early music, one that he was careful to control from the mid-1760s onwards.

The recapitulation opens conventionally with the first subject announced by the violin but, rather than writing the expected exact repetition by the harpsichord, Haydn turns to E minor and provides a paraphrase of the first subject in that key before proceeding with the recapitulation in a more regular way. Structural surprises of this sort were to form an increasingly characteristic and resourceful part of his musicianship and this particular example is the forerunner of many surprises at this stage of a recapitulation. The possible origins of this unexpected change of mode in Trio no. ɪɪ lie in a common procedure in the second subject areas of contemporary sonata forms. Haydn, like Christoph Monn, Wagenseil,

Vanhal, Dittersdorf and others, often presents a portion of the second subject area in the dominant minor rather than the major. This temporary switch of mode from major to minor is transferred in Trio no. II to the beginning of the recapitulation.

The central movement is a minuet and trio, hence there is no slow movement. As was normal in the dance, the minuet is composed in two voices throughout, with the violin and cello doubling the right and left hand respectively. None of the minuets presents the minuet theme doubled in octaves in the way familiar from the early quartets. The trio, in E minor, eschews melodic appeal in favour of a sustained *alla zoppa* texture: right hand and violin a quaver behind the bass

throughout. The finale is a taut, but fleet-footed Presto in 3/8 of the type that appears in many symphonies and quartets. Its form, however, is not typical: an overall ternary pattern in which the middle section is in the minor mode and the outer sections are binary in shape.

If Trio no. 11 may be taken as representing the norm in structural patterns and stylistic details, the most atypical harpsichord trio is no. 5 in G minor, which exhibits a varied – perhaps too varied – personality. The opening movement is probably the most conservative instrumental movement Haydn ever wrote, with its dotted-note rhythms and scalic flourishes in the grand manner; if one did not know its probable date of composition, only the odd moment of harmonic stasis (bar II etc.) and the strong articulatory cadences would suggest that the work belongs to the 1750s and not the 1730s. After a stern Menuet, the trio provides an almost incompatible contrast, a lengthy melody for violin over Alberti figuration in the keyboard. The concluding Presto is a minor-key version of a typical Haydn rollick in 3/8 – one, however, that remains grimly in the minor to the end. Few Haydn compositions of any period reveal such a heterogeneous mixture of styles.

A more succesful synthesis is achieved in the opening of Trio no. 10. Its first movement is a full sonata form (with a truncated recapitulation) in which most of the thematic material is based on baroque toccata-like figuration, the combination of the formal discipline of sonata form and the free-sounding, apparently improvisatory melodic material suggesting the title 'Capriccio'.

Of the instrumental music so far discussed – harpsichord sonatas and harpsichord trios – only one autograph has survived, that of Sonata no. 13, which Haydn described as a 'partitta'. His keyboard sonatas circulated also under the titles 'divertimento', 'sonatina' and 'parthia', and his harpsichord trios as 'divertimentos', 'concertos' and 'partitas'. It would be folly to attempt rigorous definitions of what composers and copyists meant by these terms, since no consistent rationale existed to distinguish, say, between 'partita' and 'divertimento'; labels were a guide only and not legally binding, as it were, and when, later in the century, they became fewer and more precise, it was because of the pervasive desire of music publishers for uniformity rather than on account of any overriding musical considerations. In mid-eighteenth-century Austria the most common of these terms was 'divertimento', applied to the whole range of chamber-music genres: sonatas, string trios, quartets, quintets, wind-band music, mixed ensemble of strings and wind, piano trios, piano quartets, etc. Nineteenth- and twentieth-century connotations of 'light' music (e.g. Bartók's Divertimento for String Orchestra) did not exist in Haydn's Austria and most of the composer's chamber music up to the 1780s carried the appellation Divertimento.[6] Equally inappropriate is the nineteenth- and twentieth-century association of the term with orchestral music; in eighteenth-century Austria it was applied only to chamber music.

In addition to divertimentos for harpsichord with violin and cello, there are a dozen extant divertimentos for harpsichord with a larger ensemble: one for harpsichord, two horns, violin and bass (XIV:1), the remainder for harpsichord, two violins and bass. In the one autograph (now lost) of these works that survived into the nineteenth century, that of XIV:11, the work was termed a 'concertino' and was dated 1760, i.e. during the Morzin period. It is probable that most of its companions were composed at about the same time, though some may date from as much as five years later. All show an attitude to the relationship between the strings and the harpsichord consistently different from that typical of the harpsichord trios. There is little evidence of the trio sonata mentality; instead, Haydn treats the string ensemble more like a discreet orchestra, accompanying the harpsichord and having the occasional very short passage on its own. However, Haydn's use of the word 'concertino' does not signify a small-scale concerto with ritornello structures; neither does it imply demonstrative instrumental writing – on the contrary, the parts are much easier than those found in the contemporary sonatas and trios, and they are, on the whole, of shorter duration. The small scale, the nature of the scoring and the undemanding technique required mark them as a distinct sub-genre in Haydn's early output, perhaps composed for a particular clientele such as Countess Morzin and friends, who lacked the technical expertise to play Haydn's trios and the more demanding of the sonatas.

Music for mixed ensemble (without keyboard)

Haydn was engaged to compose *Der krumme Teufel* after taking part in a serenade party in the street below Frau Kurz's window; Griesinger and Dies recount further anecdotes about Haydn's participation in this charming eighteenth-century custom. Some nine extant works may, with confidence, be associated with these activities: two divertimentos (or cassations) for two violins, two violas and bass (II:A1 and II:2), two for flute, oboe, two violins, two violas, cello and bass (II:1 and II:11) and three for two oboes, two horns, two violins, two violas and bass (II:9, II:20, II:G1). A clear indication of the performing circumstances of the Divertimento in C major (II:11) is given in its sub-heading, 'Der Geburtstag' ('The Birthday'); the slow movement parades the expertise of the main instrumentalists in a set of variations on a tune that may or may not be an actual folk-song, 'Mann und Weib' ('Man and Wife'). The initial presentation of the theme is in mock-serious octave unison.

The technique and spirit of this movement are highly characteristic – straight-faced two-part writing doubled at the octave features in slow movements in many of Haydn's earliest symphonies, and the love of casual instrumental display is one that never lost its appeal. Indeed, heard alongside the works that involve the harpsichord, the mixed divertimentos are consistently recognizable as the products of a young Haydn; the ability to characterize individual themes and to shape paragraphs by changing dynamics and through accentuation is a superior resource of mid-eighteenth-century music not involving the harpsichord and it was clearly a liberating spur to Haydn's creativity; the music has blood coursing through its veins in a manner that makes some of the harpsichord writing seem lifeless.

As well as providing rewarding parts for violin, cello and oboe, Haydn writes ingratiating parts for two violas, usually playing as a pair; their nasal sound is to be heard in many of the trio sections of the minuets, providing a rare tone quality in Haydn's music that does not feature in his later output. On the other hand, the virtuoso horn writing looks forward to that found in several symphonies of the Esterházy period (e.g. nos. 9, 31, 40 and 72).

Informal serenade parties were closely associated with the Viennese environment of narrow streets and sheltered, secretive courtyards. In the small town of Eisenstadt such a tradition apparently did not exist and consequently little music of this type was composed by Haydn from 1761 onwards. A particular exception is the Cassatio in D major (II:D22), a work scored for four horns, violin, viola and bass. It is not known why Haydn wrote the work, but the sonority and virtuosity of its horn writing have much in common with that demonstrated with so much elan in the two symphonies in D major composed in 1763–5 that have four horn parts, nos. 31 and 72. The Cassatio may have been composed as an exercise to prepare the horn players for the demands of those two symphonies.

Music for wind band

Similar properties to those noted above are to be found in Haydn's early music for wind band. The date 1760 is written on one surviving autograph, the Divertimento in F major (II:15). It is reasonable to assume that a further six extant works date from the same period, probably having been composed for the Morzin *Harmonie*. They are written for a typical ensemble of two oboes, two horns and two bassoons (with genuine two-part writing for the latter rather than the bass line *a due* often found in early wind-band music). Most of the divertimentos have a symmetrical pattern of movements that is frequently encountered in Haydn's instrumental music at this time, most familiarly in the early quartets: fast, minuet, slow, minuet and fast. The individual movements, however, are much shorter than in contemporary quartets, cassations and symphonies. In fast movements the modulation to the dominant is not accompanied by a new theme, nor is there a complementary sense of thematic recapitulation when the music returns to the tonic in the second half. In slow movements brevity sometimes encumbers the natural expansion of the melodic line, though changes of instrumental colour provide some compensation.

The musical idiom of the wind-band music is, however, recognizably that which appears in enhanced form in contemporary quartets and symphonies. In the F major Divertimento (II:15) the triadic melodic patterns, the antecedent-consequent phrasing patterns, the alternation of octave unison and full harmony are techniques deployed in almost identical manner in the opening of the quartet, op. 1 no. 1, possibly composed as much as three years earlier. Another F major Divertimento (II:23) has an opening that implies a gradual crescendo to the *forte* in bar 9, rather like the opening of Symphony no. 1.

Though the Esterházy princes employed a *Harmonie*, it was separately constituted from the church and chamber musicians and Haydn was not required to compose for it. However, in the early 1760s Haydn is known to have composed three works for wind ensemble involving two clarinets rather than two oboes. Only one work survives in authentic form, a C major Divertimento for two clarinets and two horns (II:14), dated 1761. The Esterházy music establishment did not include clarinet players and it is thought that this work was composed for the dilettante player, the Polish Count Michael Casimir Oginski, who was a guest at the Esterházy palace in Vienna in 1761. It was probably Haydn's first encounter with the instrument and it is not surprising that he, like many other composers of the mid-century, treated the clarinet, pitched in C, as a substitute oboe.

String trios

Before the quartet became an established genre, one of the most popular media of the divertimento in Austria was the string trio, scored generally for two violins and bass (sometimes two violas and bass, and rather infrequently violin, viola and bass). Asplmayer, Porsile and Wagenseil all wrote prolifically for the medium, the works usually being in three movements. Haydn continued the tradition, composing thirty-four works for string trio, all in three movements and, with the exception of no. 8, all for two violins and bass. Statistically, they constitute a major part of Haydn's output to *c.* 1765, and only the thirty-five or so early symphonies can rival this commitment. Unfortunately, compared with the history of the composer's symphonies, very little precise information is forthcoming about the circumstances that led to the composition of the trios. For other genres a single dated autograph may serve to suggest when similar, undated works were composed. But not a single autograph of a string trio survives, though some extant copies can be associated with Count Morzin and Baron von Fürnberg, the minor aristocrat who commissioned Haydn's first quartets in the mid–1750s. Carpani, who published his biography of Haydn in 1812, confirms that the trios were played in the Fürnberg household and states that Haydn began composing them a year after *Der neue krumme Teufel*, that is in the late 1750s. The disposition of their entry in the *Entwurf-Katalog* suggests that Haydn composed divertimentos for string trio as late as 1767, certainly long after his op. 1 and op. 2 quartets. After 1767 the string trio never featured in Haydn's output, its place being taken over in quantitative terms by the baryton trio (baryton, viola and cello); as regards quality, the new medium of the quartet fascinated and teased the composer's mind in a way that no other chamber-music medium was ever to do, and the string trio remained for other composer to exploit, in works as diverse as Mozart's Divertimento in E flat (K. 563), Beethoven's op. 1 and Schoenberg's single trio. In the 1750s and 1760s the medium, as then constituted for two soprano voices and bass, was perhaps too familiar for even a composer of Haydn's questing temperament to exploit; harpsichord trios, the string parts of many symphonies and all church music were conceived in this voice pattern and the trio had to be reconstituted as top, middle and bass before composers discovered its potential. The thematic writing in Haydn's trios is fairly shared between the two violins with, naturally, the first violin predominating, but the bass part never enters into the thematic argument and there is never any three-part counterpoint. In Haydn's quartets distinct four-part writing is rare (except on formal occasions, as in a fugue), but he compensates by involving all four players in an ever-changing pattern of voice disposition and doubling. In Haydn's trios modern listeners miss not only the sense of gravity which the viola provides, but also this varied and consistently varying texture. Typically, Haydn's trio writing consists of either two violins versus the bass, or one violin versus violin and bass. Divertimento no. 8 is the only work scored for violin, viola and bass, and though the sonority of the ensemble benefits from the richer tenor/alto sound of the viola, the actual part-writing adheres to the same norm; indeed, in the opening movement, a set of variations on a theme, the cello has exactly the same bass line for the theme and six variations.

Many of the movements show aspects of Haydn's craft that remain tantalizingly undeveloped. The set of variations in Divertimento no. 8 is built on a binary theme eighteen bars long, in which the phrasing pattern has a careful mix of the periodic and the irregular:

$$\|: 3 + 1, 4 :\|: 2 + 2, 3, 3 :\|$$

To the listener's disappointment, the subsequent variations reinforce rather than investigate the promising ambiguities of this pattern.

The Allegro of Divertimento no. 14 is a carefully controlled sonata form structure in which irregular phrasing is only one element in a thoughtfully crafted movement.[7] Some of the salient features of the exposition are summarized below:

Divertimento no. 14

Bars	
1–3	First subject, three-bar phrase, three elements, 'a', 'b', and 'c'.
4–6	Repetition down an octave, ending with an imperfect cadence.
7–12	Transition using 'c' from first subject in imitation between violins, thus intensifying the initial one-bar sequence: dominant pedal. Link into forthcoming second subject uses semiquaver figurations based on 'c' (Haydn, in less concentrated mood, might well have used the cliché descent from dominant to tonic here).
12–17	Second subject A. Routine scale and arpeggio figuration in semiquaver triplets but with repeat of final bar to avoid over-articulated four-bar phrase.
17–20	Second subject B. Dominant minor, based on 'a' of first subject. In bars 19–20 absence of quaver rhythms in accompaniment combines with slower harmonic rhythm to reinforce dominant of A major.
21–24	Cadence theme leading to melodic peak of exposition followed by contrast of register.

Divertimento no. II in E major ends with a Tempo di Menùetto movement, 109 bars long. The final phrase in both of the main sections is preceded by a bar's rest for the three instruments which, as often in Haydn's music, calls a halt to an argument that is threatening to become diffuse or sometimes too involved; the succeeding phrase establishes anew the direction and authority of the discourse.

A total of seven works have a Tempo di Menuetto movement as a conclusion to a three-movement cycle that had opened with a slow movement, followed by an

Allegro. Other trios have a three-movement pattern in which a minuet proper forms the central movement and is flanked by two fast movements. As in Haydn's harpsichord sonatas and trios, the fast-slow-fast pattern is rare; for eighteenth-century musicians it seems to have been associated with orchestral music – overtures, symphonies and concertos – rather than with chamber music.

String quartets

The oft-quoted account by Griesinger describing the origins of Haydn's first quartets (see p. 32) was written fifty years after the event, and the importance it attaches to their composition naturally reflects the central role the genre played in the composer's own development and in his contemporary fame.

It was not false modesty that led Haydn to emphasize to Griesinger the accidental origins of the genre. Unlike the medium of the string trio, divertimentos for two violins, viola and cello were almost unknown and Haydn's examples are preceded by only a handful of works by Holzbauer, Wagenseil and possibly Richter (his op. 6). In addition, Haydn would no doubt have been familiar with the practice of performing orchestral music with one player per part and minus any wind parts, so that symphonies by Monn, Wagenseil and others effectively sounded like trios or quartets, depending on whether the original had a written-out viola part. Indeed, the invention of the string quartet was inevitable once composers had come to show a preference for four-part rather than three-part string writing in orchestral works; Haydn and the others anticipated the natural end of this historical process. Whilst Wagenseil, Holzbauer and Richter never wrote further works for the medium and their example did not begin a tradition, in Haydn's case the string quartet held a lifelong fascination, even if until the 1780s the opportunity to yield to this fascination was rare; moreover, his earliest quartets encouraged other composers such as Albrechtsberger. F. X. Dussek and later Vanhal and Ordoñez to compose divertimentos for two violins, viola and cello. Thus the long history of the string quartet may legitimately be said to have begun with those that were published as Haydn's op. 1 and op. 2; to this extent 'father of the quartet' is still an apt *bon mot*.

Griesinger's phrase, 'Haydn, then eighteen years old ...', implies that the quartets were composed in 1750. A date much later in the decade is more likely, probably from 1757 to 1759, with possibly a few works composed in the early 1760s and perhaps not for Fürnberg. Compared with the number of string trios, harpsichord sonatas and harpsichord trios, the number of quartets composed during this period is small, ten only, reflecting the newness of the genre. When, at the beginning of the nineteenth century, Pleyel published the complete quartets of Haydn, he based his printed edition of the early quartets on various eighteenth-century editions, with the result that he not only gave currency to the meaningless but still useful identifying tags 'op. 1' and 'op. 2' but also included three works that were not genuine quartets and omitted one work that was. Op. 1 no. 5 is a Symphony in B flat major by Haydn for two oboes, two horns and strings (I:107), op. 2 nos. 3 and 5 are compositions for quartet plus two horns (II:21 and 22), a popular divertimento medium. The work not published by Pleyel was a Divertimento in E flat major (II:6); it was rediscovered in the 1930s and was dubbed op. 'o'.

Traditionally, these ten early quartets have been discussed in relationship to Haydn's later quartets, an approach that invariably produces a distorted view of their significance. A more natural context is afforded by relating them to other chamber music of the 1750s and 1760s, particularly the divertimentos for string trio.

All ten quartets have five movements, an indication that Haydn to a certain extent associated the number of movements with a certain genre (three for harpsichord sonatas, harpsichord trios and string trios, and five for wind-band music and quartets). In the quartets, however, there is a strong sense of overall planning that is not consistently evident in other genres. Eight of the quartets have the following pattern, already encountered in the wind-band music: Fast-Minuet-Slow-Minuet-Fast.

The neat symmetry of the plan focuses attention on the central slow movement which becomes the most overtly expressive movement in the cycle. In style these slow movements are of a type intermittently found in all Haydn's early instrumental music: solo first violin melody spun over a persistent and routine accompaniment, e.g. repeated semiquavers in op. 1 no. 1, repeated quavers in op. 2 no. 4, and triplet quavers and semiquavers in op. 2 no. 1. The delicate colouring, the gentle affecting beauty of the melodic line (with poignant changes of octave) and the pursuit of one *Affekt* are a reminder that Vivaldi's music was well-known in Austria. The dangers of this attractive procedure becoming an unthinking formula are obvious and the slow movement of op. 'o' is one movement that falls into this trap. But other slow movements are executed with irresistible charm; in op. 1 no. 4 the second violin echoes the phrases of the first violin, 'con sordino'; in the Adagio of op. 1 no. 2 the movement is punctuated by a disarming, simple pizzicato cadence theme, and in op. 1 no. 1 the concertante movement is framed by a slow-moving chordal passage with 4-3 suspensions over a sustained tonic pedal point. Residual hints of trio sonata thinking in a movement conceived in terms of theme plus accompaniment are naturally rare and only one central slow movement, the Adagio of op. 2 no. 2, reveals this approach. Here the thematic writing is distributed between the two violins, with the viola sharing a continuo role with the cello; in fact, it would not be difficult to rescore this movement as a string trio.

Two of the quartets reverse the position of the opening first movement and slow movement. Op. 2 no. 6 abandons the concertante approach in its slow movement in favour of four variations on a regularly phrased theme; as in many of Haydn's early variations movements, there is no *minore*, but less expected is the absence also of Haydn's favourite *alla zoppa* pattern. The opening movement of op. 1 no. 3 retains the concertante approach and, like the Adagio of op. 2 no. 2, reveals a trio mentality to the scoring.

The fast movements, twenty in number, are consistently characterized. Fourteen are headed Presto and a further two Allegro assai; all are taut rhythmic movements with short bars of 2/4 and 3/8, contrasting with the measured triple time of the minuets and the relaxed time signatures of 3/4 and C found in the adagio movements. Since the purpose in those quartets that have fast outer movements (eight of the ten quartets) is to provide as strong a sense of balanced symmetry as possible, there is little attempt to differentiate between a first movement and a finale style. All the movements are binary-cum-sonata-form movements with both sections repeated. (Modern performers who repeat only the exposition in these quartets distort the proportions and misjudge the nature and disposition of the argument.) In the two quartets that switch the position of slow movement and fast movement, the central fast movement is cast in an overall ternary shape: a binary theme flanking a middle section in a contrasting key. The idiom is the same as that found in the outer sonata form movements; but, enclosed in a sectional structure, it provides a foretaste of the typical Haydn rondo (see example overleaf).

Part of the 'scherzo' effect in the passage quoted is due to the rapid alternation of parts, a new delight for eighteenth-century players who were accustomed to in-

Op.1 no.3

strumental parts that were in the nature of continuous speech rather than brisk dialogue or repartee. The potential for different internal groupings within the quartet medium is far greater than in the string trio - in crude mathematical terms, which cannot begin to reveal the whole musical truth, a total of twenty-four rather than six. Within the two rarely heard extremes of one solo line and four parts moving in SATB homophony, Haydn explores various permutations of theme and accompaniment. While the first violin is naturally the protagonist, the subordinate parts never provide a consistent accompaniment, so that those lines too form a lively part of the argument, even if, as yet, they do not say very much. In comparison with baroque chamber music and contemporary symphonies, the texture is characterized by innumerable short rests of varied duration, giving a sense of clear enunciation to the entries. For the first time in Haydn's chamber music and in the development of Classical chamber music in general, the simple and slow-moving harmonic language possesses evident power. The results of this approach are often burlesque, sometimes trite, even shortwinded, and they certainly shocked Haydn's reactionary contemporaries, who 'cried out especially over the debasement of music to comic fooling' (Griesinger). In the long term the same rhythmically alive texture was to be complemented by a vast new resource of thematically related and developed argument, with the result that subordinate parts are not merely attentive and responsive supporters but also alter the direction of the argument. Some fast movements in the ten early quartets afford a glimpse of this future. Op. 2 no. 1 opens with a pair of balancing three-bar phrases, one plus two in both cases, and

feature the accompaniment figure ♪ ♩♩♩ . This cliché rhythm integrates theme and accompaniment in a manner that is rare in the early quartets and more extensively than in any string trio; the new, imitative writing at the beginning of the development and the recapitulation sections are perceived as logical extensions of a continuing, exploratory process. In the Presto opening movement of op. 1 no. 1 the development studiously takes one element from each of the main subjects to create a new proposition.

The element of disciplined control exerted by the five-movement scheme does not permit the inclusion of lengthy Tempo di menuetto movements as featured in the string trios. All twenty dance movements are brief and in minuet and trio form, and, as in the taut fast movements, Haydn seems to revel in the challenge offered by the strict confines of the structure. Frequently the paragraph after the double bar will discuss a motif from the main melody and the following nominal repeat of the melody will be enlivened by imitation. Perhaps the most thought-provoking minuet is the second one in op. 1 no. 1, where imitative writing between the instruments at first disturbs the regular phrasing and after the double bar threatens to obliterate it.

The octave doubling in this minuet is a characteristic occasionally found in other genres - e. g. Cassatios (II:1, 20, 23, II:D8) and Symphony no. 5 - but not with the same consistency as in the ten early quartets. It aroused repeated condemnation by Haydn's critics because of its startlingly raw sonority, though to modern listeners it is totally familiar and seems to be a natural alternative to presenting minuet themes in unison. As in many of Haydn's minuets at this time, the trio sections turn most naturally to the tonic minor; they are additionally characterized by a less pronounced melodic style and a predilection for *pizzicato* textures.

The comparatively small number of divertimentos for string quartet occupy a special position in Haydn's early career. Chronologically, they do not form a point of culmination to several years of development, but Haydn's attitude to the new medium shows a level of inquiring craftsmanship that is only intermittently equalled in other chamber works. In his attitude to part-writing and thematic development Haydn reveals a tough musical intellect and a new sense of argument, one that is not incompatible, however, with geniality. To probe these qualities in a new medium Haydn used movement types and an overall movement pattern without much flexibility. Ten years later, he did not feel the need for this externally imposed constraint and was able, without forgetting the particular lessons learned in opp. 1 and 2, to incorporate the wider expressive power that his music had by then acquired. Viewed in that perspective, the early quartets emerge as carefully composed studies.

'Basso' and the bass part

On a set of six parts once owned by Baron Fürnberg six of Haydn's earliest quartets are described as 'Notturni per due Violini Violae e Basso'. While 'Notturni' is a clear indication of time of performance, the word 'basso' is apparently ambiguous. In fact most title pages of works involving string instruments in this period employ the word, whether they be quartets, harpsichord trios, mixed divertimentos, concertos or symphonies. It was a legacy of the baroque basso continuo tradition, whereby a variety of bass instruments were implied by the generic term 'basso'. As such, 'basso' meant the bass part rather than a particular instrument, and the instrument (or instruments) that played from the 'basso' part varied according to generally understood conventions. In symphonies it meant cellos, double basses and (in those works that had wind parts, but no written out bassoon part) bassoons too. In music played out of doors, such as Haydn's cassations and Mozart's orchestral serenades, it could mean string bass only with no cello.

In the first performances of Haydn's own quartets, opp. 1 and 2, Griesinger clearly states that Albrechtsberger played the cello. Yet there is ample evidence to suggest that much eighteenth-century Austrian chamber music was both conceived and played on a double bass type of instrument, known as the violone. The instrument itself had five strings (tuned F, A, D, F sharp and A) and was smaller in size and less ponderous in sound than the modern double bass. Although Haydn was undoubtedly familiar with the instrument, it is difficult to be categorical about its use in the composer's early chamber music. Most 'basso' parts in the string trios and harpsichord trios, like those of the quartets, make use of pitches lower than F, suggesting that works were written with the cello in mind. Yet the lower third of the cello's register is never extensively exploited and octave displacement of these notes is feasible without serious damage to the integrity of the line. In practice it is possible, indeed probable, that the bass part was frequently performed by the larger instrument rather than the cello.

Dance music and Scherzandos

Haydn composed several sets of minuets in the 1750s and early 1760s but only one survives in original and complete form, the twelve 'Seitenstetten' Minuets (IX:1), so called because the autograph was housed in Seitenstetten Monastery for many years. It is undated, a fact which in itself points to the 1750s as the likely period of composition. Minuets X and XI, amongst others, contain some unconvincing harmonic writing, prompting the hypothesis that the dances were composed earlier rather than later in that decade. All twelve dances are scored for two oboes, two horns, first and second violins and 'basso' (which in this case meant cello, double bass and bassoon). Only three minuets (I, V and XII) have trio sections, and here the instrumentation is reduced through omitting either or both pairs of wind instruments. As minuets that were actually to be danced, all feature regular phrasing patterns and bass lines that mark the beat. This regularity reminds twentieth-century listeners that the minuet movements included in Haydn's symphonies, quartets, etc. often make their impact by exploiting the familiarity of eighteenth-century musicians and audiences with the dance, both as active participants and as passive listeners. With the spirit of the dance an omnipresent and unavoidable phenomenon, players of the second minuet of the quartet, op. 1 no. 1, for instance, would have found the rapid succession of up-beats disturbing and enthralling.

Unlike the autograph of the 'Seitenstetten' Minuets, that of the six Scherzandos (II:33–38) has not survived, and the title derives from the entry of the works in Part V (1765) of the Breitkopf Catalogue: 'VI Scherzandi del Sigr. Gius. Hayden'. They are followed by a further set of six works described as 'Scherzandi, ô Burlesques' by an unknown author (or authors). Whereas Haydn often used the term 'scherzo' to characterize a particular movement in his music in the 1750s and early 1760s (e.g. Sonata no. 3, String Trio no. 6 and Quartet op. 1 no. 3), as a title for a complete work it is otherwise unknown. If the title is Haydn's own, he may have used it in order to distinguish these small orchestral works from the more ambitious symphonies.

The six Scherzandos were undoubtedly conceived as a set: the key scheme F, C, D, G, E, and A is characterized by a fifth relationship between individual pairs of works; they are scored for two oboes, two horns, first and second violins and 'basso', with a solo flute in every trio; all have four movements in the order fast, minuet, slow and fast; with one exception (the trio of no. 5) the trio sections and slow movements are in the tonic minor; each of the opening movements is an energetic Allegro, mainly in 2/4 time; and the finales are Presto movements in 3/8.

This schematic approach for a series of works recalls Haydn's practice in the early quartets, except that in this case the works seem to have been composed as a set, rather than singly or in pairs over a period of four or five years. Compared with the bulk of Haydn's instrumental music to *c.* 1760, their main distinguishing feature is the adoption of a four-movement pattern, the ground-plan for most of Haydn's later symphonies and quartets, and for the whole symphonic tradition down to the present day. Haydn himself had composed some four-movement works as early as 1758 (e. g. Symphony no. 37), but as a composer of instrumental music he was more accustomed to three- and five-movement patterns. The presence of the flute suggests that the Scherzandos were composed for the Esterházy orchestra rather than the smaller Morzin band. When Haydn entered the service of the Esterházy family in 1761, his first works were the attractive and showy trilogy of symphonies, 'Le matin', 'Le midi', and 'Le soir' (nos. 6, 7 and 8). No symphonies are known to have been composed in the following year, 1762.[8] Can these Scherzandos date from that year, conceived as concise experiments in a four-movement pattern? Stylistically, for that date, they contain nothing that is new: the opening binary movements and concluding 3/8 Presto movements are reminiscent of Haydn's wind-band music, the instrumentation for strings without viola is very conservative, the slow movements are for strings only and the minuets, though spirited enough, are devoid of the teasing irregularities or the grand sonority found elsewhere. Because Haydn was writing well within his own capabilities, he was able to ponder the effectiveness of a four-movement pattern. It offered greater variety than a typical three-movement scheme, with the presence of a slow movement and a minuet and the opportunity to develop differentiated first-movement and finale idioms; equally, the four-movement scheme did not have the straitjacket symmetry of the five-movement scheme. The results were six attractive orchestral works which were too lightweight to be described as symphonies. Until more evidence is forthcoming, the suggested date of 1762 is no more than an attractive proposition, but even if it turns out to be incorrect by two or three years, the Scherzandos mark an important stage in Haydn's espousal during the 1760s of a four-movement scheme for instrumental music.

Concertos

The concertos composed by Haydn in this period fall conveniently into two groups: the first, six works for organ (one a double concerto for violin and organ) composed in the early Viennese period up to 1756; the second, six extant concertos from the early 1760s, mainly composed for players in the Esterházy orchestra.

Organ Concertos: Vienna
  D major (XVIII:2), *c.* 1752–5
  C major (XVIII:10), *c.* 1752–5
  C major (XVIII:8), *c.* 1752–5
  C major (XVIII:5), *c* 1752–5
  C major (XVIII:1), *c* 1756[9]
  F major (XVIII:6), *c.* 1756

Esterházy concertos:
  Horn Concerto in D (VIId:3), 1762
  Violin Concerto in C (VIIa:1), *c.* 1761–5
  Violin Concerto in A (VIIa:3), *c.* 1761–5[10]
  Violin Concerto in G (VIIa:4), *c.* 1761–5[11]
  Cello Concerto in C (VIIb:1), *c.* 1761–5
  Harpsichord Concerto in F (XVIII:3), *c.* 1764–5

In addition, it is known that Haydn composed a further five concertos, now lost, for the Esterházy musicians: another violin concerto, a second cello concerto, a second horn concerto, a double-bass concerto and a flute concerto.

In the 1750s Haydn regularly played the organ at the Convent of the Hospitallers and at the Haugwitz Chapel in Vienna. His organ concertos were probably performed during the services, typically between the Sanctus and Benedictus movements of the mass. Their accompaniment consists of the normal church orchestra of first and second violins and basso, frequently supplemented by oboes, trumpets and timpani, though it is often difficult to establish whether these parts were composed by Haydn or by another musician. The Austrian organ of the time consisted of manuals only, without pedal board.

The concertos of the Esterházy period were, in the main, designed to be played by the gifted players Haydn had at his disposal, notably *Konzertmeister* Luigi Tomasini and the cellist Joseph Weigl. In the case of the Horn Concerto, it is possible that it was not written for one of the many Esterházy players but for Joseph Leutgeb, for whom Mozart was to write horn concertos twenty years later. In all these concertos the accompanying orchestra consists of a full four-part texture, but wind instruments are not always present, which is surprising when one recalls that not a single symphony calls for less than two oboes and two horns. Not unexpectedly, the solo parts are more overtly virtuoso than those of the organ concertos and this, coupled with the fuller orchestral accompaniment, makes them more appealing than the early organ concertos. There are, however, plenty of features in common between the two groups to enable them to be discussed together and, since Haydn was never again to devote so much time and energy to the concerto, an appraisal of the composer's attitude to the genre is most appropriately made here rather than in a later chapter.

A glance at the tempo indications of the concertos would show a preponderance of Moderato and Allegretto moderato, to a far greater extent than in any other genre, including the symphony. Moreover, the pulse of the music often emphasizes quavers, and the phrase rhythms frequently divide at the half-bar. This even-spaced tempo encourages repeated use of particular thematic types, especially dotted-note rhythms and unison writing; the compass of the organ, cello and violin ensures that C major is the favourite key; consequently it is possible to speak in terms of a Haydn C major style at this stage of his career.

The first movements employ the following basic ritornello scheme, familiar from countless concertos of the early eighteenth century.

Ritornello 1	I-V-I
Solo 1	I-V
Ritornello 2	V
Solo 2	modulating then establishing vi
Ritornello 3	→I
Solo 3	I
Ritornello 4	I

The content of the opening ritornello can be divided into constituent themes, though that sense – so distinctive in a Mozart concerto – of a procession of individually characterized themes is absent; uniformity rather than diversification is the main characteristic. As if to compensate for this low thematic profile, Haydn moves with a great sense of purpose to the dominant key in the opening ritornello in a way Mozart was normally concerned to avoid; in the case of the A major 'Melk' concerto, one third of the opening ritornello is firmly in E major. This distinct modulation to the dominant pre-empts the dramatic effectiveness of the soloist's move to the dominant in Solo 1, which is further weakened by the lack of a new and separate theme at this point. The end-result in many of Haydn's concertos is that Solo 1 seems arbitrary in direction and content in comparison with Ritornello 1, a weakness that is only partially compensated for by the virtuosity of the soloist.

Following a short ritornello section, Solo 2 steers a course that is once again usually diffuse. References back to the opening theme are followed by lengthy passages of sequential patterns using ornamental figuration that at best is but tenuously related to early themes; the organ concertos, especially, are prone to note-spinning at this point and only the Cello Concerto really escapes this censure.

The only major structural alteration that Mozart was to make to the established ritornello scheme was to do away with the ritornello that separates Solo 2 from Solo 3, so that the return to the tonic and the main theme acquired a sense of arrival akin to that experienced when the recapitulation is launched in a symphony. But Haydn retained this intervening ritornello which begins, in most cases, by presenting the main theme in the submediant minor before re-establishing the home tonic, with the redundant result that the main theme is heard twice in close proximity. The ensuing solo section repeats the main thematic material of the movement and, apart from the 1756 Organ Concerto which badly loses its way at this point, achieves a sense of cohesion not found in the foregoing solo sections. All the Esterházy concertos require cadenzas in their first movements, but none of the organ concertos provides this opportunity.

If the dominant impression of the first movements is one of formal stiffness and redundancy, then the slow movements and finales are more successful. The concertante approach that serves Haydn so well in many of his early instrumental slow movements finds its true home in the slow movements of the organ concertos and violin concertos, where it is often additionally buttressed by opening and closing ritornellos. Rather interestingly, Haydn in the C major Violin Concerto uses the charming device, noted in the slow movement of the quartet, op.1 no.1, of framing his slow movement with independent material. On the whole, however, these slow movements, though elegant, are superficial and do not have the winning melodic appeal of similar movements in the early quartets.

A brisk tempo – none slower than allegro – and a predominance of short time signatures (2/4 and 3/8) ensure that the concluding movements of the concertos have a zest that is lacking in opening movements. In the organ concertos the movements are mainly binary with central double bars; in the Esterházy concertos ritornello structures are employed, but without the restricting rigidity found in the first movements. For instance, in the Finale of the C major Violin Concerto the soloist re-appears unexpectedly in the final ritornello with a *pianissimo* statement of the main theme, followed by a *fortissimo* resumption of the ritornello.

After his early interest in the solo concerto, Haydn paid only infrequent attention to the genre; only five works survive from the remainder of his life (the *lira organizzata* concertos for the King of Naples are a special case, see p.213). Moreover, none of Haydn's early concertos achieved anything like the popularity of his quartets, symphonies or sonatas, a fact reflected in the paucity of extant sources and the number of lost works. In the second half of the eighteenth century the solo concerto had been ousted as the most popular orchestral genre by the symphony, yet the demands of players and audiences ensured a steady supply of new concertos. At the Esterházy court Haydn had at his disposal some of the finest instrumentalists in the Austrian Empire, even though the composer himself could not be included in this category. Even if Haydn's imagination, unlike that of Mozart, J. C. Bach and others, was not to be excited by his own abilities as a virtuoso performer, it cannot be said that he was uninterested in instrumental display; on the contrary, many of his symphonies contain concertante virtuoso writing that delights and astonishes the listener, and poses problems for even the most gifted players of today.

In fact Haydn's lack of interest and success in the concerto genre was due to a fundamental incompatability between the structure of the eighteenth-century concerto and the composer's musical language. He found the form restricting and not dynamic; he was not persuaded that some of the principles of sonata form could be applied to ritornello structure in order to impart a new sense of drama. Haydn revelled in the dialectic freedom of sonata form; ritornello form, on the other hand, even at the hands of the mature Mozart, cannot afford to get too involved in this argumentative, apparently impulsive process. At first Haydn was content to go through the motions of concerto writing but as his style developed he became frustrated by the lack of interaction between form and content; after the mid-1760s Haydn rarely wrote concertos.

Of the early concertos by far the most successful in performance is the Cello Concerto, rediscovered in 1961 when a set of manuscript parts from Radeňín Castle was found in the National Museum in Prague. The first movement has many of the formal features noted earlier but is enlivened by distinguished thematic writing and, in Solo 2, demonstrative writing that is vigorous rather than effete. The slow movement is in full sonata form with three ritornellos – at the beginning of the movement, between the exposition and development, and at the end. The concertante approach is relinquished in favour of genuine interplay between soloist and orchestra based on well-established themes. The concluding Allegro molto is as rousing as anything in a contemporary Haydn symphony, and the manner in which Ritornello 3 continues the development of the material rather than providing a formal link into the next section is typical of the compositional energy found in this movement and in the work as a whole.

Symphonies

Of Haydn's 106 extant symphonies over a third were composed in the short period 1758–65, first for Count Morzin at Lukavec and Vienna, and then for the Esterházy court. This production rate was not unusual for a mid-eighteenth-century composer of symphonies (not to mention earlier North German composers of cantatas), but the diversity and range of inspiration, from the profound to the whimsical, marks Haydn, even in this early part of his career, as a composer of more than contemporary interest; and of all his instrumental music to 1765 it is the symphonies that give the most consistently vivid picture of Haydn's talents. Recent scholarly interest in the symphonies of his contemporaries has offered a clearer context for the appreciation of his works and has revealed that certain features, judged unusual from the inappropriate standpoint of the late eighteenth century and the nineteenth century, were not exclusive to Haydn. Paradoxically, this wider knowledge of the eighteenth-century symphony does not diminish Haydn's stature, but reinforces it and elucidates the fertility of his imagination as well as the security of his technique.

As has been mentioned, a notable feature of Haydn's instrumental music in the 1750s and 1760s is the almost complete absence of four-movement patterns. Seen against this background, Haydn's symphonies show a decisive trend away from the three-movement pattern (fast, slow and fast) towards a four-movement arrangement (fast, slow, minuet and fast) so that by 1764–5 it had become the norm for Haydn. Most of the twelve symphonies that have three movements were composed for Morzin. Symphony no. 10 in D major has many typical features. Scored for two oboes, two horns and strings, the full orchestra is used only in the outer movements, with the central Andante being played by strings alone. The opening movement is a genuine Allegro rather than the moderato tempo often encountered in other genres. It opens with a theme that contrasts *forte* chords (with triple stops) with a *piano* continuation, a juxtaposition ultimately derived from the opera house. No one accompaniment pattern predominates, though considerable use is made of repeated semiquaver figuration (on single notes and in Alberti fashion) to impart a sense of momentum and atmosphere. The texture is reduced to strings and the dynamic to a consistent *piano* for the second subject. The development repeats rather than discusses, and the recapitulation is orthodox. The slow movement has a tempo marking of Andante, which, at this stage in Haydn's career, is a more common marking than Adagio, and wears a rather impassive face, eschewing the concertante approach in favour of a regularly phrased theme shared between second and first violins who sometimes play in sixths. *Forte* and *piano* contrasts within a phrase are again a feature. More idiosyncratic are the *tenuto* marks on held notes (bar 6 etc., bar 68 etc.); throughout his career Haydn seems to have been concerned that long notes in the accompaniment should not 'die' in performance. The Finale is a movement type familiar from other genres: Presto, 3/8 tempo and a main theme generated by the typical rhythm

As well as avoiding opening movements in a moderato tempo, Haydn's three-movement symphonies avoid also 'tempo di menuetto' finales; that of Symphony no. 30 ('Alleluja') is a rare and late example composed in 1765. By that date Haydn had come to show a distinct preference for a four-movement design – fast, slow, minuet and fast. The inclusion of both a slow movement and a minuet (rather than the often prolix 'tempo di menuetto') provides a broader canvas on which to work – a liberating development which is also found in the symphonies of contemporaries such as Ordoñez and Hofmann.

A third approach, again found in the symphonies of Ordoñez and Hofmann, was to utilize a scheme derived ultimately from the old *sonata da chiesa*, though it would be fallacious to assume that these symphonies were any more likely to be performed in church than symphonies with other movement patterns. Symphonies nos. 5, 11, 18, 21 and 22 by Haydn all open with a self-contained slow movement followed by an allegro, a minuet and another, concluding allegro (no. 18 is a three-movement variant of this pattern: slow, fast and tempo di menuet). This was not merely a cosmetic change of order for it had a direct result affecting the quality of the slow movement; one of the earliest symphonies of this type, no. 5 in A major (*c.* 1760), is typical. The slow movement is an adagio rather than an andante and is scored for the full orchestra with charming linking motives in the horns. The opening statement and ensuing link reveal a sophisticated interaction of melodic contour, phrasing and motivic outlay.

The theme itself is six bars long but divided irregularly (3, 1 + 2), with the second phrase carefully avoiding a premature cadence at bar 5 by doubling back on itself and re-using a thematic motive, displaced down an octave, to lead to a cadence at bar 6. The opening phrase yields two motives (marked 'a' and 'b' in the example) that re-appear in later contexts, to unify apparently different melodic ideas.

As in the contemporary wind-band divertimentos, the horn parts in this movement are a tribute to the abilities of Morzin's players. When Haydn moved to Eisenstadt, his appointment was followed by that of many leading instrumentalists and his symphonies from 1761 to 1765 (and beyond) are full of extensive solo passages for flute (an instrument not available at the Morzin court), oboes, bassoons, horns, violin, cello and double bass; the only orchestral instrument not treated soloistically was the viola (trumpets and clarinets were not available). Though few Austrian orchestras could equal the virtuosity of the Esterházy players, concertante elements in the symphony were not an exclusive feature of Haydn's output; many Austrian symphonies of the 1760s and the 1770s, by Ordoñez and Vanhal for instance, have extensive solo writing for a wide variety of instruments, including viola, and it is a tradition that informs the orchestral serenades of Mozart too.

The first symphonies composed by Haydn for Prince Paul Anton Esterházy constituted a set of three works, individually titled 'Le matin', 'Le midi' and 'Le soir', the French titles, like Haydn's recently acquired preference for 'Menuet' rather than 'Minuet', being a reflection of the affected Francophile taste of the time. Unfortunately, nothing is known about the circumstances of their performance. The titles are no doubt authentic but, unlike Vivaldi's *Seasons*, the programmatic element is not a continuous, descriptive one. Only two specific events are described: the fourth movement of 'Le soir' is a storm ('La Tempesta', a favourite baroque conceit) and the six-bar introduction to 'Le matin' is obviously an evocation of sunrise, though not labelled as such. The baroque tradition of programmatic orchestral works is a clear source of inspiration for these works and in particular, a set of twelve orchestral suites by Gregor Werner entitled *Der curiose musikalische Instrumentalkalender* (1748) may have exerted a direct influence on the symphonies.[12] Though programmatic symphonies from the second half of the eighteenth century are by no means rare and there are some later examples of individual movements by Haydn stimulated by an extra-musical idea, Haydn as a composer of symphonies was always more readily stimulated by the possibilities of abstract musical argument. Notwithstanding their pictorial attractiveness, it is easy, therefore, to exaggerate the significance of these three symphonies. They were probably a diplomatic success for Haydn more because of their extensive concertante writing than because of their programmatic content which was slim. 'Le matin' has an extensive solo part for *Konzertmeister* Luigi Tomasini and shorter passages for flute, oboes, first horn, bassoon, cello and double bass. The colour of the orchestral fabric changes more frequently than in earlier symphonies, with the wind instruments frequently taking a decisive lead. Orchestral colour was also a stimulus to invention. In the first movement of 'Le matin', for instance, the first horn anticipates the recapitulation by two bars, a strange incident used over forty years later, and in more tense surroundings, by Beethoven in his 'Eroica' Symphony.

'Le midi' and 'Le soir' make even greater use of solo writing in allegro movements than does 'Le matin', and though the baroque concerto grosso is a clear historical forerunner of the texture, to modern listeners the diversity and informality of the solo writing seem comparable with much later works such as Bartók's Concerto for Orchestra.

Many other symphonies by Haydn have solo passages for violin, flute and cello, usually in slow movements, but in general the composer restrained his enthusiasm in this direction, preferring to cultivate a less ostentatious style. Only two further symphonies would warrant the description 'concerto for orchestra': no. 72, probably composed in 1763, and no. 31, dating from two years later. Both were designed primarily to demonstrate the prowess of the four horn players of the Esterházy *Kapelle*, but Haydn took the opportunity to write solo passages for other instruments too. The first movement of no. 31 (Allegro) incorporates evocative horn fanfares in its thematic material, giving rise to several contemporary nicknames for the work: 'Hornsignal', 'Auf dem Anstand' and 'alla Posta'. The second movement (Adagio) is a concertante movement in which the thematic lead is shared between solo violin, solo cello and pairs of horns. In the Trio of the Menuet flute and oboes share the limelight with the horns. The Finale is a set of variations; whereas variations were commonplace in Haydn's other instrumental music, this is the only example in the composer's symphonies up to 1765. A simple binary theme, sixteen bars long and marked 'Moderato molto', provides the material for a systematic exposition of the individual talents of the Esterházy players in the following order: oboes, cello, flute, four horns, violin, tutti and double bass. A rousing Presto coda once more thrusts the horns into the foreground of the texture and the work concludes with a repetition of the 'Hornsignal' from the first movement.

These dazzling symphonies, full of positive colours and energy, are the most obviously attractive achievement in Haydn's early career, and certainly endeared him to his colleagues and to his employer. The more perceptive of Haydn's colleagues would have recognized another, less demonstrative aspect of his symphonies, one that was not evident in the remainder of his output to date – the endeavour to stiffen the texture of the music with counterpoint. The first, very deliberate, attempt occurs in a Morzin symphony, no. 3 (*c.* 1759/60). The Menuet is a two-part canon between treble and bass that ceases only in order to articulate a cadence. The Finale is a four-part fugue that dissolves into homophony only twenty-two bars from the end; its subject is a four-note tag in steady semibreves announced simultaneously with a counterpoint in (mainly) moving crotchets.

Later in the movement, some of the contrapuntal possibilities of the theme are exploited, in two- and three-part stretto. The first movement of the symphony does not have the same contrapuntal formality, yet its main theme is conceived in two voices, a slow-moving motive in dotted minims[13] and running quavers.

These two related procedures, formal counterpoint and use of melodic tags to bind the texture together, appear in many subsequent symphonies.

Date	*Symphony*	
c. 1760	no. 11	Second movement (Allegro) features a five-note tag, a decoration of the one later used in Symphony no. 13. Recapitulation opens with stretto.
1763	no. 13	Finale. First subject and cadence theme use four-note tag now familiar from Mozart's 'Jupiter' Symphony and other later works. Used homophonically and as a constituent element in double and triple counterpoint; also in four-part stretto in coda.
1763	no. 40	Finale: *Fuga* (four parts). Fifteen-bar theme with prominent use of falling perfect interval in semibreves; plentiful imitation later in the movement.
c. 1760/64	no. 25	Finale. Sonata form. Four-note tag, some imitation at beginning of development and recapitulation.

These four-note tags have an affinity with the beginnings of some of the *cantus firmi* found in the two textbooks known to have been studied by Haydn, Mattheson's *Der vollkommene Kapellmeister* and Fux's *Gradus ad Parnassum*, and the strict rhythmic differentiation between theme and counterpoint often shows the legacy of species counterpoint training. According to Dies, Haydn studied Mattheson and Fux in the early 1750s, yet it was not until *c.* 1760 that the results of this contrapuntal application were employed more generally, giving Haydn's compositions a sense of measured control that is rare in music of the early Classical period. This desire to broaden the stylistic outlook of his music through the incorporation of counterpoint was to continue throughout the 1760s, most self-consciously in the *Missa* 'Sunt bona mixta malis', and reached an apotheosis of assimilation in the quartets of op. 20.

Haydn in 1765

By the end of 1765 the Esterházy *Kapellmeister* Gregor Werner was seriously ill and the promise that Haydn would assume the duties of full *Kapellmeister* would shortly be fulfilled. His master, Prince Nicolaus, had provided him with the responsibilities and the facilities that allowed his music to gain in assurance, craft and flair; the building of the summer palace at Eszterháza with its two opera houses (one for marionette operas) was well under way and doubtless Haydn was eagerly anticipating the challenges that the new facilities would provide. Haydn's string trios, quartets, symphonies and church music circulated extensively in Austria, and publishers in Paris, Amsterdam and London had already issued trios, quartets and symphonies by the composer – the tentative beginnings of a wider, international fame. At the age of thirty-three, Haydn could now look into a future that was not only comfortable, but exciting.

Fifteen years earlier, even basic comfort had been unattainable. His development had been unusual as well as difficult. Though Haydn was a competent violinist and keyboard player, he was no virtuoso performer and therefore, unlike his friend Dittersdorf and others, could not broaden his musical horizons through travel. Of the major composers in the history of Western music Haydn was one of the least travelled in his formative years; probably the longest journey he undertook was from Vienna to Mariazell, a distance of some eighty miles. His formal training had not been conducive to early mastery either. St Stephen's, the cathedral of the capital city, had as its musical head Georg Reutter, a prolific and formidable composer of church music. But it seems that he neglected his teaching duties: 'In the Choir School there was no instruction in musical theory, and Haydn recalled having received only two such lessons from the worthy Reutter' (Griesinger). Apart from the short period when he acted as accompanist in Porpora's household, Haydn was largely self-taught, using the traditional textbooks of Mattheson and Fux, and, later, the writings of Johann Philipp Kirnberger. Since Haydn travelled very little, the range of the music he heard in the 1750s and 1760s was correspondingly limited: that of Asplmayer, Bonno, Gluck, Hasse, Holzbauer, Monn, Porsile, Reutter, Richter, Sammartini, Tuma, Wagenseil and Werner was some of the most familiar to him. From the diverse idioms of these composers Haydn painstakingly moulded his craft and his art. He was not a solitary figure in the quest for a new synthesis of form and style in the 1750s and he was probably reasonably acquainted with the efforts of Carl Ditters (later von Dittersdorf), with whom he played serenades in the streets of Vienna and with whom he kept in touch for many years, and his own brother, Michael. Few compositions by J. S. Bach and Handel penetrated into the Austrian domains and their names do not figure in any pertinent documentary material. However, one composer above all others was accorded a special position by Haydn – Carl Philipp Emanuel Bach (1714-88).

The second surviving son of J. S. Bach worked exclusively in North Germany, from 1740 in Berlin and from 1768 in Hamburg. Haydn singled out the composer's first six keyboard sonatas as having a special influence on his own development (cf. p. 27). In Griesinger's biographical account, Haydn is quoted thus: 'I did not leave my clavier until I had played them through, and whoever knows me thoroughly must discover that I owe a great deal to Emanuel Bach, that I understood him and have studied him with diligence.' This apparently direct acknowledgment of an artistic debt is, as A. Peter Brown has pointed out, replete with problems. Its placing in Griesinger's biography suggests that Haydn became acquainted with Bach's music in the early 1750s, but there is circumstantial evidence to suggest that it occurred rather later, perhaps in the 1760s. 'First sonatas' implies the 'Prussian' Sonatas, published in 1742, but other sets also designated as 'opus 1' were also in circulation. Haydn also admired C. P. E. Bach's famous treatise *Versuch über die wahre Art das Clavier zu spielen* (Essay on the True Art of Keyboard Playing), published in two parts in 1753 and 1762. The technical parts of the treatise, dealing with ornaments, intervals, thorough bass etc., Haydn would have found conveniently methodical, but the treatise is especially notable for its active encouragement of a performance style (and, by implication, composition) that was strongly characterized, romantic even. 'Play from the soul, not like a trained bird,' he exhorts the keyboardist, and elsewhere: 'A musician cannot move others unless he too is moved.' Having mastered the basic technique, Haydn writes music from the 1760s onwards which acquires, to borrow Bach's word, 'soul'. His music in the 1760s affords many striking similarities of gesture and technique (e. g. the impassioned slow movement of Symphony no. 12, the 'Acht Sauschneider' capriccio and the opening of the Finale of Sonata no. 16) and these occur with greater frequency in later years, but C. P. E. Bach's influence was more general than specific and Haydn paid him the artistic compliment of emulation rather than mere imitation. Bach was a more rigorous craftsman than most of the composers known to Haydn and his music, like his writings, reveals a wilful creative energy. Before Haydn became widely acquainted with the music of Mozart in the 1780s, Bach afforded the only instance of an artistic talent he could unfailingly respect and revere.

III
The fairy-tale castle at Eszterháza, 1766–1780

BEFORE HE SUCCEEDED his brother as reigning prince, Nicolaus Esterházy was in the habit of spending many months of each year at a remote hunting lodge called Süttör, on the south side of the Neusiedlersee. Süttör was a marshy and decidedly unhealthy spot: it was therefore a particularly eccentric idea on the part of Prince Nicolaus to choose it as the site for a large castle. Possibly the castle's existence was to prove 'mind over matter'; but whatever the reason, Eszterháza (known in German as 'Esterhaz' or 'Estoras', the latter being Haydn's usual spelling) was a very rich man's whim. Its cost was astronomical – 13 million gulden – and it was very large (126 rooms); but although it was called 'le petit Versailles de l'Hongrie' as early as 1784, it did not owe its existence, as was (and is) widely believed, to the Château de Versailles, which Prince Nicolaus visited in 1767, when Eszterháza was already nearly completed, but to Austrian prototypes, particularly Schönbrunn Castle in Vienna. Ultimately, both Schönbrunn and Eszterháza owed a great deal to French models (Prince Nicolaus even commissioned the French architect Mourette to draw up a plan for the new castle in 1764); French taste dominated Austrian thought throughout this period.

The hunting lodge or small castle at Süttör was designed by Anton Erhard Martinelli and construction began c. 1720; the building was later incorporated into Eszterháza. It is probable that this second stage of the castle's construction, which was entrusted to Johann Ferdinand Mödlhammer, was initiated when Nicolaus succeeded his brother as Prince in 1762. By 1765, a new architect was at work, and it was he who became responsible for the final result: Melchior Hefele (not 'Hefeles'), formerly Captain of the Hungarian Guard in Vienna and Member of the I. R. Academy. Details of Eszterháza's construction may be studied in the admirable book by Pal Voit, *Der Barock in Ungarn* (Budapest 1971, pp. 88ff.), where Hefele's later career – which included magnificent buildings in Passau, Pressburg (now Bratislava) and Szombathely – may be profitably studied.

Eszterháza was very long in the building: in the autumn of 1768 the opera house was inaugurated with a performance of Haydn's new opera, *Lo speziale*; the marionette theatre was inaugurated a few years later, in 1773. However, it was not until 1784 that Nicolaus Esterházy considered his amazing creation, a fairy-tale castle rising from the surrounding swampland, to have been truly completed: it was in this year that he caused two 'guides' to the castle to be published, one in French entitled 'Excursion à Esterhaz en Hongrie' and the other in German, *Beschreibung des Hochfürstlichen Schlosses Esterháß im Königreich Ungern* [sic], which is considerably longer. (Perhaps the actual point at which Nicolaus considered his castle to be finished was the opening, in 1784, of the large cascade in front of the main building.) Visitors flocked to see this Hungarian wonder, which included a Chinese pavilion (where Haydn and the musicians, in Chinese attire, had played for Empress Maria Theresa in 1773); a coffee house; a temple dedicated to Fortune and another dedicated to Venus; a rose garden; a menagerie; and a 'princely hunting lodge' known as Monbijou.

Haydn's singers and orchestra varied greatly in the years (1766–90) during which Eszterháza was in full operation. Although he was tremendously flexible, adapting his scores to local exigencies (sometimes two bassoons, sometimes one, and so on), some curious details emerge: there were, for example, two clarinet players who were in residence from the end of 1775 to the end of February 1778; yet there is not a single authentic score by Haydn of this period to include clarinets. Did Haydn not like clarinets? The same applies to the harp player, Johann Baptist Krumpholtz, in residence for several years (1773–6), for whom Haydn appears to have composed nothing. Since Haydn also composed no harp concerto for Krumpholz's even more famous wife, who was a regular soloist throughout the 1791 season of the Haydn-Salomon concerts in London, it must tell us something of Haydn's attitude towards the instrument (though, to balance this, Haydn must surely have intended for Madame Krumpholtz the lengthy harp solo in one of Orfeo's arias in *L'anima del filosofo*, his London opera of 1791 that never saw the light of the stage).

To give an idea of the varying size of Haydn's forces, we may compare those used for Haydn's *La canterina* at Pressburg in 1767 with pay-lists from 1775 and 1790. In February and March 1767, Haydn's orchestra consisted of two oboists (also using cors anglais), one bassoon player (probably used with the continuo group), three horn players (of whom two were also violinists, used as such – see below), four violinists and viola players, one violoncello and Haydn as harpsichordist. But in a recently discovered bill (see *H-S*, IV, 249) we see that Haydn engaged locally, at Pressburg, two horn players and a double-bass player. Hence he had at least six violin and viola players, counting the substitute horn players. Moreover, there were at Pressburg among Esterházy's troupe, the stage-designer (Le) Bon, four female singers and two male singers. On 1 March 1767, a double-bass (and bassoon) player was engaged permanently at Pressburg. In December 1775, there were no fewer than twenty-seven musicians and singers, as a document in the Esterházy Archives, Budapest (A. M. XIII, 800), shows (see opposite).

In concerts, Haydn played the violin: this we know from a report of a visiting diarist in 1772, who was at Eszterháza and wrote, 'Haydn joua du violon' (*C&W*, II, 177), whereas in the opera house he played harpsichord continuo. Otherwise, there were five singers: this was one year before the operatic side of Eszterháza suddenly began to dominate, and the results of this development are demonstrated graphically in the 1790 pay-list. In the 1775 list, No. 20, Peczival, was also a trained timpani player; of the four horn players named (Oliva, Pauer, Franz, Dietzl), two could always be used as violinists or in the viola section. Hence Haydn's orchestra in December 1775 consisted of two oboes, two clarinets, two bassoons, two (four) horns, timpani, four (counting Haydn) first violins, three second violins, two violas, one cello and one double bass.

By the end of September 1790, the last pay-list of the band at Eszterháza, quite a different constitution can be noted: after 'Capellmeister Haidn', there were the singers Bologna, Sassi, 'Polcelli' (Polzelli), Benvenuti, Zecchielli, Melo, Braghetti, Prizzi, de Paoli, Martinelli, Majeroni, Amici, Ung(e)richt and Specht – a very large ensemble of fourteen singers, who were just preparing to stage Mozart's *Le nozze di Figaro*. In the orchestra there were now seven violinists and viola players (eight with Haydn), two cellists and one double-bass player; in the wind section were one flautist, two oboists, three bassoonists (the third being the timpani player) and four horn players (two of whom could also be used in the upper string section); there were also a manager and a regular copyist. Haydn's strings could now number, with the two horn players and himself, ten violinists and violists (or, on an av-

Specifications Quittung [receipt], according to which the following chamber musicians received their salaries *pro Decembris* 1775 ...:

		Fl.	Xr.
1.	Capellmeister Josephus Haydn mpria	48	50
2.	Soprano Barbara Dichtler	16	40
3.	ditto Maddalena Friberth	41	40
4.	Tenor Carlo Friberth	25	—
5.	Leopoldo Dichtler	28	—
6.	Bass singer Christian Specht	37	30
7.	Violinist Luigi Tomasini	40	12½
8.	ditto Joseph Burksteiner [*sic*]	20	—
9.	ditto Joseph Hoffmann	16	40
10.	ditto Johann Dietzl	16	40
11.	Violoncellist Xavier Marteau	42	42½
12.	Hunting horn player Joseph Oliva	42	42½
13.	ditto Franz Pauer	38	32½
14.	ditto Carl Franz	27	30
15.	ditto Joseph Dietzl	32	57
16.	Oboist Carl Chorus	32	57
17.	ditto Zacharias Pohl	28	47
18.	Bassoonist Carl Schiringer	32	57
19.	ditto Johan Hinterberger	32	57
20.	ditto Caspar Petziwal [*sic*]	20	—
21.	Harpist J. Krumpholtz	25	—
22.	Soprano ⎤ Josephus Haydn mpria [who signed for them	10	26
23.	Alto ⎬ in their absence; they were the church singers at Eisenstadt.]	10	26
24.	ditto ⎦	10	26

[There follows some increases applying to Nos. 11, 12, 15, 16, 18, and 19, each of whom received 50 Fl. for their double households. [Add: six entries of 10 Fl. 50 xr. each]

		Fl.	Xr.
25.	Bassoonist Ignatz Drobney	25	40
26.	Clarinettist Reimund [*sic*] Griesbacher	25	—
27.	ditto Anthon Griesbacher	25	—

Summa:... 847 fl. 03 xr.

---

erage operatic night, four firsts, three seconds, two violas). As to its quality, the brilliant German composer Joseph Martin Kraus (1756–92), who visited Eszterháza in 1783, thought (as did everyone) the climate vile, the taste of the theatre vulgar and the Prince 'most condescending' (which latter word is used, of course, in its eighteenth-century connotation). 'The orchestra is what you would expect under the direction of a Haydn – therefore one of the best. It is in fact not larger than 24 men, but makes on outstanding impression. – The first two violinists and the cellist are Italians – the rest are almost all Bohemians ...' (*C&W*, II, 478). Another witness was the Venezuelan revolutionary, General Francisco de Miranda, the friend of Washington and Hamilton in America, who visited Eszterháza in 1785 and wrote in his diary (26 October):[1]

... the famous Hayden [*sic*], for whom I was carrying letters, accompanied me directly and showed me the whole of the Palace ... The theatre which performs the whole year round costs him [the Prince] 30,000 florins a year, and the actors' salaries are for life – in the evening went to the opera, saw the Prince, his niece, and his mistress, vulgar woman ... the representation cold – the orchestra twenty-four instruments, Hayden played the harpsichord [*el clave*]. ...

[Two days later, 28 October, we read:] The next day early Hayden came and we went together in a coach sent by the Prince to see the garden ... talked a lot about music with Hayden, and he agreed with me about the merit of Boccherini ...

The most interesting detail in that diary entry is 'the representation cold': possibly to a Latin temperament, Haydn's interpretation of an opera by Cimarosa or Paisiello may have seemed frigid and intellectual.

By the time Eszterháza was at its cultural zenith, there was a long, regular season of opera and theatre, the latter given by strolling players (*Wandertruppen*) who came to stay at the castle for several months each year. Some of these troupes were famous, such as that led by Carl Wahr, who performed Shakespeare plays in translations commissioned by Prince Nicolaus. Obviously much of the repertoire was of an ephemeral nature, but that would also have been true of many much larger and more important centres such as London or Paris. It is difficult for us to judge the standard of Haydn's ensemble. Although everyone was of one opinion about the excellence of the orchestra, the vocal ensemble was (as we have just seen) thought rather cool by one visitor and second-rate by a visiting British nobleman, Henry William Paget, 1st Marquess of Anglesey (1768-1854), who was making the Grand Tour in 1788 and in the late autumn visited Eszterháza,

one of the most magnificent chateaus possible, belonging to the Prince D'Esterhazy ... He has an immense establishment and tho' economising to a great degree, spends about £50,000 a year. Those strangers who choose to be presented to him he lodges & receives with every mark of attention & hospitality. Those who go incognito are furnished with carriages to see the Parks, Gardens &c. He has an Italian Opera & German Play who perform alternatively. The Theatre which is the most elegant and handsomest I ever saw he built himself. Tho' the Opera is not of the first rate, yet they are very tolerable – and the excellence of the Orchestra, of whom Haydn, the illustrious Haydn is at the head, makes amends for the moderate Vocal Performers. He has a great collection of curiosities of countries – and a tolerable Gallery of Pictures. I am no connoisseur but I found some strikingly good. All this I admire, but I cannot forgive the superfluous magnificence of having a body of Guards, in the midst of his own most peaceable harmless tenants. The Chateau is of an immense extent, he has capital rooms for 50 masters with their servants – I could not help remarking the overflow of Clocks and immense great Glasses – of the former there are above 400, many of which are richly set in diamonds. Notwithstanding all this Plasnewydd or Beau Desert [Paget's British estates] are a Paradise to it, according to my taste.[2]

Although the Esterházy Archives provide a uniquely detailed and authentic group of documents concerning court life and the musicians who played such an important role there, one of the aspects on which little information is provided concerns the concerts or 'academies' given in the beautiful music room situated on the first (American, second) floor. This was the room designed *a priori* for concerts, and it was, interestingly, much smaller than the large hall in Eisenstadt Castle (not designed with music in mind, of course) and caused Haydn to compose orchestral music quite different from that which he had destined for Eisenstadt. The whole atmosphere of the Eszterháza music room was more intimate and especially well suited to the small orchestra over which Haydn disposed: hence a work like Symphony no. 67 (*c.* 1778), with its delicate solo passages and filigree scoring, is perfectly suited to Eszterháza, while the bold, organ-like scoring of Symphony no.13's beginning (1763) seems designed for the large and generous acoustics of Eisenstadt. There is, however, one document which sheds at least some light on the kind of music being given at Eszterháza in the 1770s. It is a list for the season 1778, which was reproduced in its entirety in *C&W* (II, 94-8).

In January, when the season started (23rd), there were plays but also on the

30th, a concert, the programme of which included a symphony, an aria sung by Madame Poschwa, a flute concerto played by Hirsch, an aria sung by the tenor Dichtler, a 'sonata by Mr Luigi' (i.e. Tomasini, the leader), a symphony by Vanhal, arias by Messrs Prandtner and Bianchi, ending with another (unnamed) symphony. The operas started in February with Dittersdorf's *Il finto pazzo* and on 11 February there was another 'Academie' which included, apart from the usual arias, a concerto by Rosetti, a divertimento and a concertino by Pichl and a symphony by Haydn. For three days in February there was 'academia musicale nell' appartamento', presumably chamber music.

The various troupes of strolling players are listed and the entire theatrical programme, which was exactly like that of a large commercial theatre. There was also German-language marionette theatre: on 16 May Joseph Purksteiner's opera, *Das ländliche Hochzeitsfest*, and on 15 September a revival of Haydn's (lost) marionette opera *Dido*, for which the Prince had the libretto reprinted and Haydn required a number of rehearsals. Among the plays there was Beaumarchais's *Le Barbier de Sé-ville* and Goethe's *Stella*, as well as Lessing's *Minna von Barnhelm*. Among the operas, there were works by Piccinni (*La buona figliuola*), Guglielmi, Paisiello, Anfossi and Gazzaniga. When the Prince was present – and he is recorded as being away in July and August and in Vienna for the first week of September – a German play, an Italian opera or a German marionette opera was performed every night. The list gives a vivid picture, in skeleton form, of the variety of theatrical and operatic life at Eszterháza; and we must imagine a similar pattern occurring in the other years between 1776 and 1790.

One of the problems of Eszterháza was the lack of rooms to accommodate the artists, among whom were not only the musicians but, for many months each year, the visiting theatrical companies. That was why Prince Nicolaus at first forbade the wives (husbands) of his musicians to accompany their spouses when in residence. Until the music building was completed, this lack of space created a certain amount of friction, and was the origin of the famous 'Farewell' symphony late in 1772 (see p. 112), when the musicians persuaded Haydn to plead their cause, which he did with particular eloquence.

In the early years of Eszterháza, Prince Nicolaus gave a series of splendid celebrations in which music played a central role; but there were also illuminations, balls (the dance orchestra was always engaged from outside, usually from the *Thurnermeister* of nearby Oedenburg), fireworks (the trumpets and drums also engaged from outside) and crowd scenes using the local peasantry. When, from 1776, there began to be a regular operatic season at Eszterháza – previously, operas had been of a sporadic and 'festival' nature – these extravagant celebrations began to decrease in number, finally disappearing entirely as Prince Nicolaus grew old. The prince was not enamoured of Vienna and, as time went on, he confined his visits there to his annual appearance at the imperial court for the Christmas and New Year season. At the beginning of this period, Esterházy and the musicians spent the winters in Eisenstadt, moving to Eszterháza when the weather grew warmer; but gradually, the season at Eszterháza was extended so that in the 1780s, the musicians and theatrical companies remained in residence from March until mid-December. In the 1760s and 1770s, the Esterházy court made much use of Kittsee Castle on the Danube, opposite Pressburg. But as Eszterháza's importance grew, that of Kittsee diminished until in the 1780s any associations with it quietly fade out of Haydn's life.

In fact, Haydn's principal occupation at Eszterháza became, after 1776, that of an opera director or, as we would say nowadays, manager; there is no evidence that he particularly liked his new role, but we can see that he performed it with great efficiency. He was responsible for the rehearsals, the copying, the actual performances – ultimately, for everything connected with the theatre. Later he was assigned a 'director' who helped in the administration, but, even with his various assistants, Haydn's duties were crushing. We can notice the effect in his handwriting, which becomes hastier as the 1770s turn to the 1780s; the notation starts to become ever more careless in his scores and the abbreviations multiply. It is also a curious fact that although Haydn soon became one of the most experienced opera managers in music history, he seems to have remained strangely aloof from it all; his own operas become, if anything, *less* dramatic as time progresses. *L'infedeltà delusa* of 1773 has a tautness and stage 'presence' which (say) *L'isola disabitata* (1779) or *Armida* (1784) have not, at least for twentieth-century audiences. But some of his most interesting music during this period is to be found in those many insertions for the operas of 'foreign' composers – and these consist not only of arias but even include trios, such as the vivacious and fast-moving 'Lavatevi presto' from the pasticcio *La Circe* of 1789.

Prince Nicolaus's and, as far as we can tell, Haydn's taste was for *opera buffa* rather than *opera seria*, but with the performance of Giuseppe Sarti's *Giulio Sabino*, in May 1783, Prince Nicolaus seems to have been won over to *opera seria*; Haydn, too, seems to have been so impressed with Sarti's opera that it inspired him to compose his last Eszterháza stage work as an *opera seria* – *Armida* – which proved to be the most popular work ever produced in that remote Hungarian court, with a total of fifty-four performances. Haydn was undoubtedly reflecting Prince Nicolaus's judgment when the composer wrote to his publishers Artaria on 1 March 1784, 'Yesterday my *Armida* was performed for the 2nd time with general applause. I am told that this is my best work up to now.' And here we come to one of the paradoxes of life at Eszterháza, for Haydn, influenced by Esterházy's enthusiasm, actually believed *Armida* to be 'his best work up to now', an opinion shared by hardly anyone outside Eszterháza in the 1780s and certainly not shared by even the composer's most ardent admirers today. It must have been frequently difficult to retain a balanced judgment in circumstances of such total isolation; hence it is doubly amazing that Haydn was able to gauge the general European musical climate with such accuracy, and to compose work after work which proved to be the hits of their respective seasons in Paris (e. g. Symphony no. 56, three Paris editions within a few months of each other) or London (Symphony no. 53, made popular during the last season of the celebrated Bach-Abel concerts in 1781 and already arranged for 'the piano forte or harpsichord' by 1782).

In summing up these years at Eszterháza, we may turn to the most reliable of Haydn's contemporary biographers, G. A. Griesinger, who states:

Hunting and fishing were Haydn's favourite pastimes during his sojourn in Hungary, and he could never forget that once he brought down with a single shot three hazel-hens, which arrived on the table of the Empress Maria Theresa. Another time he aimed at a hare but only shot off its tail, but the same shot killed a pheasant that happened to be nearby; while his dog, chasing the hare, strangled itself in a snare. In riding Haydn never developed any skill, because ever since he had fallen from a horse on the Morzin estates [at Lukavec in Bohemia], he never trusted himself to mount a horse again; Mozart too, who liked horseback riding for exercise, was always terrified when doing so.   [19]

Prince Nikolaus Esterhazy was an educated connoisseur and passionate lover of music, and also a good violin player. He had his own opera, spoken theatre, marionette theatre, church music and chamber music. Haydn had his hands full; he composed, he had to conduct all the music, help with the rehearsals, give lessons and even tune his own piano [*Klavier*] in the orchestra. He often wondered how it had been possible for him to compose as much as he did when he was forced to lose so many hours in purely mechanical tasks. ...

Although it must be said that Haydn's outward circumstance was anything but brilliant, it nevertheless provided him with the best opportunity for the development of his many-sided talents. 'My Prince was satisfied with all my works; I received approval; as head of an orchestra, I could undertake experiments, could observe that which enhanced an effect and that which weakened it, thus improving, adding to it, taking away from it, taking risks. I was cut off from the world; there was no one in my vicinity to make me unsure of myself or to persecute me; and so I had to become original.' [17]

In Chapter I we noted the diatribe against Haydn by *Kapellmeister* Werner, written in the autumn of 1765. As if confirming that he did not take the whole affair very seriously and that his faith in Haydn remained firm, Prince Nicolaus wrote to Rahier from Eszterháza on 4 January 1766 as follows: 'This very moment I received 3 pieces [probably compositions for the prince's favourite instrument, the baryton; see pp. 108, 169] from Hayden [*sic*], and I am very satisfied with them. You will therefore see that he gets 12 ducats from the cashier's office in my name; tell him at the same time to write 6 more pieces similar to those he sent me, and also 2 Solo pieces, and to see that they are sent here at once ...' (*C&W*, II, 118).

On 3 March 1766, Werner died and it seems that Haydn, as stipulated in his contract of 1761 (clause 14), was more or less automatically appointed full *Kapellmeister*. Perhaps this watershed in Haydn's career prompted him to begin, in 1766, a great 'cantata' mass in honour of the Blessed Virgin Mary, his intercessor in all things, and for the pilgrimage church of Mariazell in Styria, where he had been welcomed by the Benedictines as a starving lad just out of choir-school. Recently it has been suggested that Haydn may actually have composed this enormous *Missa Cellensis in honorem Beatissimae Virginis Mariae* (to give the work its autograph title on the important ms. of the Kyrie discovered some years ago in Romania) for the Vienna chapter of the Styrian Priory.[3] But whatever its ultimate fate was – and there is evidence that Haydn had to replace the later movements sometime between 1769 and 1773 (on the basis of the watermarks in the Budapest fragment, which includes the Benedictus and Agnus Dei, both incomplete), perhaps because the autograph was partly destroyed by fire in 1768 – there can be little doubt that Nicolaus Esterházy, whose family were so intimately connected with the basilica at Mariazell, would have encouraged his new *Kapellmeister* in his pious endeavours.

With Werner's death, Haydn was now in charge of all aspects of music at the court, which meant primarily that he was henceforth free to compose church music. Thus a whole new horizon suddenly opened up to the composer, now thirty-four years of age and having been unable (since 1761) to compose religious music on a large scale (some Advent arias in German may have been written at Eisenstadt in the early 1760s, but even that is not certain and they may date *post* March 1766).

Haydn also celebrated his promotion by buying a little house in the Klostergasse in Eisenstadt (it is today the Haydn Museum), a few hundred yards from the castle; it was there that Haydn and his wife lived during the winter months for the next ten years.

In the summer of 1766 was celebrated at Eisenstadt the name-day of Prince Nicolaus's eldest son and heir, Anton. For the occasion Haydn produced his new *intermezzo* entitled *La canterina*, which proved such a success that the Prince ordered everyone involved to be given handsome gratuities, Haydn twelve ducats and the others each six. Presumably the work was given on a temporary stage in

the great hall; at any rate it was to serve as a kind of glorified dress-rehearsal for
the work's first 'official' performance at Pressburg the following year.

Throughout this period, Haydn was busy composing baryton trios for his
Prince, and by December 1766 he had completed twenty-four; the final six 'Divertimenti' were sent together with the following letter, probably delivered to Eszterháza by courier and recorded on 6 December:

MOST SERENE HIGHNESS AND NOBLE PRINCE OF THE HOLY ROMAN EMPIRE, GRACIOUS AND
DREAD LORD!

The most joyous occasion of your name-day (may YOUR HIGHNESS celebrate it in divine
Grace and enjoy it in complete well-being and felicity!) obliges me not only to deliver to
you in profound submission 6 new Divertimenti, but also to say that we were delighted to
receive, a few days ago, our new Winter clothes – and submissively to kiss the hem of your
robe for this especial act of grace: adding that, despite YOUR HIGHNESS' much regretted absence, we shall nevertheless venture to wear these new clothes for the first time during the
celebration of High Mass on YOUR HIGHNESS' name-day. I have received YOUR HIGHNESS'
order to have the Divertimenti I wrote (twelve pieces in all) bound. But since YOUR HIGH-
NESS has returned some of them to me to be altered, and I have noted the changes in my
score, I would respectfully ask you to let me have the first twelve you have at hand for three
days, and then the others one after the other, so that apart from the required changes, they
may be all neatly and correctly copied and bound: in this connection I would like to ask respectfully in which way YOUR HIGHNESS would like to have them bound?

Incidentally, the two oboe players report (and I myself must agree with them) that their
oboes are so old that they are collapsing, and no longer keep the proper pitch [*Tonum*]; for
this reason I would humbly point out to YOUR HIGHNESS that there is a master Rockobauer
in Vienna, who in my opinion is the most skilful for this sort of work. But because this master is continually busy with work of this kind, and since it requires an exceptionally long
time to complete a pair of good and durable oboes with an extra length of reed pipe (as a
result of which, however, all the necessary notes can be produced) – for these reasons the
cheapest price is 8 ducats. I therefore await YOUR HIGHNESS' gracious consent whether the
above-mentioned and most urgently needed two oboes may be constructed for the price
indicated. I hope for your favour and grace,

YOUR SERENE AND GRACIOUS HIGHNESS'
most humble
Joseph Haydn.

The upshot of the letter was a very pleasant surprise for its writer – a reward of
twelve ducats, on 7 December, to celebrate the completion of the twenty-four
baryton trios, just then being bound in Vienna by Josephus Aloysius Maurer (*H-S*,
IV, 248); it was the first of what would eventually comprise five such ms. collections (the fourth has survived and is in the Esterházy Archives, Budapest). There
is an interesting second point brought up in the letter: the question of the oboes
and the 'extra length'. Although there is no record of exactly when the oboists received their new instruments, we suggest that this happened by 1 September 1768,
when the famous virtuoso, Vittorino Colombazzo, was engaged. In Symphony
no. 38's Trio (an oboe solo) there is a now famous note *d flat'*, which could not
have been played on an ordinary oboe of the period but only by an instrument
with the 'extra length'; the same procedure obtains (as noted in the Introduction)
for the pedal notes for the cor anglais in the Great Organ Solo Mass, composed *c.*
1768 (or 1769). Perhaps both solo parts were composed with Colombazzo in mind:
it was the kind of device Haydn often used to bring to the special attention of
Prince Nicolaus the presence of a new player.

Prince Esterházy now took his entire court, with all the musicians, for a protracted stay in the old coronation town of Pressburg. We are informed of the

principal event, the public premiere of *La canterina* in the garden of the Primate's palace on 16 February 1767, by the diary of Prince Johann Joseph Khevenhüller-Metsch, who went with the Archduchess Marie Christine and her husband, Duke Albert of Sachsen-Teschen, to spend carnival time in Pressburg. Prince Nicolaus caused a libretto of *La canterina* to be printed on the spot, in an elegant quarto size, of which two copies (for the royal pair) were bound 'with stiff cardboard covered with velvet'. During the two months that Haydn stayed in Pressburg, he must have delivered some music that met with special princely approbation, for on 3 February the princely cashier was ordered to pay 'our *Capellmeister* ... four and twenty ordinary ducats against receipt'.

This was the year in which Haydn composed the Stabat Mater, his first vocal piece to achieve European celebrity. We have no date for the first performance, but its very small forces (oboes or cors anglais, strings and organ) suggest that it was composed with the Eisenstadt players in mind. Prince Nicolaus, this time using the Princess Elisabeth to sign the document, on 6 July 1767 ordered his cashier to give Haydn another twelve imperial ducats at Eisenstadt; perhaps this was for the Stabat Mater, though Lent would seem a more appropriate period for such a work.

Our first known reference to the Stabat Mater in fact comes in a letter from Haydn to Prince Nicolaus, by way of the Princely Secretary, Anton Scheffstoss:

Eisenstadt, 20th March 1768.

Nobly born,
Highly respected Sir!
   You will recall that last year I set to music with all my power the highly esteemed hymn, called Stabat Mater, and that I sent it to the great and world-celebrated [composer J. A.] Hasse with no other intention than that in case, here and there, I had not expressed adequately words of such great importance, this lack could be rectified by a master so successful in all forms of music. But contrary to my merits, this unique artist honoured the work by inexpressible praise, and wished nothing more than to hear it performed with the good players it requires. Since, however, there is a great want of singers *utriusque generis* in Vienna, I would therefore humbly and obediently ask His Serene and Gracious Highness through you, Sir, to allow me, [the cellist Joseph] Weigl and his wife,[4] and [the tenor] Friberth to go to Vienna next Thursday, there on Friday afternoon at the FFr.:Miseric: to further the honour of our gracious prince by the performance of his servant; we would return to Eisenstadt on Saturday evening.
   If His Highness so wishes, someone other than Friberth could easily be sent up. Dearest Mons. Scheffstoss, please expedite my request; I remain, with the most profound veneration,

Your nobly born Sir's
most devoted
Josephus Haydn, [m.] pria.

P. S. My compliments to all the gentlemen. The promised Divertimenti [baryton trios] will surely be delivered to His Highness one of these next weeks.

It is interesting that Haydn was not anxious to rely on Viennese forces but preferred to take the key soloists with him, something he was to repeat when *Il ritorno di Tobia* was given in Vienna in 1775. We also see that the composer kept his close ties with the institution that had given him one of his first positions (he had been the leader of the orchestra in the 1750s).

   In the late autumn, Prince Nicolaus decided to go to Paris: in the princely entourage were his personal secretary, his major domo, his architect, his 'Travelling Commissioner', five valets (among them a blackamoor named Zibas and a barber), his gun-master, a page, two runners and, in a separate carriage, the violinist Luigi Tomasini. Esterházy went on to Versailles, but left Tomasini in the city to study the musical life of the French capital. It is thought likely that he may have worked out a connection between Haydn and some of the French publishers; in any event, Tomasini would have seen the considerable amount of music, some of it spurious, published there under Haydn's name. The French had started publishing Haydn's symphonies and quartets in 1764, and by November 1767 they had issued six *opera* (of six works each) and half-a-dozen individual symphonies and quartets. Of all this activity, Haydn can only have been dimly aware; he certainly made no money on any of these transactions, which were conducted by Viennese copyists; Tomasini will have had much to tell on his return. For the princely return, Haydn composed Symphony no. 35, the autograph of which is dated 1 December 1767.

Early in 1768 Haydn was at work on an interesting commission from the Cistercian Abbey of Zwettl in Lower Austria, whose Abbot, Rayner I. Kollmann (abbot from 1747 to 1776) was about to celebrate the fiftieth anniversary of his entering the priesthood (17 April). A great porcelain service was ordered from Vienna (it can be seen in the Museum für angewandte Kunst there) and a cantata from Haydn in Eisenstadt, which in the event was performed at Zwettl on 15 May 1768. Since Haydn knew he could not be present at the first performance of his 'Applausus' cantata (XXIVa:6), he wrote a long letter to the monastery, in which he explained some aspects of the score ('... there is a very great difference between *piano* and *pianissimo*, *forte* and *fortissimo* ...'). The letter (*C&W*, II, 146–8) is full of interesting remarks about the work's performance. The orchestra must wait until the singer has finished his text, 'even though the score often shows the contrary' – a feature which Haydn surely had from his Italian teacher Porpora and which must also apply, although most conductors nowadays take peculiar pride in ignoring the rule, to Handel. It is absurd for the singer's cadential phrase to be contradicted by the orchestra's conclusion. Haydn also wanted two players for his viola part, 'for the inner parts sometimes need to be heard more than the upper parts'; and he wants a bassoon to double the bass, preferring a bass line with one cello, one bassoon and one double bass to one with six double basses and three cellos. Haydn also explains how the recitatives must be sung, and this is something that applies right through the eighteenth century and up to Bellini, in whose *Norma* properly trained singers (such as the late Maria Callas) continue this tradition, which is now in danger of becoming forgotten:

... I suggest that the two boys [i.e. soloists] have a clear pronunciation, singing slowly in recitatives so that one can understand every syllable; and likewise they should follow the method of singing the recitation whereby, for example,

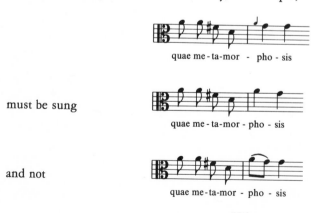

quae me - ta - mor - pho - sis

must be sung

quae me - ta - mor - pho - sis

and not

quae me - ta - mor - pho - sis

Haydn kept a copy of 'Applausus' in Eisenstadt: he must have thought it a waste to send such a large work to a remote monastery with the prospect that, after a single performance, it would disappear for ever. He therefore turned most of the work into smaller pieces of church music, in which forms the music became very popular.

Later, in July 1768, we find Haydn engaging the Oedenburg *Thurnermeister* and his apprentices to come to Eisenstadt for St Anne's Day, the name-day of Prince Nicolaus's sister-in-law, the Dowager Princess Maria Anna, *née* Marchesa Lunati-Visconti. There were five trumpeters and timpani players, probably used to accompany fireworks but also, perhaps, for use in the great hall or in the church (Haydn's band included neither instrument at this period): this document (*H-S*, IV, 49) explains how Haydn came to compose the supplementary trumpet and drum parts for such works as the *Missa in honorem B.V.M.* and Symphonies nos. 38 and 41, all three having, apparently, been composed without them. It was certainly not the only time that Haydn engaged trumpets and drums to come to Eisenstadt for some special occasion.

On 2 August 1768, a great fire destroyed most of the lower part of Eisenstadt. The Klostergasse, where Haydn lived, was particularly devastated, and the Franciscan monastery and also the nunnery (both on that street) were burned out. As well as the parish church, only nineteen houses in the lower part of town survived. The Castle, being set in its own grounds, escaped serious damage. Apart from his furniture and household goods, many of Haydn's scores were destroyed: Griesinger discusses both this disaster and a later fire of 1776, and (p. 17) tells us that 'some of Haydn's operas and other compositions were lost in the flames, and it is hardly likely that another copy exists'. One such work is possibly the *Missa* 'Sunt bona mixta malis', of which Haydn retained only the Kyrie and part of the Gloria.[5]

The municipal authorities of Eisenstadt drew up a list of the damage to each house. Haydn's repairs and losses were listed as follows:

Numerus urarialis 82 Hr. Joseph Haiden [*sic*] *Fürstl. Capellmeister*

For carpentry repairs and for materials	500 fl.
For mason's repairs and materials	160 fl.
For joiner's work [window frames etc.] and glass-maker	100 fl.
Loss of burned and ruined crops, hay, straw and furnishings	388 fl. 27 x.

Summa: 1148 fl. 27 x.

At this juncture, Haydn was practically a ruined man. 'But,' as the present-day princely Archivist Janos Harich phrased it, 'the Prince was not one to fail at such a moment, and rebuilt Haydn's house at his [the Prince's] expense: Haydn had to pay only 50 gulden for adding a new room' (*HJB*, IV, 13f., 49f.). It was a noble gesture and one more reason why Haydn considered his official position more of an asset than a liability, despite all the hard work.

On 5 August 1768, the name-day of Princess Marie Elisabeth was celebrated at Eszterháza with balls, illuminations, fireworks and with German plays given by a *Wandertruppe*, probably that of *Prinzipal* (Director) Lorenz Riersch, who was engaged to come to Eszterháza for a month. (Riersch had previously been there in May 1767.) A choir of trumpets and drums from Oedenburg accompanied the fireworks.

The grand official opening of the opera house was, of course, left to Haydn, who with *Lo speziale* (libretto: Carlo Goldoni) inaugurated the new theatre and began, in the words of Janos Harich, a quarter of a century of theatrical history. Although the handsome printed libretto of the opera specifies only 'nell'autunno dell'anno 1768' as the date of this historic occasion, we believe that a bill, signed by Prince Nicolaus and dated '29 September' (*C&W*, II, 151f.), now in the Esterházy Archives, enables us to pinpoint the opera's premiere more precisely.

As we have seen, Prince Nicolaus usually rewarded his musicians the day after an opera performance, and we may thus postulate that *Lo speziale* was first given on 28 September. The libretto was printed by Johann Joseph Siess in Oedenburg; it consists of 5 *Bögen* (40 pages) in small quarto format. Three hundred copies were printed at a cost of 5 gulden 30 kreuzer per '*Bogen*', and the copies were bound by Anna Maria Heinbeck of Oedenburg. Four copies – two for Prince Nicolaus and his wife, two for the honoured guests of the occasion, Duke Albert von Sachsen-Teschen and the Archduchess Marie Christine – were bound in rose-coloured taffeta, the rest in gold or so-called 'Turkish' paper. The title page reads:

Lo speziale / dramma giocoso / da rappresentarsi / a Esterhaz / nel teatro di S.A. il prencipe / Esterhazy / de Galantha &c &c. / nell'autunno dell'anno 1768.

> Sempronio, Speziale   Carlo Friberth.
> Mengone, Uomo di Spezieria   Leopoldo Dichtler.
> Grilletta, pupilla sotto tutela di Sempronio   Maddalena Spangler.
> Volpino   Barbara Dichtler.
> La musica è di Giuseppe Haydn Maestro di capella ...

In September that year, one of the festivities provided in connection with the visit to Eszterháza by Archduchess Marie Christine and Duke Albert – the couple lived only a half day's comfortable ride from Eszterháza, at Halbturn Castle – was a 'Masquera' in which Haydn and the musicians took part. The following enchanting document,[6] the content of which conjures up visions of a painting by Watteau, shows that Haydn and the band were attired, for this occasion, as *commedia dell'arte* musicians. The ladies noted in the company of Haydn and Friberth were possibly their wives; Magdalena Friberth (*née* Spangler) had been engaged shortly before; Haydn's 'lady' may of course have been one of the other singers.

List of items of Masque clothing for
the Court Musicians of His Highness

	Fl.	Kr.
To *Music Director Haydn:* Man's black domino, velvet waistcoat, velvet breeches, and hat with feather; one new lady's domino of glossy taffeta, velvet skirt, and lady's hat of black taffeta	4	0
„ *Herr Friberth*: Green and red Dutch peasant costume;	4	0
similar female costume, with curls;	1	8
One man's black domino with Jabot and breeches	2	0
1 domino curls and beard		51
„ *Herr Franz*: 1 wealthy Milord [costume] and curls	2	34
„ *Herr Kiefel* [Ignaz Küffel]: 1 English peasant [costume];	2	0
curls and gloves	1	8
„ *Herr Luigi* [Tomasini]: 1 domino and fancy waistcoat	2	0
„ *Herr Victorini* [Colombazzo]: 1 domino with fancy waistcoat;	2	0
curls, beard and 1 pair gloves	1	25
„ *Herr Jos. Weigl*: 1 domino and fancy waistcoat;	2	0
curls, beard and 1 pair gloves	1	25
„ *Herr Specht*: 1 domino and fancy waistcoat;	2	0
curls, beard and 1 pair gloves	1	25

For the fireworks and balls, the *Thurnermeister* of both Eisenstadt and Oedenburg were engaged to supply musicians – trumpets and kettledrums and '11 persons for the ball' (thus a larger group than the usual two violins and bass).

A few days before Christmas, Haydn had occasion to address an official petition to Prince Nicolaus, and wrote to Anton Scheffstoss as follows:

Nobly born,
Highly respected Sir!
   I send you herewith my petition to His Highness, reading as follows: Your Serene Highness, etc.
   Your Illustrious and Serene Highness graciously gave me to understand, not long hence, that not only was the Rent Collector Frantz Nigst found superfluous as a violinist, but also Joseph Die[t]zl as a member of the band; and moreover I was ordered to demand the 2 uniforms from the former. Concerning the former, i.e., Franz Nigst, I must respectfully persuade Your Highness, and admit myself candidly, that the second violin section in all the operas hitherto produced was, with him, in the best possible hands, because he is the only one capable of leading the seconds: therefore if he were dismissed, one would fear for the future on account of the mistakes which would creep in – that is, unless Your Highness were minded graciously to engage another permanent second violinist, or to have one come from Vienna when we produce operas. Because there are no other players for the seconds except the horn players [Joseph] Frantz and [Carl] May, with whom one is really not properly equipped. It is true that if the whole band goes to Esterház next year, he could not be in Esterház permanently on account of the rent office, but nevertheless it is my humble opinion that he should be brought to Esterház when the Imperial and Royal Court, or other high dignitaries, are present there. I humbly ask Your Highness, moreover, graciously to allow him the yearly 50 gulden, and also the winter and summer clothes (in which he has already seen service in Esterház). Joseph Die[t]zl is in my opinion especially necessary in the choir-loft if the whole band goes off to Esterház, so that the customary church services can be held by him, his *praeceptor* and the boy choristers who are in his apprenticeship. I hear from many people that he cannot possibly support himself with his position as schoolmaster. I ask you humbly to grant him in your graciousness enough so that he can live.

   In case you find anything imprudent in the above, please kindly let me know of it at once. I flatter myself that through my petition and through your confirmation of it, something may have an effect on His Highness.
   Apart from wishing you best greetings for the coming Holidays, and a happy farewell to the old and welcome to the new year, I am,

Highly respected Sir,
Your obedient servant,
Joseph Haydn [m.] pria.

Eisenstadt, 22nd December 1768.

Haydn was successful in the case of Dietzl, but not immediately with Nigst, who on 30 December petitioned the Prince as follows:[7]

... I had to learn from the Bookkeeping Department and also from Capellmeister Haydn that not only am I dismissed as violinist with my previous yearly salary of 50f but also that I am to return the summer uniform, given to me in grace and worn all last summer, together with the winter uniform, recently given but nonetheless already worn.
   I am not aware of having done anything wrong, so that this sad sentence crushes me to the ground, especially as ... I have suffered greatly through the fire and the new rules of the town and, God knows, I am in no condition to buy a suit of clothes out of my present salary ... [He relies on Prince Nicolaus's generosity and goodness.]

The petition was refused, but Nigst continued to play first violin in the church choir at Eisenstadt (without fee); finally, in August 1771, he was reinstated at 25f. p.a.
   In August 1769, there was another visit to Eszterháza by the Hungarian Palatine, Duke Albert of Sachsen-Teschen, and Archduchess Marie Christine. Again,

there was a masquerade, with masks for the eyes and 'domino masks', some with beards. We read the intriguing note: 'then, for the H: Capell Meister once again 2 domino masks for the Opera' and sixteen masks for the actors and actresses of the Catherina Rössl Troupe which was this year in residence. The new opera was Sacchini's *La contadina in corte* (also referred to by its alternative title, *La contadina ingentilità*).[8]

On 1 August Prince Nicolaus did a very curious thing: he engaged a professional baryton player named Andreas Lidl. When the Prince himself was such an avid player, one can only imagine that he especially liked to play baryton duets – hence Lidl in addition to the horn player Carl Franz, who was also a baryton player: was it, perhaps, not entirely accidental that Franz left the court only a few months later? It was probably also about this time that the following events, recorded by the composer's biographers Griesinger and Dies, were taking place. In their accounts we read:

> The baryton was … the favourite instrument of Prince Nicolaus Esterhazy. Haydn, wanting to give his Prince a pleasant surprise, practised on the baryton without anyone noticing it, and one evening he quite unexpectedly gave a concert on it. The Prince was rather offended, saying that Haydn wanted to usurp his position with regard to that instrument, and from that hour Haydn never touched the baryton again.   [Griesinger, 19]

> The Prince loved music and he himself played the baryton, which in his opinion should be limited to one key only. Haydn could not be certain of that because he had only a very superficial knowledge of the instrument. Nevertheless, he thought it must be playable in several keys. Unknown to the Prince, Haydn conducted an investigation into the instrument's capabilities, and he acquired a liking for it; he practised it late at night because he had no other time, with a view to becoming a good player. He was, of course, often interrupted in his nocturnal studies by the scolding and quarrelling of his wife, but he did not lose his patience and in six months he had attained his goal.

> The Prince still knew nothing. Haydn could not resist a touch of vanity any longer. He played in public before the Prince in a number of keys, expecting to reap enthusiastic applause. But the Prince was not in the least surprised and took the whole thing in his stride; he merely remarked: 'You are supposed to know about such things, Haydn!'

> 'I quite understood the Prince,' said Haydn to me, 'and though I was at first hurt by his indifference, nevertheless I owe to his curt rejoinder the fact that I gave up my intention of becoming a good baryton player. I remembered that I had already gained some reputation as a *Kapellmeister* and not as a practising virtuoso. I reproached myself for half a year's neglect of composition, and I returned to it with renewed vigour.'   [Dies, 58]

On 17 September 1769 another grand ball was held at Eszterháza, for which *Thurnermeister* Planckh of Oedenburg supplied sixteen musicians. We also have the detailed bill from the Castle Tavern (*H-S*, IV, 294), showing what the musicians were given to eat – and a very handsome menu it was – the day after (perhaps they were given princely refreshments while they played during the evening of the 17th): there was soup 'for 16 persons', 'beef with red beets, a dish with vegetables and meat, 6 pairs of frying chickens with salad', and wine and bread 'for everybody'. A month later (15 October), there was another splendid celebration, with Planckh again supplying sixteen musicians but 'Extra for the trumpets and timpani during the fireworks'. They were fed, on that day, with 'Eingemachtes' (veal in a sauce), geese, wine and bread; for lunch the next day there was soup, beef with horseradish sauce, vegetables with meat, 'Eingemachtes', wine and bread – all on a very generous scale.

In March 1770 Prince Esterházy arranged for his entire opera company to give a guest performance of Haydn's *Lo speziale* in the palace of Baron von Sumerau in the Viennese suburb of Mariahilf; apparently there was no room large enough in the Esterházy Palace in the city. The performance, according to a review in the *Wiener Diarium*, was so successful that it was repeated 'in the form of a musical academy', i.e. a concert performance. Possibly the lovely second version of Grilletta's 'Caro Volpino amabile' was composed for this Vienna revival of *Lo speziale*.

On the eve of St Anne's Day, 25 July 1770, there was a grand *Fest* at Kittsee Castle in honour of Prince Nicolaus's sister-in-law. Haydn and his *Kapelle* were present wearing newly designed summer uniforms, with the usual additional forces brought in from outside, as specified in a recently discovered bill (*H-S*, IV, 308) signed by the Eisenstadt *Thurnermeister* and addressed 'To His Highness Prince Esterhasi for 20 music persons in service in Kitse [*sic*] as agreed 3f. per person with my own person double makes f 63— / for 1 choir of trpts and timpani [f] 4 / f 67 / 30th July 1770'.

This document may explain a curious printed account of this incredible event, written by one G.F. von Rotenstein, in which we read that among the guests were Joseph II, Empress Maria Theresa, Archdukes Ferdinand and Maximilian, Duke Albert of Sachsen-Teschen, Prince Charles of Lorraine and Princess Charlotte. Rotenstein describes the castle at Kittsee ('... looks like a fortress', but 'the rooms in the castle are handsome, especially the hall in the middle', still extant, and where the concerts were given). As the distinguished guests arrived, the princely grenadiers and so forth were on parade, and lining the handsome stairs up to the great hall (on the first floor) were 'the whole princely music corps, 36 in number'. Even allowing for all the singers, it would seem difficult to arrive at this figure unless we take into account all the large number of supplementary musicians engaged from Eisenstadt – we have seen above that there were twenty. But did the *Thurnermeister* and his apprentices receive Esterházy livery for the occasion?

Grand though the occasion at Kittsee must have been, the musical highpoint of the year 1770 was the first performance of Haydn's new opera *Le pescatrici*, given to celebrate the marriage of Prince Nicolaus's 'dear niece', Countess Lamberg, to Count Poggi (*recte*: Pocci). The festivities at Eszterháza lasted three days and were reported in identical wording in both the *Wiener Diarium* and the *Preßburger Zeitung* – a 'press release' from Eszterháza, perhaps? The first performance of the new opera was on Sunday, 16 September, after the wedding (which took place in the princely chapel at 5 p.m.). The opera was 'performed with all possible skill and art by the princely singers and instrumentalists, to universal and well deserved applause.' 'Herr Hayden [*sic*]', continues the newspaper report, 'whose many beautiful works have already spread his fame far and wide ... had the honour to receive the most flattering praise from all the illustrious guests.' There was a ball on the Monday with 400 guests, for which the Oedenburger *Thurnermeister* and his apprentices provided eighteen men for the dance music, as well as a choir of trumpets and timpani for the fireworks. Three theatrical painters and the Court Opera tailor from Vienna were imported for the occasion. Next day, at 6 p.m., the opera was repeated 'to not less generous applause than at the first performance'. The libretto was printed in 200 copies, but not one is known to have survived.

It was in 1770 that the young painter Ludwig Guttenbrunn came to Eszterháza to work, and became Frau Haydn's lover. We have this interesting piece of information from the composer himself, who told it to G.A. Griesinger in November 1799. The Guttenbrunn portrait of Haydn,[9] which Breitkopf & Härtel thought to include with their *Œuvres Complettes* of Haydn as a frontispiece, was now in Frau Haydn's possession. '... Guttenbrunn was once, said Haydn, her lover' and that was why she clung to the picture, which she later took with her to Baden.

One of the composer's own friends was a lady-in-waiting to Princess Grassal-kovics in Pressburg; perhaps Haydn met her during the extended visit which he and the musicians made there in 1767. We know of 'Mademoiselle Catherine Csech' only because she was left 1,000 gulden – a vast sum of money – in Haydn's will dated 1801. Possibly the 'bad weather' mentioned by Haydn in a bill dated 16 May 1769 (*C&W*, II, 158) was not the only reason for him to tarry in Pressburg for three days.

We now turn to a petition addressed by Haydn to Prince Nicolaus in December 1770:

SERENE HIGHNESS AND NOBLE PRINCE OF THE HOLY ROMAN EMPIRE, GRACIOUS AND DREAD LORD!

In order to purchase my house, I had to borrow 400 gulden in cash some years ago, and now this capital has been recalled. Since I do not have the sum, I wanted to take out an-other loan in this amount (on which I would pay interest) to repay the debt. But I could not find any creditors here in Eisenstadt, and inasmuch as I have to repay this loan soon, I would humbly ask Your Highness graciously to allow me to have these 400 gulden, against a receipt from the cashier's office, whereby the 50 gulden I receive quarterly from that source (of which the first payment is due to me by the end of January 1771) would be with-held until such time as the whole debt is repaid. I most humbly commend myself to your fa-vour and grace,

> YOUR SERENE HIGHNESS'
> most humble
> Josephus Haydn.

Prince Nicolaus agreed and on 6 January 1772 instructed his Chief Cashier Zoller to advance Haydn the money (*C&W*, II, 170), yet another instance of the prince's boundless generosity to his *Kapellmeister*.

Haydn seems to have become seriously ill in 1770. He himself placed this illness in connection with the Stabat Mater, written at the time of his recovery; this ver-sion was related by him to his friend Latrobe, but as we have noted, the Stabat Ma-ter was composed in 1767. The fact that Haydn was ill *c*. 1770 is attested by two sources: (1) in 1771, his brother Johann Michael applied for and was granted leave by the Archbishop of Salzburg 'to visit his sick brother' (in fact, the visit did not take place, hence we may presume that Michael Haydn heard of Joseph's recovery before he set out); (2) the following episode recorded in Griesinger's biography (p.18):

About the year 1770, Haydn succumbed to a fever [*hitziges Fieber*], and the doctor had strictly forbidden him, during his slow recovery, to occupy himself with music. Soon after-wards, Haydn's wife went to church, and before she left the house she gave strict instruc-tions to the maid not to let her master go near the piano. Haydn was in bed and pretended to have heard nothing of this order, and hardly had his wife left than he sent the maid out of the house on some errand. Then he rushed to his piano. At the first touch the idea for a whole sonata came to him, and the first section was finished while his wife was still in church. When he heard her returning, he hastily retreated to his bed, and there he wrote the rest of the Sonata, which he could not identify for me more precisely than that it had five sharps.

The 'sonata' was probably the lost B major Piano Sonata no.23. If Haydn wrote a work to 'celebrate' his recovery, it might have been the gravely beautiful Salve Re-gina in G minor of 1771 (XXIIIb:2), also in the Virgin's honour.

On Good Friday (29 March) 1771, Haydn conducted an important performance of his Stabat Mater in the Basilica Maria Treu of the Piarists (the Piaristenkirche), in the Vienna suburb of Josephstadt. For this performance Haydn gathered together no less than sixty musicians, and the annals record that there was a very large congregation. Haydn liked to perform choral works with large forces, and this is the first time in his career that we have documentary evidence to that effect. All his other oratorios, from *Il ritorno di Tobia* (1775) to *The Seasons* (1801), would be performed with large forces.

On 24 June 1771, there was a dreadful affair in the Eszterháza Castle tavern, a real brawl between the cellist Xavier Marteau and the oboist Zacharias Pohl[10] – it was preceded, as one might surmise, with a lot of wine and dice-throwing – in the course of which Pohl lost the use of an eye. The file in the Esterházy Archives is voluminous, with long reports by the witnesses, but it was solved in a decent and dignified way by Haydn and the Prince. The eventual contract by which the whole affair was settled reads:

> *Contractum inter Zachariam Pohl et Xaverium Marteau*
> *Musicos, vi cujus hic ob laesum Musici Pohl oculum ad respondas*
> *in curam habitans expensas semet obligat.*

This day on the date and year recorded below is herewith set down and agreed the following settlement and contract between the Princely Esterházy oboist, Zacharias Pohl, and the Princely Esterházy bass-player, Xavier Marteau, because of the scandalous brawl between them which occurred on the 24th of the previous month of June in the Eszterháza Castle Tavern, whereby Zacharias Pohl lost his right eye; to wit:—

Whereas, according to the statements of both parties and various witnesses, it may be surmised that Xavier Marteau did not purposely intend to inflict this damage with his ring on the eye of Zacharias Pohl, but on the other hand, Zacharias Pohl is not entirely guiltless, both parties have therefore agreed, in the presence of *Herr Kapelmeister* Hayden [*sic*], to the following settlement: that Xavier Marteau shall recompense Zacharias Pohl for the costs of the cure and trip arising from the above-mentioned damage, in the amount of forty-nine gulden 13 kreutzer, within six months, at the rate of 8 gulden $17\frac{1}{6}$ kr. per month, of which the first 8 fl. $17\frac{1}{6}$ kr. are to be paid on the first of January 1772; but Zacharias Pohl, because of the indemnification here given him as a result of the damage to his eye, shall not and cannot demand anything at any time from Xavier Marteau.

As witness thereto both parties have set their hands and their customary seals. Eisenstadt, the 21st of December 1771.

> L.s. Zacharias Pohl, mp
> *hochfürstlicher Hautboist.*
> L.s. Xavjer Marteau
> *hochfürstlicher Bassetist.*
> In my presence: Josephus Haydn, mpria
> *Hochfürstlicher Capellmeister* L.s.

Haydn's constant concern for his musicians at Eisenstadt and Eszterháza reached a kind of climax in the year 1772. On 9 January we find him writing to the princely secretary, Anton Scheffstoss, thanking him for all his 'kind efforts on behalf of my wishes' and asking his help to secure for the cellist Xavier Marteau 'the 6 cords of wood, 30 lbs. of candles, and 30 gulden lodging money which should be his, and which his Highness promised me to give him ...'. This letter (*C&W*, II, 175) produced results almost at once, for on 14 January the Prince issued a decree granting the desired items to Marteau (*C&W*, II, 175n.). Meanwhile, however, a small but, for the musicians, ominous little note dated 10 January from Rahier to the Prince reads:

... I have communicated to all the musicians by word of mouth your high order of the 8th, that none of the wives and children of the musicians except for the wives of Haydn, Fribert[h], Dichtler, Celini [*sic*] and Tomasini are to be allowed to be seen at Eszterház, and there was no one who did not agree to the terms of that high order ...

This decree was not simply the result of ill-will on the part of the Prince but of a real lack of space at the castle. If one were to have a regular season of a dozen actors and actresses, there would hardly be room for all the wives and children of the musicians; and some of the exceptions, such as Magdalena Friberth and Barbara Dichtler, were singers in their own right. But that was not all. A document in the Archives shows that Prince Nicolaus further intended to reduce the size of the orchestra and to cut the salaries of the remaining musicians (*HJB*, VIII, 35). The stage was being securely set for the 'Farewell' Symphony at the end of 1772.

The story of the 'Farewell' Symphony has been told many times, and even Haydn's contemporaries had several versions (which may be seen in *C&W*, II, 180-2, 758 f.). Basically, what happened seems to have been as follows: the musicians, threatened with dismissal or reduction in their salaries, were further distressed at their enforced separation from their wives. They 'went to Haydn and asked for his advice', relates Griesinger. Haydn thereupon composed the 'Farewell' Symphony – it appears from the documents that it must have been during the second part of November – in which, during the Finale, the musicians exit, one after the other, blowing out their candles and stealing away, until only two violins (Haydn and Tomasini, presumably) are left. 'The Prince and his company understood the point of this pantomime at once, and the next day came the order to leave ...' (Griesinger, 19).

We may assume that the court was at Eisenstadt to celebrate the Prince's name-day on 6 December. Haydn had won a diplomatic coup with his great new symphony, whose merits (apart from its programmatic connotation) will have been recognized by the profound connoisseur for whom it was composed. As a sort of 'thank-offering' Haydn had the equally charming idea of composing a new mass, which he entitled on the autograph 'Missa Sancti Niccolai' and dated 1772 'In Nomine Domini'. When Prince Nicolaus celebrated his name-day in the Castle Chapel the princely Church Choir and *Kapelle* will perhaps have surprised him completely with a new setting of the mass by Haydn. The original parts, now in the Esterházy Archives, show signs of enormous haste: Haydn himself copied out some of the pages and wrote the Latin text in others, helping Joseph Elssler Sen., whose knowledge of Latin was probably less profound than Haydn's (facsimile in the score published by Faber Music).

It was in 1772 that the Empress Maria Theresa wrote to the Archduchess Maria Beatrix in Milan, 'Pour les instruments il y a un certain Haydn qui a des idées particulières, mais cela ne fait que commencer' – a sentiment that makes one wonder if, musically speaking, she understood what was happening under her own nose, as it were.

It was also the year in which Count Ladislaus Erdödy, a member of the noble family with which Haydn had many contacts of various kinds, sent Ignaz Pleyel to study with the master. In time, Pleyel became very famous, earning praise from Mozart ('. . . Good – and fortunate for music, if Pleyel will in time be able to replace Haydn for us!').[11] On the other hand, he also perfected a pseudo-Haydn style which would do great damage to the original by debasing the whole currency.

The year 1773 is famous for the first performance of what was to prove Haydn's most successful opera, *L'infedeltà delusa*, written to celebrate the Dowager Princess Maria Anna's name-day at Eszterháza on 26 July. After the performance, for which 200 copies of the libretto were printed by Siess in Oedenburg, the castle and park were illuminated, and then there was a masked ball at which Archduchess Marie Christine and Duke Albert appeared unexpectedly and incognito. There were also marionette plays, put on by the Georg Habentinger Troupe.

The highpoint of the year was the state visit by the Empress Maria Theresa to Eszterháza on 1 and 2 September. Prince Nicolaus caused a pamphlet in French to be published, describing the visit in detail (facsimile, *C&W*, II, 190–6). The royal entourage, which included Archduchess Marie Christine and Duke Albert, as well as Archduke Maximilian (later to be Beethoven's patron) and the Archduchesses Maria Anna and Elisabeth, was feted with the usual illuminations and fireworks, as well with many musical events. It had originally been planned to revive *Acide* – perhaps it was thought that an *opera seria* would be more appropriate for such an occasion – but at the last minute *L'infedeltà delusa* was substituted 'avec beaucoup de succès' and with a special mention of Haydn, '... dont les talens sont connus dans toute l'Europe ...'. The opera was given in the early evening of 1 September, and afterwards the Empress was taken to the Chinese Pavilion, where Haydn and the orchestra, all attired in Chinese costumes, gave a concert. The next day, the new marionette theatre was opened with Haydn's *Philemon und Baucis*, preceded by a prologue (of which most of the music is lost). At the end of the opera there was an allegorical paean to the Habsburg dynasty (this too, has not survived): 'Happiness clasped the Imperial arms with one hand, and with the other showered Plenty upon the Nation from her cornucopia' (*Preßburger Zeitung*). Haydn shot three hazel-hens which the Empress ate. When Prince Nicolaus introduced his *Kapellmeister* to the Empress, Haydn reminded her of the thrashing she had ordered he be given (when still a choir-boy) for clambering on the scaffolding of Schönbrunn Castle (for Dies's account, see p. 25 above).

Prince Nicolaus later rewarded the five singers who had performed in the opera with ten ducats each 'but Capell Meister Haydn thirty, and the scene-painter Grundemann also thirty ducats' (*C&W*, II, 199).

On 26 February 1774, the Viennese publisher Joseph Kurzböck announced the publication of six harpsichord sonatas by Haydn, dedicated to Prince Nicolaus. They had been composed the previous year, and their publication in this fashion was an important milestone in their composer's career. Hitherto, most of the music published under Haydn's name had appeared abroad (especially in Paris) and without his participation. Now, he was trying to reap some of these profits himself, and although such publication was, strictly speaking, forbidden by the terms of his contract (1761) with the princely house, the dedication to Prince Nicolaus shows that Haydn was now being allowed much more freedom in this respect. In a few years, a new contract would remove this limitation altogether.

In 1774, the Carl Wahr Troupe was again in residence at Eszterháza, and that summer Haydn wrote incidental music to a play in their repertoire, a German translation of Jean François Regnard's *Le distrait*. This incidental music, which Haydn soon turned into a symphony (no. 60, called 'Il distratto' or, in German, 'Der Zerstreute'), proved to be one of his greatest successes. In a report from Eszterháza dated 30 June, the *Preßburger Zeitung* relates that 'connoisseurs consider it [the incidental music] a masterpiece' (*C&W*, II, 205 f.).

From the pages of a Viennese theatrical journal,[12] we learn many interesting details about the opera performances and the marionette theatre at Eszterháza. The latter was now (in 1774) under the direction of Carl von Pauersbach, and apart from his own plays, they also gave two marionette operas, *Genovefens 1. Theil* and *Genovefens 2. Theil* (1st and 2nd Parts), the music probably compiled by Haydn but not composed by him. *La contadina in corte* (possibly by Sacchini or Piccinni) and Haydn's *L'infedeltà delusa* were in the repertoire, soon however to be joined by two more Haydn revivals: 'About the Opera we have the following to report, *viz.*: on 25th September there was an *opera seria* entitled *Acide*. The music was by Hr. Joseph

Hayden. On the 26th there was a comic opera, *La canterina*, the music also by Hr. Hayden. This opera was excellently acted and sung, so much so that the whole ending had to be repeated.' Of this revised *Acide*, only fragments have survived (but including some complete numbers, among them a beautiful bass aria, 'Tergi i vezzosi rai').

The next year, 1775, saw Haydn's first major commission for Vienna since he had composed *Der (neue) krumme Teufel* more than twenty years earlier: the oratorio *Il ritorno di Tobia*. The charitable organization that sponsored it was the Tonkünstler-Societät, a group of musicians founded in 1771 by Court *Kapellmeister* Florian Leopold Gassmann to provide pensions for the widows and orphans of their members. Since its foundation it had given two double performances annually, one just before Christmas and one during Lent. Following the old Viennese court tradition, the Society sponsored oratorios in the Italian language, in the intervals of which a concerto was usually performed; there were, upon occasion, other instrumental insertions. One of the specialities of the organization was the very large size of the group – some 180 performers.

To ensure that the work was performed according to Eszterháza standards, Haydn took along three of his own vocal soloists and two instrumental players, the leader Luigi Tomasini and the principal cellist, Marteau (probably to ensure a smooth rendering of the *secco* recitatives, with Haydn at the harpsichord). The author of the libretto was Luigi Boccherini's brother, Giovanni Gastone, who had come to Vienna to join other members of the family.

The work was 'a general success ... Especially his choruses glowed with a fire that was otherwise only in Händel', wrote a Viennese paper (*C&W*, II, 215). The Society took in the large sum of 1,712 gulden; the artists, of course, gave their services *gratis*. The Society repeated the work in 1784, for which occasion Haydn composed two additional choruses, one of which achieved lasting fame in an arrangement as a Latin church piece, 'Insanae et vanae curae', with slightly altered orchestration.

At Eszterháza, the principal event of the year 1775 was the state visit by Archduke Ferdinand and his consort, Beatrice d'Este. For this occasion Haydn composed a new opera, *L'incontro improvviso*, with text by the adroit singer Carl Friberth. Haydn was able to recruit not only trumpets and timpani from outside but also extra percussion players for the 'Turkish' music in the overture and also later in the work. The first performance was on 29 August, and the *Preßburger Zeitung* thought 'the idea and plot ... comic in the extreme, the music, as is customary with Haydn, excellent' (*C&W*, II, 218). After the opera there was a *souper* and a masked ball in the Chinese ballroom, where the *Preßburger Zeitung*'s correspondent counted 1,380 guests. The next day, in the marionette theatre, there was a performance of Ordóñez's *Alceste*, and the day after, the Wahr Company performed *Le distrait* with Haydn's incidental music. In the evening there was a gala illumination and swarms of 2,000 Hungarian and Croatian peasants, swinging banners, sang their national folk-songs. As dawn broke, and the revellers returned to their rooms or their carriages, the park was softly illuminated by innumerable green lampions. It was the last, and possibly the greatest, of the *feste* held at Eszterháza Castle. From 1776, Prince Nicolaus would institute a regular operatic season with performances of works by many foreign, and mostly Italian, composers; Haydn continued to write works for the stage, of course, but the whole organization was to undergo a complete change.

With the initiation of a regular operatic season, librettos were printed, and these give us a very valuable insight into what was actually sung (and what Haydn altered, for not all scores and parts have survived, though, most are, fortunately, still in the Esterházy Archives in Budapest). The season included Gluck's *Orfeo*, Ditters(dorf)'s *Il finto pazzo per amore*, Sacchini's *L'isola d'amore*, Piccinni's *La buona figliuola*, Ditters(dorf)'s *Lo sposo burlato* and also his *Il Barone di Rocca Antica*. Among the marionette operas in the repertoire was a new work by Haydn, *Dido* (first performance in March, music lost) and possibly *Die Feuersbrunst*, which has come down to us in an imperfect late manuscript (now in the Yale University Library). Pleyel, Haydn's talented pupil, was given a chance to display his compositional skills with a marionette opera, *Die Fee Urgele* (November 1776), of which the whole autograph score (with the characteristic high-C horns of Eszterháza fame) has survived.[13] Count Erdödy was so pleased with his protégé's progress that he presented Haydn with two horses and a carriage. Haydn petitioned Prince Nicolaus for hay and oats for the horses; these he was granted, as well as a place to stable the horses (*C&W*, II, 307).

The year 1776 is important because it brought forth Haydn's Autobiographical Sketch, intended for an Austrian periodical. It was addressed to a 'Mademoiselle Leonore', about whose identity there has been considerable speculation (was it in fact the lady who would become Madame Lechner, wife of the Prince's economic advisor?). The document has been reproduced many times (*C&W*, II, 397ff.), and here we may single out some of the more interesting points. Concerning his formative years, Haydn draws particular attention to the fact that, after his dismissal from St Stephen's Cathedral, he eventually 'had the good fortune to learn the true fundamentals of composition from the celebrated Herr Porpora' (cf. p. 26). Haydn also singles out Hasse's praise of the Stabat Mater, composed in 1767. 'In the chamber-musical style I have been fortunate enough to please almost all nations except the Berliners', obviously a sore subject on which Haydn then proceeds to elaborate (Dittersdorf wrote that Haydn should defend himself 'against their hard words'). But the most interesting aspect of the sketch is its omissions – three operas and an oratorio are listed in detail, but there is not a word about symphonies, sonatas, trios or string quartets, on which Haydn's by then considerable reputation was based.

On 17 July 1776, another terrible holocaust ravaged Eisenstadt, destroying within two hours the town hall, the Franciscan church and monastery, the brewery and this time the parish church; 104 houses were destroyed and sixteen people died. Once again the Prince rebuilt Haydn's house and altogether paid out more than 7,000 gulden to owners of damaged or destroyed property. Haydn's house was less badly damaged in this than in the previous (1768) fire, and it cost Esterházy 450 gulden to repair it. Now that Haydn was living for most of the year at Eszterháza, he may have thought it a disadvantage to have almost his entire capital tied up in a house at Eisenstadt that he hardly used, and in 1778 he sold it. We do not know if Haydn was in Eisenstadt when the fire happened, but probably he was at Eszterháza. No doubt many autograph scores perished in this conflagration.

In 1777, the Carl Wahr Troupe again returned to Eszterháza, and it is thought that for one of their plays, a German translation of Charles Simon Favart's *Les trois sultanes*, Haydn composed the incidental music which was later turned into Symphony no. 63, known (from its slow movement) as 'La Roxelane', the leading female part in the play. To complete the symphony, Haydn used the overture to *Il mondo della luna* (the opera written for the celebrations connected with the marriage of the Prince's second son, Count Nicolaus, to Countess von Weissenwolf, in August), also composed that year. The opera repertoire was now broadened to include Gassmann's *L'amore artigiano*, Haydn's own *Il mondo della luna*, Paisiello's *La*

Frascatana, Ditters(dorf)'s *Arcifanfano Rè de' Matti*, and two works from the 1776 season, Dittersdorf's *Il Barone di Rocca Antica* and Sacchini's *L'isola d'amore*.

As Haydn was preparing *Il mondo della luna*, the entire marionette theatre gave guest performances in Vienna at Schönbrunn Castle. They performed two works, apparently, directed by Pauersbach: Haydn's (lost) *Hexen-Schabbas*, which he had composed some years earlier; and *Alceste* by Ordoñez. It is not entirely clear from the documents if Haydn was present or if he remained in Hungary, supervising the rehearsals for his new opera; but it seems likely that he was not in Vienna at the time.

In 1778, we find the following Italian operas newly produced at Eszterháza: *La sposa fedele* (Guglielmi?, Sarti?), Piccinni's *L'astratto*, Anfossi's *Il geloso in cimento* and Gazzaniga's *La locanda*. Five operas already in the repertoire were repeated. Of the marionette novelties, we might mention *Das ländliche Hochzeitsfest* by the Esterházy violinist, Joseph Purksteiner, and a revival of Haydn's *Dido*, for which new libretti (dated 1778) were printed and distributed. The theatrical season was getting longer, too: in 1778 it lasted from January to December; the Wahr Troupe had left and Prince Nicolaus engaged no less than four different theatrical companies to amuse him with German plays.

When Haydn had given the Tonkünstler-Societät his oratorio *Il ritorno di Tobia* in 1775, both he and the society had been pleased with the favourable reception it was given. Now, four years later, a formidable battle developed between Haydn and the society. Apparently the society decided in November 1778 to demand of Haydn, as part of his admission requirements, that he compose a new work whenever the society wished (*gratis*, of course). Haydn protested, as might be expected, and the society gave in and he was made a member. Now, in the middle of January 1779, the society changed its mind and decided after all to require Haydn to deliver new compositions whenever the society wished. Haydn was understandably furious and resigned,[14] asking that his very large entrance fee (368 fl. 10 kr.) be returned to him. This breach would be healed only in 1798, but meanwhile Haydn continued to undertake commissions for the society, including the large-scale revision of *Il ritorno di Tobia* in 1784.

The Eszterháza opera season of 1779 included Paisiello's *Le due contesse*, Astaritta's *I visionarj*, Haydn's *La vera costanza*, Anfossi's *Metilde ritrovata*, Gazzaniga's *L'isola d'Alcina*, Sarti's *Le gelosie villane*, Naumann's *La villanella incostante*, Franchi's *Il finto cavalier Parigino*, Piccinni's *L'incognita perseguitata* and Felici's *L'amore soldato*. The final work of the season was another new Haydn opera, *L'isola disabitata*, given on Prince Nicolaus's name-day, 6 December. There may have been still more operas given this year, but the evidence is inconclusive (*C&W*, II, 416 f.). As if the production of two new Italian operas of his own was not enough, Haydn also found the time to compose his last German marionette opera (music lost), *Die bestrafte Rachbegierde*, given in the autumn.

In March 1779, the violinist Antonio Polzelli and his nineteen-year-old soprano wife, Luigia, were engaged; she was to become Haydn's mistress and he was probably the father of her son, Alois Anton Nicolaus ('Antonio'). Her presence at Eszterháza can hardly have contributed to the stability of Haydn's shaky marriage.

Later in the year, we have the following description of a serious fire at Eszterháza, as reported in the *Preßburger Zeitung*:

Wednesday, 24 November 1779.

From Eszterház we receive the unpleasant news that last Thursday the 18th at 3:30 a.m. a dreadful fire broke out in the world-famous Chinese ball-room, which because of its magnificence, taste and comfort was so admired by all visitors. As a result, the adjoining water works with the tower, and the theatre, which was so excellently appointed and which contained not only a grand box for the Prince but also two comfortable side-boxes for the other guests, were entirely destroyed. The fire was dreadful to behold and glowed now and again the next day, because the ball-room was mostly painted with varnish and in the theatre was stored a large quantity of wax lights. The fire must have burned in the roof for some hours, because the whole of the valuable roof was in flames, and also the beautiful walls were almost consumed by the time the fire was discovered. – The origin of this unexpected occurrence was as follows: as is well known, the 21st inst. was the day set for the exalted marriage of Count Forgátsch with the noble Countess Miss Graschalkowitz. For this celebration the stoves in the ball-room were to be previously lit. There were also two Chinese stoves therein which were more for show than for actual use. They were neverthless lit despite all previous warnings. They probably exploded from the heat and thus the fire spread. It would have spread even further if not for the wise order to remove the roofs of the nearby buildings, and for the fact that heavy rains and strong winds lessened the fire's effect and finally extinguished it. The damage, according to several eye-witnesses, is estimated to be more than 100,000 gulden. Two beautiful clocks; the magnificent theatrical costumes; all the music collected at great effort and expense; the musical instruments, including the beautiful harpsichord [*Flieg*] of the famous *Kapellmeister* Haiden [*sic*] and the concert violin of the virtuoso Lotsch [Luigi Tomasini] – all were lost to the flames, which reached their height at 8:00 a.m. His Highness the Prince, despite the inclement weather, was at once present at a time when a speedy rescue seemed distant.

Since various high persons had already arrived for the festivities, a brand-new opera [*L'amore soldato*] was given in the marionette theatre on the 21st.

The opera troupe transferred to the marionette theatre and the marionette theatre – its activity was sharply diminished in any case by the absence of Pauersbach who had left a year earlier – moved into the pavilion in the garden. Haydn lost many works in this fire – certainly all the marionette operas except *Philemon und Baucis* and *Die Feuersbrunst*, and the performance material of the Italian operas up to *L'isola disabitata*: the fragments of the autographs that have survived were probably by pure accident in Haydn's rooms (*Acide*, *La canterina*, *Lo speziale*, *Le pescatrici*, *L'infedeltà delusa*, *L'incontro improvviso*, *Il mondo della luna*). The material for *L'isola disabitata* was obviously in Haydn's own rooms for revision: otherwise there would have been no premiere on 6 December. It seems, moreover, that the orchestral parts of all Haydn's Esterházy symphonies (1761–November 1779) also perished.

However, the Prince was not a man to allow even a holocaust to interrupt his theatrical activities, and on 18 December – only a month later – the ceremony of laying the foundation stone of the new theatre, to be constructed from plans by Michael Stöger, was performed. To celebrate this event, Haydn completed a symphony with very original features – no. 70 in D. (cf. p. 155). Its fantastic contrapuntal finale is itself a miniature programmatic reference to the fire: it begins in D minor, evoking the terrifying aspect of the raging flames, but concludes in the major, evidently referring to the happy event for which the work was composed.

In 1779, Haydn's contract was renewed. It is not clear why it was thought necessary to do so, but one of the reasons from the composer's point of a view was the whole question of publication of his works. Obviously Prince Nicolaus now allowed his *Kapellmeister* considerable latitude in accepting outside commitments (such as the cantata commission from Zwettl Abbey or the mass composed for Mariazell) and also in the matter of publication (such as the Six Sonatas issued by Kurzböck of Vienna in 1774); but it may have been considered advisable to bring the whole contract up to date. Another reason was more topical: the death, on 15 November 1777, of the schoolmaster and Eisenstadt organist Joseph Dietzl, who had been appointed in 1773. Johann Georg Fuchs was given the post of school-master, and a year later he was given the position of organist, his duties, however, being shared with the church violinist Michael Ernst. Previously, Haydn had shared the organist's responsibilities with Dietzl, Haydn playing the organ in the winter months and Dietzl in the summer. For this Haydn was paid in kind (or a cash equivalent) and Dietzl 100 gulden in cash. Haydn's salary now amounted to 961 gulden 45 kr., making him one of the highest-paid employees of the entire Esterházy court, his emoluments being exceeded only by those of the Estates Manager and the physician in ordinary. It was a graphic illustration of the importance Prince Nicolaus now attached to the role of his *Kapellmeister*; Haydn's salary and other benefits also made it easier for him to resist the offers which, increasingly in the future, would be made to lure him away from Hungary.

The new contract of 1779 replaced the original contract of 1 May 1761 (see p. 36). In particular, not only the wording of the 1761 contract is changed but some of its provisions are now omitted, e.g. '... he shall ... take the more care to conduct himself in an exemplary manner, abstaining from undue familiarity and from vulgarity in eating, drinking and conversations ... remembering how displeasing the consequence of any discord or dispute would be to his Serene Highness ...' (from clause 3). And the whole of the old clause 4 is omitted entirely: '4. The said Vice-Chapel-Master shall be under obligation to compose such music as His Serene Highness may command, and neither to communicate such compositions to any other person, nor to allow them to be copied, but he shall retain them for the absolute use of His Highness, and not compose for any other person without the knowledge and permission of His Highness.'

Other clauses in the old contract were likewise modified and in its terse essentiality the new contract is very modern in feeling.[15]

This day, according to the day, month and year hereto appended, is ratified between H. Highness, Prince of the Holy Roman Empire, Lord and Master Nicolai Eszterházy v. Gallantha, Hereditary Count of Forchtenstein, Knight of the Golden Fleece, Comendeur [*sic*] of the Military Maria Theresia Order, Chamberlain and Acting Privy Councillor of Her Imp. Royal and Apostolic Maj., General Field Marshal, Colonel and owner of a Hung: Infantry Regiment, Captain of the Noble Hungarian Body-Guard, and likewise Acting Hereditary *Ober-Gespann* of the *Oedenburg Gespanschafft*; and *Capelmeister* [*sic*] Herr Joseph Haydn, to be considered an Officer, the following contract agreed between them.

Primo: Herr Haydn is to conduct himself in a manner which is edifying, Christian and God-fearing.

Secundo: *Herr Capell-Meister* is to treat his subordinates at all times with great goodness and forbearance.

Tertio: The party of the second part agrees to perform any music of one kind or another in all the places, and at all the times, to which and when H. Highness is pleased to command.

Quarto: The party of the second part should not, without special permission, absent himself from his duties, nor from the place to which H. Highness has ordered the musicians.

Quinto: Both contractual parties reserve the right to cancel the agreement.

Sexto: *Herr Capell-Meister* will receive every two years one winter and one summer uniform, alternately, according to H. Highness's discretion; and he will receive the following (but apart from these items he will receive nothing further either in money or in kind), to wit:

As *Capellmeister*

In cash	782 f.	30 Xr
Officer's wine in Eszterház	9	*Eimer* [kegs]
Good genuine firewood in Eszterház	6	*Klafter* [fathom cords]

As Organist

Waitz [wheat]	4	*Metzen* [3.44 litre,
Kohrn [rye]	12	miller's dry measure]
Greißl [i.e. 'Grieß' = semolina or grits]	¾	
Rindtfleisch [beef]	300	
Saltz	50	*Pfundt*
Schmaltz [lard] . . . . alles in	30	[pound = 56 dkg.]
Kertzen [candles] . . . . Estzerház	36	
Weinn [wine]	9	*Eimer*
Krauth und Rueben zusamen [cabbage & beets together]	1	
Schwein [pig]	1	*Stück* [one whole pig]
Good firewood	6	*Klafter*

Then the necessary forage for 2 horses. Finally two identical copies of this contract are to be prepared and exchanged one with the other, and all previous *Resolutions, Conventiones* and Contracts are declared null and void. Schloß Eszterház the 1st of January 779.

[signed:] Josephus Haydn mpria

Concerning the above payment in kind and the 100 fl. (which latter are not listed in the above contract) which are to be paid in Eisenstadt, there is the following condition that, when I am not able to play the organ myself in Eisenstadt, I herewith agree myself to provide, to install and to recompense an organist.

[signed:] Josephus Haydn mpria

A measure of Haydn's increasing success elsewhere may be seen in an important business connection, first documented in correspondence beginning in January 1780, between the composer and the leading music publisher in Vienna, Artaria & Company; this firm was to become Haydn's principal publisher for the next decade, a period during which his works would also be widely published abroad.

Meanwhile, the 1780 opera season at Eszterháza included a total of ninety-three performances, with the following premieres: Anfossi's *La forza delle donne*, Gazzaniga's *La vendemmia*, Salieri's *La scuola de' gelosi* and Anfossi's *La finta giardiniera*; while four operas from earlier seasons were repeated. While the new theatre was being built, these opera performances continued to be given in the marionette theatre. Hence, the marionette operas had to be pushed aside, and they now disappeared almost entirely. The construction work took much longer than expected; it had been hoped to open the theatre in October 1780, but it was in fact not ready until early in the following spring. Haydn was to compose the new opera with which the house was to be inaugurated, *La fedeltà premiata*, perhaps his greatest piece for the stage, which – when it was first performed on 25 February 1781 – proved to be an enormous success. (Subsequently the work was regularly repeated until June 1784, with a total of thirty-six performances, thus making it the fifth most popular opera ever given at Eszterháza.)

IV
Haydn's music,
1766–1780

BETWEEN 1766 and 1780, opera of various kinds came to dominate Haydn's life in a way that he could not have predicted when he first joined the Esterházy court and which, even with the extensive modern rediscovery of the composer's output, still requires a conscious effort of comprehension. He composed a total of fourteen stage works, nine Italian works and five in the German language, an impressive total which, while not matching the output of other leading composers of the day (Jomelli, Galuppi, Paisiello etc.), is remarkable when one remembers that Haydn was not exclusively a composer of opera, and that those years included far-reaching developments in the genres of quartet, symphony, sonata and church music. The years around 1770 have long been recognized as crucial ones in Haydn's career, the emotive quality that his music acquires and, in particular, the sudden concentration on the quartet genre, are clear features that cannot be ignored. Yet, important as these particular few years are, there was also over a longer period the cumulative influence of opera, less sensational in its immediate impact and producing noticeably fewer individual works of outstanding merit, but equally crucial in feeding Haydn's style and his concept of musical drama in the widest sense. It is for this reason as well as biographical prominence that this chapter begins with a survey of Haydn's operas, including five marionette operas, composed for performance at Eszterháza:

	Italian	German
1766	*La canterina*	
1768	*Lo speziale*	
1769	*Le pescatrici*	
1773	*Acide* (revised version)	*Philemon und Baucis*
	L'infedeltà delusa	*Hexen-Schabbas* (lost)
1775	*L'incontro improvviso*	
1777	*Il mondo della luna*	*Die Feuersbrunst*
1778		*Dido* (lost)
1779	*La vera costanza* (completed 1778)	*Die bestrafte Rachbegierde* (lost)
	L'isola disabitata	
1780	*La fedeltà premiata*	

Of the five German works written for the small marionette theatre, only two survive: *Philemon und Baucis*, which has a *Vorspiel* entitled *Der Götterrath* ('The Counsel of the Gods'), is a rather ponderous drama recounting the visit of Jupiter and Mercury to earth, where they bring Aret and Narcissa back from the dead; more lively and laced with much saucy Austrian dialect, is *Die Feuersbrunst*.[1] In the latter the common *Singspiel* characters (derived from those of *commedia dell'arte*), Hanswurst and Colombina, act out a charade of thwarted love, featuring at the end of Act I the burning down of Colombina's house. Spectacular incidents like this fire and the storm in *Philemon und Baucis* elicit appropriately atmospheric music from Haydn, agitated minor-key music of the type familiar from the many minor-key symphonies composed prior to the two operas. By and large, however, Haydn probably regarded the composition of these artistically unambitious, if musically opportunist, German operas as a pleasant diversion. Italian opera, on the other hand, was a different proposition, providing Haydn with the opportunity to compose in the most international of eighteenth-century musical genres. Haydn himself came to regard his Italian operas as the most significant aspect of his output in the 1770s and early 1780s. On the whole, his attitude to opera composition shows untypical caution in comparison with other genres, and the development of his operas up to 1780 was conditioned more by the improving facilities at Eszterháza and his own acquaintanceship with contemporary trends in operatic composition than by an infallible theatrical instinct. He was no Gluck or Mozart, and his operatic career is a quest for self-esteem in a genre that he and others regarded as the ultimate musical challenge, rather than the exciting self-discovery that characterizes his church music and instrumental music.

Italian opera: the texts

Of the nine new Italian works all but one, *L'isola disabitata* ('The desert island'), are comic operas. Composed for Prince Nicolaus's name-day on 6 December 1779, *L'isola disabitata* is a setting of a Metastasio text first written in 1752 for Giuseppe Bonno and subsequently set, like many Metastasio librettos, by several other composers, including Holzbauer, Traetta and Jommelli. An *azione teatrale* rather than an *opera seria*, it is in two parts, has only four characters and the entire action takes place in one locality at one time. There are only seven arias plus a concluding *coro* for the four participants. The stylized setting of the opera and the formal, impersonal utterances of the characters make it a very old-fashioned work for 1779, and the additional absence from the libretto of any epic or apparent allegorical content makes it the least attractive of the texts that Haydn had set since the Italian cantatas of the early 1760s. The young sister, Silvia, emerges as the least stereotyped figure, slightly comic in the manner of Carlo Goldoni (but without the crucial quickness of speech) in that, like Miranda in *The Tempest*, she falls in love with the first man she encounters simply because she has never before seen a member of the opposite sex. Comic glosses in a serious context are not a regular feature of eighteenth-century opera, but the reverse process, seriousness invading the essentially comic antics of a plot, was at the heart of the success of the most progressive Italian opera in the second half of the eighteenth century. The librettos of Haydn's comic operas reflect this trend in the 1760s and 1770s.

His first surviving opera, *La canterina* ('The singing girl'), is described on the autograph as 'Intermezzo in Musica' and on the printed libretto as 'Opera buffa'. The four comic characters comprise Don Pelagio (a *maestro di cappella*), Gasparina (a singing pupil), Apollonia (the presumed mother of Gasparina), and Don Ettore (a merchant's son). The characters are typical of contemporary Italian comic opera; the old man with pretensions to learning and who is the object of ridicule, the procuress mother, the innocent party of a young girl who is not so very innocent, and the intruder who unsettles a cosy domestic situation. In the early performances at Eisenstadt and Pressburg there was an additional source of amusement and comic confusion in that Apollonia and Don Ettore were sung as travesty roles by the husband and wife Leopold and Barbara Dichtler. The libretto, from an intermezzo in Piccinni's *L'Orgille*, is in two acts, both consisting of recitatives and arias culminating in a quartet; the quartet at the end of Act I coincides with the point of maximum confusion, and at the end of Act II it celebrates the successful outcome.

Haydn's next comic opera, *Lo speziale* ('The apothecary'), dates from two years later and was the first work to be performed in the opera house at Eszterháza. For this inaugural occasion Haydn chose a book by the most celebrated librettist of the day, Carlo Goldoni. *Lo speziale* had been written in 1754–5 and is an early example of a particular type of comic opera that was given the name *dramma giocoso*. Characters were divided into two groups, the traditional *parti buffe* (comic parts) and the *parti serie* (serious parts), the essentially lighthearted action gaining much variety (and, potentially through the music, profundity). Because of the still limited resources of the Eszterháza troupe, Haydn had the total number of Goldoni's characters reduced from seven to four. The characters omitted were the two *parti serie*, Lucindo and Albina, and a minor *parte buffa*, Cecchina. Though Haydn and his unknown editor retained the designation *dramma giocoso*, the libretto in its revised form was much closer to that of *La canterina*: four characters (two male, two female), a mocked profession (Haydn's second jibe at apothecaries), the innocent young girl, Grilletta, who is the apothecary's pupil and the object of amorous attention by the stranger, Mengone. In addition, Goldoni's libretto has the equally typical disgruntled servant and much of the plot features disguise. The adaptation of the Goldoni original is skilful and one does not miss the *parti serie*. Moreover, in comparison with *La canterina*, *Lo speziale* benefits from the talents of the librettist, especially in the quick-witted repartee and unfailingly comic portrayal of eccentricity.

Haydn's next opera, *Le pescatrici* ('The fisherwomen'), is also based on a Goldoni *dramma giocoso*, from 1752, two years before *Lo speziale*. This time Haydn was able to retain Goldoni's seven characters: five *parti buffe*, fishermen and women; and two *parti serie*, Lindoro, a prince from Soriento, and Eurilda, a fisherwoman, respectively a bass and alto. Against the petty intriguing of the fisherfolk the prince appears magnanimous and enlightened, while Eurilda appears oddly aloof and uneasy amongst her companions; it transpires that she is a princess and the lost heiress to the kingdom of Soriento. Haydn's opera was composed to celebrate the marriage of Prince Nicolaus Esterházy's niece, Countess von Lamberg, to Count Pocci, and Goldoni's *dramma giocoso* could not have been a more appropriate choice, with its deft combination of lighthearted entertainment, a marriage made in heaven and a dignified affirmation of noble breeding.

Goldoni's libretto features plenty of banter, but none at the expense of the nobility. However, the libretto of Haydn's next opera, *L'infedeltà delusa* ('Deceit outwitted'), shows no such reservations. The original author was Marco Coltellini (1719–1777), chiefly noted for his serious librettos and his association with Traetta. *L'infedeltà delusa* is described as a 'burletta per musica' and the characters are not divided into two distinct social groups. All are peasants and, as in many comic operas, there is some cruel humour at the expense of certain stereotyped figures: the ambitious but gullible father (Filippo), an old hag, and a punctilious notary whose bureaucratic concern to dot i's and cross t's precludes any human feeling. The last two are disguises assumed by Vespina ('little wasp') who, like Despina ('little despot') in *Così fan tutte*, is a careful manipulator of the plot. She further disguises herself as the Marquis of Ripafratta, a favourite character in Italian comedy who appears in Goldoni's *Mirandolina* (as a priggish misogynist) and *Il mercato di Malmantile*. Coltellini's *burletta* was probably written before 1758. Even though the book had been altered only slightly, his name does not appear on the printed libretto issued for the Eszterháza performances, probably because, in the year preceding Haydn's setting of the opera, Coltellini had achieved notoriety with a biting satirical attack on the Empress Maria Theresa. The Empress herself attended

an early performance of *L'infedeltà delusa* at Eszterháza (see p.113), and Haydn must
have known that he was sailing dangerously close to a particularly chill wind when
he set the following text in Act II, scene 6:

Il Marchese, son io di Ripafratta, che ha feudi, e marchesati, baronie, e principati, e che di
nobiltade a centinaja numera i quarti, e gli misura a staja. Non basta, sappi che al mio ser-
vizio ho paggi ed ho staffieri, lacchè, mozzi di stalle e cappe nere ed un mondo di bestie, e
di persone, e che, se a questa porta t'ardirai d'accostarti più mai, io ti farò morir sotto un
bastone.
(I am that Marquis of Ripafratta who has fiefs and marquisates, baronies and principalities
and who numbers in hundreds the quarterings of his nobility and measures them by the
bushel. Moreover, know that in my service I have pages and I have stirrup-holders, lackeys,
stable-boys and black-capes [chaplains] and a world of cattle and people and that if you ever
dare to approach this door again I will cause you to meet your death by the cudgel.)

Each of Haydn's four remaining comic operas is described as a *dramma giocoso*,
and though none of the extant copies of the librettos used at Eszterháza lists the
characters separately as *parti serie* and *parti buffe*, in practice the division is always
clear. In *L'incontro improvviso* ('The unforeseen encounter') the serious roles are
Prince Ali and Princess Rezia; in *Il mondo della luna* ('The world of the moon'), Fla-
minia and Ernesto; in *La vera costanza* ('True constancy'), Ernesto and Baroness
Irene; and in *La fedeltà premiata* ('Fidelity rewarded'), Celia (Fillide) and Fileno. In
the printed cast-lists audiences could often identify the serious roles in advance by
noting the absence of imaginative descriptions like those usually given to the
comic characters; thus, in *La vera costanza*, the Marchese Ernesto is described simply as a friend of the Count, while the Count himself is an 'eccentric and fickle
young man, secretly married to Rosina' ('giovine volubile estravagante, sposo
segreto di Rosina'). A third, intermediate category is often discernible in *dramma
giocoso*, the *parti di mezzo carattere*, characters whose actions (and music) are more
equivocal; the lovers Clarice and Ecclitico in *Il mondo della luna* are of this type.

As always, Haydn chose librettos that had been successfully set by other composers, skilfully adapting them to the particular requirements of the Eszterháza
personnel. *L'incontro improvviso* was a translation from the French libretto of
Gluck's last and most ambitious *opéra comique*, *La recontre imprévue*, first performed
in Vienna in 1764.[2] Haydn had ample opportunity to visit Vienna in that year while
Prince Nicolaus was attending the coronation in Frankfurt of Joseph II as King of
the Holy Roman Empire; the choice of libretto for his first large-scale *dramma giocoso* may reflect his experience of the Gluck opera. In Gluck's work a disproportion-
ate amount of the action is occupied by a deranged French painter named Vertigo.
In Carl Friberth's adaptation for Haydn this character is dropped, though one of
his arias is allotted to Prince Ali in Act III ('Ecco un splendido banchetto').

Il mondo della luna was one of Goldoni's most popular librettos, first written for
his artistic partner, Galuppi, in 1750; Haydn's setting includes some revisions but
the plot and characterizations constitute a prime example of Goldonian *dramma
giocoso*.[3]

La vera costanza was a libretto by Francesco Puttini that had recently been set by
Anfossi (1776). Haydn's choice was not a happy one and the textual changes made
by Pietro Travaglia, the Eszterháza set designer, stopped short of rectifying its de-
ficiencies. Much of the action is slow-moving as well as complex, too much moti-
vation is taken on trust and, above all, the dialogue lacks the sparkle and wit typical of Goldoni and Coltellini.

For the re-opening of the Eszterháza opera house (rebuilt after the 1779 fire)
Haydn selected a libretto previously set by Cimarosa under the title *L'infedeltà*

fedele, changing its title to *La fedeltà premiata* in order to avoid confusion with his own *L'infedeltà delusa*. Cimarosa's opera, too, had been composed to celebrate the opening (in 1779) of a new theatre, the Teatro del Fondo in Naples; the librettist was G.B.Lorenzi.[4] In that opera two of the characters, Viola and Vazzachio, sing in Neapolitan dialect; in Haydn's opera Viola is omitted, though some of her characteristics are incorporated into the person of Nerina, while the part of Vazzachio is completely rewritten for the newly created role of Lindoro.

By the last quarter of the eighteenth century *dramma giocoso*, particularly as pioneered by Goldoni, had acquired a range of characterization and sophisticated dramatic irony that was a long way from the unrelievedly comic atmosphere of the older intermezzo, *opera buffa*, *scherzo in musica* etc. Other aspects of the drama, particularly its setting and stagecraft, reflect this infusion of seriousness. Haydn's operas show these developments. *La canterina*, *Lo speziale* and *L'infedeltà delusa* are set in more or less everyday surroundings with little visual spectacle. *L'incontro improvviso*, however, is set in Turkey, a favoured locality in opera of the second half of the eighteenth century, providing opportunities for elaborate scenery, costumes, ceremony and, of course, 'Turkish' music.[5] *Le pescatrici*, *La vera costanza*, *Il mondo della luna* and *La fedeltà premiata* all require the kind of fantastic settings and elaborate stagecraft that had formerly been the prerogative of *opera seria*, including the arrival of ships, action in rocky caves and temples, and, in *La fedeltà premiata*, the appearance (*deus ex machina*) of a beneficent god. Unlike contemporary *Singspiel*, the purpose was not parody but the provision of a stimulating mixture of seriousness and lightheartedness, and it is a measure of the distance and direction that *dramma giocoso* had travelled that *La fedeltà premiata* is closer to Metastasian *opera seria* in its unreal, Arcadian setting than it is to the Tuscan landscape of *L'infedeltà delusa*, an association that prompted the description '*dramma giocoso pastorale*'.

This new seriousness further manifests itself in the gentle moralizing tone of Haydn's later comic operas. All Haydn's Italian operas conclude with the entire cast assembled on stage; what they declaim shows a distinct eighteenth-century trend towards pointing the moral. In *La canterina*, for instance, the sentiments expressed are simple ones of general rejoicing:

> Si viviamo tutti quanti 　　(And so we all live
> e finiam in lieti canti 　　　and end in merry songs
> per poter allegri star. 　　　so as to stay cheerful.)

By the time of *La vera costanza*, over a decade later, the sentiment is gravely prescriptive:

> Benché gema un'alma oppressa, mai non perde la speranza;
> se conserva la costanza, se la regge la virtù.
>
> (Though an oppressed soul may lament, it never loses hope
> if it preserves its constancy and is ruled by virtue.)

In *La fedeltà premiata* the action is resolved by rewarding the loyalty of the two *parti serie*, Celia and Fileno, celebrated in a concluding chorus.

> Quanto più diletta e piace, 　　(How much more we enjoy peace,
> quanto cara è quella gioia, 　　how precious is the joy
> preceduta dalla noia 　　　　preceded by the worries
> d'un incomodo dolor. 　　　　of trouble and grief.)

As a genre, *dramma giocoso* had evolved a structure that encouraged the pointing of a moral: the first two acts related the story leading to the point of dénouement, while Act III was much shorter, often in the nature of an epilogue, and consisted typically of a love duet and the concluding *coro*. Act III of *Il mondo della luna*, which is not an extreme case, lasts only about thirteen minutes, as compared with Acts I and II, each lasting some 75 minutes.

The increased scope of comic opera as shown in Haydn's own involvement with the genre over a period of fifteen years is best exemplified by comparing a skeleton list of the distribution of musical numbers in the first and last operas in the period, *La canterina* and *La fedeltà premiata*. Act I of *La canterina* begins with an ensemble, proceeds with two arias and concludes with a group presentation; Act II focuses attention on two characters before concluding with an ensemble.[6] One character, Don Pelagio, emerges as the most commanding figure; the status of the singing teacher is enhanced by his delayed arrival and by the fact that subsequently he never leaves the stage.

DISTRIBUTION OF CHARACTERS AND NUMBERS WITHIN OPERAS

La canterina (1766):

	Act I No.					Act II No.			
	1	2	3	4	5	6	7	8	9
Don Pelagio (T)		x	x	x	x	x		x	x
Gasparina (S)	x			x	x		x	x	x
Apollonia (S)	x			x	x			x	x
Don Ettore (S)	x			x	x			x	x

La fedeltà premiata (1780):

	Act I No.											
	1	2	3	4	5	6	7	8	9	10	11	12
Celia (S)								x			x	x
Fileno (T)						x			x			x
Amaranta (S)	x	x								x		x
Perrucchetto (B)			x									x
Nerina (S)	x					x						x
Lindoro (T)	x	x										x
Melibeo (B)	x			x								x
Diana (S)												

	Act II No.										Act III No.	
	13	14	15	16	17	18	19	20	21	22	23	24
Celia								x		x	x	x
Fileno		x					x			x	x	x
Amaranta									x	x		x
Perrucchetto					x					x		x
Nerina			x							x		x
Lindoro										x		x
Melibeo	x									x		x
Diana												x

(No. 16 = CHORUS; No. 18 = CHORUS; Act III No. 24 = AND CHORUS)

In *La fedeltà premiata*, though clear traces of this broad scheme of ensemble-aria-ensemble are to be found, the greater number of characters adds immeasurably to the dramatic tension. Deft manipulation of the plot ensures that each character is presented to the audience as a soloist before assuming a part in the cumulative ensemble. In Act I, after the initial chorus (containing a solo section for Amaranta), the principal characters are each allotted an aria (or a portion of an aria) in turn: Lindoro, Amaranta, Perrucchetto, Melibeo, Fileno, Nerina and Celia. The last named is to be one of the memorable characters in the opera and her first appearance is skilfully delayed; she is the subject of two arias (2 and 6), before herself appearing in a new scene, described as 'Boschetto: Celia guidando le pecorelle' ('A grove: Celia tending her sheep'). Act II shows a similar desire to distribute arias fairly with the additional resource of a hunting scene featuring a chorus (16, 17 and 18). Act III has the typical duet and concluding chorus, but the subject matter is a telling inversion of that typical of most third acts. Rather than being united happily in love, Celia and Fileno remain the victims of misunderstood circumstances and motives, and, with personal pride momentarily overriding affection, exit on opposite sides of the stage, leaving everything to be resolved in the following recitative.

Not all of Haydn's chosen librettos reveal the same craft in their presentation of characters and development of plot; the opening acts of *L'incontro improvviso* and *Il mondo della luna*, for instance, both have two successive arias for the same character (respectively Calandro and Buonafede). On the other hand, the rigid distribution of arias as between *prima donna*, *seconda donna* etc., which emasculated the plausibility of many old *opere serie*, is not to be found, and any weakness perceived is the result of a librettist's unwillingness (or inability) to manipulate the story-line rather than being endemic to the genre itself. The freedom allowed to the librettist placed an onerous responsibility on the composer.

Italian opera: the music

Haydn's arias in the nine Italian operas under consideration include a fair number of eighteenth-century stereotypes: a serenade and drinking song in *L'infedeltà delusa*; a catalogue aria in *L'incontro improvviso*; and arias that make use of onomatopoeic sounds, such as that of the apprentice apothecary Mengone in *Lo speziale*, the gibberish 'oriental' language of Calandro in *L'incontro improvviso* and Buonafede's whistling in *Il mondo della luna*. The serenade in *L'infedeltà delusa*, sung by Nencio, is in 6/8 time with pizzicato strings imitating a guitar; the music includes a warming progression on the word 'cor' ('heart') that lifts the aria out of its charming routine (see example).

The role of Nencio was sung by Leopold Dichtler, who took part in all Haydn's operas. His roles never require much in terms of coloratura but, to modern ears, they have an astonishingly wide range. The example above contains a high C (one of several in the aria); in the same aria Nencio is required to sing also a low B flat – a range of over two octaves. In *La canterina* Dichtler took the travesty part of Apollonia, which suggests that he used the head voice much more frequently than modern opera singers do.

Haydn makes particularly effective use of a further operatic stereotype: the blustering fast-moving aria in a minor key. As in many operas of the period, the minor key is used typically only once during the course of an evening, usually to evoke agitated emotions such as anger, fear and confusion, sometimes coupled

with a scenic element such as a storm; these arias are clearly a legacy of the baroque *Affekt* principle. *La canterina, Lo speziale, Le pescatrici, L'infedeltà delusa* and *La vera costanza* each contain one such example. Depending on the dramatic context, the emotion can be either empty bluster, as in Volpino's Presto G minor aria in Act I of *Lo speziale*, or genuine anguish, as in Rosina's F minor aria in Act II of *La vera costanza*. Perhaps Haydn's most telling use of this convention occurs in *La fedeltà premiata*. The minor key is first heard at the appearance of the ridiculous Count Perrucchetto. Billed as a 'man of extravagant temper', he bursts, breathless, onto the stage having, apparently, been set upon by robbers; he feels faint and only the thought of a bottle of wine revives him. The Presto tempo, the pounding quavers, the forzando accents and the abrupt contrast of dynamics all contribute to the musical caricature.

One of the conventions of *opera seria* despised by progressive musicians and librettists was that of the exit aria, whereby action and music contrive to allow the singer to leave the stage at the end of a rousing aria to tumultuous and flattering applause. As comic opera expanded its expressive horizons, rather than scorning the practice, it came to appreciate its usefulness, either for dramatic realism or for mocking parody. Haydn's operas contain examples of both types, especially in the four large-scale operas beginning with *L'incontro improvviso*. There are two examples of exit arias that take the form of an *aria di guerra*, in both cases the analogy is the centuries' old one of fighting a war and wooing a girl. In *L'incontro improvviso* Prince Ali, one of the *parti serie*, has an *aria di guerra* in D major, scored for oboes, horns, trumpets, timpani and strings; a resplendent concluding tutti precedes his departure. Count Errico, a *buffo* part in *La vera costanza*, has his *aria di guerra* in C major, scored for oboes, bassoons, C alto horns (as substitute trumpets), timpani and strings. Like Prince Ali's aria, this has impressive long notes in the vocal line and fanfare figuration in the accompaniment. Count Errico has the additional feature of a preceding accompanied recitative that provides instant musical responses to the mention of drums, marching and sundry military commands. The subsequent aria continues in this lighthearted vein but by the end the atmosphere has lost all sense of a *buffo* musical jape; what began as parody has been transformed into the serious. The change begins in the central adagio section, in which the Count becomes enraptured by his own description of the very person - Rosina – whom he is meant to be mocking. His ambivalence is genuine and his consequent confusion real; a Presto conclusion in C minor is as powerful as it is unexpected.

Although dramatic and musical conventions play an important part in shaping the direction of Haydn's operas, it should not be thought that they contain only serenades, *arie di guerra*, exit arias etc. At their best, Haydn's arias are capable of rising above the obvious or the conventional. Sandrina's three arias in *L'infedeltà delusa* make a lasting impression. She is billed as a 'ragazza semplice' ('an ordinary girl') who is in love with Nanni; however, her father Filippo wishes her to marry a wealthier man by the name of Nencio. After an initial ensemble which hints that intrigue may disturb the lambent evening air, Sandrina, the victim of this intrigue, is the first solo voice to be heard. Her 'semplice' nature is conveyed by 3/8 time and a regularly phrased melody doubled literally by the first violins, conventional techniques associated with such characters (Zerlina's 'Vedrai, carino' in Mozart's *Don Giovanni* is a familiar example). As she questions her father about her future, her questions are accompanied by strings and Filippo's evasive reply by wind instruments.

In her first full aria she tells Nanni that her father has forbidden them to meet. Her distress and muted anger are well suggested by the Presto tempo, melodic material that moves mainly in quavers and a dynamic level of *piano* with occasional thrusts to *forte*. The fifteen lines of the text are set across a sonata form design, as explained below:

Line		
1	Che imbroglio è questo!	(O what a tangled web is this!
2	Che vuoi che ti dica?	What would you that I say?
3	Che vuoi che ti faccia?	What would you that I do?
4	Il padre nemico	An unfriendly father
5	mi sgrida, e minaccia	Scolds and threatens me
6	s'io parlo d'amarti	If I speak of loving you,
7	s'io dico di sì.	If I say yes.
8	Comanda, e mi dice	He commands me and tells me
9	che ha trovo il marito,	That he has found the husband
10	che opporsi non lice,	Whom I must not reject,
11	ch'è meglio partito.	Who is the best possible match.
12	Io devo lasciarti,	I must leave you,
13	non posso parlarti,	I may not speak to you
14	e crepo d'affanno	And I gasp for breath.
15	Ti basti così.	Let this suffice.)

The exposition, development and recapitulation are laid out as follows:

EXPOSITION

lines 1–7	lines 8–11	lines 12–15, 2–3	lines 4–7
bars 1–18	bars 19–27	bars 28–39	bars 40–58
First subject	Transition	Second subject A	Second subject B
I (A major)	V/E	V	V

DEVELOPMENT

lines 12, 10, 4, 3, 4, 8, 10, 9, 11, 3, 2, 3, 2, 1
bars 59–90
V, vi, IV
V/A major

RECAPITULATION

lines 12–15, 2–3	lines 4–7, 4, 8, 10, 11	lines 2–3, 12–15
bars 92–103	bars 104–115	bars 116–142
Second subject A	Second subject B	First subject and coda
I	I	I

In the exposition three distinct melodic lines are associated with a phrase of the text; in the development Sandrina's increasing confusion is mirrored by the fact that the text too is repeated out of sequence; in the recapitulation she regains some composure by singing the text largely in its original order, though beginning with the second subject and concluding with the first subject. Haydn employs this so-called 'mirror' recapitulation in many of his arias but not in his contemporary instrumental music.[7]

Sandrina's final aria is the penultimate number of the opera and is in a totally different mood. Following the presentation of the 'ragazza semplice' and her genuine, if still naive, confusion, the audience is given a heart-warming portrayal of an individual who although she has come to accommodate the thought of marrying the rich Nencio, would still prefer the life of a country girl. Much of the preceding action in Act II had been comic, even burlesque, as Vespina, in a series of disguises, had unfolded her complicated plan to ensure that Sandrina marries Nanni; Sandrina is unaware of these conspiracies and her final aria focuses attention on her plight before the happy dénouement.

È la pompa un grand'imbroglio	(Ostentation is a great complication
per un'alma, che disprezza	For a soul that despises
fasto, onor, e la ricchezza.	Honours, pomp and riches.
Io non cerco, ed io non voglio	I neither seek nor wish
che la pace del mio cor.	But for peace in my heart.)

The five lines of the text are once more set in a sonata form design but with none of the complex interaction between text and structure that characterized 'Che imbroglio'. The text is sung three times, corresponding to the exposition, development and recapitulation sections of the overall design. The predominant impression is of the porcelain beauty of the vocal line, from broad cantabile to gentle, almost musing coloratura on the closing phrase 'che la pace del mio cor'. The orchestra has a richness of sonority that is not often encountered in Haydn's operatic music: in particular the parallel moving thirds in the middle of the texture are highly suggestive. By the end of the aria Haydn's sympathetic music has ensured that Sandrina has outgrown her 'ragazza semplice' designation; she has acquired a new dignity.

In *L'infedeltà delusa* all the recitatives are *secco*, except for some orchestral passages in the recitative that precedes Vespina's Act II aria, 'Ho un tumore in un ginocchio'. Elsewhere in his operas Haydn uses *recitativo accompagnato* in the customary fashion: first, to designate the social status of a character (both Prince Lindoro in *Le pescatrici* and Prince Ali in *L'incontro improvviso* make their initial entries in *recitativo accompagnato*); secondly, for particularly telling dramatic incidents, such as Buonafede's belief that he has been transported to the moon (*Il mondo della luna*). Beyond these usages Haydn reveals a developing interest in deploying orchestral recitative more extensively in order to break down the usual predictability of number opera. *La canterina* provides an early example of this interest, though without affecting its essentially lightweight mood. The first aria, sung by Apollonia, never reaches a formal close but moves directly into *secco* recitative, then four bars of *accompagnato*, and then back to *secco*. Next, Don Pelagio, the singing teacher, ostentatiously demonstrates the technique of recitative singing in a lengthy accompanied recitative – seventy-two bars for only thirty words! After a demonstration aria, Don Pelagio and Gasparina, his pupil, sing the same orchestral recitative together. Later composers (and librettists) of comic opera would probably regard the whole scene as slow-moving, yet, in Haydn's development, the extensive use of *recitativo accompagnato* prefigures similar usage in three operas composed over a decade later, *La vera costanza, L'isola disabitata* and *La fedeltà premiata*.

In *La vera costanza* accompanied recitative is first used to precede the Count's *aria di guerra*, both to suggest his status and to colour the comic imagery. In Act II, at the height of the two lovers' difficulties, three scenes in close proximity (6, 8 and 9) make use of accompanied recitative. In the first of these Rosina, who is a fisher-girl and not an aristocrat, utters a series of rhetorical questions concerning her plight: 'Who will give me aid? What can I hope for? What do I know?' Rather than punctuate each clause with appropriate orchestral gestures, as the composer would have done earlier in his career, Haydn re-utilizes the same orchestral phrase throughout, varying its length, melodic detail, harmonic direction and tonality, but ensuring that attention is drawn repeatedly to Rosina.

In Scene 8 the Count draws a parallel between his search for Rosina and that of Orpheus for Euridice. His thoughts are accompanied by snatches of conventional pastoral music, two flutes in thirds over a pizzicato accompaniment (for this section Haydn was content to use music from Anfossi's *La vera costanza*). Scene 9 returns to Rosina, now completely resigned to her fate. The entire scene is accompanied by strings alone and consists of an orchestral recitative, an aria in E major and a second orchestral recitative, each flowing uninterruptedly into the next, and in its unconstrained way suggesting the dejection of the character. Taking the broadest view of music history, the continuity of the scene and the way it coalesces into an aria both recalls Monteverdi and foreshadows nineteenth-century opera, Italian as well as German. Some of Haydn's inspiration may have come from the reform operas of Gluck, particularly *Orfeo* and *Paride et Elena*, which likewise seek to achieve continuity through dramatic use of recitative.

Following *La vera costanza*, Haydn's next opera was the idiosyncratic *L'isola disabitata*, composed probably in the autumn of 1779. Having, in the course of fifteen years, composed comic opera on an ever more ambitious scale, Haydn's choice of a serious libretto, an *azione teatrale* by Metastasio, comes as an unexpected development. Divided into two parts, the opera has only four singers compared with the seven of *La vera costanza*. If, as seems likely, Haydn was directed towards a serious topic, he used the opportunity to continue his experiments with integrating aria and recitative; as in the *azione teatrale* by Gluck, *Orfeo ed Euridice* (which Haydn had conducted in the 1776 season), accompanied recitative is used throughout. Many of the recitatives are very lengthy (over a hundred bars is not unusual) and the arrival of a formal aria is often long awaited. The slow delivery of a serious text and the reserved emotions of the participants give rise to a laboured musical drama, especially noticeable after the fleet music and varied emotions of the preceding comic operas. As if in compensation, Haydn introduces some instances of thematic cross-references to help articulate emotions, an extension on a broad scale of the recurring motto phrase noted in Rosina's recitative in Act II of *La vera costanza*. The subsequent single repetition of a theme may not have the impact of a nineteenth-century reminiscence theme, nevertheless the measured *tremolo* that accompanies Costanza's and later Gernando's reading of the same chiselled inscription is a startling anticipation of Weber or Verdi.

La fedeltà premiata reveals the results of these experiments in the more appealing genre of *dramma giocoso*. Amaranta's first aria, in which she feigns love of Melibeo, is interrupted without warning by an orchestral recitative that heralds the sudden entrance of the breathless Count Perrucchetto, who then sings his agitated G minor aria. (In Cimarosa's opera *L'infedeltà fedele*, Amaranta's lines and the offstage 'strepito' are set in *secco* recitative.) As in *La vera costanza*, a sequence of accompanied recitative and aria units (i.e. *scena*) is reserved for the middle of Act II. Three occur in succession, sung by Fileno (tenor), Celia (mezzo soprano) and Amaranta (soprano). Within these scenes there is some limited use of musical cross-reference. Fileno carves a message in a tree, which is subsequently read in a similar musical fashion by Celia. In Celia's recitative an entrancing melody played on the flute over a pizzicato accompaniment is associated with Fileno, now 'Ombra dell' idol mio' ('spirit of my beloved'); it returns as the main melody of the subsequent aria.

One of the celebrated features of comic opera in the second half of the eighteenth century (as pioneered by Goldoni and Galuppi) was the ensemble or chain finale, a series of musical sections running one into another to form continuous stretches of music uninterrupted by recitative; the librettos were skilfully engineered so that all (or nearly all) the cast would take part, the result forming the dramatic highspot in each of the first two acts. Haydn's comic operas both reflect and promote this development. In his operas up to and including *Il mondo della luna* the maximum number of constituent sections is four, with two or three being quite typical. An early approach, used in Act II of *Lo speziale* and in Acts I and II of *Le pescatrici*, consists of the alternation of two tempi, fast and slow, with associated music. More conducive to shaping a dramatic climax are those finales that feature a gradual increase in tempo and in which three clear stages are apparent: suspense; reaction; and either a freezing of the action until its continuation in the following act, or resolution and conclusion. The finale of Act I of *Lo speziale* provides an early example. In an Andante moderato, 2/4 tempo the orchestra conjures up a mood of comic intrigue with short phrases, simple diatonic harmony and avoidance of immediate modulation. (Similar music can be heard at the beginnings of several finales by Haydn, including those in Act II of *L'infedeltà delusa* and Act I of *L'incontro improvviso*, and it is the nearest that Haydn comes to projecting that sense of childish glee and anticipation which characterizes Mozart's mature operas.) Each character sums up the situation in turn, the two lovers Mengone and Grilletta, and then the apothecary Sempronio. Sempronio's departure to fetch a map, so that he can pompously assume the role of international diplomat, signals a change of tempo to Allegro, time-signature to 3/4, and the beginning of the second stage of the ensemble. While Sempronio is out of the room, Mengone and Grilletta converse freely; Sempronio's return is signalled by a six-bar crescendo. He studies the map, decides that he needs a compass and leaves once more. But this time there is no orchestral crescendo to signify Sempronio's return and he arrives unexpectedly, giving vent to his surprise and anger in a passage of octave unison. The exchanges of dialogue become brisker, Haydn adds *tremolo* strings to heighten the tension and, at the point of maximum tension, rather like the modern TV series that seeks to hold the viewer in suspense until the next episode, the action freezes. The tempo changes to Presto and the time-signature to 6/8 for all three to display their annoyance.

This carefully paced finale is 222 bars long and involves three of the four characters in the opera. In the later operas with larger casts and more elaborate plots the finales are naturally longer and the results more exciting. The most dramatically engrossing of Haydn's chain finales occur in *La vera costanza* and *La fedeltà premiata*, both of which include for the first time changes of tonality to complement the changes of tempo. Acts I and II of *La vera costanza* have eight sections each (the greatest number of sections in any Mozart opera is fifteen, in Act II of *Così fan tutte*); they are 633 bars and 651 bars long, accounting for approximately a quarter and a third of their respective acts.

The finales of *La fedeltà premiata* have respectively ten and six sections and, with the benefit of a tauter libretto, are more forceful in their impact; that of Act I (see table) is particularly compelling, providing moments of theatrical *frisson* that few eighteenth-century composers could equal and only one could surpass.

La fedeltà premiata: Finale of Act I

Key	Tempo	Time signature	Maximum number of singers in ensemble	A	L	M	C	N	P	F
B flat	Vivace assai	C	3	x^e	x	x^e				
G	Adagio	3/4	1		x		x			
g	Presto	2/4	1		x		x^e			
E flat	Presto	6/8	4	x	x	x			x^e	x
C	Vivace assai	C	5	x	x	x	x		x	
A flat	Adagio	¢	1			x	x		x	x
g	Presto	2/4	6	x	x	x	x		x	x
B flat	Presto	¢	7	x	x	x	x^e	x	x	x
g–V/B flat	Vivace	3/4	6	x	x	x		x	x	x
B flat	Presto	¢	6	x	x	x		x	x	x

(Characters*: columns A L M C N P F)

* Abbreviations of characters: A = Amaranta; L = Lindoro; M = Melibeo; C = Celia; N = Nerina; P = Perrucchetto; F = Fileno.

x^e: character exits at end of section.

The immediately striking aspect of the organization of this finale is its daring key scheme. Beginning and ending in B flat, it is governed, not by fourth or fifth relationships between sections, but by a chain of falling thirds from B flat through to A flat major in the sixth section; a semitone descent to G minor then precedes a rise of a third back to the tonic B flat major. Strictly ordered as it seems to be, this scheme cannot be regarded as an *a priori* conception applied to the music regardless of dramatic relevance. On the contrary, the broad movement downward in thirds helps to sweep the action forward to its unpredictable climax, a battle between satyrs and shepherds that frustrates Amaranta's machinations when they are about to succeed. On a local level, the mediant contrast between each section reinforces changes of mood and sudden incident: from aggressive B flat to the sorrow of Celia (G major), the return of Amaranta (E flat major), the dragging in by the arm of Celia (C major), and the pitiful first appearance of her lover, Fileno (A flat major). G minor is given special importance as the only minor key in the scheme. First used when Celia refuses Lindoro's advances, it reappears twice, when Fileno is told that Celia is to be forced to marry Lindoro and again when the satyrs enter.

In broad musical and dramatic terms, the finale divides into two parts of five sections each. The first contains the greater number of entries and exits of individual characters and culminates in a C major quintet, given due emphasis by virtue of a long dominant peroration. It strikes a balance between action and the focusing, in the Adagio, on the misfortune of Celia. The second part of the finale begins by concentrating on the other maligned party, Fileno, before Nerina enters, pursued by satyrs, and the action moves relentlessly to the musical climax of a sextet. As in many contemporary operatic finales, by Haydn and others, the characters demonstrate their shared feelings (if for different motives) at the end of the act through a series of imitative entries.

In addition to the tonal structure, tempo and number of participants, the poetic metre and rhyme-scheme play an important part in the structure of the finale. The two static sections, the adagios in G and A flat major, have regular scanning and rhyming schemes, as does the final section. Elsewhere, to mirror the greater activity, metre and rhyme are less consistent. One final aspect of this resourceful finale deserves to be highlighted, and that is the telling use of the customary format of an eighteenth-century operatic duet. Most of Haydn's operas contain duets that utilize the plan of melodic line sung by one partner, same melodic line sung by the other, dialogue and, finally, duet writing in 'perfect harmony' of thirds and sixths, often in a quicker tempo.[8] The format of sections two and three correspond to this pattern, but the sentiments do not. Celia, her heart fluttering (repeated demisemiquavers in the orchestral accompaniment), thinks of Fileno rather than of Lindoro, the person she is addressing; the dialogue is brief and the sentiments unrequited rather than affectionate; and the quick section turns curtly to the minor as Celia slaps Lindoro on the face and leaves.

The success of the ensemble finale encouraged many librettists and composers to adopt a similar procedure at the beginnings of operas, termed '*Introduzione*', and all Haydn's operas from *Le pescatrici* onwards reflect this development. There are opening ensembles in *Le pescatrici* and *Il mondo della luna*, and, in *L'infedeltà delusa* and *La fedeltà premiata*, a three-part design, of two ensembles (chorus in the later opera) enclosing an aria.

Apart from *La fedeltà premiata*, Haydn reveals little interest in large-scale tonal planning of his operas and though most begin and end in the same key, three of the largest, *L'incontro improvviso*, *La vera costanza* and *Il mondo della luna* disdain even this easily applied feature. In the case of *La fedeltà premiata* there is an impressive attempt to make the wide-ranging key scheme, from B major in a sharp direction to E flat in a flat direction, revolve around D major; no fewer than eight of the twenty-four musical numbers (including the overture) are in this key. Elsewhere in the operas, sonority rather than any broader structural consideration determines the choice of key: thus, A and E major are associated with tranquil or amorous scenes, E flat major with resigned pathos, B flat major with brisk, neutral moods and C major with brilliance or pomposity.

One of the most frequently quoted contemporary criticisms of Mozart's operas is that uttered by Joseph II to Dittersdorf concerning *Die Entführung aus dem Serail*, 'Too fine for our ears, and an immense number of notes'. A few lines later in this smug dialogue between emperor and composer, Haydn's operas are criticized for the same reason, musical complexity. Too much has been made of Joseph II's censure of Mozart, since – as the remainder of the conversation implies – such criticism was frequently applied to many an opera. Jommelli and Piccinni, for instance, were other composers similarly attacked, and Haydn himself, in 1795, was to criticize Bianchi's *Aci e Galatea* for the same reason. Haydn's basic opera orchestra is, naturally, the same as in his symphonies: two oboes, two horns and strings, with bassoons present as continuo instruments at first, later as fully independent parts.

Other instruments are present as alternatives or extras. The flute is often associated with pastoral scenes and, by extension, often portrays innocence; two cors anglais are required in single numbers in *La canterina*, *Le pescatrici* and *L'incontro improvviso*. Turkish percussion instruments are *de rigueur* in *L'incontro improvviso*, timpani are needed in *L'infedeltà delusa* and *La vera costanza*, and trumpets and timpani in *Il mondo della luna* and *La fedeltà premiata*.

Italian opera: some conclusions

Haydn thought very highly of his operas, regarding them as more significant than his instrumental music. In 1781, three months after the premiere of *La fedeltà premiata*, he received a letter from the Director of the Concert Spirituel in Paris (*C&W*, II, 446–7) informing him of the successful performances of the Stabat Mater and expressing surprise that he 'was so singularly successful' as a composer of vocal music. Haydn's comment to his Viennese publisher, Artaria, was one of genuine self-esteem: 'but I wasn't at all surprised, for they have not yet heard anything. If they only could hear my operetta [*sic*] *L'isola disabitata* and my most recent opera, *La fedeltà premiata*, I assure you that no such work has been heard in Paris up to now, nor perhaps in Vienna; my misfortune is that I live in the country.'

This pride reflects a sense of artistic fulfilment that goes beyond the pleasurable satisfaction of earning his employer's plaudits and the regard of fellow musicians. Justifiably, Haydn may have felt that he was moving towards a new synthesis of operatic conventions in *La vera costanza* and *La fedeltà premiata*, drawing on the traditions of Italian comic opera and some of the techniques of dramatic continuity associated with Gluck's reform operas. Perhaps the task was too ambitious, the diverse elements too incompatible, particularly for a composer who lacked an overwhelming dramatic instinct. Between them, *La vera costanza* and *La fedeltà premiata* reveal a vast range of material, the comic, the serious, the moralistic, conventional arias, chain finales, increasingly imaginative orchestral recitative, evocative settings of caves as well as stereotyped shepherds' groves. With the notable exception of *The Creation* and to a limited extent the six late masses, Haydn was not the type of composer capable of controlling a whole range of influences and re-channelling them to form a personal *Gesamtkunstwerk* along the lines of Bach's Mass in B minor, Beethoven's *Missa Solemnis* and, of course, Mozart's operas. Haydn's richest achievements were the results of consistent tilling of a single furrow; by temperament he was an inquisitive explorer rather than a masterly synthesizer. It is for this reason that the earlier, less ambitious operas, such as *La canterina*, *Lo speziale* and *L'infedeltà delusa* are more successful in performance than the later works, even though the music, *qua* music, is less resourceful. (*Le pescatrici* is difficult to judge, since approximately one-third of the music has not survived.) *L'infedeltà delusa*, in particular, moves fluently through a series of engaging and dramatic arias and only the anti-climactic finale disappoints; if only Haydn could have found time to revise this finale later in the 1770s!

Haydn's next opera, *L'incontro improvviso*, dating from 1775, is the first of the large-scale works and, despite the 'Turkish' ambience (actually Cairo) and the colourful music, the opera is dramatically very slow-moving, the scale of individual numbers threatening the continuity of the story-line so that, eventually, there seems to be little interaction between music and drama. To a less damaging extent, similar criticisms can be levelled at *Il mondo della luna* and *La vera costanza*; both have moments of genuine theatre and the former has the advantage of a typically delightful libretto by Goldoni.

Haydn's final *dramma giocoso*, *La fedeltà premiata*, is dramatically the most absorbing and fluent of the large-scale works, with a feeling that the music is always relevant to the narrative. There are vexatious problems of plausibility, however: especially the appearance of the satyrs and Diana's last-minute resolution, in perfunctory accompanied recitative, of the many intricacies of the plot. In general the pastoral setting, traditional and full of its own resonances, appears unconvincing because it is not allowed to flourish as an artifice or an allegory; neither is it sufficiently ridiculed to succeed as a parody. Consequently, Haydn's *dramma giocoso* tends to fall between two stools: the setting could be that of an opera by Handel or Hasse, and the music is the product of half-a-century's quest for realism. It is no accident that none of Mozart's mature operas is set in groves with roving nymphs and shepherds.

Musically splendid and, at their best, dramatically absorbing, the operas of Haydn to 1780 reveal a mixed sense of human characterization. The superficial qualities of the buffoon, the pretentious, the haughty, the deceitful are well caught, especially if there is an element of caricature. Complex emotions are normally the prerogative of female characters, for instance Sandrina in *L'infedeltà delusa*, Rosina in *La vera costanza* and Celia in *La fedeltà premiata*. Their respective would-be and eventual lovers – Nanni, Count Errico and Fileno – are, in comparison, palely drawn (especially the first two) though, again, there is a persistent tradition of ineffectual lovers in eighteenth-century opera, including Don Ottavio in *Don Giovanni*. As regards the manipulators of the various plots (Vespina, Ecclitico, Baroness Irene and Amaranta), they remain conventionally and entertainingly humorous without exposing any deeper levels of cynicism or unsettling malice.

In even the most concentrated discussion, comparison of Haydn's operas with those of Mozart is difficult to suppress. Revealing as such comparisons can be, they are historically unfair when one remembers the chronology and particularly the pace of operatic development in the eighteenth century. Comic opera was evolving at an unprecedented rate in the period 1760–90, ever willing to embrace new ideas. By 1780 Haydn was fully up with the times and, in some respects, more adventurous, even if his geographical situation meant that he could not be part of the mainstream of European operatic development. Haydn, by c. 1780, had every reason to be proud of his achievement in a field which he, like all contemporary musicians, regarded as the most significant. It was Haydn's historical role to change that belief and to assert the primacy of the symphony. As for opera, it was left to Mozart in the following decade to capitalize on its recent development, one in which Haydn had played an interesting and often ambitious part.

Church music and oratorio

With the death of Gregor Werner in 1766, Haydn assumed the duties of full *Kapellmeister*, including the supervision of church music at the Esterházy court. Though the next decade produced a succession of fine individual works – five masses, a cantata, Stabat Mater, Salve Regina, an oratorio, as well as some smaller church music and derivative *contrafacta* – only two works, the so-called Great Organ Solo Mass of 1769 and the *Missa Sancti Nicolai* of 1772, were written for the Esterházy court. Haydn's contract of 1761 forbade the accepting of outside commissions without the approval of the Prince, yet in respect of church music the composer seems to have been allowed to cultivate such contacts; Prince Nicolaus was evidently not very interested in church music and allowed the facilities for its performance to decline. Haydn, however, was impatient to compose vocal music on a larger scale than his career had so far permitted, and the *Missa Cellensis in honorem B. V. M.* (1766), Stabat Mater (1767), 'Applausus' Cantata (1768) and the oratorio *Il ritorno di Tobia* (1774–75) were all the products of this desire. Scale was not the only attraction. The variety of works and style explored in this period is unequalled at any other time in his career and seems to be the product, if not of a long-term strategy, then certainly of *ad hoc* planning. He had recently composed a Te Deum, and now he was able for the first time in his career to compose a *missa longa* (or *missa solemnis*), the *Missa Cellensis*; then followed a setting of the demanding text of the Stabat Mater, a mass in the severe *a cappella* style (the *Missa* 'Sunt bona mixta malis'), a celebratory cantata on a moralistic text (the 'Applausus' Cantata) and a Salve Regina. It would be gratifying to discover whether Haydn declined the composition of a second Te Deum, a second *missa longa*, a second Stabat Mater etc., preferring to wait until a new challenge came his way. Three further masses were composed, the Great Organ Solo Mass, the *Missa Sancti Nicolai* and the Little Organ Solo Mass (1777?), but these, too, are strongly individual works. In this music Haydn's religious character becomes glowingly apparent: instinctive and unquestioning in faith, yet celebratory and reverent rather than naive, and one that seeks devotion through the contemplation of beauty. The result is the most aptly Catholic music between the sixteenth century and Bruckner.

The first in this series of works, the *Missa Cellensis*, owes its name to its association with the baroque pilgrimage church at Mariazell (Zelle = Celle), the destination of many Catholic pilgrims through the ages, including in the 1750s Haydn himself. As one of the principal shrines in Austria, it was replicated in several 'Mariazell' chapels in Vienna and it is possible that Haydn's mass was composed for Vienna rather than for Mariazell (which lacked a strong musical tradition). Until the rediscovery of a portion of the autograph in 1975, the work was known as *Missa Sanctae Caeciliae*, a spurious title originating in the nineteenth century.

The mass lasts some seventy minutes (compared with the fifteen or so of the early F major setting) and is of the type that is now described as a 'cantata mass'; eighteenth-century Austrians would have categorized it as a *missa longa* or *missa solemnis*. It is scored for four solo voices, SATB choir and an orchestra of two oboes, two trumpets, timpani, four-part strings and continuo; the Benedictus has parts for two horns (possibly not authentic) and written-out bassoon parts. The main key, C major, and the associated tone colour of trumpets and timpani make it a particularly jubilant work. The text is subdivided to form a large number of separate movements or sections – hence the term cantata mass – with more extended use of vocal soloists than is normally the case in settings of the Ordinary. Thus, after a Largo introduction, itself an indication of scope, the Kyrie is divided into three parts: an Allegro of unceasing vigour that moves with ease between choral homophony and counterpoint, all accompanied by dashing figuration in the violins; an Allegretto in A minor for the Christe eleison, a tenor solo with short choral confirmations; and a Vivace choral fugue in C major for the return of the Kyrie eleison.

To bind together the longest section of the mass, the Credo, Haydn uses a well-established procedure in eighteenth-century settings, that of reiterating the initial affirmative word 'Credo' ('I believe') several times during the course of the movement. This technique is also used in two masses by Mozart (K.192 and K.257) and, most memorably, by Beethoven in the *Missa solemnis*. Haydn would have known this procedure from settings by Caldara, Fux, Holzbauer, Wagenseil and others. In the *Missa Cellensis* it is always sung by the soprano soloist in florid semiquavers in a choral context that is predominantly syllabic.

Also an indication of scale and the concomitant need to provide decisive points of climax is the use of fugue. In addition to the Kyrie, there are four further fugues: the customary ones at the end of the Gloria and Credo, and less expected ones for the 'Gratias' and the 'Dona nobis pacem'.

Haydn had not composed a mass for seventeen years and he clearly relished the traditional challenge of composing a work that incorporated a wide range of idioms and techniques. The later case of Mozart's Mass in C minor does not form an exact parallel but is, nevertheless, revealing. After several years of being obliged to compose masses for an unsympathetic employer, Mozart was able in 1782–3 to compose a mass on an unprecedentedly large scale, embracing an even wider range of idioms than Haydn's *Missa Cellensis*. In Haydn's case the work is simultaneously a summing up of the early C major style (the main theme of the Credo could appear quite happily in an organ concerto from the 1750s), a compendium of contemporary techniques of mass composition and word setting (e.g. the traditional word-painting for 'laudamus te' and 'crucifixus') and an anticipation of stylistic developments that became general in later years (e.g. the orchestral scoring of the Benedictus). Before the rediscovery of a portion of the autograph, carrying the date 1766, the disparity of style, the sheer size and the absence of a comparable work combined to perplex scholars, and dates ranging from 1769 to 1781 had been put forward for its composition. Lately it has been suggested, plausibly, that the extant mass is a composite of two portions written at separate times: Kyrie, Gloria, Credo and Sanctus in 1766; Benedictus, Agnus Dei and Dona nobis pacem composed in 1773, possibly to replace an earlier setting of these sections.[9] This argument accommodates some uncomfortably conflicting bibliographical evidence, as well as the stylistic range of the mass. Even if the work is a composite, it only reflects within one work the general, very deliberate diversity found in Haydn's church music at this time.

The Stabat Mater is on an equally large scale but its tone is different and, exploited with greater consistency, forms a more satisfactory whole. It was composed in 1767, possibly for performance at Eisenstadt; Good Friday and the Feast of the Seven Dolours on 15 September were both customary dates for performances of the Stabat Mater. Musical settings of this text, the depiction of the Virgin Mary at the foot of the cross, were comparatively rare, if only because of the largely unvaried nature of the text which evokes sorrow without the drama and imagery encountered in other liturgical texts. The settings by Pergolesi and Domenico Scarlatti were known throughout Europe and within Austria those by Gassmann and Vanhal were equally well known. The nature of the text's appeal for Haydn may be perceived in the opening sentences of a letter written in March 1768 to the Esterházy administration requesting leave of absence for himself and other musicians to take part in the second performance of the work, on Good Friday at the church of the Barmherzige Brüder in Vienna (see p. 103).

Primacy of the words may well have been a more compelling challenge here than in the composition of the *Missa Cellensis*, which owes much to convention. Both in broad conception and telling detail Haydn's setting of the Stabat Mater is an impressive work of contemplation and devotion, and though, ironically, it achieved fame for Haydn in the concert halls of Paris und London, this is a work that benefits from the congenial setting of a baroque Catholic church to a greater extent than perhaps any other liturgical work by the composer.

The preponderance of music in a slow tempo (seven complete movements and the beginning of an eighth) is to be expected, less so the extensive sound of the minor key, particularly when one recalls how rare that sound is in the earlier part of Haydn's career. The work begins in G minor and charts a tonal course that includes five further movements in the minor: G minor, E flat, C minor, F, B flat, F minor, D minor, B flat, G minor, E flat, C minor, C, G minor to major. The major-key movements are all in flat keys so that when the final movement moves from G minor to G major, the brightness of the latter provides the perfect sonority for the 'glory of heaven'. Remembering Haydn's use of the minor key elsewhere in his œuvre at this time – Gasparina's aria in *La canterina* for instance – the striking aspect of its appearance in the Stabat Mater is the way it avoids the cliché or the superficial. Only the bass aria, 'Flammis orci ne succendar' ('Lest I burn in the flames of hell') and the contralto aria 'Fac me vere tecum flere' ('Make me truly weep with thee') deserve this criticism, the former an operatic aria, the second a *concertante* melody over a persistent accompaniment. A couple of the major-key movements also appear uneasy in their tone, a total of four movements out of thirteen preventing this work from being a masterpiece of the greatest distinction. Haydn's response to the opening lines of the text represents the best of this work. The music of the tenor solo (bars 15ff.) is preceded by an orchestral ritornello that opens in a similar way. The contrast between the octave unison opening and the harmonized response that turns to the Neapolitan sixth for the word 'dolorosa' ('sorrowful'); the descending chromatic scale; the strong orchestral response to 'crucem' ('cross'); the two different motifs for 'Lacrimosa' ('tearful'); and for 'pendebat' ('was hanging') still syncopation over a harmonic accompaniment that has lost its direction: all these are carefully considered responses that combine to exhibit a sensitivity typical of the work as a whole.

When Haydn wrote his letter concerning the Vienna performance of the Stabat Mater he had probably just finished the composition of a third ambitious vocal work, the 'Applausus' Cantata, commissioned by the Cistercian abbey of Zwettl to celebrate the fiftieth anniversary of the taking of vows by their abbot, Rayner I. Kollmann. 'Applausus' was a generic term used to describe laudatory works of this type and Haydn's cantata is part of a long tradition of works written to commemorate similar events. In a sense his cantatas for Prince Nicolaus were of the 'Applausus' variety; the text of the present work, rather than being in the secular Italian of the Esterházy cantatas, is in venerable Latin and is a largely allegorical discourse between the four Cardinal Virtues, Temperance, Prudence, Justice and Fortitude, with a fifth persona, Theologia, representing learned Christian doctrine. The text, probably written by one of the Zwettl monks, praises the goodly life of the monastery, the generous spirit of the abbot and asks for the bounteous blessing of God. Like the Esterházy cantatas, it exploits to the full the musical resources of the abbey for this special occasion: orchestra with trumpets and timpani and, in several movements, two viola parts (rarely encountered in Esterházy works), arias for the five characters, obbligato harpsichord and violin, and a concluding chorus. In idiom the music is fully up to date, with echoes of the composer's symphonies and operas, though the widespread use of large da capo structures checks the natural impetus of the music.

The year 1768 also witnessed the composition of a mass, described by Haydn in his *Entwurf-Katalog* as 'Missa sunt bona mixta malis'. The work remained lost for over two hundred years, with successive generations of Haydn scholars having to content themselves with the tantalizing D minor incipit given in the *Entwurf-Katalog* (later reproduced in the *Haydn-Verzeichnis*). In 1955 it was learned that the autograph of the Kyrie and part of the Gloria had been sold by Artaria to Novello early in the nineteenth century. Two anomalies surrounded the history of the work. Why were there no contemporary manuscript copies such as exist in profusion for

most of Haydn's masses, and why had not Novello published the work? The rediscovery of the autograph in December 1983 provided the most exciting event in
modern Haydn scholarship since the discovery of the C major Cello Concerto in
1961. It explained the anomalies but posed many new and intriguing questions.

The manuscript consists of eight bifolios (sixteen leaves) and contains a Kyrie
movement and the Gloria up to the end of the clause 'Gratias agimus tibi propter
magnam gloriam tuam'; a perfect cadence in A minor is followed by a double bar
and five blank pages. Clearly Haydn halted work on the autograph score for some
reason, even if preliminary work had been carried out for any of the remainder of
the text. The work is described on the title page as 'Missa/a 4^{tro} voci/alla cappella',
with 'Sunt bona mixta malis' underlined (these words having been added to the
right of the first line at a later stage). Underneath and to the right are the composer's signature and date: 'Del giuseppe Haydn mpria/$\overline{768}$.' It is scored for SATB
with a figured bass part for 'Organo' containing thematic leads as in other continuo parts by Haydn. Stylistically, it is written in *stile antico*, more specifically
'stylo à capella' as described by Fux in his *Gradus ad Parnassum*. Though Fux's
principles were drily codified from the study of Palestrina's music, *stile antico* in
general was honoured more in the breach than in the observance, increasingly so
as the century wore on and composers made use of anachronistic sequence, chromatic and cadential harmony. The limited appeal for Novello of an atypical Haydn
work written in an archaic style and, moreover, incomplete is obvious, and he sold
the autograph without publishing it. In the eighteenth century the incomplete nature of the work meant that it could not be readily performed in a church service;
Haydn naturally refused to release the work and consequently no copies were
made. The composer may have intended to finish the work at some time but in old
age he sold the manuscript to his Viennese publisher, Artaria.[10]

Why did Haydn compose the work in the first place and why was it apparently
never completed? Compositions in the *a cappella* style were frequently performed
during Advent and Lent, either newly-composed or from older repertory. Fux,
Caldara and Reutter all wrote in this idiom, in 1762 Michael Haydn composed his
Missa Sanctae Crucis (described on the autograph as 'a 4 Voci in contra punto'), and
Joseph Haydn himself in later life composed two further *a cappella* works, the 'Li-
bera me' (XXIIb:1) and the 'Non nobis domine' (XXIIIa:1), both, incidentally, in
the same key, D minor.[11] More immediately relevant to Haydn and the Esterházy
court was the large number of *a cappella* works by the late *Kapellmeister*, Gregor
Werner, pointing to a strong local tradition: *Missa Lydia*, *Missa pro Quadragesima
alla Capella*, *Missa Quadrages*, *Missa S. Dominici*, several Salve Regina settings and
smaller works.[12] In the 1760s Haydn was evidently keen to explore the whole spectrum of contemporary church music and the *Missa* 'Sunt bona mixta malis' was
part of a process that had already produced works as different as the *Missa Cellensis*
and the Stabat Mater. If Haydn had intended the work to be performed in Lent
1768, it is possible that he had to put it aside in order to complete the 'Applausus'
cantata. This was altogether a hectic year for Haydn. In addition to 'Applausus', he
is known to have composed the opera *Lo speziale* and Symphony no. 49 ('La passione'), and many other works that cannot be dated accurately may be assigned to
this year, including symphonies, baryton trios and keyboard sonatas. The few
weeks after the premiere of *Lo speziale* in October seem to have been the only time
in the year when Haydn was not engaged on a major project and perhaps the mass
was intended for Advent rather than Lent.

Before we consider the significance of the title 'Sunt bona mixta malis', the content of the work should be appraised. In the *alla breve* first movement the phrases

'Kyrie eleison', 'Christe eleison', 'Kyrie eleison' are announced in turn in a similar way, in the form of a four-part fugal exposition that continues in a contrapuntal fashion before culminating in stretto. Two brief interludes for organ separate the three main paragraphs, making conventional use of sequential patterns. The opening subject (see example) and the subsequent subsidiary motif to the word 'eleison' (bar 30 etc, anticipated in bars 13–14) seem unnerving anticipations of passages

from the opening movement of Mozart's Requiem, but as in Haydn's use of the so-called 'Jupiter' motif, these contrapuntal subjects and others in the mass are part of a shared musical heritage; the opening motif occurs, for instance, in Mozart's Misericordias (K.222).

Formal counterpoint plays a less pervasive part in the Gloria. It contains two expositions on the phrases 'Laudamus te' and 'Gratias agimus tibi', each subsequently leading to skilful overlapping of entries. Elsewhere the texture is either freely contrapuntal in a reduced number of parts, as in the carefully judged climax to the Gratias, or predominantly homophonic, as in 'Et in terra pax' which, often in Haydn's masses, is sung in a low, as it were, 'terrestrial' register. Two continuo links precede the two fugal expositions and, like those in the Kyrie, make perfunctory use of sequence.

Perhaps the most intriguing aspect of the composition is its title, 'Sunt bona mixta malis' ('good things mixed with the bad'). Titles were often applied to masses in the eighteenth century, as in earlier times, to demonstrate some particular association; the Werner titles given above are typical. In Haydn's case *Missa Cellensis*, *Missa Sancti Nicolai*, *Missa Sancti Bernardi de Offida* and other titles were applied by the composer and their meaning is clear. That of 'Sunt bona mixta malis' is more elusive. In earlier centuries masses based on pre-existing musical material, plainsong, chanson, motet etc., often recorded the name of the source in the title. Parody masses, however, were scarcely known in eighteenth-century Austria. The phrase itself is a metrical proverb, the first half of the hexameter 'sunt bona mixta malis, sunt mala mixta bonis', a classical commonplace.[13] Haydn himself was clearly familiar with the proverb and the second half appears in one of his interviews with his biographer, Griesinger: 'Of his own works he said, "Sunt mala mixta bonis"; there are good and bad children, and here and there a changeling has crept in'.[14] There are several instances in Haydn's output of autograph scores or authentic printed editions containing votive, semi-cryptic or jocular annotations in Latin or German in addition to the customary 'In Nomine Domini' and 'Fine Laus Deo', e.g. the Latin phrases that occur at the end of individual quartets in op. 20 (see p. 165), 'in Schlaff geschrieben' on the Horn Concerto, 'Dieses war vor gar zu gelehrte Ohren' on Symphony no. 42, and 'fatto a posta' and 'nihil sine causa' on Baryton Trio no. 109. The added phrase 'Sunt bona mixta malis' is very much in this vein, being a gently sceptical remark applied to a composition that is wholly untypical of the composer's style. It also suggests why the mass may have been left unfinished. In contrapuntal technique, this is the most concentrated and deliberately ingenious work that Haydn had hitherto composed. Having completed the Kyrie and a third of the Gloria – five separate fugal expositions with succeeding developments – Haydn may have become less sure of the work's value as a composition and the prospect of composing four further movements in the same restricting vein may have seemed a less absorbing challenge than when he embarked on the mass.

There is some further evidence to support the view that Haydn's learned Latin remark was a comment on an effort to compose in a learned style. The composer's own copy of Fux's treatise, *Gradus ad Parnassum*, contains several annotations including marginal remarks such as 'bene – melios', 'male', 'Lic: non bona'; 'sunt bona mixta malis' is very much in this schoolmasterish vein. Unfortunately, the volume did not survive the Second World War and doubts have since been expressed about the status of the annotations. Even if it were demonstrated beyond doubt that the annotations were not by Haydn, this would not affect the essential argument that the proverb constitutes a critical remark.

There is one telling piece of bibliographical evidence that weakens the hypothesis that the work was left unfinished. The *Missa* 'Sunt bona mixta malis' was entered with its incipit (misquoted, incidentally) in the usual way in the *Entwurf-Katalog*. Haydn regarded this catalogue as an aide-mémoire to his output (incipits, but not always, and instrumentation inconsistently noted) and included only completed work. If the mass was left unfinished, it represents the only incomplete (as opposed to lost) work to have been entered in the catalogue. Indeed, very few fragments of discarded works by Haydn survive, in comparison with many by the mature Mozart. However, the evidence is not necessarily conflicting and can be made compatible by the following hypothetical chain of events: the mass was left unfinished for whatever reason; Haydn intended returning to it at a later date; untypically, he recorded its incipit in the *Entwurf-Katalog* and retained the autograph.

The modern discovery of the mass confirms, in an extreme manner, the stylistic turmoil that Haydn's music was undergoing in the late 1760s. Increased use of counterpoint and the minor key are two particular features that broaden the emotional scope of his music, features that are demonstrated in a severe form in this mass in *stile antico*. In reality, 1768 was for Haydn an *annus mirabilis* of stylistic diversity, including works as different as the comic opera *Lo speziale*, Symphony no. 49 ('La passione') and the *Missa* 'Sunt bona mixta malis'.

Most of the autograph of Haydn's next mass, the so-called Great Organ Solo Mass, is lost, but the work circulated widely in the composer's own day. Again the circumstances of its composition are unknown. Modern scholarship has proposed *c.* 1768–9 as the date of composition; perhaps, in view of the amount of other work accomplished in 1768, 1769 is more likely. The predominant tone of the mass is unique: personal rather than conventionally festive (as in the *Missa Cellensis*) or distinctly objective (as in the *Missa* 'Sunt bona mixta malis'). In the key of E flat major (comparatively unusual for a mass), the work's restrained, gently plangent effect derives from two complementary aspects. The orchestra consists of two cors anglais, horns and strings, with a few solo passages for organ.[15] In his music at this time, the cor anglais was favoured by Haydn for providing occasional tone colour, and works as diverse as Symphony no. 22 ('The Philosopher'), the Stabat Mater, *La canterina*, *Le pescatrici* and *L'incontro improvviso* make effective use of the instrument. As in Symphony no. 22, the cors anglais play throughout the mass (oboes being omitted from the scoring). In this carefully cultivated sonority the cheerful interjections of the concertante organ prevent the music from becoming inappropriately morose. Secondly, the mass is notable for the way it cultivates a melodic style that is less stereotyped than that of the *Missa Cellensis* and, especially, the *Missa* 'Sunt bona mixta malis'. The vocal entries in the Kyrie take the form of a fugal exposition on a subject that has as its principal feature a succession of rising fourths, a common characteristic of fugue subjects which Haydn had already used elsewhere ('In Paradisi gloria' in the last movement of the Stabat Mater and the 'Christe' in the *Missa* 'Sunt bona mixta malis'). Here, however, the *piano* dynamic and the displaced accents impart a ruminative rather than assertive quality to the line. Many of the later themes in the mass also feature this rising interval more or less prominently (see examples opposite).

Controlling the emotional boundaries of a work through similarly shaped themes is a practice that begins to figure in Haydn's music at the end of the 1760s; the C minor quartet, op. 17 no. 4, is a better-known instance of the same technique.

Haydn's next two works of church music continue this introspective trend. A Salve Regina (XXIIIb:2) in the distinctive key of G minor is scored for four solo voices, strings (with viola) and concertante organ. Composed in 1771, probably as a

pious thanksgiving after his recent illness, its small forces were dictated by the personnel available in the Eisenstadt chapel; it was in 1771 that the singer Eleonora Jäger petitioned the Prince to maintain the basic complement of church musicians at four singers, two violinists and an organist. Later in the century, the vocal parts of the Salve Regina were divided into solo and tutti by an unknown musician, disturbing the subdued melancholy of the work.

The *Missa Sancti Nicolai* was first performed in 1772 on Prince Nicolaus's name-day (6 December). With the approach of Advent, the Kyrie projects a suitably pastoral idiom: a flowing 6/4 tempo (the alternative 6/8 had more lively associations for Haydn) complemented by a simple harmonic style and a predilection for vocal lines that move in parallel thirds. Since this music reappears verbatim for the Dona nobis pacem the pastoral idiom forms the final impression too. Elsewhere, dramatic gestures are rare, and the work achieves a smooth integration of soloists and choir, one not exemplified in the *Missa Cellensis* or the Great Organ Solo Mass.

Haydn's final mass in this period is known as the 'Little Organ Solo Mass'. Haydn's title, *Missa Brevis Sancti Joannis de Deo*, refers to the patron saint of the Barmherzige Brüder (Order of the Brothers of Mercy); the chapel of their hospital in Vienna had been the venue for the second performance of the Stabat Mater. They also ran a hospital in Eisenstadt and it is surmised that the *Missa Brevis* was written for the Eisenstadt chapel. Scored for SATB choir (soprano soloist in the Benedictus only), two violins, basso continuo and obbligato organ, the mass is perfunctorily polytextual, the Gloria and Credo consisting of only thirty-one and eighty-two bars respectively. Haydn, however, was not a composer who allowed unpromising circumstances to stifle experiment and the shared eleven-bar Amen conclusion to the Gloria and Credo and the treatment of the Agnus Dei and Dona nobis pacem combined as one section are novel and attractive features. Unusually, Haydn's autograph is not dated; the mass was probably composed in the mid-1770s.

Since 1771 the Tonkünstler-Societät in Vienna had organized bi-annual oratorio performances, at Christmas and during Lent, for the benefit of widows and orphans of musicians. The performances were given *gratis* by musicians from the churches and palaces of Vienna; correspondingly, the oratorios were often composed on an unusually large scale. In the 1770s Gassmann, Dittersdorf and Bonno had all written oratorios for this organization, and its concerts had become highlights in the musical calendar of a city where music-making outside the palaces of the nobility, the churches and the opera house was still undeveloped. For the 1775 Lent performances an oratorio was commissioned from Haydn; the result was *Il ritorno di Tobia*, Haydn's most ambitious work to date, in any genre.

The text was written by Giovanni Gastone Boccherini, brother of Luigi, and narrates the story of the blind Tobit as given in the Apocrypha. Haydn, who had no experience of such compositions, was not well served by Boccherini. The text is prolix, sometimes confusing, has little sense of drama and even the moralizing lacks conviction; Haydn's music could do very little to rectify these grievous shortcomings. Rather like the opera *L'incontro improvviso* composed in the same year, the total product is less than the sum of its parts, a series of effective individual movements that for the most part do not form a dramatic narrative. Nearly ten years later, in 1784, Haydn, now a vastly more experienced composer of large-scale dramatic music, prepared a second version of *Il ritorno di Tobia*, severely pruning several of the arias and imparting much needed dramatic impact by the addition of two choruses midway through the two parts, respectively 'Ah, gran Dio' and 'Svanisce in un momento'. The arias were nearly all da capo or dal segno movements on an immense scale: for instance, Sarah's first aria consists of two sentences, 'Del caro sposo son fra le mura, e m'assicura la sua virtù. Ma in te ripongo, mio Dio, le speme, che d'ogni bene fonte sei Tu' ('I am within the walls of my dear husband and his virtue protects me. But, my Lord, I again place my hope in You, as You are the source of all good'); the aria has 275 bars of Allegro moderato music in common time, with a central section in Adagio, 3/4 time. The Allegro moderato contains several bursts of coloratura, more showy than that found in Haydn's operas and often not a little arbitrary.

Symphonies

Despite the considerable demands made on his time and energy by church music and opera, Haydn composed over three dozen symphonies between 1766 and 1780, largely concentrated in the first ten years of this period; from 1775 onwards the composition of the series of operas for performance at Eszterháza afforded little opportunity for new symphonic writing.

The orchestra which Haydn had at his disposal remained essentially the same as in the early Esterházy period; as before, the number of horns fluctuated between two and four and a flute player was not always on hand. Trumpets, however, were more readily available, brought in from the town of Oedenburg (Sopron), equidistant from Eisenstadt and Eszterháza. With the solitary exception of Symphony no. 26 ('Lamentatione'), Haydn turned his back for ever on the three-movement pattern of his early symphonies, though this pattern continued to be used by many of his contemporaries. Similarly, Symphony no. 49 in F minor ('La passione') of 1768 is the solitary example of the *sonata da chiesa* format that had often been encountered in the early 1760s. Taking the broadest view of Haydn's symphonic development in this period, the works confirm the trend discerned in the pre-1765 period of striving for an integrated and balanced four-movement pattern of fast, slow, minuet and fast. Such a scheme produced a common sequence of tempo headings in this period: Allegro (often qualified by 'con brio' or 'di molto'), Andante, Menuetto and Presto. A handful of works have a slow introduction, more likely to occur in symphonies that originated as theatre music (e.g. no. 50 is the assumed overture to the lost marionette opera *Der Götterrath*, and no. 60, a six-movement work, was composed as incidental music to the play *Der Zerstreute*).

One particular genus of symphony is exploited in this period, the extrovert C major type with trumpets and/or C alto horns and timpani. No less than eight such symphonies belong to this period – nos. 38, 41, 48, 50, 56, 60, 63, and 69 – a distinct category to which Haydn would add only a few more works in the 1780s and 1790s. It was, too, a sonority that appears consistently in church music (the Te Deum and *Missa Cellensis*) and opera (*La vera costanza* and, in the 1780s, *Orlando Paladino* and *Armida*). No. 56, composed in 1774, is typical of the C major works. The descending *forte* arpeggio of the opening theme is a recurring feature in symphonies of this period, in works as emotionally diverse as nos. 45 ('Farewell'), 62 and 70. In no. 56 the two-bar descent leads to a *piano* passage for strings alone, whose deceptively unremarkable content provokes vigorous discussion in the development and a charming digression in the recapitulation. The first subject is completed by some more *forte* fanfare material (see overleaf).

In these C major symphonies Haydn is not averse to repetition and the creation of clear, self-contained paragraphs, procedures he was anxious to avoid elsewhere in his instrumental music, especially in quartets and sonatas. The narrative of the first movement of Symphony no. 56 is organized into clear paragraphs: a transition characterized by voluble measured tremolo in the violins, a new second subject with typically bass-light accompaniment followed by further climactic writing for full orchestra. The development section (see pp. 149–50) makes telling use of the lower auxiliary figure of bars 7 and 8: first, in the treble register as part of a *piano* phrase that is juxtaposed with a *fortissimo* rising arpeggio and, secondly, in the bass to underpin dominant harmony of F major, then E minor.

The rhetorical pause that concludes this paragraph is a feature often found in Haydn's symphonies of this time and, again, is one that does not figure to the same extent in quartets and sonatas. The development then moves forward with an extended *forte* passage derived from the transition. The approach to the recapitulation is via the mediant rather than the dominant; *piano* then *pianissimo* dynamics aid the feeling of expectancy, fulfilled by the return of full orchestra, *forte* dynamic, first subject and C major. In the recapitulation the lower auxiliary figure provokes a harmonic digression of twelve bars, a chain of sequences making concentrated use of the single most important motif in the first movement (opposite).

Partial expansion of this area of sonata form is typical in Haydn's sonata forms of this period and the technique of exploiting the latent potential of what, at first hearing, seems to be an insignificant chromatic note is one of the major resources of Haydn's symphonic thinking, producing results that range from the whimsical to the dramatic. It is this kind of intellectual sophistication that separated Haydn from his contemporaries, the product of inspired craftsmanship that imparts incident to the slow harmonic rhythms of the classical style. As a compositional technique it is one that Haydn passed on to Beethoven: the chromatic F natural and C sharp that redirect the progress of the recapitulation sections of the first movements of the latter's 'Ghost' Trio (op. 70 no. 1) and the 'Eroica' Symphony, respectively, are two well-known instances.

Trumpets and timpani are omitted from the Adagio and the violins are muted, the latter feature typical of Haydn's symphonies in the 1760s and 1770s. As in many of the earlier Esterházy symphonies, there is a strong concertante element, here featuring the bassoon and oboes.

Among the chief splendours of the C major symphonies are the minuets which make optimum use of the sonority of Haydn's full orchestra; in no. 56 there is, in addition, a reflective quality produced by the many passages in a *piano* dynamic.

The Finale is a rousing Prestissimo with much tonic and dominant posturing and racing triplet rhythms. The approach to the recapitulation is once again via a third relationship, but realized with a ribald humour that is in keeping with the high spirits of the movement: a lengthy passage of aggressive A minor heralds two bars of dominant preparation for D minor; a false start to the recapitulation begins *piano* in D minor before the full orchestra enters, *forte* or *fortissimo*, in the correct key with the first subject. The formerly silent fourth beats are now filled in with fanfare figuration to add even greater momentum to the movement. The first movements of Symphonies nos. 35 and 48 do something similar at the beginning of their respective recapitulations, an audacious horn scale in no. 35 and growling semiquavers in lower strings in no. 48.

The lineage of these C major symphonies in Haydn's own development and in Austrian music in general is a clear one, stretching back to the trumpet and drum *intrade* typical of the baroque period and culminating in the masterpieces of Haydn's own Symphony no. 97, Mozart's 'Linz' and 'Jupiter' Symphonies and Beethoven's First Symphony. More idiosyncratic in conception and individual in impact are the seven symphonies in a minor key composed by Haydn in this period, Symphonies in the minor by Haydn's contemporaries are extremely rare before the mid-1760s and in Haydn's case, Symphony no. 34, dating from *c.* 1766, is the first in a remarkable series of works that also includes: nos. 26 in D minor, 39 in G minor, 44 in E minor, 45 in F sharp minor, 49 in F minor and 52 in C minor. The latest of these seven is the C minor work dating from *c.* 1773, so that within a period of some seven years Haydn had composed seven symphonies in the minor, whereas none had been written in his first seven years as a composer of symphonies and none was to be composed after *c.* 1773 until the beginning of the next decade, with no. 78 in C minor.

The principal attraction was the untapped reservoir of evocative sonority that the minor key in combination with the slow harmonic rhythm of the classical style could offer. Haydn deliberately explored the properties of the minor keys, C, D, E, F, and G, and of the principal minor keys only A and B were not used (Haydn never composed a symphony in either of those two keys). His exploration of new sonorities even led him to compose one symphony (no. 45) in the rare key of F sharp minor, necessitating the construction of new crooks for the horns.

The inspirational influence of Gluck's D minor music in the ballet *Don Juan* has already been noted (see p. 63). By 1770 Haydn had composed several operatic arias in the same vein, usually one per opera, and the mood of these, ranging from the blustering to the genuinely anguished, is reproduced on occasion in these minor-key symphonies. For instance, the finale of Symphony no. 39 and the first movement of no. 52 reveal a sure indebtedness to the opera house. But theatricality is not the main characteristic of the symphonies. Each one is different, an individual exploration of sonority that does not rely exclusively on atmosphere for its effect. The enduring intensity of the expression is often the product of considerable intellectual resource, affecting every aspect of composition from balance of movements to local detail of harmony; unlike the C major works, what is striking about the minor-key works is how different they are one from another and how wide-ranging they are in their technique. Haydn's 'Trauer' and 'Farewell' symphonies (nos. 44 and 45), in particular, are two early masterpieces in the long history of the symphony, integrated in mood and purpose in a way which no other composer had yet managed.

The 'Trauer' has the four-movement pattern of fast, minuet, slow and fast, in which all but the trio of the Menuet and the Adagio are in E minor. Throughout, the thematic argument has rigour and force, with the outer movements being genuinely monothematic in the sense that the sonata forms are governed by a well-nigh continuous discussion of their respective first subjects; in both cases it is an octave unison phrase that provides the generating material. The sixty-bar minuet places a similar emphasis on thematicism, a 'canone in diapason' at a bar's distance (later two bars) between violins and basso doubled intermittently by appropriate instruments; again the opening, a laconic one-bar phrase, generates all the thematic material of the movement. In contrast to the tense, occasionally brusque, E minor of these movements, the trio of the Menuet and the slow movement, both in a relaxed, submissive E major, form the ideal complement to the surrounding E minor.

Heard alongside the compact 'Trauer', the 'Farewell' Symphony sounds expansive, even impassioned. Even so, perhaps its well-known programme (producing the disconcerting last movement) has too often limited the response of listeners, and concealed the perfect proportions and infallible pacing of the work as a whole. Haydn lays less emphasis on dense thematic argument in this symphony than in the 'Trauer' and, instead, uses a wide, carefully controlled tonal and harmonic vocabulary. The first three movements are all in different keys, successively F sharp minor, A major and F sharp major. The same sequence is repeated in the Finale: F sharp minor for the sonata form Presto, A major for the ensuing Adagio, turning to F sharp major for the last forty bars. The first movement, with its widely spaced thematic line over relentless quavers, plays a determining part in this total design by deploying A major, the relative major, in a highly unorthodox way. Expositions of minor-key sonata forms by Haydn and his contemporaries normally move towards the relative major. In this case, after securing A major (bars 29–30), Haydn moves deliberately away from this conventional relationship to establish the dominant minor, C sharp, for the remainder of the exposition. This enables the development section to begin in a blaze of A major with a repetition of the first subject, for which Haydn, significantly, reserves his first *fortissimo* marking in the movement.

All Haydn's music *c.* 1770 gains in expressive force through a wider harmonic vocabulary, diminished sevenths, secondary dominant harmony and, a special favourite, Neapolitan sixths in a minor key. A particularly distinctive chromatic inflection is that of the flattened submediant degree in a major context; it had long been used as the root of an augmented sixth chord, and now it is also used as the third of the minor subdominant chord and, even simpler, unharmonized. Examples abound, in the symphonies especially. One forceful example occurs in the Menuet of the 'Farewell', when violas and bass instruments enter unprepared with a D natural in bar 3:

This brief extract also illustrates a favourite orchestral texture of Haydn – bare, two-part writing for first and second violins; Haydn is no longer dependent on orchestral padding to maintain forward momentum. Certainly, there are plenty of passages in a full orchestral scoring that make use of routine accompaniment figuration – the first movement of the 'Farewell' is especially fully scored – but Haydn now has the confidence to reduce the orchestral fabric to a thinner sound in order, as here, to emphasize an untoward element in the argument. In this sense the orchestral scoring of these works departs from the norm of full texture from bass to treble as found in the composer's operas and church music and reveals Haydn's experience of part writing in his quartets, without ever approaching the continuous manipulation of parts found in that genre. Another aspect of this confidence in the self-sufficiency of the argument is the increased part which silence now plays in the rhetoric of the music, e.g. in the first movement of the 'Farewell' and in the finale of Symphony no. 52. Argumentative thematic lines, reduced textures and use of silence combine in no. 39 to produce a remarkable opening that almost brings the symphony to a halt before it has properly begun.

Although these new aspects of Haydn's creative craft are most memorably displayed in the minor-key symphonies, it should not be thought that the major-key symphonies are inferior. Nos. 59 in A major and 46 in B major, in particular, have an energy and inventiveness on a par with the minor-key symphonies. No. 46 reveals many of the same characteristics: unusual key, widely-spaced, four-note motif that figures throughout the first movement, two-part texture, routine orchestral figuration alongside thematic writing, a finale that unexpectedly breaks off, in this case in order to incorporate a partial restatement of the Menuet, and, in the Presto return, some quizzical pauses.

From 1774 onwards the output of symphonies declines as does their originality. They are never less than entertaining, but are less inclined to experiment or to provoke. Whether Haydn felt that, at its most resourceful, his symphonic idiom was in danger of becoming too individual, sometimes even arcane, is not known; certainly his heavy involvement with opera made very different demands on his musical personality, ones that were reflected in the facility of symphonies such as nos. 61 in D (1776) and 68 in B flat (*c.* 1774–5). Throughout the history of the symphony composers have had to seek a compromise between becoming too symphonic and presenting an appealing face, reflecting the origins of the genre in the theatre. In the early 1770s Haydn, as well as Mozart in works like the two A major symphonies (K.114 and K.201), had come face to face with this central dilemma. For the remainder of the decade Haydn was, to a large extent, content to present an appealing face, disregarding the dramatic tension that he had demonstrated could be present in the genre. Despite the heavy demands of opera composition and performance, it is not unreasonable to assume that Haydn did ponder about the future direction of the symphony – had he been Wagner, Schoenberg or Hindemith, he would have exercised such thoughts in print – and Symphony no. 70, composed at the end of the decade, seems to sum up his quandary. It is dated 18 December 1779 (Prince Nicolaus's birthday) and was probably first performed in the same month as that other musical oddity, *L'isola disabitata* (cf. p. 116).

The two main keys of the symphony, D major and D minor, sum up the opposing worlds of the work: D major, used for the Vivace first movement and the Menuet, conjuring up the public face of Haydn, as used in Symphonies nos. 42, 53, 61 and 62 and in the overture to *L'incontro improvviso*; D minor, used for the slow movement and for the Finale, the intellectualizing side of Haydn's make-up, as in the quartet, op. 9 no. 4, the 'Lamentatione' Symphony and the *Missa* 'Sunt bona mixta malis'. The slow movement is a set of variations on two alternating themes in these two keys, a scheme probably invented by Haydn and used for the first time in a symphony in no. 53; it is more productive of contrast than single variation movements. The movement is proudly labelled 'Specie d'un canone in contrapunto doppio'. Two-part writing with octave doubling had been a feature of symphonic slow movements from the Morzin days and Symphony no. 47 also contains double or invertible counterpoint, but the dry severity of this example is unprecedented, especially effective in context after the D major of the rousing first movement and of the second, complementary theme.

The Finale extends the expressive contrast even further without attempting a synthesis. It begins hesitatingly in D minor, contrasting a five-note crotchet motif on repeated D's in a high register with cadential harmonies in the lower register.

After a pause Haydn unleashes 117 bars of counterpoint labelled 'a 3 soggetti in contrapunto doppio' ('on three subjects in invertible counterpoint'); the principal component is the repeated-note figure heard at the beginning of the movement. Using invertible counterpoint to intensify an argument had been a resource since *c.* 1770 (e.g. bar 28 etc. and bar 121 etc. in the finale of the 'Trauer') and in the 1780s triple counterpoint is often encountered in development sections. Yet the ferocity of this contrapuntal outburst would not be equalled in the composer's symphonies until 1794, in the three-part canon in the development of Symphony no. 102's first movement. Moreover, unlike the later symphony, this paragraph remains stubbornly unintegrated into the broader sweep of the movement; following a return to the hesistant opening, the music turns to the major key in what could have become a concluding peroration on the triple counterpoint material. Instead Haydn chooses to end the movement with repeated D's, *piano*, *pianissimo* and, finally, *forte*: an unexpected, tongue-in-cheek ending to an eccentric, uncomfortable work.

String quartets

During the 1760s the father of the quartet found himself in the ironic position of being an onlooker as other composers developed and popularized the genre. In Austria, Albrechtsberger, Franz Dussek, Ordoñez and Vanhal all wrote for the medium in the 1760s, while Boccherini, with the publication of his op. 1 in Paris in 1767, had embarked on a career during which he was to contribute with great elegance to the genre. Although Haydn did not compose new works until near the end of the decade, his earliest quartets were available throughout Europe, in manuscript copies in Austria and Italy, and in printed form in France, Holland, England and North Germany, so laying the solid foundation of his later international fame. His duties at the Esterházy court never required him to compose quartets, and so time had somehow to be found in the busy schedule of his life. Between 1769 and 1772 a lull in the composition of church music and opera provided such an opportunity; the quartets, opp. 9, 17 and 20, are bounded on the one side by the Great Organ Solo Mass and *Le pescatrici*, and, on the other, by the *Missa Sancti Nicolai* and *L'infedeltà delusa*. Unlike the so-called opp. 1 and 2, the quartets were composed in sets of six: op. 9 probably in 1769–70 (the autographs are lost), opp. 17 and 20 in 1771 and 1772 respectively.[16] There is no reason to doubt the traditional association of these quartets with the technical prowess of Luigi Tomasini, leader of the Esterházy orchestra; opp. 9 and 17, in particular, have many passages of double stops in a low register, perhaps a speciality of the player. He must have been a very sympathetic player too, one who had the utmost confidence in his composer and who was able to lead an ensemble which articulated the novel musical demands made by their *Kapellmeister*. The Tomasini quartet had the privilege, and were up to the challenge, of being at the cutting edge of stylistic development.

All eighteen quartets have a four-movement pattern, rather than the five-movement pattern of the early quartets. In the 1760s Haydn had established the primacy of four-movement patterns over three- and five-movement patterns in instrumental music, and its adoption in the quartet genre is a reflection of this process. But any theory that links this feature without qualification to the composer's four-movement symphonies founders on the fact that, beyond this basic similarity, the movement pattern and characteristics of the quartets are noticeably different. The minuet is placed second in fifteen of the eighteen quartets, not third as in the vast majority of contemporary symphonies. The reason for this distinct difference, apparent throughout Haydn's quartets though never so acutely as *c.* 1770, lies in the nature of the first movement. Many of Haydn's symphonies of the period, designed for a less attentive audience, open with Allegro movements in a flowing 3/4; to follow these with a minuet in the same metre would afford little contrast. In the quartets, however, the first movement is usually broader and more studied, typically a 'Moderato' movement in common time; a minuet in triple time provides stronger contrast than a slow movement. Opp. 9 and 17 show this pattern most evidently, but op. 20 nos. 1, 2 and, perhaps, 5 demonstrate this thinking too. Significantly, two of the three quartets of op. 20 that have the minuet placed third rather than second also have brisk first movements marked Allegro di molto: 3/4 in no. 4; and 6/8 in no. 6. As their third and fourth movements these fifteen quartets normally have an adagio (or largo) and a presto (or allegro di molto) in 2/4, both legacies of equivalent movements in the early quartets but now assuming roles as stages in a journey rather than units in a neat symmetrical pattern. Also inherited from the early quartets is the notion – found in op. 9 no. 5 and op. 17 no. 3 – of beginning a quartet with a set of variations on an andante theme. More prophetic is the element of set planning, with each opus containing a quartet in the minor key (two in op. 20), reflecting Haydn's recent predilection for the mode, and one quartet that begins with a 6/8 movement.

In a lesser composer than Haydn the even pace of the moderato first movements could have yielded music of unremitting blandness. Though not all the movements have the intensity of the D minor quartet (op. 9 no. 4), the fascination of the C minor (op. 17 no. 4) or the rhythmic incisiveness of op. 20 no. 2, none is bland. What distinguishes these quartets from their predecessors is the manner in which initial thematic ideas control the unfolding of subsequent paragraphs, even when, as in opp. 9 and 17, the ideas themselves often seem unpromising and their scoring unremarkable. Op. 17 no. 2 opens with a four-bar theme in the first violin over an accompaniment of repeated quavers followed by sustained notes.

The decoration at the beginning of bar 2 draws attention to its main melodic characteristic, the move from dominant to tonic and then to leading note; this pattern, sometimes curtailed to a rising fourth or falling fifth, features in all the material of the movement. The harmonic context of this thematic pattern remains the same throughout, except for one strategically placed instance. The development begins as if it were setting out on a third verbatim statement of the first subject but the decoration now lands on an E flat rather than the E natural, redirecting the music towards G minor and sequential development of the principal figure; the brief crescendo to *forte* emphasizes this modification.

Harmonic re-orientation working in combination with a three-note motif plays a more pervasive part in op. 17 no. 4. The quartet begins with the first violin announcing the notes E flat and G, as if the work is going to be in E flat major; it is only in bar 2, when the first violin moves to C and the other players enter on a C minor chord, that we realize the work is going to be in C minor. (Knowing beforehand that the work is in C minor does not detract from this ploy. It would require a perverse suppression of musicality to hear the first E flat as a mediant rather than a tonic.) Reduced to two notes, the figure occurs throughout the texture, in a manner that foreshadows symphonies such as nos. 45 and 46, but when extended to three notes and played initially without accompaniment it invariably leads to new harmonic directions, summarized in the next example as 'a', 'b', 'c', 'd', 'e' and 'f'. At the end of the development, or what seems to be the end of the development (bar 78), a move to an F minor chord encourages the postponement of the recapitulation by fourteen bars ('g' in the example).

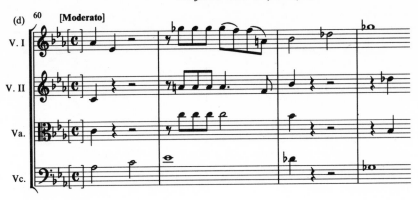

In the D minor quartet (op. 9 no. 4), the finest quartet in that set, thematic development is replaced entirely by harmonic development directed by the insistent rhythms of bars 2 and 3. In the development the theme is presented twice, first in G minor then in A minor, each initiating a new harmonic journey. With rich Neapolitan harmonies, pauses and volatile dynamics, this is a highly rhetorical movement. Musical rhetoric, like any other, can easily degenerate into bombast, especially in recapitulation sections. The compression of this section from thirty-two bars to twenty ensures that the movement remains compulsive throughout.

One of the cardinal differences between opp. 9 and 17, on the one hand, and op. 20, on the other, lies in the scoring. It is rare for any instrument other than the first violin to take the thematic lead in the first movements of opp. 9 and 17 and the subsidiary parts are not averse to routine accompanying figuration, particularly at the beginnings of paragraphs to establish momentum. In op. 20, however, there is a consistent, often wilful attempt to share material between instruments, including the Cinderella of Haydn's chamber music since the earliest string trios, the cello. The first subject of op. 20 no. 2 is a *locus classicus* of emancipated scoring: three-part counterpoint with the cello taking the thematic lead. Op. 20 no. 1 is less frequently quoted because the individual lines are not as clearly separated, but it is equally democratic (see example opposite).

Again using a three-voice texture as its starting point, the first paragraph has ten different scoring patterns. The development sections of both these quartets contain extended dialogue between first violin and cello, indicative of the stronger sonority of op. 20 in general.

The first movement of the quartet in D major, op. 20 no. 4, displays a masterly assimilation of rhetoric, sonority, equitable scoring and symphonic language. Rather like the first Allegro of Mozart's Symphony no. 39, the easy delivery of the music in triple time belies its extreme sophistication. The first subject is thirty bars long: five six-bar phrases over a tonic pedal that establish, firstly, three crotchets as a generating motif and, secondly, in the last phrase (marked by a drop from *piano* to *pianissimo*) a propensity for gentle harmonic surprise. Later, ostensibly contrasting melodic material is all brought within the orbit of this first subject through combination and juxtaposition. During the course of the development the opening of the first subject appears four times to initiate discursive paragraphs pivoted around B minor. Five beats of silence precede a fifth statement, a *fausse reprise* in G major; though common in contemporary symphonies – the first movement of Symphony no. 51 affords a striking parallel – this dramatic device does not otherwise feature in the quartets of this time. As in the D minor quartet, the repeated use of the first subject in the development of this D major quartet means that the recapitulation is shortened to avoid redundancy. Throughout the movement there is a tone of persuasive eloquence which is as characterful as the energetic or flamboyant tone of the best of contemporary symphonies.

The minuets of Haydn's earliest quartets had been singled out for special criticism by several mid-eighteenth-century commentators because of the octave doubling of the main theme, 'father and son begging', as one critic put it.[17] In opp. 9, 17 and 20 this scandalous sound is conspicuous by its comparative absence; only the minuets of op. 9 nos. 3 and 5 are characterized by it. Maybe Haydn himself felt octave doubling already constituted a personal cliché and that in works as enterprising as these quartets he should avoid such sonority. One of its virtues had been the steely strength of the resultant tone colour and it is perhaps especially surprising that the vibrant textures of op. 20 should not make use of this technique. Haydn, however, finds new resources of sonority in the minuets of op. 20: in no. 1, contrast of register, dynamic and harmony versus unison; and, in no. 2, double stops.

Disturbing the expected phrase patterns of the minuet also occurs in opp. 9, 17 and 20. The imitative entries of the G major minuet, op. 17 no. 5, recall the similar disruptive entries in the second minuet of op. 1 no. 1, but the most exciting example is the 'Minuet alla Zingarese' of op. 20 no. 4. Though notated, naturally, in 3/4, the violins in fact sound in 2/4 throughout the minuet; the viola and cello, also, effectively play in 2/4 but with the accent a beat later. The lusty conflict of metre and accent is exaggerated by liberal *sforzando* markings. The trio, in contrast, could not be more straightforward: scalic cello passages with the simplest of accompaniments, all in the regular phrase structure of 4 + 4 + 4 + 4.

Less spectacular, but also indicative of the need to avoid minuets that sound short-winded, is the frequent practice, especially in opp. 9 and 17, of avoiding an emphasized cadence after four bars; several minuets reach the double bar with no intervening punctuation. The wish for continuity may also have prompted Haydn in op. 17 nos. 3 and 5, and in op. 20 nos. 1 and 2, to do away with the second half repeat of the trio in favour of a lead-back into the da capo of the minuet. In two of the quartets, op. 17 no. 2 and op. 20 no. 2, the relationship between minuet and trio is even closer in that both trios take their melodic cue from the last bar of the respective minuets.

In comparison with the many innovations found in other movements, the slow movements of opp. 9 and 17 are conservative. Solo violin over a repetitive accompaniment is the principle, though executed with less rigidity than in the ten early quartets. There are some contrasting passages, such as the recitative in op. 17 no. 5, and the slow improvisation that precedes the aria of the violin in op. 9 no. 2. Tomasini's brilliant technique encouraged Haydn to allow several opportunities for brief cadenzas.

In op. 20, only no. 6 contains a slow movement in this format, the other movements being more individually conceived. That of no. 2 is headed 'Capriccio' and consists of a forceful recitative – *accompagnato*, in which the players act as soloists and orchestra – followed by an arioso in E flat that merges into the succeeding minuet. It is rare for a Haydn quartet movement to be stimulated by an extra-musical idea, but the powerful rhetoric and dialogue of this movement may well be an exception. Or perhaps the movement is best viewed as a logical extension of the recitative and aria pattern found in op. 17 no. 5 and intermittently in earlier instrumental music (e.g. Divertimento in C [II:17] and Baryton Trio no. 52).

To date, three quartets by Haydn had begun with variation movements; op. 20 no. 4 is the first to place the pattern second in the design, indeed the first example of a conventionally placed slow movement in variation form in any genre by Haydn. The eighteen-bar theme makes poignant use of appoggiatura harmony and in the second half a four-bar crescendo during which all the parts move in parallel motion to a liberating augmented sixth. For the first time in Haydn's chamber music the cello is entrusted with a thematic lead in a variation (no. II). A final repetition of the theme leads to an extensive coda that effectively breaks the phrasing and dynamic pattern established in the movement.

No less distinguished and more original in conception is the slow movement of op. 20 no. 1 in A flat major. It is marked 'Affettuoso e sostenuto' and unfolds in a smooth 3/8 metre with a consistently full four-part texture and little discernible articulation. Beethoven is known to have copied out the op. 20 quartets in 1793/4, but this tranquil movement seems to prefigure late rather than early Beethoven. More consciously, this movement seems to have been the stimulus for the slow movement of Mozart's E flat major quartet (K.428).

In opp. 9 and 17 the typical finale consists of a brisk Presto in 2/4, with repetitive accompanying quavers and showy first violin writing for Tomasini; occasionally good spirits incorporate genuine comedy, as in the protracted *Eingang* for two violins that leads into the recapitulation of op. 17 no. 1, and the off-key beginning to the recapitulation of op. 9 no. 3. In the two minor-key quartets, op. 9 no. 4 and op. 17 no. 4, the main theme is distributed evenly between the instruments in tense interplay. The more forward-looking op. 20 set contains a couple of finales reminiscent of those in opp. 9 and 17: that of the E flat quartet is a 2/4 Presto and the G minor distributes its principal thematic material between the instruments.

Op. 20, especially the first movements, often shows Haydn using a three-part texture distributed fairly between the four players; the complete fugues that form the last movements of three quartets in op. 20 (nos. 2, 5 and 6) are a natural extension of this attitude. The fugues have often been described as a conscious return to the baroque, as if the classical style were admitting to some stylistic weakness by having a good old-fashioned fugue. But this hopelessly misrepresents the music itself, ignores its context in Haydn's development and in that of contemporary Austrian music in general. Haydn's public would not have regarded a fugue in chamber music as strange or unusual since there was a strong tradition of fugal writing for small ensembles, exemplified by Haydn's predecessor, Werner, and, in the 1760s, in literally dozens of quartet fugues by Gassmann. This is a forgotten, largely sterile repertory to which others, like Ordoñez and Albrechtsberger, were later to contribute, and it contains nothing to rival the spontaneity of Haydn's op. 20 fugues, particularly those in C and A major. This spontaneity had been hard won, the result of a decade of conscious assimilation of contrapuntal procedures. At the same time Haydn was striving, in the quartet genre, to involve all four players in the argument, a process that also culminated in the six quartets of op. 20. Thus the fugues in op. 20 form a natural, unforced conclusion to their respective quartets, testimony to Haydn's unique achievement *c.* 1770, whereby classical homophony could move without any sense of dislocation to polyphony.

The least Classical sounding fugue is that of the F minor quartet, op. 20 no. 5. The principal theme of this 'Fuga a due Soggetti' is a commonplace eighteenth-century type featuring a falling diminished seventh; subject two and other complementary figuration make sure that the movement never sounds stolid.

In the A major quartet (no. 6) the fugue is on three subjects, the principal one of which has a passing resemblance to the second theme in the F minor work. With its capricious energy, the movement is in a vein of high comedy. The C major fugue of op. 20 no. 2 is a contrapuntal *tour de force*, a fugue on four subjects. In conception the main theme owes something to the common fugal (or ground bass) type of a descending chromatic line, but in realization this prototype is immediately forgotten as octave displacements and the intricate counter-rhythms of subject two transform its character. Subjects three and four are less distinctive in thematic profile but their rhythms ensure that they stand out in the four-part texture.

Many of the fugal procedures present in the vocal fugues of the 1760s are apparent in op. 20 too: five-stage exposition with a redundant fifth entry, stretto and move towards homophony near the close. The differences are crucial, however, explaining the modernity of the sound. The number of themes, two, three and four, rather than the single theme associated with a text, ensures that they sound less formal; the quartet is never a substitute SATB choir. The modulatory range of the fugues is more extensive than in the vocal fugues, reaching A flat minor in the F minor fugue. In op. 20, too, Haydn frequently inverts the principal thematic line, always proudly labelling it 'al rovescio', and the inversion also is treated in stretto. Finally, and not the least significant, there is in the fugues a complete absence of self-conscious declamation because Haydn marks them to be played 'sempre sotto voce'.

The six quartets of op. 20 represent a clear advance on those of opp. 9 and 17, though only a year separates the completion of op. 17 and op. 20. In comparison with the ten early quartets, opp. 9 and 17 have a new authority, and individual movements can stand comparison with anything in Haydn's quartet output. However, viewed as complete works, the quartets, including the two in the minor, are weakened by stereotyped concertante slow movements. In op. 20 each quartet has an individual total personality and where standard procedures are used, such as the concertante slow movement of no. 6 or the Moderato through to Presto pattern of no. 1, they contribute to the individuality of the work and not to a debilitating uniformity. In terms of range of subject matter and mood, the quartets of op. 20 are unprecedented – from the lighthearted *scherzando* of no. 6 to the pathos of no. 5 in F minor – and these qualities are the product of a compositional technique of commanding assurance. That Haydn too was excited by his achievement is demonstrated by the annotations he appended to the end of each quartet of op. 20. Only no. 5 contents itself with the usual 'Fine Laus Deo', while the others are wonderfully effusive in their gratitude: no. 1, 'Soli Deo et Cuique Suum'; no. 2 'Laus omnip: Deo' and 'Sic fugit amicus amicum', no. 3; 'Laus Deo et B:V:M: cum S° S^{to} [Sancto Spirito; sc. Spiritu]'; no. 4, 'Gloria in excelsis Deo'; and no. 6, 'Laus Deo et Beatissimae Virgini Mariae'.[18]

Keyboard music

As distinct from the private, self-fulfilling world of the string quartet, Haydn's keyboard sonatas reveal a diversity of outlook that mirrors their varied function. Between 1766 and 1780 Haydn composed some thirty-one sonatas, eighteen of which were published. Six sonatas from the late 1760s are lost, possibly destroyed in the 1768 fire at Eisenstadt. Their incipits, recorded in the *Entwurf-Katalog*, provide succinct reminders of Haydn's interest in colouring by choice of unusual keys in this period. There is a work in D minor, Haydn's favourite minor key in the late 1760s, and one in B major, foreshadowing Symphony no. 46 (the sonata is probably the work which Haydn later recalled composing while recovering from an illness). Unusual and emotive keys feature too in extant single sonatas of the time. Sonata no. 31 is in the rare key for the mid-century, and for Haydn in general, of A flat major and its slow movement is in a richly clothed D flat major, while Sonata no. 32 is a two-movement work in G minor.

Sonatas nos. 31 and 32, like many others, display a consistent interest in enriching and varying the texture of the keyboard writing. Only rarely (e. g. second subject of the first movement of no. 30) does Haydn depart from the general principle that thematic writing is entrusted to the right hand and accompaniment to the left, but the texture is now a fuller three-part one rather than the two parts of earlier sonatas and, with the customary absence of prolonged routine keyboard figuration, produces a sense of thoughtful speech rather than the automatic patter typical of much contemporary keyboard music. Like the op. 20 quartets, the sonatas revel in contrasts of register; for instance, in no. 31 the second subject begins two octaves away from the close of the transition and in no. 30 the slow movement is in effect a duet between soprano and bass, one of the most operatic movements in all of Haydn's sonatas.

A significant formal innovation occurs in the finale of Sonata no. 30. It is a sectional rondo, ABACA plus coda, in which the main theme is varied on each return. The varied rather than exact return of the theme is a characteristic feature of C. P. E. Bach's keyboard music and, remembering Haydn's avowed admiration for the composer, it seems that Haydn's use of it derives from the North German composer's six *Sonaten mit veränderten Reprisen* (Wq. 50) which date from 1758–9, when Haydn was working on his earliest quartets, but did not circulate in Vienna until 1767. In the first five sonatas by Bach it is the repeat of the two constituent parts of the binary pattern that is varied. The sixth sonata consists of a single movement, a rondo in C minor in which recurring C major episodes are based on the main theme to make the following scheme: $ABA^1B^1A^2$. In his preface Bach states that the varied reprises of sonatas 1–5 represent a regularization of performance practice that often produced, in artless hands, tasteless frippery. Unlike Bach, Haydn no longer wrote binary first movements and his sonata form movements usually have structural changes that would make mere decoration arbitrary. The result is that Bach's principle of varied reprise is usually applied to less dynamic, sectional constructions such as rondo form. Thus the rondo returns featured in Sonatas nos. 30, 34 and 37 and Symphonies nos. 42, 51 and 55 are all varied. Haydn also takes up the scheme outlined in Bach's sixth sonata to create the highly characteristic variations on two alternating themes. The first example in Haydn's music occurs in the first group of sonatas known to have been composed as a set. Nos. 36–41 (XVI:21–26) were composed in 1773 and published in Vienna in 1774, thus becoming the first publication of Haydn's music supervised by the composer. The publication was dedicated to Prince Nicolaus Esterházy. The second sonata, in E major, has as its finale a Tempo di Menuet consisting of two alternating themes that are varied; the first major and cantabile, the second minor and severe. Unlike the varied rondo, alternating variations were not featured immediately in other genres; the first symphonies to use the pattern date from near the end of the decade (nos. 53 and 70).

The E major sonata, like all of Haydn's instrumental works in E (major and minor), retains the tonic throughout, changing only the mode. Moreover, this is a characteristic of the set as a whole – only the C major sonata changes tonic for the slow movement – and repeats an approach found to a certain extent in the op. 20 quartets, where four of the six works retain the same tonic throughout. Haydn's contemporary interest in canon is also demonstrated in this published set of keyboard sonatas. The Tempo di Menuet of no. 40 is a canon throughout, while the second movement of no. 41 is a transposition up a tone of the Menuet al Roverso and Trio al Roverso of Symphony no. 47.

Haydn's next sonatas, nos. 42–47 (XVI:27–32), were completed by 1776 when they were entered in the *Entwurf-Katalog* as '6 Sonaten von Anno 776'; only no. 44 survives in autograph, dated 1774, suggesting that Haydn took at least two years to complete the set. He did not arrange for their publication, possibly because they contain some unusual, even eccentric movements which the composer may have thought unsuitable for the traditional amateur market. From the flamboyant orchestral first subject that opens no. 44 no-one could have predicted the fantasia-like second subject, especially its conclusion. The recapitulation of the first movement of no. 45 in A never reaches a formal close, but leads via two dramatic pauses to an Adagio featuring melodic *fioriture* over a wide-ranging staccato bass. This F sharp minor movement cadences in E in preparation for the finale in A, a routine set of six variations on a minuet theme. In Sonata no. 46 in E major it is the central Allegretto that yields a surprise: a conservative chorale prelude-like movement in E minor, complete with lengthy dominant pedal. Finally, in Sonata no. 47, one of only four instrumental works in B minor by Haydn, the concluding Presto is a volatile mixture of virtuosity, harmonic surprise and rhythmic vehemence – not the sort of music to ingratiate itself with 'le beau sexe'.

Haydn's final group of sonatas in this period, nos. 48–52 and 33 (XVI:35–39, 20), was published by Artaria in 1780 and carries a dedication to Caterina and Marianna von Auenbrugger, daughters of the physician and scholar Leopold von Auenbrugger. In Haydn's own words, the sisters possessed 'genuine insight into music equal to that of the greatest masters'.[19] Though the composer knew the capabilities of the dedicatees, the six sonatas vary enormously in technical and interpretative demands. Little technical ability and even less 'genuine insight' are needed to play the first of the set, no. 48 in C, whose opening movement is platitudinous to the point of embarrassment. Other sonatas, however, such as no. 50 in D and especially the two minor-key works, no. 49 in C sharp minor and no. 33 in C minor, require considerable interpretative and technical skill. No. 33 had been composed, or perhaps partly composed, in 1771 and is one of the very finest sonatas by Haydn. It is likely that other sonatas in the set, too, were composed long before 1780 and that the publication represents a compilation of individual works, rather than a set composed specifically for the Auenbrugger sisters. There is evidence to suggest that no. 52 was written in haste in order to complete the set. The first movement is a rondo with variations (ABA¹CA² coda) whose principal theme is the same as that of the middle movement of no. 49, which is a set of variations on two alternating themes (ABA¹B¹A²coda). Haydn thought it necessary to forestall any criticism and at his suggestion the following *Avertimento* (in Italian) was printed in the score; it understates the correspondence, but the justification is, nevertheless, a reasonable one, and one that would have appealed to *Kenner* rather than to *Liebhaber.*[20]

Among these six sonatas there are to be found two movements which begin with a few bars of similar meaning, viz. the Allegro scherzando of Sonata no. 2 and the Allegro con brio of Sonata no. 5. The composer gives notice of having done this on purpose, changing, however, in each of them the continuation of the same opening.

The title page of this first edition is of further interest in that it specifically mentions the piano: 'Sei sonate per il Clavicembalo o Forte Piano'. Earlier editions of keyboard works, catalogue entries and extant autographs never go beyond the generic word 'cembalo' ('keyboard'), implying harpsichord, piano or (less common in Austria) clavichord. Haydn became acquainted with the piano in the early 1760s and the Capriccio: 'Acht Sauschneider' (XVII:1) may have been written specifically for the new instrument. Though precise documentary evidence is lacking, the composer seems not to have acquired a piano until the mid-1780s, probably a Schantz. The sonatas up to the 1780 publication are generally free of dynamic markings and other expressive markings realizable only on the piano, yet the few that do exist, together with the richer and more varied texture of the music itself, suggest that Haydn thought increasingly in terms of the piano, if only idealistically. Sonata no. 44 (1774), for instance, contains '*f*' and '*p*' markings on alternate notes, a '*p cresc. f*' passage, and a few *tenuto* markings. Sonata no. 33 in C minor is an even more interesting case. The partial autograph dates from 1771 and is clearly headed

'Sonata p[er] il Clavi Cembalo', but it contains several dynamic markings appropriate to the piano, including '*f*' and '*p*' on alternate quavers. For the publication nine years later Haydn made changes reflecting the greater sustaining power of the piano; in the first bar the original accompanying figure [musical notation] | is changed to [musical notation] | and 'tenuto' is added to the colourful dominant ninth chord that precedes the second subject.

The sonata possesses a strength of personality that makes it the first in a distinguished line of C minor keyboard sonatas by each of the principal figures in the Viennese Classical School, Haydn, Mozart, Beethoven and Schubert. In Haydn's own career the sonata is fully the equal of the best of his contemporary music such as the op. 20 quartets and the 1772 symphonies, and though many of its features are to be found in earlier and later sonatas of the period, no other sonata quite matches the authority of this work. The two balancing four-bar phrases of the opening theme culminate in a Neapolitan sixth chord. Neapolitan sixth harmony is a favourite resource in themes in Haydn's minor-key music of the 1760s and 1770s, e. g. the opening of the Stabat Mater, the 'Et incarnatus est' in the Great Organ Solo Mass, the Gloria of the *Missa* 'Sunt bona mixta malis', the opening theme of the quartet op. 9 no. 4 and of the finale of op. 20 no. 3 and the first subject of Sonata no. 49. In Sonata no. 33 the chord is carefully deployed, being conspicuously absent from the remainder of the movement, including the recapitulation where Haydn characteristically tautens the argument by making one new paragraph where two (the first subject and the transition) had existed in the exposition. The Neapolitan sixth returns to make a magnificent impact in the recapitulation section of the finale; instead of the two bars (37–38) of subdominant and supertonic harmony of the exposition, there is now a five-bar diversion on to the flattened supertonic. As in the op. 20 quartets, there is a unity of medium and message in this sonata that makes it unrealizable by any instrument other than the piano: in the first movement the explosive, densely textured second subject that follows after the romantic conclusion to the transition; the Alberti figuration which imparts drive to the development rather than routine momentum; the wide-ranging bass line of the second movement; and the expressive hand-crossing of the finale all benefit from the nuanced power of the piano.

Brief mention should be made of three other keyboard works composed between 1766 and 1780 – two sets of variations and a duet sonata. The first set of variations (XVII:2) exists in two versions: twenty variations in G and a shorter version of twelve in A. Initially composed no later than 1771, it was not published until 1788 or 1789. Also published at that time was another set of strophic variations (XVII:3), using an adapted version of the minuet from the E flat quartet, op. 9 no. 2; this set of twelve variations also dates from the early 1770s. Finally, there is a two-movement sonata (XVIIa:1) for harpsichord duet ('cembalo' in the *Entwurf-Katalog*), Haydn's only keyboard duet. The title 'Il maestro e lo scolare', though not authentic, is an accurate indication of its didactic purpose as an eighteenth-century bicinium. The first movement is a laboured set of seven variations in which, phrase by phrase, the *secondo* ('il maestro') demonstrates and the *primo* ('lo scolare') imitates; the second is a Tempo di Menuetto in which the main theme is played in tenths by 'scolare' and 'maestro'.

Music for the baryton

The baryton – a string instrument descended from the viola da gamba – enjoyed an idiosyncratic vogue from the end of the seventeenth century to the beginning of the nineteenth. Prince Nicolaus Esterházy took up the instrument in the 1760s and became moderately proficient on it. Similar in shape and size to the bass viol, it had a fretted fingerboard with six or seven gut (sometimes silk) strings. Behind the fingerboard there was a second set of wire strings whose primary function was to vibrate in sympathy with the bowed notes, creating a hazy resonance; in addition the thumb of the left hand could be used to pluck selected sympathetic strings. The tuning, as well as the number of strings, varied according to preference. The Prince's instrument had a maximum of seven main strings, though in practice the lowest was not used. The sympathetic strings could be ten in number, though the highest seems not to have been used.

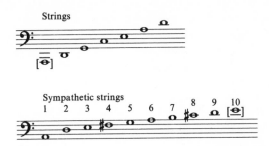

The instrument was treated as the principal voice notated in treble clef but sounding an octave lower; plucking of sympathetic strings was indicated by appropriate numbers placed above or below the notated pitch. As *Vice-Kapellmeister*, Haydn was reprimanded in 1765 for not devoting himself wholeheartedly to the composition of music for his employer's instrument. Some baryton music predates this reprimand but most of it, over 160 single works, was composed between 1765 and 1778, including three concertos, duets (with cello or a second baryton), trios, a quartet, quintets and octets. Some of this prodigious quantity of music, including the concertos, is lost, the most substantial legacy being the 126 trios scored for baryton, viola and 'basso', in this case the cello. (In nos. 89–91 a violin replaces the viola.) At first, Esterházy's limited technique meant that works were composed only in D and A major, and two-thirds of the trios are in one or other of these keys; later, as the Prince became more proficient, keys such as C and F were also used. In comparison with the remainder of Haydn's contemporary output, from solo keyboard to opera, the predominant impression made by the trios is a rather faceless one, and even the fascination of the instrument palls after a while. One cannot fail to admire Haydn's stoicism even when that quality is present in the music itself. A few trios re-use material from other works (e. g. the minuet and trio movement of no. 52 is derived from Symphony no. 58) and a couple of works quote directly from contemporary operas, 'Che farò senza Euridice' from Gluck's *Orfeo* in no. 5 and 'Che visino delicato' from Haydn's *La canterina* in no. 29. Haydn took care not to overtax his prince, hence only one movement, the trio of the minuet of no. 107, makes use of the obvious aural gimmick of theme and accompaniment being played by the baryton alone. Solo plucked strings are usually introduced with discretion, charm and, occasionally, humour, as in the second movement of no.147. Naturally, the prince's instrument is given the lion's share of the thematic writing, but the viola writing too is rewarding, especially in the trio section of minuet movements and often at the beginning of development sections; indeed, extended solo viola writing is more often encountered in the baryton trios than in Haydn's contemporary quartets. The trios are nearly all in three movements, not the fast-slow-fast associated with the early symphonies and concertos, but various patterns employing a minuet as a middle movement or finale, slow-fast-minuet, slow-minuet-fast, fast-slow-minuet and fast-minuet-fast.

Between 1764 and 1768 hardly six months would elapse without Haydn composing a new baryton trio, and the characteristics of the genre provide a useful perspective for similar features revealed intermittently but with greater individuality elsewhere. There are many strophic variation movements, usually on 2/4 themes in an adagio or moderato tempo. As in the symphonies and quartets, there are no *minore* variations (Variation IV in Trio no. 73 begins as a *minore* but turns to the major), even though such a contrast of mode is commonly used between minuet and trio and locally in the binary-cum-sonata forms. In the earliest examples of variations movements the cello is restricted to an *ostinato* bass line from one variation to the next but towards the end of the 1760s, as in the opp. 9, 17 and 20 quartets, the cello is liberated and, even though it rarely takes the thematic lead, its part too is varied. In Trio no. 60, probably composed in 1768, the third variation has the cello moving in wide-spaced arpeggios, anticipating the texture of the finale of the quartet, op. 54 no. 2. This variation is followed by the routine 'Thema da Capo', with no separate coda; Haydn's provision of a coda to break the established orbit of the theme in the quartet, op. 20 no. 4, acquires a new significance when viewed against this normal practice.

Concertante slow movements, as one might expect, are common. Trio no. 52, probably composed in 1767, opens with such a movement and, like the quartet, op. 17 no. 5, composed four years later, incorporates recitative passages. In minuets, octave writing in the presentation of the main theme is common. Also to be found are trios related thematically to their companion minuets; that of no. 87 in A minor, takes as its starting point a major version of the opening phrase of the Menuet while that of no. 91 takes as its cue the last four beats of the Menuet. There are two examples of canonic minuets. The two-part (plus a false entry) 'Canone' in the trio of no. 5 (1764) is probably the earliest example in any genre by Haydn. Trio no. 94 (1771-2?) is proudly headed 'Menuet, Canone in Diapente', i.e. a canon at the fifth between baryton (doubled at the written octave by viola) and cello; the trio continues the texture with the viola now doubling the cello in thirds, effectively providing a canon at the third and fifth simultanously. The canon is a notable anticipation of that found in the Credo of the 'Nelson' Mass of 1798.

Several baryton trios contain Presto finales that use the scheme first noticed in the early D major quartet, op. 1 no. 3. No. 69 is typical. It has the broad ternary plan of A in the tonic, B in the minor and a 'Da Capo fino alla Segno' of A. 'A' itself is an asymmetrical binary shape in which, however, the first part ends in the tonic and the second half begins with contrasting material in the dominant before proceeding to an exact reprise of the main theme:

$$\underset{\text{I}}{\text{a}} \; :\|: \; \underset{\text{V-V/I}}{\text{b}} \; \underset{\text{I}}{\text{a}} \; :\|$$

The thematic idiom, the construction of the theme in three stages and the principle of alternation of theme and contrasting section are clear harbingers of rondo form as developed on a broader scale in the sonatas and symphonies of the 1770s.

Equally striking are the numerous finales that make use of fugal techniques: nos. 11, 33, 40, 53, 67, 71, 75, 81, 97, 101 and 114. Up to and including no. 81 these trios pre-date the composition of the op. 20 quartets, so providing a proving-ground for the fugal finales of that opus and further evidence of Haydn's preoccupation with fugal technique in the 1760s. Although they do not usually carry headings, many of the finales could have been labelled 'Fuga a due soggetti', that is two themes announced simultaneously and thereafter used in invertible counterpoint. After a threefold exposition – 'redundant' entries are rare in the baryton trios – the texture becomes less contrapuntal than in op. 20, though counterpoint is later resumed; moreover, there is no display of learned artifice such as stretto and inversion as encountered in op. 20. Perhaps the most distinctive influence on op. 20 of the baryton trios was not one of contrapuntal technique. Haydn's peculiar *sotto voce* marking in op. 20 may have represented an attempt to recreate in another medium the reclusive, rather austere sonority of brisk fugal texture played by the baryton trio. Trio no. 101, which may be exactly contemporary with the op. 20 quartets, has a finale that is more ambitious in terms of fugal technique than most baryton trios, even if it is still less consummately masterly than op. 20: it is headed 'Finale Fuga a 3 soggetti in contrappunto doppio' and the contrapuntal texture is maintained throughout (see example below).

Though some of these trios circulated in versions for two violins and 'basso', there was no market beyond Eisenstadt and Eszterháza for the original versions. Yet Haydn never seems to have become tired of the work, his happy temperament

turning a task that might have been a burden to his own advantage, so that he as well as his prince was gratified. The baryton trios enshrine a fundamental paradox in Haydn's personality: he was the last major composer who saw no conflict between being a dutiful *Kapellmeister* and an innovative creative artist. In the next decade he was to outgrow this fruitful dependence, with enormous effect on his music, but he never turned his back on it, much less decried it.

From stylistic diversity to stability

Anyone studying the output of Joseph Haydn in the fifteen-year period covered by this chapter cannot fail to notice the extraordinary burst of creative energy that occurs in the earlier part of the period, from 1766 to 1773, undoubtedly the most critical years in Haydn's career. There was the challenge of new genres such as opera, church music of all types and baryton music, the return to the quartet medium, and the continued exploration of the symphony and the keyboard sonata. In addition to this diversity of genres, Haydn explored an unparalleled range of stylistic idioms from the most glibly Italianate to the cerebral. Much of his music, chiefly quartets, symphonies and church music, has a dramatic impact that can stand comparison with anything that Haydn was to produce later in his life but is, nevertheless, unique to this time. An obvious indication of this new spirit in Haydn's music is the high proportion of compositions in the minor key: the Stabat Mater, *Missa* 'Sunt bona mixta malis', Salve Regina, four out of eighteen quartets, two sonatas and no less than seven symphonies. Another is the pervasive use of imitative texture, whether it be the formal counterpoint of church music or the liberal, argumentative textures of quartet, sonata and symphony. Haydn's expressive range can now encompass the impassioned frailty of Sandrina in *L'infedeltà delusa*, the comfortlessness of the 'Trauer' Symphony, the poignancy of the Stabat Mater and the absorbing discourse of the D major quartet, op. 20 no. 4.

The period *c.* 1770 is frequently referred to as the years of *Sturm und Drang* (storm and stress), because of the obvious parallels between certain rhetorical features in the music and similar characteristics in the slightly later movement in German literature. In music the term has come to be predominantly associated with restless, agitated music in a minor key featuring some or all of the following: *tremolando*, nervous repeated quavers, wide leaps in thematic lines and declamatory use of pauses and silence. The term is useful to describe the idiom heard in the first movements of Symphonies nos. 39 and 45 ('Farewell') and especially its occurrence in music by several of Haydn's contemporaries, including Vanhal, Ordoñez, Michael Haydn and the young Mozart. In Haydn's case use of this meaningful term has had two unfortunate results. Rather like the uncritical use of the word 'impressionism' to describe Debussy's music, it implies a consistent sameness in the music, whereas the most striking feature of Haydn's music at this time, especially in comparison with that of his lesser contemporaries, Vanhal and Ordoñez, is its diversity and the individuality of each work. Secondly, it tends to draw attention exclusively to the minor-key works, to the detriment of works in the major, such as the D major quartet (op. 20 no. 4), the Great Organ Solo Mass, the A flat major sonata (no. 31) and the symphonies in A and B major (nos. 59 and 46). There was a broadening of expressive horizons in Haydn's music at this time, of which *Sturm und Drang* minor-key music formed only a part, albeit a highly characterful one.

It is known that Haydn suffered from illness at the end of the 1760s and the beginning of the 1770s. The sheer amount of physical labour would have crushed a lesser spirit, the self-imposed intellectual challenges and the general contemplation of the direction his music was taking as he approached his fortieth birthday must have taken their toll on the composer's well-being. These years were truly critical ones. From 1773 to the end of the decade Haydn's development was more evenly paced and more uniform in its direction. Church music and quartets played little or no part, opera exerted its influence on his instrumental music and there is a less spectacular production of striking individual works. Yet, though the second half of the period is overshadowed by the self-evident and enduring achievements of the earlier years, the period from 1773 onwards should not be dismissed summarily as a reaction, a calm, as it were, after the *Sturm und Drang*. These were the years during which Haydn unostentatiously laid the foundations of his later popularity. Under the guiding control of opera his instrumental music wore a cheerful, populist face and he began especially to explore the potential of two highly approachable forms then much in fashion, variations and rondo. Symphonies such as no. 55 in E flat and no. 61 in D palpably do not have the expressive power of their predecessors, but in technique and general demeanour they are recognizably the antecedents of the Paris and London symphonies of the 1780s and 1790s.

V

The last years at Eszterháza, 1781–1790

ALTOGETHER, 1781 must be reckoned a crucial year in Haydn's career, for not only did it see the première of *La fedeltà premiata* (his most interesting opera hitherto), but the composer was also on the threshold of achieving wide dissemination of his works, which would be published by Artaria in Vienna and by firms abroad (eventually to include publishers in Lyon, Paris, London, Berlin and Speyer). Haydn was now discovering the pianoforte as a modern and expressive keyboard instrument, and he was about to return - by the end of 1781 - to composing string quartets, a field left fallow since his opus 20 of 1772. His fame was now truly international, and he had become the most popular composer in Europe.

In 1783, one Austrian journal reported that, ten years earlier, Haydn was playing the 'Piano-forte' (as opposed to the harpsichord) at Eszterháza; however, with the visit to the castle in February 1781 of the greatest Austrian piano-maker of the day - Anton Walter (who made Mozart's piano now exhibited in the Mozart Museum in Salzburg) - we realize that Walter must have supplied one of his own fortepianos, for why else would he have been engaged now to work for '12 days repairing the clavier and harpsichord instruments'? It was probably no accident that in 1780 Artaria had published, as 'Op. 30', Haydn's six keyboard sonatas 'Per il Clavicembalo o Forte Piano' (cf. p. 167) dedicated to the Auenbrugger sisters. The final work of the set, the famous C minor sonata (no. 33), although composed as early as 1771, features dynamic marks that are more suited to the new piano than to the harpsichord.

By now Prince Nicolaus Esterházy was growing old, and one of the things he had given up was playing the baryton; or at any rate after 1778 he no longer required Haydn to compose for the instrument. But if the Prince's personal appetite for practical music-making had diminished, he seemed to need a longer and larger operatic season each year at Eszterháza. The culmination of this trend was reached in the 1786 season with 125 performances of seventeen different operas, nine of them premieres. Although *opera buffa* still dominated the repertoire, the Eszterháza première of Giuseppe Sarti's *Giulio Sabino* in 1783 started a new vogue for *opera seria* which resulted *inter alia* in Haydn's own *Armida* a year later. Whether this slightly altered focus was the result of a whim on Prince Nicolaus's part, or whether it actually represents Haydn's own aspirations, can not now be determined: possibly both parties became interested in serious or heroic opera at the same time. The final tally of opera performances given at Eszterháza between 1781 and 1790 is 880, an impressive figure by any standards (for details see the lists in *C&W*, II), involving three new works by Haydn himself (*La fedeltà premiata, Orlando Paladino* and *Armida*) and operas by twenty other composers, culminating in preparations - in the summer of 1790, the year of Prince Nicolaus's death - for the staging of Mozart's *Le nozze di Figaro*. In addition to opera, Prince Nicolaus and his guests were regularly entertained with theatrical performances by seasonal visiting companies, from 1781 to 1785 the Diwald Troupe, followed by the Johann Mayer Company (1786, 1788-90) and the Johann Lasser Company (1787).

As more and more of Haydn's energies were being required in the Eszterháza opera house, he was simultaneously in constant demand abroad, both in person and for his music, especially in Germany, France, Spain and England. The first of these countries to wish his presence in person was England, and for an expected concert season in 1782-3 the composer wrote Symphonies nos. 76-78. We have no details why the visit never materialized, but it is easy to surmise that Prince Esterházy was very unwilling to let his *Kapellmeister* leave on that occasion. (Later Haydn would write, on another occasion, '... the refusal is always couched in such polite terms, so polite in fact that I just don't have the heart to insist ...'; *C&W*, II, 741f.), and it must always have been in the back of Haydn's mind that he owed much to that Prince, not least for his having twice rebuilt his little house in Eisenstadt, after the disastrous fires there ('He swore to the Prince to serve him till death should bring to a close the life of the one or the other, and never leave him even should he be offered millions'; Dies, 73f.).

The English even thought it might be a good idea to kidnap the composer, as a report in *The Gazetteer & New Daily Advertiser*, 17 January 1785, suggests:

There is something very distressing to a liberal mind in the history of *Haydn*. This wonderful man, who is the Shakespeare of music, and the triumph of the age in which we live, is doomed to reside in the court of a miserable German Prince, who is at once incapable of rewarding him, and unworthy of the honour. *Haydn*, the simplest as well as the greatest of men, is resigned to his condition, and in devoting his life to the rites and ceremonies of the Roman Catholic Church, which he carries even to superstition, is content to live immured in a place little better than a dungeon, subject to the domineering spirit of a petty Lord, and the clamorous temper of a scolding wife. Would it not be an achievement equal to a pilgrimage, for some aspiring youths to rescue him from his fortune and transplant him to Great Britain, the country for which his music seems to be made? ...

But if there seemed for the moment no way to persuade Haydn to visit London, there need be no abatement of his music; and during the late 1780s, the composer's symphonies, sonatas and quartets were published with ever-increasing frequency. Haydn was now in contact with many foreign publishers: his correspondence with William Forster in London has survived, and so have some of his letters to J. G. Sieber in Paris and (a recent discovery) to John Bland in London. From various pieces of evidence we know that Haydn was also in correspondence with J. J. Hummel in Berlin (the firm also operated in Amsterdam), and probably with Guéra in Lyon (where textually accurate prints of some of his music appeared).

Perhaps the most flattering offer came from Paris: to compose six new symphonies for the Concert de la Loge 'Olympique', a fashionable Masonic Lodge; the organization was led by Claude-François-Marie Rigoley, Comte d'Ogny (1757-90) who offered Haydn 25 louis d'or for each of the six proposed symphonies, 'a sum which appeared colossal to Haydn', and a further 5 louis d'or for the publication rights. The six works, nos. 82-87, became very popular in Paris, and Haydn sold them all over again to Artaria and to Forster in London. The composer was often thought to be avaricious, and on this subject we have a fascinating report from a young composer, Joseph Martin Kraus (1756-92), of whom Haydn thought very highly. Kraus went to Eszterháza, where he performed his own magnificent Symphony in C minor (now at last beginning to be recognized as the masterpiece it is):

18 October 1783: Eszterháza. I fulfil my promise to write again from a place where I have thoroughly enjoyed myself ... The Prince here was most condescending towards me, and from the monetary standpoint something would surely be there for me if I had time and inspiration – and if I could stand the Hungarian way of life better ... The theatre is built with enormous luxury – but with little taste and still less reflection. The orchestra is what you

would expect under the direction of a Haydn – therefore one of the best. It is in fact not larger than 24 men, but makes an outstanding impression. – The first two violinists and the cellist are Italians – the rest are almost all Bohemians. In Haydn I got to know a right good soul, except for one point – that's money. He simply couldn't understand why I didn't provide myself with a drawer full of compositions for my trip, so as to be able to plant them whenever necessary. I answered quite drily that I wasn't cut out to be a Jewish salesman. *Satis!* Sterkel wrote him and asked for some arias for his sister and offered as an equivalent several arias from his Neapolitan opera; Haydn shook his head, for that wasn't ringing coin of the realm! It's a curious thing with most artists. The closer one examines them, the more they lose the halo with which the Messrs. Amateurs and critics invest them. My compliments to my dear Hoffstätter . . .[1]

But the trouble was, Haydn really had no capital except for the little sum he had saved (and banked with the princely establishment) when he sold his house in Eisenstadt: the report in Griesinger (23) that Haydn 'had in 1790 hardly 2,000 gulden' is quite correct. Contrary to much speculation on the subject, Haydn made hardly more money than Mozart after 1787. And Haydn's attitude will have been 'pecunia non olet' – and quite right too!

Consequently, these foreign commissions were doubly welcome. Did Prince Esterházy know about all of them? Was Haydn allowed total freedom for foreign orders? We shall probably never know, but it may be assumed that Esterházy permitted Haydn to do as he pleased so long as the operatic establishment at Eszterháza did not suffer (which is why the composer could hardly leave during the season, and that meant about eleven months of each year).

Following the 'Paris' symphonies, Haydn composed the five remaining symphonies between no. 87 (the last of the six 'Paris' works) and 93 (the first numerically, though not chronogically, of the London series) all for Paris – nos. 88–92. Nos. 88 and 89 he gave to Johann Tost, the leader of the second violins at Eszterháza, to take to Paris along with the six string quartets, op. 54/55. Haydn sent Symphonies nos. 90–92 to Comte d'Ogny, the latter two with handwritten dedications to his French benefactor. Haydn also sold copies of these works to Prince Krafft Ernst of Oettingen-Wallerstein, a German admirer who lived in Wallerstein (Bavaria).

Haydn composed the six 'Paris' symphonies in 1785 and 1786, and it must have been in the latter year that he received the interesting commission to write music for the Good Friday ceremonies at the Grotto Santa Cueva near Cádiz in southern Spain. When Haydn later sent the score of the vocal version to the publishers Breitkopf & Härtel in 1801, he dictated the following foreword to his go-between, G. A. Griesinger:

About fifteen years ago [1786], I was requested by a canon of Cádiz to compose instrumental music on *The Seven Last Words of Our Saviour on the Cross*. It was customary at the Cathedral of Cádiz to produce an oratorio every year during Lent, the effect of the performance being not a little enhanced by the following circumstances. The walls, windows, and pillars of the church were hung with black cloth, and only one large lamp hanging from the centre of the roof broke the solemn darkness. At midday, the doors were closed and the ceremony began. After a short service the bishop ascended the pulpit, pronounced the first of the seven words (or sentences) and delivered a discourse thereon. This ended, he left the pulpit, and prostrated himself before the altar. The interval was filled by music. The bishop then in like manner pronounced the second word, then the third and so on, the orchestra following on the conclusion of each discourse. My composition was subject to these conditions, and it was no easy task to compose seven adagios lasting ten minutes each, and to succeed one another without fatiguing the listeners; indeed, I found it quite impossible to confine myself to the appointed limits.[2]

Abbé Maximilian Stadler, who was a friend of both Mozart and Haydn, happened to be with Haydn when he received the commission from Cádiz. In his autobiography Stadler relates:[3]

He also asked me what I thought of it all. I answered that it seemed to me advisable that over the words an appropriate melody should be fitted, which afterwards should be performed only by instruments, in which art he was in any case a master. He did so, too, but whether he had intended to do so anyway, I do not know.   [Pohl II, 215]

We have confirmation of the Stadler part in the proceedings from the Diaries of Vincent and Mary Novello, who visited Vienna in 1829:

Stadler was with Haydn when he received the commission to write the seven Adagios – and as he seemed comparatively at a loss to proceed in introducing sufficient variety in writing seven Adagios directly following each other, it was the Abbé Stadler who advised him to take the first words of the text and write a melody to each which should be the leading feature of each movement; he followed the Abbé's advice and with a success that requires no eulogy from me.[4]

Another series of interesting commissions came from Naples, where Haydn's music was scarcely known; it was from Norbert Hadrava, Secretary of Legation at the Austrian Embassy, who was a musical partner of King Ferdinand IV. They played the *lira organizzata* (see p. 213) and Hadrava commissioned double concertos or *notturni* from various foreign composers, including Gyrowetz, Sterkel and Pleyel. Haydn wrote a whole series of music with two *lire* for Naples – five concertos and eight notturni have survived, all presumably composed between 1786 and the late autumn of 1790. (Haydn actually met Ferdinand IV when the latter was in Vienna in 1790. He was very annoyed when Haydn said that he was leaving for England the next day: 'What! You promised to come to Naples', but in the end, after keeping Haydn waiting for an hour, provided him with a letter of recommendation to the Neapolitan Ambassador in London, Prince Castelcicala, who in January 1791 promptly invited Haydn to dine. 'Princes have long arms,' as Handel used to say . . .)

———————

This period is remarkable for the lengthy business correspondence Haydn conducted with Artaria in Vienna, and for his interesting letters to the wife of Prince Esterházy's physician, Peter von Genzinger. Maria Anna von Genzinger was a talented musician and played the piano well enough for Haydn to write for her the difficult Piano Sonata no. 59 in E flat (1790). Haydn's letters to her (quoted in *C&W*, II) are amusing sad, witty and civilized; they show us hitherto unrevealed aspects of the composer's character. Perhaps Haydn was a little in love with Maria Anna, who obviously fulfilled a feminine need hardly supplied either by Frau Haydn or, since her arrival at Eszterháza in 1779, by the soprano, Luigia Polzelli.

Recently, an important letter from Haydn to the London music publisher, John Bland, has come to light. Bland went to Vienna to enter into arrangements with the principal composers, including Mozart and other masters; he also went especially to Eszterháza to visit Haydn, who contracted to compose three piano trios with flute or violin accompaniment for his new British publisher. The letter, dated 12 April 1790, reads:

Mon tres cher Ami!

I received your letter of 16th March on 10th April, in good order, through the courtesy of our Master of the Equerry: I would ask you for the future, however, please to seal your letters to me since I have important reasons for your so doing.

A week from today I shall deliver the second piano sonata, and the third as soon as possible. When this happens you shall also receive a brand-new and very beautiful cantata for Herr Salamon [*sic*], to whom I present my most sincere compliments and whom I thank for his greetings: since he is so generous as to propose a fee for me of forty ducats for this cantata. I should like to show my gratitude and apart from the cantata I shall send him a brand-new and magnificent symphony, but with this condition, that Herr Salamon retain this symphony only for himself and therefore not give it to anyone, and neither sell it nor much less cause it to be engraved:

This symphony and the cantata, together with your piano sonatas [*sic*], I intend to send from here in a week. However, I also trust that H[err] Salamon will keep his word about the 40 ducats. This cantata is for the voice of my dear Storace, whom I kiss many times. The cantata *Ariadne on Naxôs*, however, I intend later on to orchestrate for a full band and then I shall send it to you.

Please just be patient. I shall make it a point of honour to deserve your valued friendship. I am very much looking forward to the watch, but the man who brings it should be very careful not to have any difficulties with the customs and to be sure that the watch is not damaged. I have received the razors in good condition and also the 30 ducats from H[err] Oliver, for which I thank you very much. Concerning the portraits you ask for, you must be patient until I arrive in Vienna. I shall then be able to satisfy you. Meanwhile I am your most sincere

> Friend and Servant
> Joseph Haydn
> mpria

The 'sonatas' are the three trios for flute, or violin, violoncello and pianoforte (XV:15–17). It is possible that the new cantata for Signora Storace (who had participated in Haydn's *Il ritorno di Tobia* when it was revived in Vienna in 1784) was 'Miseri noi, misera patria', which has come down to us in two ms. sources, both in the Library of Congress, Washington, D.C., one being the typical score on 'small post paper' by an Esterházy copyist with holograph corrections by Haydn (including the addition of a second flute part): this score came from England, and is certainly one of the vocal works Haydn either sent there, or conducted himself when he was in London - very probably both. The new symphony was no. 92, composed in 1789, and later known as the 'Oxford'. As matters turned out, Haydn did not send the symphony but took it with him to England when Salomon came to fetch him in the autumn of 1790. Perhaps the most interesting part of the letter from the biographical standpoint is the mention of the (British) razors, which of course confirms the story of Bland coming upon Haydn while the latter was shaving badly ('I would give my latest quartet for a good pair of razors.'). Bland promised to supply the razors and Haydn gave him the 'Razor' quartet (op. 55 no. 2), as well as the autograph of the cantata *Arianna a Naxos*. We cannot, of course, determine which works, if any, Haydn actually gave Bland: but the story of the razors appears, on the evidence of this letter, to be true. It is also valuable to know that Haydn kept Anna Maria ('Nancy') Storace in fond remembrance and, even more important, that he was in friendly connection with the great German impresario. J. P. Salomon, who was, a few months later, to play such a decisive role in Haydn's life.

Sometime about the middle of the 1780s, Haydn and Mozart became firm friends; in the surviving documents, the first evidence of this friendship comes in a letter of 22 January 1785, wherein we learn that 'last Saturday he [Wolfgang] had his 6 Quartets, which he has sold to Artaria for 100 ducats, played to his dear friend Haydn and other good friends . . .';[5] of course, they must have met earlier, possibly at the Tonkünstler-Societät concerts on 22 and 23 December 1783, when works by

Haydn and Mozart were performed – the latter played a piano concerto (only on 22 December) and Adamberger sang his new 'Misero! o sogno!' (K.431).

This historic friendship has been the subject of endless discussion and speculation (the documentation may be studied in *C&W*, II, 508–16). In this survey we have preferred to quote only two documents, one by Haydn in answer to a commission from Prague to compose a new opera, and one by Mozart (the dedication to Haydn of the six quartets, K.387 etc.); before doing so, however, one might add that there is considerable reason to think that Mozart was perhaps instrumental in persuading Haydn to join the Freemasons, which the older man did at the Lodge 'Zur wahren Eintracht' in Vienna on 11 February 1785.[6] Later in that year, Haydn's Lodge got into serious trouble (as a result of Emperor Joseph II's reforms) and most of the leading members, including the Master, Ignaz von Born, resigned; there is some speculation, too, that Prince Nicolaus, himself a high-ranking Mason – he was Master of Ceremonies in Mozart's own Lodge 'Zur (neu)gekrönten Hoffnung' in 1790, not only joined Mozart in persuading Haydn to become a Mason, but that Esterházy, in whose lodge were four members of the family,[7] may have had his own, semi-private Lodge in Eszterháza (similar to the beautiful eighteenth-century Lodge at Rosenau in Lower Austria, discovered after World War II, which was also not part of the St John's organization of Lodges, with its centre in Vienna). But the fact is that – for whatever reason – Haydn attended only the one meeting of his Lodge in Vienna.

The following two documents reveal, more than any others, the depth of the mutual admiration that existed between Haydn and Mozart. In September 1785, Mozart wrote (in Italian):

To my dear friend Haydn:

A father, having resolved to send his sons into the great world, finds it advisable to entrust them to the protection and guidance of a highly celebrated man, the more so since this man, by a stroke of luck, is his best friend. – Here, then, celebrated man and my dearest friend, are my six sons. – Truly, they are the fruit of a long and laborious effort, but the hope, strengthened by several of my friends, that this effort would, at least in some small measure, be rewarded, encourages and comforts me that one day, these children may be a source of consolation to me. – You yourself, dearest friend, during your last sojourn in this capital, expressed to me your satisfaction with these works. – This, your approval, encourages me more than anything else, and thus I entrust them to your care, and hope that they are not wholly unworthy of your favour. – Do but receive them kindly and be their father, guide, and friend! From this moment I cede to you all my rights over them: I pray you to be indulgent to their mistakes, which a father's partial eye may have overlooked, and despite this, to cloak them in the mantle of your generosity which they value so highly. From the bottom of my heart I am, dearest friend,

Vienna, 1st September 1785

Your most sincere friend,
W. A. Mozart

For his part, Haydn wrote to Franz Roth (or Rott) in Prague, replying to a request for a new comic opera:

December 1787[8]

... You ask me for an *opera buffa*. Most willingly, if you want to have one of my vocal compositions for yourself alone. But if you intend to produce it on the stage in Prague, in that case I cannot comply with your wish, because all my operas are far too closely connected with our personal circle (Esterház, in Hungary), and moreover they would not produce the proper effect, which I calculated in accordance with the locality. It would be quite another matter if I were to have the great good fortune to compose a brand-new libretto for your theatre. But even then I should be risking a good deal, for scarcely any man can brook comparison with the great Mozart.

If I could only impress on the soul of every friend of music, and on high personages in particular, how inimitable are Mozart's works, how profound, how musically intelligent how extraordinarily sensitive! (for this is how I understand them, how I feel them) – why then the nations would vie with each other to possess such a jewel within their frontiers. Prague should hold him fast – but should reward him, too: for without this, the history of great geniuses is sad indeed, and gives but little encouragement to posterity to further exertions; and unfortunately this is why so many promising intellects fall by the wayside. It enrages me to think that this incomparable Mozart is not yet engaged by some imperial or royal court! Forgive me if I lose my head: but I love the man so dearly. I am, &c.

Joseph Hayden [*sic*].

N.S. My respectful compliments to the Prague Orchestra and all the virtuosi there.

Suddenly, in 1790, the fairy-tale world of Eszterháza was at an end. Prince Nicolaus, after two operatic evenings in September, went to Vienna, possibly to attend the triple marriage at the Viennese court (Archduchess Marie Clementine married the Crown Prince Francis of Naples, the Neapolitan Princess Maria Teresa married Archduke Francis, later the Emperor; and the Neapolitan Princess Ludovica Louisa married Ferdinand, Grand Duke of Tuscany) which took place on 19 September; some days later, on the 28th, 'after a short illness', Nicolaus died. His son and successor, Prince Anton, dismissed the exorbitantly expensive opera troupe, the orchestra and the visiting players. Haydn received a noble life pension of 1,000 gulden p.a., Luigi Tomasini (the leader) and Leopold Dichtler (the faithful tenor singer) pensions of 400 and 300 gulden, respectively. Haydn fled to Vienna, leaving so hurriedly that he found he had forgotten many important scores (which he probably collected in 1792 and 1793). Eszterháza now became a kind of glorified hunting lodge and was used only for the occasional house party.

From Dies we learn that 'Count Graschalkowiz' (*sc.* Prince Grassalkovics) offered Haydn a position as *Kapellmeister*, but Haydn 'showed his attachment to his Prince and refused, and an unusual occurrence provided him with the occasion to persuade Prince Anton to reverse his decision and to re-engage the whole wind-band section of the dismissed orchestra' (Dies, 119). Apparently this was done for the Coronation festivities of Leopold II at Pressburg, where on 15 November the joint wind bands of Esterházy and Grassalkovics played with such success that they were persuaded to make a guest appearance at the Tonkünstler-Societät concert in April 1791 (with a work for twenty-one wind instruments by Druschetzky).[9]

Meanwhile, the impresario Johann Peter Salomon, who had often tried to lure Haydn away from Hungary to England, was in Cologne on his annual tour of the Continent to recruit singers for his coming concert season in London, when he read in the newspapers of Prince Nicolaus Esterházy's death. He immediately set off for Vienna and one evening a visitor was announced to Haydn, and in walked Salomon with the (later) famous words, 'I am Salomon of London and have come to fetch you. Tomorrow we will arrange an *accord*.'[10] Haydn also had an understanding (as we have seen) to go to Naples at the invitation of Ferdinand IV – the composer thought he might have become a celebrated opera composer if he had gone to Italy. But Salomon was a persuasive gentleman and Haydn obviously liked him from the first. Haydn said to Salomon, according to Dies (81), 'If my Prince approves of the idea, I will follow you to London.' Haydn had always informed Salomon in previous years, when the latter had pressed him to come to England, that he could not break his word to Prince Nicolaus. Now, however, there was no compelling reason not to go, but difficulties there certainly were. We read in a contemporary source:

Never would Salomon have been able to lure Herr Hayden [*sic*], that great and inimitable genius, away from the quiet atmosphere of his homely and modest existence; and persuade him to seek – under whatever pretext – permission from his then Prince, Anton Esterházy, for leave of absence, were it not for your happy letter to General Jerningham [the British Ambassador], which to the general astonishment of this city, worked miracles. Everyone who knew the philosophical character of this first of virtuosi was astonished at this unexpected decision. What thanks, on the part our musical world, are your due, my dear friend, for your recent visit to Vienna and for this wonderful, fortunate letter.[11]

On 8 December, Salomon had signed the 'accord' with Haydn and was able to write to England and have a notice to that effect inserted in the *Morning Chronicle*. Subsequently, in March 1791, it appears that plans were afoot to ask both Mozart and Haydn to compose music for the forthcoming coronation in Prague of Leopold II; but Haydn (who was already in England when the invitation came) refused: 'Wo Mozart ist, kann sich Haydn nicht zeigen' ('Where Mozart is, Haydn cannot show himself'). We are told

that Beethoven, although a great admirer of Mozart, was not himself sufficiently advanced to excite much of Mozart's attention, but that Haydn and Mozart were like Brothers. Mozart delighted in Haydn's writing and owned repeatedly that he was much indebted to him in forming his style. Stadler said that on his first arrival at Vienna and becoming acquainted with Haydn's work, Mozart naturally changed his manner of composing.

Haydn was not a great Pianoforte player (his best instrument was the Violin) – but he delighted in hearing Mozart play the pianoforte. Haydn owned Mozart's superiority and said, 'he was a *God* in Music'. (Stadler exclaimed to me 'Mozart est *unique*; il etoit universel et savoit *tout*'). Mozart and Haydn frequently played together with Stadler in Mozart's Quintettos; particularly mentioned the 5th in D major, singing the Bass part

the one in C major and still more that in G minor.[12]

Griesinger (22) reports on the last meal that Salomon, Mozart and Haydn had together:

Mozart said, at a merry meal with Salomon, to Haydn: 'You won't stand it for long and will soon return, for you aren't young any more.' 'But I am still vigorous and in good health.' answered Haydn ...

It was at this gathering that Salomon proposed an arrangement whereby Mozart would come to England in due course, after Haydn had returned to Vienna (Pohl II, 250), and on similar terms to those already agreed for Haydn. From Dies we learn further that

Especially Mozart took pains to say, 'Papa!' (as he usually called him), 'You have had no education for the great world, and you speak too few languages'. – 'Oh!' replied Haydn, 'my language is understood all over the world!' [The travellers fixed their departure] and left on December 15, 179[0] ... Mozart, that day, never left his friend Haydn. He dined with him, and at the moment of parting, he said, 'We are probably saying our last adieu in this life.' Tears welled in both men's eyes. Haydn was deeply moved, for he applied Mozart's words to himself, and the possibility never occurred to him that the thread of Mozart's life could be cut by the inexorable Parcae [Fates] the very next year.   [81f., 83f.]

On 15 December, then, Haydn and Salomon set forth, travelling via Munich and Wallerstein (where Haydn conducted Symphony no. 92), then to Bonn and Calais; and on New Year's Day, 1791, Haydn crossed the stormy English channel and saw the white cliffs of Dover welcoming him to what was to prove the greatest adventure, and the happiest half-decade, of his entire life.

VI
Haydn's music,
1781–1790

THE MOST SIGNIFICANT revision in Haydn's terms of employment as defined in the new contract of 1 January 1779 was the omission of the fourth clause of his original contract of 1761, whereby Haydn had been under permanent obligation 'to compose such music as His Serene Highness may command, and neither to communicate such compositions to any other person, nor to allow them to be copied ... and not compose for any other person without the knowledge and permission of His Highness'. Some of Haydn's large-scale choral works, the first *Missa Cellensis* and the 'Applausus' Cantata for instance, had been commissioned by outside bodies and Haydn, no doubt, had sought Prince Esterházy's permission.[1] But from 1779 on Haydn was a free agent, able to compose and sell his music in the wider world and able to profit, financially as well as artistically, from his already considerable reputation. This change of contract had coincided almost exactly with the founding of the publishing firm of Artaria & Co. in Vienna, the set of six sonatas dedicated to the Auenbrugger sisters, nos. 48–52 and 33, being the first of many publications of Haydn's music by that firm. The composer also established business contacts with more distant firms; in London, Forster, Bland and Longman & Broderip; in Paris, Boyer, Imbault, Nadermann, Sieber and Le Duc; in Berlin, Hummel; in Leipzig, Breitkopf; and in Speyer (near Frankfurt), Boßler.

During the 1780s Haydn was to receive requests for works from many foreign countries, including Italy, Spain, France, Germany and England, as well as invitations to travel abroad. Some requests for new compositions – such as an opera for Prague, a set of quartets for Spain, works for the Concert Spirituel in Paris – and an invitation to appear in the Professional Concert series in London were not to be fulfilled, but they are an indication of the substantial change that occurs in Haydn's relationship with the outside world during this decade. Although the composer still spent most of his time at Eszterháza, he was no longer – as he himself put it – 'cut off from the world',[2] and his originality was now being fed by the heady realization that he was composing for an infinitely wider audience. However, his principal occupation at Eszterháza remained the direction of the opera, reaching a peak in 1786 with 125 performances of seventeen different works. Compared with his own output of five new Italian operas in the period 1774–80, Haydn composed only two – *Orlando Paladino* and *Armida* – during the 1780s. As regards symphonies, between 1781 and 1790 Haydn composed nineteen works, yet only five of these were composed for his employer, Prince Nicolaus, the last by 1784; the Prince's insatiable appetite for opera had reduced the frequency of 'academies'. Certainly the Prince's enthusiasm for the baryton had ceased and no baryton trios were composed in the 1780s. Thus, it would be fair to conclude that most of Haydn's music in the 1780s was written either directly for an outside patron or with a view to a wider dissemination through publication; of the comparatively few works he composed exclusively for Prince Nicolaus, the most notable included operatic music for performance by the members of the flourishing and now very experienced Eszterháza company.

Operas, insertion music and cantatas

The composition of *Orlando Paladino* was a rushed affair. The origin of the libretto was an opera by Guglielmi, first performed in London in 1771. For subsequent performances in Prague in 1775, and probably Vienna in 1777, the original libretto by Badini was heavily revised by Nunziato Porta and the score contained some of the London original alongside new numbers by Guglielmi and music by Piccinni, Paisiello and Jommelli. From 1781 Nunziato Porta was employed at Eszterháza as Director of Opera, and the following summer he proposed the production of the revised Guglielmi *Orlando Paladino*. Almost at once, it was learned that the Russian Grand Duke Paul and the Grand Duchess intended visiting Eszterháza in October; clearly a new opera composed for this occasion by the *Kapellmeister* would be in order, especially since the Grand Duke had already been impressed by some Haydn quartets (probably op. 33). It is indicative of Haydn's hectic circumstances at this time and his quiescent critical faculty that he should have agreed to set anew the Porta version of *Orlando Paladino*. In the event, the ducal visit was cancelled; the opera was first performed on Prince Nicolaus's name-day, 6 December 1782.

In the eighteenth century this opera achieved the widest circulation of any Haydn stage work. Despite its contemporary popularity, this opera cannot be said to have the sustained interest of *La fedeltà premiata*, for the work lacks both the wit and the charm of its predecessor. The debunking of the fabled heroism of Orlando and Rodomonte, King of Barbary, is pungent enough, but there is little humanity left to fill the void, with the result that in the final *Coro* the drawing of the moral on the rewards of fidelity seems unmotivated. In deference to its subject matter, the opera is termed a *dramma eroicomico*, a subdivision of the generic *dramma giocoso*. In practice *Orlando Paladino* reveals many familiar features of the *dramma giocoso*. Six of the characters fall naturally into two groups, serious and comic –

Parti serie	*Parti buffe*
Angelica, Queen of Cathay (S)	Rodomonte, King of Barbary (B)
Medoro, her lover (T)	Pasquale, Orlando's groom (T)
Alcina, sorceress (S)	Eurilla, shepherdess (S)

– while Orlando, the Paladin knight, is a *mezzo carattere*, part-comic, part-serious. He is much talked about in Act I but his first appearance occurs only in Scene 8. By this time his qualities of heroism and valour have been pre-empted by similar characteristics in King Rodomonte and Queen Angelica and, worse, have been ridiculed by the absurd antics of the groom, Pasquale. It is difficult, therefore, for Orlando to make a credible impact. Haydn reserves his first accompanied recitative for Orlando, but the recitative's recurring thematic idea paints an unexpectedly forlorn picture of this alleged tyrant. This promising, if surprising aspect of Orlando's personality is not expanded upon. The ensuing aria fails to flesh out the character, while in the subsequent ensemble his actions display a lively comic aspect. In the space of a few minutes at the end of Act I it is too late to fuse these very different elements into a credible human figure. In Act II the process is repeated almost identically: apart from a brief appearance in the opening *secco* recitative, Orlando does not appear until near the end of the act. The libretto suggests an angry, confused and eventually frightened man, but Haydn's response is an atmospheric accompanied recitative that leads, again, to an anti-climactic aria. Orlando's most convincing (as opposed to merely entertaining) music occurs in Act III, in yet another accompanied recitative and aria, a carefully controlled depiction of the knight as he wakes from a magic sleep.

The weaknesses in the characterization of this central figure are typical of the opera as a whole: the number of constituent elements, often attractive in themselves, fail to combine to form a convincing drama. In particular, there is a surfeit of arias, like Orlando's first, in which the character is dejected and sees little or no hope in the future. Sandrina's 'È la pompa un grand' imbroglio' in *L'infedeltà delusa* is a precursor of this tender mood, but when the tempo is a slow one, the sound of the flute prominent and the setting imaginary rather than real, it is rather Gluck who springs to mind. In the Act II finale of *La vera costanza* Rosina had exhibited this distinctive poignancy; in *Orlando Paladino* there are five such numbers (or sections within chain finales); much of Angelica's music is in this vein.

The two lowly characters, the shepherdess Eurilla and the groom Pasquale, are more appealing, especially the latter who is a proto-Leporello with a nice line in self-recommendation; his four arias include an *aria di guerra* ('Vittoria, vittoria') and two catalogue arias, one recounting his extensive foreign travels, the other his equally extensive musical abilities.

After the development that had taken place in Haydn's chain finales between *L'incontro improvviso* and *La fedeltà premiata*, the two chain finales of *Orlando Paladino* are disappointing, exhibiting little sense of mounting tension, though the incorporation of accompanied recitative into the chain is a new and undeniably effective departure. For the concluding *Coro* of Act III Haydn followed Guglielmi's example, writing a rondo in which the assembled cast declaim the moral to the main theme and the individual characters present their own viewpoint in the episodes.

On 18 June 1783, six months after the premiere of *Orlando Paladino*, Haydn mentioned in a letter to Artaria that he was 'just now composing a new opera seria'; *Armida* was given its first performance on 26 February 1784. The printed libretto described the work as a 'dramma eroico', and this was Haydn's first full-length serious opera. The whole course of development of Italian comic opera in the 1770s and 1780s is characterized by increasing seriousness, in Haydn's case, as in his contemporaries, revealed by personalities, situations and settings that could have come directly from *opera seria*. That the Esterházy court had become receptive to serious opera is shown by the productions of Gluck's *Orfeo* in 1776 and of Haydn's own *azione teatrale*, *L'isola disabitata*, in 1779. *Opera seria*, however, did not figure regularly in the Eszterháza repertoire until the 1780s and even then it did not supplant *dramma giocoso*. Having composed *L'isola disabitata*, Haydn was perhaps further inclined to try his hand at a full *opera seria* following the successful performances at Eszterháza of Sarti's *Giulio Sabino* in May 1783, less than a month before he alluded to his own new work in his letter to Artaria. Haydn's *opera seria* was written for the same singers as those who performed *Giulio Sabino*, has similarities of construction and the occasional telling musical echo.[3]

Haydn's source for the libretto of this popular operatic subject was an opera by Antonio Tozzi entitled *Rinaldo*, performed in Venice in 1775. The libretto, by an unknown author, was modified in detail by Porta, though the customary six singers and three acts of *opera seria* were retained; equally typical, there are no chain finales. The opera is set in Palestine at the time of the Crusades and takes as its theme the superior call of duty on behalf of Christendom over the sweet voice of love – a sturdy ethic alien to the world of *dramma giocoso* and a dilemma Haydn himself would hardly have thought possible. Human comedy is naturally absent from the libretto, though in the opera the character of Zelmira, sung by the soprano Costanza Valdesturla (who had previously created the roles of the nymph Nerina in *La fedeltà premiata* and the sorceress Alcina in *Orlando Paladino*), presents a personable character as the protagonist of love. The stage settings of palace, mountain, garden and forest, the references to valour (albeit serious rather than comic), the appearance of nymphs and the magic transformation of scenes would not have seemed novel to members of the Eszterháza audience familiar with *La vera costanza*, *La fedeltà premiata* and *Orlando Paladino*; indeed, at one point during the preparation of the sets it was proposed that materials from *La fedeltà premiata* and *Orlando Paladino*, as well as from Sarti's *Giulio Sabino*, be used in order to save money.

The opera opens, not with the typical *Introduzione* of *dramma giocoso*, but with a sequence of recitatives and arias for some of the main characters, Rinaldo, Idreno and Armida. The entry of the valiant Ubaldo, commander of the Christian forces, is announced by a stage band of two clarinets (a startlingly new sound in Haydn's music), two horns and two bassoons. The subsequent accompanied recitative initiates a continous stretch of recitative and aria that reflects Haydn's abiding interest in providing musical continuity: the first recitative leads to an aria whose concluding orchestral ritornello is deflected into a second accompanied recitative; this, in turn, leads directly to a *secco* recitative for the arrival of the knight Clotarco. In Act II there is an unbroken sequence of five numbers, and the bulk of Act III consists of a sequence of seven numbers; in both cases orchestral conclusions to arias merge with succeeding accompanied recitatives. In the absence of chain finales, these lengthy chains of aria and recitative do much to create dramatic consistency, though towards the ends of acts one misses the inimitable sense of climax and dénouement associated with *dramma giocoso*. The presence of large stretches of continuous music also prevents the opera from sounding like an impersonal series of concert arias, especially necessary since many of the arias demand a virtuosity, often featuring a cadenza, that is more ostentatious than usual in Haydn's operatic writing.

The lack of comic relief such as that which contributes humanity to Haydn's earlier operas is partly compensated for by the new vividness of mood and scene-painting found in this opera. The following passages are representative: the return to the tonic in Ubaldo's first aria, with its new 'hairpin' dynamic (also found in *Orlando Paladino*), chromatic harmony and sustained wind notes; the chromatic harmonies associated with deceit in Clotarco's only aria, 'Ah si plachi il fiero Nume'; the exaggerated orchestral accents that convey Rinaldo's torment in his Act II aria, 'Caro, è vero'; and most memorably, the scene in the forest in Act III which, though it makes use of familiar musical conventions (pastoral music with flute and stirring *Sturm und Drang* music), is a gripping mixture of the magical and the personal, anticipating a major obsession of the German Romantics.

Before *Armida* Haydn's operatic overtures had been typical of contemporary practice in that they sound suitably theatrical, sometimes anticipating a particular atmosphere, as in *L'incontro improvviso* and *La fedeltà premiata*; in *Armida*, however, the overture is directly related to the opera, quoting material from the first scene of Act III. After *Armida*, Haydn did not compose a single further stage work for Eszterháza, even though operatic activity was to dominate his duties for seven more years until the death of Nicolaus in 1790. Given the productivity of the previous decade, three or more new operas could have been expected in this later period. Biographical evidence suggests, however, that Haydn was becoming less sure than formerly of his status as an opera composer; at the very least there is a new ambivalence towards the genre. In 1787 he refused to write an *opera buffa* for Prague, partly to avoid comparison 'with the great Mozart', yet in the same year he was proposing to compose *opera seria* for London, one of several references to a project that eventually materialized in the shape of *L'anima del filosofo* in 1791. As well as Haydn's own unsureness in the genre, there was no large-scale *Fest* held at Eszterháza in the second part of the decade that might have required the *Kapell-meister* to write a new opera. Meanwhile, Haydn had found that the world outside Eszterháza was more interested in his instrumental music from which, moreover, the increasingly commercially minded (but never artistically cynical) composer could supplement his income. It took this contact with the outside world and its ever-increasing interest in the composer's instrumental music to rid Haydn of his traditionalist belief that opera constituted the basis of international esteem.

Although operatic activity continued unabated at Eszterháza up to 1790, the apparent statistical decline from a maximum of 125 performances in 1786 to ninety-two in 1789 and sixty-one in 1790 is misleading, since Prince Nicolaus was away in July 1789 and the 1790 season was cut short by the Prince's death, thus accounting for some fifteen 'lost' performances in 1789 and thirty in 1790. Revivals of Haydn's own operas, such as *La fedeltà premiata* and especially *La vera costanza*, required adjustments to suit the new cast. Indeed, the bulk of Haydn's operatic work, apart from time-consuming rehearsals, lay in making other composers' work suitable for performance by the Eszterháza company. Haydn's amendments to the operas of Dittersdorf, Gassmann, Salieri, Anfossi, Sarti, Paisiello, Righini, Piccinni, Cimarosa and others are largely practical rather than artistic; redistributing clarinet parts, transposing arias to suit different vocal ranges and adjusting linking recitatives. The excision of repeated passages, especially coloratura, shows a desire to quicken the pace of the drama, as does the apparently ruthless, but very common, practice of changing a tempo marking from Andante to Allegro. For some operas new arias and a few ensembles were composed to suit the capabilities of the singers. Many of these so-called insertion arias were composed for the limited talents of Luigia Polzelli and show Haydn's customary flair for the composition of simple soubrette arias. The increasing number of such arias composed in two sections, slow then fast, confirms a trend that is discernible in his operas from *L'incontro improvviso* to *Armida*.

In the 1780s Haydn allowed many extracts from his operas to be published for use outside the opera house: collections of arias arranged for voice and keyboard, several overtures and some of the larger vocal numbers with full orchestration. For instance the cantata, as it was now called, 'Ah come il core mi palpita', that is Celia's accompanied recitative and aria from the second act of *La fedeltà premiata*, was published by Artaria in 1783 and was performed several times during Haydn's first visit to London.

'Miseri noi, misera Patria' is another cantata for soprano and orchestra, composed not làter than 1786 but not published in Haydn's lifetime; it is possible that this was written as a concert aria, since no suitable operatic context has been found. The text, by an anonymous poet, relates the horror caused by a fire in a city being attacked by an unspecified conqueror – a typical *opera seria* situation reminiscent of the burning of the Capitol in Metastasio's *La clemenza di Tito*. The leading singer of serious roles at Eszterháza in the 1780s was Matilde Bologna (Celia in *La fedeltà premiata*, Angelica in *Orlando Paladino* and the title role in *Armida*), and the cantata may well have been composed for her. It has three stages: an accompanied recitative with a recurring theme that suggests fortitude in adversity rather than the selfpitying despair which is often encountered in *dramma giocoso*; an arioso section (Largo) with orchestral figuration expressive of groans, sobs and sighs; and a two-part aria (Largo assai – Allegro moderato) in which forceful coloratura demonstrates that personal valour remains unaffected by the surrounding destruction.

Music for voice and keyboard

In 1789–90 Haydn composed an extensive cantata for voice and harpsichord (or piano) entitled *Arianna a Naxos* which, according to a letter to John Bland of 12 April 1790, he intended orchestrating.[4] The cantata was published in its original form by Bland and performed several times in London in 1791, but Haydn seems never to have carried out his intention to orchestrate it. In its extant form, however, it is clear that the cantata was conceived orchestrally, for the declamatory accompanied recitative section and, especially, the final F minor Presto of the aria sound undernourished in the keyboard format. A more effective, if restrained, combination of voice and keyboard is to be found in Haydn's first Lieder, which date from the early part of the decade.

In a society in which sophisticated cultural taste had been dominated by French and Italian traditions, the German Lied arrived late in Austria, coinciding with Joseph II's attempts to create in his country a new German consciousness, the most tangible sign of which was the founding of the German theatre in 1776 and *Singspiel* in 1778. Also in 1775, the first Lieder by an Austrian composer appeared – *Deutsche Lieder* by Joseph Anton Steffan, one of the court composers. During the following decade there was a steady stream of native Lieder by Hoffmann, Fribert, Koželuch and, of course, Mozart. Haydn played a part in this cultural development, though his own contribution is at least as significant in personal terms, being a particular instance of the effect of wider social and cultural contact on his output. Haydn sought the literary advice of Franz von Greiner, a government official and notable man of letters, who supplied him with suitable texts. The two sets, of twelve Lieder each, were published by Artaria in 1781 and 1784 and dedicated to another figure in Viennese society, Francisca Liebe von Kreutzner, whose father commissioned the second *Missa Cellensis* (see p. 189).

Haydn was concerned that both sets of Lieder should have 'light and shade' (letter to Artaria of 18 October 1781) and, within the prescribed limits of the medium, there are jolly songs in a rhythmic 2/4 pulse reminiscent of *Singspiel*, e.g. 'Der Gleichsinn', and more reflective songs, such as 'Das Leben ist ein Traum' ('Life is a dream') which gives the impression of being a chamber version of an operatic scene by the composer. More novel in their sentiment are the delicate protestations of love, songs that are far removed in mood from the wry cunning of the average 'ragazza semplice' of Italian *opera buffa*. 'Cupido' (see example opposite), 'Der erste Kuß' ('The first kiss') and 'Minna' are representative of this new delicacy, of the urban drawing room rather than of the countryside; it was a vein which Haydn was to cultivate with particular distinction in the next decade, not only in the English Canzonettas but in instrumental music too.

All the songs are strophic and, with a few significant exceptions, are written on two staves only, with the right hand doubling the voice. The scoring for keyboard is simpler than in contemporary sonatas and trios, though many of the ritornellos and interjections go well beyond the perfunctory. In addition to the twenty-four songs for Artaria, Haydn composed three single songs, 'Beim Schmerz, der dieses Herz durchwühlet', 'Der schlaue und dienstfertige Pudel'[5] and 'Trachten will ich nicht auf Erden'. The last-named song and 'Trost unglücklicher Liebe' from the first Artaria set go beyond simple charm, and demonstrate the appeal of the new medium to Haydn.

Today, Haydn's Lieder of the period 1781–90 cannot hold their own against the accepted masterpieces of the Romantic period, but this fact should not be allowed to obscure their importance in the composer's own development. They were yet

'Cupido'

Weißt du, mein klei-nes Mäg-de-lein, wer wohl Cu-pi-do ist?

another productive element in his long career and an element that was to influence his music in general (which was not the case with Mozart). The road from 'Cupido' to the first movement of the quartet, op. 76 no. 5 (see example, p. 355), is a long one, but the two are, nevertheless, related.

Sacred music (vocal and instrumental)

Prince Nicolaus seems to have had little interest in religious music. There was no chapel at Eszterháza for which music was required, and he not only allowed the church music establishment in Eisenstadt to decline but did not encourage Haydn's special gifts as a composer of church music. After the magnificent series of church music in the late 1760s and early 1770s, Haydn composed nothing of comparable significance until 1782. In the winter months, when the court returned to Eisenstadt, Haydn played the organ in the chapel but the *Kapelle* relied for its repertoire on the existing large library and the occasional new work by the violone player, Carl Schiringer.

Haydn's first opportunity in ten years to compose a substantial mass arose in 1781–2 when Anton Liebe von Kreutzner, a retired military man living in Vienna, commissioned a mass to be performed at the pilgrimage church at Mariazell. Thus Haydn's second *Missa Cellensis* (XXII:8) was composed in 1782. Like the first, it is in C major, the most popular key for Austrian masses. It is an assertive, forthright work, scored for the same forces of oboes, bassoons, trumpets (or horns), timpani, strings, continuo, SATB choir and soloists. Although less ambitious than the first *Missa Cellensis* and often conventional in its response to the text, it is by no means a conservative work and many of its most striking features reflect Haydn's general development in the intervening years.

The Kyrie opens with a short Adagio introduction, as did the earlier mass, but here the idea of homophonic chords with instrumental support is intensified by the repeated semiquavers of the accompaniment, the gradual increase in volume to *fortissimo* followed by a *diminuendo* (notated by the new 'hairpin' dynamic) and a final affirmative *fortissimo*.[6] The ensuing Kyrie is marked Vivace, the first of many similar markings in the mass that impart a distinctive energy. The movement is in three parts, showing an indebtedness to monothematic sonata form.

> *Exposition: Kyrie eleison*
> bar 9: first subject; soprano solo, later choir; I
> bar 48: second subject (derived from first subject); choir; V
>
> *Development: Christe eleison*
> bar 74: first subject; alto solo, later choir; V–vi
>
> *Recapitulation: Kyrie eleison*
> bar 100: first subject; choir; I
> bar 116: second subject; choir; I
> bar 136: coda; choir; I

The manner in which trumpets re-enter at the beginning of the recapitulation and in which the movement culminates in a pause before proceeding to the coda is reminiscent of similar techniques used in the symphonies of the 1770s.

The Gloria has the familiar broad approach of two fast sections enclosing a slower section beginning with the clause 'Gratias agimus tibi' and ending with 'miserere nobis'; the outer sections make use of full forces, the middle portion has reduced orchestration and soloists. Within the first section a more integrated attitude to thematic writing is apparent, with the clause 'glorificamus te' signalling a return to the music of the opening. The Credo, too, adheres to the customary three-part design, with a change to slow tempo and soloists for the 'Et incarnatus est' followed by a return to a fast tempo and full forces at 'Et resurrexit'. Here, again, there is an unorthodox musical recapitulation and, in keeping with the straightforward atmosphere of the work as a whole, the ten clauses from 'Et resurrexit tertia die' to 'qui locutus est per Prophetas' are set polytextually, the voices uniting for the first two words of the phrase 'et unam sanctam catholicam'. The central slow portion shows interesting adaptations of two old features. The 'Et incarnatus est' is sung by the customary solo tenor in the minor key (including the familiar blush on Neapolitan harmony), but it is a sign of the widening tonal range of Haydn's music in this period that this A minor section should modulate to the harmonically remote distance of C minor, in which key it stays.[7] The setting of the 'Crucifixus' recalls that in the Great Organ Solo Mass in the use of non-diatonic melodic lines (here adumbrating part of a whole-tone scale) held together by secondary dominant harmony; as in the opening of the mass, repeated semiquavers impart a sense of awe. The jaunty 6/8 fugue associated with the text 'et vitam venturi saeculi' ('and the life of the world to come') seems an inappropriate evocation of the after-life, but the certainty of this vision is typical and is an impulse that will recur in the corresponding section in several of the late masses.

The Benedictus is the oddest movement in the mass. Rather than being the customary lyrical movement, it begins in a severe G minor with dotted rhythms, trills, suspensions and a descending bass line, almost like a baroque aria. In abridged sonata form, the movement's second subject is more conventional in mood. The movement was taken, with some minor adjustments, from Act II of *Il mondo della luna* where, sung by Ernesto, it had expressed the sentiment that the course of true love does not run true. Condemning the use of the aria in the mass, simply because of its secular origins, would be to ignore a practice common in music up to the nineteenth century; far better to note that, like the Benedictus movements in the *Missa in angustiis* and the 'Harmoniemesse', this is a deliberately unsettling movement, the hope of a life in Christ being counterpoised by a sense of mystery and fear.

The year following the composition of the second *Missa Cellensis* saw the beginning of the so-called *Josephinische Verbote*, the reforms introduced by Emperor Joseph II in successive decrees that restricted the use of instrumentally accompanied music in church to Sundays and stipulated holy days, part of a wider political and economic plan to reduce the status of the church in Austria and to re-affirm its fundamental role of 'bettering humanity', as the Emperor put it. In a period when Haydn might have welcomed further outside commissions along the lines of the *Missa Cellensis*, the new restrictions certainly limited such opportunities, yet the affect on Haydn's career is easily exaggerated. Instrumental music was far from being banned in church and Prince Nicolaus's lack of interest in church music remained a prime reason why Haydn did not compose any more liturgical works in the 1780s.

That Haydn himself was fully convinced of the emotive power of instrumental music in church is shown in the *Seven Last Words of our Saviour from the Cross*, composed in 1786 in the middle of an increasingly liberal decade in Austria. Both as a musician and as a traditionally minded Austrian Catholic, Haydn may well have viewed with some concern the new restrictions on church music and the accelerated decline in the number and the wealth of the monasteries, for though he dabbled with fashionable Freemasonry, becoming a member in 1785, the composer remained a committed and orthodox member of the Church. If he had misgivings about recent trends, *The Seven Words* seems to re-assert the potency of his faith and the part music can play in affirming that faith. Certainly Haydn held the work in special regard.

The work was composed in response to a request from a canon in Cádiz for music to accompany the annual Passion celebration on Good Friday. The first Spanish performance probably took place on Good Friday 1787. Following the declaiming of the text and a ten-minute discourse on each of the seven last words, Haydn's instrumental music accompanied the adoration of the bishop before the Cross. In addition to the seven 'sonatas', as he termed them, Haydn provided an *Introduzione* and, to conclude, *Il terremoto*, a depiction of the earthquake that convulsed Calvary (Matthew, xxviii, 2).

Apart from *Il terremoto*, Haydn's task of encouraging contemplation and veneration without, as he later told Griesinger, 'fatiguing the listeners' was a difficult one. To a certain extent the Stabat Mater, with its many slow movements, had given Haydn valuable experience for this task of composing eight successive slow movements, though, of course, the earlier work had the important advantage of a text to aid comprehension on the part of the listener. Though *The Seven Words* is devoid of text, the 'Words' themselves are strongly suggested in the music in that each opening theme is a musical realization of the rhythms of the spoken Latin. When the work was published by Artaria, Haydn went to great pains to ensure that the text was underlaid in the first violin part; for the listener this association would have registered subliminally. The 'leitmotifs' recur through each respective slow movement in a manner normally encountered in allegro music in Haydn's symphonies. Although each movement is thematically independent, there are plenty of melodic and rhythmic correspondences (falling thirds, dotted rhythms and appoggiaturas) to prevent them from sounding disparate; one of the many ways in which *Il terremoto* interrupts and destroys the carefully nurtured atmosphere is by using thematic material completely unrelated to that of previous movements. The thematic and harmonic language has a resourcefulness not previously encountered in a large-scale sacred or orchestral work. Power and anguish are evoked by chromatic harmony and wide-ranging modulation, the poignancy of the situation by the many passages of diatonic harmony, routine accompaniment and easy cantabile. The orchestra consists of two flutes, two oboes, two bassoons, four horns, two trumpets, timpani and strings, and the scoring is skilfully varied, from dangerously light textures to a massive sonority new in Haydn's music. The introduction and seven sonatas are the aural equivalents of the paintings and sculpture of rococo Catholic churches, inducing tranquil thought and peace of mind. The earthquake, which is a reminder of the original great drama and, in general, of the part played by inexplicable physical phenomena in religious belief, is realized by an orchestra of one flute, two oboes, two bassoons, four horns, two trumpets, timpani and strings playing 'Presto e con tutta la forza', suggestive of Verdi's later markings. The C minor movement concludes with the unprecedented dynamic demand of *fff*.

String quartets

Between 1781 and 1790 Haydn completed twenty-five quartets: four sets of six and a single quartet. Op. 33 was completed late in 1781, op. 42 (the single work), in 1785, and then, in a burst of creativity reminiscent of the period *c.* 1770, three sets in four years – op. 50 in 1787, opp. 54/55 in 1788 and op. 64 in 1790. As before, none of these works was produced as part of Haydn's duties as *Kapellmeister*; but if self-motivation occasioned these quartets, it was not the rarified, rather exclusive type that had earlier produced opp. 9, 17 and 20. Haydn was now fully conscious of the popularity of the genre, and his quartets fom op. 33 onwards show a continuing regard for their likely wider success. He was closely involved in the sale and/or publication of all the quartets, and this awareness of a wider public conditioned their content. Conditioned, but not determined, for Haydn was never to reach the sterile position of composing what he thought the public wanted; the quartets reveal an intellectual rigour and energy that is as commanding as it is inexhaustible, yet there is, too, an approachability, a wit and a charm. It is still a private world, but not the world of a recluse.

The combination of immediate appeal and consummate craftmanship is most apparent in the first set of six, op. 33 (III:37–42), completed in December 1781 and published the following April by Artaria. Before publication Haydn sent a number of letters (three have survived, but probably more were sent) to potential patrons offering pre-publication manuscript copies. The one sent to Prince Krafft Ernst Oettingen-Wallerstein is typical in its general tone and its business particulars.

I take the liberty of humbly offering Your Serene Highness, as a great patron and connoisseur of music, my brand-new *a quadro* for 2 violins, viola and violoncello *concertante* correctly copied, at a subscription price of 6 ducats. They are written in a new and special way, for I have not composed any for 10 years. The noble subscribers who live abroad will receive their copies before I issue them here. I beg for your favour, and a gracious acceptance of this offer, and remain ever, in profound respect ...

This is certainly sales talk, not couched in the sycophantic prose of many eighteenth-century letters or dedications to patrons, but in an unambiguous mixture of matter-of-fact business talk and a desire to please. As such, it is typical of many letters of the period written by the increasingly astute composer: the letter of 27 May 1781 to Artaria *re* Lieder, '... I assure you that these Lieder perhaps surpass all my previous ones in variety, naturalness and ease of vocal execution'; 15 June 1783 to Boyer concerning *The Seven Words*, 'Each sonata, or rather each setting of the text, is expressed only by instrumental music, but in such a way that it creates the most profound impression even in the most inexperienced listener.'; 29 September 1782 to Artaria *re* overtures, 'At last I can send you the five Symphonies you wanted, neatly and correctly written and also well constructed ...'; and 29 March 1789 to Artaria *re* the Fantasia in C, partially quoted on p. 207. However, Haydn's letter announcing the quartets was no empty sales talk, for the claim that they were written 'in a new and special way' ('auf eine ganz neue besondere Art') is a reasonable one, reflecting a fresh approach after nearly a decade during which no quartets were composed. As a consequence of the new wider audience there is a new popularity, a less self-conscious exploitation of the medium. This is most immediately apparent in the general tone of the quartets in C, E flat and G and it is not surprising that these have acquired the nicknames of 'Bird', 'Joke' and 'Compliments' (or 'How do you do'). Even the now customary single work in a minor key, in this case B minor, avoids the dark mood of earlier quartets in the minor. Equally indicative of the 'new and special way' is the use of the word 'Scherzo' for the dance movement rather than 'Menuet' and, in the finales, the favouring of rondo and variation form rather than sonata form and fugue.

In the absence of the autograph manuscripts, which have not survived, the Artaria first edition has to be taken as the principal authority for the composer's intentions. In that publication those movements which could have been expected to carry the headings 'Menuet' and 'Trio' bear the title 'Scherzo' and for the separate enclosed section no title at all, not even 'Alternativo' which Haydn was to use in op. 76 no. 6.[8] The title 'Scherzo' itself had frequently been used by Haydn in the earlier part of his career to denote movements of a lively, jesting, occasionally whimsical type – attributes very much in evidence in op. 33. Although the scherzos are minimally faster than the average minuet (certainly a danced minuet), they are certainly not early examples of the one-in-a-bar movements associated with Beethoven, Schumann, Bruckner etc. By using the structure and proportions of the customary minuet and trio Haydn teased the listener with disruptions of metre, pulse and phrasing in a manner foreshadowed in earlier minuets for quartet, but never with the same concentrated application. The scherzos of the quartets in C and B flat are the nearest to the conventional minuet and trio, though the extreme contrast of register and sonority between scherzo and contrasting section in the C major quartet and the nine-bar period that opens the contrasting section in the B flat work are whimsical enough. In the scherzo movements of nos. 1 and 6 the approach is more provocative, with apparently regular phrasing patterns in the leading melodic line being undermined by subversive entries in other parts; in revealing contrast, the 'trio' sections are blandly regular in their phrasing. The most extreme case of 'scherzoid' thinking occurs in the G major quartet, the first quartet in Artaria's publication and probably also the first to be composed.

The opening four-bar phrase is deprived of any sense of normality by the conflicting 2/4 rhythms of the first violin; the second phrase proceeds regularly until the expected tonic in bar 8 is replaced by a silent bar, and followed by a *piano* cadence into bar 10. The mixing of two pulses continues after the double bar and the fact that the 'trio' has simple phrasing patterns whilst, at the same time, making thematic reference to the Scherzo serves to emphasize the irregularity of the main section.

Two principal characteristics of Haydn's instrumental music composed between op. 20 and op. 33 had been the increased use of rondo and variation movements, sectional structures that are, in general, more accessible than sonata form and fugue. The finale movements of op. 33 reflect and promote this popularizing trend, with only one, that of the B minor quartet, in sonata form. Three are rondo structures, nos. 2, 3 and 4, and two, nos. 5 and 6, are variations movements.[9] In schematic terms the rondos are all of the simple ABACA type, two episodes separating three statements of a crisp, light-hearted theme. However, Haydn is careful to avoid the inherent dangers of too much material and too little development. In nos. 2 and 3 the episode returns a second time (i.e. ABAB²A) and in nos. 2 and 4 there is strong integration of main theme and episodes. The concluding 'joke' in the E flat quartet has been commented upon many times but its effect never palls: a portentous Adagio halts the progress of the Presto and then, after a pause, the constituent phrases of the main theme are played separated by a bar's silence and followed, after three bars' rest, by the first phrase, *pianissimo*.

The two finales in variations form use structures developed in the 1770s: no. 5 has a set of strophic variations, and no. 6 a set of variations on two alternating themes, one in the major and one in the minor, the first of which always returns verbatim, as in a rondo.

For the first time in his quartets Haydn finds an alternative to the melody-plus-accompaniment approach for slow movements. No. 5 is the only quartet to employ this long-serving technique, perhaps because it was probably the first of the set to be composed. Traces of the texture can be found also in no. 6 with its *messa di voce* entries for the first violin, but in the remaining four quartets the instruments are treated with the equality found in surrounding movements. The Adagio ma non troppo of the 'Bird' quartet (no. 3) is a *locus classicus* of string quartet writing in a slow tempo, with its beautifully judged chordal spacing, easy sense of forward movement and well-paced harmonic climax; the melody too is distinctive, one of the earliest examples in Haydn's *œuvre* of a cantabile hymn-like theme, a new warm dimension to Haydn's melodic style. Perhaps the most idiosyncratic slow movement is the Largo of no. 2; the main theme is presented in two voices, viola and cello, this being Haydn's first lengthy viola solo in a quartet and a duet scoring that is directly indebted to the baryton trios of the previous decade. The practice of beginning a slow movement in two parts only was to be another recurring feature in Haydn's later quartets. The exploitation of a contrasting tessitura on the repeat of the melody is typical of op. 33 in general, but the forceful dynamics that characterize the secondary idea in no. 2 are completely unexpected; seventeen markings in eight bars, the *pianissimo* forming a written-out echo, and the melodic dénouement making affecting use of Haydn's recently acquired 'hairpin' *diminuendo* marking. This movement, like others in op. 33, proves that lyricism and a slow tempo need not preclude rhetoric.

Commentators on op. 33 have always focused on the new thematicism in the works, *thematische Arbeit* ('thematic working'), the use of consistently recurring motifs so that there is little irrelevance; every stage, almost every phrase is made germane to the argument. Some of the scherzo movements embrace this principle, e.g. that of no. 6, but it is the first movements that demonstrate this attitude most typically. Over a century later, Webern was to write apropos Schoenberg's first quartet – in which context one could with complete justification substitute Haydn's name for that of Schoenberg:

It is marvellous to observe how Schoenberg creates an accompaniment figure from a motivic particle, how he introduces themes, how he brings about interconnections between the principal sections. And everything is thematic! Every thread of the music's texture, including the accompaniment details, has a thematic basis. It is total thematicism.

The first movements of nos. 2 and 4 are the most ruthless in their avoidance of new material; neither has anything which could be called a second subject, the tension of the exposition in no. 2 being released by four bars of passage work, in no. 4 by a cadence theme that uses the same motivic ingredients as earlier themes (thirds and turns). It is not surprising, therefore, that these movements are far shorter than any in op. 20 (ninety and eighty-nine bars of common time). But the extent of this impressive thematicism in op. 33 can be exaggerated and can seem to be the only important element in the first movements. There is, for instance, far more use of repeated quaver figuration in subordinate parts in op. 33 than in op. 20, giving momentum at crucial moments, relaxation at others and always throwing into relief the important foreground of the music. Frequently, as in the first subject of no. 1, background becomes foreground, occasionally, as in the second subject of no. 2, foreground becomes background, but Haydn is always conscious of the distinction between the two in a way which was not apparent in op. 20.

Changing the harmonic perspective and exploiting ambiguities are two resources developed in sonata forms in Haydn's symphonies in the 1770s (e.g. the punning on augmented sixth versus dominant seventh in the development section of the first movement of no. 55). In op. 33 such procedures are deployed knowing that the intimacy of the medium produces a manifold gain in subtlety. In no. 1 the oft-quoted initial ambiguity between D major and B minor is only one of many notable harmonic features: the first four-bar phrase is succeeded by a careful building-up of a supertonic seventh chord instrument by instrument which, when repeated two phrases later, is intensified to a Neapolitan sixth, leading to the first perfect cadence in the movement. In the recapitulation the two passages are differently treated; the opening is harmonized unambiguously in B minor and the Neapolitan chord produces a powerful harmonic digression, with forceful double stops. In the deceptively superficial 'Bird' quartet, the chattering quavers that precede the entry of the first subject are consistently used to redirect the harmonic course of the music: at the beginning C major, then D minor, then apparently B flat; at the beginning of the development, down a fifth to F. At the juncture of the development and beginning of the recapitulation the repeated quavers result in a displacement of thematic recapitulation and the return to the tonic in the following way: the quavers arise out of an E minor context, are superimposed with the G of the recapitulated first subject, then change to a dominant chord before finally reaching the tonic three bars into the first subject. The second phrase too has new harmonic clothing, the quavers providing dominant harmony rather than the tonic harmony of the exposition.

Although the quartets of op. 33 have an immediate appeal that goes beyond that of opp. 9, 17 and 20, and although many of the features are novel to the genre, the broad structural framework established in the earlier quartets persists in this set: four movements with the slow movement placed third rather than, as in most symphonies, second, and a broad progression from an Allegro moderato first movement through a dance movement and a slow movement in a leisurely tempo (Adagio or Largo) to a concluding Presto in duple time. Only two works, nos. 5 and 6, depart from this grand plan. In these works the slow movement comes second, probably because the first movement in both cases is in a new tempo in Haydn's quartets – Vivace assai; another feature of these two works is that they retain the same tonic throughout. It was the new approach that was to form the basis of further development in the genre.

Haydn's quartets had always spearheaded his wider reputation: they constituted his first published music in France, England, North Germany and Holland, whilst the thematic catalogues of the Leipzig publisher Breitkopf reveal Haydn to be the most popular composer of quartets (followed by Vanhal, Pleyel, Boccherini and Cambini). The composition of op. 33 and the quest for patrons in Switzerland, Wallerstein and elsewhere testify to Haydn's recognition of this wide popularity. From 1783 to the end of the decade Haydn maintained regular contact with two Spanish aristocrats, the Countess-Duchess of Benavente and Osuna and the Duke of Alba, regularly supplying them with copies of his latest instrumental music. In a letter to Artaria written in April 1784, Haydn mentioned that he was working on three 'very short' quartets 'of three pieces [movements] only; they are intended for Spain'. The works have not survived. A year later, he composed a single quartet in D minor (III:43) which, though certainly shorter than any in op. 33, still has four movements; nevertheless, it is possible that some of the Spanish music was incorporated into this work. At first it was not published by Artaria but by his rival, Hoffmeister, whose normal business practice was to issue chamber music as single works. Thus, Haydn's D minor quartet fitted neatly into Hoffmeister's scheme and it appeared in January 1786. Hoffmeister was unorthodox also in that he did not use opus numbers; the familiar designation, op. 42, dates from the nineteenth century.

The quartet itself may be less ambitious than op. 33 and later works, yet it is beautifully shaped and immaculate in its scoring. Contrasting with the relaxed dialogue of the first movement and the Menuetto, the Adagio has a rich sonority; its thematic progress too is notable, the main theme being followed by an elaboration of constituent phrases, demonstrating that Haydn's monothematicism can embrace lyricism. The quartet ends with an up-dated version of the taut Presto finales of opp. 9 and 17: imitative two-strand counterpoint which is now comic rather than sober in effect. An entire musical personality is enshrined in this deceptively simple work.

Apart from this single extant work, Haydn composed no other quartets between 1781 and 1787, his time being taken up with symphonies and *The Seven Words*. The next set of quartets, op. 50 (III:44–9), was composed and published in 1787. With Haydn's agreement, Artaria dedicated the publication to Frederick William II of Prussia, a keen and accomplished cellist who was a regular purchaser of Boccherini's music and who later commissioned Mozart's three 'Prussian' quartets (K. 575, 589, 590). Though Haydn approved the dedication to the royal cellist, he – unlike Mozart – did not set out to flatter the king with lengthy passages of concertante writing; the eloquent main theme of the Andante più tosto Allegretto of op. 50 no. 3, the main theme in the Poco Allegretto of no. 1 and the statement of the fugue subject in the finale of no. 4 constitute the only significant cello solos.

Op. 50 incorporates as many new features as op. 33, without abandoning either the thematically and harmonically integrated texture or the popular guise. All the quartets have four movements, with the slow movement placed second. The scherzos of op. 33 are replaced with minuet movements which do not seek to disturb the phrase patterns of the dance, though their thematic and harmonic sophistication makes them far removed from the ballroom; as for the trios (the term is revived), Haydn consistently uses them to intensify the mood of their companion minuet, rather than to provide pleasant contrast. The opening movements avoid the moderate pace, common time approach in favour of a brisk tempo (Allegro con brio and Allegro spiritoso) and/or duple or triple time. The slow movements in the set, perhaps reflecting the slow movements of the contemporary 'Paris' symphonies, are mainly variations movements: strophic in no. 2, with rondo-like returns of the main theme in no. 3, and on two alternating themes in no. 4. Finally, there are no concluding rondos; with the exception of no. 4, which is a fugue, the finales are all 2/4 movements in sonata form. Thus, while op. 33 was of great significance in pointing Haydn's quartet writing in a new direction, it is clear that the composer did not regard the set as a blueprint for later essays in the genre. Haydn's intellectual fascination with the medium was apparent in his very earliest quartets, reaching fruition (after two or three years of concentrated work) in op. 20, and thereafter each new set was to explore this mastery with new techniques and principles, so that to highlight one set as being more significant than another is to risk undervaluing many individual works: it was Haydn's unparalleled achievement, and it is our problem of comprehension, that each set is significant, and almost every work a rigorous investigation of the possibilities of the medium.

In op. 50, the second quartet, in C major, is representative of the main trends of the set and one of its strongest works. The first movement shows the full resourcefulness of Haydn's creativity in the genre. The argument is based on two very different main subjects: the first characterized by chromaticism and rhythmic strength, the second by a rich harmonic digression. The nine-bar opening cleverly employs *fz* accents to emphasize the abrupt shifts of melodic accent, the secondary dominant harmony (bar 5) and the melodic peak in bar 7.

The continuation to bar 20 is regular in phrase structure, allowing scales and arpeggios to establish the dominant and tonic securely. The transition (bar 21) contains the first modification of the main theme, when the F and E of the fourth and fifth bars are harmonized with diminished rather than secondary dominant harmony. The semiquaver scales now provide an affirmation of the dominant of G, in preparation for the principal second subject. The comfortable, chattering quaver accompaniment and the diatonic, tonic-dominant harmony of this theme are undermined by a phrase structure that perversely avoids the four-bar; equally perversely, the theme never reaches an unequivocally resolved cadence. It is this passage of cadence avoidance that leads to a new feature in Haydn's quartets and his music in general: the harmonic digression from the principal key. As a set the op. 50 quartets are harmonically more sophisticated than any previous set, particularly in the use of secondary dominant harmony. Perhaps it was the close reading of Mozart's quartets that encouraged this widening of the harmonic spectrum; certainly there are some passages, such as the harmonization of the descending chromatic line in the minuet of no. 1, that demonstrate the influence unequivocally. Harmonic digression during the course of the exposition – in the phrase so often used by Tovey, 'the purple patch' – is a feature of the first movements of Mozart's A major quartet (K. 484) and the 'Hoffmeister' quartet (K. 499), but when Haydn uses the device the results are usually quite un-Mozartian – compressed and insecure rather than colourful and relaxed. In op. 50 no. 2 a consonant D natural becomes a dissonant D sharp, which is enharmonically altered to a consonant E flat, leading the music first to A flat and then to F minor. The thematic material of this digression refers back, almost casually, to the transition. To re-establish the tonic of G major and to return the music to its predominant forthright mood, the second theme of the second subject takes the form of a repetition of the first subject, fully scored and firmly anchored to a tonic pedal. The theme is played by the second violin, another new feature of op. 50 that may derive from Mozart (thematic statements in Mozart's mature quartets, particularly second subjects, are often led by the second violin).

The development has two stages: an intense exploration of the first subject, and a more relaxed presentation of the transition and second subject material. Polyphony features in the first stage as the first subject is accompanied by a new countersubject, each instrument entering in turn. From bar 132 the theme is treated in inversion, the chromatic harmony and the plethora of entries producing a dense texture; it is in passages like this that the Classical style sowed the seeds of its own destruction. The second stage of the development is harmonically stable, preparing for a statement of the first phrase of the second subject in A minor, then in F major. Using the motif of the turn from this theme, the music then moves towards the dominant of C for the recapitulation. In the recapitulation the first and second subject areas are presented verbatim so as to accommodate the new development that takes place in the transition. Rather than the transition, twenty-two bars in length, that had begun as a counterstatement and concluded with routine preparation, the recapitulation has an entirely new paragraph. Twenty-nine bars long, it consists of overlapping statements of the first subject in paired entries, initially in its original guise and then in inversion; a *calando* marking and two pauses are needed to restore equilibrium.

The principal second subject in the first movement shows how easily Haydn's sense of drama can now accommodate the simple and the apparently offhand. Profundity is certainly the last word to describe the slow movement, which emerges as a parody of a serenade. Thirty years earlier, Haydn would have disdained the plodding accompaniments and the short-breathed phrases. Here, fortified by the experience of writing slow operatic arias, they produce an ironic interlude in the middle of so much cerebration.

The third movement, a minuet and trio, is, once again, a tough one, testing accepted premises of musical continuity and structure in a manner suggestive of Beethoven in his keyboard bagatelles. The Menuet extends the usual three stages of its structure – theme to double bar, development and restatement – to four by adding an eighteen-bar coda. The reason for this extension is to be found in the tonal course charted by the movement. The texture is completely free of padding, each phrase beginning with a single line joined by chromatic harmony to articulate a cadence; the cadence at the double bar is in C major. After the double bar the music moves to D minor and reaches a harmonic and rhythmic cul-de-sac at bars 18 and 19. Another five bars of D minor lead directly into the repetition of the main theme in C major. Thus, in a C major movement, the only other key which has been established is D minor and the absence of any preparation for the return of the tonic makes the reprise of the theme an unsettled one. What Haydn does, in effect, is to have a double reprise: the first concluding with an interrupted cadence, the second (led by the violin) being heard over a dominant pedal in order to secure C major. The trio, likewise, avoids formal conventions but with an added touch of humour. Its thematic material, a rising C major arpeggio, is obviously derived from the minuet; the first section presents the material in the form of a dialogue between the violins over stepwise descending harmony. After the double bar, as if to emphasize the lack of tonal preparation in the minuet, the material rests securely on a dominant chord. But beware; when Haydn is apparently at his most naive he is often also at his most resourceful, and here – instead of the routine reprise – there is a new, farcical chain of events, two false starts (one *forte*, the other *piano*), a silent bar, a third beginning led by the cello, and, finally, an eight-bar 'reprise', except that the dialogue is now heard above a stepwise ascending bass rather than descending. Whereas the minuet had dealt with the problem of a tonally insecure reprise, the trio does the opposite, overcoming a preparation that was too secure.

In the absence of an emotionally committed slow movement, the minuet provides the turning point in the work, the minuet itself referring back to the serious-minded first movement, the trio anticipating the light-hearted energy of the finale. Marked Vivace assai, the last movement is a sonata form of incessant bravura, involving all four players in fast-moving repartee covering the total span of the ensemble, from the bottom C of the cello to a climactic top C, five octaves higher. Most of the thematic material of the movement can be traced back to the first two bars.

Finale: Vivace assai

Indeed, the cello figure 'z' is already a derivation of 'x'. Two later manifestations of the material are given in bars 50 ff. and 104 ff. (shown opposite).

Harmonic and tonal surprises would be out of place in this fast-moving music, and the wide-ranging modulation pattern of the development is held firmly in place by conventional preparation and departure. In this helter-skelter movement

a well-placed secondary theme (the second theme of the second subject area) provides the only element of contrast:

The individual character of the C major quartet is by no means unique in the
op. 50 set, the F sharp minor quartet, for instance, inhabiting a very different
world, ultimately one of impersonal pathos. Uniqueness is a clear sign of artistic
maturity and, though features like the wider harmonic vocabulary owe something
to Mozart, the end result is completely unlike anything in Mozart. Typically, in
Haydn's music of this period, harmonic sophistication does not produce melancholy, but reinforces the sinewy textures. This quartet occupies a world of forceful
argument, parody, wit and bravura and, significantly, the kernel of the work is not
a soulful slow movement but a thought-provoking minuet.

Haydn's next set of quartets was composed a year after op. 50, probably during
the summer and autumn of 1788. Johann Tost, the leader of the second violins at
the Esterházy court, was entrusted with securing their publication in Paris, where
they appeared in June 1789 under the Sieber imprint. However, the frequent assertion that Tost was their dedicatee cannot be traced further back than Aloys Fuchs's
catalogue of Haydn's music compiled in the early nineteenth century; it was probably a mistake occasioned by the fact that Tost was the dedicatee of op. 64. The
Sieber publication divided the six works into two sets of three each, op. 54
(III:57–9) and op. 55 (III:60–2), as did the subsequent Artaria publication in Vienna
with which Haydn was directly involved, and that by Longman & Broderip in London. Though the six works were composed in a matter of months and conceived as
a group, their publication in two parts is possibly an indication by the composer
and his two publishers of the unparalleled variety of approaches found within

these six quartets, which have less in common with each other than any other set of six works by the composer, an early instance of that individuality which was to lead to the eventual demise of the concept of a set of six. In the late 1780s Paris was still the music-publishing centre of Europe and Haydn may have composed opp. 54/55 in a deliberately diverse manner in order to capture the attention of the receptive French market. The parallel with the 'Paris' symphonies is a suggestive one; they, too, are strongly individual works intended to impress the Paris public with the range of Haydn's abilities. A month after the publication of opp. 54/55 in Paris, the Bastille was stormed, a single event that unleashed the pent-up forces of the French Revolution. For Haydn, still at Eszterháza, it meant the French capital was no longer the allurement it had been. *Zeitgeist* theories often encourage opportunist remarks of the most irresponsible kind, and writers on Mozart and the French Revolution have usually restricted themselves to misunderstanding the revolutionary aspect of *Le nozze di Figaro*. In Haydn's case commentators have been more cautious, perhaps unnecessarily so, since no one could deny that there is, for instance, in the C major and F minor quartets, op. 54 no. 2 and op. 55 no. 2, a new dramatic urgency, all the more powerful for being articulated by four single players. The sources of that idiom form the principal preoccupation of the present discussion; the way that idiom suggests the spirit of the time is an indication of Haydn's stature as an artist.

The C major quartet is the fourth in a distinguished series of quartets in this key by Haydn, and the third to be composed within eight years. Like its two immediate predecessors, its opening has tremendous thrust, with two balancing five-bar phrases separated by a general pause; following a second general pause, the music explodes into A flat major and the third clause of the first subject. In the recapitulation Haydn deflates the abruptness of this opening by filling in the general pauses with *pianissimo* crotchets in the first violin. But despite this gesture, the turbulent energy of this opening movement is not to be subdued until the finale. The second movement is a dark Adagio in C minor, in which the melody is smothered with rhapsodic decoration by the first violin (decorative descant writing for the first violin is a recurring feature in opp. 54/55) and the movement moves directly into the Menuetto, an elision between movements last employed in op. 20. The C major minuet encloses a C minor trio that is an anguished compression of the material of the minuet. All this intensity and power are then distilled in the finale, which is not the C major, 2/4 movement in a brisk tempo that might be expected, but another Adagio in which a gentle melodic line is heard over the simplest of accompaniments, a movement of touching simplicity which, had it been late Beethoven, would have been labelled 'cantante e tranquillo'; a Presto interruption suggests a conventional unbuttoned ending, but the Adagio returns to form the most appropriate resolution to this spellbinding work.

Another re-thinking of the conventions of emotional balance and movement types occurs in op. 55 no. 2, the so-called 'Razor' quartet.[11] For the first time in Haydn's quartets the composer interchanges the position of slow movement and first movement in a four-movement scheme (a design last used by him in a symphony twenty years previous – in no. 49, 'La passione'), though the formally more varied keyboard sonatas and trios of the time, which often begin with a slow movement, would have reminded Haydn of the scheme. The probable reason for the use of this plan in this quartet may be sought in the construction of the slow movement itself: an imposing set of variations on two alternating themes in F minor and major, the second theme being a paraphrase of the first. While variations on alternating themes, one in the major and one in the minor, had been a long-standing resource, the deriving of the second theme from the first represents the final element of sophistication; the slow movement of Symphony no. 82 (1786) anticipates this unified approach without achieving the same overall sense of cohesion. Moreover, the quartet movement has a definable harmonic relationship with the following Allegro, of a type rarely encountered in contemporary sonatas and trios; whereas in Symphony no. 49 the relationship had been motivic, here it is primarily harmonic. The melodic peak of the F minor theme is a D flat, harmonized with a Neapolitan chord that is maintained for the following two bars; in the Allegro the gruff sixteen-bar first subject is followed by a counter-statement on the Neapolitan G flat major, one of the many stark contrasts of tonality in this movement.[12] As in most of Haydn's quartets in a minor key from the very earliest in op. 9, the recapitulation is highly compressed, thirty-six bars instead of seventy-six; less usually, it is in the tonic major throughout, the major key and the preceding lengthy dominant preparation being sufficient to quell the harmonic rigours of the exposition and development. The remaining movements, too, reflect the influence of the first: minuet in F major, trio in F minor, and a sonata-form finale in F major.

Although the force and energy of the C major and F minor quartets make them the most commanding works in the set, other quartets, whose demeanour seems placid in comparison, also contain many innovations. It might seem strange to call the octave writing of the minuet of op. 54 no. 3 an innovation, but this is a scoring Haydn had not employed since its scandalous first appearance in the very earliest quartets; from op. 54/55 onwards octave scoring in minuets is rediscovered, and is used to impart definition to other movements as well. In op. 55 no. 1 the slow movement contains as part of its thematic material a written-out cadenza, heralded in the customary fashion by a six-four chord and concluded by a trill on the dominant, an attractive feature perhaps suggested by the quartets of Vanhal, in which it is common. In the rondo finale of the same work, the first reprise of the main theme in fast-moving quavers is accompanied by two new contrapuntal lines, providing a texture reminiscent of that exploited in the baryton trios and the op. 20 quartets.

Perhaps for the first time since op. 17, Haydn's next and final set of quartets of the decade shows more consolidation than new features. Op. 64 (III:63–8), his third set of quartets in four years, was composed in 1790 and dedicated to Johann Tost. Haydn was at work on the set in the autumn of that year, and László Somfai has suggested that the stronger profile of the last two works, the 'Lark' and no. 6 in E flat major, is attributable to the composer's swiftly changing circumstances occasioned by the death of Prince Nicolaus, the arrival of Salomon and the hastily arranged trip to London.[13] Certainly, after the works had been performed in the Hanover Square Rooms in 1791, Haydn placed these two quartets at the beginning of the publication by Bland in 1792. Meanwhile, the set had been published in Vienna by the new firm, Magazin de Musique, and it was this publication that established the now familiar order.

In addition to lacking the obvious innovations of the previous sets, the works of op. 64 withdraw from the forceful, almost expressionist world encountered in opp. 50 and 54/55. The works are certainly not introverted, neither are they unimaginative, but there is an easy-going amiability and a marked tendency to re-examine and re-use old ideas. Op. 64 no. 2, in B minor, like its great predecessor, op. 33 no. 1, begins with the first violin as if it were going to be in D major and only when the other instruments enter is it clear that the quartet is going to be in B minor. The movement has the tempo marking of Allegro Spiritoso and, as in all

Haydn quartets that begin with a brisk first movement, the slow movement comes second. In this Adagio ma non troppo in B major, the continuous sound of stopped strings creates a warm sonority that contrasts with the sharply etched sonority of the first movement. Haydn feared that the slow-moving Alberti figuration of the second violin part presented particular problems for the player and wrote in the autograph 'In quest' Adagio raccomando al Violino Secondo una bona e sicura intonazione' ('In this Adagio I recommend good and secure intonation to the second violin'). The principle of the movement is that of variations, but not of the regular kind; within the binary theme repeats of phrases are themselves written out and varied and when large-scale repetition occurs (bar 35 onwards and bar 69 onwards), these internal repeats are omitted. The thematic material itself is consistently marked by the use of a four-note motif in a manner which Haydn had first deployed in fast movements of symphonies; indeed the motif is a stock one featuring a falling seventh, as used in the first movement of Symphony no. 3.

The remaining slow movements are more orthodox. That of no. 1, placed third rather than second in the design because the first movement is an Allegro moderato, is a set of strophic variations on an F major theme that encompasses a modulation to the rich key of A flat major; the remaining movements are clear-cut ternary patterns with, normally, some thematic relationship between the sections.

With one exception, the minuet movements of op. 64 continue the general attitude apparent since the scherzos of op. 33: regular phrasing patterns but in a through-composed movement that has the minimum of literal repetition. The spirit of the dance invades the minuet of no. 1, with its octave writing, and of no. 4, with its off-beat accompaniment. The minuet of the B minor work is unusual in that it is the first (with the partial exception of that of op. 54 no. 1) to return to the asymmetric, disruptive phrasing of the scherzos of op. 33. The minuet opens with a five-bar phrase, the extra bar being the third (a repetition of the second). This ear-catching bar then figures prominently in the unpredictable unfolding of the remainder of the minuet: a nine-bar phrase concluding in D major; overlapping two-bar phrases in a concentrated development section; six bars of dominant preparation; an altered reprise of the theme to make a seven-bar phrase; a bar's rest; and, finally, an eight-bar conclusion with harmonic intensification (Neapolitan, augmented sixth, diminished seventh to cadence). The B major trio, in contrast, is as sweet and smooth as a Tokay wine.

The finale movements of the last two quartets to be composed are different from the other four: that of no. 5 ('Lark') is a *moto perpetuo*, two D major sections in a *piano* dynamic enclosing a D minor section in *forte*; the finale of no. 6 is one of only six rondo movements in Haydn's quartets after op. 33.[14] Perhaps these two deliberately 'popular' movements were composed with the London audience in mind. The remaining quartets, nos. 1–4, have Presto movements in duple time, but in sonata form, with less extensively demonstrative first violin parts and, significantly, *piano* or *pianissimo* endings rather than the loud conclusions of nos. 5 and 6. There is too a notable interest in beginning development sections in remote keys; those of the C major and G major quartets both begin in the flat submediant.

Keyboard music (solo and ensemble)

Following the publication by Artaria in 1780 of seven keyboard sonatas, it might have been expected that Haydn would continue to compose and publish solo sonatas for the eager amateur market. The surprising aspect of Haydn's extensive contact with publishers in the 1780s is the dearth of such sonatas; only six original works were composed – a set of three and three single works. However, stimulated by the new publishing opportunities, Haydn renewed his acquaintanceship with the keyboard trio after a break of twenty years, the decade producing fourteen works. The keyboard sonatas and trios composed earlier in the decade are less ambitious than one might have predicted from the 'Auenbrugger' sonatas of 1780, but towards the end of the decade Haydn managed a better balance between the consumer and the questing composer and, even if individual works do not approach the high standards of contemporary quartets and symphonies, they do provide a clear foretaste of the masterly sonatas and trios of the 1790s.

Nothing is known about the history of Sonata no. 53 in E minor (XVI:34), beyond the fact that it was published in London in 1784. The most original movement is the first, a Presto in sonata form in 6/8 time, an unsmiling, precise movement unique in Haydn's output. (Given the unusual atmosphere, many performers cannot resist the obvious temptation of playing the wide bass arpeggios and the parallel sixths in an expansive, Brahmsian manner.) A highly florid Adagio leads directly into a rondo finale. Haydn's next three sonatas, nos. 54–56 (XVI:40–2), were published as a set in the same year – 1784 – and dedicated to Princess Marie Hermenegild Esterházy (*née* Liechtenstein), recently married at the age of fifteen to Prince Nicolaus's grandson, Count Nicolaus, later Prince Nicolaus II. All three sonatas have two movements only; there is only one movement in sonata form, the opening one of no. 55 which, despite some unexpected harmonic touches, relies too heavily on triplet figuration. More absorbing are the variations movements that open nos. 54 and 56, two of many such movements in sonatas and trios of the 1780s and the testing ground for the opening movement of the quartet, op. 55 no. 2 ('Razor'). Sonata no. 54 alternates major and minor variations, the minor theme itself being a compressed paraphrase of the harmonic progress of the major theme. Though marked 'innocente', like the best soubrettes in *dramma giocoso*, the movement becomes rather less so as it proceeds. The variations in no. 56 are of the strophic variety, on a theme that is twenty bars long and itself prone to rhapsodic impulse.

Five years after the publication of these sonatas, Haydn successfully negotiated with Breitkopf of Leipzig for the publication of a single work, no. 58 in C major (XVI:48), the most impressive sonata of the decade. The first movement is a set of variations on two alternating themes, the second in the minor being a compression of the first; the whole movement makes notable use of dynamic nuances and contrasting keyboard sonorities. The second movement is a rondo, showing the distinct influence of Haydn's symphonic rondos, e.g. in Symphonies nos. 88 and 89. There is the same lightweight beginning before the 'tutti' enters at bar 31, the form ABACA is the same as that used in the rondo of Symphony no. 88; the preparations for the returns of the theme are full of bustling activity and comic suspense; and the piano writing itself does its best to imitate a Haydn orchestra with trumpet punctuation and timpani rolls and high woodwind *pianissimo* anticipations before the return of the theme.

The final sonata of the decade, no. 59 in E flat major (XVI:49), also contains many fine things, but without the same unity of purpose and design; the Finale, marked Tempo di Minuet, is especially disappointing. The autograph manuscript carries a dedication to 'Signora Anna de Jerlischek', that is Maria Anna Gerlischek, housekeeper to Prince Nicolaus and later Johann Tost's wife. But it was another lady, one of great sympathy and sensibility, who occasioned the composition of the work. Maria Anna von Genzinger's intuitive understanding of Haydn's music is well documented in their correspondence (cf. p. 177), and this is the composer's tribute to her. The work has a quiet expansiveness that occasionally suggests more ardent emotions. The long preparation for the recapitulation in the first movement makes telling use of ♩♩♩ | ♪ in different registers, though for modern listeners comparison with the equivalent passage in Beethoven's Fifth Symphony is difficult to suppress.

As well as incorporating variations movements in most of his sonatas and trios, Haydn also composed and published simple sets of variations. Three sets were either composed or first published at the end of the decade; sets in A (formerly G) and E flat both composed in the 1760s and 'VI Variations faciles et agréables' in C major (published in 1791 by Artaria). Haydn also arranged for the Capriccio: 'Acht Sauschneider', composed in 1765, to be published, the renewed familiarity with this early work leading to the composition of a second work in a similarly free rondo pattern. Haydn wrote to Artaria in March 1789 that 'In a moment of most excellent good humour I have written a quite new Capriccio for the pianoforte whose tastefulness, singularity and special construction cannot fail to win applause from connoisseurs and amateurs alike'. When the work was published in September, it carried the title 'Fantesia' [*sic*]. It is a Presto, 3/8 movement of great verve and virtuosity with much of the brilliance of the contemporary C major sonata. As in the 'Acht Sauschneider' work, all the episodic material is derived from the principal theme. The harmonic scheme is of unprecedented daring, incorporating sections in B flat major, E flat major and E flat minor, and on many occasions routine tonal preparations are ironically deflected to remote destinations. The upward-moving chromatic lines in strident octaves that feature in the C major Sonata no. 58 appear again in the unbuttoned coda of the Fantasia, where they are joined by three downward *glissandi* in the right hand (much easier on an eighteenth-century piano than on a modern instrument).

More numerous than solo works for the keyboard are trios for piano, violin and cello, a medium which, apart from one isolated work of *c.* 1772 (no. 17 in F; XV:2), Haydn had ignored for two decades. During that time the piano trio or, more properly, the sonata for the pianoforte with the accompaniment of violin and cello, had become as popular as the solo keyboard sonata itself. Like the sonata, the keyboard trio was aimed at the amateur rather than the professional player, though in the late 1780s and especially in the 1790s the artistry of individuals associated with Haydn's works in these genres encouraged compositions that show little intellectual or technical concession to the limited abilities of the average dilettante.

Accompanied sonatas were especially popular in London where Schroeter, Vento, Ricci and the imported works of Johann Schobert (*c.* 1735–1767), who was active in Paris, had provided the market with a steady supply. It was Haydn's contact with the English publisher William Forster that led him anew to the genre. To follow the successful publication of several symphonies (nos. 70, 74, 77 and 78) Forster requested some piano trios. Haydn subsequently sent Forster three trios, two of which were actually by Pleyel, the authentic work being the Trio in G major, no. 18 (XV:5). Two further sets of three works appeared in London: nos. 19, 20 and 21 (XV:6–8); and nos. 22 (XV:9), 17 (a revised version) and 23 (XV:10). Most of these works were printed in Vienna also, by Artaria and by Hoffmeister.

The market intended is clearly reflected in the brevity of the works; in two or three movements rather than the standard four movements of quartet and symphony. Three works, nos. 18, 19 and 21, conclude with a leisurely Tempo di Menuetto, inappropriate in the more serious or more flamboyant world of quartet or symphony. The sonata forms have little zest for argument and there is considerable reliance on routine accompaniment figuration. The fine opening of no. 23, with its well-judged use of a diminished fifth chord (see below), is, unfortunately, untypical of the bulk of the movement.

The carefully wrought part-writing and the consistent use of the opening motif shows the influence of the composer's quartets; the subsequent lapse into triplet figuration is disappointing even if one admits that the opening had not been especially suited to the medium. The scoring for the string instruments adheres to the accompanied sonata principle and shows no fundamental change of attitude from that exhibited in the trios of the 1750s and 1760s; the cello is firmly wedded to the left hand of the keyboard, while the violin is allowed more independence. In the first movement of Trio no. 22 the three instruments, unusually, are given equal status; in the second movement Haydn returns to normal practice. Whereas in matters of scoring Haydn was for some reason reluctant to stretch the capabilities of the player, in terms of musical content, especially in his well-developed sense of comic incident, there are passages that could not have been composed by anyone else. The development in the first movement of Trio no. 19 in F major establishes a related key, G minor, by a very circuitous route. More provocative is the ternary finale of no. 20 in D major: the middle section ends in the mysteriously remote key of E flat major; E flat becomes a repeated unharmonized D sharp, is absorbed into

the key of B major, whose dominant chord (F sharp major) then provides a mediant preparation for the return of D major.

Four further piano trios date from the end of the decade, a set of three, nos. 24–26 (XV:11–13), published by Artaria in 1789 and a single work, no. 27 in A flat major (XV:14), published by the same firm the following year. Notwithstanding the primitive scoring, these four trios make fewer concessions to the traditional market. The outer movements of no. 25 in E minor demonstrate how passage work can be contained within the rhetoric of the movement rather than debilitating the argument. The rondo, especially, proclaims that a piano texture can be as thrilling as a full orchestra. More distinctive to the keyboard idiom is the number of themes in these trios that begin with arpeggio grace notes, not itself a new feature in Haydn's instrumental writing (especially for violin), but one that imparts a distinct elegance and command to these works.

The tonal and harmonic language of the trios mirrors the new extended boundaries probed in contemporary quartets and symphonies. The second movement of no. 26 is a sonata form (Allegro spiritoso, 3/4) in C major; the recapitulation contains a daring excursion to E flat in the transition, and the coda begins in A flat. The first movement of no. 24 in E flat major, rather like Symphony no. 84, has a *fausse reprise* before embarking on tense further development; the subsequent true recapitulation is compressed to only thirty-five bars, compared with the seventy-five bars of the exposition.

The most telling use of tonal drama, with consequences for the entire work, occurs in Trio no. 27 in A flat. The first subject is twenty-four bars long (see below).
Beautifully proportioned, it has three broad sentences, the symmetry of the first
two broken by *piano* interjections in a quicker harmonic rhythm (bar 5 and bar 11)
and the third sentence divided into two parts by an interrupted cadence. The first
six bars with now different, more argumentative consequences provide material
for the second subject, but it is the manner in which the theme re-appears in the
development that is novel. Following routine preparation on the dominant of
F minor and then B flat minor, a silence of two bars precedes a section in G flat
major based on transition material. G flat major is then treated as the dominant of

C flat major and in its enharmonic equivalent of B major (Haydn changes the key signature) the music launches into an almost complete statement of the lengthy first subject; only halfway through the third sentence does the music veer away from B major and towards further development. After this excursion to distant tonalities, fifteen bars of dominant preparation are needed to re-establish the tonic, preparation that is 'spelt' in G sharp minor. In the recapitulation the second subject version of the main theme is omitted. The Adagio is notated in E major (really F flat major to the A flat of the first movement), the first time in any instrumental genre that Haydn does not choose the opposite mode or a directly related key. Though this colourful choice of key had been presaged in the chain finales of *La fedeltà premiata*, in Haydn's instrumental music it grew naturally out of the extended tonal and harmonic vocabulary of the 1780s, and in this particular Trio from the harmonic adventures of the previous movement. Mediant relationships within and between movements were to fascinate Haydn for the rest of his life, and it was a feature of his style that fired the imagination of the young Beethoven. In Haydn's case it added a new sense of colour and drama to his music that complemented and sometimes interacted with more traditional relationships.

The slow movement, in E major, of Trio no. 27 itself is a ternary pattern with a middle section in E minor; the final section moves towards the dominant chord of G sharp minor in an 'attacca subito' preparation for the rondo in A flat, thus repeating the tonal preparation for the recapitulation in the first movement.

In 1790 Haydn also composed three trios for piano, flute and cello (nos. 28-30; XV:16, 15, 17) for the London publisher, John Bland. Far less absorbing than the contemporary A flat trio (no. 27), they are, nevertheless, works of charm and finesse, especially rewarding for the flute, an instrument for which, from Symphony no. 6 ('Le matin') through the operas to the late oratorios, Haydn always wrote with particular sympathy. The Andantino più tosto Allegretto of the D major trio is the last of three distinctive siciliano movements in D minor composed by Haydn in this decade, the others being found in Piano Trio no. 20 and, the greatest of them all, in the quartet, op. 50 no. 6; all three bear a cousinly resemblance to the finale of Mozart's quartet in that key (K.421), itself suggested by the finale of Haydn's op. 33 no. 5 in G.

Miscellaneous orchestral music

During the 1770s and 1780s Haydn composed copious quantities of dance music, much of it to be played at Eisenstadt and Eszterháza and much of it now lost. Performances are known to have taken place also in Vienna and Pressburg and, further, there is documentary evidence that Haydn composed dance music for the Countess-Duchess of Benavente and Osuna (Madrid) and for Prince Krafft Ernst Oettingen-Wallerstein. The commissioned dances are, unfortunately, among the many lost sets of dances composed by Haydn. Of the four sets that have survived two were published by Artaria in the mid–1780s: 'A collection of ballroom minuets' (*Raccolta de Menuetti Ballabili*; IX:7) and Six Allemandes (IX:9). While providing the occasional foretaste of the minuets of the 'Paris' symphonies, they lack the melodic appeal as well as the sophistication of the symphonic minuets. Interestingly, the keys of the Six Allemandes are ordered in a sequence of descending thirds (B flat, G, E flat, C, A and then a fall of a fifth to D), a colourful procession that was to feature in future sets of dances by Haydn.

At the beginning of the 1780s Haydn composed two concertos, his first essays in the genre for nearly twenty years, the Cello Concerto in D major (VIIb:2), the autograph of which was dated 1783, and the Piano Concerto (XVIII:11), also in D major, first published by Artaria in 1784. The latter became Haydn's most popular concerto in his lifetime, published by eight firms in five different countries. Its precise date of composition is unknown; recently, on the basis of a contemporary memoir, it has been suggested that it was played by Fräulein von Hartenstein, a pupil of Leopold Koželuch, at a private concert in Vienna on 20 February 1780.[15] The Cello Concerto, on the other hand, is one of the comparatively few instrumental works of the decade directly associated with the Esterházy court; rather unusually, it did not circulate widely. Tradition has it that the concerto was composed for Anton Kraft, the principal of two regular cellists at the court in the 1780s, a tradition which in the nineteenth century led to the belief that it was actually composed by Kraft. Only the rediscovery of Haydn's autograph in 1951 finally scotched this fable. However, this D major work is an uncomfortable composition for the 1780s, displaying, particularly in the first movement, those same misjudgements of dramatic timing that devitalize most of Haydn's early concertos. Compared with the lively first movement of the Piano Concerto, that of the Cello Concerto proceeds laboriously in Allegro moderato, common time (not *alla breve*, as in many contemporary works); the lengthy second ritornello (i.e. before the development) is only one of many longueurs in this movement. The Adagio in A major is more successful: three statements of a main theme, separated by episodes that are extensions or variants of the theme. Yet this movement suffers in a comparison with the Adagio of the Piano Concerto, where rhapsodic decoration adds a feeling of spontaneity absent from the Cello Concerto; the harmonic writing too is more sophisticated in the Piano Concerto. Since Haydn had last composed a concerto, rondo form had become enormously popular with composers and public alike, hence these two works conclude with such movements. The Piano Concerto has a 'Rondo all'Ungarese' whose main theme is based on a dance melody from Bosnia and Dalmatia; drone accompaniments, syncopations, *acciaccature* and swirling trills feature throughout. The rondo of the Cello Concerto does not have this prior advantage of a distinct atmosphere and, in comparison, sounds staid and melodically short-winded.

The Cello Concerto is unique in Haydn's instrumental music of the 1780s (with the understandable exception of the lira organizzata works discussed below) in that it was not published soon after its composition (in fact only after twenty years). Part of the reason for this is that cello concertos had a much more restricted market than did concertos for piano or violin, not to mention symphonies and quartets. Even so, given Haydn's stature as a composer and his knowledge of the publishing industry, he could surely have arranged for its publication. Perhaps he recognized the work's weaknesses. The autograph clearly states Haydn to be the composer (the usual signature 'di me giuseppe Haydn mp. 7̄8̄3'), but there may be more to the attribution to Kraft than can be settled definitively by reference to the autograph. Earlier in his career, sometime in the period 1773–6, Haydn is alleged to have assisted Krumpholtz, then a harp player at the Esterházy court, in the composition of ritornellos for a harp concerto (his op. 6 no. 2) and this practice of an experienced composer helping a performer-composer fashion a concerto is mentioned too in Adalbert Gyrowetz's autobiography.[16] At the very least, Kraft would have advised Haydn on the practicalities of the solo part, and possibly his contribution was even more extensive, perhaps including the basic thematic material.

Works for lira organizzata

In 1786, one of the busiest years in Haydn's long career, he received a strange commission from Ferdinand IV, King of Naples, one of the most eccentric and colourful monarchs of the time. He was a Bourbon, and his wife, Maria Carolina, was the daughter of the Empress Maria Theresa, but neither the king's ancestry nor his marriage could explain his strange social behaviour which was at best embarrassing, at worst uncouth. Ferdinand, however, was not unkind or despotic and was genuinely loved by his subjects; the fact that he learned to play one of their instruments, the *lira organizzata*, was a reflection of his eccentricity and sociability and not – as in the case of Marie Antoinette and her farm – an act of self-conscious escapism; this particular king happened to be a *lazzarone*. The *lira organizzata* was developed from the hurdy-gurdy and, when activated by a keyboard and a revolving wheel, could emit four types of sound simultaneously: a melody from a row of small wooden pipes, a melody from stopped strings, a drone string bass and, finally, several freely vibrating sympathetic strings. The strings and pipes could be uncoupled and played alone. Its complicated mechanism meant that it could be played in only three keys, C, F and G. In the period 1786–7 it is thought that Haydn composed six concertos for two *lire*, two horns, two violins, two violas and cello, of which five have survived (VIIh:1–5). They were, apparently, well received by Ferdinand and were followed in the period 1788–90 by nine Notturni, of which eight (II:25–32) have survived, scored for two *lire*, two clarinets in C (violins in II:27), two horns, two violas and 'basso' (cello and/or double bass). It might have been thought that at this stage in his career Haydn would have had little desire to compose fifteen works for a musically limited instrument to be played in a distant part of Europe. No financial details of the commission are known, but even if the rewards were negligible, Haydn may have felt that cultivating this contact with Naples would provide him with an opportunity to travel to Italy; but, following Prince Nicolaus's death in September 1790, Haydn's other foreign contacts were to provide him with more attractive proposals.

Haydn probably never heard the *lira organizzata* and the works restrict themselves to notating the melodic line, though the occasional drone passage in the accompaniment – a general stylistic development in Haydn's music in the 1780s (e.g. Piano Concerto in D and Symphony no. 82) – is an appropriate complement to the leading instrument. All the works are in the available keys of C, F or G, with slow movements in the subdominant, dominant or the same tonic major. Development sections and episodes in rondos are similarly limited in their modulation, the former, particularly in the concertos, being very brief in comparison with contemporary instrumental music, and the latter, in the extreme case of the rondo of the first concerto (VIIh:1), restricting themselves to the tonic minor and major. It is difficult to be categorical about whether these works should be played with one player per part or orchestrally. The title 'concerto' for the first five extant works and the frequent repeated quaver accompaniment suggest a small orchestra, but the extant parts are unusually specific in denoting only cello for the bass part; the Notturni, on the other hand, display a more varied texture and less dependence on orchestral figuration, suggesting that perhaps Haydn had a large chamber ensemble in mind. That both sets of works can be played soloistically or orchestrally is an appropriate indication of their content; they possess neither the rhetoric and flamboyance of contemporary symphonies nor the intricate argument of the quartets and certain sonatas and trios.

The first movements of the concertos avoid the large unwieldy ritornello structures of Haydn's previous works with that title; the brisk tempos, the amiability of the melodic material and the persistence of repeated quaver figuration in the bass ensure that the works do not have the stolid quality of earlier concertos. The two *lire* usually duet in thirds or sixths, or answer each other in close dialogue. Concerto no. 5, the second of the F major works, opens with a theme based on the same motif that Haydn had used in the finale of Symphony no. 3, but, unlike that symphony and later allegro movements with prominent rhythmic contours, this concerto movement makes little attempt to unify its progress through persistent use of the motif, which indeed, makes only one further appearance, in the concluding ritornello of the movement. This, by the way, is the only concerto not to have a cadenza before the final ritornello.

Three of the extant concertos have andante slow movements in siciliano style, rather like the slow movement of Symphony no. 84. Also indebted to a contemporary symphony is the slow movement of concerto VIIh:3 which, like Symphony no. 85 (see p. 221), is a sectional Romance (*Romanze* in the symphony) in *alla breve* time. The Adagio ma non troppo of VIIh:2 is a transcription of Haydn's Cavatina, 'Sono Alcina', composed as an insertion aria for Gazzaniga's opera *L'isola d'Alcina*, revived at Eszterháza in 1786. With the exception of VIIh:3, which has a finale marked Tempo di menuetto, the Notturni have lively rondos whose principal subjects often recall the 'Paris' symphonies, but whose subsequent treatment does not exhibit the same élan as those works. The second episode in the finale of VIIh:1 takes the form of another cavatina for *lire* and strings and is possibly another transcription from an opera, so far untraced.

Seven of the eight extant Notturni are likewise in three movements, the first in the set (II:25) having an additional prefatory *Marcia*, and cavatina-type slow movements and rondo finales again feature. The most fundamental difference between the concertos and the *Notturni* lies in the allegro first movements which are sonata forms, encouraging the greater instrumental interplay (usually between pairs of instruments) found in these works. Equally absorbing is the wider harmonic palette of these works, which in allegro and slow movements shows a repeated fondness for deflections onto the flattened submediant. Perhaps the least expected movement is the finale of no. 5 (II:29), a *Fuga* on two subjects, a texture Haydn had not employed in his instrumental music for nearly a decade; the fugal texture is maintained throughout the movement and is composed against the background of sonata form without, however, allowing the inherent drama of that form to figure.

Clearly in Haydn's total output the works for *lire organizzate* occupy a position analogous to that of the baryton music. But the analogy is not a complete one, for in the case of the works for *lire* Haydn borrowed extensively from them for later compositions; together with the unrevived opera *Il mondo della luna*, they constitute the main source of Haydn's self-borrowing. The slow movement and the finale of concerto VIIh:5 provided material for the equivalent movements of Symphony no. 89; the Romance of VIIh:3 found a spectacular home as the slow movement of the 'Military' Symphony (where the heading is understandably dropped); and most (possibly all) of the Notturni were revised for performance in London during the composer's first visit, when the *lira* parts were entrusted to flute and oboe and the clarinet parts to violins.

Symphonies

Apart from the Cello Concerto, all Haydn's instrumental music considered thus far in this chapter owed its composition to the composer's contact with the outside world. A similar situation exists in the case of the symphonies. Up to the 1780s, over seventy symphonies had been composed for performance at the Morzin and Esterházy courts. All circulated freely in manuscript copies in the Austrian Empire (and occasionally beyond) and most were published in Paris and Amsterdam; Haydn derived little or no income from this wider distribution. In the 1780s the position was completely reversed. Of the nineteen symphonies composed, only five were for the Esterházy court; the remainder were composed for London and Paris, with a tight rein kept on commission fees and publication opportunities. The outstanding characteristic of Haydn's symphonic output in the 1780s is the way it responds to this imaginary public at large; the six 'Paris' symphonies and nos. 88 and 92 are not courtly or monastic works played for the enjoyment of only a handful of onlookers, but works of grandeur composed for large orchestras and a mass audience. Public concert life in Vienna in the 1780s lagged behind that of London and Paris and few performances of Haydn symphonies are known to have been given in that city. The stimulus to the composer's creativity came solely from reports of those musicians who had travelled to more distant cities. The products were several symphonies that represent a distinct peak in the development of the genre; less idiosyncratic, perhaps, but more powerful than the symphonies of the early 1770s, they, together with Mozart's 'Prague' (K.504) and his last three symphonies (K.543, 550 and 551) constitute the fulfilment of some sixty years of development. In the process the symphony had made the critical move from exclusive palace or monastery to the public concert hall, which would be the setting for its future development.

Perhaps the first symphony of the decade is no. 73 in D major, a work with trumpets and drums. Haydn's last D major symphony had been no. 70 with its strange juxtaposition of severe D minor counterpoint and D major jollity. No. 73, composed before 1782, is a less ambitious work. The finale consists of the overture to *La fedeltà premiata*, now given the title 'La Chasse', an instance of re-using instrumental music from his operas that may have prompted the revision and publication of the six overtures by Artaria in 1786;[17] the slow movement is an adaptation of the simple 2/4 tune of the contemporary Lied, 'Gegenliebe' ('Mutual love'). The first movement is rather more thought-provoking in that its first subject consistently avoids beginning on the tonic (or dominant) chord, the three-quaver anacrusis figure being used in the development section to channel the music towards unpredictable goals. The potential offered by an off-key beginning may owe something to the recently completed quartet, op. 33 no. 1, and it is a resource that Haydn was to turn to again not only in the quartet genre, but also in the symphonies, e.g. nos. 81 in G and 86 in D.

No. 81 is one of three further symphonies that Haydn wrote initially for the Esterházy court, the others being nos. 79 and 80; Haydn arranged the publication of all three by Forster of London and by Artaria of Vienna. Like no. 73, these symphonies contain many agreeable passages but without the sense of a commanding personality. Listeners will be intrigued by the glimpses of the future glories of Haydn's 'Paris' and other symphonies: the rondo finale of no. 79, with its main theme doubled by bassoon; the rhetorical opening of no. 80 in D minor which, like Haydn's next symphony in the minor, no. 83 ('La poule'), makes dramatic use of silence; and the Andante of no. 81, in which the theme is doubled at the octave by the flute, reflecting its source in Haydn's operas and foreshadowing its final autumnal flowering in the slow movement of the 'Oxford' Symphony (no. 92). The symphonies also contain characterful features intrinsic to each particular work. For instance, in the first movement of no. 80 the tension is relaxed in a last-minute second subject, which sets out to be two balancing four-bar phrases but perversely manages a total of only seven. A silence of two bars follows the exposition before the same theme launches the development in, of all keys, D flat major. Only at the end of the recapitulation is the theme allowed to become two balancing four-bar phrases.

Symphonies nos. 76, 77 and 78 were written in preparation for Haydn's planned visit to London in 1783. Though the visit never came about, the symphonies were published in that city by Forster, continuing a business relationship that had already been flourishing for two years. Haydn sold the symphonies also to the Paris publisher, Boyer, and it is in a letter to Boyer that the following remarks occur: 'Last year I composed three beautiful, elegant and by no means over-lengthy symphonies, scored for 2 violins, viola, basso, 2 horns, 2 oboes, 1 flute and 1 bassoon [*recte*, 2 bassoons] – but they are all very easy, and without too much *concertante* for the English gentlemen, and I intended to bring them over myself and produce them there ...'

Indeed *concertante* parts are rare in these three symphonies and nearly all wind solos, such as the ones in the finale of no. 78, are doubled by the strings. In this respect Haydn was being unnecessarily cautious, for the London wind players – as Haydn's later symphonies were to demonstrate – were the equal of any. It is not known whether anyone such as General Charles Jerningham, British ambassador to the Court in Vienna, or the impresario Sir John Gallini (who visited Vienna in 1786) advised Haydn on English taste, but it seems unlikely. These symphonies are all in Haydn's customary four movements, whereas the symphonies of J. C. Bach and others then writing for London audiences show an overwhelming preference for three. The harmonic rhythm of the first movement of no. 76 is unusually leisurely for Haydn and recalls J. C. Bach's Symphony in E flat (op. 9 no. 2), yet the moment in the development (bar 105) when a *pianissimo* A flat major chord is approached as the dominant of D flat and quitted as the subdominant of E flat is something that would never have occurred to the elegant London Bach. Minor-key symphonies were rarely heard in the London of J. C. Bach and Carl Friedrich Abel: Haydn's own *Sturm und Drang* symphonies arrived there ten years after their composition, Bach composed only one symphony in the minor and Abel none. Thus, no. 78 in C minor would have come as something of a shock to English audiences; the first movement is a notable precursor of *the* London Symphony in C minor, no. 95, composed a decade later. However, the remainder of the symphony fails to provide a convincing integration of its diverse moods, the C major Menuetto and the conclusion to the rondo Finale being gratuitously joyful. Attractive though these symphonies are, they do not begin to match the supreme quality of the works he was to compose for Paris. It was with these symphonies, begun in 1785, that the genre returned to centre stage in Haydn's output, a position it was to maintain for the next ten years.

The commission for six symphonies came from the Concert de la Loge 'Olympique' in the winter of 1784–5 and Haydn composed nos. 83, 87 and possibly 85 in 1785, and nos. 82, 84 and 86 in 1786; the first performances of all six took place in 1787. The oldest concert-giving body in Paris was the Concert Spirituel, in whose programmes Haydn's name had figured regularly since 1778; as well as his symphonies, the Stabat Mater was frequently performed. From 1769 to 1781 this body had been rivalled by the Concert des Amateurs, under the direction of F. J. Gossec and then of Joseph Boulogne de Saint-Georges. In January 1781, probably because of financial difficulties, the Concert des Amateurs was dissolved and its place as a rival to the Concert Spirituel was taken by two organizations, the Société du Concert de l'Emulation and, more important, the Concert de la Loge 'Olympique'. Promoted under the aegis of a Freemasons' lodge and directed by Saint-Georges, the concerts were first held in the lodge's own premises, but their popularity was such that from 1786 they were held in the guard room at the Palais des Tuileries. The Concert de la Loge 'Olympique' systematically gathered together the best players in Paris, allowing them to become nominal members of the Freemasons' craft. The size of the orchestra is not known, but it is unlikely to have been less than its predecessors and rivals. In 1785 that of the Concert Spirituel numbered fifty-seven players, and Michel Brenet notes that the Concert des Amateurs had consisted of forty violins, twelve cellos, eight basses and the usual complement of wind instruments.[18] Paris had established a tradition of forceful and elegant orchestral playing nurtured by the enthusiasm of the audience and the virtuosity of the players and, though Mozart had in 1778 been caustically dismissive of their vaunted abilities, there is no doubt that Parisian orchestras were amongst the very best in Europe in the 1770s and 1780s. For the recently established Concert de la Loge 'Olympique' the commissioning of symphonies from Europe's leading composer was a sure way of establishing primacy over its rival, the Concert Spirituel, and it is an indication of the desire as well as the wealth of the organization that they agreed to pay Haydn 25 louis d'or per symphony (compared with the 5 louis d'or which Mozart had reported was the normal fee for a symphony in 1778). Haydn more than repaid their artistic judgment and financial investment.

No correspondence between Haydn and the Concert de la Loge 'Olympique' has survived and there is no way of knowing whether the Parisians gave Haydn any indication of duration or character for his symphonies. Haydn would have heard plenty of reports of Parisian musical taste from musicians who had visited the city, including Mozart. For his symphony for the French capital Mozart had composed a three-movement work (K.297) for the full available forces of double wind (including clarinets), timpani and strings. Three-movement symphonies were as common in Paris as four-movement works, but Haydn probably felt more secure with a four-movement design, especially as his imagination as a composer of minuets was apparently limitless. In terms of instrumental forces, Haydn was reticent; he did not take the opportunity of including clarinets, though he had recently written for them in *Armida* and was soon to write for them in the Notturni for the King of Naples. In the six symphonies Haydn remained content to use the instruments he knew well: one flute (not two), two oboes, two bassoons, two horns and strings plus, in the C and D major works (nos. 82 and 86), two trumpets and timpani.

Three of the 'Paris' symphonies open with a slow introduction, immediately impressing the listener with the depth of sonority found in these works. Some of Haydn's earlier introductions restrict themselves to polite formalities, those in the 'Paris' symphonies have a new sense of power, whether it be due to the slow-moving thematic lines of no. 84 in E flat, the dotted rhythms and scales of no. 85 in B flat or the forceful scales over repeated quavers in no. 86 in D. Perhaps the scales are Haydn's version of the *coup d'archet*, about which Mozart was so cynical but which he nevertheless incorporated to splendid effect in the first subject of his 'Paris' Symphony. Mozart's cynicism pricked Parisian conceit by suggesting that 'They all begin together, just as they do in other places'; in Haydn's case there is no need to look further than the finale of Act I of *La fedeltà premiata* for examples of forceful scale passages. In no. 85 scale passages appear also in the subsequent Vivace, revealing the only slow introduction in the 'Paris' symphonies which foreshadows the thematic content of the ensuing movement. In all three cases the fast movements begin *piano* in a light texture which, particularly in nos. 84 and 85, wryly deflates the grandeur of the introduction. Those symphonies that begin without an introduction have *forte* or *fortissimo* first subjects that are unsurpassed in rhetorical power anywhere in Haydn's symphonic output, including the later London works. That of no. 82 ('L'ours') is divided into three parts: a *fortissimo* C major arpeggio in the manner of a Mannheim rocket; a *piano* consequent phrase, harmonized and scored for strings only; and twelve bars of vigorous *forte* fanfares for the full orchestra. This opening derives its splendour from the long tradition of C major symphonies in Haydn's output – that of no. 56 (p. 148) is close in content – invigorated by the theatricality of the C major arias in his operas; only three years separate *Armida*, with its heroic C major music, from this symphony, and the opera was being regularly performed at the time of no. 82's composition. Symphony no. 56 had been one of Haydn's most popular symphonies in France, being printed by three different publishers. To include this C major work in the commissioned set of six was a typically astute move on Haydn's part; there could be no better instance of the difference in temperament between two great composers, Mozart's 'Paris' Symphony was written with apparent cynicism, Haydn's 'L'ours' to capitalize on established popularity.

Re-invigorating a trusted and favoured style that had already proved popular in Paris is an approach that informs Symphonies nos. 83 and 87, too. The energy of no. 87 in A major, with its repeated-note figuration in the first subject, is reminiscent of that of the 'Feuer-Symphonie' (no. 59), composed in the late 1760s and published in Paris in 1772, though without the edgy nervousness of the earlier work.[19] Symphony no. 83 in G minor takes its stimulus from the minor-key symphonies of *c.* 1770, though again its energy is suited to the concert hall rather than to the

Eszterháza *sala terrena*. The first subject of no. 83 divides into three parts and – like its great predecessor, no. 39, published in Paris in 1773 – includes several stunning silences, but the first subject of no. 83 is declaimed in *fortissimo* rather than a timid *piano* (see example below).

The first four-bar phrase has two figures that generate most of the material of the movement: 'a', a four-note motif (as in many symphonies of the 1770s) with an appoggiatura (C sharp) of searing power as the third note; and 'b', dotted rhythms. The sense of spaciousness which Haydn's music has acquired through his extensive contact with opera is revealed in the controlled manner in which bars 12–16 reduce the tension of the opening: 'a' produces further harmonic asperity in the transition as it moves to establish B flat major.

In comparison with his contemporaries, Haydn often surprises the listener with the content of the second subject, and the 'Paris' symphonies offer a representative sample of this variety. Nos. 84, 86 and 87 return to re-investigate their first subjects, whereas no. 85 in B flat daringly thrusts the listener from the dominant of F major into F minor and a direct quotation from the 'Farewell' Symphony (published in Paris in 1775). No. 83 in G minor, like no. 82, has a new idea, far more lightweight than Haydn would have allowed himself in previous years, but which is masterfully brought into the orbit of the first subject by the dotted-note accompaniment heard during its repetition. The 'clucking' oboe encouraged the French in the nineteenth century to apply the nickname 'La poule' to the symphony, an instance of the public patronizing Haydn's whimsy without recognizing its latent symphonic power.

In the development section of no. 83's first movement modified statements of the first and second subjects precede an exploration of 'a': a new running counterpoint is provided, and Haydn occasionally avoids a dissonant third note, as hitherto, by supplying a consonant secondary dominant harmony. The preparation for the recapitulation shows a new aspect of Haydn's symphonic language, a distancing of perspective before the recapitulation returns the listener to the predominant mood. This control of aural perspective, incorporating the relaxed in order to project the urgent, is another feature that can be related to Haydn's experience in the opera house. The recapitulation of no. 83 moves to G major at the beginning of the transition without diluting the overall power of the movement. The coda, for the first time in the movement, modifies the third note of 'a' from C sharp to D sharp and another, slight, distancing of perspective occurs before the *forte* cadence theme.

When Mozart composed his 'Paris' Symphony, he – on his own admission – misjudged Parisian taste in the slow movement and was persuaded to substitute a new one. Haydn, again, manages to cultivate his audience without any condescension, using variations movements in three of the symphonies. The theme of no. 85 is a French song, 'La gentille et jeune Lisette', a pretty Allegretto theme that is the subject of four decorative variations: the simple, repetitive melodic idiom encouraged Haydn to use for the first time in his career the heading *Romanze*, though in its German rather than French spelling. Variations on tuneful melodies serve as the slow movements of two further symphonies: no. 84, a strophic set but with a free *minore* section; and no. 82, on alternating major and minor themes, the first re-peated verbatim like a rondo theme, the second a paraphrase of the first. The coda of no. 84 includes an ensemble cadenza for the woodwind, probably a deliberate at-tempt to evoke the spirit of the *symphonie concertante*; the feature is found near the end of the slow movement of no. 87 too. The sound of a flute or bassoon doubling the melody at the higher or lower octave respectively occurs regularly in these movements and, though the scoring had been typical since the end of the 1760s, it occurs with particular consistency in the 'Paris' symphonies. The bassoon 'shad-ow', especially, is such a distinctive feature of Haydn's orchestration, imitated in the nineteenth century by Brahms (e.g. in the slow movement of his Second Piano Concerto), that it is worth pondering its origins.

Many concertos by the celebrated flautist and composer Johann Joachim Quantz (1697-1773) contain melodies doubled at the lower octave by bass instru-ments and, apparently, it was a feature of the symphonies of another North Ger-man, Johann Gottlieb Graun (1702/3-1771).[20] But Haydn was more likely to have been acquainted with several Gluck operas of the 1760s, in which the bassoon has an *ad libitum* part, strengthening the vocal line; Haydn's fondness for this tone col-our may well stem from this source. In addition, Haydn would have stumbled on the scoring accidentally. His own early symphonies often included a theme played in octaves between violins and cellos (the slow movement of no. 84 returns to this scoring) and in those works that had *colla parte*, rather than obbligato, bassoon parts the colouring would have arisen naturally.

Symphony no. 86 in D major is a work that has more in common with the later D major symphonies composed for London (nos. 93, 96 and 104) than with its com-panions. The slow introduction and the minuet lend it a thoughtfulness that is alien to nos. 84, 85 and 87. As for the slow movement, given the delicate superficiality of most of the 'Paris' slow movements, it comes as something of a surprise: Largo, rather than Andante or Allegretto, it is a movement of measured eloquence, with a rich harmonic palette. Haydn headed it 'Capriccio', an indication of its unortho-dox form; it gives the impression of a controlled improvisation centred on strate-gic re-appearances of the opening idea with its distinctive *crescendo-decrescendo* swelling of orchestral tone.

One of the fascinating aspects of Haydn's quartets in the 1780s is the way in which the composer manages to bring the minuet up to the same level of sophisti-cation as the surrounding movements without, at the same time, losing sight of the dance. Intricacies of phrasing, ambiguities of harmony and extensive thematic argument such as feature in the quartets are clearly too complex for direct use in the symphony, a lesson Haydn had appreciated from his earliest days. However, the minuets and trios of the 'Paris' symphonies never rely entirely on orchestral grandeur for their effect. The longest and most elaborate Minuet movement is that of no. 86, with ninety bars (sixty-two for the Minuet proper and twenty-eight for the Trio). Two areas of expansion occur in the Minuet: eighteen bars of develop-ment at that point (bar 21) where a reprise of the principal theme would have been expected, and a twelve-bar coda appended to the reprise. At one stage Haydn con-templated placing the Trio in D minor, a further indication of the sense of com-parative gravity of this symphony. Perhaps Haydn felt that this key would have en-couraged the work towards introversion; certainly, the existing D major Trio, with its violin line doubled by bassoon over a pizzicato accompaniment, has a more straightforward demeanour. The shortest and least complicated Minuet is that of no. 84, with a total of only fifty-four bars. The steady flow of four-bar phrases makes it a foot-tapper's delight until shortly after the reprise of the theme, when the flow is cruelly halted by an unexpected silence; the dynamic drops to *piano*, the melody seems unsure of its direction and the phrasing becomes disjointed. A *forte* two-bar phrase concluding with an emphatic cadence regains the former poise. The minuet of no. 86 had been notable for its thematic development and that of no. 84 for its thwarting of expected phrasing patterns. Unexpected tonal events feature in no. 82. The Trio, in C major, is longer by two bars than the Minuet and has the typical lightweight scoring in a *piano* dynamic; a rather solemn pause prepares for the expected reprise of the main theme. What follows, however, is an entirely new melodic paragraph in a rich sounding E flat major, beginning *forte*; eight bars of dominant preparation are then needed to precede the reprise proper in C major.

Given the contemporary popularity of the rondo and the fact that many symphonies by French composers conclude with a movement in that form (e.g. Pleyel's symphonies published by Imbault from 1785 onwards), it is surprising that only one of Haydn's 'Paris' symphonies, no. 85, has a rondo finale.[21] Its scheme could be reduced, brutally, to ABACAB, which has the merit of suggesting a sonata rondo but which obscures the ceaseless flow of the music, its thematic economy and wit. For perhaps the first time in his symphonies Haydn displays that perfect sense of proportion allied to infectious energy that figures in the rondo movements of the op. 33 quartets. The second subject, 'B', is derived from the first bar of 'A', and 'C' is a vigorous development section beginning with a favoured technique, combining the theme with a new running accompaniment, the two parts being subsequently inverted. The paragraphs that prepare for the two returns of 'A' are irresistible, revealing that sense of comic suspense that is part of Haydn's new mastery of perspective in these symphonies: the first return has eight bars of dominant preparation with overlapping thematic entries played by oboe and first violin while the second has eighteen bars of dominant preparation with major ninths (G) turning to minor ninths (G flat), a hushed *pianissimo*, a written-out *ritenuto* and a pause.

The remaining five finales are all high-spirited sonata forms, providing well-judged conclusions to their respective symphonies. No. 86 has a good deal of thematic argument derived from the initial rhythm of ♪♩♩♩ (as in no. 80) and a theatrical deflection from the tonic D major to B flat major in the recapitulation that is entirely unpredictable; no. 82 features a drone bass as the ever-present accompaniment to its first subject, which gave rise to the work's nickname 'L'ours' (i.e. a 'bear' dance), and has the courage to end with an audacious timpani entry, *fortissimo*, against the prevailing *forte*; and the finale of no. 83 is a good-humoured movement in G major, in 12/8 time, whose development section becomes intensely dramatic, an appropriate change of mood back to the beginning of the symphony, ensuring an overall cohesion that had been absent from the two recent minor-key symphonies, nos. 78 and 80. The final movements of nos. 84 and 87 are less strongly profiled than their companions, though the charm of no. 84 is deceptive. Again it is preparatory sections and unexpected events in the recapitulation that produce the sophistication in no. 84. Following a transition that establishes the dominant of B flat with considerable confidence, the music, instead of moving directly into the second subject, is deflected into a passage of slow-moving harmonies in B flat minor, *pianissimo*. This interpolated material recurs at the end of the development, now vastly expanded to provide a new outlook onto the forthcoming recapitulation. The first subject in the recapitulation is affected by this introspection, dwelling *pianissimo* on the concluding phrase.

Haydn followed up the success of the 'Paris' symphonies with five more symphonies between 1787 and 1789. These too have a French connection. The violinist Johann Tost was entrusted with the selling of Symphonies nos. 88 and 89 to a French publisher, and Haydn undeniably had this receptive market in mind when he composed them in 1787. Nos. 90–92 were composed as a group of three works in 1788 and 1789, probably for the Concert de la Loge 'Olympique'; certainly, nos. 91 and 92 (the latter dubbed the 'Oxford' in 1791) were dedicated to Comte d'Ogny who, since 1786, had been a leading member of the Loge 'Olympique'; copies of all three works were simultaneously despatched to Prince Krafft Ernst Oettingen-Wallerstein in order to satisfy that nobleman's desire for three new Haydn symphonies.

Posterity has been right in its selection of two works, nos. 88 and 92, as the best of the five and, along with nos. 83, 85, and 86, they constitute some of the finest examples of the Classical symphony. The remaining symphonies, nos. 89, 90 and 91, are less characterful, often relying on previous works for their inspiration. In no. 89 this is literally the case, since the slow movement and the finale are reworkings of movements from a *lira* concerto in F (VIIh:5). No. 90 in C major shows the particular influence of no. 82 ('L'ours'), as opposed to the generic influence of the C major tradition; the slow movement is a set of alternating variations in F major and minor and the Menuet re-uses the tonal plan of the Trio of no. 82 (i.e. with the digression from C to E flat major). Similarly the influence of no. 84 in E flat can be heard in no. 91 in the same key, in the triple-time slow introduction and in the finale which recalls the first movement of no. 84. Although these symphonies lack the unity of purpose of their predecessors and contemporaries, there are, as always, some individual features that reveal Haydn's perpetually inventive musicianship. The slow movement of no. 91 is a set of strophic variations on a theme in B flat major that includes an idiosyncratic modulation to D flat major (anticipating the similar structure of the theme in the slow movement of the quartet, op. 64 no. 1), and the finale of no. 90 has a boldly restructured recapitulation with quizzical use of unexpected silence and a mosaic display of melodic and rhythmic motifs.

In addition, nos. 88 and 92 contain new features, notably the expressive slow movements, but it is their overall authority that sets them apart. Both are in G major and the first two of a quartet of distinguished symphonies in that key composed by Haydn between 1787 and 1794; indeed, many would say that nos. 88 and 92 possess more durable qualities than the later 'Surprise' and 'Military' Symphonies. It is a curious fact that the nineteenth century saw few attempts at a symphony in the key of G major, and it was not until Dvořák's Eighth Symphony (completed in 1889) that a fifth masterpiece was added to Haydn's four.

Nos. 88 and 92 are both scored for an orchestra of one flute, two oboes, two bassoons, two horns, two trumpets, timpani and strings, and both move towards a witty finale in 2/4 time (rondo in no. 88, sonata form in no. 92); however, their point of departure and subsequent progress heading to á witty finale are very different. No. 88 is a forceful and at times very dramatic work; no. 92, lighter, reflective, yet full of undemonstrative subtleties. The slow introduction to no. 88 is a measured formal preparation for the Allegro movement; that of no. 92, though only four bars longer, seems more eloquent and provides the first instance (second if one includes no. 85) of a slow introduction adumbrating the profile of the first subject of the subsequent allegro; Haydn also increases the harmonic tension between introduction and allegro by concluding the former with an augmented sixth chord, beginning the latter with four bars of dominant and allowing the resolution to the tonic to coincide with the first tutti in bar 5.[22]

For his slow movements Haydn eschews variations in an andante tempo in favour of a Largo in no. 88 and an Adagio in no. 92. Both include trumpets and timpani: in no. 88 they appear for the first time in the slow movement to add weight to the sonorous *fortissimo* interjections that feature amongst the broad sentences of the movement; in no. 92 they reinforce the drama of the contrasting middle section in D minor. The pattern of the slow movement of no. 92 is an easily comprehended ternary one, while that of no. 88 is less stereotyped, everything revolving around statements of the main theme, as in the *Capriccio* of no. 86. The minuet movements follow the customary plan with lighter scoring in the trios contrasting with the full sonority of the embracing minuets; the Trio of no. 92 replaces the expected solo line with a discourse based on a syncopated *sforzando* figure that ruffles the 3/4 pulse, an idea perhaps suggested by a brief passage in the Trio of no. 91 and certainly re-explored in the Trio of the quartet in B flat, op. 64 no. 3, composed the following year. While the ebullience of the two finale movements provides a similar climax to each of these symphonies, it would be a rash person who would suggest that they were interchangeable. This broad plan of seeking various routes to a similar destination was to serve Haydn well in the 'London' symphonies.

Haydn and Mozart

The eleven symphonies that Haydn had composed since 1785 are contemporary with Mozart's final four symphonies, no. 38 in D ('Prague'), no. 39 in E flat major, no. 40 in G minor and no. 41 in C ('Jupiter'). None of these masterpieces was published in Mozart's lifetime, and Paris, in particular, remained ignorant of them until some years after the composer's death. By a cruel quirk of fate, this most travelled of composers, whose musical style was genuinely cosmopolitan, never witnessed international acclaim, whereas Haydn – who had never travelled more than eighty miles from Vienna – had not only fashioned progressive musical taste throughout Europe but was about to reap the benefits of this achievement. When, in the nineteenth century, Mozart's music came to be widely appreciated, Haydn's popularity declined correspondingly: Mozart's last three symphonies were idolized and Haydn's 'Paris' and 'Oxford' symphonies well-nigh forgotten. It has taken nearly two centuries for the public to allow the greatness of both and to recognize their differences. When Mozart was composing his last three symphonies in the summer of 1788, the most recent symphonies by Haydn he could have known would have been nos. 82–87, published in Vienna by Artaria as opp. 51 and 52 in December 1787 (a few weeks before the French edition). For his three works Mozart chose the same keys as the Artaria op. 51 publication (nos. 82–84) – E flat, G minor and C major – and there are further correspondences that suggest that the older composer's symphonies spurred Mozart to new levels of inspiration. (Commentators on Mozart's music have until recently preferred to take an exclusive, romantic view of Mozart's music of this period, as being the work of a lonely creative artist struggling against adversity; however, there is no reason to suppose that Mozart had become less responsive to external stimuli – composers, performers, venues, prospect of publication etc. – than at any other time in his life.) The common ground between the 'Jupiter' (K.551) and 'L'ours' (no. 82) is obvious, for both belong to the same tradition of C major symphonies with trumpets and timpani, but the provenance of the other two symphonies is more individual. Fifteen years earlier, in 1773, when Mozart was seventeen years old, he had composed the 'Little' G minor symphony (K.183), written in clear imitation of Haydn's Symphony no. 39 and, more generally, of other minor-key symphonies by Haydn and contempora-

Haydn, Symphony no.83/II

ries such as Vanhal. Mozart's choice of the same key for his Symphony no. 40 was not prompted by the remembrance of his own early work but by Haydn's no. 83 ('La poule') and this time Mozart's response was an entirely personal, un-derivative one, exploring an emotional area that no other composer had or has since penetrated. Nevertheless, Mozart's slow movement shows a certain initial resemblance to that of no. 83 by Haydn: E flat major, andante, *piano* dynamic, string scoring (later supported by horns in the Mozart), repeated tonic notes to open the theme and gently emphasized discords (including supertonic seventh in bar 3 in Haydn, bar 2 in Mozart).

The two symphonies in E flat, no. 84 by Haydn and no. 39 by Mozart, also show some similarities in the form of points of departure for entirely different movements: a slow introduction and a minuet movement that has exaggeratedly regular phrasing patterns. The shadow of Haydn's B flat symphony, no. 85 (printed by Artaria as op. 52 no. 1), also is to be sensed in the first movement of Mozart's no. 39: adagio introduction with dotted note figuration followed by a relaxed first movement in triple time.

Personal circumstances meant that the outputs of the two composers in the 1780s emphasized different genres – opera and concerto in the case of Mozart, symphonies and quartets in the case of Haydn – thus obscuring any stylistic influences. In general, Mozart's music absorbed some of the argumentative features of Haydn's style, obviously evident in Mozart's increasing interest in monothematic sonata form in the second half of the decade, while Haydn's harmonic language was to broaden, the more familiar he became with Mozart's compositions. The give and take of influence is at its most apparent in chamber music. The indebtedness of the younger composer's 'Haydn' quartets was generously expressed by Mo-

Mozart, Symphony no.40/II

zart; Haydn, in turn, had shown his indebtedness to Mozart from op. 50 onwards. During the autumn of 1790 both men were in Vienna, Haydn from early October, Mozart from early November, and both, apparently, spent a great deal of time in each other's company in the month before Haydn departed for London. Haydn was working on a set of quartets, op. 64, which was subsequently dedicated to Johann Tost, and tradition has it that it was Tost, also, who commissioned Mozart's last two quintets, the D major (K.593) completed in December 1790 and the E flat major (K.614) completed in April 1791. Abbé Stadler reported that Haydn and Mozart frequently took part in performances of Mozart's quintets and his report specifically identifies the D major work (see above, p. 181). Certainly these two quintets are amongst the most Haydnesque music Mozart ever wrote: in their use of a slow introduction (K.593), 6/8 movements, monothematicism, thematically elaborate development sections, a 'tuneful' slow movement (K.614) and a rondo (K.614). Further, there are telling thematic resemblances between the two Mozart quintets and the two Haydn quartets in D and E flat major, respectively. The main theme of the opening Allegro of Mozart's quintet in D recalls that of Haydn's 'Lark' quartet (op. 64 no. 5), while the rondo of the E flat Quintet is reminiscent of the equivalent movement in op. 64 no. 6, suggesting that each knew the other's most recent compositions intimately. Has there ever been a more fruitful month in the history of music?

VII
Haydn in England,
1791–1795

FOLLOWING THE SUDDEN CHANGE of his circumstances in the autumn of 1790, Haydn might have gone to Naples (where he had been invited by King Ferdinand IV), or to Paris (where his music was immensely popular), or to some petty court in Germany (perhaps even to Berlin, where the King of Prussia, Frederick William II, was an admirer of his music); or he might have stayed in Austria, as *Kapellmeister* to Prince Grassalkovicz in Pressburg (at Esterházy's death, the Prince had been anxious to engage the composer). In the event, London was by far the best choice for Haydn: it might not have been the undisputed musical capital of Europe (with Mozart still alive in Vienna, that city had a strong claim to such a title), but in the years 1791–5 it was musically the most interesting centre; and more than that, it was in every sense a free city in the country blessed with the greatest amount of freedom, political and personal, anywhere in the world at that time, except perhaps for the United States of America (then, however, a musical desert). Haydn had a very strong instinct not only for survival but for choosing the right step in his career, and his choice of England as his home for the next five years - with the exception of his brief sojourn in Austria in 1793 - was to prove brilliantly successful. The English loved him and he loved the English; it was as simple as that.

Haydn did not record his impressions of the white cliffs of Dover when he arrived there, after the (for him) novel experience of a sea voyage, on New Year's Day 1791; but he does have a great deal to say about London, that huge metropolis and Haydn's first experience of a major city (Vienna was still no more than a large town, enclosed within protective medieval walls). London's population in 1801, when the first official census was made, was 1,114,644; and ten years earlier it must have been very close to a million.

Within a week of his arrival in London, Haydn wrote to Maria Anna von Genzinger in Vienna as follows:

London, 8th January 1791.

Nobly born,
Gracious Lady!
I hope that you will have received my last letter from Calais. I should have written you immediately after my arrival in London, but I wanted to wait a few days so as to be able to write about several things at once. So I can tell you that on the 1st inst., New Year's Day, after attending early mass, I boarded the ship at 7:30 a.m. and at 5 in the afternoon I arrived, thank God! safe and sound in Dower [*sic*]. At the beginning, for the first 4 whole hours, we had almost no wind, and the ship went so slowly that in these 4 hours we didn't go further than one single English mile, and there are 24 between Calais and Dower. Our ship's captain, in an evil temper, said that if the wind did not change, we should have to spend the whole night at sea. Fortunately, however, towards 11:30 o'clock a wind arose and blew so favourably that by 4 o'clock we covered 22 miles. Since the tide, which had just begun to ebb, prevented our large vessel from reaching the pier, 2 smaller ships came out to meet us as we were still fairly far out at sea, and into these we and our luggage were transferred, and thus at last, though exposed to a medium gale, we landed safely. The large vessel stood out to

sea five hours longer, till the tide turned and it could finally dock. Some of the passengers were afraid to board the little boats and stayed on board, but I followed the example of the greater number. I remained on deck during the whole passage, so as to gaze my fill at that mighty monster, the ocean. So long as it was calm, I wasn't afraid at all, but towards the end, when the wind grew stronger and stronger, and I saw the monstrous high waves rushing at us, I became a little frightened, and a little indisposed, too. But I overcame it all and arrived safely, without (excuse me) vomiting, on shore. Most of the passengers were ill, and looked like ghosts, but since I went on to London, I didn't feel the effects of the journey right away; but then I needed 2 days to recover. Now, however, I am fresh and well again, and occupied in looking at this endlessly huge city of London, whose various beauties and marvels quite astonished me. I immediately paid the necessary calls, such as to the Neapolitan Ambassador and to our own; both called on me in return 2 days later, and 4 days ago I lunched with the former – N.B. at 6 o'clock in the evening, as is the custom here.

My arrival caused a great sensation throughout the whole city, and I went the round of all the newspapers for 3 successive days. Everyone wants to know me. I had to dine out 6 times up to now, and if I wanted, I could dine out every day; but first I must consider my health, and 2nd my work. Except for the nobility, I admit no callers till 2 o'clock in the afternoon, and at 4 o'clock I dine at home with *Mon.* Salomon. I have nice and comfortable, but expensive, lodgings. My landlord is Italian, and also a cook, and serves me 4 very respectable meals; we each pay 1 fl. 30 kr. a day excluding wine and beer, but everything is terribly expensive here. Yesterday I was invited to a grand amateur concert, but I arrived a bit late, and when I showed my ticket they wouldn't let me in but led me to an antechamber, where I had to wait till the piece which was then being played in the hall was over. Then they opened the door, and I was conducted, on the arm of the *entrepreneur*, up the centre of the hall to the front of the orchestra, amid universal applause, and there I was stared at and greeted by a great number of English compliments. I was assured that such honours had not been conferred on anyone for 50 years. After the concert I was taken to a handsome adjoining room, where a table for 200 persons, with many places set, was prepared for all the amateurs; I was supposed to be seated at the head of the table, but since I had dined out on that day and had eaten more than usual, I declined this honour, with the excuse that I was not feeling very well, but despite this I had to drink the harmonious health, in Burgundy, of all the gentlemen present; they all returned the toast, and then allowed me to be taken home. All this, my gracious lady, was very flattering to me, and yet I wished I could fly for a time to Vienna, to have more quiet in which to work, for the noise that the common people make as they sell their wares in the street is intolerable. At present I am working on symphonies, because the libretto of the opera is not yet decided on, but in order to have more quiet I shall have to rent a room far from the centre of town. I would gladly write you in more detail, but I am afraid of missing the mail-coach. Meanwhile I am, …

> Your Grace's
> most sincere and obedient servant,
> Joseph Haydn.

Haydn was now established in quarters at 18 Great Pulteney Street, where Salomon also lived; in addition, Haydn had a room at the famous music shop of Broadwood's, which was opposite, and there he could compose. But he found it difficult to concentrate amidst the noise of the city and later in the season he took rooms in Lisson Grove, then a quiet suburb with cows grazing in nearby fields.

Johann Peter Salomon, the remarkable impresario, violinist and composer who brought Haydn to England, was born at Bonn (christening: 20 February 1745); later, in 1770, Beethoven was also born in the very same house. After a successful career in Germany, Salomon emigrated to England where he made his debut as a violinist at Covent Garden Theatre on 23 March 1781. He was at first associated with the Professional Concert but later formed his own concert series, at which one of his specialities was the performance of string quartets.

In Haydn's London there was opera or a subscription concert every night of the week. Salomon's series was held at the Hanover Square Rooms, and among the other concert halls regularly in use were Freemasons' Hall, the Rooms in Tottenham Street, the Crown and Anchor in the Strand, and Willis's Rooms in King Street, St James's. The Opera was held at the King's Theatre, which later contained a magnificent concert hall (usually called the 'New Room') where Haydn's last three symphonies were first performed (using an orchestra of sixty players).[1] Sir John Gallini's rival opera company, supported by the Prince of Wales, was at the Pantheon, and it was there that Haydn's new opera, *L'anima del filosofo*, was to have been staged; as it happened, Haydn's most popular vocal work, the *Maccone* for Sir John Gallini, was given there many times during the 1791 season (Haydn called it *Maccone*; it was a seven-part Catch and is, alas, lost). The two principal concert series were the Professional Concert (Hanover Square, Mondays) and the Haydn-Salomon series (Hanover Square, Fridays). Haydn was, of course, expected to provide numerous new works for the Friday concerts, but he could also supply as 'new' works several symphonies (no. 90 and the soon very popular no. 92, to be nicknamed the 'Oxford'), a set of six quartets (opus 64, composed in 1790), and some of the notturni for the King of Naples (*c.* 1788–1790), as well as vocal works not known in England (such as 'Ah, come il core' from *La fedeltà premiata*, which Haydn offered as a concert aria, and the Cantata *Arianne a Naxos*). Apart from a new aria for the singer Davidde, 'Cara deh torna in pace' (lost), and the *Maccone* for Gallini, Haydn composed two new symphonies, nos. 96 ('Miracle') and 95, both specifically signed and dated London 1791, for Salomon's first season. The new opera *L'anima del filosofo*, which was based on the Orpheus legend (and was later published in fragments as *Orfeo ed Euridice*), had a libretto by Carlo Francesco Badini, a clever Italian journalist who had settled in London, and who was a rival of Mozart's librettist, Lorenzo da Ponte; he contributed regularly to various newspapers and, like Da Ponte, was something of a scandalous figure.

Haydn was soon swept into the musical and social life of the capital. He made friends with men and women of widely diverse social backgrounds and nationalities; be became a popular figure and his comings and goings were soon noted by the daily press. Among his influential friends was Dr Charles Burney, composer, writer, and father of the famous novelist, Fanny Burney (who later married a French émigré named D'Arblay); Burney welcomed the Austrian composer with a long poem, published as 'Verses on the Arrival of the Great Musician Haydn in England. Price one shilling.' An announcement in the *Public Advertiser* of 7 January 1791 whetted its readers' appetites thus:

MUSICAL ARRANGEMENTS FOR EVERY DAY IN THE
WEEK, THROUGH THE WINTER SEASON.

Never could this country boast of such a constellation of musical excellence as now illuminates our fashionable hemisphere. No one Metropolis can exhibit such a union of Masters as London now possesses: and therefore as Music will be the chief pleasure of the season, we shall endeavour to give faithful representation of the Performances.

The Meeting, which through the condescension of the Prince of Wales, was to be held yesterday at Carlton House, may finally arrange the great affair of the rival Operas; but there is no doubt from the auspices, but that it will be settled to give the Opera a national establishment.

In the meantime our Readers may be pleased to see what will be the arrangements of musical pleasures for the week; even if the coalition of the two Operas should not take place.

We shall announce whatever change may be made; at present they stand as follow:

SUNDAY. – 	The Nobleman's Subscription, is held every Sunday at a different House.

MONDAY. –   The Professional Concert – at the Hanover-Square Rooms – with Mrs. Bil-
              lington.
TUESDAY. –   The Opera.
WEDNESDAY. – The ancient music at the rooms in Tottenham Street, under the Patronage
              of their Majesties.
   — -   The Anacreontic Society also, occasionally, on Wednesday.
THURSDAY. –   The Pantheon. – A Pasticcio of Music and Dancing, in case that the Opera
              Coalition shall take place; if not, a concert with Madame Mara and
              Sig. Pacchierotti.
   — -   Academy of Ancient Music, every other Thursday, at Freemason's Hall.
FRIDAY. –   A Concert under the auspices of Haydn at the Rooms, Hanover Square,
              with Sig. David.
SATURDAY. –   The Opera.

This is the arrangement for each week throughout the season; and so full is the town of eminent professors in every department of the science, that there may be a double orchestra found of admirable performers, so as to open two places of musical entertainment every evening.

> If Music be the food of Love, play on,
> Give me excess of it; that surfeiting,
> The appetite may sicken, and so die.' –
>   SHAKESPEARE.

On 15 January, we read the important announcement (in the *Public Advertiser*, the *Gazetteer*, etc.) of the forthcoming Haydn–Salomon concerts:

HANOVER SQUARE. MR. SALAMON [*sic*] respectfully acquaints the Nobility and Gentry, that he intends having TWELVE SUBSCRIPTION CONCERTS in the Course of the present Season. The first of which will be on Friday the Eleventh of February next, and so continue on the succeeding Fridays. Mr. HAYDN will compose for every Night a New Piece of Music, and direct the execution of it at the Harpsichord.
    The Vocal as well as Instrumental Performers will be of the first Rate, and a List of them will appear in a few Days.
    Subscriptions, at Five Guineas, for the Twelve Nights, to be held at Messrs. Lockhard's, No. 36, Pall-Mall.
    Tickets transferable Ladies to Ladies, and Gentlemen to Gentlemen.

A Court ball was held at St James's on 18 January, Queen Charlotte's birthday. Haydn was present, and from that evening his future in London's aristocratic society was assured. The *St James's Chronicle* reported the occasion, and a similar report in the *Daily Advertiser* (20 January) informs us that 'A remarkable Circumstance happened on Thursday Evening'.

In the Ball-Room at St. James's: Haydn the celebrated Composer, though he has not yet been introduced at our Court, was recognized by all the Royal Family, and paid them his silent Respects. Mr. Haydn came into the Room with Sir John Gallini, Mr. Wills and Mr. Salomon. The Prince of Wales first observed him, and upon bowing to him, the Eyes of all the Company were upon Mr. Haydn, every one paying him Respect.

Haydn came to know a great many members of the aristocracy. King George III, who was a much more astute and sensitive man than is often realized, asked him to stay in England; and in 1795 the Queen offered Haydn a suite in Windsor Castle. Haydn was entertained many times by the Prince of Wales, his brother, the Duke of York and especially the handsome Duchess of York. The composer soon became immensely popular; he spent weekends in beautiful country houses, and his hosts obviously found him a delightful guest. Haydn's special friend and patron was Lord Abingdon, who took the composer around with him.

Haydn was no snob, however. He said, with great pride, 'I have been in the company of emperors, kings and many great gentleman, and I have received many a compliment from them: but I do not wish to live on terms of intimacy with such persons and prefer to be with people of my class' (Griesinger, 55). In England, Haydn found a middle class much older-established, much richer, and with much more influence than in his native Austria. The aristocracy may have been the ones to send Haydn fifty guineas for a ticket to his benefit concert but it was the solid (in those days not stolid) middle class who flocked to Haydn's and Salomon's concerts, cheered their lungs out after hearing the 'Military' Symphony and avidly bought up Haydn's piano trios and English canzonettas. It was from this same large segment of British society that Haydn drew the many friends whose names are to be found in his London notebooks.

Even before the Salomon concerts began (after several delays) on 11 March, Haydn was already leading a frantically busy life. Apart from his 'guest appearances' at concerts, Haydn also gave lessons 'to various people on the fortepiano, and every lesson was paid for by a guinea' (Griesinger, 35). Said Haydn; 'Da machte ich große Augen' (ibid.; a colloquial translation would be, 'My eyes popped out of my head').

Salomon had the following announcement printed several times in the *Public Advertiser*:

HANOVER-SQUARE. MR. SALOMON respectfully acquaints the Nobility and Gentry, that his CONCERTS will open without further delay on Friday next, the 11th of March, and continue every succeeding Friday.

PART I.
Overture - Rosetti.
Song - Sig[nor] Tajana.
Concerto Oboe - Mr. Harrington.
Song - Signora Storace.
Concerto Violin - Madame Gautherot [Composed by Viotti].
Recitativo and Aria - Signor David [Composed by Rusi].
PART II.
New Grand Overture [i.e. Symphony] - Haydn.
Recitative and Aria - Signora Storace.
Concertante, Pedal Harp and Pianoforte - Madame
Krumpholtz and Mr. Dusseck,
Composed by Mr. Dusseck.
Rondo - Signor David [Composed by Andreozzi].
Full Piece - Kozeluck [*sic*].
Mr. HAYDN will be at the Harpsichord.
Leader of the Band, Mr. SALOMON.
Tickets transferable, as usual, Ladies to Ladies and
Gentlemen to Gentlemen only.
The Ladies' tickets are Green, the Gentlemen's Black.

The Subscribers are intreated to give particular orders to their Coachmen to set down and take up at the Side Door in the Street, with the Horses' Heads towards the Square.
The Door in the Square is for Chairs only.

People were curious, of course. Some thought that Haydn must by now have written himself out. Even such a great admirer as the Rev. Thomas Twining (a friend of Burney's and a fine amateur musician) had written to Burney on 15 February:

If the resources of any human composer could be inexhaustible, I should suppose Haydn's would; but as, after all, he is but a mortal, I am afraid he must soon get to the bottom of his genius-box.[2]

Twining need have had no fear: the genius-box was still bottomless. There are at least three contemporary criticisms of the concert in London newspapers, one in the *Morning Chronicle* on 12 March:

SALOMON'S CONCERT.

The First Concert under the auspices of HAYDN was last night, and never, perhaps, was there a richer musical treat.

It is not wonderful that to souls capable of being touched by music, HAYDN should be an object of homage, and even of idolatry; for like our own SHAKSPEARE [*sic*], he moves and governs the passions at his will.

His *new Grand Overture* was pronounced by every scientific ear to be a most wonderful composition; but the first movement in particular rises in grandeur of subject, and in the rich variety of *air* and passion, beyond any even of his own productions. The *Overture* has four movements – An Allegro – Andante – Minuet – and Rondo – They are all beautiful, but the first is pre-eminent in every charm, and the Band performed it with admirable correctness.

Signor DAVID exhibited all the wonders of his voice, and never surely was there heard a tenor of such riches and beauty. His first song was a *Recitativo* and *Aria*, by RUSI; and his second *a Rondo*, by ANDREOZZI.

There was an exquisite *concertante* between M. DUSSECK and Madame KRUMPHOLZ [*sic*]; Signora STORACE sung two songs in a very fine style.

We were happy to see the Concert so well attended the first Night; for we cannot suppress our very anxious hopes, that the first musical genius of the age may be induced, by our liberal welcome, to take up his residence in England.

Happily, we have another contemporary report, less reliable, perhaps, than the newspapers but interesting all the same: it is the diary of Charlotte Papendieck, whose husband, a flautist, had played in Vienna in 1779 (Haydn may have met him there) and now taught music to members of the royal family.

... The wished-for night at length arrived, and as I was anxious to be near the performers I went early. Mr. Papendiek followed from Queen's House, and I got an excellent seat on a sofa at the right-hand side. The orchestra was arranged on a new plan. The pianoforte was in the centre, at each extreme end the double basses, then on each side two violoncellos, then two tenors or violas and two violins, and in the hollow of the piano a desk on a high platform for Salomon with his ripieno. At the back, verging down to a point at each end, all these instruments were doubled, giving the requisite number for a full orchestra. Still further back raised high up, were drums, and other side the trumpets, trombones, bassoons, oboes, clarinets, flutes, &c., in numbers according to the requirements of the symphonies and other music to be played on the different evenings.

The concert opened with a symphony of Haydn's that he brought with him, but which was not known in England. It consisted of four movements, pleasing lively, and good. ...

The second act invariably opened with a new symphony composed for the night. Haydn of course conducted his own music, and generally that of other composers, in fact all through the evening.

The Hanover Square Rooms are calculated to hold 800 persons exclusive of the performers. By the beginning of the second act we concluded that all had arrived who intended to come, and though we knew that Salomon's subscription list was not full, we had hoped for additions during the evening. But no; and I regret to make this observation of my countrymen, that until they know what value they are likely to receive for their money they are slow in coming forward with it. An undertaking of this magnitude, bringing such a superior man from his own country as Haydn to compose for an orchestra filled with the highest professional skill and talent, should have met with every encouragement, first to show respect to the stranger and then to Salomon, who ... had done so much for the musical world, in this case having taken such infinite trouble and incurred so much risk.

From the evidence at our disposal, it would seem that Haydn's 'new symphony' (or, as the *Morning Chronicle* called it, 'new Grand Overture') played at this first Salomon concert was no. 92 in G, which in fact had been composed in 1789. Something of the thrill of Haydn's early concerts given with his friend Salomon may be caught in the following entry from Dr Burney's memoirs:

1791. - This year was auspiciously begun, in the musical world, by the arrival in London of the illustrious Joseph Haydn. 'Tis to Salomon that the lovers of music are indebted for what the lovers of music will call this blessing. Salomon went over himself to Vienna ... purposely to tempt that celebrated musical genius hither; and on February 25 [*sic*], the first of Haydn's incomparable symphonies which was composed for the concerts of Salomon was performed. Haydn himself presided at the piano-forte; and the sight of that renowned composer so electrified the audience, as to excite an attention and a pleasure superior to any that had ever, to my knowledge, been caused by instrumental music in England. All the slow middle movements were encored; which never before happened, I believe, in any country.[3]

The report is useful for one further point regarding the instrument from which Haydn conducted. In most of the 1791 newspapers, it is referred to as a harpsichord; but although the British continued to make powerful and mechanically the best harpsichords the world had ever seen down to the last decade of the century, Burney, a professional musician, says specifically 'piano-forte'; and it may be doubted if Haydn would have chosen the harpsichord when the new English pianos were obviously much more powerful.

The Haydn-Salomon series of 1791 turned out to be a spectacular success for everyone concerned. Haydn presented the London public with a judicious selection of vocal and instrumental pieces, most of which were immediately published by British houses (Quartets op.64, *Arianna a Naxos*, Symphonies nos.90, 92, 95 and 96). It was easy to persuade Haydn to stay on for another year, and Salomon was soon able to announce a new season 'with the assistance of Mr Haydn'. The last part of May was given over to a gigantic Handel Festival, 'by command and under the patronage of their Majesties', in Westminster Abbey. There were over a thousand performers, including the cream of all the orchestras and singers; the famous 'large double basses', 'double bass Kettle drums' (tuned an octave below the normal pitches) and double bassoons. Haydn could hear magnificent performances of *Israel in Egypt*, the Coronation Anthem 'Zadok the Priest', *Messiah* and various extracts from numerous other oratorios. He was both astonished and deeply moved by it all.

Many years later in Vienna, Haydn gave his biographer Dies one of the London notebooks. Dies (133f.) writes:

I opened it up and found a couple of dozen letters in the English language. Haydn smiled and said: 'Letters from an English widow in London, who loved me; but she was, though already sixty years old, still a beautiful and charming woman and I would have married her very easily if I had been free at the time.'
   This woman [continues Dies] is the widow [Rebecca] still living, of the famous pianist Schröter [*sic*], whose melodious song Haydn emphatically praised. ... If he was not invited elsewhere, he usually dined with her.

Johann Samuel Schroeter (1750-88) had in 1782 succeeded J.C.Bach as Master of the King's Musick. Rees's *Cyclopaedia* (1819-20) says, 'He married a young lady of considerable fortune, who was his scholar, and was in easy circumstances.' Schroeter published many works for the keyboard and Haydn owned several, which Rebecca probably gave him. It has been doubted if she was really sixty; but in any case she grew to love Haydn and certainly introduced him to a delightful group of people in London. Her first letter reads as follows:

Mrs. Schroeter presents her compliments to Mr. Haydn, and informs him, she is just returned to town, and will be very happy to see him whenever it is convenient for him to give her a lesson. James str. Buckingham Gate. Wednesday, June 29th 1791.

Both Dies and Griesinger relate how even in his old age Haydn loved women. Dies (134) writes:

He freely admitted that he loved pretty women, but he couldn't understand how it happened that in his life he had been loved by many a pretty woman. 'They can't have been led to it by my beauty.' ...

In July 1791, Haydn received the honorary degree of Doctor of Music from Oxford University. Happily, many contemporary documents tell us, in considerable detail, of the three concerts and of the ceremony itself, held in the Sheldonian Theatre, one of Sir Christopher Wren's masterpieces. Griesinger relates (34):

Dr. Burney suggested to Haydn that he should be given a doctor's degree at Oxford. The ceremony during which the degree was given took place in a cathedral [*sic*] with great solemnity; the doctors enter in procession and put questions to the candidates, if they wish to be admitted and so forth. Haydn answered what his friend Salomon told him to say. The election is put to the assembly from a raised platform; the speaker [the Public Orator of the university] enlarged upon Haydn's merits, listed his works, and to the question, would Haydn be admitted, there arose a general cry of assent. The doctors dress in a small gown with frills at the collar and they have to wear it for three days. 'I would have dearly liked my Viennese acquaintances to see me in this dress!' The Storaces[4] and some other musical friends waved to him from the orchestra. The day after the election Haydn conducted the music. 'I thank you,' he answered [in English], raising the ends of his gown. That caused much jubilation ... It happened several times to Haydn that Englishmen went up to him, looked at him from top to toe, and left him saying, 'You are a great man.'

Dies (135 f.) relates much the same story but supplies some further details:

Dr. Burney was the moving spirit: he talked Haydn into it and went with him to Oxford. At the ceremony in the University Hall, the assembled company was encouraged to present the doctor's hat to a man who had risen so high in the service of music. The whole company was loud in Haydn's praises. Thereupon Haydn was presented with a white silk gown, the sleeves in red silk, and a little black hat, and thus arrayed, he had to seat himself in a doctor's chair. ... Haydn was asked to present something of his own composition. He climbed up to the organ loft, turned to the company, took his doctoral robes in both hands, opened them at his breast, closed them again and said as loudly and clear as possible [in English], 'I thank you.' The company well understood this unexpected gesture; they appreciated Haydn's thanks and said, 'You speak very good English.' 'I felt very silly in my gown, and the worst of it was, I had to drag it round the streets for three whole days. But I have much to thank this doctor's degree for in England; indeed, I might say everything; as a result of it, I gained the acquaintance of the first men in the land and had entrance to the greatest houses.'

Haydn said this with that openness which is so characteristic of him, so that I simply could not understand how it is possible for such a genius to be so completely unaware of his own strength and to ascribe everything to the doctor's hat and nothing to his art. Self-adulation could not be seen in his words, much less any hidden pride. ...

The *Morning Herald* of 11 July describes not only of the ceremony but also the concert that evening:

On Friday morning the annual Commemoration took place at OXFORD, when the celebrated

HAYDN was admitted to a DOCTOR'S DEGREE in a manner highly flattering to him and creditable to the University, being the free gift and unanimous desire of that learned body.

Between the parts of the Latin and English oration, upon this occasion the band performed pieces adapted to the situation. On the return of the procession from the theatre, and on HAYDN's retiring, the applause which arose, was perhaps equal to any that ever attended a similar occasion.

At five in the evening the concluding Concert took place; and several performers were all well received on their entrance, particularly CRAMER, who was honoured with warm tokens of general respect.

The opening piece was the Overture from ESTHER, performed with great spirit. KELLY followed with 'why does the Go[d], etc.' from Samson, with good expression. MATTHEWS and BELLAMY, then sung 'The Lord is a Man of War' tolerably. The next in order was, a beautiful Cantata by HAYDN, who appeared in his gown and conducted it; - this charming air used to be finely sung by MARCHES[I]; therefore STORACE was injudicious in attempting it on this occasion, and indeed, obtained less applause than HAYDN's *Doctorial Robe*. The first act terminated with the Recitative 'Search round the, etc.' and Chorus 'May no rash, etc.' from Handel's Solomon by KELLY. This was repeated.

A new Overture by PLEYEL led on the second act. The composition was much admired and the Band played it with very great correct[n]ess and spirit, though they never saw it till that evening. STORACE then sung 'The Prince unable to conceal, etc.' from Alexander's Feast, with such *expressive gesture* that the young gentlemen in the *Black Gowns* were highly gratified and unanimously *encored* it. The next was a Concerto on the Violin by CRAMER, executed in his best style, and with such brilliancy that the applause was very great from all quarters. DAVID was followed with 'Comfort ye my People', but not with such success as he gave at the Abbey. This act concluded with the Chorus, 'And the Glory, etc.'.

KELLY before the third act sung an Italian Air, the music of which was not very striking; and he made as much of it as it deserved.

The last act commenced with an Overture of HAYDN, very fine, but well known. HAYDN was not present at this performance. STORACE followed with the Air 'with lowly suite' in which she was very deservedly *encored*. DAVID next sung 'Pensa che in [campo] etc.' an Air of PAESIELLO, but in too flourishing a style of execution with a want of neatness in his divisions. ...

Haydn, methodical as always in money matters, recorded the cost of the trip to Oxford in one of his notebooks (in German, of course).

I had to pay 1½ guineas for having the bells rung at Oxforth [*sic*] in connection with my doctor's degree, and ½ a guinea for the robe. The trip cost 6 guineas.

Haydn's ex-mistress Luigia Polzelli had written to him saying that her husband, Antonio, who had been an invalid for years, had died. On receiving this news, Haydn replied (in Italian):

London, 4th August 1791.

Dear Polzelli!

I hope that you will have received my last letter through Count Fries and also the hundred florins [Gulden] which I transferred to you. I would like to do more, but at present I cannot. As far as your husband is concerned, I tell you that Providence has done well to liberate you from this heavy yoke, and for him, too, it is better to be in another world than to remain useless in this one. The poor man has suffered enough. Dear Polzelli, perhaps, perhaps the time will come, which we both so often dreamt of, when four eyes shall be closed. Two are closed, but the other two - enough of all this, it shall be as God wills. Meanwhile, pay attention to your health. I beg of you, and write me very soon, because for quite some time now I have had days of depression without really knowing why, and your letters cheer me, even when they are sad. Goodbye, dear Polzelli, the mail won't wait any longer. I kiss your family and remain always

> Your most sincere
> Haydn.

Meanwhile a very unpleasant situation had arisen for Haydn, not of his own doing. To explain the circumstances, we must return to the composer's arrival in England. One of his first duties was, of course, to write to Prince Anton Esterházy: in contradistinction to the long, chatty letter to Maria Anna von Genzinger quoted above, Haydn's letter to the prince (dated 8 January) was short and formal; it tells of the new opera libretto, of the singers who had been engaged to sing it, and of Haydn's favourable reception with people of the prince's rank (the Neapolitan Ambassador, etc.). Prince Anton replied as follows:

To the Kapellmeister Hayden [*sic*]
Right nobly born
Much respected Herr Kapellmeister
It was with much pleasure that I received your letter of 8 January and the news that you arrived safely in London on the 2nd of the same month and were so well received there, at which I rejoice, as also over the opera which you have it in mind to write, and I await your news of other events there. For the rest, however, I remain with much esteem

> Your well-wisher
> A. F. E. mpria
> [= Anton Fürst Esterházy]

Vienna, 3 February 1791

Meanwhile, Haydn had started to invest some of the large sums of money he was earning in England; he entrusted 4,883 gulden to Count Fries's bank in Vienna and 1,000 gulden to Prince Esterházy's bank at 5%, as the following note from Prince Anton to his chief collector Züsser shows:

Dear Züsser.
He is [i.e. 'you are'] hereby instructed to have prepared a bond for 1,000 Gulden for Kapellmeister Haydn as from yesterday's date at 5% and to submit it to me for signature: the amount of the said 1,000 Gulden has already been paid into my hands here.
Eszterháza, 11 July 1791

Then, on 20 July, *Kapellmeister* Haydn evidently wrote to his patron informing him that he intended to stay another season in London and had signed a contract to that effect with Salomon. This letter has not yet been located in the Esterházy Archives, but Prince Anton's answer must have dismayed the composer:

To the Kapellmeister Hayden [*sic*]
It is with much pleasure that I learn from your letter of 20 July how much your talents are prized in London and I genuinely rejoice thereat: but at the same time I cannot conceal from you that your present, already extended absence has turned out to be not only very vexatious for me but also very expensive since I was compelled to have recourse to outsiders for the festivities held at Eszterháza this month.

You will not think ill of me therefore that I cannot grant you the requested extension for a further year of your leave of absence; but instead expect to hear from you by the next post the exact time when you will arrive back here again. On which, with all respect, I remain your Honour's

> Well-wisher
> A.F.E. mpria

Eisenstadt, 12 August 1791

By 17 September, when he next wrote to Frau von Genzinger in Vienna, Haydn was sure that he would be dismissed from the princely service (but in the event,

Prince Anton did not do so, though there seems to have been a rather long and ominous silence from Austria). Haydn's letter reads:

... Now, my dear good gracious lady, how is your fortepiano? Is a Haydnish thought brought to mind, now and then, by your fair hand? Does my dear *Fräulein* Pepi sometimes sing poor *Ariadne*? Oh yes! I can hear it even here, especially during the last two months, when I have been living in the country, amid the loveliest scenery, with a banker's family where the atmosphere is like that of the Gennzinger family, and where I live as if I were in a monastery. I am all right, thank the good Lord! except for my usual rheumatism; I work hard, and when in the early mornings I walk in the woods, alone, with my English grammar, I think of my Creator, my family, and all the friends I have left behind – and of these you are the ones I most value. Of course I had hoped to have the pleasure of seeing you sooner, but my circumstances – in short, fate – will have it that I remain in London another 8 or 10 months. Oh, my dear gracious lady! how sweet this bit of freedom really is! I had a kind Prince, but sometimes I was forced to be dependent on base souls. I often sighed for release, and now I have it in some measure. I appreciate the good sides of all this, too, though my mind is burdened with far more work. The realization that I am no bond-servant makes ample amends for all my toils. But, dear though this liberty is to me, I should like to enter Prince Esterházy's service again when I return, if only for the sake of my family. I doubt whether this will be possible, however, for in his letter my Prince strongly objects to my staying away for so long, and absolutely demands my speedy return; but I can't comply with this, owing to a new contract which I have just made here. And now, unfortunately, I expect my dismissal, whereby I hope that God will give me the strength to make up for this loss, at least partly, by my industry. Meanwhile I console myself by the hope of hearing something soon from Your Grace. You shall receive my promised new symphony in two months, but in order to inspire me with good ideas, I beg Your Grace to write, and to write a long letter, too, to one who is ever

> Your Grace's
> most sincere friend and obedient
> servant,
> Jos: Haydn.

Esterházy's demand for Haydn's return was caused by the fact that he had had to commission a new *opera seria* to be performed on the occasion of the Prince's installation as Governor of the County of Oedenburg; the event took place at Eszterháza on 3 August 1791 and was the last great *festa* to take place there. The festivities were commemorated in a handsome engraving showing some gypsy musicians in the right foreground – no doubt to compensate for *Kapellmeister* Haydn's absence. In the event, Prince Anton made it up with Haydn, and when they met in Frankfurt in 1792 (see p. 244), the Prince simply said, 'Haydn, you could have saved me 40,000 Gulden', reputedly the staggering price paid to stage Joseph Weigl's *Venere ed Adone* with an imported Viennese cast.

Meanwhile, in the summer of 1791, Haydn had been invited to stay at Roxford, the home of a banker named Nathaniel Brassey, near Hertingfordbury in Hertfordshire (north of London). During the quiet summer weeks at Roxford, Haydn will have composed Symphony no.93 and probably some of no.94 and no.98, which he now had to complete for the new Salomon season of 1792. By the end of September, if not before, Haydn was back in London: on 26 September 1791, he signed the guest book at Broadwood's piano shop across the street from his lodgings on Great Pulteney Street.

To a certain extent, Haydn was no longer master of his own fame. His reputation began to exist as a thing almost separate from the man. While on the one hand, like all other composers of the period, he had no control of the publication and dissemination of his music once it left his hands; on the other, he was, like all famous men, subjected to intense scrutiny. It could not be thought, of course, that everyone approved of his music; it had been in years past far too controversial for that; but as far as his music was available, it was now being played all over Europe. Even his operas, written for performance at Eszterháza, were beginning to circulate on the Continent: too late, for they were already 'old' compared to Haydn's own style *de anno* 1791 and, even more, to Mozart's brilliant works.

Early in November Haydn was invited to an official lunch given by the new Lord Mayor of London. The description of it in the First London Notebook is a brilliant piece of reportage which shows that like all aspects of England in which noise dominated, Haydn was slightly repelled:

On the 5th Nov. I was guest at a lunch given in honour of the Lord Mayor. The new Lord Mayor and his wife ate at the first table No. 1, then the Lord Chanceler and both the Scherifs, Duc de Lids [Leeds], Minister Pitt and the other judges of the first rank. At No. 2 I ate with Mr Silvester, the greatest lawyer and first Alderman of London. In this room (which is called the geld Hall [Guildhall]), there were 16 tables besides others in adjoining rooms; in all nearly 1200 persons dined, all with the greatest pomp. The food was very nice and well-cooked; many kinds of wine in abundance. The company sat down at 6 o'clock and arose at 8. The Lord Mayor was escorted according to rank before and also after dinner, and there were many ceremonies, a sword was carried in front of him, and a kind of golden crown, to the sound of trumpets, accompanied by a wind band. After dinner the distinguished company of [table] No. 1 retired to a separate room which had been chosen beforehand, to drink coffee and tea; we other guests, however, were taken to another adjoining room. At 9 o'clock No. 1 rose and went to a small room, at which point the ball began: in this room there is, *a parte*, an elevated place for the high *Nobless* where the Lord Mayor is seated on a throne together with his wife. Then the dancing begins according to rank, but only 1 couple, just as at Court on the King's Birthday, 6th January [*recte*: 4th June]. In this small room there are 4 tiers of raised benches on each side, where the fair sex mostly has the upper hand. Nothing but minuets are danced in this room; I couldn't stand it longer than a quarter of an hour; first, because the heat caused by so many people in such a small room was so great; and secondly, because of the wretched dance band, the entire orchestra consisting only of two violins and a violoncello. The minuets were more Polish than in our or the Italian manner. From there I went to another room, which was more like a subterranean cavern, and where the dance was English; the music was a little better, because there was a drum in the band which drowned the misery of the violins. I went on to the great hall, where we had eaten, and there the band was larger and more bearable. The dance was English, but only on the raised platform where the Lord Mayor and the first 4 numbers had dined; the other tables, however, were all occupied again by men who, as usual, drank enormously the whole night. The most curious thing, though, is that a part of the company went on dancing without hearing a single note of the music, for first at one table, then at another, some were yelling songs and some swilling it down and drinking toasts amid terrific roars of 'Hurrey, H[urrey], H[urrey]' and waving of glasses. The hall and all the other rooms are illuminated with lamps which give out an unpleasant odour. It is remarkable that the Lord Mayor requires no knife at table, for a carver … cuts up everything for him in advance …

Although Haydn, like any other eighteenth-century gentleman, enjoyed his glass of wine, he seems to have been shocked – and with good reason – by the amount of drinking he witnessed in London.

On 23 November the marriage took place of Frederick, Duke of York (the second son of George III), and Princess Friedericke Charlotte Ulricke (eldest daughter of Frederick William II of Prussia). The couple had already been married in Berlin, but British law required that they marry again on English soil. The ceremony took place at seven o'clock in the evening, at Buckingham House (now Palace). The Duke of York was described by Mirabeau as 'puissant chasseur, puissant buveur, et puissant homme en cordialité pour les femmes mariées, et libre comme un Seigneur Anglais'. Haydn adored the Duchess at first sight, and she was to become his faithful benefactress and patron. Everybody tried to make the girl feel at home. The handsome Prince of Wales went to greet the couple when they arrived at York House. The *European Magazine*, November 1791 (pp. 323 ff.) reports:

On their arrival at York House they were received by his Royal Highness the Prince of Wales, who came thither about twenty minutes before. The Prince received the Duchess in the Great Hall, with the elegance so peculiar to him; his Highness taking her by the hand, saluted his royal sister, and congratulated her on her arrival in the German language, which the Prince speaks with great perfection.

Next day, Haydn was invited to visit Oatlands, near Weybridge in Surrey, as a guest of the newly married couple. In his notebook Haydn wrote:

On 24th Nov., I was invited by the Prince of Wales to visit his brother, the Duc du York, at eatland [Oatlands]. I stayed there 2 days and enjoyed many marks of graciousness and honour, not only from the Prince of Wales but also from the Duchess, daughter of the King of Prussia. The little castle, 18 miles from London, lies on a slope and commands the most glorious view. Among its many beauties is a most remarkable grotto which cost £25,000 Sterling, and which was 11 years in the building. It is very large and contains many diversions, *inter alia* actual water which flows in from various sides, a beautiful English garden, various entrances and exits, besides a most charming bath. The Duke bought this country estate for some £47,000 Sterling. On the 3rd day, the Duke had me taken 12 miles towards London with his horse and carriage.

The Prince of Wales wants my portrait. For 2 days we played music for 4 hours in the evening, that is, from 10 o'clock till 2 o'clock in the morning, then we had supper and went to bed at 3 o'clock.

The portrait mentioned was to be executed by John Hoppner and is one of the best-known likenesses of Haydn; it is in the Royal Collection.[6] He refers to it again when writing a long report to Frau von Genzinger in Vienna, dated 20 December:

... I must take this opportunity of informing Your grace that 3 weeks ago I was invited by the Prince of Wales to visit his brother, the Duke of York, at the latter's country seat. The Prince presented me to the Duchess, the daughter of the King of Prussia, who received me very graciously and said many flattering things. She is the most delightful lady in the world, is very intelligent, plays the pianoforte and sings very nicely. I had to stay there 2 days, because a slight indisposition prevented her attending the concert on the first day. On the 2nd day, however, she remained continually at my side from 10 o'clock in the evening, when the music began, to 2 o'clock in the morning. Nothing but Haydn was played. I conducted the symphonies from the pianoforte, and the sweet little thing sat beside me on my left and hummed all the pieces from memory, for she had heard them so often in Berlin. The Prince of Wales sat on my right side and played with us on his violoncello, quite tolerably. I had to sing, too. The Prince of Wales is having my portrait painted just now, and the picture is to hang in his room. The Prince of Wales is the most handsome man on God's earth; he has an extraordinary love of music and a lot of feeling, but not much money. *Nota bene*, this is between ourselves. I am more pleased by his kindness than by any financial gain. ...

Now, gracious lady, I would like to take you to task a little, for believing that I prefer the city of London to Vienna, and that I find the sojourn here more agreeable than that in my fatherland. I don't hate London, but I would not be capable of spending the rest of my life there, even if I could amass millions. I shall tell Your Grace the reason when I see you. I look forward tremendously to going home and to embracing all my good friends. I only regret that the great Mozart will not be among them, if it is really true, which I trust it is not, that he has died. Posterity will not see such a talent again in 100 years! I am delighted that Your Grace and your family are well. I have enjoyed excellent health up to now, thank God! but a week ago I got an attack of English rheumatism which was so severe that sometimes I had to cry aloud. I hope soon to get rid of it, however, inasmuch as I have adopted the usual custom here of wrapping myself in flannel from head to foot. I must ask you to excuse the fact that my handwriting is so poor today. ...

Unknown to Haydn, Mozart had died in Vienna on 5 December. When the full details reached London, he was stunned; he never got over Mozart's loss and in later years tears would spring to his eyes whenever he saw one of the composer's sons. Haydn knew that Mozart's brother-Mason, Johann Michael Puchberg, the banker, had a special relationship with the young composer. Early in 1792 – the letter has survived only in fragments – Haydn wrote to Puchberg in Vienna:

London, January 1792.
... For some time I was beside myself about his [Mozart's] death, and I could not believe that Providence would so soon claim the life of such an indispensable man. I only regret that before his death he could not convince the English, who walk in darkness in this respect, of his greatness – a subject about which I have been sermonizing to them every single day. ... You will be good enough, my kind friend, to send me a catalogue of those pieces which are not yet known here, and I shall make every possible effort to promote such works for the widow's benefit; I wrote to the poor woman three weeks ago, and told her that when her favourite son reaches the necessary age, I shall give him composition lessons to the very best of my ability, and at no cost, so that he can, to some extent, fill his father's position ...

Haydn must have remembered, with a stab of pain, how he and Mozart and Puchberg ('I am inviting only Haydn and yourself') had listened first to piano rehearsals and then to the orchestral rehearsals of *Cosi fan tutte* in January 1790. Haydn will probably not have known the extent of Mozart's debts to Puchberg (1,000 gulden, equal to Haydn's salary in 1790). On 14 January 1792, Haydn wrote a long letter (in Italian) to Luigia Polzelli, who had by then obtained a position in the opera house at Piacenza:

My dearest Polzelli! This very moment I received your letter, and hasten to answer it. I am relieved that you are in good health, and that you have found a position in a little theatre; not so much because of the payment but to have the experience. I wish you every possible success, in particular a good role and a good teacher, who takes the same pains with you as did your Haydn. You write that you would like to send your dear Pietro to me; do so, for I shall embrace him with all my heart; he is always welcome, and I shall treat him as if he were my own son. I shall take him with me to Vienna. I shall remain in London until the middle of June, not longer, because my Prince and many other circumstances make it imperative that I return home. Nevertheless I shall try, if possible, to go to Italy, in order to see my dear Polzelli, but meanwhile you can send your Pietro to me here in London; he will always be either with me or with your sister,[7] who is now alone and who has been separated quite some time now from her husband, that beast. She is unhappy, as you were, and I am very sorry for her. I see her but rarely, for I have a lot to do, especially now, when the Professional Concert has had my pupil Pleyel brought over, to face me as a rival; but I'm not afraid, because last year I made a great impression on the English and hope therefore to win their approval this year, too. My opera was not given, because *Sig.* Gallini didn't receive the licence from the King, and never will; to tell you the truth, the Italian opera has no success at all now, and by a stroke of bad luck, the Pantheon Theatre burned down just this very day, two hours after midnight. Your sister had been engaged in the last piece; I am sorry for all of them.

I am quite well, but am almost always in an 'English humour', that is, depressed, and perhaps I shall never regain the good humour that I used to have when I was with you. Oh! my dear Polzelli: you are always in my heart, and I shall never, never forget you. I shall do my very best to see you, if not this year, then certainly the next, along with your son. I hope that you won't forget me, and that you will write me if you get married again, for I would like to know the name of him who is fortunate enough to have you. Actually I ought to be a little annoyed with you, because many people wrote me from Vienna that you had said the worst possible things about me, but God bless you, I forgive you everything, for I know you said it in love. Do preserve your good name, I beg you, and think from time to time about your Haydn, who esteems you and loves you tenderly, and will always be faithful to you. Write me, too, if you have seen and spoken with anyone who was formerly in Prince Ester-házy's service. Goodbye, my dear, that's all for this evening: it's late.

Today I went to see your dear sister to ask her if she would be able to put up Pietro in her house. He will be received with the greatest pleasure; he can sleep there and have his meals there, too, since I always eat out and am invited out every day; but Pietro can come every day to me for his lessons – I live only a little way from your sister's. I give your sister a bit of money, because I am very sorry for her; she is not exactly poor, but she has to be very economical. I shall clothe your son well, and do everything for him. I don't want you to have any expense on his account; he shall have everything he needs. I shall certainly leave for Vienna in the middle of June, but I shall take the route *via* Holland, Leipzig and Berlin (in order to see the King of Prussia); my Petruccio will always be with me. I hope, however, that up to now he has been an obedient son to his dear mother, but if he hasn't been, I don't want him, and you must write me the truth. I don't want to have an ungrateful boy, for then I would be capable of sending him away at a moment's notice. Your sister embraces you and kisses you thousands and thousands of times. Write me often, dear Polzelli, and remember that I shall be always your faithful

Haydn.

Haydn and Salomon had been so successful in their 1791 season that it was to be expected that rival organizations would be jealous. The directors of the Professional Concert series, having tried without success to lure Haydn away from Salomon, had persuaded Haydn's star pupil, Ignaz Pleyel, to come to London as the principal composer for their organization's 1792 season. It is hard for us today to appreciate how popular Pleyel's music – which is now all but forgotten – was in 1792. Indeed, Pleyel was more popular in parts of Europe than his master, and publishers vied with each other for Pleyel's latest compositions, which were clever but superficial imitations of the Haydn manner – a watered-down version of the original, but easier on the minds, ears and fingers of many young ladies in London, Paris, Berlin and Vienna. Mozart had thought very highly of Pleyel and imagined that one day the pupil might supplant the master; so we must realize that Pleyel was a formidable, potentially even dangerous, rival to Salomon and his series. Haydn alludes to the pressures on him in a letter to Frau von Genzinger dated 2 March 1792:

... there isn't a day, not a single day, in which I am free from work, and I shall thank the dear Lord when I can leave London – the sooner the better. My labours have been augmented by the arrival of my pupil Pleyel, whom the Professional Concert have brought here. He arrived here with a lot of new compositions, but they had been composed long ago; he therefore promised to present a new work every evening. As soon as I saw this, I realized at once that a lot of people were dead set against me, and so I announced publicly that I would likewise produce 12 different new pieces. In order to keep my word, and to support poor Salomon, I must be the victim and work the whole time. But I really do feel it. My eyes suffer the most, and I have many sleepless nights, though with God's help I shall overcome it all. ... Pleyel's presumption is sharply criticized, but I love him just the same. I always go to his concerts, and am the first to applaud him. I am delighted that Your Grace and the family are well. Please give my kind respects to all of them. The time is drawing near when I must put my trunks in order. Oh! how happy I shall be to see Your Grace again, to show you how much I missed you and to show the esteem in which, gracious lady, you will ever be held by

Your most obedient servant,
Jos: Haydn.

At the sixth Salomon concert,[8] on 23 March, Haydn's Symphony no. 94 in G (soon to become known as the 'Surprise') received its first performance. Next day, the *Oracle* stated:

The Second Movement was equal to the happiest of this great Master's conceptions. The surprise might not be unaptly likened to the situation of a beautiful Shepherdess who, lulled to slumber by the murmur of a distant Waterfall, starts alarmed by the unexpected firing of a fowling-piece. The flute obligato was delicious.

Griesinger elaborates on this slow movement in his biography (32):

I asked [Haydn] once in jest if it were true that he wrote the Andante with the kettledrum beat in order to awaken the English public that had gone to sleep at his concert. 'No', he answered me. 'Rather it was my wish to surprise the public with something new, and to make a début in a brilliant manner so as not to be outdone by my pupil Pleyel, who at that time was engaged by an orchestra in London (in the year 1792) which had begun its concert series eight days before mine. The first *Allegro* of my symphony was received with countless bravos, but the enthusiasm reached its highest point in the *Andante with the kettledrum beat. Ancora, Ancora!* sounded from every throat, and even Pleyel complimented me on my idea.'

Haydn was clearly seeing a good deal of Rebecca Schroeter in his free moments. On 6 March they were together in the evening. Her letter the next day shows that their relationship had crossed a certain line and become a real love-affair.

March 7th 92.
My D: I was extremely sorry to part with you so suddenly last Night, our conversation was particularly interesting and I had [a] thousand affectionate things to say to you, my heart was and is full of TENDERNESS for you, but no language can express HALF the LOVE and AFFECTION I feel for you, you are DEARER to me EVERY DAY of my life. I am very sorry I was so dull and stupid yesterday, indeed my DEAREST it was nothing but my being indisposed with a cold occasion'd my Stupidity. I thank you a thousand times for your concern for me, I am truly sensible of your goodness, and I assure you my D. if any thing had happened to trouble me, I wou'd have open'd my heart, & told you with the most perfect confidence. Oh, how earnes[t]ly [I] wish to see you, I hope you will come to me to morrow. I shall be happy to see you both in the Morning and the Evening. God Bless you my love, my thoughts and best wishes ever accompany you, and I always am with the most sincere and invariable Regard my D:
  My Dearest I cannot be happy
till I see you if you know,
do, tell me, when you will come

Mrs Schroeter liked to write notes the last thing before retiring so that her servant could deliver them the following morning. On 1 June she wrote:

My D[r] I beg to know HOW YOU DO? hope to hear you[r] Head-ach is ENTIRELY GONE, and that you have SLEPT WELL. I shall be very happy to see you on Sunday any time convenient to you after one o'clock – I hope to see you my D[r] L on tuesday as usual to Dinner, [crossed out: "and all (?night ?p.m.) with me"] – and I shall be much obliged to you if you will inform me what Day will be agreeable to you to meet M[r] M[tris] and MISS STONE at my house to Dinner, I shou'd be glad if it was either Thursday or Friday, whichever Day YOU PLEASE to fix, I will send to M[r] Stone to let them know. I long to see you my D[r] H, let me have that pleasure as soon as you can, till when and Ever I remain with the FIRMEST attachment My D[r] L:
              most faithfully and affectionately
                        yours [etc.]
Friday June ye 1st 792.

However, she soon disappears as a letter writer from Haydn's life. If further letters existed, were they perhaps copied into Haydn's Fourth London Notebook (which has survived incomplete)? Or did the fact that during his second visit to Engla in 1794-5, Haydn lived in Bury Street, St James's, only a short walk fre Mrs Schroeter's house, remove the need for their corresponding? She actually pears later in Haydn's 'official' biography; to her are dedicated three of his great Piano Trios, opus 73, in 1795; and she is known to have been a subscriber to *Creation*. She also helped Haydn with an important contract in 1796 in which s appears as a witness. Recently, a previously unknown letter has come to light which it is seen that Haydn was in constant touch with Rebecca Schroeter after returned to Austria. It is a letter to J. G. Graeff, a collaborator in the Hayd Salomon concerts both as flautist and composer, of April 1797. Haydn wrote German) referring to business matters:

… I had willingly written all this to Mme. Schroeter; but I can not yet explain myself c rectly in the English language, and I also lack the time. Mme Schroeter should only have goodness to address her letter directly to Vienna and I shall see that it is delivered me … [*HJB* XIII.

Just before he left England, Haydn was given a dinner party by no less a fig than James Boswell (25 June 1792; the guests seem to have included Sir John Gall and the Earl of Exeter).[9] And on 20 June, when Boswell had asked Dr Burney dine, the latter declined, saying that 'I have been long engaged to dine w Dr Haydn and all the Musical graduates that are in town, on that day.'

Not long before, on 10 April, Haydn had written to Prince Anton Esterházy, forming him of his plans to return to Austria:

Most Serene Prince of the Holy Roman Empire,
Gracious Lord and Sire!
    Since I must leave England in a short time, I hasten to place my entire faithful servi in all matters - as far as I shall be able to fulfil them - at Your SERENE HIGHNESS' dispos Our concerts will be finished at the end of June, after which I shall begin the journey ho without delay, in order to serve my most gracious Prince and Lord again. I am, in huml submission,

Your SERENE HIGHNESS'
Most humble Joseph Haydn, m.p.,
Capellmeister.

Haydn travelled back to Vienna via Bonn (July 1792), where he met a talent young man who was viola player in the Electoral Orchestra and who had co posed in 1790 two spectacular cantatas ('On the Death of Joseph II'; 'On the Elev tion of Leopold II to Emperor'); one of these (or possibly both) was submitted Haydn. The older composer was impressed and it was agreed that Beethoven, th aged 22, would accompany Haydn when he returned to England the followi year. In November 1792, Beethoven came to Vienna to begin his studies (in cou terpoint and harmony) with Haydn but, as we know, the 1793 visit to Engla never materialized.

From Bonn, Haydn journeyed to meet his Prince at Frankfurt-am-Main whe on 14 July, Leopold II was crowned Holy Roman Emperor. A few days later Hay went to discuss publishing affairs with Bernhard Schott in the town of Biebrich the Rhine; but Schott was never to become one of Haydn's personal publishe On 24 July, Haydn arrived back in Vienna and took up his old quarters on t Wasserkunstbastei No. 992, at Herr Hamberger's (this historic house, now d stroyed, was to be Beethoven's residence some years later). No Viennese new paper recorded Haydn's arrival.

If Viennese newspapers were reticent about Haydn's presence in the Imperial and Royal capital city, there was a general awareness of the triumphs achieved by Austria's leading composer while in England. Perhaps the most touching honour of all was a pyramid-shaped monument erected in 1793 by Count Harrach, the Lord of Rohrau, where Haydn had been born sixty-one years earlier. Count Harrach, upon being asked by Dies to explain how the monument came into being, wrote the following in a letter, which Dies quotes (140f.):

… The reason why I had a monument to Haydn placed in my garden was none other than the fact that, having come of age, I wanted to reorganize the flower-, vegetable-, fruit- and pheasant-gardens round my castle – a total of some forty *Joch* [= 16·83 hectares, or about 41½ acres] – into, I won't dare say an English park, but at least a proper promenade, in the planning of which economic restrictions had of necessity to play a certain part.

I thought it right and proper, and also honourable for my park, to erect a monument for the so famous J. Haydn in the castle grounds which encompassed his birthplace. Haydn was then in England [so the plan must have been made in 1791 or 1792] and was but little known to me and had no idea of my undertaking; and it was not until two or three years later that he happened to hear that this monument in Rohrau existed and without my knowing it went to see it …

Haydn offered, in 1804, to make provision in his will to ensure that after his death the monument would continue to be cared for, and Count Harrach, not to be out-done, offered to subscribe a trust fund of 500 or 600 Gulden to see that the monument was protected. In any event, it is now in Haydn's birthplace, beautifully restored by the Lower Austrian Government.

On 13 November Haydn wrote what would prove to be his last letters to Frau von Genzinger; she died a little over two months later – not yet forty-three years of age – on 20 January 1793.

Gracious Lady!
Apart from wishing you a Good Morning, this is to ask you to give the bearer of this letter the final big Aria in F minor from my opera, because I must have it copied for my Princess. I will bring it back myself in 2 days at the latest. Today I take the liberty of inviting myself to lunch, when I shall have the opportunity of kissing Your Grace's hands in return. Meanwhile I am, as always,

> Y[our] G[race's]
> Most obedient servant,
> Joseph Haydn.

Haydn had loved Frau von Genzinger perhaps more than he dared show in his letters. She had occupied a special place in his heart that neither *la* Polzelli nor even Rebecca Schroeter could replace.

Among Haydn's many friends in England was a family with which he was – to judge from the following letter in the composer's idiosyncratic English – in regular contact; although it is not possible to identify the recipient, the letter may have been sent to the Brassey family mentioned above. Writing from Vienna in December 1792, Haydn indicates that he was finding it advisable to postpone his second trip to London planned for the following year; the reasons for this no doubt included the difficulty he was having with the polypus in his nasal cavity (a long-standing problem). Haydn's letter – the longest extant example written by him in English – was discovered in a country house in the north of England in 1980:[10]

Dear Sir!
I got your beloved letter at due time: with my Prince I am a little more reconcield, but hinderme many other circumstances not to see dear friend for this year, for I am in so bad

circumstances, with my poor Nose, that I am obliged to undertake an operation, it gri
me in the Hearth, and how much I loss by it, you may imagine yourself, but I must sub
to the fate, I hope you will remain as formerly my friend. I rejoie very much, that my ha
some and good Mother Susana has changed her state, and that she got from me wishes h
and by her deserving a so good, and greatly respectable Father in Law, I wish from all
heart, that my Dear Mother may at my arrival next year present me a fine little Brother
Sister. God bless you, and your Family. I assure you to are always.

       Dear Sir

                      your Sincerely and obliged servant
                      Joseph Haydn.

   P.S. my compliment to all your good friends.

In addition, however, the Napoleonic Wars soon made it doubtful whether Hay
would be able to return to England in time for the new concert season in 1793, a
when on 21 January Louis XVI of France was guillotined it seemed that Europe
history had entered a new phase. Even before this new and dangerous situati
arose, Prince Anton Esterházy had been all against Haydn's undertaking a furth
visit to England (Haydn had 'acquired enough fame for himself'), and for the m
ment, the old composer acquiesced. He busied himself with many activities:
November 1792 he wrote Twelve Minuets and Twelve German Dances (IX:11 a
12) which were performed with a huge orchestra (the original parts have survive
including double woodwind (4 flutes, 4 oboes, etc.) and sixteen (or for the Min
ets ten) first violins. These were the greatest sets of dances he had hitherto co
posed, and are rivalled in strength, sophistication and beauty only by the Twent
Four Minuets for orchestra (1795–8?; IX:16). Haydn spent the summer months
1793 at Eisenstadt, taking his pupil Beethoven with him, and in the autumn
wrote to inform Maximilian Franz, Elector of Cologne and Beethoven's patro
that the young man 'will in time fill the position of one of Europe's greatest co
posers, and I shall be proud to be able to speak of myself as his teacher.' That su
mer of 1793, Haydn purchased a pretty little house in the Viennese suburb
Gumpendorf, where he intended to retire; it is now the Haydn Museum
Vienna.

   In June, from Eisenstadt, Haydn had to write to the tiresome Polzelli abo
money (as usual) and other devious manipulations of his ex-mistress:

Dear Polzelli!
   I hope that you will have received the two hundred florins [Gulden] which I sent *t*
Sig. Buchberg [Puchberg] – and perhaps also the other hundred, a total of 300 florins
wish I were able to send more, but my income is not large enough to permit it. I beg you
be patient with a man who up to now has done more than he really could. Remember wh
I have given and sent to you; why, it's scarcely a year ago that I gave you six hundred flc
ins! Remember how much your son costs me, and how much he will cost me until such
day as he is able to earn his own daily bread. Remember that I cannot work so hard as I ha
been able to do in the years past, for I am getting old and my memory is gradually getti
less reliable. Remember, finally, that for this and many other reasons I cannot earn a
more than I do, and that I have no salary other than the pension from my Prince Nicola
Esterházy (God rest his soul), and that this pension is barely sufficient for me to keep bo
and soul together, particularly in these critical times. ... At present I am alone with yo
son in Eisenstadt, and I shall stay here for a little while to get some fresh air and have
little rest. You will receive a letter from your son along with mine; he is in good health, a
kisses your hand for the watch. I shall stay in Vienna until the end of September, and ther
intend to take a trip with your son, and perhaps – perhaps – to go to England again for
year; but that depends mainly on whether the battleground changes; if it doesn't, I shall

somewhere else, and perhaps – perhaps – I shall see you in Naples.[11] My wife is still sick most of the time, and is always in a foul humour, but I don't really care any more – after all, this woe will pass away one day. Apart from this, I am much relieved that you, for your part, are a little more relieved about your dear sister. God bless you and keep you in good health! I shall see to it that you receive what little I can offer you, but now you really must be patient for a while, because I have other onerous debts; I can tell you that I have almost nothing for all my pains, and live more for others than for myself. I hope to have an answer before you leave for Naples. ...

While in Vienna during 1793, Haydn gave two public performances of his new London works. The first was at the Small Redoutensaal on 15 March and it included three of the London Symphonies; it was a great success ('Il etoit charmant', writes Count Zinzendorf in his Diary). At the end of the year, the Tonkünstler-Societät invited Haydn to conduct their annual Christmas concert. Although Haydn had long not been 'on speaking terms' with the society, he agreed and gave his 'madrigal' *The Storm* (XXIVa:8), originally composed with English words for the Salomon series of 1792 and now offered in a new German translation, possibly by Baron Gottfried van Swieten, who would, in due course, provide the libretto for each of the late oratorios; he also conducted a chorus from *Il ritorno di Tobia* and three of the London Symphonies (no.94 certainly, no.95 probably, and a third, unidentified, work). The daughter of Haydn's old friend, *Hofrat* Franz von Greiner, Caroline (later married Pichler, a court official) wrote some appalling dedicatory verses to commemorate the performance of Haydn's 'six new Symphonies written in England'. The *Wiener Zeitung* wrote:

Haydn himself conducted the orchestra, which consisted of over 180 persons, and the excellent performance moved the public, which appeared in large numbers, to show its complete satisfaction by often repeated and vigorous demonstrations of its undivided approval.

Eventually, Haydn persuaded his benign Prince Anton Esterházy to allow a new English trip; Baron van Swieten lent his travelling coach, and the composer, taking his valet and excellent music copyist, Johann Elssler,[12] set off for London on 19 January 1794. On his arrival (5 February), he installed himself at No.1 Bury Street (St James's), near Rebecca Schroeter, whose house at No. 6 James Street, Buckingham Gate, lay an easy ten minutes' walk via St James's Palace and The Mall, along St James's Park. On his return, Haydn brought with him a complete new symphony (usually referred to as 'Overture') to be performed at the first Salomon concert; this was no. 99 in E flat, the first symphony in which he used clarinets. The 1794 concert series was to have opened on 3 February, but in the event was postponed for a week partly owing to Haydn's arrival having been delayed. The following announcement was placed by Salomon in several London newspapers (*Oracle*, *Public Advertiser*, *Morning Chronicle* etc.) during January:

MR. SALOMON'S CONCERT, HANOVER-SQUARE.
MR. SALOMON most respectfully acquaints the Nobility and Gentry, that his CONCERTS will open on Monday the 3rd of February next, and continue on every succeeding Monday (Passion and Easter Week excepted).

Dr. HAYDN will supply the Concerts with New Compositions, and direct the Execution of them at the Piano Forte.

Principal Vocal Performers are, MADAME MARA, and Mr. FISCHER, one of the King of Prussia's principal opera Singers, who never appeared in this Country before.

Principal Instrumental Performers, who will play Concertos and Concertantes on their respective Instruments, are – Violins, Signor Viotti and Mr. Salomon – Piano Forte, Mr. Dussek – Oboe, Mr. Harrington – German Flute, Mr. Ash[e]. – Pedal Harp, Madame KRUMPHOLTZ.

Besides other distinguished Performers, who will appear occasionally.

Subscriptions at Five Guineas for the Twelve Concerts received, and Tickets delivere
at Messrs Lockarts, Maxtone, Wallis, and Clark, Pall Mall.

The Ladies' Tickets are blue, and transferable to Ladies; and the Gentlemen's are r
and transferable to Gentlemen only.

Four daily newspapers reviewed the first concert of Salomon's series; the who
of London's non-operatic musical attention was now centred on this series, t
Professional Concert having ceased to exist after an abortive 1793 season. On
February the *Morning Chronicle* reported:

SALOMON'S CONCERT.

This superb Concert was last night opened for the season, and with such an assemblage
talents as make it a rich treat to the amateur. The incomparable HAYDN, produced an Ov
ture of which it is impossible to speak in common terms. It is one of the grandest efforts
art that we ever witnessed. It abounds with ideas, as new in music as they are grand and i
pressive; it rouses and affects every emotion of the soul. – It was received with rapturo
applause.

VIOTTI produced a new Concerto, in which his own execution was most delicate a
touching; nothing could be more exquisite than his tones in the second movement. V
have no doubt but both these pieces will be called for again; for they are to be rank
among the finest productions of which music has to boast.

DUSSEK had also a new Concerto on the *piano forte*, in his best manner; and Madar
MARA sung divinely.

Symphony no. 99 was repeated at the second concert (17 February), and the crit
of the *Morning Chronicle* singled out the beautiful woodwind playing in the famo
solo wind section of the second movement: but '... indeed the pleasure the who
gave was continual; and the genius of Haydn, astonishing, inexhaustible, and su
lime, was the general theme.'

Apart from the new symphonies, Haydn brought to Salomon the new quarte
(opp. 71 and 74), which this great leader performed during the course of the seaso
and which were subsequently published in London. In the fourth conce
(3 March), Haydn conducted the première of his newest symphonic masterpiec
no. 101 ('Clock'), which was received with jubilation. Both the first and secon
movements had to be repeated – 'It was HAYDN: what can we, what need we sa
more?', concluded the *Morning Chronicle*; while the *Oracle* noted of this symphor
that 'the connoisseurs admit [it] to be his best work.'

In the eighth concert (31 March), Haydn conducted the first performance of th
third of his new symphonies, no. 100 in G (the 'Military') which, as the criticisn
were soon to show, would be the greatest success of his whole career, surpassir
even the popularity of the 'Surprise': he had somehow caught the spirit of the da
in a miraculous way. The *Morning Chronicle* of 9 April reported:

... Another new Symphony, by Haydn, was performed for the second time; and the midd
movement was again received with absolute shouts of applause. Encore! encore! encore! r
sounded from every seat: the Ladies themselves could not forbear. It is the advancing
battle; and the march of men, the sounding of the charge, the thundering of the onset, th
clash of arms, the groans of the wounded, and what may well be called the hellish roar
war increase to a climax of horrid sublimity! which, if others can conceive, he alone ca
execute; at least he alone hitherto has effected these wonders.

The review obviously refers to bars 152 ff. of the Allegretto; 'the climax of horri
sublimity' describes the ominous timpani roll (bars 159 f.) and the ensuing tut
(bar 161).

Salomon's last concert of the season took place on 12 May; it is now clear from the criticisms that men in London realized more than ever before that these concerts were continually creating musical history, and it must have occurred to more than one astute mind that these great Haydn symphonies were in fact entering the permanent repertoire on the night of their respective débuts. Haydn had been persuaded to remain another season, and this fact was apparently announced to the, no doubt delighted, audience on 12 May.

One reason why Haydn may have shown himself willing to stay on in England had been the news of the death of Prince Anton Esterházy ('from a sudden bursting of a pus sac in his rib-cage'). In such circumstances there seemed to be no reason why Haydn should not settle permanently in England – his professional future was, after all, assured – and there is every evidence to suggest that he was seriously considering the prospect during the season of 1794. However, at this critical juncture in his career Haydn received an all-important letter containing the intentions of Prince Anton's successor, Nicolaus II, who was visiting Italy; the letter, which has not survived, was sent from Naples, as Dies (155f.) records:

About half a year after Haydn's arrival in London, a letter was sent him in the name of the [then] reigning Prince Nicolaus [II] Esterházy (who was at that time travelling through Italy) from Naples, which contained the news: 'The Prince has appointed Haydn as his *Kapellmeister*, and wishes to restore the whole band again.' Haydn received this news with the greatest pleasure. He had entertained for a long time the warmest sympathy for the Princes Esterházy; they had offered him his daily bread and (what was more important) given him the opportunity of developing his musical talents. Haydn saw, of course, that his income in England was large, and that it by far exceeded that in his fatherland. Moreover, it would have been easy for him to secure any kind of well-paid position there [in England]. Since the death of Prince Anton, he was a completely free man; nothing bound him to the princely house except love and gratitude. It was those things, however, that silenced every opposition and persuaded him to accept the offer of Prince Nicolaus with joy and, as soon as his commitments in London were fulfilled, to return to his native country.

There were probably three important reasons which motivated Haydn's decision to return: (1) The pace at which he lived in England was simply too quick for a man of over sixty to be able to keep up for any length of time. (2) The Terror in France was approaching its ghastly climax, and the war was going badly for the Allies: on 10 July the French occupied Brussels, in August Trier (Trèves) which they successfully defended against Allied counter-attacks, and in October they attacked Holland and drove out the English troops. In view of all this, Haydn thought it was best to be in his own country and where his own native language was spoken (he never achieved fluency in English). (3) Haydn knew that in his old age, he would be taken care of by Prince Esterházy, that he would never starve or lack for bodily comforts.

For the moment, however, Haydn stayed on. Apart from attending London festivities, he was anxious to see more of England, and in the summer of 1794 he travelled widely. In July, after visiting Hampton Court, he went on to Portsmouth. He had come to love ships, and among his friends in England were several sea captains, one of whom had given him a memorable lunch on board an East India merchantman in August 1791. From Portsmouth, the composer crossed the Solent to the Isle of Wight. In August he went with two friends to Bath, where he stayed at Perrymead, the house of the famous Italian-born castrato, Venanzio Rauzzini, for whom Mozart had composed 'Exsultate, jubilate' (K.165) in Milan in January 1773. In his notebook, Haydn recorded his impressions in some detail:

On 2nd August 1794, I left at 5 o'clock in the morning for Bath, with Mr Ashe and Mr Cimador, and arrived there at 8 o'clock in the evening. It's 107 miles from London. The Mail Coach does this distance in 12 hours. I lived at the house of Herr Rauzzini, a *Musicus* who is very famous, and who in his time was one of the greatest singers. He has lived there 19 years, supports himself by the Subscription Concerts which are given in the Winter, and by giving lessons. He is a very nice and hospitable man. His summer house, where I stayed, is situated on a rise in the middle of a most beautiful neighbourhood, from which you can see the whole city. Bath is one of the most beautiful cities in Europe. All the houses are built of stone; this stone comes from quarries in the surrounding mountains; it is very soft, so soft, in fact, that it's no trouble to cut it up into any desired shape; it is very white, and the older it is, once it has been taken from the quarry, the harder it gets. The whole city lies on a slope, and that is why there are very few carriages; instead of them, there are a lot of sedan-chairs, who will take you quite a way for 6 pence. But too bad that there are so few straight roads; there are a lot of beautiful squares, on which stand the most magnificent houses, but which cannot be reached by any vehicle: they are now building a brand-new and broad street.

N.B. Today, on the 3rd, I looked at the city, and found, half-way up the hill, a building shaped like a half-moon, and more magnificent than any I had seen in London. The curve extends for 100 fathoms, and there is a Corinthian column at each fathom. The building has 3 floors. Round about it, the pavement in front of the houses is 10 feet broad for the pedestrians, and the street as wide *a proportione*; it is surrounded by an iron fence, and a terrace slopes down 50 fathoms in successive stages, through a beautiful expanse of green; on both sides there are little paths, by which one can descend very comfortably.

Every Monday and Friday evening all the bells are rung, but apart from this, you don't hear many bells being rung. The city is not thickly populated, and in summer one sees very few people; for the people taking the baths don't come till the beginning of October, and stay through half of February. But then a great many people come, so that in the year 1791, 25,000 persons were there. All the inhabitants live off this influx, without which the city would be very poor: there are very few merchants and almost no trade, and everything is very dear. The baths are by nature very warm; one bathes in the water, and one also drinks it – generally the latter. And one pays very little: to bathe it costs 3 shillings at all times. I made the acquaintance there of Miss Brown, a charming person of the best *conduit*; a good pianoforte player, her mother a most beautiful woman. The city is now building a most splendid room for guests taking the cure.

A touching story concerning Rauzzini is recounted by Dies (127 f.):

Rauzzini had in his garden a monument to his best friend, who had been snatched from him by death. In the inscription, he lamented the loss of such a true friend, &c., and concluded his lament with the words: 'He was not a man – he was a dog.'

Haydn secretly copied this inscription and composed a four-part canon to the words. Rauzzini was surprised: he liked the canon so much that he had it incised on the monument, to the honour of Haydn's and the dog's.[13]

Another personal touch is revealed in the compliment paid to Haydn by Dr Henry Harington, a composer then living in Bath, who wrote a poem of praise, 'What Art expresses'; on receiving this tribute, Haydn promptly set it to music. This episode inspired Muzio Clementi to observe:

The first doctor [Harington] having bestowed much praise on the second doctor [Haydn] the said second doctor – out of doctorial gratitude – returns the first doctor thanks for a favour received, and praises in his turn the said first doctor most handsomely.

From Bath Haydn went on to visit Bristol, and three weeks later the indefatigable composer went to visit Sir Charles Rich at Waverley Abbey, near Farnham in Surrey – 'I must confess that whenever I looked at this beautiful wilderness, my heart was oppressed at the thought that all this once belonged to my religion' (Haydn's Diary).

Haydn now came more and more to the attention of the royal family. In the Fourth Notebook, he wrote:

On 1st February 1795, I was invited by the Prince of Wales to attend a musical soirée at the Duke of York's, which the King, the Queen, her whole family, the Duke of Orange &c. attended. Nothing else except my own compositions was played; I sat at the pianoforte; finally I had to sing, too. The King, who hitherto could or would hear only Handel's music, was attentive; he chatted with me, and introduced me to the Queen, who said many complimentary things to me. I sang my German song, 'Ich bin der Verliebteste'.[14] On 3rd Feb., I was invited to the Prince of Wales'; on 15th, 17th and 19th Apr. 1795, I was there again, and on the 21st at the Queen's in Buckingham House.

There are many descriptions of this soirée, which must have been one of the highpoints of Haydn's whole life. By far the most interesting description is by William Parke.[15]

... At the end of the first part of the concert Haydn had the distinguished honour of being formally introduced to His Majesty George III., by His Royal Highness the Prince of Wales. My station at the time was so near to the King, that I could not avoid hearing the whole of their conversation. Amongst other observations, His Majesty said (in English) 'Doctor Haydn, you have written a great deal.' To which Haydn modestly replied, 'Yes, Sire, a great deal more than is good.' To which the King neatly rejoined, 'Oh no, the world contradicts that.'

After his introduction, Haydn, by desire of the Queen, sat down to the pianoforte, and, surrounded by Her Majesty and her royal and accomplished daughters, sung, and accompanied himself admirably in several of his *Canzonets*. The gracious reception Haydn experienced from the King was not only gratifying to *his* feelings, but flattering to the science he professed; and while it displayed the condescension and liberality of a great and good monarch, it could not fail proving a powerful stimulus to rising *genius*.

Meanwhile, Salomon had come to a momentous decision: he was going to relinquish his concerts and merge forces with the Opera. In a very long open letter to the Press, he gives his reasons for so doing, the principal one being the difficulty of finding singers willing to cross the English Channel. Thus, the great Salomon concert series seemed to be at an end (in fact, however, he was able to start them up again in 1796). Haydn was not particularly worried, since the new organization had obviously approached him at once and secured his services. The Opera Concert series of 1795 was led by the great violinist and composer Giovan Battista Viotti, who fled from France to England in 1793; he was at the head of a very large orchestra of sixty players, and it was for this splendid group that Haydn composed his last three symphonies, no. 102–104. The first of these was the *pièce de résistance* of the first concert (2 February), while the 'Drum Roll' Symphony (no. 103) was first played at the fourth concert (2 March) and 'excited the deepest attention'. Coincidentally, that very night, in Vienna, Beethoven made his début at a concert given by Prince Lobkowitz and 'made everyone sit up and listen' (Zinzendorf, Diary).

The big event of the London season was Haydn's benefit concert on 4 May, perhaps the greatest concert of his life. At this spectacular event, two new pieces by Haydn were played for the first time: Symphony no. 104, 'The 12th which I have composed in England', wrote Haydn on the autograph, perhaps with a certain sense of destiny; and the beautiful *Scena di Berenice* for Brigida Giorgi Banti, one of the great cantatas of the age and the model for Beethoven's *Scena* 'Ah, perfido!' composed a year later in Prague. Some of the greatest singers in the world participated, not only *la* Banti but also Anna Morichelli, her great rival, and Giovanni Morelli. At such elegant concerts in London, the principal performers dressed with great formality, and eye-witnesses recall Haydn playing 'at a concert in tie wig, with a sword at his side'.[16]

After this spectacular benefit concert, which brought the composer 4,000 Gulden in cash, Haydn continued to appear, not only at the Opera Concert (which extended its season by two concerts), but at the benefit concerts for his friends, such as Sophia Corri (now Mrs Dussek), the violinist Hindmarsh or the flautist Andrew Ashe ('The house was quite full', wrote Haydn in his diary); these concerts took place in late May and early June.

On 16 May, Haydn was a witness at the marriage between Therese Jansen and Gaetano Bartolozzi at St James's Church, Piccadilly. The other witnesses were Charlotte Jansen, Gaetano's father Francis (Francesco) Bartolozzi, the famous engraver, and Maria Adelaide de la Heras. Haydn composed his last three piano sonatas (nos. 60–62; XVI:50–52) in 1794 for Miss Jansen and would later write three piano trios for her.

For the next two months Haydn lived quietly in London, supervising publications of his latest works, e.g. three piano trios, nos. 35–37 (XV:21–3) dedicated to Princess Marie Hermenegild Esterházy; they appeared in London on 13 June. He was also completing various new pieces, such as the final six English Canzonettas, and three piano trios (including the celebrated 'Gypsy Rondo') dedicated to Mrs Schroeter. He made a catalogue of his works composed in England which he put into one of his notebooks: it enumerates what Haydn called '768 sheets', a sheet meaning a bifolium (four pages), i.e. a total of over 3,000 pages – and almost every work a masterpiece. It was a staggering achievement for a man in his sixties.

On 15 August, Haydn left England, never to return. Griesinger (23) tells us that the composer

made through his three-year sojourn in England some 24,000 Gulden, of which about 9,000 were used for the trips, for his stay, and for other costs. ... Haydn often repeated that he first became famous in Germany through England ... [p.35]. [He] considered the days spent in England the happiest of his life. He was everywhere appreciated there, it opened a new world to him, and he could, through his rich earnings, at last escape the restricted circumstances in which he had grown grey.

Haydn's British friends would still remember him with affection many years after he had left the country. Writing in Rees' *Cyclopaedia* long after the composer's death, Dr Burney reminds his readers that '... it is well known how much he contributed to our delight, to the advancement of his art, and to his own fame, by his numerous productions in this country, and how much his natural, unassuming and pleasing character, exclusive of his productions, endeared him to his acquaintances and to the nation at large.'[17]

VIII
Haydn's music,
1791–1795

HAYDN'S NAME had been introduced to the London public in 1765, when six quartets published by Hummel of Amsterdam were advertised under the garbled name of 'Haydri'. During the 1770s Joseph Haydn's name became familiar to English musicians principally as a composer of quartets, but his popularity was not really established until the 1780s when, as a result of the business association between William Forster and the composer, his symphonies became available in substantial numbers. The firm of Longman & Broderip acted as English agents for Artaria and in this way many Viennese publications, too, were sold in London. Enterprise on the part of English publishers coincided with increased opportunities for composers of symphonies. For nearly twenty years J. C. Bach and Abel had dominated instrumental music in London, mainly through the annual series of subscription concerts, held between late January and April, in which their own symphonies formed the chief attraction. Bach died on 1 January 1782, Abel five years later in 1787, and there were no clear local successors. As early as the autumn of 1782, concert promoters attempted to persuade Haydn to travel to London, and his symphonies nos. 76-78 were composed for a planned visit in the following season. When, in 1790, after repeated attempts to entice him and countless rumours of his expected arrival in London, Haydn was finally able to accept the invitation of Salomon, he was about to take on the role created by J. C. Bach and Abel, that of a composer in residence, appearing in person at each of the subscription concerts, sitting at the keyboard from where he helped the leader to direct the performance.

As had been the case in the Bach–Abel concerts, the composer's own symphonies were to form the main feature of Salomon's concerts and, consequently, were the main component of the contract between Salomon and Haydn. The composer wrote six new symphonies for the first London visit, nos. 95 and 96 for the 1791 season and nos. 93, 94, 97 and 98 for the 1792 season. When Haydn returned in 1794, he provided Salomon with three new symphonies for that season, nos. 99-101; finally, in 1795, when Salomon's role as promoter was taken over by the Opera Concert, Haydn provided three symphonies, his last, nos. 102–104. In addition, in 1791 he composed an opera, *L'anima del filosofo*, to be performed at the rebuilt King's Theatre (gutted by fire in 1789) and in 1792 a *symphonie concertante* (which Haydn called simply 'Concertante'). Quartets from the op. 64 set were played in the 1791 and 1792 seasons and, recognizing their popularity with the players as much as with the audience, Haydn composed a set of six new quartets, some of which were played during the course of the 1794 season. Six quartets, twelve symphonies, a *symphonie concertante* and an opera form an impressive output over five years and, at the most mundane level, are a tribute to Haydn's untiring industry in an environment that was completely new. But, as Haydn's own catalogue of music written in and for England reveals,[1] these works constitute only a proportion, some sixty per cent, of his output during this period. Other works composed for English individuals and publishers include piano sonatas, piano trios, military marches, songs, a concert aria and a whole range of sundry vocal items (from arrangements of Scottish folk-

songs to a projected ode). A few items in Haydn's list have not survived, such
some further concert arias, dances and a setting of the national anthem describe
simply as '1 God save the King 2 sheets'. Haydn's busy life as the Esterházy *Kape
meister* had prepared him for this rigorous schedule: London provided him wi
the artistic stimulus.

English commentators of the time often linked Haydn's name with that of the
idol, Handel, typically as the 'two first composers of the ancient and moder
school'.[2] For a brief period in the 1790s, English audiences adopted Haydn as the
own. Fifty years earlier, Handel, at the age of nearly sixty, had begun the most e
duringly successful period of his career with the composition of oratorio; in 1791,
a similar age, Haydn was about to embark on the composition of works that lik
wise marked a new dynamic stage in a long career.

Symphonies

Salomon had met Haydn in Vienna in early December 1790; by 2 January 1791 th
composer was in London. The speed with which the agreement between them w.
made represented a coup for Salomon the impresario: for Haydn this unexpecte
turn of events, only three months after the sudden death of Prince Nicolau
meant that he had no opportunity to prepare new works for the beginning of th
concert season, planned for 11 February. (In the event the first concert was twic
postponed, and finally took place on 11 March. Although Salomon's difficulties i
organizing the series caused the delay, the situation should not be regarded as e.
ceptional; postponing the advertised first concert had become something of a gan
bit, frequently practised by Bach and Abel, to arouse expectation.) Haydn had tw
months, therefore, in which to acclimatize himself to the new musical enviro
ment and, rather like contemporary composers of opera, he was able to compos
his music with some knowledge of the performers and of the audience. He intro
duced himself at the first subscription concert with a performance of Symphon
no. 92, composed in 1789 and later dubbed the 'Oxford', which had not yet bee
published in England. The two new symphonies he composed for the 1791 sea
son, nos. 96 and 95, show Haydn cultivating his audience with considerable music.
diplomacy.

No. 96 in D major, probably the first of the two, seems a deliberate attempt t
recreate the brilliance of Symphony no. 53, also in D major, the composer's best
known symphony to date in London. Between no. 53 and no. 96 Haydn's sympho
nies had, of course, broken new ground, represented principally in the 'Paris' sym
phonies. These works were known to London audiences and no. 96 adopts man
of their characteristics, as well as some from nos. 88 and 92. The now standard fea
ture of a slow introduction is included, moving to the minor and adumbrating th
shape of the first subject, as in the 'Oxford' Symphony; the slow movement is de
liberately lightweight and includes a written-out ensemble cadenza (with a de
lightfully intrusive E flat appoggiatura in the bass at the trilled cadence) as i
no. 84 in E flat; the reprise of the theme in the minuet is expanded as in no. 86 i
D; and the rondo finale uses an ABACA pattern as in no. 88 in G. No. 86 in D ex
erts a particular influence on the first movement of no. 96, in the use of martia
rhythms and a flamboyant *fortissimo* deflection of the harmony shortly before th
close.

No. 95 is also very conscious of its precursors, though here the symphony rep
resents a fusion of the minor-key and the C major symphonic traditions. For this
Haydn's last symphony in a minor key, the choice of C minor may again have bee

deliberate, evoking the sound of no. 78, composed for the earlier projected visit to London, an affinity made more evident by the similarity of their opening motif. The earlier C minor symphony, like other post-*Sturm und Drang* works in the minor, had attempted unsuccessfully to resolve minor and major within one work. While Symphony no. 83 in G minor had demonstrated new powers of assimilation, no. 95 represents an even more convincing resolution of conflicting atmospheres. It would be perverse to label the C minor to major progress of no. 95 as tragedy to triumph, but Beethoven's Fifth Symphony, completed over fifteen years later, is nevertheless indebted to this work. Beethoven's Fifth was to capture the anguished imagination of many nineteenth- and twentieth-century composers, Brahms, Tchaikovsky and Shostakovich, to name only three; Haydn's resolution has the cooler demeanour of the Age of Reason.

As the only London symphony in the minor key, no. 95 is also the only one without a slow introduction, the first movement beginning with a *fortissimo* assertion of a five-note figure that is to recur throughout. But this is not a single-minded movement, the evenly phrased second subject indicating the contrast that is an essential part of this symphony. At the equivalent point in the recapitulation C minor changes to major and the first movement ends in a mood of unequivocal affirmation. Following a strophic set of variations in E flat major in an andante tempo, the Menuet returns the listener to C minor, not through immediate assertion (as in the first movement) but with a tentative four-note phrase in a *piano* dynamic for strings alone, a rare example in a London symphony of a minuet that does not begin with a tutti and *forte*. The finale is a sonata-rondo in C major, a key heralded at the end of the first movement and in the Trio. It turns to the minor only once, in a mock-serious outburst in the development section. Though obviously indebted to the long series of C major symphonies, this finale outdoes them all in sophistication, including for that matter the later no. 97. The main theme is disconcertingly inactive, with its *piano* dynamic, held notes and slow, mainly diatonic harmony. The arrival of the first tutti provides the explanation in the form of a passage of invertible counterpoint featuring, as one of its thematic components, the opening idea of the rondo. The contrapuntal writing itself, which is to recur as the second subject (or B) and in the development (or C), shows the abiding influence of species counterpoint training and its bravura presentation the undeniable influence of Mozart's 'Jupiter' Symphony (see example overleaf).

Like the symphonies of the previous decade, nos. 95 and 96 rejoice in the bold sonority of the late Classical orchestra: two flutes (one in no. 95), two oboes, two bassoons, two horns, two trumpets, timpani and strings. Trumpets and timpani are used in all twelve London symphonies, including many of the slow movements. Haydn was evidently impressed by the abilities of individual players in London, and wrote attractive solo passages for the oboe in no. 96, cello and (briefly) violin in no. 95. This trait, which recalls Haydn's practice in the 1760s when he had been excited by the Esterházy personnel, was to be developed in the subsequent London symphonies.

In the following season, Haydn presented nos. 93 and 94, composed in 1791, and nos. 98 and 97, composed in the early months of 1792. All four show a new sense of audacity, Haydn's ready response to the acclaim he was receiving and a reflection of his and his audience's predilection for the mildly shocking; the most celebrated example is the sudden *fortissimo* chord that interrupts the progress of the Andante of Symphony no. 94 ('there the ladies will jump', as he told Gyrowetz).[3] Though an extant sketch for this movement shows that the 'surprise' was in fact an afterthought, it and other features are not altogether new: the 'semplice'

Symphony no. 95/IV

tune with its distinctive *tenuto* markings has the gait of some of Haydn's songs of the 1780s, especially 'Gegenliebe'; the format of this slow movement is like that of no. 95, strophic variations; and both the surprise and the *brioso* fifth variation are reminiscent of the slow movement of Symphony no. 85. No. 93 has its own piece of audacity in the slow movement that is on a par with the famous surprise, a *fortissimo* bottom C from bassoons that smartly puts an end to six bars of directionless music. Haydn's first two symphonies for London had been cautious in their slow movements, both andante. Perhaps the particular reception accorded to the 'Ox-

ford' Symphony, with its Adagio movement with forceful trumpets and timpani, encouraged Haydn to compose the similarly characterized Largo of no. 93.

Less than a year separates the two D major symphonies, nos. 96 and 93, yet the latter is a very different work from Haydn's first symphony for London. The slow introduction in D major turns magically to the Neapolitan E flat before moving on to the tonic minor. The relaxed first subject is not foreshadowed in the introduction but, consciously or otherwise, is a re-working of the opening phrase of the rondo of Haydn's previous symphony, no. 95. The symphony traverses a wider

emotional spectrum than no. 96, from the thoughtful to the grandiloquent. Th
Menuetto [*sic*] is a masterpiece of thematic evolution and colourful orchestratio
Rather than featuring a solo instrument, the Trio alternates *forte* fanfares and *pia*
answering phrases in the strings, the harmonic direction of the latter being as ol
lique as the heralding fanfares had been straightforward. In the Trio, Haydn omi
the customary first repeat, a notable first example of a practice that was to becon
common in later symphonies. The finale is a sonata rondo of unceasing rhythm
energy and vivid orchestral colouring including, in the last few moments of th

symphony, a *fortissimo* declamation of the opening motif (with the grace notes) on oboes, bassoons, horns and trumpets – a splendidly raucous sound. The main theme itself is full of harmonic surprise, to delight the connoisseur and tantalize the impatient. The first sixteen bars (see overleaf) divide into four four-bar phrases, 'a', 'b', 'a' and 'b¹'. Phrase 'a' rests on tonic harmony and 'b' begins on diminished harmony on A sharp before leading to a half-close on the dominant; the second 'b' cleverly begins on the same bass note but now spelt as a B flat and harmonized as a first inversion chord to lead the music back to D.

The second part of the theme is equally teasing. It begins with imitative passages at the distance of a bar coming to rest on a dominant chord followed by a pause, as if in preparation for the return of the opening. Instead of the expected reprise, what ensues is a version in the minor key of the opening phrase, before the dominant is once again established and the section concludes with the second half ('a' and 'b¹') of the opening section.

This D major symphony received its premiere at the first concert of the 1792 season, on 17 February, after which Haydn recorded in his notebook that the Largo was encored. Of the several reports in the London press, that of *The Times* gives the clearest idea of the impression this symphony made.

Such a combination of excellence was contained in every movement, as inspired all the performers as well as the audience with enthusiastic ardour.

Novelty of idea, agreeable caprice, and whim combined with all *Haydn's* sublime and wanton grandeur, gave additional consequence to the *soul* and feelings of every individual present.

The 'sublime and wanton grandeur' of Symphony no. 93 had clearly succeeded in capturing the attention of the London audience at the beginning of the season; the composer's next symphony to be performed, no. 98, was quite different, less sensational and Haydn's most personal London symphony to date. In this work he used trumpets in B flat for the first time in his career and, at the age of sixty, created a new sonority that was to be as potent in the remainder of his career as the keys of D and especially C major had been hitherto. The slow introduction begins immediately in the minor, rather than in the major, with stern octave phrases that are di-

Symphony no. 98/I

rectly related to the first subject of the Allegro. That, however, is completely different in mood, the contrast typifying the impressive control of tension and relaxation that is apparent throughout this movement. In earlier years, the Allegro might have been a taut, hard-driven movement, probably dominated by its opening three-note figure. This sonata form movement is monothematic in the sense that the second subject in the dominant key draws on the first subject, but the exposition avoids over-exploiting the main idea; passages in slower harmonic rhythm with pedal points, such as that which delays the first tutti, and especially that which precedes the codetta, contribute immeasurably to the new poise of the music (see example above and overleaf).

The three-note figure asserts itself in the development section, controlling the direction of the music as the texture rids itself of the old theme plus accompaniment layout. The use of running quavers in counterpoint against the minims of the main theme is a favoured technique in development sections by Haydn, and

one that again reaches back to species counterpoint training. Here the quaver
come to dominate the texture as the music moves firmly towards G minor; at thi
point Haydn, once again, skilfully reduces the activity of the music, in preparation
for the recapitulation. In terms of length the recapitulation is nineteen bars shor
ter than the exposition, but this cold statistic conceals a process of compression
and then of expansion; the tutti following the first subject takes the music to a
point midway through the second subject area, omitting most of the transition and
the second subject version of the first subject; thereafter the process is one of con
trolled expansion involving bars 114ff. (see example) and a coda of forty-two bars
based on the first subject.

   Having first won over his audience with evenly paced slow movements includ
ing trumpets and timpani and having followed these with a slower movement also
with trumpets and timpani (the Largo of no. 93), Haydn now feels confiden
enough to compose a deeply committed Adagio without those instruments. The
thematic reference to 'God save the King' in the first two phrases is probably de-

liberate, an attraction to compensate, as it were, for the absence of trumpets and timpani. On 19 February, eleven days before the premiere, Haydn had heard the melody played by a wind band 'in the street during a wild snowstorm'.[4] In the symphony it provides an entrée into a movement of great poignancy, one suffused with a frankness and simplicity of gesture increasingly typical of Haydn in his later years. Haydn had heard of the death of Mozart in December 1791, and many commentators have opined that this movement represents Haydn's tribute to his memory; certainly the scoring, accompaniment patterns and occasional melodic nuance recall the slow movement of the 'Jupiter' Symphony, while the almost Verdian *forzato* appoggiaturas in bars 23–24 suggest a more anguished expression of grief.

Compared with the rhythmic vigour of the minuets of the previous London symphonies, especially nos. 93 and 94, that of no. 98 has a certain restraint, only permitting itself an unorthodox, though very fluent, modulation to A flat major after the double bar. Restraint, too, is the hallmark of the finale, the vein of comedy never becoming brash. The movement is a presto sonata form in 6/8, of a character

and type that owe nothing to Mozart. The comedy is held in check until the deve
opment begins in an unprepared A flat major (again!), with the second subjec
played by a solo violin over a simplified accompaniment. The music is then d
rected towards a second statement (with flute) in A major. A lengthy *fortissim*
tutti comes to rest on a pause on an octave D; the solo violin refuses to treat thi
emphasized note in the conventional way, as a dominant or a mediant, but instea
treats it as the leading note of E flat major. From this tonality the solo violin hes
tatingly leads the music into the recapitulation, a passage that, judged from th
evidence of extant sketches, caused Haydn some trouble. A substantial coda is ap
pended to the movement, beginning with a laboured version of the main them
(Più moderato) and culminating in one more statement of the main theme which
to our surprise, is accompanied by semiquaver arpeggios on the pianoforte, ai
irresistible jest which, when played by the composer at the work's premiere oi
2 March 1792, must have delighted the audience. The concluding mood of the sym
phony is very different from that in which it had begun and, in a very persona
way, this progression of mood is as impressive as that which had figured in no. 9
in C minor.

Haydn's final symphony in his first visit, no. 97 in C major, was completed rap
idly in March-April 1792 and probably first performed at the composer's benefi
concert on 3 May. For this end-of-season occasion Haydn composed a symphon
that he knew would thrill his audience, a bold, aggressive work, his last in a long
series of symphonies in the key of C major. In general approach there is nothing
startlingly new about this symphony: it has a slow introduction, a set of variations
incorporating a rousing passage for trumpets and timpani in the *minore* section, a
fully scored minuet with solos for oboe and violin in the lilting trio and a rondo
(ABACA) finale. Haydn, however, takes the opportunity to try out several new
ideas. Most obvious is the glassy sonority produced by the *al ponticello* marking ir
the third variation in the Adagio. The slow introduction ostensibly reverts to olde
practice by not even hinting at the minor and not foreshadowing the content ol
the first subject; Haydn instead presents a new relationship between introductior
and principal section, the first subject entering *fortissimo* after the *piano* of the in
troduction (the reverse of the usual procedure) and the diminished seventh har
monies associated with the melodic line foreshadowing the codetta (later coda)
material rather than first subject material. In the Menuetto Haydn dispenses with
all the usual repeat marks (except for the customary instruction 'Menuetto da
capo') so that, by writing the movement out in full, he can vary the content a little.
Finally, the coda to the rondo is unprecedentedly theatrical, a virtual compendium
of Haydn's resources at this stage in an orchestral rondo, containing harmonic
surprises, contrasting dynamics, pauses, *pizzicati* and a wide range of orchestral
sounds from tutti playing *fortissimo* to a single line: a marvellously self-confident
and brilliant conclusion to Haydn's first London visit.

In the eighteenth months that separated the two London sojourns Haydn was
able to take stock of his achievement and prepare for the second visit. He was now
fully acquainted with the taste of the English public, having first cultivated and
then enhanced it, so that in Vienna, away from the draining bustle of English life,
he was able to consider his plans for the 1794 and, more vaguely, 1795 seasons. In
1793, Haydn composed Symphony no. 99 and portions of nos. 100 and 101, complet
ing the last two in London. Nos. 100 and 101, the 'Military' and the 'Clock', play on
the London audience's liking for the simple, easily remembered characteristic –
no. 93 had had the bassoon bottom C and the fanfares, no. 94, the surprise; and
no. 98, the keyboard solo and the allusion to the national anthem. Now, no. 100 in-

troduces percussion instruments (triangle, cymbal and bass drum) in the slow movement and the finale, the former being an extreme example of the slow movement with 'noisy' interlude as cultivated in the first visit. At a time when London was the haven for countless refugees from Robespierre's Reign of Terror in France, and England had joined Austria, Holland, Spain in the war against that country, Haydn's clear intention was to evoke the terrifying sound of battle. To this end he used a march-like movement from one of the notturni for the King of Naples (VIIh:3), retaining the wind scoring and adding specific musical allusions to battle, namely an actual army call, the Austrian General Salute.[5] Haydn's 'Military' Symphony is one of the earliest, and certainly one of the most distinguished, in a long series of battle works generated by the Napoleonic Wars. When the symphony was first performed in London on 31 March 1794, the second movement was encored; when the symphony was repeated on 7 April, the reporter of the *Morning Chronicle* was hardly able to control his imagination (see above, p. 248).

The slow movement of no. 101, also, is pictorially conceived, with the accompaniment imitating the steady tick of a clock; this movement and the first were encored in the first performance. The remaining London symphonies do not include such obvious graphic features as the 'Military' or the 'Clock', and Haydn must have recognized the dangers inherent in this approach. Certainly, when the 'Military' Symphony was reviewed in the *Allgemeine Musikalische Zeitung* in 1799, its critic, tempering praise with caution, uttered remarks that may already have occurred to Haydn in 1794.

It is somewhat less learned, and easier to take in than some of the other newest works by him, but it is just as rich in new ideas as they. The effect of surprise cannot perhaps be pushed further than it is here, when in the second movement we are utterly surprised by the full Janissary music in the minore – up to that point one had no idea that these Turkish instruments were part of the symphony's scoring.

Symphony no. 99 and the three symphonies for the 1795 season, nos. 102–104, eschew the 'effect of surprise' and the last three, in particular, show a concentration of musical intellect that makes them the most serious-minded and solid of the twelve London symphonies.

A novel sound in the works composed for the second London visit is that of clarinets, featured for the first time in Haydn's symphonies. In 1791, the composer had scored for clarinets in his (unperformed) opera *L'anima del filosofo*, but although the instruments were regularly heard in England in operas and in the Pleasure Gardens, they were not yet standard members of the concert orchestra. But of Haydn's last six symphonies only no. 102 in B flat does not use the instrument. Given the assurance with which Haydn writes for other woodwind instruments, the clarinet writing in the symphonies is disappointing. Haydn must have had little confidence in the particular players, for their solo passages in no. 99 (especially in the development section of the first movement) and no. 103 (the Trio) are covered by other instruments; the only occasions when they are heard unsupported are in brief passages in the finale of no. 99.[6] Solos for other wind instruments remain as frequent as ever and, in addition, Haydn shows a new penchant for the sound of a woodwind choir, announcing the first subject in the first movement of the 'Military', frequently leading the march in the same symphony and playing a colourful role in the first, second and fourth movements of no. 104.

During the period between the two London visits Haydn composed a set of quartets, opp. 71 and 74, that show a consistent interest in the juxtaposition of keys a third apart. Interest in mediant relationships surfaces in the six last symphonies

too, though not to the same extent. At one point the G major of the slow movement of the 'Clock' switches without preparation to a rich E flat major; the first
movement of the 'Military', also in G, contains a deflection to B flat major (beginning of development) and E flat major (second subject in recapitulation); and
Haydn's last symphony, no. 104 in D, contains a Trio in B flat major. The first of
the symphonies associated with the second visit, no. 99 in E flat major, is exactly
contemporary with the opp. 71 and 74 quartets and contains several instances of the
juxtaposition of keys a third apart.[7] The Adagio introduction moves dramatically
towards an unresolved *tenuto* C flat; this is interpreted as a B natural – the old English word for a pun, a clinch, is very apt here – and the music moves through E minor before coming to a rest on a pause on a G major chord. This apparent end to
the introduction is followed by a sustained chord on the dominant seventh of the
home tonic, E flat. The slow movement is in the key of G major, the first and only
time in a symphony in a major key that Haydn used a third-related tonality for a
slow movement; it is affirmed by another of those heart-warming initial phrases
first noticed in no. 98. In this ternary-shaped movement, Haydn cleverly replicates
the effect on the return of the theme, by allowing the middle section to come to
rest on a B major chord, a major third above G major. The Menuetto is in E flat
major but its Trio is in C major, a link between the two keys being provided by the
repeated G's in the oboes, a simple device which Schubert and Dvořák were to
make their own. To get back to the E flat of the minuet, Haydn provides an eighteen-bar transition.

Haydn's slow introductions continue to grow in profundity and consequence in
the six last symphonies. Only that of no. 102 confines its field of influence to the
first subject of the following movement. That of no. 99 presages the mediant interest that is to figure throughout the symphony, while the tonic and dominant (D
and A) emphasis of that of no. 104 outlines the profile of the main themes of the
entire symphony. Similar, though less pervasive, thematic relationships between
introduction and remainder of the symphony can be heard in no. 100 and no. 101.

Symphony no. 103 in E flat major was first performed on 2 March 1795 and in
this, his penultimate symphony, Haydn is at his most commanding. The slow introduction opens with a lengthy timpani roll before unison bassoons, cellos and
double bass (the last named written an octave higher so that it sounds at the same
pitch as the other instruments) guide the music towards a perfect cadence in
B flat, a process repeated to lead back to the tonic. Ominous, unsupported thematic writing in the lowest register of the orchestra is a sound that the nineteenth
century was to make very much its own (e.g. Beethoven's Triple Concerto, Schubert's 'Unfinished' Symphony), but it must have sounded extremely novel in an
age accustomed to thematic writing in the treble register; the day after the première, the *Morning Chronicle* noted 'The Introduction excited the deepest attention'.
As if to draw attention to this new sonority, the next two phrases move to the opposite end of the pitch spectrum, treble sounds joined at the cadence by bass
instruments. A full, four-part sonority then leads the music to a pause on the
dominant of C, with weighty *forzato* emphasis on the first note of the semitone interval, A flat to G. The Allegro con spirito opens in a *piano* dynamic with a theme
that begins with the same semitone, this time rising, G to A flat. The ensuing tutti
(bars 47 ff.) shows the new density of orchestration in the second set of London
symphonies. From the 'Paris' symphonies onwards, Haydn had often written independent parts for cellos and basses, employing separate staves in many cases (e.g.
the 'Oxford' Symphony); here independent cello and bass parts form only one enriching element. There are four layers of sound, each doubled at the octave: first

Symphony no. 103/I

violins doubled by violas and flutes; second violins doubled by cellos and, in simplified form, by oboes; and basses, bassoons and timpani supported by horns and
trumpets. The boisterous energy of the orchestration plus the incisive rhythms of
6/8 contribute to a new classical sonority, a notable forerunner, along with the first
movement of no. 101, of the first movement of Beethoven's Seventh Symphony.
The second subject of the 'Drum Roll' also takes its generating interval from the
slow introduction, the expansive sixth of the second and the third bars of the
opening thematic line. The development section has three broad stages and is
amongst the most arresting in all of Haydn's symphonies. First, fragments of the
first subject are treated in imitation, leading to an imperfect cadence in C minor.

Silence follows, then violas and cellos play the thematic material of the introduction in 6/8 and in the prevailing tempo Allegro con spirito – a startling, bizarre reminder of the *fons et origo* of the movement. Another pause precedes an equally remarkable passage. The strings, underpinned by a sustained A flat in the basses, prepare for D flat major with a fragment of the main theme, then at that point when the sustained note moves to a B flat and the listener expects preparation for E flat and possibly the recapitulation the music is pushed back to D flat and to a statement of, not the first, but the second subject – a spellbinding passage of musical prestidigitation carried out in a fraction of the time it takes to explain it (see example, pp. 267–9).

As often, the first part of the recapitulation is compressed so as to allow for later expansion. The second subject has a new accompaniment, the formal horn-call

figure that is to feature in the last movement and an imitative entry in the oboe. A series of *fortissimo-decrescendo* passages theatrically unsettles the progress of the movement, finally bringing it to rest on a diminished chord. What follows is a literal repetition in adagio of twelve bars of the introduction, a dramatic masterstroke. Before the listener has time to re-orientate himself, he is thrust back into the main tempo and a lively conclusion to this breath-taking movement in which impulse and intellect play a dazzlingly complementary role.[8]

The Andante più tosto Allegretto is a well-judged counterbalance to the activity of the first movement, a set of variations on two alternating themes, in C minor and C major. Three of the first six London symphonies had employed variations for their slow movements (nos. 94, 95 and 97) but no. 103 is the only example in the second series of symphonies. Unlike the earlier examples, it is the more elaborate form of alternating variations on two themes, the second being a paraphrase of the first. This solitary example in the London symphonies gains much from the integration of the form achieved in the 'Razor' quartet and, especially, the Andante con variazioni in F minor for piano composed in 1793. Haydn's laconic C minor theme, with its intrusive F sharp, is presented in two-part counterpoint; the C major theme, on the other hand, is opulently scored with wind instruments, parallel thirds and well-judged trills over a reiterated pedal note. Each theme has two variations which emphasize their differences, in spite of their fundamental similarity. A coda in C major is grandly deflected to E flat major, a reminder of the home key of the symphony, before returning to C major.

The key of a E flat major is re-asserted with great aplomb by the full orchestra at the opening of the Menuet, skilfully avoiding a debilitating perfect cadence into the eighth bar in favour of an imperfect cadence and two echoes in the wind section of the Scotch snap figure of the melody. The central 'development' section consists of two stages: a *piano* modulation to G flat major and *forte* two-part counterpoint in E flat minor. In the reprise of the main theme Haydn replaces the imperfect cadence with an interrupted cadence, has a quizzical *piano* echo of the last phrase down a step onto diminished harmony, before, finally, launching into an affirmative extended cadence of six bars' duration. The Trio is *piano* throughout and, in contrast to the Menuet, remains in and around the tonic of E flat.

The finale is a *tour de force* of thematic and harmonic argument in which the merest scraps of material produce paragraphs of tremendous tension and fire. Behind its dexterity one may again sense, as in no. 95, the stimulus of the last movement of Mozart's 'Jupiter' Symphony; two of the main motives have a rhythmic resemblance to those used by Mozart.

(a)   **Haydn, Symphony no.103/IV**

(b)   **Mozart, Symphony no.41/IV**

Within Haydn's own development this sonata rondo is the crowning achievement to nearly thirty years of experimentation with the rondo. Spaciousness of design that, for instance, delays the first tutti until bar 73 goes hand in hand with thematic economy which, in this movement, means that every phrase is related, and obviously so, to the principal material.[9]

In his old age, Haydn was to make some telling remarks to his biographer, Griesinger, concerning his compositional method. 'Once I had seized upon an idea, my whole endeavour was to develop and sustain it in keeping with the rules of art. In this way I tried to keep going, and this is where so many of our new composers fall down. They string out one little piece after another, they break off when they have hardly begun, and nothing remains in the heart when one has listened to it.' While these observations on thematic economy and logical development apply most obviously to sonata form in instrumental music, other forms and media in Haydn's maturity also embrace these principles. One of the outstanding glories of the London symphonies, especially the last three, is the presentation of a vigorous argument, rhetorical and persuasive, throughout the four movements and in a highly approachable and absorbing manner.

By coincidence, Haydn's first and last symphonies for London, nos. 96 and 104, are both in D major, the first cautious and representative of Haydn's talents at the time, the last, composed only four years later, masterly in every aspect. The London public of the last decade of the century deserves part of posterity's gratitude for eliciting this expansion of expressive boundaries in Haydn's last twelve symphonies. The music reflects the atmosphere of *fin-de-siècle* London: assured, disputatious, intriguing, eccentric, open-minded yet sensitive. Haydn respected and nurtured his public, they, by adulation, encouraged him to a degree and in a manner no other city could have done (and certainly no individual) to further his propensity for musical argument and entertainment. By a further coincidence Haydn's last symphony shares the key of D major with his very first, composed nearly forty years earlier for Count Morzin. The progress from a three-movement work lasting ten minutes and composed for a small, exclusive audience to a four-movement work lasting over thirty minutes composed for a large audience is an endlessly fascinating one and constitutes one of the most awesome and inspiriting achievements in the history of music.

Miscellaneous orchestral and ensemble music

Although the English public had developed a fondness for concertos in their concert programmes, there is no record of a projected 'London' concerto by Haydn, possibly because traditionally – in London as elsewhere – concertos and other works for soloist and orchestra were performed by their composers. Haydn's violin playing had never equalled that of Salomon or Viotti and his piano playing did not have the technical facility of Dussek and Cramer.[10] Haydn was, however, persuaded to compose a work in the related genre of the *symphonie concertante*, his solitary essay in this hybrid genre and one which was played several times in the course of the two London visits. Its composition was prompted by the presence in London of Ignaz Pleyel. A pupil of Haydn in the early 1770s, Pleyel had worked for some time in France, where he had established himself as a leading composer of *symphonies concertantes*, this genre being as popular as the symphony in the French capital. Pleyel's quartets and symphonies were published regularly in London from the middle of the 1780s onward, and two *symphonies concertantes* (one in E flat for violin, viola, cello, oboe and orchestra, and one in B flat for violin and viola and orchestra) were well known there. Pleyel's engagement by the Professional Concert for the 1792 season was seen by the composer as a means to advance his opportunist career, and by the promoters as a counter-attraction to Haydn. Salomon's relationship with the rival Professional Concert was based on long-standing antipathy and the composition by Haydn of a *symphonie concertante* was, from Salomon's point of view, clearly intended to devalue the one aspect of the rival series which could be rightly claimed as different. The work was first performed on 9 March 1792.

Though the genre of the *symphonie concertante* was new in Haydn's œuvre, concertante writing had been always been a feature of the composer's symphonies, especially in the early Esterházy period; in London, Haydn had already written many individual orchestral solos for the violin, cello, oboe and bassoon – the solo instruments in the *symphonie concertante* (I:105). In addition, during the first London visit, Haydn had arranged most of the notturni, originally composed *c.* 1788–90 for the King of Naples, for concert performance in London, and the easy-going instrumental interplay of those works formed useful experience prior to the composition of the *symphonie concertante*. It is not surprising, then, that Haydn's handling of his four soloists and their relationship with the orchestra have a facility that is lacking in most of his solo concertos. The violin (Salomon) tends to dominate the finale with its mock-serious recitative passages and unbuttoned virtuosity rising to *c''''*, yet the overall impression is one of charming dialogue. Apart from the 6/8 slow movement, whose main theme is from the same stable as that of the slow movement of Symphony no.95, and the distinctive deflection to D flat major in the development section of the first movement, the language and gesture of the three-movement work are not those of the composer's symphonies, the evolutionary and dramatic instincts of the master symphonist being successfully suppressed in favour of an easy-going geniality. A decade earlier, Haydn's contact with Paris, the home of the *symphonie concertante*, had yielded only symphonies. Haydn's late, solitary essay in the other genre shows what a characterful contribution he could have made in that area too.

During his two visits to London, Haydn composed five brief marches, four in the conventional wind-band key of E flat major, for a variety of organizations. For the newly created Derbyshire Cavalry Regiment he composed two marches scored for two clarinets, two bassoons, two horns, trumpet and serpent, with provision for the customary optional (and improvised) percussion parts. In his catalogue of works composed during the London visits Haydn mentions a 'March for the Prince of Wales' (which is probably VIII:3), scored for the same forces as the Derbyshire marches. A second version of this march exists as the March for the Royal Society of Musicians, composed for the society's annual dinner to which Haydn was invited in 1792. For this refined, indoor occasion the serpent was omitted and strings and two flutes added. Only eight bars of a fifth march (VIII:7) exist and it is possible that Haydn never completed it. This handful of martial pieces, by the leading composer of the day, is indicative of the bellicose times. Haydn pointed the association further when, following the success of the 'Military' Symphony, he arranged its sensational slow movement for military band, dropping one flute and one trumpet and adding a serpent to provide a sixteen-foot bass line to the ensemble.

In his catalogue of his London music the composer also included works composed during the seventeen months from August 1792 to January 1794 when he was in Austria. Compositions like the opp. 71 and 74 quartets and Symphony no. 99 were written specifically with London in mind and others, like the F minor variations for piano, with half an eye on the English market. The only item mentioned in the list which was written for performance in Vienna rather than London is '24 Minuets and german dances', composed for the ball of the Pensionsgesellschaft bildender Künstler (Fine Arts Pension Society) held in November 1792 in the Redoutensaal of the Hofburg. Haydn's total of '24' refers to the minuets and German dances together, twelve minuets (IX:11) and twelve German dances (IX:12). The orchestra in the main dance hall numbered nearly fifty players, a larger orchestra, therefore, than Haydn had in London during his first visit, and the dances are grandly scored for two flutes (piccolo in Trio of no. 7), two oboes, two clarinets, two bassoons, two horns, two trumpets, timpani and strings (without violas). There are some solo clarinet lines in trio sections but these, like most of the wind solos in the dances, are doubled by strings, Haydn's standard practice when he was unsure of the capabilities of players. The first five dances are arranged in a sequence of descending thirds – D, B flat, G, E, and C – a juxtaposition soon to manifest itself in the quartets of opp. 71 and 74 and symphonies nos. 99, 100 and 101.

It was during this seventeen-month interlude between the London visits that Haydn also composed or arranged most of his pieces for musical clock (*Flötenuhr*). Since 1780, the librarian of the Esterházy family had been Pater Joseph Niemecz (1750–1806), a member of the Barmherzige Brüder who, in addition to being a competent musician, had a penchant for constructing mechanical organs designed to form the base of a clock and usually (but not necessarily) activated by the mechanism of the clock. The largest of the three surviving Niemecz organs has a compass of three and a half octaves from *g* to *d'''*. Haydn's first music for a Niemecz organ dates from the end of the 1780s, when he composed several short pieces for a recently built organ. During 1792 and 1793 he provided music for two further organs, to make a total of thirty pieces.[11] In all cases, as well as composing new pieces, Haydn adapted existing music, including the Trio of Symphony no. 85 ('La reine'), the finale of the 'Lark' quartet and Buonafede's aria 'La ragazza col vecchione' from *Il mondo della luna*. In two instances, the mechanical organ versions are contemporary with and perhaps may even predate more familiar versions, the finale of quartet op. 71 no. 2, and the minuet of the 'Clock' Symphony, and one wonders in the case of the latter whether the famous slow movement was prompted by the association between mechanical organ music and clocks.

Miscellaneous vocal music

Haydn had been invited to London primarily as a composer of symphonies and of opera and the period 1791–95 was to see his last essays in these two international genres. Haydn never contemplated a further opera after the disappointment in 1791 of not having *L'anima del filosofo* performed, and in the case of the twelve symphonies he surely regarded them as the culmination of a lifelong endeavour. They were the result of exhilarating stimuli that were unlikely to occur again in the composer's lifetime. If the content of the symphonies and the opera demonstrate that in his early sixties Haydn's outlook was an ever-broadening one, the readiness with which he embarked on the composition of various vocal works in the English language confirms this extraordinary intellectual energy. He composed songs, canons, catches, glees and settings of psalms, arranged national folk-songs and wrote choral pieces for the concert hall, all minor works which collectively explored a new resource of technique and aesthetic that contributed directly to the composition of the two late oratorios, *The Creation* and *The Seasons*.

The composer's first attempt at setting English words arose out of unpredictable circumstances. The London publisher, William Napier, who had issued a few symphonies and quartets by Haydn but with whom he had had no formal business connection, was declared bankrupt in the spring of 1791. To help Napier re-establish his business, Haydn agreed to provide accompaniments to two volumes of 'Original Scots Songs', the first appearing in 1792 and the second three years later. Between 1791 and 1795 Haydn arranged 150 songs for Napier, who remained in business until, coincidentally, the year of Haydn's death, 1809. There was a well-established market for these songs in Georgian Britain, and it must have given countless amateurs satisfaction to be able to sing arrangements of folk-songs by a composer whose symphonies they so admired. Haydn's arrangements for Napier cost him the minimum of effort: the melodies – the 'folk' pedigree of some is dubious, many having been newly composed by contemporary musicians – are doubled by the right hand of the keyboard, as in Haydn's early Lieder; there are no preludes, interludes or postludes; the violin part is accompanimental throughout and the bass part is figured to encourage a realization of the mainly two-part keyboard texture.

More representative of the composer's craft is the work known as 'Dr Harington's Compliment' (XXVIb:3). Dr Henry Harington, M.A., M.D., was an amateur composer whom Haydn met in Bath in the summer of 1794. His 'compliment' was to present Haydn with a song that set the following stilted couplet: 'What Art expresses and what Science praises / Haydn the Theme of both to Heaven raises' Haydn returned the compliment by using the song as a basis for a brief set of four variations for soprano, chorus (one or more singers per part) and keyboard. It was published in German (with a new text) by Breitkopf & Härtel in 1806 and it is perhaps not over-fanciful to suggest that the publication of this homely work may have sown the seed for Beethoven's grandiloquent Choral Fantasia, composed two years later.

While Dr Harington is relatively unimportant, the Earl of Abingdon's name figures prominently during Haydn's English stay. He had been a notable supporter of public concerts in London for two decades, first of the Bach-Abel concerts and then of the Professional Concert, and had been a leading figure in trying to attract Haydn to the English capital in the late 1780s. An amateur flute player and composer, he presented Haydn with the vocal parts of nine catches and three glees, to which Haydn duly added an accompaniment to be played by harp or piano. The Earl of Abingdon subsequently arranged for their publication as *Twelve Sentimental Catches and Glees*, an eminent contribution to an already extensive market. The texts of the catches (i.e. rounds) and glees introduced Haydn to the favourite figures of the English pastoral – Phillis, Strephon and Corinna – and to its wan and languid affectations; the text of no. XI reads 'Farewell, my Flocks once tender care, / Your bleating sounds have lull'd mine ear; / No longer can I with you stay, / For love commands me Far away'. The settings themselves, for three male voices, are rather short-breathed and lack the sparkle and humour of the best of eighteenth-century catches and glees.

The Napier folk-song arrangements, 'Dr Harington's Compliment' and the *Twelve Sentimental Catches and Glees* are chips from the workshop produced, one imagines, in moments of comparative relaxation after the strenuous demands of symphonic (and operatic) composition. Undoubtedly, however, they gave Haydn some confidence to embark on completely original works in this, to him, new language; two sets of six 'Original Canzonettas', later supplemented by two single songs, 'The spirit's song' and 'O tuneful voice'. Most of the texts are by the poetess Anne Hunter, who was a favoured companion of Haydn during his London visits. Her most characteristic poetic vein is the heightened sentimentality of 'My mother bids me bind my hair', 'Pleasing Pain' and 'O tuneful voice', but she could invoke also the sombre, as in 'The spirit's song', and proclaim the jauntily patriotic, as in 'The sailor's song'. It was Anne Hunter who selected the remaining texts, including 'She never told her love' from Shakespeare's *Twelfth Night*. Equally crucially, she must have nurtured Haydn's limited poetic sense, for these songs are resourceful in a way that is only fitfully demonstrated in the German Lieder of the previous decade. Although the beautifully arched melodic line of 'My mother bids me bind my hair' owes little to Italian opera, the magical initial entry of the voice during, rather than after, the concluding cadence of the piano introduction in 'O tuneful voice', 'The spirit's song' and 'She never told her love' is reminiscent of similar entries in Haydn's operas (e.g. Costanza's 'Ah, che in van per me pietoso' in *L'isola disabitata* and the duet 'Qual contento' in *Orlando Paladino*). The piano scoring has a sense of part-writing and harmonic imagination in, for instance, 'Recollection' and 'Despair' that shows the practised craft of the composer of quartets, always anxious to avoid the commonplace. Also reminiscent of Haydn's instrumental music is the effective use of pauses, whether emphatically rhetorical, as in 'The sailor's song', or wonderfully pensive, as in 'The wanderer'. Most of the songs are strophic settings (typically two verses), others, such as 'Fidelity' and 'The spirit's song', are either through-composed or ternary in shape. Perhaps as a result of Anne Hunter's guidance, Haydn often repeats concluding phrases (sometimes, a few words) to provide a characteristic air of gentle musing.

The London visits also saw the composition of some English-language canons; an appropriately learned but not (as so often) arid 'Canon cancrizans a tre' (three-voiced retrograde or crab canon) to the text 'Thy Voice, O Harmony, is Divine' (XXVIIb:46), composed as a thank-offering for his honorary doctorate at Oxford; and the amusing 'Turk was a faithful dog' (XXVIIb:45), prompted by an inscription on a dog's grave in Bath. It is odd that Haydn should have written his first vocal canons in England rather than in Austria where the singing of canons was a favourite social pastime. Apart from two English-language canons, Haydn composed forty-five German canons between 1791 and 1799, setting a variety of texts. The dates of most of these are imprecise but it is known that the set of canons on the Ten Commandments (*Die heiligen zehn Gebote*; XXVIIa:1–10) were composed in London. Written for between three and five voices, these canons strike an intriguing mixture of poses, from the intonation-like third commandment, 'Du sollst Sonn- und Feiertag heiligen' ('Thou shalt keep the Sabbath a holy day') to the wrily ribald setting of the sixth commandment, 'Du sollst nicht Unkeuschheit treiben' ('Thou shalt not yield to lewdness'), which doubtless reflects the composer's own attitude to the sin of adultery.

Whereas the Ten Commandments were designed for performance at home, Haydn's settings of six English psalms were to be performed in church, constituting the composer's only music for the Protestant Church. In 1794 Haydn was one of a group of composers asked to contribute to a new collection of psalm settings edited by the Rev. William Dechair Tattersall and using the metrical versions of the Rev. James Merrick. Composed for the meagre musical resources of the average English parish church, they are scored for three voices only, soprano, alto and bass. A few of the settings have some desultory imitation but the predominant approach is homophonic, relying on easily sung melodic lines. The setting of verses from Psalm 69 uses the melodic line of the canzonetta 'Pleasing pain', but it is the melodic anticipations of later works that catch the attention of the informed listener; the two E flat settings (verses from Psalm 31 and Psalm 61) prefigure many E flat movements in the later oratorios and masses, while the many correspondences between the setting of Psalm 50 and the closing chorus of Part I of *The Creation*, 'The heavens are telling', provide a direct indication of the part English musical tradition would play in that work (see examples overleaf):

Public concerts in London, as elsewhere in Europe, featured vocal as well as instrumental items, Salomon's concerts typically including four vocal items, usually recitatives and arias from contemporary operas by Paisiello, Sarti, Bianchi etc., and occasionally a lighter, Pleasure Garden song. Haydn's own 'Ah come il core' from

Psalm 50

La fedeltà premiata was sung and, in addition, he composed at least five concert arias, of which only one survives. For his benefit concert near the end of the 1795 season Haydn provided a 'New Scene' for the Opera Concert's leading soprano, Brigida Giorgi Banti. The text selected was from an *opera seria* by Metastasio, *Antigone*, originally written for Hasse in 1744 and familiar to London opera audiences from Giordani's opera, first performed in 1774, and from several *pasticcio* versions. In Act III, Scene 7, Berenice, abandoned by her lover, Demetrio, and despairing of her fate, vacillates between anger and sorrow before concluding that only death can remove 'L'eccesso del dolor' ('the surfeit of sorrow'). Haydn drew on his con-

The Creation, No. 13

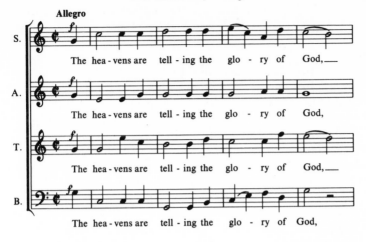

siderable experience of similar operatic situations and there are persistent reminders of Angelica's solo scene in Act III of *Orlando Paladino*, Celia's in Act II of *La
fedeltà premiata* (already known to London audiences) and, particularly, Rosina's
scene in Act II of *La vera costanza*; like the last-mentioned, the *Scena di Berenice*
(XXIVa:10) culminates in an intense aria in F minor. The preceding recitative and
arioso sections have a dramatic urgency that had eluded Haydn in previous *scene*,

Miseri noi (XXIVa:7) and *Arianna a Naxos* (XXVIb:2). It is derived in no small part from an adventurous harmonic language contained within an equally wide-ranging tonal scheme (D major, B flat, C, E and E flat to the dominant of F minor for the aria).

Vocal music in subscription concerts in London did not normally extend to choral works partly, as Haydn explained in a letter to Maria Anna von Genzinger (24 April 1792), because of the difficulty of obtaining boy choristers to perform on prescribed days. Outside subscription concerts, however, choral music featured prominently in concert life, in concerts for charity, in the oratorio season during Lent and in the celebratory Handel festivals. Haydn's extensive writing for chorus in the opera *L'anima del filosofo* had shown the composer's ready response to the new musical opportunity, and in June 1791 he was able to attend several concerts of Handel's music in Westminster Abbey where he heard the Coronation Anthem 'Zadok the Priest', extracts from *Israel in Egypt, Esther, Judas Maccabaeus, Deborah* and *Messiah*, as well as various instrumental works by the composer. In the course of the next four years Haydn was to hear many more works by Handel, usually in the large-scale performances that then constituted the Handelian tradition, and the strong impression the music made on Haydn was supplemented by noting the veneration which was lavished on the earlier composer. Not surprisingly, there were rumours that Haydn himself was engaged on an oratorio, but with his commitment to the composition of symphonies it is difficult to see how Haydn could have found the time in London to tackle such a large-scale project; however, the denial of opportunity made the attractiveness of the idea even stronger and to a large extent it explains the consuming enthusiasm with which *The Creation* was to be composed in 1796–8.

Haydn did find the time to compose one item of choral music, *The Storm* (XXIVa:8), and to embark on another, the *Invocation to Neptune. The Storm* was a setting of words by Peter Pindar (the pen-name of John Wolcot) evoking the favourite eighteenth-century poetic notion of a storm followed by calm. Scored for SATB choir, two flutes, two oboes, two bassoons, two horns, two trumpets, timpani and strings, it was first performed on 24 February 1792. The main part of the chorus is reminiscent of another storm chorus by Haydn, also in D minor, 'Svanisce in un momento' from the 1784 version of the oratorio *Il ritorno di Tobia*. The aggression of the D minor storm is followed by the calm of D major, a repose effectively captured by pauses in the otherwise even flow of the music. The choral writing itself is unambitious and no more difficult than any of the choruses in the opera *L'anima del filosofo*. As a clear harbinger of the descriptive music in the two late oratorios, especially the storm in *The Seasons*, it is a pointer to the aesthetic world of those two oratorios.

A more intriguing work is the fragment of what is usually referred to as an incomplete oratorio: an aria in F major and a chorus in D major (XXIVa:9), composed during the second visit to London. The autograph of these two substantial items, which is in the British Library, does not have a title page but carries an explanatory note, dated 1821, by Henry Hill, a founder member of the Philharmonic Society:

This original Manuscript was Composed By the celebrated G. Haydn when in England in the year 1794 at the desire of the Earl of Abingdon, & by His Lordship given to I. Monzani who now presents it to the Noble Directors of the British Museum, as a scarce specimen of that unrivalled Master's hand writing. It consists of a Song & Chorus – & were intended to form a part of an Oratorio, and is all He ever did towards its completion. The Poetry is from Selden's Work on the Sovereignty of the Sea – 1821.

The Selden volume mentioned in this annotation is John Selden's *Mare Clausum*, a Latin treatise first published in 1635 in London, a treatise that, in the manner of the day, united fact and wishful fancy in order to assert England's natural right to sovereignty of the sea. Haydn's text, however, comes not from Selden's treatise, but from additional prefatory material supplied by an English-language translator, Marchimont Nedham (or Needham), for an edition that first appeared in 1652. There are six stanzas, of which Haydn set only two, in the form of a bass aria and a chorus.

Aria:
Nor can I think my suit is vain,
That Land the Sea should now maintain;
Since retribution's due.
For England hath great wealth possess'd
By Sea's access; and thereby blest
With plenties not a few;
Which, next the virtue of thy watchful eyes,
Will her secure from foreign miseries.

Chorus:
Thy great endeavours to increase
The Marine Power, to confess
Thou act'st some great design!
Which had Seventh Henry done, before
Columbus launch'd from Spanish shore,
The Indies had been thine.
Yet do thy seas those Indian mines excel
In riches far. The Belgians know it well.

Pohl[12] and subsequent authors have followed Henry Hill in describing the work as an 'oratorio', encouraged by the fact that there were rumours during the second visit to England that Haydn was working on an oratorio. The crudely xenophobic text, however, is clearly not suitable as the subject matter of an oratorio and Henry Hill's remarks in that context could be dismissed were there no further evidence. However, Pohl also mentions that Haydn stopped working on the 'oratorio' when he learned that three other composers (Graf, Fischer and Pleyel) had previously set the text. Nothing is known about the Fischer and Pleyel settings, but the libretto for the Graf version has survived in the British Library;[13] it carries the heading 'Invocation of Neptune, and his Attendant Nereids to Britannia on the Dominion of the Sea' which, in shortened form ('Invocation of Neptun[e]'), is the title Haydn used when noting the work in his catalogue of music written for London. The setting by Graf was performed on 19 May 1784 (not 1785, as stated by Pohl), when it was advertised in the newspapers as 'An Ode, with grand Chorusses'.[14] Graf's ode was a contribution to the persistent vein of patriotic music in eighteenth-century England that included works such as Arne's masque, *Alfred* (with its 'Rule Britannia'), Barthélemon's 'Victory Ode to Admiral Keppel', Dupuis's 'Ode to the Genius of Britain' and many other works. Haydn's setting of the text was clearly intended by the Earl of Abingdon to form part of this tradition and we should follow the Graf version in terming it an ode rather than an oratorio. The undocumented assertion by Pohl that Haydn stopped working on the ode when he learned of the earlier settings is unconvincing; after all, Haydn, like other composers, set existing texts as readily as newly written ones. It is more likely that the Earl of Abingdon's imprisonment for three months in February 1795 following a libel case prevented the arranging of the intended concert and Haydn simply abandoned the work, having composed approximately a third of it. From the evidence of the Graf libretto, the finished ode would have consisted of three, perhaps four, further numbers – two arias (or an aria and a duet or trio) and opening and closing choruses, forming a work of about thirty to forty minutes' duration.

The completed numbers indicate that Haydn planned a work of considerable impact. They are scored for a full 'second visit' orchestra: one flute, two oboes, two clarinets, two bassoons, two horns, two trumpets, timpani and strings. Neptune's surviving aria is an imposing one. In F major, it opens with the wind band led by clarinet declaiming the melodic material over repeated pizzicato crotchets in the strings. The following chorus in D major begins with an eighteen-bar introduction with much trumpet fanfare figuration, before embarking on a fugue of great vigour and, in its final pages, uplifting excitement. Haydn's music far transcends the appalling and sometimes obscure text and the fact that he never completed the work is disappointing. Along with the 'Military' Symphony, the reference to 'God save the King' in the slow movement of Symphony no. 98 and 'The sailor's song', it reveals a new aspect of Haydn's personality, the grateful patriot. England first elicited this distinctive and ready response and it was to become ever more prevalent in Haydn's later music: the incidental music for the play *Alfred or the patriotic King*, the Hungarian National March, the *Volkslied* 'Gott erhalte Franz den Kaiser', the cantata 'The Battle of the Nile', the *Missa in angustiis* ('Nelson' Mass) and the *Missa in tempore belli*. Mozart's death in 1791 meant that he was never exposed to this new fashion, and his personality was such that he probably would have remained indifferent to it. On the other hand much of Beethoven's output was conditioned by it, either directly (*Egmont* music) or subsumed into a general 'heroic' idiom (Seventh Symphony, 'Archduke' Trio).

Italian opera: *L'anima del filosofo*

That Haydn should have accepted a commission to compose an opera for London is, at first sight, unexpected. After all, his last opera, *Armida*, had been composed as long ago as 1783, and a few years later he had turned down the offer to compose an *opera buffa* for Prague, firstly because his operatic experience was entirely based on his work at Eszterháza and, secondly, because he recognized the superior talents of Mozart. In London, Mozart's operas were still unknown, hence comparisons could not be made; in addition there was a new theatre and a new audience; but perhaps the principal reason why Haydn accepted Sir John Gallini's commission was the feeling that he was fulfilling a long promise. In 1787, negotiations between Sir John Gallini and Haydn had been based on 'concerts in Hanover Square' and a 'new opera'.

To assist the composer in this enterprise, Gallini engaged the services of the most experienced librettist in London, Carlo Francesco Badini, who had lived in London for over twenty years and had written comic and serious librettos for Pugnani, Vento, Giordani and Anfossi. Badini seems to have begun work on the libretto before Haydn arrived in London, and that there was no collaboration between poet and composer is clear from Haydn's letter to Prince Anton Esterházy of 8 January 1791: 'The new opera libretto which I am to compose is entitled *Orfeo*, in 5 acts, but I shall not receive it for a few days. It is supposed to be entirely different from that of Gluck ... Incidentally, the opera is supposed to contain many choruses, ballets and a lot of big changes of scenery. ...'

The choice of subject was a brave one. Gluck's opera with additional items by

J. C. Bach was well-known in London, having received over thirty performances between 1770 and 1785; Haydn, too, knew the Gluck opera intimately from the performances of the work he had given at Eszterháza in 1776. The subject was an attractive one, but, as Haydn's letter makes clear, the content of the opera is very different from that of Gluck's masterpiece. Beginning at an earlier point in the legend than does Gluck's opera, Act I presents Orfeo and Euridice as lovers, concluding with Creonte's reluctant consent to their marriage. Act II presents the death of Euridice, and it is from this point that the stories of the two operas run in parallel for a while, but with several differences of detail. In his grief, Orfeo consults a Sybil who arranges that he be allowed to enter the Underworld in order to bring back Euridice. Their reunion ends tragically when Euridice accidentally walks ahead of Orfeo, breaking the condition that they should not set eyes on each other until they have left the Underworld; she is again lost to Orfeo. In Gluck's opera Orfeo's second grief is relieved when Amore, the God of Love, brings Euridice back to life. Haydn's opera, however, eschews this typical happy ending of eighteenth-century opera; Orfeo is poisoned by the followers of Bacchus and, in a *coup de théâtre*, is borne away on the waters to the island of Lesbos, while his adversaries are drowned in a storm.

Gluck's opera benefits immeasurably from beginning with Euridice's first death, allowing the theme of conjugal love to be presented consistently and the eventual happy resolution as a just fulfilment; Haydn's text lacks this consistency, making the presentation of a tragic ending seem a haphazard conclusion. It was to take Italian opera several decades to learn how to deal effectively with tragic endings and it was certainly expecting too much of Haydn's limited sense of the theatre to accomplish this in 1791. Instead of glorifying conjugal love, Badini's text repeatedly attempts to draw the rather grim moral from Orfeo's misfortunes, hence the title *L'anima del filosofo* ('The spirit of the philosopher'). At one point King Creonte utters the following: 'Non è stupor che giunge il disperato affetto d'un valor fedele a così grave eccesso; chi perde il caro ben, perde sè stesso.' ('It is no surprise that the desperate feeling of faithful valour reaches such a grievous extreme; he who loses his well-beloved loses himself!'.) One does not imagine such stoic sentiments appealing to Haydn, the composer of *Singspiel* and *dramma giocoso*. On a more local level, Badini's text is as lacking in dramatic pace and conviction as any previously set by Haydn. Major incidents, such as Euridice's final departure, occur in *secco* recitative (including a gratuitous quotation of Gluck's 'Che faro'), Orfeo's journey to the Underworld is remarkably free of incident and the action is frequently absurd. Haydn, as always, was content to rely on the judgment of others when it came to fashioning a libretto and here, despite the eminence of the author, he was badly served.

Like Gluck's *Orfeo*, Haydn's opera contains extensive writing for chorus, which assumes in turn the roles of monsters, lovers, spirits, Furies and followers of Bacchus. In the second half of the eighteeth century *opera seria* made increasing use of chorus, and in London Sacchini's operas had been noted for their choral writing, prompting contemporary commentators to remark that the composer was trying to fuse Handelian oratorio with Italian opera. In *L'anima del filosofo* there are thirteen choral numbers. Some are conventionally operatic, simply setting the scene (the music of the chorus of lovers in Act II was taken directly from *Orlando Paladino*); many, however, constitute the most powerful music in the whole opera. The concluding number is a choral storm during which the fading cries of the drowning Bacchae are heard and Orfeo's departure is suggested by a long drawn out *diminuendo* and a gradual thinning of the texture.

The central role of Orfeo was written for the celebrated tenor, Giacomo Davidde, then a leading figure in London's musical scene. It is a demanding part, since
the character is on stage for most of the action; Orfeo has three big arias and many
accompanied recitatives. His second aria, 'In un mar d'acerbe pene', avoids the aggressive coloratura that is featured elsewhere and is an expressive portrayal of despair; in its more thoughtful moments it turns to a theme first heard in the overture. Euridice's arias are similarly demanding and affecting but our picture of her
is limited since she sings nothing of any consequence after Act II. She, like Orfeo,
has many accompanied recitatives that lead into arias. However, given the frequent fusion of accompanied recitative and aria in Haydn's last opera, *Armida*, the
absence of any similar, prolonged stretches of music from *L'anima del filosofo* is disappointing.

In addition to emphasizing the dissimilarity between his and Gluck's opera and
the featuring of the chorus, Haydn's letter to the Prince indicates that several ballet sections were to be included. There is no mention of a ballet in Haydn's score
and it is probable that, as was frequently the case, the music for the ballet was
composed by someone else. In fact, during March 1791, under Gallini's auspices, a
ballet entitled *Orpheus and Euridice* was performed at the King's Theatre, the composer of most of the music being František Václav Tomeš (Thomisch), an immi-
grant Bohemian composer whose name (as Tomich) appears in Haydn's First London Notebook in a list of resident composers. It is likely that Tomeš's ballet was
intended to be included in Haydn's opera and that only when Gallini's difficulties
became intractable was it performed separately.

The new opera was in rehearsal when it was learnt that the King had refused
Gallini a licence for his theatre and hence the opera could not be performed. For
Haydn this was a sad, ignominious end to an operatic career that had begun in the
mid-1750s with the *Singspiel, Der krumme Teufel*. In *L'anima del filosofo* Haydn reveals
some of the strengths of his operatic craft, namely highly characterized individual
moments and a ready sense of the graphic, but weaknesses appear in accentuated
form. Badini's diffusely constructed text with its heavy burden of serious moralizing gives little opportunity for the theatricality that had sustained the best of
Haydn's operas, *L'infedeltà delusa* and *La fedeltà premiata*, so that dramatic continuity is at best intermittent, at worst implausible.

Solo piano music

Four solo keyboard works date from this period, a set of Variations in F minor
(XVII:6) from 1793 and three sonatas (nos. 60–62) from the second London visit.
On the autograph and in his London catalogue, Haydn called the F minor Variations a 'sonata', and it is possible that at one stage the composer intended the variations to form the first movement of a larger work, rather like the variations that
had opened the two-movement C major sonata of 1789 (no. 58); but the strength
and scope of the movement may have caused Haydn to recognize its self-sufficiency. Following on the example of the F minor alternating variations that had
opened the 'Razor' quartet (op. 55 no. 2), it is a work of commanding assurance and
sensitivity, certainly the finest set of keyboard variations between Bach and Beethoven and one that is by no means overwhelmed by either the 'Goldberg' or the
'Diabelli' variations, despite their greater size and scope. The first theme demonstrates a perfect integration of melody and accompaniment, the twenty bars sharing material between the right and left hand, while simultaneously exploring the
full sonority of the contemporary piano; the theme reaches a perfectly judged

climax on a Neapolitan chord (rather like the 'Razor' quartet theme). The haunting quality produced by the repeated dotted rhythms of the main theme must have had an influence on Schubert, for the beginning of his Fantasia in F minor for piano duet cultivates a similar mood. The alternating theme in F major ingeniously avoids sounding spry by basing its harmonic framework on that of the F minor, by making some thematic allusions to it and, crucially, by being shorter (twenty bars as opposed to twenty-six). There are two variations on each of the themes before an unprecedentedly large coda of eighty-three bars brings the movement to a close. The coda begins conventionally with a reprise of the main theme up to the phrase that has the Neapolitan sixth; that chord is emphasized and heralds a re-markable passage of parallel first inversion triads rising chromatically – the source is the first bar of both themes – to break the harmonic mould of the theme.

The subsequent return to the tonic, F minor, is accompanied by a full keyboard sonority, the first *fortissimo* marking in the movement and repeated emphasis on a top F, the highest note of Haydn's piano. Following the *fortissimo* passage, which is maintained for fifteen bars as the texture becomes more rhapsodic, the final section is an immaculately controlled restoration of composure, affirming F minor as the tonic and making repeated allusion to the dotted anacrusis figure.

The F minor variations were dedicated to the 'most esteemed' ('Stimatissima') Babette von Ployer, a former pupil of Mozart. It was another lady pianist, Therese

Jansen, who elicited at least one, probably all three of Haydn's last sonatas for the instrument. Born in Aachen, Jansen settled in London, received lessons from Clementi and, in turn, became one of the most sought-after teachers in London. In 1795 she married Gaetano Bartolozzi, son of the well-known engraver Francesco Bartolozzi. Already the dedicatee of sonatas by Clementi (his op. 33) and Dussek, Jansen was also to receive the dedication of Haydn's last three piano trios, nos. 43–45. The three solo sonatas – nos. 60 in C, 61 in D and 62 in E flat – contain ample evidence of Jansen's technique, including chains of parallel thirds and octave passages. The latter contribute inestimably to the bold sonority evident in these sonatas, often reproducing the 'noisy' atmosphere that commentators found in the composer's London symphonies. In a few sonatas in the previous decade Haydn had often shown a willingness to produce a kind of raw bravura in his piano writing; the last three piano sonatas, perhaps prompted by the stronger sonority of the English fortepiano as well as Jansen's technique, sees the culmination of this trend in Haydn's keyboard music.[15] The opening of the very last sonata, with its arpeggiated full chords, contrast between *forte* and *piano*, double thirds in the treble followed by a *decrescendo* into a *piano* passage in the alto register of the keyboard, is a particularly masterly integration of medium and message, unrealizable on anything but the piano. More idiosyncratic are the two 'open pedal' markings in the first movement of Sonata no. 60, two *pianissimo* passages that are to be played with the dampers raised, creating a gentle blurring of harmonies, an interest in keyboard tone colour that Beethoven was to pursue (e.g. the end of the slow movement of the B flat Piano Concerto and the first movement of the 'Moonlight' Sonata).

In matters of dramatic content and form, the sonatas show the influence of trends in other genres: the three-chord opening of no. 60 (also present in altered form in nos. 61 and 62) catches the attention in the same way as the opening chords of the opp. 71 and 74 quartets, though their function here is never solely introductory as in the quartets; the command of harmonic climax, use of decoration and contrasting of texture between sections in the E major slow movement of no. 62 profits from the E major slow movement of the 'Rider' quartet (op. 74 no. 3); and the finales of nos. 60 and 61 follow the example of certain minuets in the London symphonies by writing out the repeats (unlike the symphonies, however, these movements are not termed minuets and do not have a dance-like gait). The strength of the musical argument in no. 60 and, even more so, in no. 62 is irresistible. The E major slow movement of no. 62 is flanked by two movements in E flat, a blinding contrast of keys, but one that is carefully absorbed into the work as a whole; the development section of the first movement had featured a paragraph beginning in E major (after a pause on the dominant of C minor) and the beginning of the finale is a remarkable exercise in tonal disorientation. First, an eight-bar period is heard above a tonic pedal (the very beginning suggests E minor rather than E flat), then up a tone on F which, in normal circumstances, would have enhanced the tonic but here only adds to the confusion; finally, in desperation as it were, Haydn resorts to a *forte* passage of alternating dominant and tonic harmony with bravura passage work to successfully establish the tonic. This large-scale integration of two immensely remote tonalities was to fascinate Beethoven, and his C sharp minor quartet, op. 131, is likewise fashioned to deal with the conflict of keys a semitone apart.

Piano trios

In terms of the number of individual works the only genre to rival the twelve London symphonies is that of the piano trio: ten works composed in London between 1793 and 1795 and first published there; three works composed by 1796 and published in London; finally, two works written shortly after the second London visit, but published in Vienna. The date of composition of many of the trios is conjectural since, with the exception of no. 41 and a portion of no. 42, the autographs are lost, having been presented in most cases to the original dedicatees.

Work	Date	Date and place of publication
no. 31	1792–93?	1794, London
nos. 32–34	1793–94?	1794, London
nos. 35–37	1794–95?	1795, London
nos. 38–40	1795?	1795, London
no. 41	1795	1803, Vienna
no. 42	1796?	1797, Vienna
nos. 43–45	1796?	1797, London

In many ways these trios are the most neglected works of the period, and probably of Haydn's entire output. A couple of piano trios from the end of the 1780s had shown that Haydn was eager to invest the genre with a gravity that he had only intermittently displayed in the solo keyboard sonatas of the period. The fifteen trios continue in this vein and, indeed, contain developments of style and symphonic thinking not found elsewhere in his contemporary output. Traditionally, the quartet medium had always drawn from Haydn the most consistently private and thoughtful music; in the 1790s, as quartet playing moved from the chamber to the concert hall, the piano trio, in several respects, assumed the role of musical initiate and confidant.

There is the possibility that the first trio of the period, no. 31 in G, was originally a violin sonata, the most obvious candidate for identification with the 'Sonata in g' listed in Haydn's London catalogue. A two-movement work, this trio is an exception amongst the other fourteen, in that it conspicuously lacks the creative flair displayed in them. The series begins in earnest with nos. 32–34, printed by Longman & Broderip and dedicated to 'Madame la Princesse Douarière Esterhazy née Hohenfeldt', widow of the recently deceased Prince Anton. They are three well-contrasted works, making varied use of a balanced three-movement structure. No. 32 in A major begins with an expansive Allegro moderato initiated, as in the contemporary quartets of opp. 71 and 74, by three introductory chords; the development section contains a bewitching modulation from the dominant of F sharp minor to the dominant of E flat which, in turn, is treated as an augmented sixth leading to a 6-4 D minor chord. Haydn's harmonic language is often at its most fluently sophisticated in these piano trios, eschewing the drama and grandeur of similar procedures used in symphonies and even quartets (see example overleaf). The scoring in this example is representative of this group of trios: two-part keyboard writing often enriched to three and four parts, a cello line that follows the bass and a violin part that is essentially subordinate but takes the lead occasionally. The central slow movement, as often in the trios of the previous decade, leads directly into the third movement and is the first of four distinctive andante 6/8 movements in these late trios. The finale is a bouncing 3/4 movement with syncopations and comic acciaccaturas, a clear forerunner of the rondo 'in the Gypsies' stile' of no. 39.

Trio No. 32/I

During the London period Haydn turned comparatively infrequently to the minor mode, one symphony out of twelve (no. 95), the customary one quartet in a set of six (op. 74 no. 3) and the F minor keyboard variations. In the fifteen piano trios, however, there are four works that set out from a minor tonic. The first is no. 33 in G minor, which opens with an alternating set of variations which, unlike the F minor variations, draws a rather inscrutable quality from the minor key, a characteristic that goes back to the 1760s. A highly decorated Adagio ma non troppo in E flat leads into a sonata form Presto that begins in G minor and turns to the major at the recapitulation.

In the final trio of this set it is the central slow movement that catches our attention. An Andante cantabile in G major, it is flanked by two movements in B flat major, an example of the third relationship that fascinated Haydn at this time. The layout of the movement too is telling. It is a set of three variations laid out in a manner that recalls string quartet scoring: the theme is announced by the left hand alone in two voices, the equivalent of viola and cello (as at the beginning of the slow movements of quartets, op. 33 no. 2 and op. 50 no. 3); for the first variation the left hand repeats the melody and bass as before, while the right hand adds an intermittent commentary (as in the slow movement of quartet, op. 64 no. 1) and the violin doubles the melody at a higher octave. This strict part-writing continues for the remainder of the movement, imparting a textural strength rarely found in Classical keyboard variations.

Haydn's next set of three trios, nos. 35-37, again were dedicated to a member of the Esterházy family, 'Madame La Princesse Marie Esterhazzy [*sic*] née Princesse Leichtenstein [*sic*]', wife of the new reigning prince, Nicolaus II, and previously (in 1784) the dedicatee of three piano sonatas (nos. 54-56). The minor-key work in the set, no. 37, is in D minor and follows the scheme of the earlier G minor trio, a set of alternating variations in D minor and major (with a very prominent 'Lydian' fourth in the melody – the work was composed in the same period as the 'Drum Roll' Symphony), a decorative Adagio ma non troppo and a lively sonata form finale which, unlike that of no. 33, is entirely in the major. Closer in spirit to contemporary symphonies is no. 35 in C major, the first of two brilliant and vivacious late trios in that key. It opens with a short six-bar introduction in 6/8 with the unusual indication 'Adagio pastorale'; the following Vivace Assai, still in 6/8, immediately destroys any sense of the pastoral with its rhythmic high spirits and voluble piano writing, using many of the quasi-orchestral sonorities of the C major piano sonata. The thematic lead in the slow movement, Molto Andante, is shared between the violin and the right hand of the keyboard in a rather stiff, formal way; in his piano trios Haydn never attempted the deft interweaving of parts typical of his quartets, that task of complementing phrase and sentence structure through scoring in the medium of the trio being left to Beethoven. Though the 2/4 Presto finale has many characteristics of contemporary rondo finales in symphonies – tempo, time signature, rhythmic patterns, silences, anticipations of theme, and carefully prepared 'tutti' climaxes – it lacks the rondo form itself, probably because of the smaller dimensions (here 193 bars, over 300 being typical in a symphony).

As in the previous set of trios, there is one work that makes use of mediant relationships between movements. No. 36 in E flat reproduces the contrast of colour between movements evident in Symphony no. 99, likewise an E flat major work enclosing a slow movement in G major. As in the symphony, the Poco Adagio moves naturally from delicate pathos to more forceful emotions, engendered by a wonderfully measured harmonic climax that presages Schubert.

Five months after the appearance of trios nos. 35–37, a further set of three was published, nos. 38–40, dedicated to Rebecca Schroeter. The minor-key work, no. 40, is in the unusual key of F sharp minor and stands comparison with other F sharp minor masterpieces by Haydn, the 'Farewell' Symphony and the quartet, op. 50 no. 4. Unlike the other trios in the minor mode, this one does not turn to the opposite mode for its conclusion. Instead, F sharp major is heard in the slow movement, which is a transposition up a semitone of the slow movement of Symphony no. 102 (the repetition of the opening paragraph is omitted) and, though one inevitably misses the weight of Haydn's orchestra and the way individual instruments are used to pick out strands in the chromatic writing, the Adagio cantabile succeeds in its fundamental purpose of providing contrast to the surrounding F sharp minor. The finale, marked Tempo di Minuetto, includes a Trio section in the major but its overall earnestness is intensified by some questing harmonic writing. The emotional world of this work is a very private one and, in the output of an increasingly public composer, it is one of the few works that show any sign of the late-period introversion familiar to us in the careers of J. S. Bach, Beethoven and, to a certain extent, Brahms and Schumann.

Trio no. 39 in G major opens with a set of alternating variations in an andante tempo, follows it with a movement in E major and concludes with a dashing rondo (described in the first edition as 'in the Gypsies' stile'), the only rondo in these late trios. The first work in the set, no. 38, is in D major and, unlike the two C major trios (nos. 35 and 43), inclines towards the intimate rather than the orchestral. The first movement includes a number of reflective pauses, often heralding a harmonic area a third away.

Following two sets of three works each, Haydn next composed two single works. Nothing is known about their inception, except that no. 41 was composed in 1795 and no. 42 before November 1796. Trio no. 41 features the familiar approach of opening with a slow movement in variations form, here the very sophisticated mixture of variations and rondo that can be summarized as ABA^1CA^2 (B is a major theme derived from A, A^1 is a literal repeat, C is a contrasting section and A^2 is an ornamented version of the main theme). The choice of key is audacious, E flat minor, with the contrasting section (C) placed in B major (i.e. C flat major). This grimly powerful movement is followed by a ternary Allegro in E flat major whose middle section decisively recalls B major.[16] Trio no. 42 occupies a different emotional world, is more conventional in its formal outlay, but no less absorbing in its bar-to-bar progress. A broad Allegro moderato in E flat major is followed by an Andante in C major that leads to a concluding Presto. Again, all three movements feature harmonic creativity of the most challenging kind, the second subject area in the first movement being particularly beguiling with its off-key approach and minor-key interpolation. The trio was first published in 1797 in Vienna and extensively advertised in later years; Schubert must surely have known and played the work which is as seminal for his style as Haydn's quartets and symphonies were for Beethoven's.[17]

Haydn's final three trios (nos. 43–45) were conceived as a set and published in London in 1797; it is possible that they predate no. 42 and perhaps no. 41. The set does not contain a work in a minor key but the other standard characteristic – beginning a work with a variations movement in a slow tempo – is present in no. 45 in E flat major. On this occasion the movement is ternary in shape, ABA¹, in which B is in E flat minor and A¹ is a decorated version of the opening A. Once again in a piano trio, B major is brought into juxtaposition with E flat, in the central slow movement marked Andantino ed innocentemente. This leads directly to the finale, an ebullient sonata form 'in the German style', that is a speeded up one-in-a-bar waltz with some completely disruptive cross-rhythms. The pensive middle movement in no. 44 in E major, marked Allegretto, recalls the similar movement in Piano Sonata no. 46 in E: over a continuously unfolding bass line that gives the feeling of an ostinato, the right hand declaims a wide-ranging melody; two-thirds of the way through the movement the texture is inverted. The first trio in this last set, no. 43, is the most high-spirited Haydn ever wrote and probably the most difficult for the pianist, a tribute to Therese Jansen's technique. She must, too, have been a great artist to bring off the rhythmic wit and sparkle of the outer movements. Initially, the A major Andante in 6/8 adopts the sentimental stance of an English canzonetta in 6/8, later proceeding to an impassioned middle section in A minor. In range of emotions, from the profound to the comic, these late piano trios are fully the equal of better-known contemporary works; that they also contain aspects of Haydn's musical personality not apparent in quartets and symphonies is yet more testimony to the continuing fertility of the composer in his mid-sixties.

String quartets

During the 1780s London concerts regularly included quartets in their programmes, such as the works of Vanhal and, especially, Pleyel and Haydn. During the 1791 Salomon season, five performances of three Haydn quartets (from the recent op. 64 set) were given, as well as chamber works by Koželuch and Pleyel; in 1792 Salomon's concerts included a performance of a Haydn quartet and chamber works by Gyrowetz and Cambini. For the second visit Haydn composed a new set of quartets, the so-called opp. 71 and 74.[18] Two were performed in the 1794 season and Haydn probably intended that the others should be performed in Salomon's concerts the following season; however, the change of management in 1795 from Salomon to the Opera Concert encouraged programmes with a stronger vocal content, hence no quartets were performed in that season. The audience for Haydn's quartets performed in the Hanover Square Rooms numbered about eight hundred people, and the genre was now heard in mixed programmes that contained symphonies, other orchestral music and operatic arias. To have played works with the harmonic and motivic intricacy and ingenuity of opp. 33 and 50, or the very individual character of the op. 42 quartet and the 'Razor' quartet (op. 55 no. 2) would have been to risk losing the attention of his audience, and possibly alienating them. Opp. 71 and 74 are, consequently, composed with an audience of *Liebhaber* in mind, woven on a broader loom, with a stronger fabric and a bolder pattern. Typical features of this approach are: virtuoso writing, primarily for the first violin but involving other instruments too; an increased use of routine accompaniment patterns (e.g. repeated quavers) providing a clear contrast between foreground and background in the music; a pervasive tunefulness in the main themes of all movements; a forthright harmonic language that, for instance, is as likely to juxtapose

contrasting tonalities as to modulate from one to the other; a clear sense of paragraphing in the music; first movements that avoid allegro moderato indications in
favour of brisker tempos; and finale movements that are usually in two in a bar
(2/4 or 6/8) and provide an exciting conclusion. Many quartets from the previous
decade (e.g. the 'Lark') anticipate these features but none applies them with the
same consistency as the six quartets of opp. 71 and 74.

Haydn's opp. 71 and 74 also reveal the influence of the *quatuor concertant* tradition, that is quartets composed with the prime purpose of demonstrating the technical prowess of the players rather than the composer's masterly control of thematic and harmonic material. Cambini and Pleyel were only two among many

composers of this type of quartet, chattering and vapid to modern ears (and no doubt to Haydn's ears too), but well suited to holding the attention of an audience in a hall. The quartets of Haydn's former pupil, Pleyel, were extensively played and published in London and passages such as that quoted above (pp. 290–1), from his third 'Prussian' quartet (published in Paris, Vienna and London in the 1780s), are common and anticipate similar passages in opp. 71 and 74:

Haydn's achievement in opp. 71 and 74 was to combine this approach with a modified form of his traditional symphonic attitude to produce six strongly individual works. There was another factor that contributed to the new assertiveness of these quartets. London had a long tradition of virtuoso violin players, Giordani, Cramer, Barthélemon and, of course, Salomon; also of cello players, Cervetto, Crosdill and Damen (Haydn's cellist in the first performances of opp. 71 and 74). All these were accustomed to performing in front of an audience. In response to this ambience, London string players had started to use a stronger bow, concave rather than convex in shape. This bow was perfected in the mid-1780s and is today usually called the Tourte bow, but it had been preceded by several transitional forms that continued to be used into the nineteenth century. Whether transitional or Tourte, concave bows with their greater tension imparted more attack and edge to the sound and had greater sustaining qualities, ideally suited to the strongly profiled sonorities of opp. 71 and 74.

As in all Haydn's sets of quartets since op. 9, the composer includes a work in the minor; op. 74 no. 3, in G minor, is only his second quartet in this key. It is representative of the new approach in these London quartets. Instead of beginning immediately with the first subject of the sonata form, Haydn, in all six quartets, calls the attention of his audience with some introductory material. Op. 71 no. 2 (in D) has the only slow introduction as such, an Adagio of four bars; op. 71 no. 1 (in B flat), op. 71 no. 3 (in E flat) and op. 74 no. 1 (in C) have between one and five preludial multi-stopped chords before their respective first subjects enter – a clear influence of symphonies such as nos. 74, 81 and 89. Whereas none of these chordal introductions establishes any kind of thematic relationship with the following main body of the movement, the G minor quartet, along with op. 74 no. 2, has passages that are clearly prefatory, if only because of the extended octave unison writing, yet they are also to be integrated into the body of the movement. The opening eight-bar gesture of the G minor quartet (see example) is followed by eight beats

of silence, allowing the first subject to enter *piano* and to begin in the lowest register of the medium before moving gradually upwards. After the strong character of
the opening, this material seems distinctly unpromising, but it contains the essential ingredients of most of the ensuing argument, the leading rhythm 'a' and the
apparently throwaway triplet ending, 'b'. A potentially debilitating cadence in
G minor is avoided as the music moves away from the tonic, making use of motifs
'a' and, especially, 'b' to establish B flat major; a feeling of expectation is created by
the high range of the first violin part and by two bars (42, 43) of what is in effect
2/4 metre. The waltz rhythms and the succession of four-bar phrases marked by
emphatic cadences make the second subject easily memorable:

Here, too, Haydn carefully avoids the arbitrary or the redundant; the source of the triplet accompaniment is obvious and the rising sixth of the melody together with the repeated notes of the second and third beats provide a discernible point of contact with 'a'. Unusually for Haydn in the medium of the quartet, this eight-bar theme is repeated verbatim in the second violin, with the triplets transferred to the first violin. The triplets figure also in the crisp two-bar cadence theme.

Energetic triplet quavers run a continuous course through most of the development and are joined by an unexpected return of material from the introduction – a simple, dramatic stroke that even the most inexperienced or casual listener could appreciate. The development charts a direct tonal course from C minor to E flat and then back to C minor. At this point the triplets disappear and the harmony becomes less active as the thematic material anticipates the first subject. Perhaps earlier in his career Haydn would have allowed the end of the development to merge imperceptibly with the beginning of the recapitulation, but here, as in all these London quartets, he is anxious to present his audiences with clearly articulated paragraphs; this development, therefore, ends *fortissimo* with a pause on a diminished seventh. The recapitulation, in terms of order and presentation of events, is regular, only the transition is expanded so that the triplet quavers and *sforzando* accents can now affirm G minor.

Slow movements for four players were clearly the most difficult to compose for a public performance, especially since the slow movements of Haydn's symphonies had earned particular esteem with audiences because of their contrast between easy tunefulness, played by a reduced orchestra, and impassioned declamation, projected by a full orchestra (usually with trumpets and drums). Such a flamboyant contrast was not available in the quartet genre and, equally, Haydn could not reproduce the exclusive world of some slow movements from the quartets of the 1780s; to have gone even further back to the concertante approach of his quartets up to op. 20 would have seemed *passé* in the 1790s. Two slow movements are variations on simple, tuneful themes in an andante tempo, those of op. 71 no. 3 and op. 74 no. 2. The G minor quartet, op. 74 no. 3 (the 'Rider'), adopts a bolder approach, a ternary Largo assai. The slow movement of op. 64 no. 5 (the 'Lark'), composed in the autumn of 1790, shares some general features but the differences are those that make the slow movement more accessible and, paradoxically, more profound. The Adagio of the 'Lark' quartet is placed in the dominant major, a conventional relationship between first and slow movement; the Largo assai of the G minor quartet, however, is heard in E major, providing a gorgeous contrast with the G minor to major of the first movement. Whilst the theme of the 'Lark' has a distinct atmosphere of the opera house about it, with its expressive appoggiaturas, chromatic passing notes and occasional repeated quaver accompaniment, the melody of the 'Rider' quartet suggests a more corporate form of singing, a hymn. No hymn tune, however, can match Haydn's masterful control of chord spacing (especially in the move to the *fortissimo* German sixth), dynamics and register. Like the slow movement of the 'Lark', the contrasting section is in the tonic minor and derives its material from the principal section (first four notes in inversion); the gradual move to the augmented sixth pinpoints this general relationship. The return of the main theme is decorated in both quartets; in the G minor two bars of measured *tremolo* near the beginning of the second half of the theme provide a further, exquisite intensification of mood.

At first, the Menuet in G major avoids approaching the tonic chord with undue emphasis, its final arrival at bar 23 signalling a lengthy passage of tonic and dominant harmony in a *forte* dynamic and an active texture. This passage, which replaces the expected reprise of the opening theme, also contains the thematic seeds of the Trio, the repeated D's. The Trio in G minor continues the gradual adjustment of mood from the beautiful E major of the slow movement to the forceful G minor that is to figure in the Finale.

Only two of the opp. 71 and 74 quartets invite comparison with contemporary symphonies through their use of rondo form in the finale – op. 71 nos. 2 and 3. The remainder, including the G minor, adopt a strongly characterized sonata form where, in addition to the clear sense of paragraphing, the music makes even greater demands on virtuosity and powers of projection than in the first movements. The Finale of the G minor is particularly graphic: an Allegro con brio tempo marking, abrupt contrasts between *forte* and *piano*, repeated quavers and semiquaver passage work all help to explain the nickname the 'Rider', the only London quartet, compared with six of the symphonies, to acquire a sobriquet. The second subject area is equally forceful with a particularly bold contrast of register, from a high B flat to a low B natural nearly three octaves away. As in the first movement, there is in the Finale a relentless momentum but, instead of the thematic integration of the first movement, here exaggerated contrast is signified in the development by three histrionic pauses. Some of the melodramatic fever of the movement disappears when the recapitulation turns, at the beginning of the second subject, to the tonic major; the work, consequently, ends in a mood of incisive brilliance rather than near-tragedy.

Haydn and Beethoven

Beethoven's name has already been mentioned several times in passing. The twenty-two year old composer had arrived in Vienna in November 1792 and, until Haydn departed for his second visit to London in January 1794, he was a composition pupil and frequent companion of the older composer. Although, when still in Bonn, Beethoven had already composed ambitious and impressive large-scale works, such as the cantatas on the death of Joseph II and the accession of Leopold II, in Vienna he was able to bring himself fully up to date with the recent achievements of the most progressive living composer. In 1793, he was able to hear performances of Haydn's latest symphonies and during the year he witnessed the composition of some symphonies for the second London visit, the F minor keyboard variations, the piano trio no. 34 and the opp. 71 and 74 quartets. Beethoven's formal lessons consisted of the usual species counterpoint and canon writing which, as always in even the most prodigiously gifted composer, gave increased assurance in the basic craft of making the notes work; nevertheless, the long-term impact of acquaintance with Haydn's most recent music and with his mental processes was even more important. The three piano trios of Beethoven's op. 1, the piano sonatas op. 2, the First Piano Concerto and, later, the First Symphony and the first set of quartets (op. 18) show a wilful, sometimes very self-conscious attempt to assimilate the taut strength of Haydn's symphonic language (in the broadest sense), and the younger composer's indebtedness is apparent in every aspect: orchestration, dynamics, tempo markings, motivic elaboration, harmonic ambiguity and increased sophistication of simple forms such as variations and rondo. Of particular interest to Beethoven was a recent development in Haydn's instrumental music, the use of third-related keys for slow movements and/or trios. Haydn's piano trio no. 27, composed at the end of the previous decade, had been notable for placing the slow movement in the flat submediant (A flat to E major) rather than the customary E flat major for this tonic. During 1793, Haydn was at work on five compositions that likewise use mediant relationships: Symphony no. 99 in E flat – slow movement in G; quartet, op. 74 no. 1 in C – Trio in A; op. 74 no. 2 in F – Trio in D flat; op. 74 no. 3 in G minor – slow movement in E; and piano trio no. 34 in B flat – slow movement in G. This resource, wholly untypical of Mozart's instrumental music, fascinated Beethoven, and many of his compositions of 1794–95 feature it: the piano trio, op. 1 no. 2 in C – slow movement in E; piano sonata, op. 2 no. 3 in C – slow movement in E; piano concerto no. 1 in C – slow movement in A flat; and in one of his many revisions of the piano concerto in B flat, the so-called no. 2, Beethoven actually began a new slow movement in D major to replace the existing one in E flat. During the very time when Beethoven was composing these works, Haydn was in London and, in a series of piano trios, further exploiting this stimulating resource.

As an artist of immense creative energy, Beethoven soon attained self-sufficiency, yet much of the broadening of his language and structure represents a logical development or enhancement of Haydn's own practices. The older composer's return to Vienna in 1792 had initiated a major step forward in Beethoven's development; the period after Haydn's second visit to England was to prove equally fruitful.

IX
The late years in Vienna, 1796–1809

ON 8 SEPTEMBER 1795 the following announcement was printed in the *Preßburger Zeitung*:

> According to letters from Hamburg, the princely Esterházy *Kapellmeister*, Herr Joseph Haydn, that universally esteemed and indeed very great composer whose excellent compositions are everywhere received with the greatest approbation, arrived there from London on the 20th of last month, continuing his journey to Vienna the next day.

After Haydn's return from his second triumphal visit to England, the city of Vienna was to be his principal place of residence until his death in 1809. Haydn's new patron, Prince Nicolaus II Esterházy, found Vienna attractive – unlike Nicolaus I, who had preferred the isolation of Eszterháza Castle in Hungary. Eszterháza was now completely abandoned, and the best furniture and pictures were removed to Vienna or to the family castle in Eisenstadt, where Nicolaus II spent the summers and from which the huge Esterházy estates were managed.

In summer, Haydn would follow the Esterházy court to Eisenstadt, and while there he had quarters near the castle; but otherwise he lived in Vienna and became the doyen of musical life there. During the period 1795–1802 Haydn's only formal duty as *Kapellmeister* was to compose a new setting of the mass each year for performance in Eisenstadt to celebrate the name-day of Nicolaus II's wife, Princess Marie Hermenegild; the result was the series (with the exception of the year 1800) of six great masses. In 1796, Haydn's *Capelle* included the princely *Feldharmonie* (wind band), consisting of pairs of oboes, clarinets, bassoons and horns, and a small group of voices, strings and another bassoon player who usually played timpani.

It would be pleasing to record that Haydn's late years were spent in the employ of a prince whose instinct for music was of the kind displayed by Nicolaus I; but, alas, not only was Nicolaus II basically unmusical, but personal relations between the prince and his *Kapellmeister* were, in the beginning, somewhat strained. Evidence of this is to be found in a number of episodes. Most revealing is a story concerning an orchestral rehearsal, probably *c.* 1795–6, at which Haydn was conducting; the prince entered and made a criticism, whereupon Haydn replied – in the presence of all the musicians – 'Your Highness, that is my business.' Nicolaus, white with fury, strode from the room. Another aspect of the prince's attitude towards the venerable composer recalls Haydn's position in the early years of his service with the Esterházys, when he was addressed in the third person (e.g., 'He will conduct a symphony tomorrow.'). This mode of address, appropriate to a lackey, had long since been dropped under Nicolaus I, and Haydn justifiably objected to its use; it now required the good offices of Princess Marie Hermenegild – with whom Haydn had always been on the best of terms and to whom he had dedicated three piano trios while absent in England – to restore a dignified form more suited to a Doctor of Music of Oxford University and one who had not long before chatted *tête-à-tête* with the King and Queen of England. As time went on, relations be-

tween the prince and his *Kapellmeister* improved, but Nicolaus was at best a difficult and unsympathetic man.

Now that Eisenstadt was again the centre of the Esterházy administration, elaborate plans were drawn up for rebuilding the rather ugly castle, and the architect's
plans are impressive; but Charles de Moreau was able to realize only a very small
part of his plans (e.g. the handsome stables in front of the building). Here is how
an Englishwoman, Martha Wilmot, described Eisenstadt in 1828:[1]

26th [September, 1828].

... Eisenstadt, Prince Esterházy's celebrated Chateau, surrounded by lands, woods, and
every possible luxury, save that of good taste was our next station. The town is a very poor
one, ill-paved and dirty. Even the Chateau stands in a square the pavement of which is
enough to break the springs of a carriage, altogether it was very desolate looking, and grass
grew (amidst the stones and large flags) before the door ... There are soldiers guarding the
entrance, and a great deal of military parade and pride but a desolate appearance about the
place, however, when his Chateau is thrown open during the hunting season, which sometimes happens, he can receive and accommodate with their attendants, 80 visitors. The bed-
rooms too, are in general, excellent, and some very handsome. The reception rooms are nothing remarkable considering the great scale of everything, except the grand banqueting
room, and this is 180 feet long ... here 300 guests dine sometimes, sometimes plays are acted
by performers from Vienna, and in short it is a noble piece ...

Apart from the castle, where Haydn gave concerts (on a large scale in the Great
Hall, now known as the 'Haydnsaal'; on a smaller scale in some of the attractive
rooms on the first [American, second] floor), our musical interest in Eisenstadt
must concentrate on the Bergkirche (Mountain Church); it was there that Haydn –
with one major exception – conducted the first performances of his last six
masses. The first performance of the 'Nelson' Mass (*Missa in angustiis*; XXII:11)
took place in 1798 in the parish church (now Cathedral) of St Martin on Sunday, 23
September. Haydn himself probably played the many organ solo parts on the great
organ – now beautifully restored – built in 1778 by J. G. Malleck, who in 1797 also
built the present organ in the Bergkirche. The great flowering of Haydn's choral
style is reflected as much in these masses as it is in his late oratorios. The masses
are scored for a large orchestra and the usual four-part complement of soloists and
choir with supreme skill and audacity, but basically they remain lasting tributes to
Haydn's belief in the order of the universe and the omnipresent and beneficent influence of God's goodness. On this aspect of Haydn's character Griesinger (53ff.)
tells us:

Haydn was very religiously inclined, and a devoted follower of the religion in which he
grew up. In his heart he was most firmly convinced that all human destiny lies under God's
guiding hand; that God is the rewarder of good and evil; that all talents came from above.
All his larger scores begin with the words 'In nomine Domini' and close with 'Laus Deo' or
'Soli Deo gloria'. 'If, when I am composing, things don't go quite right,' I heard him say, 'I
walk up and down the room with my rosary in my hand, say several Aves, and then the
ideas come again.' ...

A natural consequence of Haydn's religiosity was his modesty; for his talent was not of
his own doing but a gracious gift of Heaven, for which he considered he must show himself
grateful.

Haydn's pupil, Sigismund von Neukomm (in his day a highly successful composer), commenting on a passage in Dies's biography concerning the so-called
'Creation' Mass of 1801, states:[2]

The newer Masses by Haydn, against which the critics have been ruthlessly opposed because of their more elegant and less ecclesiastical style, were composed in Haydn's last and

glorious period and each year for the birth- or rather the name-day of his deeply respected patroness the Princess Esterházy, for whom a Mass in an attractive, elegant style would have more value than a learned or more serious work.

In Vienna the amount of musical activity was, if anything, even greater than in the era of Haydn's youth; but now the nobility could ill afford the full orchestras they had employed in Haydn's youth; instead they had wind bands which were used for *Tafelmusik*. One popular kind of repertoire for this *Feldharmonie* was the transcription of operas, and many such arrangements, even of Mozart's operas, have survived (also in the Esterházy Archives at Eisenstadt). There were two op-era orchestras in the city, one for the German and one for the Italian repertoire; most of the singers were primarily engaged for the one or for the other, seldom for both. Haydn, and later Beethoven, drew upon this pool for their benefit concerts. Of the private orchestras, apart from the Esterházy *Kapelle*, perhaps the most famous was that of Prince Lobkowitz, at whose concerts Haydn and, later, Beet-hoven appeared regularly. The leading public concerts were still the Easter and Christmas double evenings by the Tonkünstler-Societät, which – after the long es-trangement referred to above – asked Haydn to become an honorary officer. These concerts were usually in the form of an oratorio, with concertos or other music be-tween the sections. Haydn later came to be their principal benefactor, performing *The Seven Words* (choral version), *The Creation* and *The Seasons* for the bi-annual concerts of the Society and bringing in huge sums of money for musicians' widows and orphans. In fact Haydn's principal public appearances – apart from the first performances of his oratorios – were now devoted to charity.

When Haydn returned from London, he and Beethoven frequently gave con-certs together, Beethoven as piano soloist and Haydn conducting his London sym-phonies. Beethoven was, of course, no longer Haydn's pupil, and the young man's relationship to his former teacher was highly ambivalent. On the one hand he dedicated to Haydn his newest piano sonatas (opus 2, 1796), on the other he is said to have told Haydn, 'I never learned anything from you' – hardly an objective statement.

The first official collaboration between Haydn and the Imperial and Royal Li-brarian, Baron Gottfried van Swieten (who had probably unofficially furnished the German text of *The Storm* in 1793), was a new version of *The Seven Words*, which Haydn had composed for Cádiz in 1786 as a purely orchestral work. Now, a decade later, Haydn added new instruments to the orchestra (e.g., clarinets and trom-bones), made other revisions, and added a new instrumental interlude for solo wind band, an extraordinary and chilling Largo in which the double bassoon ap-pears for the first time in Haydn's scores – clearly a reminder of that instrument's presence in the great Handelian festivals of London.

Readers of the *Wiener Zeitung* were informed on 14 January 1797 that

His I.R. Majesty has graciously condescended to receive with every mark of approbation the very considerable financial contributions to the war effort made since the year 1793 by Prince Niklas [*sic*] Esterházy von Galantha, Councillor, Major-General, and the First Lieu-tenant of the Noble Hungarian Bodyguard ... and has now seen fit to confer on [Prince Esterházy] the Grand Cross of the Order of St Stephen ...

Haydn, of course, was hardly in a position to make large financial gifts to help in the war effort against Napoleon; but he was able to make a contribution more lasting than any gift of money. For this is the period in which Haydn composed his gravely beautiful 'Volcks Lied' ('People's Song'), later known as the Austrian (and still later the German) national anthem.

One version of the *Volkslied*'s origin comes from Anton Schmid, Custodian of the Austrian National Library in Vienna, who wrote in 1847:

As far as the reasons for which the wonderful Haydn Song was composed, we may present to our readers the following plausible circumstances, which several of the finest composers in Vienna, some of whom are dead and some still alive, remembered from those times and communicated to us.

In England, Haydn came to know the favourite British national anthem, 'God save the King', and he envied the British nation for a song through which it could, at festive occasions, show in full measure its respect, love and devotion to its ruler.

When the Father of Harmony returned to his beloved *Kaiserstadt*, he related these impressions to that real friend, connoisseur, supporter and encourager of many a great and good one of Art and Science, Freiherr van Swieten, Prefect of the I.R. Court Library, who at the time was at the head of the Concert Spirituel (supported by the high aristocracy) and likewise Haydn's particular patron. Haydn wished that Austria, too, could have a similar national anthem, wherein it could display a similar respect and love for its Sovereign. Also, such a song could be used in the fight then taking place with those forcing the Rhine; it could be used in a noble way to inflame the hearts of the Austrians to new heights of devotion to the princes and fatherland, and to incite to combat, and to increase, the mob of volunteer soldiers who had been collected by a general proclamation.

Freiherr van Swieten hastily took counsel with His Excellency, the then President of Lower Austria, Franz Count von Saurau ...; and so there came into being a song which, apart from being one of Haydn's greatest creations, has won the crown of immortality.

It is also true that this high-principled Count used the most opportune moment to introduce a *Volksgesang*, and thus he called to life those beautiful thoughts which will delight connoisseurs and amateurs here and abroad.

He immediately ordered the poet Lorenz Haschka to draft the poetry and then requested our Haydn to set it to music.

In January 1797, this double task was resolved, and the first performance of the Song was ordered for the birthday of the Monarch.

On 30 January 1797, Saurau wrote to the Bohemian authorities in Prague as follows:

Nobly born Count!
Your Excellency will be aware of the effect on the populace caused by the well-known English song [*Volkslied*]: God save the King; and how for a long time it has admonished that people to a common defence against foreign foes.

The Song which is herewith enclosed, written by Haschka and set to music by the famous Haydn, will be sung by the people in all theatres of Vienna on 12 February, and I take the liberty of sending it in confidence to Your Excellency, in order that the Song, if you judge it to be a good idea, may be sung that same day also in Prague; and may the wishes of the whole populace for the continued welfare of His Majesty resound on that day!
I remain with every respect,
Your Excellency's
obedient servant
Saurau.

On 14 June 1797, the Swedish diplomat Frederik Samuel Silverstolpe writes to Stockholm:[3]

... A few days ago I went to see Haydn again, who now lives right next to me, since he gave up his customary winter and spring lodgings in one of the suburbs [Gumpendorf] and moved a whole quarter-of-a-mile away. On this occasion he played to me, on the piano, violin quartets which a certain Count Erdödi has ordered from him and which may be printed only after a certain number of years. These are more than masterly and full of new thoughts. While he played, he let me sit beside him and see how he divided the various parts in the score ...

It was becoming the custom for someone to commission a series of (say) quartets from a composer; these quartets remained the exclusive property of the commissioner for a certain period of time (usually a couple of years), after which the composer was free to have them published or to reap whatever other reward he could from the music. Prince Lobkowitz was to 'purchase' Beethoven's 'Eroica' Symphony on such terms, and it was for him that Haydn composed his last completed string quartets, op. 77 (1799). Before then, Count Apponyi had made a similar arrangement with the composer for the six quartets of opp. 71 & 74 (1793) and Count Erdödy for the famous series of op. 76 (1797?), as noted by Silverstolpe. The new quartets from op. 76 were performed in September 1797 at Eisenstadt, on the occasion of a visit by the Viceroy of Hungary, Palatine Archduke Joseph. The diary of Joseph Carl Rosenbaum describes the festivities:[4]

Wednesday, 27th: The Viceroy arrived in Eisenstadt at about 12 noon. His approach was announced by the thunder of cannon, which lasted until he arrived and was received in the castle. ... It was a most ceremonious reception, a brilliant demonstration of the greatness of Prince Esterházy. At midday there was a banquet in the grand hall; places were laid for 800 persons, on two tables. As toasts were drunk, trumpets and drums sounded from the balcony of the hall, and cannon fired in the garden of the castle ...
Thursday, 28th: At about 10 a.m. the Viceroy, in the company of the Prince and several cavaliers ... went hunting ... At midday a banquet was held in the small hall. In the afternoon the citizens of the town, then the princely citizens and the Jewish community, all with their superiors, and the musicians, gathered on the square and welcomed the Viceroy with a display of flags and with music ... The town parson, the magistrate and the town council then went into the small hall where they were received by the Viceroy who thanked them for the particular attentions which had been paid him. New quartets by Haydn were played, [one of them] based on the song *Gott erhalte Franz den Kaiser*, and a seven-year-old boy by the name of Böhm played the violin, earning unanimous applause. At the Viceroy's departure, cannon were fired and trumpets and drums resounded from the balcony of the castle.

During this final period, although Haydn still had his own house in the Viennese suburb of Gumpendorf (Kleine Steingasse No. 73), in the cold winter months he took a *pied-à-terre* in the inner city so that he would not have to make the lengthy journey back to the suburbs late at night. Later, after he had given up this *pied-à-terre*, he lived entirely in Gumpendorf; in an undated ms. (now in the Mozarteum, Salzburg) written after the composer's death, Haydn's faithful servant Johann Elssler set down a record of the living habits of his aging master:

Daily Schedule of the late Herr v. Haÿdn
In the summertime he rose at half-past six. The first thing he did was to shave, which he did for himself up to his 73rd year. After shaving, he got dressed completely. If a pupil were present, he had to play the lesson he had been assigned on the piano [*Clavier*] to Hr. v. Haÿdn as he was dressing. The mistakes were at once corrected, the pupil instructed about the reasons thereof, and then a new task was assigned. For this one and a half hours were required. On the dot of 8 o'clock breakfast had to be on the table, and right after breakfast Haydn sat down at the piano and improvised, whereby at the same time he worked out the sketch of the composition; for this, a daily period from 8 to 11:30 in the morning was required. At 11:30 visits were paid or received; or he took a walk until 1:30. From 2 to 3 o'clock was the hour for lunch. After lunch Haydn always concerned himself with some small domestic task, or he went into his small library and read a book. At 4 o'clock Haydn returned to musical affairs. He took the sketch which had been prepared that morning and put it into score, for which task he took three to four hours. At 8 p.m. Haydn usually went out, but came home again at 9 and either sat down to write scores or took a book and read until 10 o'clock. The hour of 10 o'clock was supper time, which consisted of bread and wine. Haydn made it a rule not to have anything else except bread and wine in

the evening, and he broke the rule now and then only when he was invited out for dinner. At table Haÿdn liked light conversation and altogether a merry entertainment. At half past eleven Haÿdn went to bed – in old age even later. –. The wintertime made no appreciable difference in the daily schelude except that Haÿdn got up in the morning half an hour later, otherwise everything was as in the summer. In old age, mainly during the last 5 to 6 years of his life, physical weakness and illness disturbed the above schedule. The active man could, at last, find no occupation. In this latter period Haÿdn used to lie down for half an hour in the afternoon.

Silverstolpe reported on a visit he made to Haydn in 1797, at which time the composer had rented lodgings in the Krugerstraße in order to facilitate consultations with his librettist for *The Creation*, Gottfried van Swieten (see below):[5]

During the conversation which followed, I discovered in Haydn as it were two physiognomies. The one was penetrating and serious, when he talked about anything exalted, and only the expression 'exalted' was enough to show him visibly moved. In the next moment this atmosphere of exaltation was chased away, quick as lightning, from his everyday expression, and he became jovial with a force that showed on his features and which then passed into waggishness. This was his usual physiognomy; the other one had to be induced. – As I left him, he said, 'Do you know that this house has something remarkable about it: here, and just in these very rooms, we lost Mozart; what a gap that has left for us!' – I felt that I stood on hallowed ground.[6]

Just before Haydn left England, his friend and 'manager' J. P. Salomon had pressed into the master's hand a handwritten libretto entitled 'The Creation'. It had been intended for Handel, but he had not composed it. Haydn had been profoundly moved by his Handelian experiences in England, and he had the idea that the old baroque oratorio form could be given new life, particularly as regards the new school of orchestration, of which he was one of the founders and leaders. When Haydn returned to Vienna, he and Gottfried van Swieten first collaborated on *The Storm*, then on the revised *Seven Words*; now van Swieten adapted the libretto of 'The Creation' and translated it into German, in such a way that Haydn could also use the original English text in parallel.

In a letter from Johann Georg Albrechtsberger to his and Haydn's erstwhile pupil, Ludwig van Beethoven, we have the first written reference to Haydn's new oratorio:

Vienna, 15 December 1796

My dear Beethoven!

For your name-day [*recte*: birthday] tomorrow, I wish you all the best. God give you health and happiness and grant you much luck. If you, my dear Beethoven, should have a free hour, your old teacher invites you to spend it with him. It would give me great pleasure if you would bring the Trio with you, we could rehearse it straight away, and since I now have more time I will start directly making the scores.

Yesterday Haydn came to me, he is carrying round in his head the idea of a big oratorio which he intends to call 'The Creation' and hopes to finish it soon. He improvised some of it for me and I think it will be very good.

Don't forget to look in tomorrow and meanwhile hearty greetings from

Your Johann Georg Albrechtsberger.

In another extract from Silverstolpe's report on his visits to Haydn in 1797, we read:

When summer began Haydn moved back to his own home in the suburb of Gumpendorf, ... When I entered the room I heard a parrot calling 'Papa Haydn!' In one of the rooms to the right one often saw the great man with his undistinguished features getting up from his work, but also sometimes remaining seated at it until the visitor was quite close. There it was that he showed me the Aria from *The Creation* ['Rollend in schäumenden Wellen'/'Rolling in foaming billows'] which describes the sea moving and the waves breaking on the shores. 'You see,' he said in a joking tone, 'you see how the notes run up and down like the waves: see there, too, the mountains that come from the depths of the sea? One has to have some amusement after one has been serious for so long.' – But when we arrived at the pure stream, which creeps down the valley in a small trickle, ah! I was quite enthusiastic to see how even the quiet surface flowed. I could not forbear putting an affectionate hand on the old and venerable shoulder and giving it a gentle squeeze, as he sat at the piano and sang with a simplicity that went straight to the heart.

It must have been about June 1797 that Haydn reached the halfway mark in composing *The Creation*. We learn from Griesinger (54f.) that

His patriarchal, devout spirit found particular expression in *The Creation*, and therefore this composition must have been more successful than if it had been written by a hundred other masters. 'It was not till I completed half of my composition that I noticed that it had turned out well; I was also never so devout as during that time when I was working on *The Creation*; every day I fell on my knees and asked God to give me strength to enable me to pursue the work to its successful completion ...'.

Later, when the time came for rehearsals of *The Creation* preceding its first performance at the Palace of Prince Schwarzenberg in the Mehlmarkt, we are informed by Silverstolpe:

This work was first given on 30 April 1798. I was among the audience, and a few days beforehand I had attended the first rehearsal. At the latter Haydn was surprised afterwards by a present. Prince Schwarzenberg, in whose rooms the work was prepared and later also performed, was so utterly enchanted by the many beauties of the work that he presented the composer with a roll containing one hundred ducats, over and above the 500 that were part of the agreement. – No one, not even Baron van Swieten, had seen the page of the score wherein the birth of light is described. That was the only passage of the work which Haydn had kept hidden. I think I see his face even now, as this part sounded in the orchestra. Haydn had the expression of someone who is thinking of biting his lips, either to hide his embarrassment or to conceal a secret. And in that moment when light broke out for the first time, one would have said that rays darted from the composer's burning eyes. The enchantment of the electrified Viennese was so general that the orchestra could not proceed for some minutes.

We have seen Haydn almost at the summit of his career with the first, semi-private performance of *The Creation*; we say 'almost' because the actual summit may be reckoned the first public performance in 1799. On 20 February 1799 the *Allgemeine Musikalische Zeitung* carried the following from a Viennese correspondent:

... We shall get this masterpiece [*The Creation*] performed here in public and at a ceremonious occasion. On 19 March it will be given in our Court Theatre. The orchestra will consist of 180 persons. The aristocracy pays for the costs of the performance, so that the whole income goes to the composer. And that this will be respectable you can see from the fact that now, at present writing, not a box more is to be had. We are just now beginning to know and appreciate our Father Haydn; ...

Johan Frederik Berwald, the Swedish child prodigy (born 1787) who was touring Europe at this period, reported on the occasion in his memoirs:[7]

... As early as 4 o'clock in the afternoon, our temporary servant came and said we should hasten to the theatre, because it was besieged by a large number of people, even though the concert was not to start until 7 o'clock. When we entered, we saw that the stage proper was set up in the form of an amphitheatre. Down below at the fortepiano sat *Kapellmeister*

Weigl, surrounded by the vocal soloists, the chorus, a violoncello and a double bass [as continuo]. At one level higher stood Haydn himself with his conductor's baton. Still a level higher on one side were the first violins, led by Paul Wranitzki and on the other the second violins, led by his brother Anton Wranitzki. In the centre: violas and double basses. In the wings, more double basses; on higher levels the wind instruments, and at the very top: trumpets, timpani and trombones. That was the disposition of the orchestra which, together with the chorus, consisted of some 400 persons. The whole went off wonderfully. Between the sections of the work, tumultuous applause; during each section, however, it was still as the grave. When it was over, there were calls, 'Father Haydn to the front! Father Haydn to the front!'; which crowned the celebration. Finally the old man came forward and was greeted with a tumultuous *Applaudissement* and with cries, 'Long live Father Haydn! Long live music!' Their imperial majesties were all present and joined in the 'bravo' calls. ...

Haydn had entered the hearts of his countrymen in a way and to an extent that no composer had done previously. It is really almost as if *The Creation* was man's hope for a peaceful future (uncertain, at best, in 1799) and man's consolation for a clouded present. That it brought real comfort, consolation and joy to thousands of Viennese and, very soon, other Europeans, is clear from every document that survives. Never in the history of music, not even Handel with his *Messiah* (hardly known, for example, in France, Spain, Italy, or Russia), had a composer judged the temper of his time with such success.

Before Haydn went to England in 1790, his principal publisher had been Artaria of Vienna; and Artaria – though 'sleepy' (Haydn) – was still entrusted with such essential publications as the quartets, op. 76. But a new publisher now entered Haydn's horizon and gradually became all-important: Breitkopf & Härtel of Leipzig. Haydn came into intimate contact with this firm *via* a middle-man, the composer's later biographer, Georg August Griesinger, who was sent to Vienna in 1799 as a tutor to the Saxon Ambassador's son and who subsequently became Secretary of Legation at the Embassy. Much of our knowledge about Haydn's activities comes from this three-way relationship. In a letter from Haydn to the Leipzig firm (then directed by Christoph Gottlob Breitkopf, and later, after 7 April 1800 – when Breitkopf died – by Gottfried Christoph Härtel), we read:

Vienna, 12th June 1799.

Dearest Friend!

I am really very much ashamed to have offended a man who has written so often and honoured me with so many marks of esteem (which I do not deserve), by answering him at this late date; it is not negligence on my part but the vast amount of BUSINESS which is responsible, and the older I get, the more business I have to transact daily. I only regret that on account of growing age and (unfortunately) the decrease of my mental powers, I am able to dispatch but the smallest part of it. Every day the world pays me compliments on the fire of my recent works, but no one will believe the strain and effort it costs me to produce them: there are some days in which my enfeebled memory and the unstrung state of my nerves crush me to the earth to such an extent that I fall prey to the worst sort of depression, and thus am quite incapable of finding even a single idea for many days thereafter; until at last Providence revives me, and I can again sit down at the pianoforte and begin to scratch away again. Enough of this!

Yesterday Herr Griesinger brought me the 2nd, 3rd and 4th volumes of our immortal Mozart, together with the musical periodical. Please let me know how much I owe you for them, and to whom I should give the money here in Vienna.

The publication of both these things does you great credit, I WOULD ONLY WISH, AND HOPE, THAT THE CRITICS DO NOT DEAL TOO SEVERELY WITH MY CREATION. ...

Meanwhile, my dear friend, I remain, with every esteem,

Your obliging and obedient servant,
Joseph Haydn

Meanwhile, Haydn – who had always liked the company of young people
helped talented musicians who came to his notice. One such was Friedrich Ka
brenner, who, in 1796, had been travelling from Prague to Vienna, accompanied
his father. In a memoir published in 1824[8] we read that

... he unexpectedly met Beethoven, whom he took in his carriage to Vienna. There t
young K. was introduced to the great Haydn, who was so much delighted with his talen
that he requested his father, whenever he thought proper, to send the lad back to [Austri
and he would gratuitously superintend his musical education.

Kalkbrenner went on to Italy but returned to the Austrian capital about 1799. Tl
memoir continues:

Haydn ... gave him some subjects on which to exercise his talents in counterpoint. Havi
examined these, Haydn, with his characteristic modesty, said to him, 'my dear Frederi
you have not yet made sufficient progress in this difficult art, and I must therefore take y
to a master who knows more about this matter than you or myself.' He accordingly led hi
to Albrechtsberger, and introduced him as the son of a friend, in whose welfare he felt
particular interest. Albrechtsberger immediately received him as a scholar and made him
through a regular series of study, in order to form him thoroughly in his art. ... [Havi
completed his course with Albrechtsberger,] he returned to his studies under Haydn, fro
whom he received instruction during the remainder of his stay at Vienna, which was nea
two years. In the first quartet he attempted to write under this great master – the you
artist thought he must put forth all his learning as well as all his imagination, and when
produced it, anticipated that he must inevitably receive no usual quantity of praise. Tl
moment Haydn cast his eyes upon it, he exclaimed – hey day! what have we here! Calmu
Siberian, Cossack, Croat – all the barbarians of the world jumbled together – he laugh
heartily, but tempered his severity with some commendation – telling him that there was
far too much fire, but that it was better to have too much than too little, and that time ar
experience would bring his exertions to more favourable issue. During his stay with Hay
he was employed upon many of those popular Scottish airs, which are published
Mr. Thompson, of Edinburgh – and the immortal work of *'The Creation'* being brought ou
under the author's own direction, young K. played the violin at its representation. In h
conversations, Haydn was very fond of referring to the time which he passed in Englan
and recounted all the circumstances that attended him there with manifest pleasur
strongly recommending K. to visit that country at some future period.

Another young composer who joined the Haydn circle in Vienna at the turn
the century was Antoine Reicha, born in 1770, the same year as Beethoven, and
member of the Electoral Court orchestra in Bonn in 1790. A memoir, written i
French, recounts Reicha's experiences:[9]

There was I, freshly arrived in Vienna with some twenty-five louis in my pocket ... Tl
next day I went to the theatre and they stole my twenty-five louis which I had neglected
change during the day into the banknotes which were then the usual currency in Austria.
consoled myself by revisiting the famous Joseph Haydn who then lived in Vienna, an
whom I had seen in Bonn on his first journey to England and whom I had seen again i
Hamburg on his return from England [in 1795].
When I paid him my first visit in Vienna, he was at his piano, trying out the accompan
ment of a Scottish song. I dared to express my astonishment that he had the patience to o
cupy himself with such bagatelles; he answered me that it helped him to retain the art
modulation; he was more than seventy years old. We soon became good friends and lat
his door was opened more or less only to persons I presented to him.
Haydn was no longer of an age to give regular courses of lessons; but all I wanted was
listen to him discussing the art of composition, because for some time I had no long
needed lessons in harmony, counterpoint and fugue. Actually our lessons were convers:
tions, but no less valuable to me because of that. ... It was I who introduced to Haydn th

secretary of state Monsieur Maret [Comte Maret-Bassano], the writer Monsieur Etienne [Charles Guillaume Etienne, 1777–1845] and Messieurs Cherubini and Baillot [the violinist Pierre Baillot], as well as many other persons who were in Vienna at the time of the Battle of Austerlitz ...

Throughout Haydn's married life, his wife, Maria Anna, remains a rather shadowy figure. In fact one of the few concrete documents associated with her is her last will and testament, which she drew up in Vienna on 9 September 1799, when her husband was still at Eisenstadt. The document is not without interest, particularly since she made Haydn her residuary legatee. Far be it from us to attempt an analysis of the ills of the Haydn's marriage, but Maria Anna may have been something less of an ogre than she has been made to appear in the Haydn literature. That she was uneducated may be seen from the incredible spelling and grammar of her will, alas untranslatable in this respect, yet it is in fact a rather sympathetic document. She suffered from severe arthritis, and died at Baden in March 1800. She had been boarding with Anton Stoll, Chapel Master of the parish church at Baden, for whom Mozart had composed the *Ave verum Corpus* (K.618) and with whom Haydn was on intimate terms.

Hardly had Haydn's wife been laid to rest, when the composer's past once again rose to meet him in the person of his former mistress, Luigia Polzelli. Polzelli had at one time extracted a promise from Haydn that he would marry her as soon as he and she were free. Now that Frau Haydn had died, Luigia actually managed to extract the following promise (written in Italian) from the good-natured composer:

I, the undersigned, promise to Signora Loisa Polzelli (in case I should consider marrying again) to take no wife other than said Loisa Polzelli, and should I remain a widower, I promise said Polzelli to leave her, after my death, a pension for life of three hundred gulden (in figures, 300 fl.) in Viennese currency. Valid before any judge, I herewith set my hand and seal,

> Joseph Haydn
> Maestro di Capella di S. Alt. il Principe
> Esterhazy.
> [Haydn's seal]

Vienna, 23rd May 1800.

In reality, Haydn was no longer in the least interested in marrying the olive-skinned Italian soubrette. He was quite content to remain single and, with a few more letters to Polzelli sending her money, she fades quietly out of his life: for, having extracted this promise from Haydn, she was still free to marry whomsoever she pleased, which she proceeded to do, leaving for Italy with her new husband, Luigi Franchi, a singer. Haydn (who always expected Luigia to remarry – he had written from London to ask her to tell him the name of the one 'who is fortunate enough to have you') was probably not sorry to see the last of her. He did not forget her in his will, however, but reduced the amount of money previously promised.

The final oratorio on which Haydn and Gottfried van Swieten collaborated was *The Seasons*, based on James Thomson's popular and influential poem. If relations between Haydn and Swieten had been – as far as their different social statuses allowed – cordial, the new work soon drove them apart. Haydn considered much of the new libretto trivial and frivolous (such as 'Praise of Industry'), but nevertheless he poured a lifetime of experience into the work's composition; nor did the Swieten adaptation lack for words to inspire the old composer to his greatest efforts, but a certain pessimism now began to enter Haydn's life-enhancing philosophy. For example, he thought of 'Winter' as a portrayal of his own declining years, and perhaps we may regard that incredible orchestral introduction (now available in its original, uncut version) as being Haydn's farewell to music. A report published in Leipzig in the *Allgemeine Musikalische Zeitung*, dated 24 March 1799, reads:

Now Haydn is engaged on a new great work, which the worthy *Herr Geheimrath Freyherr* van Swieten has arranged metrically from Thomson's 'Seasons', and of which he [Haydn] has already completed the first part, 'Spring'. The curiosity of all music lovers is already stretched to breaking-point. ...

Haydn refers to the new oratorio in a letter to Ernst Ludwig Gerber, the famous German musical lexicographer:

Vienna 23rd September 1799.

... Since this subject cannot be as sublime as that of *The Creation*, comparison between the two will show a distinct difference. Despite this, and with the help of Providence, I shall press on, and when this new work is completed I shall retire ...

In practice, the winter of 1800–01 saw a change of Haydn's living arrangements. On 19 November Griesinger again wrote to Leipzig:

... Haydn will not move into town this winter as he usually does, but will remain in his house in one of the most remote suburbs. He lives more quietly there but every visit to him is an expedition in itself. 'Even if I have to spend 1 fl. every day for a *Fiaker* [carriage]', he said to me, 'it costs less than having a *pied-à-terre* in town.' Judge the domestic man from this statement. ...

In the spring of 1801 Silverstolpe wrote to Stockholm:

Vienna, 28 March 1801.

... Haydn's Seasons is finished, however, but a sickness which Haydn suffered postponed everything for so long that I think the performance will be put on next year. Too bad, for who can guarantee that the master will then be able to perform his work. He is too old. His works can only lose if they later fall into strange hands.

In the event, the performance was not postponed. Possibly the most important contemporary criticism was that written by Griesinger for the *Allgemeine Musikalische Zeitung*:

Vienna, 2 May 1801.

The Seasons, after Thomson, arranged by Baron Swieten and set to music by J. Haydn, was performed in the rooms of Prince Schwarzenberg on 24 and 27 April and on 1 May. Silent devotion, astonishment and loud enthusiasm succeeded one another with the listeners; for the most powerful penetration of colossal ideas, the immeasurable quantity of happy thoughts surprised and overpowered even the most daring of imaginations.

The very subject of this poem invites everyone to participate. Who does not long for a return of spring? Who is not crushed by the heat of summer? Who does not rejoice over the fruits of autumn? To whom is the numbing frost of winter not tiresome? The wealth of such a subject makes great demands on the poetry. But even if all are fulfilled, a special talent is required for judging musical effects, choosing the metre and for making a useful order out of the various sections, and this can only be accomplished by a poet who himself has penetrated the secrets of music. Since the reader may acquaint himself with the poem through this musical journal [footnote points out that the poem is printed as appendix No. VII], he will be in a better position to see for himself just what Haydn had to do. That he did all this to perfection, however, is the unanimous opinion of the public here. Every word, under the hands of this musical Prometheus, is full of life and perception. Sometimes the melody of the voice delights, sometimes we are shaken, as a woodland torrent that bursts over its banks, by the mighty entrance of the orchestra; now one delights in a simple, artless expression; or one admires the sumptuous richness of swift and bright harmonies. From the beginning to the end the spirit is involuntarily swept along by emotions that range from the most naive to the most artful, from the commonplace to the most sublime.

Another interesting report, dated 25 April 1801, with some valuable quotations from Haydn himself, appeared in the *Zeitung für die elegante Welt*:

... It would be more daring to wish to judge such a masterpiece on the basis of a single hearing; thus only a few general remarks here. Even during the composition, Herr Haydn stated the he would rather have composed another subject than the four seasons, for example the Last Judgment or something similar, because some ideas from *The Creation* involuntarily insinuated themselves into 'Spring'; also one noticed in the new work that some arias and choruses displayed a relationship, albeit a small one, with some numbers of *The Creation*. Who would want to blame the great master for that? *The Four Seasons*, instead, contained many passages which must move the coldest heart to the most gentle emotions, and many which are great, sublime, that sweep us along like a great river and excite one to the greatest enthusiasm. But the imitation of the cock's crowing at dawn, the gun's explosion during the hunt, seem to me to be a mistaken concept of tone-painting in music, perhaps even a degradation of this divine art.

In Dies's biography (182) we read the following:

It will not displease the reader to learn Haydn's own view in a few words. The Emperor Franz asked him, on the occasion of a performance of *The Seasons*, which product of his art he preferred, *The Creation* or *The Seasons*. 'The Creation,' replied Haydn. 'And why?' – 'In *The Creation*, angels speak and tell of God, but in *The Seasons* only Simon talks.'

To another friend, Giuseppe Carpani, Haydn said something similar. Carpani (212) writes:

The best of the criticisms was made by Haydn himself. I was present the first time this oratorio was given in the house of Prince Schwarzenberg. The applause was general, cordial and without end. But I, astonished that two parts of the work containing such variety, quantity and excellence could spring from one brain [una testa sola], hastened at the end of the concert to find my Haydn and convey to him my most lively and sincere congratulations. Haydn, as soon as I opened my mouth, cut me short and spoke the following memorable words: 'It delights me that my music appeals to the public; but I do not accept compliments about it from you. I am sure you yourself realize that it [*The Seasons*] is not another Creation. I feel it, and you too ought to feel it; but this is the reason why: in the one the characters were angels, in the Four Seasons they are peasants.' One could print tomes about a comparison between the two oratorios, but it could never be said better than in those few words of the composer himself.

Haydn decided to give the first public performance of *The Seasons* in the Great Hall of the Redoutensaal on 29 May 1801. After the triumphal first public performance of *The Creation* in 1799, Haydn must have expected a similar reception for this public première of his latest masterpiece. He was mistaken. Rosenbaum's Diary tells the whole story: 'I went ... to the Redouten Saal: *The Seasons* in a benefit performance for Haydn. It was not very well attended, a little over 700 people' – the hall hardly half filled! The fickle Viennese audiences were turning away from their darling, and Rosenbaum would also have occasion to record a similar situation when Beethoven's Ninth Symphony was given the second time to a nearly empty hall twenty-three years later.

Haydn, now an old man and infinitely weary after half-a-century of unremitting labour, gradually retired from public life, but for a few years he still continued to conduct charity performances of his three late choral works. And of course as princely *Kapellmeister*, he continued his duties, administrative and otherwise,

which meant that we have two last and glorious flowerings of Haydn's choral mu
sic: the *Schöpfungsmesse* of 1801 and the *Harmoniemesse* of 1802, first given at the Berg
kirche in Eisenstadt on 13 September 1801 and 8 September 1802, respectively. O
the second of these two celebrations of Princess Marie Hermenegild's name-da
Prince Starhemberg, an Austrian diplomat and ardent music-lover recently re
turned from London, was present and noted in his diary:[10]

Wednesday, 8 September. ... Splendid Mass, new and excellent music by the renowne
Haydn and conducted by him. ... Nothing more beautiful or better performed; after th
Mass returned to the castle. ... Afterwards, a huge and magnificent dinner ... with musi
during the meal. The Princess's health proposed by the Prince and echoed by fanfares an
cannon, followed by several more [toasts], including one to me and one to Haydn, who wa
dining with us, proposed by me.
After dinner we dressed for the ball, which was truly superb, like a Court ball. ...

Here is a picture quite different from that of even a few years earlier. Haydn, w
see, is now dining at the same table as the *Herrschaften* while the musicians pla
Tafelmusik; and a distinguished diplomat proposes the toast to Haydn. Within the
span of his career in the service of the Esterházys, then, he had seen a complete
transformation of his position – from a servant in livery to a distinguished artist in
vited to dine with the Prince, the Princess and their guests.

Haydn's relationship with his brother Michael had always been the happiest, al
though they were almost always separated from each other geographically. Now
as Joseph intended to retire, Prince Esterházy offered the position of *Kapellmeiste*
to Michael who, after some vacillation, finally decided to remain in Salzburg. Two
letters in draft are all that survive from the brothers' correspondence:

[Joseph to Michael:]

Vienna, 22 January 180

Thank you heartily for all the kind wishes which you once again showed me in your re
cent letter. I, too, wish it would be within my power to fulfil your wish about my wretched
health, which has plagued me for so long. For the last 5 months I have been subject to a con
tinual nervous weakness which renders me quite incapable of doing anything. You can eas
ily imagine how terribly this sudden change of health has depressed me, but I am not en
tirely desperate and hope to God that, when the weather changes, my previous health wil
be restored to at least half of what it once was.

[Michael to Joseph:]

[*c.* February 1804

Once again your name-day is approaching, for which I wish you, without further ado
that which is dear and valuable to you; but for my part I, too, wish for myself that you wil
continue to remember me in brotherly love. – I have long wanted to write to you about ou
musical organization (which didn't start life until the second part of January [continued in a
note at the bottom of the page:] and which you couldn't describe as jammed full) NB. The
whole organization was begun with too much enthusiasm; by the time it arrived here, it had
already got stuck. The first ones skimmed the cream off, and all that was left for us was a
watery soup. Anyway, I didn't write because I was ashamed of myself. I was astonished
when I received my contract – they had always kept me in hopes and in promises, and so
time went by. I would rather tell you the naked truth myself, before someone else tells you
about it with distortions. My entire increase in salary for the whole year consists of not more
than 150 gulden. If I could have foreseen this, I would have accepted with both hands the
generous offer of your prince. Why didn't I do so at the first opportunity! Well, *tempi pas
sati*! I must comfort myself with the general consolation: it had to happen that way and not
otherwise. But just this one thing: I remain with the innermost respect Your o[ld] b[rother]
p.p.

When Haydn retired as Prince Esterházy's *Kapellmeister*, a replacement had to be found, and after Michael had declined the offer, the difficult but talented Johann Nepomuk Hummel was engaged; in his turn he contributed several brilliant masses for Princess Marie Hermenegild, who will have relished the Haydnesque style and orchestration of these new works.

Haydn's last appearance as a conductor was in Vienna on 26 December 1803, the Feast of St Stephen. The occasion was a performance of *The Seven Words* (choral version), at 11 o'clock in the morning in the Redoutensaal, the scene of so many triumphs for Haydn, Mozart and Beethoven. The proceeds were for the poor of St Marx, a suburb in Vienna, where Mozart lies in an unmarked grave. Rosenbaum tells us 'It was very crowded. The Emperor gave 1,000 gulden.' It was the last chance for the Viennese to see in action the now frail old man who had changed the history of music.

Haydn had now retired from public life for good, living modestly in his house in Gumpendorf, watched over by the faithful Johann Elssler and other devoted servants, and the object of endless visits by admirers, both young and old. The young Carl Maria von Weber visited Haydn at about this time and afterwards wrote the following:[11]

I was at Haydn's several times. Except for the weaknesses of old age, he is still cheerful and in a good humour [*aufgeräumt*], speaks very gladly of his affairs and is especially pleased to talk to pleasant young artists: the real stamp of a great man, and all that is true of Vogler, too; only with the difference that his literary wit is sharper than the natural kind of Haydn's. It is touching to see grown-up men coming to him, and how they call him Papa and kiss his hand.

Haydn now began his final large-scale opus – not a new piece of music but a thematic catalogue of those works which 'he could approximately recall having composed from his 18th to his 73rd year', the so-called 'Elssler Catalogue' or *Haydn-Verzeichnis* (HV) of 1805. Elssler drew it up under Haydn's supervision and two copies were made, one for Breitkopf & Härtel and one which remained among Haydn's personal effects and eventually went to the Esterházy Archives (it has been published in facsimile, edited by the great Haydn scholar of our century, Jens Peter Larsen). We have documentary evidence of this project from Griesinger, who on 22 August 1804 reported to Breitkopf & Härtel that

... Haydn has stopped all work because of his health, and a quartet of which he has finished two movements is the child [*Schooßkind*] whom he now cares for and to whom he sometimes devotes a quarter of an hour. Otherwise he is now occupied with the complete catalogue of his works, which he will send you when it is finished.

On 15 April 1805, a visit of considerable importance took place at Haydn's house in Gumpendorf: the painter A. C. Dies paid his first call on the composer, whose biography he would soon undertake. Writing of this visit, Dies tells us that

Grassi [the sculptor] brought me to Haydn. It seemed to me that I did not displease him, for he came towards me, although sick for a long time and with both legs swollen, gave me both his hands, and received me with a cheerfulness that spread over his whole features and with such a penetrating look that I was surprised. This lively expression, the brownish (tinged with reddish) facial colour, the exceptionally neat clothing – Haydn was fully dressed –, his powdered wig and, the swelling notwithstanding, the boots he was wearing, and the gloves; all this made one forget any trace of illness and gave the old man of seventy-three the healthy look of a fifty-year-old, which was supported by his medium height and the fact that he was not at all heavy. 'You seem,' he said to me, 'to be surprised about my being fully dressed, though I'm still sick and weak, I can't go out and I breathe nothing but indoor air. My parents accustomed me from my earliest youth to discipline concerning cleanliness and order, and these two things have become second nature to me.' He also thanked his parents for encouraging him in fear of God and, because they were poor, they were obliged to be thrifty and hard-working. All things that one encounters very rarely in our young geniuses.   [15f.]

... I feared that Haydn's weak state of health might prevent him from further conversation. I told him to look after himself, and my friend [Grassi] and I left him, because it was in any case time for his afternoon nap. They told me that for this nap Haydn undressed completely, put on a night dress and dressing gown and then went to bed. He was strictly punctual and winter or summer he kept to the period from half-past four to five o'clock; thus he slept no more than half-an-hour. After his rest was over he dressed completely, climbed down the stairs with great difficulty and went to the housekeeper's room. There he had some of the neighbour's children come and their cheerful play delighted Haydn; their jokes made him forget his sad condition ... He admits that his spirit is weak. He cannot think, cannot feel, cannot write, cannot hear music ...   [21f.]

Dies's description of Haydn's appearance in old age, as seen through the eyes of an artist, is one of the most accurate available. By 1805 the composer was merely a shell of his former self; on 5 May, when Dies went to visit Haydn for the third time, Haydn asked to be excused. The housekeeper said, 'He is always depressed when the weather is cold, or windy, or rainy.' Our 'official' biographies of Haydn, whether by Griesinger, Dies or the hopelessly inaccurate Carpani, are vignettes of an old, depressed man; the ruin of a giant intellect whose former wit and penetrating glance could only occasionally be called from their now perpetual slumber.

In 1808, on the Feast of St Joseph – Haydn's name-day – Antonio Polzelli (second son of Haydn's former mistress, and generally thought to be the composer's natural son), a violinist in the Esterházy orchestra at Eisenstadt since 1803, conveyed congratulations to his former *Kapellmeister* on behalf of the members of the orchestra; from Haydn's answer it is not quite clear whether Polzelli and a few members of the band came to visit him or whether their greetings were conveyed in writing. Haydn's reply (of which only the signature is autograph) reads:

Vienna, 20th March 1808.

My dear Son!

Your truly heart-warming remarks and those of all the members of the Princely Esterházy band, on the occasion of my name-day, moved me to tears. I thank you and all the others from the bottom of my heart, and ask you to tell all the members in my name that I regard them all as my dear children, and beg them to have patience and forbearance with their old, weak father; tell them that I am attached to them with a truly fatherly love, and that there is nothing I wish more than to have just sufficient strength so that I could enjoy once more the harmony of being at the side of these worthy men, who made the fulfilment of my duties so pleasant. Tell them that my heart will never forget them, and that it is the greatest honour for me, through the grace of my ILLUSTRIOUS PRINCE, to be placed at the head, not only of great artists, but of NOBLE AND THANKFUL HUMAN BEINGS.

Joseph Haydn

Musical Vienna decided to honour Haydn's seventy-sixth birthday with a gala performance of *The Creation*. The Liebhaber-Konzerte (Amateur Concerts), under the sponsorship of Prince Trauttmannsdorf, put on the oratorio in their regular hall, the Aula (Great Hall) of the (old) University – the hall still exists – with Antonio Salieri as conductor, Conradin Kreutzer at the piano (he would later become a well-known operatic composer) and Therese Fischer, Carl Weinmüller and Julius Radicchi as soloists. The oratorio was to be sung in Carpani's Italian translation, and the date of the performance was set for 27 March. Griesinger relates:

I was surprised that he could make up his mind, considering his failing health, to attend the ... [concert] ... on 27 March ... He [Haydn] answered: 'Consideration for my health could not stop me. It's not the first time that I have been honoured, and I wanted to show that I'm still capable of receiving it.'

On the day appointed, Haydn was borne into the Great Hall, to the sound of trumpet fanfares and tumultuous applause, and seated next to Princess Esterházy. The cream of Viennese society was there to pay a last public homage to the Father of the Symphony (as they thought him) and of the string quartet. Salieri and Haydn embraced tenderly, surrounded by cheering crowds. Beethoven, tears streaming down his face, bent and kissed the hand of his former teacher. When the passage, 'And there was Light' was reached, Haydn (as Carpani, who was an eye-witness, relates) 'raised his trembling arms to Heaven, as if in prayer to the Father of Harmony'. At the end of the First Part, it was thought advisable to take Haydn home. Carpani describes the scene:

Two robust athletes picked up the armchair in which he was seated, and amidst the greetings, the applause and the acclamations of the whole room, the harmonious man of triumph approached the stairs; but, having arrived at the doors, he made a sign to stop. The porters obeyed and turned him round to the public; he thanked them with the usual gestures of acceptance, then, looking at heaven, and with tears in his eyes, he blessed his children.

We now come to the last surviving letter sent by Haydn; fittingly, it is addressed to his now much mellowed and indeed almost sympathetic Prince Nicolaus II Esterházy. Only the signature is autograph.

Most Serene Highness,
Gracious Prince and Lord!
    I humbly place myself at Your Serene Highness' feet for the gracious approval of my request, whereby with the utmost kindness you take over my yearly expenditures for the doctor and apothecary. By this new act of generosity Your Serene Highness has freed me from a most pressing anxiety, and thus enabled me to await the end of my earthly existence in peace and serenity. May Heaven grant my zealous wish that Your Serene Highness live in everlasting well-being and Your Gracious Highness' illustrious family in ever-increasing prosperity. I remain ever your most devoted and

> Your Serene Highness'
> humble servant
> Joseph Haydn

Vienna, 22nd December 1808.

Haydn died on 31 May 1809; his last days are graphically described by the faithful Johann Elssler in a letter to Griesinger,[12] whose last visit to the composer had been on 3 May, before leaving Vienna, then threatened by the invading French army:

> Vienna, 30th June 1809

Most nobly born
    Highly respected Herr v. Griesinger!
It has long been my intention, Sir, to give you news of the death of our beloved benefactor and father. Right after his death I went to [your] H[err] Porter and asked whether I could not send a letter to you, Sir. H[err] Porter said to me, however, that there is no possibility yet because it is not known which roads are open. Now I ask you, Sir, for your pardon and kind patience if I come so late with your request for I know that you, Sir, are always anxious to know how our good and kind Papa Haydn fares. But the confusion at that moment was too great.
    With tears in my eyes I report to you, Sir, our dear Father's death. The day that you, Sir, said good-bye to our good Papa and said, we won't see each other for a long time or perhaps we will see each other soon, just after Your Grace left the room, our good Papa said,

we really won't see each other for a long time, he started to weep and said, my dear Johann, I won't be seeing Herr v. Griesinger any more, the war business depresses me right down to the ground. We had a lot of trouble (I and cook Nannerl) to get these thoughts out of our good Papa's mind and to quiet him down, but our good Papa was too weak and altogether couldn't quite pull himself together and was always anxious about how the war was going to continue. When the Imp. French army moved into the Maria Hülfer Lienie [the outer walls of Vienna] on 10th May in the morning at a quarter of seven o'clock, our good Papa was still lying in bed. I and Nannerl were just busy getting Papa out of bed. – For the noise and confusion on the street were too great at this particular moment and we didn't have any people at our side who could comfort our good Papa; anyway as we were still busy getting the Papa out of bed, four canister-shots exploded by the Lienie, one after the other, and indeed, we kept one ball that fell into the courtyard as a souvenir, because of these explosions the door to the bedroom blew wide open and all the windows rattled, our good Papa was shocked and cried in a loud voice, 'Children, don't be afraid, for where Haydn is, nothing can happen' and trembled violently all over his body. But the whole day they were shooting from the fortress [in town], and our good Papa composed himself a bit though it was very hard for him, his nerves were hit too hard, and well! His whole body sank, but he still enjoyed his food and drink but as for walking I couldn't get our good Papa on his feet all by myself and the strongest medicines didn't help any longer. The *Kayser Lied* was still played three times a day, though, but on May 26th at half-past midday the Song was played for the last time and that 3 times over, with such expression and taste, well! that our good Papa was astonished about it himself and said he hadn't played the Song like that for a long time and was very pleased about it and felt well altogether till evening at 5 o'clock then our good Papa began to lament that he didn't feel well, but he still stayed up another half-an-hour but at 5:30, Well! Our good Papa asked to be taken right to bed and then he began to shiver a little and had a headache. All sorts of things were given him, and our good Papa felt so much better on that same evening and had quite a good night's sleep and was so well when he got up and the other things were all right too, so that of a dying moment nothing was felt. Saturday the 27th of May our good Papa asked about 8:30 o'clock to get up as usual and get dressed, but his bodily strength wouldn't allow it, and so our good Papa didn't leave his bed any more. The numbing got much worse, but so quietly and willing in everything that we were all astonished, our good Papa didn't complain of any pains, and when we asked him how he felt, was always received the reply, 'Children, be of good cheer, I'm well.'

The 29th of May we asked for a *Consillium* to be held with the permission of H[err] v. Hohenholz. The medicus Doctor Böhm was asked to come, for our good Papa needed it and he [Böhm] is also a very clever man, so the *Consillium* was held on the 30th in the morning, but despite all kinds of medicines administered, it was all of no use, and our good Papa got steadily weaker and quieter, 4 hours before his death our good Papa still spoke but then we didn't hear another sound, our good Papa had reactions and knew us 10 minutes before the end, for our good Papa squeezed Nannerl's hand, and the 31st of May in the early morning five minutes before a quarter to one o'clock our good Papa went quietly and peacefully to sleep, at his death there was no one there but me, the servants and a neighbour who also signed the will as a witness [Anton Meilinger, of 74 Kleine Steingasse]. Our good Papa is buried in God's field [cemetery] in front of the Hundsturmer Lienie, in his own grave.

The 31st March 1732 our good Papa was born, and 1809 the 31st of May was for us all the saddest day of death for ever. Our good Papa was 77 years and 61 full days old.

Otherwise everything is in the best order and everything remains until the whole business [of the legacy proceedings] starts, the Nannerl and the niece [*Mum*] of the late Papa and also the maid are still in the house, I'm with my wife and children at home and carry on as best I can in these trying times. May God help us out of our sad position, I eagerly hope to see Your Grace, God keep Your Grace in the best of health and we all kiss your hands

Your thankful
Johann Elssler m.p.
Copyist and Servant of the
late Herr v. Haydn.

N. B. I have taken my good Papa in plaster.[13]

X
Haydn's music,
1796–1803

THE FIVE-YEAR PERIOD that had embraced the two London visits transformed Haydn's relationship with his public. No longer was he a lonely creative artist reaching out to a distant, unknown audience; popularity had meant that he had become, in modern jargon, 'public property' with palpable – though never debilitating – results reflected in his musical style. London had made him aware of his status and had broadened his artistic base; in the productive years that remained following his return to Vienna, Haydn was to communicate from the commanding position of a celebrity who could address himself to civilized society throughout Europe. The two oratorios, *The Creation* and *The Seasons*, are the clearest manifestations of this new outlook, multi-faceted but unified by the intensity of Haydn's vision. They are conceived on an extensive scale and require the largest forces of any of Haydn's compositions; the subject matter – the creation of the universe and the measured course of the seasons – could not be broader. These are the works of a devout Austrian Catholic setting librettos written in Protestant England; they were inspired by the very different aesthetic of Handelian oratorio, with Haydn drawing on his own unmatched experience as a composer of symphonies, quartets and operas; first performed in German in Vienna, they were first published bilingually in German and English (indeed, *The Creation* was composed bilingually); and, within the composer's lifetime, both librettos were translated into several languages, including Italian, French, Swedish, Polish and Russian. The other outstanding achievement of this period was the series of masses associated with the name-day of Princess Marie Hermenegild Esterházy. As the only major works of the late years specifically composed for the Esterházy court, the masses clearly do not share the same broad outlook as the oratorios, yet these too reveal an awareness of the world beyond that of the Bergkirche in Eisenstadt, in their references to contemporary events and their evident desire to sustain a tautness of argument comparable to that of the London symphonies; five of the masses were published in Haydn's own lifetime (by Breitkopf & Härtel of Leipzig), a significant indication of their wider appeal. Haydn was a revered figure in Viennese musical life. For instance, between the first public performance of *The Creation* in 1799 and his death ten years later, thirty-four performances of the oratorio are known to have been given in the city, usually in aid of charity and often directed by the composer. The international composer had become a prophet honoured in his own country.

Music with text dominated this last period of Haydn's life, the principal instrumental works consisting only of the Trumpet Concerto, eight quartets (opps. 76 and 77) and two movements of a ninth (op. 103). There were to be no symphonies or piano sonatas, even though Haydn was asked to compose works in both these genres. In addition to the oratorios, the masses, the Te Deum and the folk-song arrangements, Haydn was busily occupied with providing (or supervising) revised versions of earlier compositions: a choral version of *The Seven Words*, and the enlarged instrumentations of *Il ritorno di Tobia*, the Mass in F and the Stabat Mater –

all of them enjoying a new success in the wake of the oratorios and the masses. After completing *The Seasons* in 1801, the composer frequently lamented his mental and physical exhaustion, observing poignantly that although ideas occurred to him, he lacked the powers to develop them and, later, even to remember them. Had his energies been equal to the tasks, Haydn would no doubt have composed more symphonies, sonatas, quartets and masses, as well as a third oratorio (probably to be entitled *The Last Judgment*). Except for supervising the publication, by Breitkopf & Härtel, of parts of *L'anima del filosofo*, opera does not figure in Haydn's last years. Some of the reasons for this are to be found in the factors that made oratorio composition so congenial.

The Oratorios

The precise origins of the libretto of *The Creation* are unknown and have become confused by anecdote and rumour. Haydn certainly acquired the libretto in London during his second visit and there may well have been an intention to set it for a performance organized by Salomon. The lack of time in 1794 and 1795, the change of sponsors from Salomon to the Opera Concert and no doubt Haydn's shrewd assessment that, despite his popularity in England, it would be unwise for him to enter into direct competition with the choral works of Handel, meant that not one syllable was set in London. This original English libretto is lost and may never have carried the name of its author. Certainly, Gottfried van Swieten remarked that the author was not named, but that does not necessarily contradict Haydn's later statement to Griesinger that the author was 'an Englishman by the name of Lidley'. 'Lidley' sounds suspiciously like a muddled conflation of Lidl (the baryton player who served at the Esterházy court from 1769 to 1774 and who had died in London, probably before 1789), the composer Thomas Linley Sr (1733–95) and Robert Lindley (a London cellist). In addition to being a composer, Thomas Linley had played a prominent part in the organization of the Drury Lane oratorio seasons and there is no reason to doubt the modern hypothesis that the libretto was in some way associated with him, not as its author – he had no literary skills – but as an impresario and/or potential composer.

Swieten translated the English text into German and Haydn then set both texts to music, paying equal attention to the two languages.[1] Notwithstanding the infelicities of syntax in the surviving English version, the text is a beautifully paced account of the creation of the universe, carefully blending the narrative, the descriptive and the laudatory. Three distinct sources are drawn upon: the Book of Genesis, complementary passages from Milton's *Paradise Lost* and, for many of the climactic choruses, verses from the Psalms.

The pedigree of the libretto of *The Seasons* is easier to establish, drawing directly rather than selectively on the mainstream of English literature. By an appropriate coincidence, James Thomson's epic poem, *The Seasons*, was inspired by Milton's *Paradise Lost*; it was issued in instalments between 1726 and 1728. Encouraged by its enthusiastic reception, Thomson gave free rein to his lyrical imagination in an ever more indulgent manner, with the result that the finished product consisted of over 5,000 lines. Swieten again prepared the libretto for Haydn's oratorio. As an editor, critic and translator of existing librettos, Swieten was very experienced (having, for instance, prepared the German librettos of the four Handel works newly orchestrated by Mozart, as well as translating *The Creation*), but compiling an entirely new libretto was a new and very different challenge to a man whose skills were editorial rather than creative. His chosen task could not have been more difficult. Out of Thomson's vast poem Swieten culled a libretto of some 650 lines, omitting the extravagant digressions of the poem, the passages of moralizing, and selecting only the most pertinent passages of narrative and description. In many places, Swieten compressed the rococo excesses of Thomson's poetry into succinct, unpoetic lines better suited to vocal declamation. Nevertheless, many of the descriptive passages that remain, especially in 'Summer' and 'Autumn', are still dangerously long and, given a lesser composer, might well have inhibited the independence of the music. A storm, a hunting chorus and a chorus in praise of wine ensure plenty of incident in 'Summer' and 'Autumn', while the mood of 'Spring' is more uniformly relaxed. Swieten rightly perceived that the last part of Thomson's epic, 'Winter', with its repeated descriptions of a bleak landscape, might make the expected uplifting conclusion to an oratorio unattainable. In Thomson's poem there is another storm (the third) to provide some excitement, but Swieten rejected this dramatic event in favour of two new interpolations taken from other sources, a spinning song (poetry by Gottfried August Bürger) and a 'Lied mit Chor' ultimately derived from Charles Simon Favart, being a story about a saucy girl outwitting a nobleman. These two numbers constitute the greatest departure (as distinct from omissions) from Thomson's poem, but other, less extensive changes were also made in fashioning the libretto. Reflecting its sources, the libretto of *The Creation* was shaped by choruses of praise and thanks to God, explicit Christian sentiments absent from the Thomson poem 'The Seasons'. Consequently, near the end of 'Spring' and 'Winter', Swieten added several lines of his own composition, providing the requisite element of praise and thanks. From the omissions and amendments that Swieten made to Thomson's epic it is clear that he recognized the problem of converting this vast poem into an oratorio libretto; yet, it must be said, his attempt was a noble failure for, in comparison with *The Creation*, the finished libretto lacks the careful balance between narrative and reflection and only just manages to provide sufficient material to kindle Haydn's most elevating style.

The libretto of *The Creation* is divided into the three parts typical of English oratorio. Parts I and II share a flexible approach to the description of the six days of the biblical Creation: a recitative to announce the beginning of a new day, an accompanied recitative and/or aria to evoke the most picturesque incidents and a concluding chorus of praise and thanks. The story is unfolded by three soloists, whose names, taken from Milton, were supplied by Swieten: Gabriel, Uriel and Raphael. Part III, in contrast, is a leisurely evocation of the Garden of Eden on the seventh day, the day of rest, presenting a more difficult challenge since there is no graphic incident. The bass and soprano soloists become the 'happy pair', Adam and Eve, and, to mirror their carefree existence, there is less recitative and accompanied recitative, the music being an extended tableau of solo, duet and chorus. The work ends with a general chorus of praise.

The libretto of *The Seasons* lacks the simple but strong construction that had characterized *The Creation*, with no repeated units of design to mark its unfolding. As in *The Creation*, there are three soloists (soprano, tenor and bass) who are given names by Swieten: Simon (a farmer), Hanne (his daughter) and Lukas (a young peasant). As named individuals, the three soloists obscure the distinction between narrator and participant that is present in *The Creation*. Likewise, the role of the chorus in the two oratorios is different. In the earlier oratorio the chorus takes part in the description only once (the creation of light) and never assumes an identity; its function is to provide cumulative praise – man and the angels in adoration. In *The Seasons*, on the other hand, they are sometimes participants (peasants and hunters), at other times narrators, as well as providing two general choruses of praise.

Before proceeding to the music itself, it is worth assessing the appeal the English oratorio form held for Haydn, it being as strongly suited to his temperament as opera was to that of Mozart. Its chief superiority over Italian oratorio, such as Haydn's own *Il ritorno di Tobia*, was the opportunity to write extensively and with great variety and impact for a large chorus (larger than Haydn would have had at his disposal in Eisenstadt for any of his masses). Handel's choral writing in *Messiah*, *Solomon*, *Israel in Egypt* and the Coronation Anthems had been the direct stimulus, and Haydn's appetite had been further whetted by the limited chances offered in the opera *L'anima del filosofo*, the ode *Invocation to Neptune* and the single-movement 'madrigal' *The Storm*. The second element was the opportunity for pictorial writing that the subjects of both oratorios offered, more pervasive in *The Creation* and *The Seasons* than in any one Handel oratorio but a consistent element of the genre nevertheless. The many passages describing animals and the weather in Haydn's oratorios are in the same tradition as the many pictorial incidents (battles, dancing, angels, nightingales, processions etc.) in most of Handel's oratorios and especially reminiscent of the frogs, flies, lice, locusts, hailstones and darkness in *Israel in Egypt*. From the early *Singspiel*, *Der krumme Teufel*, to the 'Clock' Symphony, Haydn had shown a disarming penchant for pictorial writing in a way that is not encountered in Mozart's output. Precedents for the descriptive passages in the two late oratorios abound: the seascapes of *Le pescatrici*, the cantata 'Destatevi o miei fidi' and *L'anima del filosofo*; the storms in Symphony no. 8 ('Le soir'), *Philemon und Baucis*, *Il ritorno di Tobia* and the English 'madrigal' *The Storm*; the streams of *Il mondo della luna* and *L'incontro improvviso*; the thunder, the turtledove and the hunt in *La fedeltà premiata*; the sunrise in Symphony no. 6 ('Le matin'); the moon in *Il mondo della luna*; the earthquake in *The Seven Words*; the monster in *Orlando Paladino*; and the Furies in *Armida* and *L'anima del filosofo*. With some notable exceptions, such as the Furies and the earthquake, these pictorial incidents, if always charming, tend to the gratuitous. In the two late oratorios, however, Haydn was presented with a context in which the pictorial was a persistent and governing element. In *The Seasons*, indeed, the composer complained that there was too much pictorialism, describing No. 18 as 'Frenchified trash' (a reference to *opéra comique*); within the space of thirty-eight bars, the text and music refer to sheep, a quail, a cricket, frogs and the tolling of the evening bell. In general, however, Haydn responded with enthusiasm to the pictorial element and, crucially, managed to contain it within the broader sweep of the narrative. He usually succeeded in making the incidents subservient to a more elevated purpose. His caustic remark about excessive pictorialism in one number in *The Seasons* constituted a tacit recognition that, in comparison with *The Creation*, pictorialism in the later oratorio was in danger of becoming not so much a means to to an end, but an end in itself.

A third element in the attractiveness of these particular librettos is the absence of human characterization. In *The Creation*, the three archangels – Gabriel, Uriel and Raphael – are narrators who, in true archangelic fashion, explain God's creation to an astonished and believing humankind. Somewhat similarly in *The Seasons*, Hanne, Lukas and Simon are archetypal peasants rather than individuals, as much part of the landscape as the storm, the hunt, the brook or, indeed, the despised frogs. Neither libretto requires strongly profiled characters, though in both cases Haydn was to make the named characters recognizably human by giving them music redolent of *Singspiel*. Clearly appropriate for Simon, Hanne and Lukas in *The Seasons*, such music is similarly appropriate for Adam and Eve in Part III of *The Creation*, cleverly suggesting the innocence and susceptibility of the first 'Mann und Weib'.

Overlaying the content of both oratorios, and of paramount importance to Haydn, was the element of rapturous wonder at the workings of the universe. To a man who habitually prefaced his scores 'In nomine Domini' and concluded them 'Laus Deo', and who found easy and unselfconscious stimulus in repeatedly setting the text of the mass, the attraction of the two oratorio librettos, larger and less constricting than that of the mass, was without precedent. Haydn was to remark to Griesinger that he was 'never so devout' as during the time he was working on *The Creation* (see p.304). The autograph scores of *The Creation* and *The Seasons* have not survived. Swieten is known to have owned both of them in 1803, when he died intestate. His belongings were subsequently sold and Haydn's scores were lost to posterity. One wonders whether, as in the case of the op. 20 quartets, Haydn may have written something more extensive than the normal opening and concluding votive annotations.

Swieten's role in the success of *The Creation* and *The Seasons* was more than that of translator and compiler. He took a direct interest in the setting of the text and provided the practical means to mount the first semi-private performances of both oratorios, and their subsequent success was as much a climax to Swieten's career as it was to Haydn's. Swieten's early professional life as a diplomat had taken him to Brussels, Frankfurt, Regensburg, Paris and Berlin, before he returned to Vienna in 1777. At his home in the Imperial Library he organized informal Sunday concerts devoted to music of an earlier epoch, and it was here that Mozart made his first sustained acquaintance with the music of Bach and Handel. Mozart also became involved with Swieten's successful promotion of large-scale choral works, principally the oratorios of Handel, an enterprise sponsored by a fluctuating group of interested noblemen who later called themselves the Gesellschaft der Associirten. Swieten was the driving force behind these enterprises, carefully editing and revising texts and deciding that, in the case of Handel, the music should be re-orchestrated to suit contemporary taste. Even before Haydn had received the libretto of *The Creation*, Swieten had attempted to persuade the composer to write an oratorio on a text by Alxinger, *Die Vergötterung des Herkules* ('The apotheosis of Hercules'), and, more fruitfully, he had provided the text of the choral version of *The Seven Words*. After the successful first performances of *The Creation* sponsored by the Gesellschaft der Associirten, it was Swieten who instigated the composition of *The Seasons*. The Haydn oratorios, therefore, were the products of two distinct Handelian traditions, both corrupt: the Austrian developed by Swieten over a period of ten years, and the British experienced at first hand by the composer in London in the early 1790s.

Swieten was also an amateur composer competent enough to have written several symphonies and two *opéras comiques*, and this limited creative ability together with his extensive, if heavily worn, knowledge of the oratorio genre encouraged him to annotate his librettos for *The Creation* and *The Seasons* with suggestions for the musical realization. Haydn was too practised and artful a diplomat to regard this as arrogance and may well have encouraged Swieten, knowing that as the composer he would have the final say. It is possible too that these suggestions represent the results of deliberations between librettist and composer, an *aide mémoire* rather that a set of instructions. The final product, in either case, shows that Haydn rejected only a minority of these 'suggestions'. Four examples must suffice here.

In *The Creation*, next to the choral lines in the first recitative, Swieten wrote 'In the Chorus, the darkness could gradually disappear; but enough of the darkness should remain to make the momentary transition to light very effective. "And there was light" must be stated only once.' Haydn followed these remarks, with memorable effect. In 'Be fruitful all, and multiply' (No. 16)[2] Swieten, casting his mind back to Handelian oratorio, suggested a walking bass accompaniment for continuo: 'Here it seems that that the bare accompaniment of the bass moving solemnly in a straight rhythm would create a good effect.' At first, Haydn followed this scheme but added divided violas and cellos after the first performance. In the recitative, No. 16, that precedes the storm in *The Seasons*, Swieten noted 'Muffled roll of the kettledrum. Perhaps the part of the recitative in which Hanne sings could be taken in tempo and accompanied with short accented or pizzicato notes, so as to have bowed instruments ready for the lightning.' Haydn included two timpani rolls and provided a pizzicato accompaniment for Hanne's music; full thunder and lightning effects are held in reserve for the ensuing chorus. Haydn ignored Swieten's most daring annotation in *The Seasons* libretto. In the wine chorus (No. 28), with obvious indebtedness to Mozart's *Don Giovanni*, Swieten suggested conjuring up the sound of separate groups of instruments playing simultaneously: 'These instruments, when they are mentioned, must also be heard, and heard until the last entrance of the chorus. But since they are not grouped in one place but are spread throughout in various groups, they must have differing melodies and differing rhythms and come forth with the one or the other melody. Thus the fiddles could have the German waltz, the drums and pipes the 'Juch-he' ['Hurrah'], the lyre and bagpipes could sometimes be heard in the *waltzes*. The *Contratempi* should be useful in suggesting the varied places of the instruments.'

The clear distinction in Parts I and II of *The Creation* between narration, commentary and praise promoted strongly differentiated functions for *secco* recitative, accompanied recitative, aria and chorus. *The Seasons*, on the other hand, because it fuses these strands and also because it reduces the prominence of laudatory texts, does not have this systematic association of musical format with text. In both works accompanied recitative is used in the standard operatic fashion to present vivid and contrasting subject matter, and to effect a gradual move from *secco* recitative to aria. Part III of *The Creation* begins with a lengthy orchestral introduction, depicting morning in the Garden of Eden, that dissolves into an accompanied recitative. This same plan is followed in the orchestral introductions to each of the four seasons, thus avoiding the formality of an overture followed by first number. It is in these German/English oratorios and not in his Italian operas that Haydn achieved a full relevance and continuity between overture and the main body of the work. Accompanied recitatives contain some of the most delightful and instantly memorable music in *The Creation*: the creation of light; the storm, the wind and the rain of the second day; the sun, moon and stars of the fourth day; and the animals, both nautical and terrestrial, of the fifth day. The immediacy of the orchestral description removes the effect from the merely charming to the strongly compelling. In No. 21, two trombones, bassoon, double bassoon and lower strings imitate the lion's roar with a fortissimo A flat that intrudes into a diatonic B flat major; the music switches to brief ascending scalic passages in A flat for the leaping tiger, changes metre to a springing 6/8 for the stag and the section concludes with punctuating chords in D flat for the 'sprightly steed'. For the less energetic animals the tempo changes to Andante and the key to a placid A major: first, cattle and sheep (this is one of several melodies in the two late oratorios that prefigure Schubert, this one is especially prophetic of 'Frühlingstraum' from *Die Winterreise*);

then swarming insects; and, to end, in an Adagio in D major, the worm. Many commentators have pointed out that the orchestral description usually precedes the vocal identification in these accompanied recitatives. This was normal practice in Italian opera, including Haydn's own; in the oratorios it is more noticeable simply because well-contrasted objects and natural phenomena rather than subtle human emotions are being described. It also has a neat logic in these works: seeing something before naming it.

The bass aria that follows this recitative includes a single pictorial incident, the two *fortissimo* entries of bassoons and double bassoon to suggest the ungainly tread of the beasts, within a movement that contemplates the universe and looks forward to the creation of man. This mixture of contemplation and visual incident is typical of most of the arias in *The Creation*, including 'Rolling in foaming billows', 'With verdure clad the fields appear', 'On mighty pens' and 'In native worth and honour clad'. Haydn's skill in absorbing the pictorial into the musical course of the aria so that it does not become obtrusive is remarkable; in the soprano aria 'On mighty pens' (No. 15), the songs of the lark and the dove and the nightingale are wonderfully integrated into an almost operatic coloratura line (example overleaf). The reflective pauses that occur in this extract are a feature of many arias in *The Creation*, but not in *The Seasons*, suggesting the oneness of the observer with the observed. The arias in *The Creation* are all on the same generous scale as 'On mighty pens' and demonstrate a varied synthesis of vocal styles: the English canzonetta with the operatic, in 'With verdure clad the fields appear'; and the *bel canto* with the folk-song, in 'In native worth and honour clad'. The vocal writing for the soloists in *The Seasons* displays even more variety. The most extended number is Hanne's *scena*, an accompanied recitative and aria, welcoming the shade in the heat of midsummer (Nos. 14 and 15). In the recitative the orchestra illustrates successively a brook, swarming bees and a shepherd's pipe. The shepherd's pipe, in the form of a solo oboe, then provides an intermittent obbligato in the following aria; but descriptive writing and coloratura are not as well integrated as in *The Creation*.

As named peasant figures, Simon, Hanne and Lukas have short arias of a type not found in *The Creation*. Simon's first aria (No. 4) is an Allegretto in 2/4 time, a businesslike description of the farmer ploughing the field and sowing the seed; the style derives from two sources, the slow movements of some of the Paris and London symphonies and, more generally, *Singspiel*; this broad affinity is shown by Haydn's incorporation of the tune of the slow movement of the 'Surprise' Symphony. Simon's next aria illustrates the rural background, a 6/8 pastoral movement with a shepherd's call on the horn as the farmer drives the cattle and sheep to the verdant hills in summer (No. 10). In 'Autumn', Simon has an ungainly aria recounting the trailing of a scent by a dog (an *accelerando* as the scent warms) and, eventually, the shooting of the prey (*fortissimo* gun shot in the orchestra). A more complex side to Simon's character is revealed only in his last aria (No. 38), the penultimate number of the oratorio, an extended metaphor on the progress of the seasons and the course of human life. This aria, in E flat major, is in two parts, a 3/4 Largo and a 2/4 Allegro molto, and is a moving portrayal of resignation tinged with resentment at the passing of time – a virtual self-portrait of Haydn at the time of its composition. Haydn avoids a formal conclusion as the music moves into a recitative and the listener is directed towards contemplating the life hereafter.

The Seasons contains only one duet (No. 22), between Hanne and Lukas; another Allegretto in 2/4 time, it follows the normal layout of an operatic duet, and concludes rapturously with the statement that love is 'the joy and bliss of life' ('des

The Creation, No. 15, 'On mighty pens'

Lebens Wonn' und Glück!'). Although there is no other duet in *The Seasons*, the fact that each of the soloists is an actor *manqué* in the drama, and consistently identified as such, encourages a ready interaction between them and the chorus in a way that would not have been relevant to the more stylized format of *The Creation*. Each season contains one example, sometimes more, of a trio with chorus in

which the three peasants first represent their community and then easily withdraw
into it. The concluding number of 'Summer' (No. 18) begins as another 2/4 Allegretto, with the three soloists commenting on the appearance of the countryside
after the storm; the main theme shares the same heritage as Papageno's 'Der Vo-
gelfänger bin ich ja'. After the sound of the evening bell, the three soloists lead

the singing of a hymn to evening. The simple measured style, the key of E flat major and, not least, the prominence of the clarinet in the orchestral accompaniment provide a further aural reminiscence of *Die Zauberflöte* (e.g. the Finale of Act II).

These elements of *Singspiel* are present in *The Creation* too and help, especially, to explain the course of Part III which, to many listeners, has always been the most problematic part of the oratorio. In Parts I and II there are no duets and the three narrators combine on only three occasions: briefly, as a textural contrast, in the final chorus of Part I, 'The heavens are telling'; to describe the earth, heaven and the seas in No.18; and, as an extended interlude, between the two final choruses of

Part II. In the last-mentioned instance the moderate pace, the key of E flat and the prominent sound of the clarinet again bring to mind *Die Zauberflöte*. In Part III, ensemble writing and, more important, interaction between vocal groupings play an increased and crucial role. In the first duet of Adam and Eve (No. 30) the chorus interject soft chanting words of praise, emphasized by dotted rhythms in the wind scoring and, later, *piano* rumblings in the timpani; the whole section displays a masterly deployment of moderately full forces within a *piano* dynamic, in technique and atmosphere foreshadowing the Benedictus of Beethoven's *Missa Solemnis*. The following section, 2/4 Allegretto, suggests a more earthbound view of the marvels of the universe, as the chorus echo and summarize the views of Adam and Eve. The transition from the elevated to the patently fallible is completed in Nos. 31 and 32, which are laden with dramatic irony of a kind infrequently encountered in Haydn's operas. With a melodic reference back to 'Achieved is the glorious work', Adam pompously declaims 'Now follow me, dear partner of my life. Thy guide I'll be ...'; Eve's entry is in the voluptuous key of the flattened submediant (G flat to Adam's B flat) and her music concludes with a little flourish on the word 'pride' ('Freude', 'happiness', in the German text). The subsequent duet is an operatic love duet like that of Hanne and Lukas in 'Autumn', and perhaps the most wickedly tongue-in-cheek that Haydn ever composed; the concluding Allegro has the rhythms and regular phrase lengths of a *contredanse* and is led by those most suggestive of instruments, the horns, and the many pauses in the section imply a personal fulfilment that complements the perfection of nature as presented in Parts I and II. Through the medium of *Singspiel*, Haydn's view of the world is reassuringly fallible and contains no hint of moral censure.

The outstandingly novel feature of the music of the oratorios is the extensive use of the chorus. It was this aspect of Handel's oratorios that had captured Haydn's imagination in London and he himself suggested their primacy over the composer's arias when he told Griesinger that 'Handel was great in his choruses but mediocre in his song'. Nevertheless, it is easy to exaggerate the influence – as opposed to the example – of Handel, on the choruses of *The Creation* and *The Seasons*. There are many features of Handel's choral writing that do not appear in Haydn's oratorios: the homophonic, adagio summing-up to a contrapuntal allegro chorus, the *alla breve* chorus in motet style and the type of choral writing that presents slow-moving homophony against a pulsating background. The prime attraction was a broadly dramatic one, the availability of a large body of singers capable of broad pronouncement, and, if there is one aspect of Handel's craft that impressed Haydn, it is the rhythmic vitality of such choruses. 'Awake the harp' from *The Creation* has been called Handelian, perhaps because the biblical text tends to suggest comparison with choruses such as 'Tune your harps' from *Judas Maccabaeus*, 'Awake the trumpet's lofty sound' from *Samson*, and 'Your harp and cymbals sound' from *Solomon*. Handel's influence may be glimpsed too in 'Achieved is the glorious work' which, with its reiterated 'Hallelujahs' and well-judged move to a 4-2 chord (see example, pp. 327–9), suggests comparison with the conclusion of the second Coronation Anthem, 'The King shall rejoice' (see example, pp. 330–2). Haydn's cadential harmony and orchestration ensure, however, that his writing is completely personal. The pedigree of the text of *The Creation* makes such comparisons inevitable; they are certainly less obvious in *The Seasons* and perhaps only the final chorus of that work, particularly the fugue 'Uns leite deine Hand', comes remotely near to sounding Handelian.

72

63

Another English source lies behind the most exciting chorus in *The Creation*, 'The Heavens are telling the glory of God'. The undeniable influence of Haydn's settings of English Psalms on this movement – itself a setting of the first two verses of Psalm 19 – has already been noted (see p. 275); the initially homophonic scoring, four-square phrasing, diatonic harmonic language and restricted vocal tessitura all reflect this background. A quasi-operatic change of tempo to Più Allegro signals an extended passage of imitation, based on the first two phrases of the chorus, culminating in a thrilling passage built over a chromatically rising bass. This conclusion to the fourth day and Part I of the oratorio stands in place of the fugue that might bave been expected at the same point in a Handel oratorio. Indeed, the oratorio as a whole reveals a well-judged and carefully integrated use of fugue. The first instance occurs in 'Awake the harp', based on a wide-spaced subject and featuring some exciting stretto; the second occurs in the chorus 'Achieved is the glorious work' that concludes Part II, where again it emerges out of a homophonic texture; at the end of Part III comes Haydn's third and most extended fugue, to the words 'The Lord is great; his praise shall last for aye' (subject) and 'Amen' (countersubject). In this concluding fugue the influence of Haydn's contemporary masses is evident; the fugue at the end of the Gloria of the *Missa Sancti Bernardi de Offida* (1796) divides the text in a similar fashion, 'in gloria dei Patris' (subject) and 'Amen' (countersubject). This third fugue in *The Creation*, like the others, moves to homophony towards the close and, for the second time in the oratorio, features long held octave notes in the chorus against rhythmic and harmonically changing accompaniment, ending in a *fortissimo* release of tension.[3]

As with the writing for the solo voices, the choral writing in *The Seasons* displays more variety, but not always the same conviction. The first chorus is typical of the different approach, a lightweight, 6/8 Allegretto welcoming spring, with separate passages for women and menfolk – a frequent division of forces in *The Seasons* and one never found in *The Creation*. In tone, the nearest thing in the earlier oratorio is the A major chorus that announces 'a new created world' (No. 2). The progress of the second chorus in 'Spring' is also typical of many in *The Seasons*, an extended homophonic opening – this time a prayer – that leads to a fugue. Many of these openings, for instance in nos. 8 and 18, are of great intrinsic beauty, an atmosphere that is rather marred by the artificiality of their concluding fugues, as if Haydn was compensating for the length of the text by presenting well-argued fugues to maintain the progress of the oratorio as a whole. The B flat major chorus that concludes 'Spring' is a clear attempt to produce a second version of the final chorus of *The Creation*, but it does not generate quite the same excitement. Haydn complained about the text of the first chorus in 'Autumn' (No. 20), observing drily that it had never occurred to him to set 'industry' ('Fleiß') to music; the fugal texture is not maintained and the movement as a whole may be seen as an attempt to draw upon the C major energy of 'The heavens are telling', even to the extent of climactic chromatic writing over a rising bass (bars 196–206).

The choral writing in *The Seasons* is at its most convincing when the chorus is required to act as participants – peasants and hunters – rather than proponents of general truths. Two numbers in 'Autumn' provide an extended role for the chorus and constitute a *tour de force* in any performance. The first, No. 26, describes a hunt and the second, No. 28, is in praise of wine, both numbers, being as graphic as anything in nineteenth-century opera. The musical chase is the crowning glory to a lifetime of preoccupation with 6/8 hunting music, usually in sublimated fashion but previously given full vent in *La fedeltà premiata* and in the symphony, no. 73, derived from it. The hunt for the stag is recounted, stage by stage, by the onlookers, women and men, separately and together. The chorus is punctuated by a series of authentic horn calls taking the listener from the 'search' (bars 1–6) to the 'kill' (bars 117–120 and 129–132); in an extravagantly colourful score Haydn even notates *forte* grace notes for trombones (effectively short *glissandi*) to suggest the exhausted stag.

Following the excitement of the hunt comes the equally extensive chorus in praise of wine. Its opening has a recurring cadential phrase –

– featuring a leap to an emphasized *sforzando* note (a stage presention would no doubt provide a clashing of steins at this point). As the wine begins to have its effect, the music modulates, and this note is harmonized in no less than seven different ways, using the resourcefulness that Haydn had first explored in his quartets and symphonies: root of subdominant, fifth of supertonic, part of diminished seventh, third of dominant, fifth of dominant, seventh of dominant and fifth of subdominant. The middle section of the chorus is an increasingly confused dance, the orchestra providing onomatopoeic representation of the fife, the drums, the fiddle, the hurdy-gurdy and the bagpipes (this is the passage Swieten suggested should feature several dances in contrasting tempos). More wine is called for and the participants attempt a fugue, only to take refuge in a 6/8 harmonic rendering of the subject; the babble increases as triangle and tambourine join in, and the movement ends with a boisterous reference to the phrase quoted above. All this is a long way from Handel.

Many felicities of orchestral scoring in the two oratorios have already been mentioned and, certainly, few oratorios since Haydn have managed to demonstrate a massiveness of sonority as well as local individual, sometimes even idiosyncratic, colouring. The size of Haydn's orchestra reflects Vienna's own tradition of generously scored oratorios, performed at the bi-annual Tonkünstler-Societät concerts, as well as the composer's experience of hearing the bloated Handel performances then customary in London. *The Creation* requires three flutes, two oboes, two clarinets, two bassoons, double bassoon, two horns, two trumpets, three trombones, timpani, strings and continuo (fortepiano). The forces needed for *The Seasons* are even more numerous: one piccolo, two flutes, two oboes, two clarinets, two bassoons, double bassoon, four horns, three trumpets, three trombones, timpani, triangle, tambourine, strings and continuo (fortepiano). For the first semi-private performances of the works, sponsored by Swieten's Gesellschaft der Associirten, choir and orchestra probably numbered no more than 120 (precise evidence relating to individual performances has not survived) but the later public performances often had forces of *c.* 400, extant orchestral parts suggesting that wind instruments were doubled and perhaps even tripled. Passages such as the creation of light, the grand opening to the final chorus of *The Creation* ('Sing the Lord ye voices all! / Utter thanks, ye all his works / Celebrate his pow'r and glory! / Let his name resound on high!) and the storm in *The Seasons* must have been imposing beyond belief. Haydn's scoring for smaller combinations of instruments is equally telling: the introduction to Part III of *The Creation* (three flutes and pizzicato strings); the introduction to 'Winter' (strings, woodwind and horns); and the accompanied recitative 'Be fruitful all' in *The Creation* (divided violas and cellos plus double bass). Haydn uses the clarinet with greater freedom than he had achieved during his second London visit and the timpani writing is especially fascinating. In only one respect does the orchestration ignore previous experience: there is no extended writing for woodwind ensemble of the type consistently found in the London symphonies.

Haydn's harmonic language is at its most extensive in these two late oratorios, possessing a variety and range that are beyond those normally encountered in the contemporary masses. There is the firm diatonicism of the opening of 'The heavens are telling' and the last number of 'Summer' (No. 18) and, at the opposite end of the spectrum, the weaving chromaticism of the introduction to 'Winter'. The 'Representation of Chaos', the orchestral introduction to *The Creation*, shows these extremes within one movement. From C minor the introduction moves to E flat, marked by a passage that is as diatonic to that key (apart from some minor ninth appoggiaturas) as the previous C minor section had been chromatic. The chromaticism of the C minor section is remarkable and, as extant sketches reveal, cost Haydn a great deal of labour. The chromatic lines, the lengthy appoggiaturas, the avoidance of the expected cadence (because, as Haydn pointed out, 'there is no form in anything yet') have encouraged comparison with Wagner's *Tristan und Isolde*. Haydn's source for passages such as the following example (a) from near the end of the movement may be found in slow movements of his quartets and symphonies, e.g. the passage (b) that leads the Andante of Symphony no. 104 from D flat major back to G major; both passages use sequence and descending chains of diminished sevenths.

The influence of the instrumental music of the London period is apparent also in the unorthodox modulation schemes of many individual numbers. Whereas none of the movements in the oratorios has the enharmonic modulations encountered in the London piano trios, the choice of tonal goal is often unexpected, capturing the attention in much the same way as an interestingly told narrative. For instance, Simon's first aria in C major (No. 4), after moving routinely to C minor, has a large paragraph in E flat major. The celebrated entry of bassoons and double bassoon to suggest the tread of the beasts in 'Now heav'n in all her glory shone' directs the music from the key of D major to F major. Simular modulations, to the major key on the flattened mediant, occur in the trio with chorus, 'So lohnet die

Natur den Fleiß' (No. 20) in *The Seasons* and, via the tonic minor, in the trio 'On thee each living soul awaits' in *The Creation*.

Apart from *La fedeltà premiata*, Haydn had never displayed an interest in shaping a large work, such as an oratorio or an opera, with a broad key structure. In *The Creation* there is an impressive control over choice of key, partly governed by traditional associations but also providing a firm and absorbing sense of an onward journey. The most frequently heard key is C major, used first for the blaze of the first light and then in Nos. 4, 13, 24 and 30. Up to No. 24, 'In native worth and honour clad', there is a persistent trend to push the music sharpwards from this neutral base as A major and D major are used (Nos. 2, 6, 10, 12, 18, 19 and 22); in this respect it is interesting that Haydn's sketches indicate that he first considered setting No. 13, 'The heavens are telling', in D major before deciding on C. From No. 24 onwards the process moves in the opposite direction, flatwards, as B flat and attendant keys first compete with C and then replace it as the final tonic of the work (Nos. 26, 27, 28, middle portion of 30, 32 and 34 are in B flat or its close relatives, E flat and F; B flat had been foreshadowed in No. 8, F in No. 15). This broad process of attempting to move upwards from C to a key a tone higher only to fall to a key a tone lower suggests the imminent Fall from Grace in such a potent manner that remarks about whether it was deliberate or not seem irrelevant. Perhaps the clinching piece of evidence is the choice of key for the beginning of Part III, the Garden of Eden. E major is the sharpest key in the entire score, is used only once and is the furthest point away (tritone) from B flat.[4]

The Seasons does not have such an apparent overall sense of tonal progression, though the final key of C major is a convincing point of rest; firstly, because it is the most frequently encountered key in the work and, secondly, because within 'Winter' it is heard as the resolution of the C minor of the orchestral introduction.

The starting point for the composition of *The Creation* had been the shared desire of Haydn and Swieten to emulate the achievement of Handel. In that aim they certainly succeeded, as the two oratorios constitute one of the few highpoints in the history of the genre between Handel and Elgar, but they are hardly Handelian. They do not feature strongly portrayed characters such as Saul or Jephtha; nationalist sentiments, whereby the victorious Israelites of *Saul*, *Jephtha* and *Israel in Egypt* could be associated with the assertiveness of Augustan England, were entirely absent; and the abiding presence of a God that can sustain a people in strife, that too is absent from Haydn's oratorios. Handel's mixture of characterization, nationalism and the religious formed a distinctive aesthetic which English contemporaries soon recognized as being to them more powerful and relevant than was that of Italian opera. In Haydn's oratorios the ingredients are very different: they are Catholic in their desire to praise and contemplate; less exalted, in their attempt through *Singspiel* characterization to involve the ordinary person; and, above all, they take great pride in noting and being part of the workings of the universe, a pride borne out of intuition rather than rational explanation. At the time of his death in 1809, Haydn's library contained a copy of Edmund Burke's *A Philosophical Enquiry into the Origin of our ideas of the Sublime and Beautiful*. Its pages contain much that explains the aesthetic stance of *The Creation* and *The Seasons*.

The first and the simplest emotion which we discover in the human mind, is Curiosity. By curiosity, I mean whatever desire we have for, or whatever pleasure we take in novelty ...

The second passion belonging to society is imitation or, if you will, a desire of imitating, and consequently a pleasure in it.

... [beauty] is a name I shall apply to all such qualities in things as induce in us a sense of affection and tenderness, or some other passion the most nearly resembling these.

The passion caused by the great and sublime in *nature*, when those causes operate most powerfully is Astonishment; and astonishment is that state of the soul, in which all its notions are suspended, with some degree of horror ... the inferior effects are admiration, reverence and respect.

There are many animals, who, though far from being large, are yet capable of rousing ideas of the sublime, because they are considered as objects of terror. As serpents and poisonous animals of almost all kinds. And to things of great dimensions, if we annex an adventitious idea of horror, they become without comparison greater. A level plain of a vast extent on land, is certainly no mean idea; the prospect of such a plain may be as extensive as a prospect of the ocean; but can it ever fill the mind with anything so great as the ocean itself?

Greatness of dimension, is a powerful cause of the sublime.

... as the great extreme of dimension is sublime, so the last extreme of littleness is in some measure sublime likewise ...

Another source of the sublime is *infinity*; if it does not rather belong to the last, infinity has a tendency to fill the mind with that sort of delightful horror, which is the most genuine effect, and truest test of the sublime. *Magnificence* is likewise a source of the sublime. A great profusion of things which are splendid or valuable in themselves, is *magnificient*. The starry heaven, though it occurs so very frequently to our view, never fails to excite an idea of grandeur.

With regard to light; to make it a cause capable of producing the sublime, it must be attended with some circumstances, besides its bare faculty of shewing other objects. Here light is too common a thing to make a strong impression on the mind, and without a strong impression nothing can be sublime. But such a light as that of the sun, immediately exerted on the eye, as it overpowers the same, is a very great idea. Light of an inferior strength to this, if it moves with great celerity, has the same power; for lightning is certainly productive of grandeur, which it owes chiefly to the extreme velocity of its motion. A quick transition from light to darkness, or from darkness to light, has yet a great effect. But darkness is more productive of sublime ideas than light.

Such sounds as imitate the natural inarticulate voices of men, or any animals in pain or danger, are capable of conveying great ideas; unless it be the well-known voice of some creature, on which we are used to look with contempt. The angry tones of wild beasts are equally capable of causing a great and awful sensation.

Whenever the wisdom of our Creator intended that we should be affected with any thing, he did not confine the execution of his design to the languid and precarious operation of our reason; but he endowed it with powers and properties that prevent the understanding, and even the will, which seizing upon the senses and imagination, captivate the soul before the understanding is ready either to join with them or to oppose them.

Miscellaneous sacred compositions

Before beginning work on *The Creation*, Haydn prepared a choral version of *The Seven Words*, which was probably first performed in Vienna on 26 March 1796 under the aegis of the Gesellschaft der Associirten. Haydn had been prompted into undertaking this unusual task after hearing a vocal version of his work in Passau, prepared by Joseph Friebert. Friebert may have been the author of the German text, too, which amplifies the sentiment of the terse Latin headings of the original; for *Il terremoto* (the Italian title was retained) the text was taken from the poem, 'Der Tod Jesu', by K. W. Ramler. In his customary manner, Swieten edited and improved the 'Passau' text and Haydn improved on Friebert's setting. The drama and pathos of the original are not diminished by the addition of words but the ease with which the original orchestral version encouraged contemplation is perhaps compromised by the literalness of the words and undermined by their syllabic delivery. Occasionally, too, the words alter the melodic character of the original, as in the many anacruses added to the melody of No. 5 and the unavoidable emphasis on longer note values in the otherwise busy texture of *Il terremoto*. The presence of a choir in the overall texture means that the orchestration is sometimes reduced to avoid overdoubling; in particular, Haydn found that he needed only two horns rather than the four of the original. Two trombones are added, doubling the alto and tenor lines in *forte* passages. In order to affirm the importance of the choir, Haydn precedes Nos. 1, 2, 3, 4, 6 and 7 with brief, four-part *a cappella* introductions declaiming, in German, the title of each movement. Before No. 5, Haydn inserts a new movement, seventy-one bars long, for wind band, a chilling A minor preparation for the A major of the following movement. (Could this A minor wind-band sonority have been the subconscious stimulus for the equally chill first chord of the slow movement of Beethoven's Seventh Symphony?) The vocal version of *The Seven Words*, like the revised versions of *Il ritorno di Tobia*, the Mass in F and the Stabat Mater, was able to profit from the popularity of Haydn's two late oratorios, *The Creation* and *The Seasons*. It was published by Breitkopf & Härtel in 1801 and in this version became widely known in the nineteenth century.

Also well known in the nineteenth century was Haydn's second setting of the Te Deum (XXIIIc:2), probably composed in the autumn of 1799. Marie Therese, wife of Emperor Francis I, was an enthusiastic admirer of Haydn's music, amassing a small library of his recent works (often acquired directly from the composer) and singing the solo soprano part in private performances of some of the late masses and the two oratorios. According to a letter from Griesinger to the firm of Breitkopf & Härtel – a letter that initiated the publication of the Te Deum – that work was composed at the request of the Empress. Although it retains the customary three-part division of the text, as shown in Haydn's early Te Deum, this C major work has the new assertiveness developed in the many choruses in that key in *The Creation* and *The Seasons*. Wagner once implied that Haydn's orchestration possessed a 'sensitive coarseness',[5] a description that is especially suited to the orchestral texture of this work which avoids warm sonorities in favour of highly rhythmic figuration, punctuated by rests and pointed by pungent chromatic harmony (especially diminished sevenths). This approach may have emanated from the decision to base the opening on the Te Deum plainchant. This first line is boldly declaimed by the full orchestra and then, equally boldly, by the choir in octave unison. Bruckner undoubtedly knew this work and when he came to write his own Te Deum in C in 1884, he provided his own type of 'sensitive coarseness', as well as incorporating the plainchant in the melody. For Haydn, this C major movement, like the many choruses in that key in *The Creation* and *The Seasons*, owes a clear debt to the C major sonority (with trumpets and timpani) that Haydn had so frequently drawn upon in earlier compositions: in the Lauda Sion, in several masses and symphonies and in the military arias in *Orlando Paladino* and *Armida*. The extra rhythmic zest and orchestral brilliance that are added here are perhaps due to Haydn's experience of hearing Handel's music in London; certainly, the final bars of the Te Deum show a marked resemblance to the end of the concluding chorus of Handel's *Israel in Egypt*.

A very different, but equally representative, item of church music, 'Non nobis, Domine', probably dates from this period. Described by Haydn in the *Entwurf-Katalog* as 'Offertorio in Stillo a Capella', it is another contribution to the repertoire in the *stile antico* usually sung during Lent and Advent. Although the autograph is lost, circumstantial evidence suggests that the work belongs to this late period of renewed involvement with sacred music. Like the *Missa* 'Sunt bona mixta malis' of 1768, this offertorium is in a severe D minor and opens with a fugal exposition before sequential material leads the music in new harmonic directions. However, unlike the early mass, this offertorium is more integrated in its thematic course and leads to a powerful homophonic climax.

Masses

Between 1796 and 1802 Haydn composed six settings of the mass, his most sustained period of sacred composition since the late 1760s and early 1770s. The first three settings had titles applied by the composer himself and the remaining three were soon to acquire nicknames; the nicknames are given in parentheses in the following list.

Missa Sancti Bernardi de Offida ('Heiligmesse')	B flat	1796
Missa in tempore belli ('Paukenmesse')	C	1796
Missa in angustiis ('Nelson' Mass)	D minor	1798
Mass ('Theresienmesse')	B flat	1799
Mass ('Schöpfungsmesse')	B flat	1801
Mass ('Harmoniemesse')	B flat	1802

The six masses were performed in celebration of the name-day of Princess Marie Hermenegild Esterházy, wife of Nicolaus II, usually on the first convenient Sunday on or after 8 September, the Feast of Our Lady. For Haydn it was a happy return to Marian observance, since earlier in his career he had dedicated two masses to the Virgin Mary. The performances normally took place in the Bergkirche in Eisenstadt, but precise details of date, work and venue are not available for every occasion, and in some cases the evidence is conflicting. There is a possibility that the first work in the series was the *Missa in tempore belli*, but it is more likely that this was written first to be performed at the Piaristenkirche in Vienna, on 26 December 1796, to celebrate the admittance into the priesthood (the *Primitiae*) of Joseph von Hofmann, and then used for the name-day celebrations in Eisenstadt the following September. The *Missa in angustiis* probably received its first performance on 23 September 1798, not in the Bergkirche but in the Eisenstadt parish church (Stadtpfarrkirche). The 'Theresienmesse' was probably first performed on 8 September 1799, but no absolute proof is available. The 'Schöpfungsmesse' was hurriedly composed, and was first performed on 13 September 1801; the last of the series of name-day masses, the 'Harmoniemesse' was first heard on 8 September 1802. Haydn – by then a very tired old man of seventy – now relinquished this formal duty and in later years it was discharged by Hummel and, in 1807, by Beethoven (the Mass in C, op. 86).

Although the purpose of these masses was to celebrate in a semi-private service the name-day of a member of a family in whose service Haydn had remained for forty years, the masses are in no other sense local or provincial works. Although the lure of the genre to a man of Haydn's religious disposition was as strong as ever, the composer does not retreat into a private world tinged with nostalgia. On the contrary, the masses are as progressive in their approach and technique as *The Creation* and *The Seasons* and, whilst they have firm roots in the Austrian tradition of church music, Haydn, as ever, takes that as a stimulus rather than a substitute for new ideas.

The clearest indication of the outward-looking nature of these masses is to be found in Haydn's titles for two of them: 'Mass in time of war' and 'Mass in straitened times'. During his time in London, Haydn had experienced at second hand the effects of the French Revolution. In this last period of his life, his own country, Austria, was directly and continually involved in the conflict with the France of Napoleon. Haydn's symphonies were performed in charity concerts to aid the war effort, he composed the *Volkslied* 'Gott erhalte Franz den Kaiser' to raise national morale and, in 1801, he was asked to write a cantata to celebrate the Treaty of Lunéville. There was no escape from the atmosphere of war and it impinges directly on the Esterházy masses.

In the summer of 1796, Austria had been forced to cede most of its Italian territories to Napoleon, whose troops now threatened Austria itself. In the *Missa in tempore belli* the Agnus Dei opens calmly in F major, ominous *piano* timpani strokes disturb the mood, choir and orchestra repeat the opening in an anguished C minor before *fortissimo* trumpets, oboes and bassoons pierce the texture with their relentless fanfares. Further *piano* timpani strokes feature near the end of the Agnus Dei before more triumphant, but equally military wind figuration initiates the Dona nobis pacem.

By the time Haydn came to compose the *Missa in angustiis*, a large part of Austria was under French rule and Napoleon was engaged in his Mediterranean campaign which, quite unexpectedly, ended in his defeat at the hands of Nelson in the Battle of Aboukir. Haydn's mass, in the austere key of D minor, is scored for the uncompromising forces of three trumpets, timpani, strings and organ. The fanfare figuration that opens the work sets a typically foreboding mood and the Kyrie eleison, with its dashing solo soprano part, is the most theatrical setting of that text in Haydn's output. In the D major Gloria and Credo, Haydn's use of the trumpets is noticeably reticent in comparison with equivalent passages in the other late masses; he is clearly keeping them in reserve. The 'Et incarnatus est' consists of the customary lyrical section in a major key (G) and in a relaxed tempo (Largo); when the clause 'Crucifixus etiam pro nobis sub Pontio Pilato' ('And was crucified also for us under Pontius Pilate') is reached, the music turns to G minor and trumpets and timpani enter with six bars of fanfares on the single note D, a striking association of Pontius Pilate with the war-mongering and equally anti-Christian Napoleon. Unusually, Haydn does not set the Benedictus movement in a contrasting key, the use of the tonic D minor being a signal for further unorthodoxy. Trumpets and timpani play a prominent part in the customary long orchestral introduction and, near the end, threaten to change the demeanour of the music entirely before a *pianissimo* cadence theme returns us to the opening mood. Later in the movement, when the choir and orchestra reach the same point again, instead of the *pianissimo* resolution of tension, there is a full confrontation between fanfare trumpets and the declaimed text of 'Benedictus qui venit in nomine Domini' ('Blessed is he that cometh in the name of the Lord'). Significantly, after this confrontation, neither D minor nor insistent trumpet scoring is featured in the remainder of the mass; even in the most dire circumstances Haydn retained the happy confidence of the eighteenth-century whereby well-founded optimism was never to give way to disconsolate despair. To these implicit references to contemporary events listeners, then and now, might have added other less sustained but equally dramatic passages in other masses: the first entry of the trumpets and timpani in the Adagio introduction of the 'Theresienmesse', the trumpet and timpani parts in the 'Dona nobis pacem' of the same mass and the tutti fanfare that announces the same section in the 'Harmoniemesse'.

Each of the six masses is scored for SATB choir and a nucleus of four soloists (also SATB), sometimes expanded to six for a particular section, an extra soprano and bass in the *Missa Sancti Bernardi de Offida* and an extra soprano and tenor in the 'Harmoniemesse'. The orchestral forces are differently constituted for each mass, revealing a range of colour unusual in the genre, before or since. Practicalities, as always, governed Haydn's choice. In Eisenstadt, he had at his disposal the church forces, sadly depleted since the 1760s, of strings and organ. Nicolaus II, in 1794, had reconstituted the Grenadiers' band, forming a basic ensemble of two oboes, two clarinets and two bassoons, and these were available to Haydn until 1798, when the players were dismissed. Two years later, wind players became available again when the prince added to the complement of church musicians. Three trumpet players were available from 1797 onwards. In addition to this changing complement of strings and sundry wind instruments, Haydn could supplement his forces with specially engaged players as and when necessary, trumpets, clarinets or flute. The issue of scoring is complicated by Haydn's provision of additional parts for later performances, and complicated beyond resolution when the task was carried out by others, with or without Haydn's approval. The most traditionally scored mass is the *Missa in tempore belli*, for two oboes, two clarinets, two bassoons, two horns, two trumpets, timpani, strings and continuo. Its bright C major sonority is firmly of the Austrian tradition which, even eleven years later, Beethoven in his Mass in C was to find a stimulus. Haydn later elaborated the clarinet and horn parts and added a flute, the last-named making a typical contribution to the 'Qui tollis' by doubling the solo cello at the higher octave in the choral passage.

The least traditionally scored, at least at first hearing, is the *Missa in angustiis*, with its three trumpets, timpani, strings and organ, though it brings together several traditions: the small church ensemble of strings and organ and the tradition of trumpets and timpani fanfares articulating the progress of the service. It is, too, Haydn's third 'Orgelsolomesse', following the *Missa in honorem B.V.M.* of 1768–9 and the *Missa Brevis Sancti Joannis de Deo*, in that the organ part is sometimes written out and contributes tellingly to the orchestral scoring, as in the 'Qui tollis' portion of the Gloria; however, the tense atmosphere of this mass means that there was no opportunity for an extended organ obbligato as in the earlier masses. Later, full wind parts were added to the mass by Haydn's successor at Eisenstadt, Johann Fuchs, and also by Breitkopf & Härtel for their publication.

The remaining four masses are all in B flat major, and feature the usual strings and continuo, together with a varied complement of wind instruments: the *Missa Sancti Bernardi de Offida* has two oboes, two clarinets, two bassoons, two horns (authenticity uncertain), two trumpets and timpani; the 'Theresienmesse' has two clarinets, two bassoons, two trumpets and timpani; the 'Schöpfungsmesse' has two oboes, two clarinets, two bassoons, two horns, two trumpets and timpani; and the 'Harmoniemesse' is so called because it makes full and comparatively prominent use of a complete 'wind band' (*Harmonie*) of one flute, two oboes, two clarinets, two bassoons and two horns, as well as two trumpets and timpani. In these four masses in B flat with trumpets, Haydn creates a new sonority to replace that of the traditional C major, and the fact that he chose this key for his last three masses shows its attraction. Contemporary musicians, too, noted this novel feature. Friedrich Rochlitz, in a review of the Breitkopf & Härtel publication of the *Missa Sancti Bernardi de Offida*, wrote that 'the composer has understood how to achieve the most shining effects through a great deal of reflection and long experience; the nobility and pious attributes of the work are effected by devices not apparent at first glance – of which we would draw attention to only one feature, namely that in those movements of the mass in B flat, the trumpets and drums (not used exactly sparingly) are, *because of their low pitch*, of the greatest strength, dignity and gravity.'[6] Haydn had first used trumpets in B flat in three of his London works, the

Symphonie concertante (I:105) and Symphonies nos. 98 and 102 where, as Rochlitz's phrase 'strength, dignity and gravity' indicates, the resulting sound is quite different from the B flat sonority found in Haydn's earlier music, viz. that imparted by B flat alto horns in many symphonies and operatic numbers. B flat trumpets are also used in *The Creation* and later both Beethoven and Schubert were to write symphonies in B flat with trumpets (nos. 4 and 2 respectively).

In his approach to broad structure and detailed word-setting, Haydn's late masses reveal the same constructive attitude of tradition fortified and expanded. The composer is everywhere concerned that the traditionally more relaxed moments in the mass should not threaten the momentum of the whole and that the musical argument should never be diffuse. New techniques, aimed at making the music more unified than was typical of contemporary masses, are in evidence throughout. Some of the progressive, symphonic features adumbrated in the *Missa Cellensis* of 1782 are now expanded, but it is Haydn's unequalled experience as a composer of instrumental music that principally contributes to the musical authority of these works; their indebtedness is as much to the Paris and London symphonies as to Haydn's earlier masses.

The Kyrie movements of four of the late masses begin with a slow introduction and in all six there is a sense of return at the recapitulation (tonic chord, tutti scoring and principal theme), the point where the phrase 'Kyrie eleison' returns after the 'Christe eleison'. Featured in the *Missa Cellensis* of 1782, this relationship between the Kyrie movement and the first movement of a symphony is now probed further, always in a flexible manner, selecting only those procedures deemed necessary for a particular movement. In the *Missa in tempore belli* the ten-bar Largo introduction foreshadows the shape of the principal theme of the succeeding Allegro in the manner of the London symphonies, ending in the tonic minor; the following Allegro moderato begins in a light scoring with the principal subject, a florid elaboration of the figure announced in the Largo. The Allegro moderato can be described as an abridged monothematic sonata form: first subject; second subject (derived from first subject) in G major, announced by the alto soloist; a short bridge passage during which the text 'Christe eleison' is sung; and a compressed recapitulation (no second subject) initiated by the soprano soloist.

Though the 'Theresienmesse' applies techniques familiar from first movements of symphonies more extensively, it would, again, be misrepresenting the act of composition to state simply that it appropriated the form of the first movement of a symphony, even if one allowed that such an abstract entity existed in the first place. The ample Adagio introduction, twenty-six bars long, contains two motifs rather than one, the first of these introduced by the orchestra, the second by the alto soloist.

When the tenor enters with 'b', the music is deflected to B flat minor and remains in that key, ending with a relaxed dominant pedal. The Allegro begins with an active fugal exposition on 'c' in the example, fashioned out of 'a'. As the music moves away from the tonic, the contrapuntal texture is gradually relaxed in preparation for the second subject, 'Christe eleison', sung by the soloists and based on 'b'; this elicits a lively descant from the solo soprano. The chorus re-enters to begin a brief development section based on 'a' and associated text. The return to the tonic is affirmed in the usual way, by the entry of trumpets and timpani. It is from now on that any exact parallel between symphonic sonata form and this movement breaks down, though the remainder of the movement is as efficient in balancing the exposition in duration, tonality and re-presentation of thematic material as any symphonic recapitulation. The Allegro is halted, unexpectedly, for a return of the opening Adagio which presents the original form of the two principal subjects of the movement. In procedure, but not of course in rhetoric, this movement suggests what Haydn might have explored had he composed any further symphonies; like Symphony no.103 ('Drum Roll'), it features a literal repetition of material from the slow introduction, a feature too of many Beethoven sonata forms, but neither Haydn nor Beethoven was to write an instrumental slow introduction that foreshadowed two principal ideas.[7]

The Gloria movements of the six late masses follow the familiar pattern of three broad stages: two brisk tempos predominantly featuring the choir, framing a slow selection in a contrasting key that features soloists. The change of tempo occurs either at the clause 'Gratias agimus tibi' (*Missa Sancti Bernardi de Offida*, 'Theresienmesse' and 'Harmoniemesse') or at the clause 'Qui tollis peccata mundi' (*Missa in tempore belli*, *Missa in angustiis* and 'Schöpfungsmesse'); the return to a brisk tempo coincides always with the clause 'Quoniam Tu solus sanctus'. In the opening sections Haydn is content to follow well-tried procedures to set off the contrasts of the text: *fortissimo*, highly rhythmic texture for 'Gloria in excelsis Deo' ('Glory to God on high'), a *piano* dynamic and less active rhythm for 'et in terra pax hominibus bonae voluntatis' ('and on earth peace to men of good will'). The four complementary exclamations, 'Laudamus Te, benedicimus Te, adoramus Te, glorificamus Te' ('We praise Thee, we bless Thee, we worship Thee, we glorify Thee'), are usually set in a single musical paragraph culminating, in the *Missa Sancti Bernardi de Offida* and the 'Theresienmesse', in an extended setting of the last clause 'glorificamus Te'. There may be no new techniques as such, but the fervour of these sections is unprecedented in Haydn's masses. In the middle, slow sections of the Gloria, the *Missa in tempore belli* and the 'Theresienmesse' are the least progressive works, in that their easy lyricism is of a type (but not of a quality) frequently encountered in earlier masses; elsewhere in these late masses the melodic writing is more restrained and there is a greater integration of soloists with one another and with the choir. In the 'Schöpfungsmesse', the Gloria thwarts expectations in an audacious manner akin to that frequently demonstrated in the London symphonies. The Allegro tempo, the *alla breve* metre, together with the choral scoring and *forte* dynamic, are maintained beyond the clause 'Gratias agimus tibi'. Listeners now have a right to expect a change of tempo at the standard alternative point, the 'Qui tollis'; instead, they are greeted with an orchestral quotation, in the prevailing tempo, of the contredanse theme from Adam and Eve's duet in *The Creation*, associated with the text 'The dew-dropping morn, Oh how she quickens all!'; the instrumentation, too, is the same. The bass soloist enters and repeats the thematic line to the words 'Qui tollis peccata mundi' before the choir, in a dramatic change of tempo, sing 'Miserere nobis', Adagio and in 3/4 time. One does not know which is the more amusing, the innuendo of the secular quotation, the sudden realization that the composer has 'forgotten' to change the tempo or the indignation of the choir with its outburst of 'Miserere'. Griesinger's account (which mistakenly locates the passage in the Agnus Dei) provides a somewhat reticent explanation of the passage. 'In the mass that Haydn wrote in 1801 it occurred to him in the *Agnus Dei qui tollis peccata mundi* that frail mortals sinned mostly against moderation and purity. So he set the words *qui tollis peccata, peccata mundi* to the trifling melody of the words in *The Creation*: 'The dew-dropping morn, Oh, how she quickens all!'. But in order that this profane thought should not be too conspicuous he let the *Miserere* sound in full chorus immediately afterwards. In the copy of the mass that he made for the Empress, he had to alter the place at her request.' This alteration has survived; Haydn's only change was to write a new melody, the tempo and underlying harmony remain the same, thus merely obscuring rather than removing the mischievous impropriety.

Ending the Gloria movement with a fugue was a standard practice in Classical settings of the text, useful to re-establish a sense of integration in a movement that can easily sound sectional and diffuse. Following the precedent of the 'Mariazeller' mass, Haydn does not conclude the Gloria movements of the *Missa in tempore belli* and 'Theresienmesse' with a fugue, though both, like the 'Mariazeller' mass, feature some imitation on the word 'Amen'. The *Missa Sancti Bernardi de Offida* follows the lead of the 'Great Organ Solo Mass' in having two complementary subjects, one to the text 'in gloria dei Patris' ('in the glory of God the Father') and 'Amen', though the course of the fugue reveals a new power equal to that of the similarly constructed final fugue of *The Creation*. In the last two masses, the 'Schöpfungsmesse' and the 'Harmoniemesse', the subjects of the fugues are richly chromatic without ever sounding tortuous.

Many of the masses display an interest in re-using thematic material at later stages in the Gloria where, traditionally, a new musical setting would have been expected. In the 'Harmoniemesse' the statement 'glorificamus Te' signals a return to the opening theme of the movement to complete the first section of the Gloria; in the 'Theresienmesse' the music associated with 'Qui tollis peccata mundi' returns at 'Qui sedes ad dexteram Patris'; and, in the same movement, the phrase 'in gloria dei Patris' is set to the same music as that heard at the beginning of the section, where it had been sung to the text 'Quoniam tu solus Dominus'. The *Missa in angustiis* has several such incidents of thematic recall: the phrase

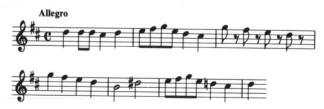

is heard four times as a short punctuating ritornello theme or modulating rondo theme: 'Gloria in excelsis Deo', 'Gratias agimus tibi', 'Domine, Fili Unigenite' and 'Quoniam tu solus sanctus'. There is a second thematic reference back when the concluding 'Amen' section repeats material first heard near the beginning of the Gloria movement to the text 'et in terra pax hominibus'.

The Credo movements reveal a similar combination of the new with the tried and tested. All have the familiar three-stage plan: an opening section in a fast tempo; a middle section, beginning with the clause 'et incarnatus est', in a slower tempo, a contrasting key and with a more indulgent ratio of music to words; and, from 'Et resurrexit tertia die' to the end, a return to the home key and to a fast tempo. Except for that of the *Missa in angustiis*, all the Credo movements end with a fugue (the final section of the 'Schöpfungsmesse' is consistently imitative rather than fugal). Possibly the reason why the Credo of the *Missa in angustiis* does not end with a fugue is because the first part of the movement, seventy-seven bars of Allegro con spirito, is laid out in the form of a strict canon at the lower fifth; sopranos and tenors anwered a bar later by altos and basses. Haydn composed most of his canons during the 1790s and the development section of the first movement of Symphony no.102 and the minuet of the quartet, op.76 no.2, are two other instances that reflect this contemporary interest. The 'Et incarnatus est' of the *Missa Sancti Bernardi de Offida* actually employs an existing secular canon (XXVIIb:44), setting the words 'Gott im Herzen ...' ('God in the heart and a good wife on the arm, / The one makes us holy, the other one warm'); in its new context the three successive entries over a simple pizzicato accompaniment with the discreet doubling of clarinets produce a passage of the most elevated beauty. Earlier in the same movement, several of the thematic statements had begun with a descending arpeggio, a simple way of unifying the progress of the music. The Credo of the *Missa in tempore belli* takes thematicism a step further by beginning as a fugue rather than with the normal homophonic statement against a busy orchestral accompaniment.

Attention has already been drawn to the heightened inspiration of the 'Crucifixus' of the *Missa in angustiis*, as well as the 'Et incarnatus est' of the *Missa Sancti Bernardi de Offida*. Indeed, all these central sections of the Credo movements in the late masses vie with each other in quality of material and richness of word-painting. The canon of the 'Et incarnatus est' in the *Missa Sancti Bernardi de Offida* is announced by voices and instruments in E flat. For the following 'Crucifixus' Haydn switches sonorities completely, to two tenors and bass accompanied by lower strings in the dark key of E flat minor, the material of the thematic line is a distillation of the canon. In the 'Schöpfungsmesse', the 'Et incarnatus est', led by the soprano soloist, is placed in G major, a bright sound in the middle of a B flat major movement. Haydn writes out the organ part, indicating that a flute stop should be used, perhaps an aural projection of the frequently encountered visual image of the dove as the Holy Ghost. The ethereal sound of the organ flute stop drops out of the scoring at the 'Crucifixus', the bass voice enters and the music swings round to B flat for the choral entry with the words 'sub Pontio Pilato'.

All the Sanctus movements retain the usual division into two parts, a slow tempo for 'Sanctus, Sanctus, Sanctus, Dominus Sabaoth' ('Holy, Holy, Holy, Lord God of Hosts') and a fast tempo for 'Pleni sunt coeli et terra gloria Tua. Osanna in excelsis' ('Heaven and earth are full of Thy glory. Hosanna in the highest'). The 'Sanctus' portion is more likely to veer towards the mysterious rather than the jubilant, with a penchant for homophonic statements. The Sanctus of the *Missa in angustiis* opens with a *piano - forte - piano* expansion and contraction of tone, the apex of the volume coinciding with an arpeggiated chord on the organ and a single note on trumpets and timpani. A beat-marking 'Pleni sunt coeli' is followed by an imitative setting of the 'Osanna'.

After the brief, musically undeveloped Sanctus movements, the Benedictus movements provide a complete contrast. Traditionally, the Benedictus movement has always been the most relaxed in any Austrian setting of the mass, espousing extended lyricism and a gently ecstatic mood that made this movement the musical highpoint of any setting. In Haydn's six late masses this primacy is threatened, first by the beauty of many of the 'Et incarnatus est' settings in the Credo movements and, secondly, by Haydn's occasional modification of the traditional response to the text. Most of the Benedictus movements are placed in a contrasting key (E flat in the *Missa Sancti Bernardi de Offida* and the 'Schöpfungsmesse', G major in the 'Theresienmesse') and feature an expansive orchestral introduction; however, in keeping with the musically argued nature of these masses as a whole, there is no concession to charm in the shape of obbligato writing. In the *Missa in tempore belli*, the *Missa in angustiis* and the 'Harmoniemesse' Haydn probes the unsettled mood first encountered in the Benedictus of the 'Mariazeller' mass. That of the *Missa in angustiis* is the most overtly disturbed. In the *Missa in tempore belli* the 6/8 Benedictus starts in a wavering C minor before changing to C major. This ambivalent response is taken further in the Benedictus of Haydn's last mass, the 'Harmoniemesse', a highly eccentric movement that replaces the simple joy of belief with a sense of nervous awe. The sonata form movement is marked 'Molto allegro' and the first subject *'pianissimo'*; the theme is subsequently sung in hushed octave unison and is always heard over an unrelaxed running bass of quavers. The most radical modification of standard procedures in the Benedictus movements occurs at the point when the phrase 'Osanna in excelsis' returns. Only two masses, the *Missa in angustiis* and the 'Harmoniemesse', repeat the 'Osanna' music from the Sanctus, providing the usual jolt. In the remaining Benedictus movements the return of the 'Osanna' sentence is integrated into the musical flow of the Benedictus enabling that movement to reach a fulfilling musical conclusion. This novel modification is another indication of Haydn's desire to impose a new musical coherence on the procedures of the Classical mass.

After the contrasting keys of most of the Benedictus movements, the Agnus Dei movements provide a tangential approach to the home key of the works, re-established in readiness for the beginning of the 'Dona nobis pacem'. The Agnus Dei sections are all in a slow tempo, but the choice of initial key exposes two different approaches to the setting of the text, 'Lamb of God, who takest away the sins of the world'. The B flat minor of the *Missa Sancti Bernardi de Offida* and the G minor of the 'Theresienmesse' produce a dark, impassioned mood; in the B flat minor of the the first mass one should not underestimate the element of *Augenmusik* as the players and singers struggle with the five flats of the key signature. The remaining masses approach the tonic from a major key, F major to C major in the *Missa in tempore belli*, a bright G major in the D minor of the *Missa in angustiis* and an even more luminous G major in the last two masses in B flat. The associated mood is one of composure, a certainty of response anticipating the forthright mood of the ensuing 'Dona nobis pacem' section. It is these major-key sections that profit most clearly from the slow movements of the composer's London symphonies; the three G major movements, all Adagio, with their simple phrasing patterns, melodic decoration, careful part-writing and general air of candour, could easily be adapted as instrumental slow movements. Indeed, the Agnus Dei of the 'Harmoniemesse' opens like the slow movement of Symphony no. 98. The same mood, produced by the same means, features, appropriately, in the 'Bittgesang' in Part I ('Spring') of *The Seasons*. Later (January 1806), Haydn told his biographer, A. C. Dies:

> I prayed to God not like a miserable sinner in despair but calmly, slowly. In this I felt that an infinite God would surely have mercy on his finite creature, pardoning dust for being dust. These thoughts cheered me up. I experienced a sure joy so confident that as I wished to express the words of the prayer, I could not suppress my joy, but gave vent to my happy spirits and wrote above the *miserere*, etc. Allegro.

Most of Haydn's earlier masses had shown this 'sure joy' in their 'Dona nobis pacem' ('Grant us Thy peace') sections, and the composer felt no need to change this sincere, uplifting response in his last six masses. The 'Dona nobis pacem' of the 'Schöpfungsmesse' is unusual in that it begins as a fugal exposition, making the mood graver than is typical. The predominant dynamic is *forte*, the texture is full and there are liberal repetitions of the words' 'Dona nobis', yet in all these late masses Haydn avoids the glib jubilation of the 'Great Organ Solo Mass' by withdrawing towards the end of the movement into *pianissimo*, often complemented by one or more of the following features: longer note values, slower harmonic rhythm, interrupted cadences, pauses, pizzicato accompaniment and solo vocal writing. The subsequent concluding *forte* passages are all the more convincing for these reflective passages.

Haydn had begun his career with the composition of masses; various circumstances had then ensured that his only sustained occupation with the genre was from 1768 to *c.* 1775. It is fitting that, at the end of a long and richly diverse career, this deeply religious composer should have returned to the genre and produce six works of outstanding individual distinction. The *Missa Sancti Bernardi de Offida* is a carefully proportioned work, effective in its word-painting and unfailingly tuneful. Indeed, it owes its nickname 'Heiligmesse' to the fact that the Sanctus incorporates an old German hymn, 'Heilig, Heilig, Heilig', in its fabric. The *Missa in tempore belli* makes more extended use of soloists in an altogether more flamboyant work, with its rich contrasts of key and orchestral colour. Flamboyance becomes gripping theatricality in the *Missa in angustiis*, perhaps the most novel work of the six. Apart from the extra-musical references, the instrumentation and the many symphonic features, the mass cultivates a new attitude to the shaping of thematic lines, previously associated with the beginnings of Gloria and Credo movements only; they are primarily declamatory rather than being self-contained melodic entities; for instance, in the Kyrie the choir does not have a single melody, the only lyrical idea being entrusted to the orchestra (bar 11 etc.). Following the surprising juxtaposition of C and A major in the *Missa in tempore belli*, the last three masses all display a similar relationship in the juxtaposition of B flat and G major; the 'Schöpfungsmesse' is especially wide-ranging in its modulatory schemes (e.g. B flat to D flat in the Kyrie). Of these three, perhaps the 'Theresienmesse' is the least consistently impressive; the C major 'Gratias' section and the first section of the Credo are not on the same level of inspiration as the Kyrie and the Benedictus. The very last mass, the 'Harmoniemesse', like many of its predecessors, achieves an easy integration of solo and choral writing and combines this with a majestic orchestral sonority; the opening Kyrie, especially, is a movement of consummate power and authority.

It is this inspired control over diverse material and stimulus that marks the masses as among the highest artistic achievements of the Classical period, being at their best fully the equal of *The Creation*, the London symphonies and the best of the quartets. With the exception of the quartets, whose intellectual content has always been apparent to all, Haydn's music has suffered from a blinkered critical attitude, one that tends to patronize the 'Papa Haydn' aspect and seriously undervalue the composer's profundity. The six late masses have borne more than their share of criticism, having been variously castigated as 'uncomfortable compromises'[8] and 'works of tedious dignity with a senatorial tone',[9] and their cause has not been helped by superficial treatment in performances (fast tempi, clipped rhythms, scant regard to word-painting etc.) or, in the case of the 'Nelson' Mass, over-inflated renderings (as much the fault of the work's heroic nickname as of the unauthentic instrumentation noted above). There are artistic riches to be recovered.

Miscellaneous secular vocal music

The composition of masses to celebrate the name-day of Princess Marie Hermenegild Esterházy constituted Haydn's principal remaining official duties in the final period of his life, but they were not the only products of the family's *Kapellmeister*. He also composed some incidental music for plays performed at the Esterházy court by visiting companies, isolated pieces of music that, in the main, cannot be performed outside their original context. For an unidentifiable comedy in the French language Haydn composed an accompanied recitative (XXX:4), with spoken interjections in dialogue, beginning 'Fatal amour, cruel vainqueur' ('Fatal love, cruel conqueror'). It is possible that this unknown play was performed during the six-week season of plays and German opera provided at Eisenstadt by the Johann Karl Stadler troupe in September and October 1796. They performed also *Haldane, König der Dänen*, a translation and adaptation of Alexander Bicknell's tragedy, *The Patriotic King; or Alfred and Elvida*.[10] Haydn provided three numbers (XXX:5): a lively 6/8 opening chorus in C major to celebrate the Danish victory; an aria for the Guardian Spirit ('Schutzgeist') and a duet for Alfred and Odun, Earl of Devon. The most substantial number is the aria, an Adagio in common time in E flat major, accompanied by a *Harmonie* of two clarinets, two horns and two bassoons. It takes the form of a dialogue between the Guardian Spirit and the disconsolate Elvida, the latter a spoken part. The key, the leisurely tempo, the warmth of the sentiment and the prominent use of the clarinets provide the first instance of many such movements in late Haydn, from the 'Et incarnatus est' of the contemporary *Missa Sancti Bernardi de Offida* to movements in *The Creation* and *The Seasons*.

Two years later, in 1798, Haydn composed a concert aria in Italian which was probably first performed at the traditional two Christmas concerts of the Tonkünstler-Societät in the same year. Rather than the customary operatic text, the aria sets Petrarch's twenty-eighth Sonnet, 'Solo e pensoso i più deserti campi/vo mesurando a passi tardi e lenti', a text apparently suggested to Haydn by a Russian Grand Duke (identity unknown). Petrarch's sonnet, one of the many inspired by his love for Laura, is a dignified picture of a lonely figure 'bereft of joy' ('d'allegrezza spenti'), but inwardly aflame, who finds solace in solitude. Haydn's aria has a customary two-part structure, Adagio and Allegretto, the change of tempo occurring at the end of the octave of Petrarch's sonnet; though the sonnet concludes in resolution, Haydn's Allegretto and the ebullient operatic ending are conventional in comparison with the deep personal feeling of the words. The setting is accompanied by a small orchestra of two clarinets, two bassoons, two horns and strings.

Nelson's visit to Eisenstadt in September 1800 was the occasion for Haydn's last original vocal work for solo voice (XXVIb:4). Nelson and Lady Hamilton were accompanied on their journey by one Cornelia Knight who, after Nelson's victory at the Battle of Aboukir, had written an ode entitled 'The Battle of the Nile'. During the visit of the Nelson entourage to Eisenstadt, Haydn set ten of the seventeen stanzas for voice and piano, the first performance apparently being given by Lady Hamilton accompanied by Haydn. The jingoistic text, in the manner of Nedham's *Ode to Neptune*, is set as an accompanied recitative and aria. A powerful C minor piano introduction sets the despondent scene before the 'Sons of Neptune' and 'Britannia's Hero' lead 'Kingdoms to free from servile dread'. The aria becomes a paean in praise of Nelson, set in Haydn's favourite key of B flat major and featuring a recurring martial phrase. The rhetoric is empty and Haydn's setting cannot improve on Knight's long-winded poetry. Haydn had made a much more distinguished and lasting contribution to patriotic music in the *Volkslied* 'Gott erhalte Franz den Kaiser', which was and remains the only national anthem written by a composer of the first rank.

'Gott erhalte' (XXVIa:43) was composed in 1797, in the period immediately after the *Missa in tempore belli* and though clearly inspired by the British anthem, 'God save the King' (Haydn's own setting of this anthem is lost), it was conceived as an Austrian rejoinder to the recently composed *La Marseillaise* of France. Possibly prompted by the ubiquitous Gottfried van Swieten, the Austrian government set the project in motion by commissioning a text from Lorenz Leopold Haschka (1749–1827). Haschka's four verses were then set by Haydn, originally as a single line accompanied by piano and then a single line accompanied by an orchestra of one flute, two oboes, two bassoons, two horns, two trumpets, timpani and strings. The British and French anthems may have prompted the Austrian anthem, but Haydn's music is a good deal more distinctive than either of its predecessors. The tempo – Poco adagio – is a familiar one from many slow movements, a slow *alla breve* to be felt in two, not four, beats; and the measured, undecorated melodic line supported by simple, but firm harmony has counterparts in many slow sections in the late masses and oratorios. Not surprisingly, the anthem has been extensively dissected by generations of musicians who have pointed out similarities between it and anything from plainsong, through Croatian folk-song, to the 'Alleluja' of Mozart's 'Exsultate, jubilate' (K.165); what these observations reveal is not an indebtedness, much less the use of musical clichés, but Haydn's ability to compose a theme whose resonances contribute to rather than affect its durability.

Three German songs (XXVIa:44-6) date from this period, 'Als einst mit Weibes Schönheit', 'Ein kleines Haus' and 'Antwort auf die Frage eines Mädchens'. All three follow the example of the latest of Haydn's English canzonettas, 'The spirit's song' and 'O tuneful voice', in being through-composed, though none has the intensity of emotion of the English songs and the piano writing, in comparison, is modest. In each case the poet is unknown. More absorbing, if simpler, are two Italian duets for soprano and tenor with piano accompaniment (XXVa:1 and 2), composed in 1796. The text of the duets is by Badini, the librettist of the ill-fated opera *L'anima del filosofo*, and the composer probably acquired it in England; it is possible that the two separate duet texts, 'Saper vorrei se m'ami' and 'Guarda qui che lo vedrai', came from a single opera that cannot now be identified. In both, Nisa and Tirsi are two lovers who, in the usual operatic fashion, move from circumspect dialogue to unanimity of thought and deed. Though the ambience and musical language of Haydn's two duets are those of Italian opera, thus constituting a touching farewell to an idiom which had dominated so much of the composer's life, there are some sophisticated touches that make the duets more suited to the salon than to the theatre. Both duets have two tempos, slow and fast, but neither duet adheres slavishly to the routine of proposition, answer, dialogue and, in a fast tempo, homophonic writing. In 'Saper vorrei se m'ami' the happiness of Nisa and Tirsi is celebrated by the singing of a canon, another instance to set alongside examples in the masses and the D minor quartet (op. 76 no. 2) of the influence of Haydn's many canons composed in the 1790s.

Also begun in 1796 was a project that occupied the composer intermittently for the next three years. Haydn intended composing twenty-four German part-songs on sacred and secular texts; nine were composed in 1796 and four more over the next three years. Haydn never fully realized his intentions and the thirteen

(XXVc:1–9 and XXVb:1–4) were published by Breitkopf & Härtel in 1803. Like 'Dr Harington's Compliment' and the *Twelve Sentimental Catches and Glees*, these part-songs are written for voices (usually four-part, a few three-part) with piano accompaniment (indicated as figured bass in nos. 1–9, written out in nos. 10–13). For perhaps the only time in his life Haydn took the trouble to seek out poetry which he knew would elicit a characterful response, and in range of subject matter and in the alertness of the setting these German songs are far superior to the English examples. No. 3, 'Alles hat seine Zeit', is a drinking song in which snatches of thematic material are tossed between the participants, the singers coming together for the crucial phrase 'ich bin wieder klug mit dir' ('Now I'm sensible with you again'); the clause 'wenn ich schwärme' ('when I revel') is set in imitative bursts of semiquavers. The alternation of imitation and homophony, always prompted by the words, is a consistent feature of these songs. No. 5, 'Der Greis' ('The old man'; XXVc:5), makes use of the same technique in a slow tempo and, allied to some unexpected modulations (A major to D minor, for instance), provides a touching portrayal of declining powers and the welcome release of death; Haydn used the opening four bars of the soprano line as a musical inscription on his visiting card, 'Hin ist alle meine Kraft; alt und schwach bin ich' ('Gone is all my strength, old and weak am I'). The last two songs have sacred texts, a sonorous song of praise to God ('Aus dem Danklied zu Gott') suggesting the influence of the English Psalms, and an evening hymn to God ('Abendlied zu Gott'), set in Haydn's most responsive E major. Haydn told Griesinger that the part-songs were written 'con amore'; certainly they are the most durable and touching of the smaller vocal items of the late period.

The very different distinction of being the last music composed by Haydn belongs, however, to his arrangements of Scottish and Welsh folk-songs. The 150 folk-songs that Haydn had arranged for the publisher William Napier during his visits to London had proved enormously popular and in 1799 the Edinburgh entrepreneur George Thomson, Clerk to the Board of Trustees for the Encouragement of Arts and Manufactures in Scotland, contacted Haydn requesting further arrangements. Three years later, another Scotsman, William Whyte, also commissioned arrangements from Haydn. For these two men, Haydn supplied over 250 settings of Scottish and Welsh folk-songs between 1799 and the winter of 1804–5. Initially, Haydn found the task an absorbing one, a pleasant diversion from the intellectual and physical effort expended in the composition and many performances of the two oratorios. In a letter to Thomson dated 5 December 1801, Haydn wrote '... I have taken great pains to satisfy you, and to show the world how far a man can progress in his art, especially in this genre of composition, if he is willing to exert himself; and I wish that every student of composition would try his hand at this type of music'. Some of Haydn's pupils did indeed 'try their hand' and over two dozen of the 'Haydn' arrangements are now known to be the work of a pupil, Sigismund von Neukomm. It is likely that other arrangements, particularly the later ones, were the work of other pupils. On the whole, the arrangements are far more resourceful than those done for Napier. The right hand of the piano usually doubles the vocal line, but the accompaniment of keyboard, violin and cello is conceived as a full piano trio texture with independent introductions and postludes (or 'symphonies', as they were called). 'Wha wadna be in love' is a lively setting of the Scottish tune, 'Maggy Lauder', while 'The live long night' ('All through the night'), one of the few duets, is an example of the many fetching arrangements of slow melodies.

Miscellaneous instrumental music

In November 1800, Prince Nicolaus II re-engaged a complement of wind players which, in combination with the orchestra of the *Chor-Musique* in Eisenstadt, enabled Haydn to compose for full orchestra in his last two masses. A couple of months after the first performance of the 'Harmoniemesse' in 1802, Haydn composed, for the meagre sum of one florin, the *Hungarischer National Marsch* (VIII:4) for the Esterházy wind band. The basic octet of pairs of oboes, clarinets, horns and bassoons is supplemented by one trumpet, an increasingly common addition in wind-band music at the turn of the century. The march, thirty-two bars long and without trio, is a brisk Allegretto with forceful harmonies.

Nothing is known about the composition of Haydn's Twenty-four Minuets (IX:16), which survived only in a single and undated set of manuscript parts. The orchestral requirement of piccolo, two flutes, two oboes, two clarinets, two bassoons, two horns, two trumpets, timpani, 'Turkish' percussion and strings without violas points to the 1790s, and the emancipated use of the clarinet, in particular, to the later years of that decade. The orchestration has the variety of colour and sonority found in the London symphonies, with independent cello and double-bass parts, grand C and D major movements for full orchestra that contrast with minuets for a reduced orchestra. The practicalities of the dance meant that Haydn could not indulge in the structural sophistication of the minuets of the London symphonies or the propensity for third-related modulations within movements found throughout his music in this late period, but the arrangement of the minuets into a set shows a characteristic liking for colourful contrasts of key.

The least likely composition of Haydn's old age is the Trumpet Concerto (VIIe:1) of 1796. Haydn never felt entirely at ease in the concerto genre and his previous solo concerto, the D major work for cello of 1783, is one of his weakest compositions. As for the solo instrument in this, Haydn's last orchestral work (with the possible exception of the Twenty-four Minuets), the choice of the trumpet would have been unthinkable for most of Haydn's career. The decline of the clarino technique in the mid-eighteenth century had meant that extended solo writing for the instrument was an evocative memory to be recalled by the older generation of musicians; probably the last Austrian concerto for clarino trumpet had been written by the young Mozart in 1768 (the work is unfortunately lost). It was Anton Weidinger, a trumpeter in the Viennese Court Orchestra, who ensured that Haydn returned to the concerto to write what is possibly his best work in the genre. Since the early 1790s Weidinger had been experimenting with an 'organized trumpet' ('organisirte Trompete'), that is a trumpet with five or six holes in the bore covered by padded keys, the opening and closing of which enabled all the chromatic notes between the notes of the natural series to be played. Weidinger became a celebrity, travelling throughout Europe to demonstrate his invention; it was copied by many instrument makers and superseded only by the valved trumpet. Although Haydn composed his concerto in 1796, Weidinger did not play this new work, by the leading composer of the day, in public until March 1800; perhaps his technique was not quite up to the demands of the work at the time of its completion. The concert also included two other compositions featuring the organized trumpet, an aria by Süssmayer and a sextet by Kauer. Koželuch and Hummel were two further composers who wrote for the instrument, the latter's concerto now rivalling Haydn's in public popularity.

Haydn's concerto, like Hummel's after it, provides a resourceful display of the traditional brilliance of the instrument, together with its new lyrical capabilities.

Haydn includes three very brief entries of the solo instrument in the opening ritornello (the first a single note), pitches that do not require the use of the added keys; when the solo section begins with the first subject (see example), the keys are put to immediate use, six of the notes in the first phrase (ringed) would not have been possible on a natural trumpet in E flat.

In matters of form, this first movement shows little influence of Mozart's magnificent series of piano concertos composed in the previous decade. Haydn retains the orchestral ritornello between the development and the recapitulation sections, though here it is not a weakness since the dominant preparation benefits directly from similar sections in the composer's symphonies. More individual is the interpolation in the recapitulation (bars 140 etc.) of a new passage, enabling Weidinger to flaunt his skill in negotiating contrasting registers and rapid scalic passages.

As in many of the concertos for the *lira organizzata*, composed ten years earlier, Haydn follows the Allegro of the first movement with a lyrical slow movement in siciliano style, though the amplitude of the melody reminds the listener that the work is contemporary with *The Creation* and the *Missa Sancti Bernardi de Offida* (the gentle *sforzando* accents on off-beats are a particular feature also found in, for instance, the slow movement of Symphony no. 104 and 'With verdure clad the fields appear' from *The Creation*). There is an effortless modulation to C flat major in the middle section of this A flat movement, and the new chromatic capability of the trumpet is again put to particularly effective use when it doubles the bass line in the oscillation of dominant and augmented sixth harmonies that precedes the reprise of the main theme. The Finale (Allegro) is a sonata rondo that exhibits, alongside well-motivated virtuosity, some of the élan of the sonata rondos of the London symphonies, but without attempting to rival their far-ranging powers of surprise, suspense and invention.

String quartets

Haydn began work on the six quartets of op. 76 in 1796, composing them at the same time as *The Creation*, and probably finished them by early autumn of 1797. They were not published until 1799, by Longman & Broderip in London and by Artaria in Vienna. The latter publication dedicates the set to Count Joseph Erdödy, who had commissioned the works. In the same year, 1799, Haydn began work on a second set of quartets, but of these he managed to complete only two works and to compose a slow movement and a minuet of a third. Another patron, who was to figure even more conspicuously than Erdödy in Beethoven's career, Prince Lobkowitz, commissioned this set. The two quartets completed were published in 1802, by Artaria in Vienna and by Clementi in London (possibly a year later). The incomplete third quartet in D minor, composed in 1803, was published by Breitkopf & Härtel in 1806 as 'op. 103'. At the end of this melancholy last publication of a portion of a quartet, Haydn appended his musical visiting card: 'Hin ist alle meine Kraft, alt und schwach bin ich'. All that remains of a further movement in this D minor work is a sketch for a bass line (reproduced below), which was probably the beginning of an allegro (the common time suggests a first movement rather than a finale).

Chance circumstances had given rise to Haydn's first quartets forty years earlier and at various times in his career he had returned to the genre, on each occasion making a novel contribution to its development, and always enhancing his understanding of the special qualities of the Classical style. Opp. 76 and 77 continue this approach, opening up new paths of development rather than being works of consolidation or valediction. Although, in comparison with other genres, much of the musical communication is exclusive, a dialogue between initiates, it is all too easy to over-emphasize this aspect. Haydn was conscious that he was writing for a contemporary public and not, as Beethoven was to feel, for posterity, and those musicians who were privileged to know the late oratorios and masses, as well as Haydn's previous quartets, could find the same approachable, all-embracing humanity.

Here, some of the distinctive features of the opp. 71 and 74 quartets composed for London are retained or modified. The first movement of op. 76 no. 1 in G major opens with three prefatory *forte* chords but, rather than the full textured theme in a *piano* dynamic that usually followed such introductions in opp. 71 and 74, there now follows a single melodic line played by cello. Only a composer of Haydn's confidence could risk a theme of such devastating simplicity: four bars to dominant, answered by four bars to tonic. The two phrases are then repeated in two-part counterpoint. At the beginning of the development, the single line is enlivened by a running quaver accompaniment, a scoring that is repeated at the beginning of the recapitulation. Elsewhere in these late quartets, *forte* chords are used in a manner found in the London piano sonatas, that is, integrated into the thematic material of the movement (finales of op. 76 nos. 3 and 5 and the first movement of op. 77 no. 1). The forceful sonority of opp. 71 and 74 is apparent too in many of the opp. 76 and 77 quartets. Indeed, the first movement of the 'Emperor' quartet (op. 76 no. 3) is obviously orchestral in its 'padded' scoring, far more so than any quartet in opp. 71 and 74. In their tonal language, the opp. 71 and 74 quartets had been the first group of works, as distinct from single works, to proclaim the strong contrast of keys a third apart. Such contrasts, a pervasive feature of Haydn's style in his late period, inform many of the opp. 76, 77 and 103 quartets. Op. 76 no. 5, in D major, has a slow movement in F sharp major; op. 76 no. 6, in E flat, has its slow movement in B major; op. 77 no. 1, in G, places both the Adagio and the Trio of the minuet movement in E flat major; and op. 77 no. 2, in F, has the Trio of the minuet in D flat major and the slow movement in D major. The fact that op. 77 no. 2 includes movements in two different third-related keys is indicative of the ever-expanding tonal horizons of these quartets. Within movements, far-reaching modulations occur in the slow movements of op. 76 no. 6, and op. 103 and the finale of op. 76 no. 1. The Adagio of the E flat major quartet (op. 76 no. 6) is headed 'Fantasia' and is divided into two complementary parts. The first, notated without a key signature, consists of successive statements of the main theme, usually announced in regular phrase lengths and traversing a wide tonal terrain: B major, C sharp minor, E major, E minor, G major, B flat major, B major and A flat major. Three of the statements are preceded by an introductory single line, and one by preparatory chords. In the second half of the movement, in which Haydn uses a key signature, the texture is more polyphonic, the phrasing, consequently, less obvious and the modulation pattern more conventionally centred on the tonic. The movement finishes with a tonic chord with a third on top, a pitch, D sharp, that is then enharmonically emphasized as repeated E flats at the beginning of the following Menuet.

Enharmonic modulation occurs extensively in the late quartets, usually accomplished by full scoring. In the development section of the first movement of the F major quartet (op. 77 no. 2), however, enharmonic modulation is largely accomplished by single lines whose harmonic implications are clear. The tonic note of E flat is re-spelt as the leading note of E minor, emphasized by Haydn's indication 'l'istesso tuono' ('the same pitch').

In addition to the use of third-related keys and enharmonic modulations, Haydn makes forceful and novel use of an older technique, the contrast of mode. In the exposition of three sonata form movements from op. 76 nos. 1, 3 and 4, Haydn finds new vitality in a resource found in much of his earliest music and that of his precursors and contemporaries; part of the second subject area is placed in the dominant minor rather than in the dominant major. There are a few sonata forms by Haydn from the 1780s and 1790s that turn to the dominant minor, e.g. the first movements of three symphonies ('La Reine', 'Oxford' and 'Surprise'), but three instances within a single opus are evidence of a new and particular enthusiasm. The opening sonata form movement of the Piano Trio in B flat (no. 42), probably composed in 1796, also includes a passage in the dominant minor, and it is possible that this rediscovered resource was prompted by Beethoven's use of it in two of his op. 2 sonatas, the A major and the C major, published in 1796 and dedicated to Haydn. Haydn, however, extended the major-minor contrast so that it featured in other movements too. The Trio of the minuet in op. 76 no. 3 and the slow movement of op. 76 no. 4 both make poetic use of the change of mode. More startling are two major-key quartets from op. 76, nos. 1 and 3, which include finale movements that move from the tonic minor to the tonic major, the introduction of the minor sonority at this late stage in the progress of the works providing a new sense of seriousness where, earlier in his career, Haydn would have turned to light comedy. The control of ever-changing moods is especially impressive in the G major quartet (op. 76 no. 1), with its energetic triplets and extended tonal scheme; when G minor does give way to G major at the beginning of the recapitulation, it is a moment of complete surrender and Haydn's supreme powers of assimilation even allow him then to end with a flippant coda, featuring a derivation of the main theme over a pizzicato accompaniment.

Op. 76 no. 2, in D minor, owes much of its tough, uncompromising nature to its opposition of D minor and D major. After a first movement in D minor, one of Haydn's most radical essays in sonata form, the slow movement is in D major and begins with a fifteen-bar(!) theme

$$\|: 2 + 2 :\|: 2 + 3 + 1 + 1 + 2 + 2 :\|$$

played by first violin over an alternating accompaniment of *pizzicato* and *arco*. The design of the movement is Haydn's favourite ABA, in which the return of A is varied and a coda added, and B turns to the tonic minor and derives its thematic material from A. The keys of D minor and D major are brought into even closer proximity in the following Menuet; the ruthless 'Witches' canon is succeeded by a Trio that begins in D minor and switches to D major, a moment of brutal conflict that encapsulates the tension of the work as a whole. The D minor Finale is given added spirit and rigour by the many 'Hungarian' inflections, Lydian fourths, glissandi, drone harmonies and double stops; the music finally turns to the major after the beginning of the recapitulation.

For Haydn D minor had always been a key that encouraged severity and aggression rather than passion, and, on the evidence of the Menuet of op. 103, these were qualities that Haydn desired to pursue, once again, in a quartet. In earlier, more productive times, D minor had often allowed Haydn to release a certain grim, studious side to his personality; in his old age he could not summon the resources to complete another work in this difficult vein.

The rigour of the D minor quartet in op. 76 is enhanced also by the pervasive use of the motif of a fifth: omnipresent (usually falling) in the first movement, it features in the remaining three movements too, delineating the contours of the melodic material. Likewise, the B flat major quartet, op. 76 no. 4, makes consistent use of a motif (this time a semitone and a third) in all its movements so that the apparently different thematic material is perceived to derive from the same source. In the opening sonata form movement of the D minor quartet the recurring motif controls the discourse and enables Haydn to do away with the clear paragraphing associated with opp. 71 and 74 and employed elsewhere in opp. 76 and 77. In the first movement of op. 77 no. 1, close thematic argument based on the most unassuming of themes allows Haydn to devise a recapitulation that is a complete re-composition rather than a modified re-statement of the exposition.

The opening sonata form movements of the two op. 77 quartets show that Haydn had lost none of his creativity in the form, but the use of variations movements to open the cycle in two of the op. 76 quartets is an indication that perhaps this alternative approach would have become more prevalent had Haydn completed any further quartets. These two quartets, no. 5 in D major and no. 6 in E flat, are also the two works that feature the bold contrast of key in the ensuing slow movement, the tonally static variations allowing F sharp major and B major, respectively, to make maximum impact. These two works look back to the 'Razor' quartet, op. 55 no. 2, and even further back to quartets dating from *c.* 1770, op. 9 no. 5 and op. 17 no. 3. More recent encouragement for opening movements that were not in sonata form (albeit in a three-movement scheme) may have come from the piano trios of the London period and after. The D major movement of op. 76 no. 5 takes as its broad pattern the ABA approach already mentioned in connection with the slow movement of the D minor quartet. Another D major movement, the finale of op. 71 no. 3, may have been an additional stimulus; both are in 6/8 and have a coda in a faster tempo. The notable aspect of op. 76 no. 5, however, is the liberal attitude to the structure of the Allegretto main theme.

The opening eight-bar period, A^1, cadences in the tonic; it is followed, apparently by a decorated repeat (A^2), but one which is deflected at the end of its eight bars to B minor; four bars return the music to D major and a third version of A (A^3), more firmly anchored to D major at its cadence than A^1. The central section is an extended *minore* derived from the rhythms and melodic contours of the opening section. The return of the opening section begins with A^2, newly decorated; A^3 avoids resolving the cadence and prepares for the extended coda in a faster tempo, Allegro; the repetitive diatonic harmonies and routine figuration of the coda gradually alter the mood from lyricism to a sort of bright agitation.

The first movement of op. 76 no. 6 is a strophic set of variations on material that replaces melodic appeal with a sturdy harmonic framework, articulated by short two-bar phrases. Like its more famous companion, the variations movement in the 'Emperor' quartet, the theme is then stated verbatim by different instruments. The dotted figuration and trills of Variation no. 3 provide a rare aural reminiscence in Haydn's instrumental music of Handel, but it is the conclusion to the movement that attracts greatest attention: a fugue based on the main theme, the beginning of a broad historical tradition of fugal conclusions to variations movements that was passed on to Beethoven and then – fortified by the rediscovery of Bach's use of the procedure in his C minor Passacaglia (BWV 582) – employed by Mendelssohn, Brahms, Reger and others.

The E flat major quartet has other points of contact with Beethoven; the theme has similarities with that of the variations movement in Beethoven's 'Harp' quartet, op. 74; the minuet contains similar 'harp' figuration (bars 35ff.); and the *Alter-*

357

nativo is built on a scalic theme, rather like the minuet of Beethoven's First Symphony. But, as has been suggested in the case of the dominant minor interpolation in a major-key exposition, the flow of influence was two-way and, indeed, it is often difficult to establish who was the originator of a particular feature. The minuets of op. 76 no. 1 and op. 77 nos. 1 and 2 are all marked 'Presto' and are clearly to be played in one-in-a-bar. Haydn did not head the movements 'Scherzo', despite their apparent indebtedness to the scherzos found in Beethoven's op. 1 piano trios and op. 2 piano sonatas. However, in tracing the origins of these one-in-a-bar movements, one should also remember the finale movements of two of Haydn's London piano sonatas, nos. 60 and 61, which have the formal pattern as well as the pulse of a scherzo. The period 1793–1801, delimited by Beethoven's arrival in Vienna to receive lessons from Haydn and the composition of *The Seasons*, witnessed a process of mutual influence which was even more potent than that which had occurred between Haydn and Mozart a decade earlier, and any exhaustive record would have to take account of the following characteristics of opp. 76 and 77: mediant and other extended tonal relationships, thematic argument, variations as an alternative to sonata form first movements, monothematic sonata form, canon, one-in-a-bar dance movements, tempos that accelerate towards the ends of movements, as well as numerous details of thematic construction and textural outlay. Perhaps not the least of the frustrations of Haydn's old age was that he was unable to take further part in this artistic exchange with a composer thirty-eight years his junior.

That Haydn delayed the publication of the unfinished D minor quartet until 1806 is a pathetic reflection of the composer's frequently voiced lament that he had, spasmodically, the energy to invent ideas but lacked the physical stamina to attend to their potential. His dealings with Breitkopf & Härtel, the drawing up of the *Haydn-Verzeichnis*, the interviews with his two earliest biographers, Griesinger and Dies, and the visits of people as varied as the Swedish diplomat Silverstolpe and the composer Cherubini encouraged Haydn, perhaps for the first time in his life, to pause and reflect on his achievement. For nearly half a century his music had been the touchstone against which everyone tested their progress. Merely to catalogue his immense accomplishments in the genres of sonata, quartet, symphony, mass and oratorio is to risk restricting its range in order to aid our dazed comprehension. It may also mask the more fundamental achievement, the complete mastery of a new and rapidly evolving language, its vocabulary, grammar and syntax, to found a tradition that has dominated the course of musical history for the better part of two centuries. Haydn told Griesinger that he knew no more appropriate epitaph for his life's work than 'Vixi, scripsi, dixi'. The humour, simplicity and directness of that statement are typical of the man, its sentiments even more so. Many composers have lived and written, some almost as much or more; few have spoken with such assurance.

Notes on the text

INTRODUCTION

1 In the original operatic production there was perhaps no third movement, and, after the slow movement, the opera itself began with its D major 'set piece'. The third movement of this and other Haydn overtures of the period, e.g. *Lo speziale* and *L'infedeltà delusa*, were probably added when the composer published a group of these overtures with Artaria & Co. in 1782, for use in concerts.
2 Emily Anderson (trans. and ed.), *The Letters of Mozart and his Family* (London 1966), II, 833.
3 I. F. Runciman, *Old Scores and New Readings* (London 1899), 92.
4 In 1984 the new CBS recording of the Trumpet Concerto, with Wynton Marsalis as soloist and conducted by Raymond Leppard, was the best-selling classical record in the U.S.A. for a period of six months.
5 Cornelia Rost, 'Nur den Gesangstext', *Die Deutsche Bühne*, 55. Jahrgang, no.7 (July 1984), 6–11.
6 In preparing the biographical chapters, especially those on Haydn's visits to England and on his late years in Vienna, we have drawn also on the summaries in H. C. Robbins Landon, *Haydn: a documentary study* (London and New York 1981; now out of print).

CHAPTER I

1 Haydn never used his first given name.
2 For the full text see *C&W*, II, 397ff.
3 *Leaves from the Journals of Sir George Smart* by H. Bertram Cox and C. L. E. Cox (London 1907), 3; cf. *C&W*, III, 247f.
4 Haydn did, however, remain attached to the Servite Order; it was in the Vienna Chapter of the Order that his *Missa brevis* in F was 'rediscovered' in 1805. Cf. *C&W*, V, 338f.
5 'Joseph Haydn und Karl Joseph Weber von Fürnberg', *Unsere Heimat*, Jg 5 (July 1932), 190ff.
6 Abbé Stadler's *Materialien zur Geschichte der Musik unter den österreichischen Regenten* (ÖNB, Codex S.N. 4310), quotations from folios 104v., 105r.
7 H. M. Schletterer, *Johann Friedrich Reichardt ...*, (Augsburg 1865), 61. See also Otto Biba, 'Nachrichten zur Musikpflege in der gräflichen Familie Harrach', *HJB*, X (1978) 36ff., esp. 38f.
8 The part of the Esterházy Archives ('EH') now in Budapest is divided into two sections: the 'Acta Musicalia' and 'Acta Theatralia' in the Music Department of the National Széchényi Library (Országos Széchényi Könyvtár); and documents

preserved in the Hungarian State Archives (Magyar Országos Levéltár) in Buda. These documents are readily available to scholars. The other part of the Esterházy Archives is in Austria, mostly in Forchtenstein Castle and under the control of the present prince. It is very difficult, and for most scholars impossible, to gain access, but fortunately one of the few institutions to be permitted such access is the Joseph Haydn Institut, Cologne.
9 EH, Budapest, Magyar Országós Levéltár, p.131, fol.1546.
10 The playing order for the four horn parts was: Carl Franz (I), Franz Reiner (II), Johann Knoblauch (III), and Thaddeus Steinmüller (IV). See *H-S*, IV, 188f.

CHAPTER II

1 E.g. Reutter, *Missa S. Caroli* (1734); Michael Haydn, Mass in A minor, *Missa Sancti Josephi*; and Mozart, 'Coronation' Mass (K.317).
2 This passage may remind listeners of similar passages in J. S. Bach, Handel and, prophetically, the 'Rex tremendae' in Mozart's Requiem; but Haydn's source was the choral music of Reutter and Tuma, where it is often encountered.
3 See pp.86–9.
4 'Nespola' is the fruit of the medlar tree. The word was often used pejoratively, e.g. 'succia nespole' (*nespole* sucker), to describe someone with a protruding chin or a speech defect. 'The Marchioness Nespola' is thus a satirical title.
5 The first two phrases of Symphony no. 20 are thematically almost a supertonic gambit, but they are supported by full harmony.
6 In 1788 Mozart called his wonderfully resourceful string trio (K.563) a divertimento. He was merely being correct, if by this time rather old-fashioned.
7 The disappearance of the autograph is particularly frustrating here. Given the attention this movement devotes to all aspects of composition, especially phrasing and consistently applied interval patterns, it is not unreasonable to assume that Haydn showed similar care in the application of dynamics and other performance marks. The only extant manuscript source is devoid of dynamic marks for the entire work.
8 Symphony no. 9, which may have been composed in 1762, probably started life as an overture.
9 Haydn added the date later in his career.
10 This work was rediscovered in 1949 when a manuscript copy was found in Melk Abbey; it is often dubbed the 'Melk' concerto.

11 Doubts have been expressed about the authenticity of this work. The solo part is less demanding than those of the other concertos. It is possible that this concerto dates from before 1761.
12 Modern edition of the Werner in *Das Erbe deutscher Musik*, vol. 31 (Kassel, 1956).
13 Mozart used a minor version of the same motive in his 'Little' G minor symphony (K.183).

Chapter III

1 *Viajes Diarios 1750–1785* (Carácas 1929), I, 435.
2 *One-Leg, the Life and Letters of Henry William Paget, First Marquess of Anglesey, K.G. 1768–1854* by the Marquess of Anglesey, F.S.A. (London and New York 1961), 34f.
3 Cf. Otto Biba, writing in the catalogue of the Haydn exhibition held at Eisenstadt in 1982, *Joseph Haydn in seiner Zeit*, 142–51. See also James Dack, 'The Dating of Haydn's *Missa Cellensis* ...: an Interim Discussion', *HJB*, XIII, 97–112.
4 Weigl had joined the band in June 1761; in 1764 he had married the daughter of Scheffstoss.
5 Autograph dated 1768, recently discovered and sold at Christie's, London, in March 1984; for details of the work see p. 140.
6 From EH, Forchtenstein Castle; see *C&W*, I, 626.
7 *H-S*, IV, 272f.
8 Cf. *H-S*, IV, 289; *C&W*, II, 158.
9 One of the two versions is reproduced in colour in *C&W*, II, pl. III; the other in H. C. Robbins Landon, *Essays on the Viennese Classical Style* (London 1970).
10 Marteau was a cellist in the band, 1771–8; Pohl had been engaged in 1769 and remained with the *Capelle* until his death in 1781.
11 *Mozart-Briefe*, III, 311.
12 *Historisch-kritische Theaterchronik von Wien*, 3 vols. For relevant extracts see *C&W*, II, 206–11.
13 Now in the ÖNB, Vienna.
14 For the text of his letter see *C&W*, II, 418ff.
15 Cf. *C&W*, II, 42–3.

Chapter IV

1 The work, minus the dialogue, survives in only one late eighteenth-century score, and some commentators have doubted its authenticity.
2 See Bruce Alan Brown, 'Gluck's Rencontre Imprévue and its Revisions', *Journal of the American Musicological Society*, XXXVI (1983), 498–518.
3 See Michael Brago, 'Haydn, Goldoni, and *Il mondo della luna*', *Eighteenth-Century Studies*, 17 (1983–84), 308–32.
4 See Friedrich Lippmann, 'Haydns "La fedeltà premiata" und Cimarosas "L'infedeltà fedele"', *Haydn-Studien*, V/1 (1982), 1–15.
5 Other 'Turkish' operas, in various languages, include: Jommelli, *La schiava liberata*; Bickerstaffe, *The Sultan or A Peep into the Seraglio*; Grétry, *La caravane du Caire*; Süssmayer, *Soliman der Zweite oder Die drei Sultanninen;* and, of course, Mozart, *Die Entführung aus dem Serail*.
In Haydn's *Lo speziale*, Volpino disguises herself as a Turk to impress Sempronio, and in *Le pescatrici* the wicked Turk, Oronte, has usurped the throne that rightfully belongs to Eurilda.
6 In Nos. 4, 5, 8 and 9 the characters more often sing separately rather than in genuine ensemble.
7 Many of Haydn's contemporaries used 'mirror' recapitulations: Mozart (K.311), Ordoñez and, most regularly, the Mannheim composers.
8 Mozart's 'Là ci darem la mano' is a well-known example. Perhaps Mozart's use of this convention has an element of parody that is lost to twentieth-century audiences (particularly if the music is performed too indulgently).
9 James Dack, 'The Dating of Haydn's *Missa Cellensis in Honorem Beatissimae Virginis Mariae:* an Interim Discussion', *HJB*, XIII (1982), 97–112.
10 The precise date is not known; 1805 is likely. See Haydn's covering letter to Artaria in August 1805 (*C&W*, V, 336).
11 Mozart's output encompasses some *a cappella* music, but none of it is associated with Salzburg or Austria in general.
12 See H. Dopf, *Die Messenkompositionen Gregor Josef Werners* (Dissertation, University of Innsbruck, 1956), *passim*.
13 See H. Walter, *Proverbia Senteniaeque Latinitatis Medii Aevi* (Göttingen, 1967), vol. 15, p. 194, no. 30705. We are indebted to Dr Nicholas Horsfall, University College, London, for this information.
14 'Von seinen eigenen Werken sagte er: "Sunt mala mixta bonis; es sind wohl und übelgerathene Kinder, und hier und da hat sich ein Wechselbalg eingeschlichen."'
15 At a later date Haydn added two trumpets and timpani to the score.
16 The opus numbers were not applied by Haydn but derive from early French editions. They were perpetuated by Pleyel in his *Collection complette des Quatuors d'Haydn* (1802).
17 See *C&W*, II, 132.
18 No. 1, 'To God alone and to each his own'; No. 2, 'Praise be to Almighty God' and 'Thus friend flees from friend'; No. 3, 'Praise be to God and the Blessed Virgin Mary with the Holy Ghost'; No. 4, 'Glory to God in the highest'; and No. 6, 'Praise be to God and the Blessed Virgin Mary'.
19 The Auenbrugger family was known to Mozart also. They first met in 1773.
20 For Haydn's correspondence with Artaria see *C&W*, II, 430f.

Chapter V

1 K. F. Schreiber, *Biographie über den Ödenwälder Komponisten Joseph Kraus* (Buchen 1928), 68f.
2 Translation in Karl Geiringer, *Joseph Haydn* (New York 1947), 77.
3 Ms. owned by the Gesellschaft der Musikfreunde, Vienna.
4 *A Mozart Pilgrimage ... in the year 1829*, ed. Rosemary Hughes (London 1955), 172.
5 *Mozart-Briefe*, III, 368.
6 For the complete available documentation on Haydn and Freemasonry, by J. Hurwitz, see *HJB*, XVI (1985).
7 See H. C. Robbins Landon, *Mozart and the Masons* (London 1982), *passim*.

8 The autograph has not survived, and the letter cannot be dated more precisely.

9 Pohl, II, 242.

10 This version is taken from *Orpheus, Musikalisches Taschenbuch*, 1841; cf. Dies, 80.

11 *Musikalische Korrespondenz der teutschen Filharmonischen Gesellschaft*, 1791, no. 7; see *C&W*, II, 751f.

12 *A Mozart Pilgrimage* (op. cit.), 170f.

CHAPTER VI

1 No relevant documentary information has come to light; perhaps, unlike the subordinate musicians, Haydn secured verbal rather than written permission.

2 Haydn's explanation for his own musical originality, as recorded by his biographer, Griesinger (p. 17).

3 John A. Rice, 'Sarti's Giulio Sabino, Haydn's Armida, and the arrival of opera seria at Eszterháza', *HJB*, XV (1984), 181–98.

4 Haydn's letter to John Bland of 12 April 1790 was rediscovered in 1982 and, amongst other things, contains proof that Haydn did sell music to the publisher in return for some razors (the quartet, op. 55 no. 2, is known as the 'Razor'): Bland also supplied a watch, *HJB*, XIII (1982), 215–16, and XIV (1983), 201–2.

5 Haydn has the odd distinction of having written two vocal compositions on canine subject matter, this Lied and, while in England, the round 'Turk was a faithful Dog'.

6 This kind of opening - homophonic chorus doubled by orchestra - was used by Beethoven in his Mass in C.

7 *Orlando Paladino* and *Armida* contain arias that change key signatures, e.g. Angelica's aria 'Aure chete' from *Orlando Paladino*, composed in the same year as the *Missa Cellensis*.

8 Later editions changed some (but not all!) the headings from 'Scherzo' to 'Scherzando'.

9 Artaria's published order of 5, 2, 1, 3, 6 and 4 produced a balanced distribution of finale forms, viz, variations, rondo, sonata form, rondo, variations and rondo.

10 Anton Webern, 'Schoenberg's Musik' (1912). Translation from Ursula von Rauchhaupt. *Schoenberg, Berg, Webern. The String Quartets. A Documentary Study* (Hamburg: Deutsche Grammophon, 1971), 16.

11 See p. 188 and footnote 4 above.

12 Beethoven must have admired this quartet, perhaps more than any other by Haydn; the tone of the Allegro as well as the Neapolitan preoccupation are echoed in the first movement of Beethoven's F minor quartet, op. 95 ('Quartetto serioso'); Neapolitan relationships feature also in the 'Appassionata' Sonata, op. 57 (F minor again); quartet, op. 59 no. 2; and quartet, op. 131.

13 László Somfai, 'An Introduction to the Study of Haydn's Quartet Autographs (with Special Attention to Opus 77/G)', in *The String Quartets of Haydn, Mozart and Beethoven. Studies of the Autograph Manuscripts*. Isham Library Papers III (ed. Christoph Wolff), (Cambridge, Mass.: Harvard University Department of Music, 1980), 13.

14 The others are: op. 54 no. 1; op. 55 no. 1; op. 71 no. 2; op. 71 no. 3; and op. 76 no. 4.

15 *JHW*, XV/2, VII.

16 For the first concerto of his op. 6 Krumpholtz had sought the aid of Pichl. 'Quelques jours après je jouai a Esterhaz devant la Cour Impériale, et le lendemain le célebre Haydn, directeur de concert, me proposa de la part du prince de rester au nombre de ses musiciens. J'acceptai avec joie, et je ne me montrai pas difficile sur l'article du traitement; heureux de pouvoir entendre et exécuter tous les jours les ouvrages du dieu de l'harmonie. Je composai un nouveau concerto, qui se trouve le premier de mon œuvre 6. Je m'adressai encore a M. Püchel pour les accompagnemens. Je fus obligé de refaire les tutti en entier, parce qu'ils n'avoient nul rapport aux motifs de ma partie principale. Le succès m'encouragea. Je fis le deuxieme concerto de cette œuvre 6, et je travaillai moi-meme les accompagnemens. Je priai M. Haydn de jeter les yeux sur mon brouillon; il ne trouve rien à corriger à ma partie principale, mais il me fit remarquer plusieurs fautes dans les accompagnemens; je donnois à un instrument ce qui appartenoit à un autre, et cette tranposition jettoit dans l'ensemble beaucoup de désordre et de confusion. Je soumis de même à son examen mes six premieres sonates, et il n'y trouva pas six notes à changer. Je composai ensuite le deuxieme concerto de mon œuvre 4, avec tous les accompagnemens, et je l'exécutai sans consulter M. Haydn.' Krumpholtz's memoirs appear in Plane (ed.), *Principes pour la Harpe par J. B. Krumpholtz* (Paris 1800). We are grateful to Ann Griffiths for drawing our attentiion to this memoir. Alfred Einstein, *Lebensläufe deutscher Musiker, von ihnen selbst erzählt.* Band III/IV: Adalbert Gyrowetz (1763-1850) (Leipzig 1915), 13.

17 The six overtures, many revised, are: *L'isola disabitata, L'incontro improvviso, Lo speziale, La vera costanza, L'infedeltà delusa* and *Il ritorno di Tobia*.

18 Barry S. Brook, *La Symphonie Française dans la seconde moitié du XVIIIᵉ siècle* (Paris: Publications de l'Institut de Musicologie de l'Université de Paris, 1962), I, 328 and 250-1.

19 This symphony is an interesting source for later ideas in two other respects: the brisk slow movement as featured in most of the 'Paris' symphonies and the thematic material of the finale, based on horn calls as in Symphony no. 103.

20 See the report from the *Wiener Diarium* (1766), quoted in *C&W*, II, 131.

21 Mozart, too, does not use a rondo in his 'Paris' Symphony; the finale is in sonata form.

22 Symphony no. 90 provides a similar, though less extensive, harmonic relationship between slow introduction and allegro.

CHAPTER VII

1 The hall at the King's Theatre, which measured 97 × 48 ft, was much larger than that in the Hanover Square Rooms, measuring 79 × 32 ft. The great hall of the castle at Eisenstadt was much larger altogether - 125 × 48 ft.

2 Roger Lonsdale, *Dr. Charles Burney, a literary biography* (Oxford 1965), 355.

3 Percy Scholes, *The Great Dr. Burney* (London 1948), II, 110.

4 The composer Stephen Storace and the soprano Anna Selina (Nancy) Storace, one of the leading singers of the day.

5 This correspondence was only recently discovered in the Esterházy Archives, Budapest, see Ulrich Tank, *Studien zur Esterbázyschen Hofmusik von etwa 1620 bis 1790* (Regensburg 1981), 285ff.

6 The portrait is reproduced in colour in *C&W*, III, pl. I.

7 Theresa Negri, soprano, who was then singing in London.

8 At the earlier concerts new symphonies by Haydn were performed for the first time as follows: 17 February (first), no. 93 – the slow movement being repeated; 2 March (third), no. 98 – the first and last movements being repeated; 9 March (fourth), the so-called Sinfonia Concertante in B flat (I:105). Haydn's 'madrigal', *'The Storm'* was first given at the second concert (24 February).

9 Evidence for this is contained in letters to Boswell from the Earl of Exeter (26 June) and Sir John Gallini (22 June); see *Yale Editions of the Private Papers of James Boswell*, Research Edition, III (ed. C. N. Fifer), London 1976, 366 (and for the Burney quotation, 365).

10 This letter is reproduced in facsimile in H. C. Robbins Landon, *Haydn: a documentary study* (London and New York 1981), 136.

11 Evidently a reference to his earlier promise made in response to the invitation from the King of Naples.

12 In order to make it possible for Elssler to make the journey abroad, Prince Esterházy had to ensure that the young man was freed from military service; this he did in a document, now in the Esterházy Archives, Budapest, dated Vienna, 14 November 1793 (shown in the Haydn Exhibition at Eisenstadt, 1982, as No. 972).

13 Canon: 'Turk was a faithful dog' (XXVIIb:45); see *C&W*, III, 268.

14 The title is a translation of 'Transport of Pleasure', from Haydn's Second Set of English Canzonettas (with words by Anne Hunter, widow of the noted surgeon, Dr John Hunter; cf. *C&W*, III, 391f.

15 William Parke, *Memoirs* (London 1830), I, 196f.

16 Samuel Rogers, *Table Talk*, Recollections, collected by Dyce, London 1856 (reprinted by Richards Press, 1952), 12; we are indebted to the late D. P. M. Michael for drawing our attention to this document.

17 Roger Lonsdale, 'Dr. Burney's "Dictionary of Music"', *Australian Musicology*, V (1979), 159–71, esp. 165.

this development. Their slow movements are both in E flat, but since both first movements end in the tonic major rather than minor, the contrast of key becomes a bold one.

8 Interrupting a movement with passages from another section or movement had been suggested in Haydn's own output by Symphony no. 46 and the quartet, op. 74 no. 3. Mozart's 'Posthorn' Serenade (K.320), the D major quintet, the overture to *Così fan tutte* and, perhaps the most potent for Haydn if only in view of the key, the overture to *Die Zauberflöte* (K. 620) all recall material from their respective slow introductions.

9 Haydn's original conclusion to the Finale was different and thirteen bars longer, featuring a modulation to E flat minor and a silence of two bars. He may have rejected this adventurous conclusion for the basic reason that it undermined the momentum of the movement.

10 In 1799 Haydn apparently intended composing a violin concerto for his friend, the well-known composer and violinist, François Hippolite Barthélemon, perhaps fulfilling a promise made in London. Nothing has survived, however; see *C&W*, III, 169.

11 Two more compositions for mechanical organ (XIX: 31 and 32) exist, but cannot be ascribed to any Niemecz organ.

12 Pohl III, 83–4.

13 Acc. no. 1870. d. 1. (110).

14 We are indebted to Dr Simon McVeigh of Goldsmiths' College, University of London, for providing the date of performance.

15 The highest note required in these sonatas is *a'''*, in the finale of no. 60, and it has always been assumed that this was a particular response to the extended compass of English fortepianos (up to *c''''*). It seems, however, that some pianos built by the Viennese maker Wenzel Schanz in the 1790s also had an extended compass, from *f'''* to *a'''* (e. g. the Schanz fortepiano in the Holburne of Menstrie Museum, Bath).

16 Some rising scale passages in the second movement of no. 41 encouraged Haydn to apply the title (later cancelled) 'Jacob's Dream' to this movement.

17 The same off-key approach and minor interpolation are to be found in the first movement of Schubert's late B flat major piano trio (D.898).

18 These numbers derive from various early editions in which the quartets were issued in sets of three: op. 71 from Pleyel, op. 74 from Artaria and from Corri & Dussek.

Chapter VIII

1 Transcribed in *C&W*, III, 316–18. Haydn noted the number of sheets used in each work; however, his system is inconsistent.

2 *Public Advertiser*, 5 December 1786.

3 See *C&W*, III, 151.

4 See *C&W*, III, 135.

5 Anthony Baines, 'The Evolution of Trumpet Music up to Fantini', *Proceedings of the Royal Musical Association*, 101 (1974–5), 2.

6 In the first published edition of no. 103 (Gombart, spring 1799) the clarinets of the autograph and the authentic manuscript parts are omitted.

7 Haydn's last two symphonies in the minor key, no. 83 in G minor and no. 95 in C minor, anticipate

Chapter IX

1 Cited in *More Letters from Martha Wilmot: Impressions of Vienna 1819–1829*, ed. the Marchioness of Londonderry and H. M. Hyde (London 1935), 323; cf. *C&W*, IV, 50f.

2 Sigismund (von) Neukomm, *Bemerkungen zu den biogr. Nachrichten von Dies* (ms. in Pohl's hand, published 1959), 30.

3 C.-G. Stellan Mörner, *Johan Wikmanson und die Brüder Silverstolpe* (Stockholm 1952), 318; for further extracts cf. *C&W*, IV, 255f. etc.

4 'The Diaries of Joseph Carl Rosenbaum 1770–1829', ed. Else Radant, in *HJB*, V (1968), 25f.

5 For the background to Silverstolpe's report, see *C&W*, IV, 250ff.
6 In reality, Haydn confused the fact that Mozart's widow, Constanze, had rooms in the same house ('Zum blauen Säbel im zweyten Stock'), at least in December 1794; Mozart did not here, but in his apartment in the Rauhensteingasse.
7 *Anteckningar utut mitt lif*; for further extracts see *C&W*, IV, 455.
8 'Memoir of Mr. Frederick Kalkbrenner reprinted from *The Quarterly Musical Magazine and Review* Volume VI (1824)', *HJB*, XII, 180–91.
9 *Opus Musicum: Notes sur Antoine Reicha, Texte présenté par Jiří Vysloužil*, Brno 1970, 12–25; the ms. memoir is headed 'Ces notes sur Antoine Reicha m'ont été données par sa fille ainée (Antoinette Reicha) le jeudi 22 février 1838. C'est la copie exacte du manuscrit de son père.' We are indebted to Peter Riethus for drawing our attention to this valuable document, not hitherto cited by Haydn scholars.
10 For the original French text see *C&W*, V, 231.
11 *Karl Maria von Weber. Seine Persönlichkeit in seinen Briefen und Tagebüchern und in Aufzeichnungen seiner Zeitgenossen*, ed. Otto Hellinghaus, Freiburg [1924], 10; Pohl III, 221.
12 Pohl III, 385ff.; for other documents relating to the composer's last days, overshadowed by the events of the Napoleonic Wars, see *C&W*, V, 387ff.
13 The death-mask of the composer, now in the Historisches Museum der Stadt Wien, Vienna, is illustrated in *C&W*, V, pls 5, 6.

CHAPTER X

1 The theory that the English was a re-translation of the German is now completely discredited. See Edward Olleson, 'The Origins and Libretto of Haydn's *Creation*', *HJB*, IV (1968), 148–66; and Nicholas Temperley, 'New light on the libretto of *The Creation*' in Christopher Hogwood and Richard Luckett (eds.), *Music in Eighteenth-Century England*, (Cambridge 1983), 189–211.
2 Individual numbers in both oratorios are identified according to the Eulenburg miniature scores. For *The Creation*, the English text quoted is that from the first edition; for *The Seasons* the German is quoted.
3 In No.19, the equivalent passage has a *crescendo* from *p* to *ff*.
4 The influence of *The Creation* and *The Seasons* on Beethoven's 'Pastoral' Symphony, both in local tone-painting and in pervasive well-being, can hardly be overstated. The key structure of *The Creation* may also have influenced Beethoven in the opera *Fidelio*, which presents a contrast between sharp and flat keys that is resolved into C; there is even a juxtaposition of E major and B flat major when, near the end of Act I, Leonore's aria 'Komm Hoffnung, laß den letzten Stern' is followed by the chorus of prisoners.
5 Cosima Wagner's diaries contain the following entry for Sunday, 28 April 1878: 'R.[Wagner] had a good night ... After lunch he talks of continuing his article, dealing with what is bad, the folklike quality which is allied to genius, the mediocre, what it is that distinguishes the "bad" from the sublime ... The military band today played some dreadful things: "Even Haydn was coarse now and again, but it has all changed so greatly, there is no longer any sensitive coarseness."', *Cosima Wagner's Diaries*, edited and annotated by Martin Gregor-Dellin and Dietrich Mack, translated by Geoffrey Skelton (New York and London 1978–80), II, 66.
6 Review in *Allgemeine Musikalische Zeitung* (1802), quoted in *C&W*, IV, 158.
7 The introduction in Beethoven's Seventh Symphony has two distinct thematic ideas in two well-established tonalities, but neither theme recurs in the body of the movement.
8 Charles Rosen, *The Classical Style* (London 1971), 369.
9 Giorgio Pestelli (trans. Eric Cross), *The Age of Mozart and Beethoven* (Cambridge 1984), 125.
10 For a detailed discussion, see *C&W*, V, 107f.

Select bibliography

Haydn studies, although not yet approaching the quantity of writing on Bach, Mozart, Beethoven or Wagner, are quickly catching up. The publications listed below embrace basic material useful to the reader wishing to explore further Haydn's life and music, and include significant recent works.

BIBLIOGRAPHICAL STUDIES

Brown, A. Peter and James T. Berkenstock, 'Joseph Haydn in literature: A bibliography', *Haydn-Studien*, III/3-4 (1974), 173-352.

Feder, Georg, 'Work-list' in 'Haydn', *New Grove Dictionary of Music and Musicians*, ed. Stanley Sadie (London 1980), vol. 8; updated version in Larsen, Jens Peter and Georg Feder, *The New Grove Haydn* (London 1982), 122-208.

Hoboken, Anthony van, *Joseph Haydn. Thematisch-bibliographisches Werkverzeichnis*, 3 vols. (Mainz 1957-78).

Larsen, Jens Peter, *Three Haydn Catalogues*, Second Facsimile Edition, with a survey of Haydn's œuvre (New York 1979).

Walter, Horst, 'Haydn: Bibliographie 1973-1983', *Haydn-Studien*, V/4 (1985), 205-93.

LIFE AND WORK STUDIES

Geiringer, Karl, *Haydn. A creative life in music*, 3rd ed. (New York and London 1982).

Horányi, Mátyás, *The Magnificence of Eszterháza* (London 1962).

Hughes, Rosemary, *Haydn*, 5th rev. ed. (London 1974).

Landon, H. C. Robbins, *Haydn: Chronicle and Works*, 5 vols. (London and Bloomington, Ind. 1976-80).

Pohl, Carl Ferdinand, *Joseph Haydn*, 3 vols. (I, II Berlin 1875/1882; III [completed by Hugo Botstiber] Leipzig 1927).

ICONOGRAPHY AND BIOGRAPHY

Bartha, Dénes, *Joseph Haydn, Gesammelte Briefe und Aufzeichnungen* (Kassel 1965).

Brown, A. Peter, 'Marianna Martines' Autobiography as a New Source for Haydn's Biography During the 1750s', *Haydn-Studien*, VI/1 (1986), 68-70.

Gotwals, Vernon (ed.), *Haydn. Two contemporary portraits*, modern ed. and trans. of biographies by Griesinger and Dies (Madison, Wis. 1968).

Hurwitz, Joachim, 'Haydn and the Freemasons', *Haydn Yearbook*, XVI (1985), 5-98.

Landon, H. C. Robbins, *Haydn: a documentary study* (London and New York 1981);

——, 'Four new Haydn Letters', *Haydn Yearbook*, XIII (1982), 213-19;

——, 'A Haydn Letter to Dr. Burney', *Haydn Yearbook*, XVI (1985), 247;

—— 'More Haydn Letters in Autograph', *Haydn Yearbook*, XIV (1983), 201-5;

—— 'New Haydn Letters', *Haydn Yearbook*, XV (1984), 214-18.

Mraz, Gerda, Gottfried Mraz and Gerald Schlag (eds.), *Joseph Haydn in seiner Zeit*, exhibition catalogue (Eisenstadt 1982).

Webster, James, 'The Falling-out Between Haydn and Beethoven: The Evidence of the Sources' in *Beethoven Essays. Studies in Honor of Elliot Forbes*, ed. L. Lockwood and P. Benjamin (Cambridge, Mass. 1984), 3-45

STYLE

Arnold, Denis, 'Haydn's Counterpoint and Fux's *Gradus*', *Monthly Musical Record*, LXXXVII (1957), 52-8.

Badura-Skoda, Eva, 'The Influence of the Viennese Popular Comedy on Haydn and Mozart', *Proceedings of the Royal Musical Association*, 100 (1973-4), 185-99.

Brown, A. Peter, 'Critical Years for Haydn's Instrumental Music: 1787-90', *Musical Quarterly*, LXII (1976), 374-94.

Cole, Malcolm S., 'Haydn's Symphonic Rondo Finales: their Structural and Stylistic Evolution', *Haydn Yearbook*, XIII (1982), 113-42.

Johnson, Douglas, '1794-1795: Decisive Years in Beethoven's Early Development' in *Beethoven Studies 3* (Cambridge 1982), 1-28.

Kirkendale, Warren, *Fugue and Fugato in Rococo and Classical Chamber Music*, revised and expanded 2nd ed. (Durham, N. C. 1979).

Mann, Alfred, 'Haydn as student and critic of Fux' in *Studies in Eighteenth-Century Music*, ed. H. C. Robbins Landon (London 1970), 323-32.

Ratner, Leonard, G., *Classic Music. Expression, Form, and Style* (New York 1980).

Rosen, Charles, *The Classical Style* (London and New York 1971);

——, *Sonata Forms* (London 1980).

Sisman, Elaine R., 'Haydn's Hybrid Variations' in *Haydn Studies*, ed. J. P. Larsen, H. Serwer and J. Webster (New York and London 1981), 509-15.

Somfai, László, 'The London Revision of Haydn's Instrumental Style', *Proceedings of the Royal Musical Association*, 100 (1973-4), 159-74.

Todd, R. Larry, 'Joseph Haydn and the *Sturm und Drang*: A Revaluation', *Music Review*, 41 (1980), 172-96.

KEYBOARD MUSIC (SOLO AND ENSEMBLE)

Brown, A. Peter, *Joseph Haydn's Keyboard Music. Sources and Style* (Bloomington, Ind. 1986).

Graue, Jerald C., 'Haydn and the London Pianoforte School' in *Haydn Studies*, ed. J. P. Larsen, H. Serwer and J. Webster (New York and London 1981), 422-31.

Newman, William S., *The Sonata in the Classic Era* (Chapel Hill, N. C. 1963).

STRING QUARTETS

Barrett-Ayres, Reginald, *Joseph Haydn and the String Quartet* (London and New York 1974).

Bloxam, M. Jennifer, 'A Sketch for the Andante Grazioso of Haydn's String Quartet "Opus 103"', *Haydn Yearbook*, XIV (1984), 129-43.

Finscher, Ludwig, *Studien zur Geschichte des Streichquartetts I. Die Entstehung des klassischen Streichquartetts. Von den Vorformen zur Grundlegung durch Joseph Haydn*, Saarbrücker Studien zur Musikwissenschaft, Bd 3 (Kassel 1974).

Keller, Hans, *The Great Haydn Quartets: Their Interpretation* (London and New York 1986).

Tovey, Donald Francis, 'Haydn' in *Cobbett's Cyclopedic Survey of Chamber Music* (London 1929), vol. I, 515-45.

Webster, James, 'The Bass Part in Haydn's Early String Quartets', *Musical Quarterly*, LXIII (1977), 390-424;

——, 'Freedom of Form in Haydn's Early String Quartets' in *Haydn Studies*, ed. J. P. Larsen, H. Serwer and J. Webster (New York and London 1981), 522-30.

Wolff, Christoph and Robert Riggs (eds.), *The String Quartets of Haydn, Mozart and Beethoven. Studies of the Autograph Manuscripts* (Cambridge, Mass., 1980).

ORCHESTRAL MUSIC

Gerlach, Sonja, 'Die chronologische Ordnung von Haydns Sinfonien zwischen 1774 und 1782', *Haydn-Studien*, II/1 (1969), 34-66;

——, 'Haydns Orchestermusiker von 1761 bis 1774', *Haydn-Studien*, IV/1 (1976), 35-48.

Landon, H. C. Robbins, *The Symphonies of Joseph Haydn* (London 1955).

Thomas, Günter, 'Studien zu Haydns Tanzmusik', *Haydn-Studien*, III/1 (1973), 5-28.

Zaslaw, Neal, 'Mozart, Haydn and the Sinfonia da Chiesa', *Journal of Musicology*, I (1982), 95-124.

MISCELLANEOUS INSTRUMENTAL MUSIC

Hellyer, Roger, 'The Wind Ensembles of the Esterházy Princes, 1761-1813', *Haydn Yearbook*, XV (1984), 5-92.

Ord-Hume, Arthur W. J. G., *Joseph Haydn and the Mechanical Organ* (Cardiff 1982).

Sisman, Elaine R., 'Haydn's Baryton Pieces and his serious genres' in *Internationaler Joseph Haydn Kongress Wien 1982*, ed. E. Badura-Skoda (Munich 1986), 426-35.

Webster, James, 'Towards a History of Viennese Chamber Music in the Early Classical Period', *Journal of the American Musicological Society*, 27 (1974), 212-47.

CHURCH MUSIC

Becker-Glauch, Irmgard, 'Neue Forschungen zu Haydns Kirchenmusik', *Haydn-Studien*, II/3 (1970), 167-241.

Brand, Carl Maria, *Die Messen von Joseph Haydn* (Würzburg 1941).

Dack, James, 'The Dating of Haydn's *Missa Cellensis in Honorem Beatissimae Virginis Mariae*: an Interim Discussion', *Haydn Yearbook*, XIII (1982), 97-112.

MacIntyre, Bruce C., *The Viennese Concerted Mass of the Early Classic Period* (Ann Arbor, Mich. 1986).

OPERA

Bartha, Dénes and László Somfai, *Haydn als Opernkapellmeister* (Budapest 1960).

Brago, Michael, 'Haydn, Goldoni, and *Il mondo della luna*', *Eighteenth-Century Studies*, 17 (1983-4), 308-32.

Branscombe, Peter, 'Hanswurst redivivus: Haydn's Connections with the "Volkstheater" Tradition' in *Internationaler Joseph Haydn Kongress Wien 1982*, ed. E. Badura-Skoda (Munich 1986), 369-75.

Geiringer, Karl, 'The "Comedia la Marchesa Nespola": Some Documentary Problems' in *Haydn Studies*, ed. J. P. Larsen, H. Serwer and J. Webster (New York and London 1981), 53-5.

Heartz, Daniel, 'The Creation of the Buffo Finale in Italian Opera', *Proceedings of the Royal Musical Association*, 104 (1977-81), 67-78.

Landon, H. C. Robbins, 'Haydn's Marionette Operas and the Repertoire of the Marionette Theatre at Esterház Castle', *Haydn Yearbook*, I (1962), 111-97;

————, 'The Operas of Haydn' in *The Age of En-lightenment 1745-1790*, ed. E.Wellesz and F.Stern-feld, New Oxford History of Music, vol. VII (London 1973), 172-99.

Lazarevich, Gordana, 'Haydn and the Italian Comic Intermezzo Tradition' in *Internationaler Joseph Haydn Kongress Wien 1982*, ed. E. Badura-Skoda (Munich 1986), 376-86.

Lippmann, Friedrich, 'Haydn's "La fedeltà prem-iata" und Cimarosas "L'infedeltà fedele"', *Haydn-Studien*, V/1 (1982), 1-15.

McClymonds, Marita, 'Haydn and his Contempor-aries: *Armida Abbandonata*' in *Internationaler Jo-seph Haydn Kongress Wien 1982*, ed. E. Badura-Skoda (Munich 1986), 325-32.

Rice, John A., 'Sarti's Giulio Sabino, Haydn's Ar-mida, and the arrival of opera seria at Eszter-háza, *Haydn Yearbook*, XV (1984), 181-98.

Thomas, Günter, 'Haydns Deutsche Singspiele', *Haydn-Studien*, VI/1 (1986), 1-63.

ORATORIO

Brown, A. Peter, *Performing Haydn's The Creation* (Bloomington, Ind. 1986).

Levarie, Siegmund, 'The Closing Numbers of *Die Schöpfung*' in *Studies in Eighteenth-Century Music*, ed. H. C. R. Landon (London 1970), 315-22.

Michel, Walter, 'Die Tobias-Dramen bis zu Haydns Oratorium "Il ritorno di Tobia", *Haydn-Studien*, V/3 (1984), 147-68.

Smither, Howard E., *History of the Oratorio. Vol. III: The Oratorio in the Classical Era* (Oxford 1987).

Stern, Martin, 'Haydn's "Schöpfung"', *Haydn-Studien*, I/3 (1966), 121-98.

Temperley, Nicholas, 'New light on the libretto of *The Creation*' in *Music in Eighteenth-Century England*, ed. C.Hogwood and R.Luckett (Cam-bridge 1983), 189-211.

Tovey, Donald Francis, 'The Creation' in *Essays in Musical Analysis*, vol.V (London 1937), 114-46;

————, 'The Seasons', ibid., 146-61.

Index

GENERAL INDEX

371

INDEX OF COMPOSITIONS BY HAYDN

Hoboken references shown in parentheses